Managing Credit Risk

Wiley Frontiers in Finance

Series Editor: Edward I. Altman, New York University

Managing Credit Risk

The Next Great Financial Challenge

John B. Caouette

Edward I. Altman

Paul Narayanan

John Wiley & Sons, Inc.

New York • Chichester • Weinheim • Brisbane • Singapore • Toronto

Copyright © 1998 by John B. Caouette, Edward I. Altman, Paul Narayanan.
All rights reserved.
Published by John Wiley & Sons, Inc.

Published simultaneously in Canada.

This publication is designed to provide accurate and authoritative information in regard to the subject matter covered. It is sold with the understanding that the publisher is not engaged in rendering professional services. If professional advice or other expert assistance is required, the services of a competent professional person should be sought.

Library of Congress Cataloging-in-Publication Data:

Caouette, John B., 1944–
   Managing credit risk : the next great financial challenge / John
B. Caouette, Edward I. Altman, Paul Narayanan.
      p.   cm.—(Wiley frontiers in finance)
   Includes index.
   ISBN 0-471-11189-9 (alk. paper)
   1. Credit—Management.   2. Risk management.   3. Financial
management.   4. Derivative securities.   I. Altman, Eward I, 1941–
II. Narayanan, Paul, 1948–   III. Title.   IV. Series.
HG3751.C32   1998
332.7—dc21   98-17660

Special thanks to

Dr. Judy Caouette
Florence Altman,
Vasantha Narayanan,

Our wives, and Ed's mother, who offered
enthusiasm and support during the writing of
this book and to the memory of

Robert J. Schwartz,

Who inspired its creation.

Contents

Preface

Revolutionary changes are taking place in the management of credit risk. When a loan was made in the past, the associated credit risk remained on the lender's balance sheet until the debt was repaid or written off. Today, the loan and the risk are just as likely to be resold and/or reconfigured for incorporation into a structured financing that serves as an intermediary between the saving and borrowing sectors. Traditionally, lenders viewed credit risk as a cost of doing business—a hazard to defend against. Today, they see credit risk as something of value that can be packaged and traded. Not long ago, lending was the preserve of banks and insurance companies. Today, rating agencies, financial guarantors, and a variety of special-purpose companies all serve as critical links in the credit chain.

Every day, new analytic tools to measure, manage, and control credit risk are created and promoted, making the present a very exciting time for credit professionals. But revolutions are also times of enormous uncertainty. How reliable are the new tools? How firm is the "science" underlying their development? Do the new techniques truly enhance an institution's ability to manage credit risk? Do they expose an institution to any new forms of risk? Finally, given the sophistication of these new tools, do senior executives still need to concern themselves with creating a sound credit culture within their institutions, or has this worry become passé?

These are among the questions that prompted us to write this book. We sought to fill a long-felt need for a comprehensive treatment of the tools and techniques currently available for managing credit risk. While a number of excellent reference books have been published on this subject (many of which we cite), these tend to emphasize classic credit analysis. Relatively few published books address the newer analytic tools, and—apart from scholarly journals—readers have few places to turn for insight into the research on which they are based. Intended both for credit practitioners and for students, our book offers a framework for understanding the key issues surrounding credit risk management today. Ultimately, it should also help practitioners choose the analytical/quantitative approach that best matches their own institution's specific needs.

Many leading credit practitioners gave generously of their time and insight to help us with this project. Several were also kind enough to review early drafts of the book and to offer their criticisms and corrections. Their thinking permeates the book. As authors, however, we take full responsibility for any errors or omissions that have crept into our presentation. Your comments on *Managing Credit Risk* are welcome. Please send them to feedback@mcr2000.com.

The following are among the practitioners we consulted: Brian Ranson of the Bank of Montreal; Robert Laughlin and Dick Levinson of Citicorp; Michael Horgan and Jack Guenther, formerly of Citicorp; William Barrett, Ann Darby, John Graham, Blythe Masters and Stephen Thieke of J. P. Morgan; Rajat Basu, David Czerniecki, the late Mike Hein, Kevin Kime, Maryam Muessel, Jan Nicholson, Phil Sherman, Dick Stuart, Mary Vermylen, Ruth Whaley, and Howard York of CapMAC (now part of MBIA); Caleb Aldrich, Howard Rubin, and David Stuehr of Standish Ayer and Woods; Andre Cappon of the CBM Group; and Paul Ross of Oliver Wyman & Company; Peter Crosbie and Stephen Kealhofer of KMV Corporation; James LaVelle, Richard Lehmann, David Meuse, John Russell, and Donald Winkler of Banc One; John Hopper of Barclays Capital; Andy Clapham of NatWest; Ross Miller of Miller Risk Advisors; Debra Perry, Lea Carty, and their associates at Moody's; Steve Lubetkin of Standard & Poor's Corporation; Neal Baron of Fitch IBCA; Harry Hummer, formerly of Chase Manhattan Bank; Camilo Gomez, Jose Hernandes, and Stephen Coggeshall of the Center for Adaptive Systems Applications (CASA); and Constance Kenneally and Robert Haldeman of Zeta Services, Inc.

We would like to thank Vellore Kishore of NYU Stern School for his able assistance in compiling the credit data sources appearing at the end of the book and Linda Lin and Chris Saxman of NYU Stern School for their research assistance. Elizabeth Jacobs at MBIA and Lourdes Tanglao at NYU Stern School provided the coordination and administrative assistance without which this book would have been delayed considerably. Editorial assistance by Jon Goldman was thorough and thoughtful. Mina Samuels from John Wiley & Sons ably prodded the process into what we hope will be a useful book for many years to come. Lastly, we wish to thank our spouses and families, whose continuing support has made it possible for us to put into words our thoughts on a topic that occupies a major part of our working day.

Managing
Credit Risk

Introduction

Credit risk is the oldest form of risk in the financial markets. If credit can be defined as "nothing but the expectation of a sum of money within some limited time," then credit risk is the chance that this expectation will not be met. Credit risk is as old as lending itself, which means that it dates back at least as far as 1800 B.C.[1] It is essentially unchanged from ancient Egyptian times: now, as then, there is always an element of uncertainty as to whether a given borrower will repay a particular loan. This book is about how financial institutions are using new tools and techniques to reshape, price, and distribute this ancient form of financial risk.

Ever since banks as we know them were organized in Florence seven hundred years ago, they have been society's primary lending institutions.[2] Managing credit risk has formed the core of their expertise. Traditionally, bankers and other lenders have handled credit evaluation in much the same way that tailors approach the creation of a custom-made suit—by carefully measuring the customer's needs and capacities to make sure that the financing is a good fit. Today's approach does not differ fundamentally from the one used by the earliest banks.

It is easier to design a suit for a customer you already know. Because of the very nature of this approach, banks have been drawn to relationship banking. Typically, they are more concerned about their relationship with a customer than they are about the profitability of a specific loan or about the effect this transaction may have on their overall loan portfolio. In recent

---

[1]Hammurabi's Code, circa 1800 B.C., is said to include many sections relating to the regulation of credit in Babylon (see Homer and Sylla [1996]). There is evidence that the Indus Valley Civilization, a riverine civilization possibly of greater antiquity than Babylonia, had trade contact with it through neighboring Melukha (see Sasson [1995]). So it is possible that concerns about credit risk go even further back in history than 1800 B.C.

[2]Siena and Piacenza are credited with being the main banking centers of Europe, preceding Florence by as many as 75 years. The Bardi, the Peruzzi, and the Acciaiulli dominated the banking scene between 1300 and 1345. All of them collapsed due to the overextension of credit, probably the first victims of cross-border lending. Their place was eventually taken over by the Medici, the Pazzi, and others, of which the Medici of Florence are the best remembered (see de Roover [1963]).

decades, this traditional approach has led to unacceptable results; banks have done a rather poor job of pricing and managing credit risk.

The counterpart to credit risk is market risk—the chance that an investment's value will change in price as a result of marketplace forces. Market risk has affected financial institutions ever since markets were created. In contrast to credit risk, however, techniques for managing market risk have undergone a radical change. Anyone who tours a large trading floor at a bank or an investment bank can see that the management of market risk has been the focus of tremendous technological development. Major breakthroughs have turned this aspect of risk management into something of a science—one that is applied to both equities and debt instruments.

This is not to suggest that market risk has been eliminated. In the case of America's savings and loan associations, for example, an entire industry quaked because of bad bets made on market trends during a period when deregulation was increasing the risks in the financial markets. As is now well known, the industry tried to grow its way out of its problems by adopting unsound funding and unsafe lending practices. Protected by the government's increased deposit insurance limit, the industry's high-stakes bets in the commercial real estate and junk bond markets constituted on-the-job training in credit and market risk, paid for by unwitting U.S. taxpayers.[3] Similar investment excesses by newly deregulated domestic financial institutions in Asian countries are believed to be a root cause of the Asian financial crisis that developed in 1997 and continues at the time of this writing. The bailout in the latter case has to come from the International Monetary Fund (IMF).[4]

Despite its shortcomings in anticipating systemic events, the science of managing market risk does nevertheless reflect late-twentieth-century knowledge and technology. For example, banks have adopted the concepts of gap management, duration, and even the theory of contingent claims. Major banks have created huge markets for interest-rate and currency swaps.

By contrast, the management of credit risk remains, to a substantial degree, a kind of cottage industry in which individual lending decisions are

---

[3]The U.S. government could have covered the market losses of troubled thrifts by writing a check for $20 billion and closing down the thrifts in the early 1980s. Instead, by allowing them to stay open, it precipitated the bailout later at an estimated cost of $166 billion (see Guttmann [1994]).

[4]The IMF economists had this to say about the Asian crisis:

As events unfolded, weaknesses in the financial sector became particularly stark in Thailand, Indonesia, and Korea, although lack of transparency delayed public realization of the scale of the problems. Inadequacies in the regulation and supervision of financial institutions—as well as limited experience among financial institutions in the pricing and managing of risk, lack of commercial orientation, poor corporate governance, and lax internal controls—all in the face of movements toward liberalization and increased competitive pressure, had contributed to imprudent lending including lending associated with relationship banking, and corrupt practices. The vulnerability of financial institutions to deteriorations in asset quality became clear in 1996–97 as a result of the economic slowdown, tighter financial policies, declines in domestic real estate and equity markets, and eventually currency depreciations that placed in difficulty customers with uncovered foreign currency liabilities. This eventually became apparent in the scale of nonperforming loans threatening the institutions' liquidity and solvency. (IMF 1997) made to order. As befits a cottage industry, there is, for the most part, no common credit language. Practitioners, academics, and regulators heatedly debate fundamental measurements such as default timing, default events, workout costs, and recoveries. There is a dearth of reliable quantitative data on financial and nonfinancial variables in the period preceding business failure as well as on recovery rates following such failure.

EVOLUTION OF CREDIT RISK IN THE ECONOMY

Credit risk is a consequence of contracted and/or contingent financial transactions between the providers and users of funds. To understand how it has evolved in modern times, we have to look at the private corporation as the vehicle of economic growth. In precapitalist societies, family and sovereign wealth were the primary bearers of credit risk. Subsequently, the formation of joint stock corporations created entities that were able to pool resources, bear economic risk, borrow money, and exist beyond the natural lives of the owners. Financial intermediaries were created to pool savings and provide them to the users of funds. Even before interest expenses were given preferential tax treatment, corporations (for example, railroads and utilities) used the debt market to raise funds from distant investors, using corporate assets or a government guarantee to secure their borrowing. The bond markets and banks were the dominant providers of debt capital (see Baskin and Miranti [1997]).

As markets grew, other providers of funds gradually took market share away from banks. Junk bonds, asset-based securities, and commercial paper displaced conventional bank financing to a significant extent. A primary reason for this was economics: According to Bryan (1993), the total cost of intermediating a security over the life of an asset is under 50 basis points, whereas the cost of bank intermediation is well over 200 basis points.

A NASCENT SCIENCE OF CREDIT RISK MANAGEMENT

In the mid-1980s, the United States experienced record defaults on bank loans and corporate bonds. When junk bond defaults jumped to over 10 percent in the years 1990 and 1991, many observers argued that both junk bond and the leveraged bank lending markets were likely to disappear. The high-yield bond markets recovered and have since reached record volumes later in the decade.[5]

Prompted in large part by very poor performance in their portfolios in the mid-1980s, practitioners of credit risk management became increasingly interested in new techniques. However, the heightened concern about credit management that emerged did not evolve into a pervasive drive to create and deploy new evaluation techniques. Nor did banks embrace portfolio management, believed to be much needed for them. Instead, this period saw the development of a few stand-alone models, continued refinement of some

---

[5]In 1997, the high-yield public bond issuance was $120 billion, and new leverage loan volume reached $197 billion.

relevant default databases (first established in the late 1980s), and a spate of surveys by regulators and consultants on existing techniques. The latter invariably reached the conclusion that in most financial institutions, credit culture and lending strategies needed to be rethought and possibly redesigned (for example, see Bryan [1988]).

Paradoxically, interest in new approaches to credit risk management has exploded during the current period when the credit markets themselves have been exceptionally benign. At this writing, the U.S. economy has been strong for more than six years, and most of the world's stock markets have been booming for a substantial period, reflecting impressive corporate growth and low interest rates. With a few conspicuous exceptions, such as Japan, Indonesia, Thailand, Malaysia, and South Korea, credit markets in most parts of the world have been well behaved. Indeed, for the last five years (1994 through 1998), well under 2 percent of total bank loans have been nonperforming, compared to an average of close to 4 percent in 1988 through 1993. Default rate on leveraged loans and junk bonds were likewise well under 2 percent for the last three years, in contrast to the 3.6 percent average for junk bonds in 1971 through 1996. Given these positive credit market statistics, the current surge of interest in new techniques for managing credit risk is surprising. Why is it happening?

The answer, we believe, may be found in the changes that have occurred in both the lending institutions and the markets in which they operate. Lending institutions have reached a stage of development where they no longer want or need to make (buy) a loan and hold it to the end of its natural life (maturity, pay off, or charge off). The reasons undoubtedly include pressures from regulators, the emergence of dynamic trading markets for loans, and the pursuit of internal objectives for return on equity. Today, banks are increasingly willing to consider shifting their credit exposure through transactions with counterparties. The markets in which banks can sell their credit assets (other than residential mortgages and consumer loans) are still fairly small and illiquid, and they are inefficient in comparison, say, with the Treasury market. Nevertheless, the market for bank loans is growing in size and liquidity. Consequently, banks and their counterparties are struggling to amass both the information and the analytical foundation necessary to value bank loans by some kind of meaningful risk/return standard. Increased competition, the drive for diversification and liquidity, and regulatory changes such as risk-based capital requirements have thus stimulated the development of many innovative ways to manage credit risk. Banks realized (yet again) from the real estate default experience of 1989 to 1991 that concentration was a critical issue. Out of this realization arose portfolio management. The contagion of the financial crisis in the Asian economies in 1997 signaled that credit risk correlation, if anything, was yet to be well understood.

Around the world, the experiences in the U.S. banking system are being repeated: European countries such as Switzerland and Sweden have gone through a similar real estate crisis. European and Japanese banks have been hurt more than the U.S. banks by concentration in lending to the Asian economies. Domestic financial institutions in the damaged Asian economies, including Japan, are looking to improve their systems for managing credit by building a new credit culture and moving toward an improved market-driven discipline. Thus, just as portfolio management appears to have arrived in U.S. and European banks, the need for credit culture is being acutely felt in the emerging economies.

INNOVATIVE PRODUCTS AND STRUCTURES

Many innovative products and structures have been developed to manage credit risk. The following are some important examples:

- *Structured finance transactions, such as collateralized mortgage obligations and asset-backed securities.* These instruments pool assets and transfer all or part of the credit risk borne by the originator to new investors and, in some cases, to one or more guarantors, as well. By means of the secondary market, investors can, if necessary, transfer the risk to yet another party.[6]
- *Exchanges and clearinghouses.* By introducing a structural hub, these entities minimize the need for every pair of contracting parties to create a separate mechanism for managing their counterparty credit risk exposure.
- *Credit derivatives, which can be layered to modify the credit risk profile of an underlying asset.* Although it is still young, the credit derivative market is growing at an impressive pace. A lender who does not want to continue to assume the credit risk from an asset no longer has to sell the asset outright. Financial instruments are being devised—some simple and some complex—that create a kind of insurance mechanism for transferring the risk of default, and, in some instances, of credit migration. For the first time ever, it is now possible to go short on credit. Furthermore, the credit risk to be bought or sold may be tailored as to amount, period, and the type of credit event. The credit derivative market will transform the business of borrowing and lending in a way that was quite inconceivable just a few years back.

CREDIT RISK IS LIKE MILK

As financial innovation has progressed, credit risk has changed in many ways. In the case of senior/subordinated securities, for example, credit risk has been segmented and redistributed. To avoid the possibility that an entire issue will be downgraded because of poor performance in an isolated segment, these structures are partitioned into separate classes (Myerberg 1996). In the dairy, milk from a cow is first separated into components and then reconstituted into various grades to suit the consumer tastes: low fat, high fat, light cream, and so on. Similarly, financial innovation has decomposed risk and repackaged it into parts that appeal to different types of investors.

---

[6]Municipal bond insurance and municpal bond banks have existed for many years, reducing credit risk through pooling and guarantees.

In this way, a single issue can attract multiple investor classes. This approach to credit risk has turned it from a *defensive* concern to an *offensive* opportunity—understanding the credit risk has made it possible to open up new channels of funds flow. The new generation of finance companies that are funded by asset-backed commercial paper are a prime example of this trend.

The number of entities participating in a credit-related transaction has grown. A structured finance transaction, for example, may include an originator, a seller/servicer, a trustee, and a guarantor. Each of these entities faces exposure from or represents exposure to some other participant. This does not mean that *total* credit risk has increased. However, because multiple parties are involved, it does mean that credit risk must now be assessed from more than one perspective. Credit risk of the underlying obligor has now been exchanged for counterparty financial institution risk, and in many instances, for market risk.

Financial engineering has created instruments with various embedded options and dependencies, each of which may expose participants to both market risk *and* credit risk. In the case of an interest rate swap, for example, potential counterparty exposure is not fixed. In some cases, it begins at zero, then increases over time, then gradually returns to zero at the maturity of the swap. Derivative transactions such as swaps require new forms of financial disclosure and accounting, and they also raise legal issues regarding enforceability. On one pretext or another, some counterparties may simply refuse to honor contractual commitments. For these reasons, rapid growth in the derivatives markets means an overall increase in credit risk.

THE GLOBAL RATE OF CHANGE IS TRULY UNPRECEDENTED

Credit risk has grown exponentially in the 1990s against the backdrop of dramatic economic, political, and technological change around the world. In decades past, geopolitical boundaries and government regulation restricted the mobility of capital. Ever since exchange rates were allowed to float in the early 1970s, financial markets have witnessed a steady progression of deregulation. This has led to increased competition between financial institutions and a blurring of the boundaries separating banks, investment banks, insurance companies, and mutual funds. There have been major changes in the geopolitical arena as well: the breakup of the U.S.S.R, the reunification of Germany, and the introduction of free-market approaches in China and the Eastern European countries. The bipolar tension between capitalism and communism has faded, and with it, much of the pressure for oversized military budgets. The spotlight is on economic growth and an improved standard of living.

Around the world, liquidity has increased. This represents an opportunity in the sense that new sources of capital have appeared. It represents a challenge, too, because new uses and users of this capital have emerged around the globe as well. Transactions take place involving currencies and entities of unprecedented variety. In many instances, credit risk must now be analyzed where parties have little or no credit history. In all, credit risk has grown more complex. At the same time, the ability of governments to guarantee and offer bailouts has diminished.

Superimposed on these geopolitical developments is the powerful force of information technology. Today, it easier than ever before to gather, pool, and retrieve data from far-flung regions of the globe. Techniques such as genetic algorithms, neural networks, and optimization models are within reach of any analyst equipped with a personal computer. Newer models and databases are leading to a better understanding of the expected financial behavior of any particular asset and its relationship to other assets. This improved knowledge may well further increase the importance of securities markets at the expense of banks. However, markets do not have the same commitment to a credit relationship that a bank may have: When the source of funds dries up overnight, a borrower cannot renegotiate the terms of the loan as easily as with a bank. Borrowers will have to manage financing sources as a portfolio of choices, each with a different price-availability profile, and learn to tolerate greater volatility in the financing arena.

Many of the techniques developed to measure and control market price risk will soon be applied to credit risk. But as in the case of market risk, tools for managing credit risk will not, by themselves, make the world a safer place. Any analytical tool is a child of the human intellect attempting to model the real world though a limited set of variables. These tools employ estimation and optimization techniques that are also inventions of the human mind. A model may capture a large proportion of the reality being modeled, but it must nonetheless omit some important aspects of it. Furthermore, a model's very existence may alter market behavior over time, rendering it less and less useful. For these reasons, participants in the financial markets will need to pay greater attention to the issue of *model risk.*

As we explain in the chapters that follow, the new financial tools are, in themselves, works in progress—useful but still imperfect. If they are accorded unwarranted authority or if they are handled without proper care and judgment, they can actually amplify—not minimize—an institution's exposure to credit risk. In the end, the effectiveness of these tools depends absolutely upon the skills, motivations, and attitudes of the people using them. That is why participants in the credit markets must pay close attention to the selection and training of their professionals, to the incentives they create for them, and to the attitudes that pervade their organizations. All of these are critical elements of a firm's risk culture. Over the coming decades, success will go to those firms that employ the right tools *and* create the right kind of culture.

The first 8 chapters of this book describe the institutional setting for credit risk: banks, insurance companies, pension funds, exchanges, clearinghouses, and rating agencies. The 16 chapters that follow introduce and discuss the tools, techniques, and vehicles available today for managing credit risk. The concluding chapter integrates the emerging trends in the financial markets and the new tools and techniques in the context of credit culture. Throughout the book, we place our primary emphasis on *practice,* introducing insights provided by *theory* as needed. Our goal is to present state-of-the-art credit risk solutions along with the perspectives of leading experts in the field who have successfully implemented them. The appendix lists the sources of hard copy and electronic information on credit risk available to the practitioner.

REFERENCES

Baskin, J. B., and P. J. Miranti, Jr. 1997. *A History of Corporate Finance*. New York: Cambridge University Press.

Bryan, L. L. 1988. *Breaking up the Bank: Rethinking an Industry under Siege*. Homewood, Ill.: Dow Jones-Irwin.

———. 1993. The Forces Reshaping Global Banking. *McKinsey Quarterly* 2:59–91.

de Roover, R. 1963. *The Rise and Decline of the Medici Bank*. Cambridge, Mass.: Harvard University Press.

Guttmann, R. 1994. *How Credit-Money Shapes the Economy: The United States in a Global System*. Armonk, N.Y.: M. E. Sharpe.

Homer, S., and R. Sylla. 1996. *A History of Interest Rates*. 3d ed. New Brunswick, N.J.: Rutgers University Press.

IMF (International Monetary Fund). 1997. *World Economic Outlook: Interim Assessment*. Washington, D.C.: International Monetary Fund.

Myerberg, M. 1996. The Use of Securitization in International Markets. In *A Primer on Securitization*, edited by L. T. Kendall and M. T. Fishman. Cambridge, Mass.: MIT Press.

Sasson, J. M., ed. 1995. *Civilizations of the Ancient Near East*. New York: Charles Scribner's Sons.

Chapter 1

Credit Risk: The Next Great Challenge for the Financial Markets

We already know . . . that there has been an irreversible application of risk management technology without which banks would not be able to design, price, and manage many of the newer financial products, like credit derivatives. These same or similar technologies can and are beginning to be used to price and manage traditional banking products.

—Alan Greenspan, Board of Governors of the Federal Reserve System

In recent decades, credit risk has become pervasive in the United States. The U.S. Treasury borrows to keep the federal government afloat,[1] and local water districts borrow to construct new treatment plants. Corporations borrow to make acquisitions and to grow, small businesses borrow to expand their capacity, and millions of individuals use credit to buy homes, cars, boats, clothing, and even food. The dramatic growth in U.S. payment volume suggests the scale of this credit explosion. In 1854, America's GNP nearly equaled the payment volume: The turnover rate was 1.5 (Perold 1995, 36). By 1983, when America's GNP was $3,547 billion and its estimated payment volume was $129,200 billion, the turnover rate had reached 36. Just nine years later, in 1992, GNP had grown to $6,560 billion, but payment volume had jumped to an estimated $513,509 billion. The turnover rate, in other words, had more than *doubled* to 78.[2] Every turn in the exponentially growing turnover rate represents the application of credit.

An element of credit risk exists whenever an individual takes a product or service without making immediate payment for it. Telephone companies and electric utilities accept credit risk from all their subscribers. Credit card issuers take this risk with all their cardholders, as do mortgage lenders with their borrowers. In the corporate sector, businesses in virtually every industry sell to customers on some kind of terms. Every time they do so, they

---

[1] While most people agree that the Treasury obligations are backed by the full faith and credit of the U.S. government and are default-risk free, foreign holders of U.S. government securities do consider the possibility of default, however slight, from time to time. See for example, Shear (1995).

[2] The payment volumes are from Bank for International Settlements (1983, 1993). The GNP figures are from *Economic Report* (1996).

accept credit risk. The credit risk assumed may be for a few hours or for a hundred years.[3]

CHANGING ATTITUDES TOWARD CREDIT

The credit explosion has been accompanied—and accelerated—by a dramatic shift in public attitudes. When Shakespeare's Polonius advised his son, "Neither a borrower nor a lender be," he was voicing the wisdom of his age. He reasoned that "loan oft loses both itself and friend, and borrowing dulls the edge of husbandry." The age of Polonius has passed, and his advice—whatever its merits—has been drowned out by the contrary opinion. He may have been wrong about friends, too. Banks continue to court borrowers who have caused them to lose money in the past! And if borrowing dulls the edge of husbandry, no one seems to mind. Any shame that once attached to the use of credit has vanished.

Even the words we use to describe credit reflect a major shift in attitude. The word *debtor* still carries connotations of misery and shame—an echo of Dickensian debtors' prisons. The word *borrower*, likewise, may still call to mind a pathetic figure going hat in hand to a powerful and possibly scornful banker. But today, we no longer need to see ourselves as debtors or borrowers: We can think of ourselves as people using *leverage*—a word with entirely different connotations. *Leverage* suggests that we are clever enough and skillful enough to employ a tool that multiplies our power. And using leverage leaves the rest of our identity intact—we do not become *leveragors* in the same way that we become debtors. Using leverage is something to boast about, not something to conceal.

From many directions, in fact, Americans are bombarded with invitations to increase their borrowing. Automobile manufacturers attract buyers with low rates on auto loans and offer leases with easy terms to customers who cannot afford a down payment. Retailers entice consumers to open charge accounts by offering discounts on their first purchases. Credit card issuers cram Americans' mailboxes with competing offers. Even credit-impaired individuals—those who once sought the protection of the bankruptcy court—are soon viewed as good credit risks because they are now debt free (*Philadelphia Inquirer* 1996, D-1). Indeed, if there is still shame in any type of consumer transaction, it currently attaches to cash. The merchant who insists that you pay for a purchase in cash may well be impugning your integrity.

This shift in attitude is just as visible in the commercial sphere. CEOs and CFOs are paid handsomely to find other people's money for their companies to leverage. The stock market, which shows little taste for under-leveraged companies, exerts steady pressure on public companies to put an appropriate level of debt on their balance sheets. Meanwhile, pension funds,

---

[3] An example of the former is the intraday risk of other banks assumed by clearinghouse banks in the CHIPS payments system. An example of the latter is the December 1996 bond issue by IBM of $850 million with a maturity of one hundred years.

insurance companies, and banks vie with one another to lend money to finance leveraged buyouts.

High-yield (or junk) bonds have existed for decades, but they were once symptomatic of "fallen angels"—formerly prosperous companies whose fortunes had declined. Today, however, issuing junk bonds is seen as a perfectly respectable strategy for companies lacking access to lower-cost forms of credit.

Even bankruptcy—at least the Chapter 11 variety—has lost much of its sting. Once avoided as a shameful and potentially career-ending debacle, bankruptcy is now widely accepted as a reasonable strategic option. Many companies have sought Chapter 11 bankruptcy as a way to obtain financing for growth, to extricate themselves from burdensome contractual obligations, or to avoid making payments that they deemed inconvenient to suppliers, employees, or others.[4] Meanwhile, individuals who choose personal bankruptcy know that their credit can be resurrected in a mere 10 years—or as little as seven years if they have completed a repayment plan under a Chapter 13 filing (Best moves 1996, 110-111).

The spectacle of Orange County's financial woes suggests that attitudes toward bankruptcy have changed in the public sphere, too. Neither the county's population nor its leaders showed much embarrassment or sense of urgency when it defaulted on its obligations. Apart from front-page stories like this, credit quality, as assessed by the rating agencies, has followed a downward trend in the public finance market. At the same time, state and local government entities have accessed the public debt market in growing numbers over the past 25 years. Seventeen states had a triple-A credit rating in 1970. Just 10 states could lay claim to this distinction in 1996 (Bureau of the Census 1997, Table 489).The causes for the erosion of municipal credit quality—taxpayer revolts and, in the cities, declining tax revenues and inflexible labor costs—may be endemic to the municipal arena, but the decline is in keeping with trends visible in the corporate market, too.

MORE NATIONS BORROW

The appetite for borrowing is truly global in scope. Sovereign obligors have come to the international financial markets in ever-greater numbers. Table 1.1 shows the growth in rated sovereign borrowers in the period 1970 through 1996.[5]

Another measure of the expansion of credit is aggregate government debt. As shown in Table 1.2, the relationship between government debt and GDP varies widely. In countries like Singapore and Israel, government credit plays a strong role in the economy.

---

[4]Examples include Braniff Airlines, Carter Hawley, Manville Corporation, Texas Air, Texaco, A. H. Robbins, and HRT Industry Inc. For a discussion of some of these examples see Delaney (1992).

[5]Moody's carried ratings for 82 sovereigns in 1996. Its rating distribution was as follows: Aaa—10, Aa—16, A—10, Baa—21, Ba—16, and B—9.

Table 1.1 Sovereigns Rated by Standard & Poor's, 1970–1996

Rating	1970	1980	1990	1996
AAA	3	13	12	22
AA			8	12
A			6	7
BBB	5		3	15
BB				3
B			1	3
Total	8	13	30	62

Source: Standard & Poor's Corporate Database 1997.

A new trend in many other developed and developing countries is privatization. Traditionally, infrastructure projects such as roads or bridges were financed by the government. This is changing rapidly. In the United Kingdom, for example, under the Private Finance Initiative, major projects, and even defense-related activities, are being shifted to private sector operators under long-term contracts remunerated by service charges. This trend is expected to accelerate in the European Union as well (*Wall Street Journal* 1997b).

Deregulated domestic financial institutions and corporations in emerging markets have been able to tap into foreign capital to finance domestic growth. The growth in the total foreign indebtedness of Asian countries affected by the financial crisis in 1997, shown in Table 1.3, came primarily from foreign private investment in these entities.

In emerging economies, the growth in borrowing is not limited to corporations and governments. Consumers in many regions are quickly learning how to pay with plastic. In developing countries from Argentina to Thailand, credit card debt is rapidly expanding. MasterCard, for example, reported that its growth in credit card dollar volume in 1995 was 25 percent in Europe, 22 percent in Asia, 36 percent in Latin America, and 22 percent in the Middle East / Africa (Mastercard 1996).

MORE DEBT, MORE RISK

Without question, the availability—and acceptability—of credit facilitates modern society. Credit enables individuals of even modest means to buy homes, cars, and consumer goods, and this, in turn, creates employment and increases economic opportunity. Credit enables businesses to grow and prosper. It allows states, cities, towns, and their agencies to meet the public's needs for schools, hospitals, and roads.

And despite today's more forgiving attitude toward bankruptcy, the risks to the creditors, in most cases, are not terribly high. Consumers know that if they fail to pay their phone or electric bills, their service will be cut

Table 1.2 GDP and Government Debt, Selected Countries, 1989–1993

		Govt debt	GDP	Debt/GDP (%)
Germany	1989	498	2,224	22.4
	1990	599	2,429	24.7
	1991	681	2,648	25.7
	1992	802	NA	—
	1993	903	NA	—
India	1989	2,486	4,568	54.4
	1990	2,926	5,355	54.6
	1991	3,312	6,161	53.8
	1992	3,782	7,028	53.8
	1993	4,463	7,864	56.7
Indonesia	1989	78,503	174,288	45.0
	1990	89,469	203,560	44.0
	1991	91,607	235,559	38.9
	1992	110,995	277,357	40.0
	1993	123,658	341,671	36.2
Israel	1989	139,388	90,067	154.8
	1990	165,199	110,413	149.6
	1991	190,499	106,327	179.2
	1992	222,990	161,292	138.3
	1993	252,818	184,117	137.3
Japan	1989	232,157	401,937	57.8
	1990	239,932	432,302	55.5
	1991	187,605	455,678	41.2
	1992	196,194	464,090	42.3
	1993	212,474	466,943	45.5
Korea	1989	14,144	149,165	9.5
	1990	14,927	179,539	8.3
	1991	16,107	215,734	7.5
	1992	17,082	240,392	7.1
	1993	18,007	267,146	6.7
Singapore	1989	47,443	61,134	77.6
	1990	54,882	69,599	78.9
	1991	62,031	76,619	81.0
	1992	69,535	83,565	83.2
	1993	71,366	95,589	74.7
South Africa	1989	86,398	250,237	34.5
	1990	98,210	283,995	34.6
	1991	113,343	320,382	35.4
	1992	143,385	347,261	41.3
	1993	184,769	395,328	46.7
Thailand	1989	433	1,783	24.3
	1990	403	2,108	19.1
	1991	335	2,437	13.7
	1992	308	2,755	11.2
	1993	267	3,086	8.7
United States	1989	2,207	5,176	42.6
	1990	2,441	5,468	44.6
	1991	2,713	5,630	48.2
	1992	3,003	5,869	51.2
	1993	3,309	6,279	52.7

Source: World Tables 1995.

Amounts in current units of domestic currency (billions). The figures are taken from country-specific tables. Govt. Debt End of Period is Item 19 in those tables, Gross Domestic Product is Item 27.

Table 1.3   Growth in Indebtedness (in US$ billions)

	1992	1993	1994	1995	1996 (est.)	1997 (proj)	1998 (proj)	92–96 growth (%)
Korea								
Foreign liabilities	44.3	50.5	66.1	92.9	125.8	155.0	175.0	29.8
Foreign assets	32.0	41.8	54.5	64.6	74.3	67.0	70.0	23.4
Net	12.3	8.7	11.6	28.3	51.5	88.0	105.0	43.0
Indonesia								
Foreign liabilities	85.3	92.3	106.0	116.5	126.3	135.0	142.0	10.3
Foreign assets	16.8	16.6	18.0	21.1	27.0	27.0	29.0	12.6
Net	68.5	75.7	88.0	95.4	99.3	108.0	113.0	9.7
Malaysia								
Foreign liabilities	27.6	36.1	33.3	37.3	42.6	50.0	59.0	11.5
Foreign assets	19.2	31.1	29.5	27.8	31.2	20.4	22.0	12.9
Net	8.4	5.0	3.8	9.5	11.4	29.6	37.0	7.9
Thailand								
Foreign liabilities	43.3	53.7	67.4	88.1	98.4	101.1	106.8	22.8
Foreign assets	23.4	30.6	36.1	45.3	44.8	27.0	22.0	17.6
Net	19.9	23.1	31.3	42.8	53.6	74.1	84.8	28.1

Source: IMF, IIF, OECD, Bank of Thailand, Bank Negara Malaysia, Bank of Korea, Standard & Poor's, and Moody's.

off. Homeowners recognize that if they stop making mortgage payments, they will lose their homes. Businesses understand that if they fail to pay suppliers, they will no longer receive needed supplies. People and companies know that their access to credit depends upon their record of performance in meeting current obligations. Since credit is vital to them, they will, by and large, do everything they can to pay their debts.

Nonetheless, every company that accepts credit in its day-to-day activities does suffer some losses. Most businesses calculate their normal loss rate and attempt to manage their credit process according to this norm. Losses of this magnitude are not a threat and are usually built into the prices companies charge for their goods and services.

When the economy is buoyant, the pervasiveness of credit may appear to be benign. In economic downturns, however, it may become a serious worry. Individuals lose their jobs and fall behind in their mortgage and credit card payments. Companies go out of business, and their creditors are forced to write off their losses. If a recession is deep enough and long enough, financial institutions begin to crumble. The more extensive the indebtedness, the greater the risk to society.

BANKS ARE FALLIBLE

Apart from the sheer volume of borrowing, credit risk is a more serious challenge today for other reasons. Major lending institutions such as commercial banks and insurance companies may no longer have the ability or the capacity to manage credit risk effectively. In the 1990s they are not the financial fortresses that they were in the past. The credit quality of these intermediaries has declined steadily over the last three decades. Other than the Federal Home Loan Banks, no U.S. bank receives a triple- A rating in Moody's Bank Credit Report Service. Just 10 out of the 127 U.S. life insurance companies possess a triple-A rating for financial strength from Moody's (Moody's 1996, 297).

Events of recent decades have demonstrated that the judgment of America's lenders is far from infallible. American banks have made serious errors in lending. While several factors converged to produce the recent bank crises, an inadequate credit policy and/or process was surely one of the most important. In lending to Latin American countries in the 1970s and to commercial real estate developers in the 1980s, banks based their decisions on their traditional credit methodology: They evaluated individual risks, and they focused on lending to customers with whom they had long-standing business relationships. These techniques failed them badly. In Latin America, as in the commercial real estate market, banks got into trouble because they selected the wrong sector, not because they chose the wrong individual risks. Some of these problems may be blamed on poor bank management, but even good management, by itself, does not make credit risk go away.

While the collapse in the Asian economies (Thailand, Indonesia, Malaysia, and South Korea) is reminiscent of the way Latin American borrowing grew in the early 80s, the causes of the financial crises in these two instances were different. In the Latin American case, according to Jack Guenther, formerly senior vice president, country risk, at Citibank, many of the difficulties experienced by those countries were due to external shocks, such as sharp declines in world commodity prices and high interest rates following the restrictive monetary policy pursued by the U.S. to control inflation at home. With the Asian economies, the problems were caused, on the one hand, by an asset bubble in real estate and, on the other, by excessive investment in productive capacity and decline in export growth. Moreover, the collapse itself was accelerated by pessimistic sentiments in the financial markets and the flight of short-term foreign capital.

CREDIT RISK IS UNDERPRICED

Available evidence suggests that, for many years, U.S. banks have systematically underpriced credit risk, especially commercial credit risk. Traditional sources of income from risk assets are less and less profitable to banks. Figure 1.1, reproduced from a study by Edwards and Mishkin (1995), illustrates this trend.

As may be seen in Figure 1.1, the pretax return on equity excluding noninterest income fell for nearly three decades following 1960, when it stood at more than 10 percent. It approached negative values in the late 1980s and early 1990s.[6] On a more conjectural level, a study by Oliver, Wyman &

---

[6]The authors of the paper acknowledge that this measurement overstates the decline because it does not adjust for the expenses incurred in generating noninterest income. Moreover, some credit-related businesses generate noninterest income.

Figure 1.1   Banking ROE Excluding Noninterest Income.

Source: Edwards and Mishkin (1995).

Co. reported in *American Banker* estimates the risk-adjusted after-tax rate of return on allocated equity for middle market loans to be in the range of 9 percent—well below the presumed hurdle rate of 13 to 14 percent that banks should be using (Rose 1992).

The reasons for inadequate pricing are varied: Some banks have treated commercial loans as a "loss leader" that induces customers to purchase other, more lucrative products from them. In addition, banks have not had good systems for measuring relationship profitability expressed in terms of return on capital. A final cause may simply be ignorance: Even today, banks lack adequate default and recovery data regarding their own corporate lending experience. In many instances, they are forced to borrow such data from the private placement and bond markets in order to understand their own business and price their loans appropriately. Even if some banks do possess this information, they may not be willing to share it with others.

WORLDWIDE BANK WOES

In Europe, bad loans have created a banking crisis of a gravity comparable to that of the United States. Because of credit losses, major banks in France and Spain have come close to failure in recent years.[7]

---

[7]Crédit Lyonnais in France and Banesto in Spain. A bank may be technically insolvent when it has a liquidity crisis or it may be definitively insolvent when there is negative net worth. A

Credit problems have been noted in the banking systems in Norway, Sweden, and Finland (OECD 1995). As shown in Table 1.4, the profitability of other major European banks has also come under pressure. In Japan, the collapse of the real estate market set off a banking crisis both deeper and longer lived than that in the United States. Bad debt in the Japanese banking system has been estimated to be in the range of $500 billion (EIU 1995, 32–33). Furthermore, according to a recent report, fragile banks and lax government supervision threaten prosperity and stability in the fast-growing economies of Asia, Latin America, and Eastern Europe. In these countries, bank capital and expertise in evaluating credit risk have not kept pace with rapid economic growth and the loss of government support pursuant to deregulation. Serious problems in the economies of Thailand, Korea, Malaysia, and Indonesia have already surfaced (*Wall Street Journal* 1997a). These countries had modeled their economies after Japan, where the government plays an important role in the resource allocation process; For example, in Korea, implicit in lending to a large conglomerate (chaebol) was a belief that the government stood behind the conglomerate. Japan has long been known for the protection that government provided to the finance and industrial sectors. Indeed, only recently did the government concede that the troubled loans in the banking system were much more than previously reported for many periods; the revised figures put them around $715 billion, much higher than previously reported.[8]

NEW TRANSACTIONS, NEW RISKS

The emergence of new kinds of financial transactions has also created greater awareness of credit risk. Financial derivatives such as interest-rate or currency swaps represent the unbundling of market risk and credit risk. An interest rate swap, for example, is typically a transaction between the following two parties: 1) a highly-rated issuer that prefers floating-rate obligations but can raise fixed-rate debt at a relatively low rate; and 2) a lower-rated issuer that prefers fixed-rate obligations but can raise only floating rate funds. Thus, a major share of the more innovative swap deals actually turns on credit risk, and it is by accepting credit risk that swap sellers derive a great proportion of their revenues.

Derivatives expand the concept of credit risk to include counterparty risk. Suppose, for example, that an auto maker A agrees to swap currencies with a bank B at some future time. On the basis of this agreement, auto maker A then signs a contract to purchase parts from offshore supplier C. If bank B subsequently fails to uphold its end of the currency swap bargain, offshore supplier C may suffer the consequences of settlement delays or worse, even though it had no direct relationship with bank B. If auto maker A is able to

---

failed institution can operate indefinitely with assistance from the regulators, and there was regulatory intervention for both of these institutions. Spain had a major banking crisis in 1978 through 1983 in which 51 banks failed (Briones, Marin, and Cueto 1988).

[8]Please refer to Chapter 22 for a discussion of country risk and the factors that are useful in analyzing it.

Table 1.4   Profitability of Major Banks in the European Union and United States: 1989 and 1992

EU	Number of reporting banks	Return on assets	
		1989	1992
Denmark	2	n.a.	−1.03
France	6	0.55	0.29
Germany	3	0.89	0.67
Netherlands	3	0.61	0.61
Spain	6	1.73	0.94
United Kingdom	4	0.04	0.29
United States	15	0.82	0.22

Source: BIS Annual Reports, 1991 and 1993.

stop its payment to the bank in time, then its principal would not be at risk. Nevertheless, this company would have to absorb any losses due to an adverse market move. In this way, counterparty risk adds a new dimension to credit risk. Companies now have exposure to third parties with whom they never entered into formal credit relationships. As society becomes increasingly interdependent, counterparty risk expands exponentially.

This is not to say that total financial risk in the economy has increased simply because there are derivative transactions; after all, derivative transactions are a zero-sum game. But derivatives entail additional financial contracting and, therefore, additional exposure to be monitored and managed by the contracting parties. Adequate standards for disclosure regarding creditworthiness have become increasingly important, and investments have had to be made in credit evaluation and monitoring structures. There are also additional risks in the interpretation and enforcement of financial contracts (see Mason 1995, 181). Default by a counterparty with a substantial aggregate exposure could lead to a chain reaction affecting many other institutions.

In fairness to derivatives, it may be argued that these systemic risks are nothing new. For example, the failure of Drysdale Securities in 1982 caused more than $300 million in losses to Chase Manhattan Bank and others in a repo transaction; at that time the Federal Reserve had to act to avert disruptions in the financial markets (see Greider 1987, 487-489). However, derivatives transactions differ from more traditional financial interactions in one key respect: They are off balance sheet. As a result, their true risks are often not visible to outsiders or, for that matter, even to insiders. It is very difficult, if not impossible, to assess a complex institution's derivative risk exposure solely from the disclosures it has made in its financial statements and the accompanying notes. In the final analysis, while derivatives may pose no incremental risk to the financial system as a whole, they do pose significant risks to participants who have not made adequate investments in people, analytics, and technology.

The emergence of asset-backed securities, like that of financial deriva-tives, forces market participants to focus more sharply on credit risk. Secur-itization entails systematically grading and segmenting these risks. The typ-ical asset-backed transaction involves a large number of variables, and understanding the correlations among them may require a high level of an-alytic sophistication. As securitization technology spreads to new jurisdic-tions and as more institutions begin to invest in residential and commercial mortgage-backed securities and asset-backed securities, financial profession-als need to know more about managing the credit risk of an obligor as it evolves over time. They also need to know more about managing *correlated* credit risk—the risk associated with separate assets that show a collective tendency to change in credit quality in the same direction.

NEW LENDERS

A new set of lenders has become increasingly important in the United States. Right after World War II, banks held 70 percent of the country's money, insurance companies 20 percent, and everyone else the remaining 10 percent. Since then, as is clear from Table 1.5, banks and insurance companies have lost market share to institutional investors—pension funds in particular—which accounted for 25 percent of assets as of 1995. This shift has accelerated in recent years.

Pension funds, mutual funds, and endowments have enormous amounts of money to invest/lend, but their preferences differ appreciably from those

Table 1.5 Relative Shares of Total Financial Intermediary Assets, 1960–95

	1960 (%)	1970 (%)	1980 (%)	1990 (%)	1995 (%)
Insurance companies					
Life insurance	19.6	15.3	11.5	12.4	12.8
Property and casualty	4.4	3.8	4.5	4.8	4.6
Pension funds					
Private	6.4	8.4	12.5	14.6	16.2
Public (state and local government)	3.3	4.6	4.9	7.4	8.5
Finance and mortgage companies	4.7	4.9	5.1	5.9	5.3
Mutual funds					
Stock and bond	2.9	3.6	1.7	6.0	12.1
Money market	0.0	0.0	1.9	4.5	4.6
Depository institutions (banks)					
Commercial banks	38.6	38.5	37.2	30.2	27.7
Savings and Loans and mutual savings	19.0	19.4	19.6	12.3	6.3
Credit unions	1.1	1.4	1.6	2.0	1.9
Total	100.0	100.0	100.0	100.0	100.0

Source: Board of Governors of the Federal Reserve System, 1997a, 1997b, 1997c, 1997d, Tables L114–L128.

of banks. Banks take in short-term deposits and have a natural predilection for making short-term loans. Institutional investors, by contrast, take in long-term money and are inclined to lend for the longer term. To a growing degree, a borrower's time frame determines whether a bank or an institutional investor will be the better source of debt capital. This bifurcation of the market is another reason why credit risk needs to be better understood.[9]

As the global economy becomes a reality, the distance between debtor and creditor is likely to grow. It is already possible, for example, for receivables from a credit card issued in Indonesia to be purchased by a fund in New York and then sold to a private banking client in Zurich. Evaluating credit risk is a matter of gathering and interpreting information, and as the distance between the borrower and the ultimate lender increases, this becomes more difficult to do.

NEW APPROACHES TO CREDIT RISK

American bankers who survived their industry's recent crisis recognize that their approach to credit risk has been deeply flawed. Today, many are actively pursuing more effective techniques for managing credit risk. Institutions such as Chase, Bank of America, and Citibank have developed global credit exposure information systems that are updated continuously so that exposure and pricing may be monitored in real time. Moving away from the traditionally held view that judging credit is fundamentally an "art," many banks are adopting new approaches. Citibank, for one, has applied an artificial intelligence system to one segment of its commercial lending business. Bank of Montreal, among others, is applying portfolio theory to the management of its commercial loans.

TECHNOLOGY TO THE RESCUE

Today, the lender community has changed, the debtor community has changed, and the circumstances of lending have changed. The process of granting credit also has changed, but at a much slower pace.

In contrast to market risk, credit risk is, by nature, the kind of low probability/high impact risk that is difficult to hedge. Good information on credit risk is not readily available, and serious academic study of it in all its aspects has just begun.[10]

---

[9]Even though theoretically a bank can lend long term by converting its natural short-term liabilities into long-term liabilities through a swap, banks continue to prefer investments of shorter duration. Whereas the increasing order of maturity is bank loans, private placements, and public bonds, the degree of liquidity follows the reverse order. This may have more to do with the life cycle of a corporate borrower. In the beginning stages, a company relies on banks for financing. As it becomes larger, the private placement markets and the public markets open up, and it has the ability to borrow long term (see Carey, Prowse, Rea, and Udell [1993]).

[10]Note that *business failure* is just one outcome, although an extreme one, in the evolution of *credit risk*. Business failure, which is a binary condition (either a business fails or it doesn't), has been studied for a long time. Credit risk, which is the fluctuating risk on the continuum of loan

In at least one respect, however, modern society is well equipped to deal with this challenge. Information technology and related analytic tools have evolved at a remarkable pace in the last 20 years. We can gather, analyze, compare, and interpret information more rapidly than any prior generation. Indeed, it is the availability of this technology that has made it possible for lenders to provide credit as widely as they have. It is realistic to expect that additional analytic tools will be developed in the years ahead, and that they will enable us to manage credit risk that is both more complex and more extensive than that of the present.

Some new risk-management approaches have already been applied, and others are still on the drawing board. However, the evolution of new techniques for managing credit risk has been uneven, and significant gaps still remain. The decade ahead should be a period of ferment, innovation, and experimentation, as new approaches are devised, tested, and put into use.

REFERENCES

Bank for International Settlements. 1983. *Payment Systems in the Group of Ten Countries.* Basel, Switzerland: Bank for International Settlements.

———. 1993. *Payment Systems in the Group of Ten Countries.* Basel, Switzerland: Bank for International Settlements.

———. Annual Report, 1990. Basel, Switzerland: Bank for International Settlements.

———. Annual Report, 1993. Basel, Switzerland: Bank for International Settlements.

The best moves if you're broke. 1996. *Business Week,* 12 August.

Board of Governors of the Federal Reserve System. 1997a. *Flow of Funds Accounts of the United States 1963–1972.* Washington, D.C.: Board of Governors of the Federal Reserve System.

———. 1997b. *Flow of Funds Accounts of the United States 1973–1981.* Washington, D.C.: Board of Governors of the Federal Reserve System.

———. 1997c. *Flow of Funds Accounts of the United States 1982–1990.* Washington, D.C.: Board of Governors of the Federal Reserve System.

———. 1997d. *Flow of Funds Accounts of the United States 1991–1996.* Washington, D.C.: Board of Governors of the Federal Reserve System.

Briones, J. J., J. L. Martin Marin, and M. J. Vazquez Cueto. 1988. Forecasting Bank Failures in Spain. *Journal of Banking and Finance, Studies in Banking and Finance* 7:127–139.

Carey, M., S. Prowse, J. Rea, and G. Udell. 1993. *"The Economics of the Private Placement Market."* Staff Study 166. Washington, D.C.: Board of Governors of the Federal Reserve System.

---

commitment, loan draw down, and loan repayment, has not been studied as much. Credit risk is also a more inclusive subject that encompasses the influence of underlying factors such as collateral, covenants, and workout costs. According to Brian Ranson of the Bank of Montreal, the commercial credit risk database being developed by Robert Morris Associates for a consortium of banks will not have sufficient sample size for meaningful analysis until at least the year 2007. This will be the first of its kind for commercial banks. Loan Pricing Corporation maintains data on commercial loan pricing, but this is believed to lack information on credit migration and recoveries.

Delaney, K. J. 1992. *Strategic Bankruptcy: How Corporations and Creditors Use Chapter 11 to Their Advantage.* Berkeley, Calif.: University of California Press.

EIU (Economist Intelligence Unit). 1995. EIU Country Report 4th Quarter 1995: Japan. London: Economist Intelligence Unit.

Economic Report of the President. 1996. Washington, D.C.: U.S. Government Printing Office.

Edwards, F. R., and F. S. Mishkin. 1995. The Decline of Traditional Banking: Implications for Financial Stability and Regulatory Policy. *Federal Reserve Bank of New York Policy Review,* July, 27–45.

Greider, W. 1987. Slaughter of the Innocents. Chap. 13 in *Secrets of the Temple: How the Federal Reserve Runs the Country.* New York: Simon and Schuster.

Lewis, A., and G. Pescetto. 1996. *European and U.S. Banking in the 1990s.* San Diego, Calif.: Academic Press.

Mason, S. P. 1995. The Allocation of Risk. In *The Global Financial System.* Boston: Harvard Business School Press.

Mastercard Prepares for a Makeover. 1996. *Credit Card Management,* May.

Moody's Investors Service. 1996. *Moody's Bond Record.* New York: Moody's Investors Service.

OECD (Organization for Economic Co-Operation and Development). 1995. *The New Financial Landscape: Forces Shaping the Revolution in Banking, Risk Management and Capital Markets.* Paris: OECD Documents.

Perold, A. F. 1995. The Payment System and Derivative Instruments, In *The Global Financial System.* Boston: Harvard Business School Press.

Philadelphia Inquirer. 1996. The Debtor's Great Escape: Bankruptcy. 29 December.

Rose, S. 1992. Why Banks Are Reluctant to Lend Money. *American Banker,* 8 April.

Shear, J. 1995. Are Foreign Investors Nervy Enough? Wall Street May Not Be Worried about the Prospect of a U.S. Default on Its Debt, but the Foreign Investors Are. *National Journal* 27 (48): 2833.

Standard & Poor's Corporate Database. 1997. Standard & Poor's, New York.

U. S. Bureau of the Census. 1997. *Statistical Abstract of the United States.* Washington, D.C.: GPO.

Wall Street Journal. 1997a. Next Economic Crisis May Stem from Woes of the World's Banks. 7 May.

Wall Street Journal. 1997b. Private Sector in Cash-strapped Nations Increasingly Finances Major Projects. 5 December.

World Tables. 1995. Baltimore, Md.: Johns Hopkins University Press.

Chapter **2**

Credit Culture

Capt. Renault: *I am shocked, shocked to know that gambling is going on here.*
Emil: *Your winnings, Sir.*
Capt. Renault: *Oh, thank you very much.*

—Casablanca

Capt. Renault exhibits two interesting traits. He feigns surprise at a transgression in which he has participated willingly all along, and he does not hesitate to take credit when the game has gone his way. These traits are not uncommon in the business world. Senior leaders often look the other way when rules are broken, and they frequently mistake luck for skill in risk taking.

Since every kind of business entails some degree of risk, every company must decide just how much risk it is prepared to take. Senior management must establish a comfort zone for risk taking and ensure that people within the organization understand it and remain within it. Outside this zone, the potential consequences of losing are more severe than the potential satisfaction from winning. Establishing a comfort zone and—more importantly—staying within it are not as simple as they may at first appear. The quest for profitable growth often puts businesses on a collision course with their risk boundaries. A few lucky companies may, for a time, be able to grow rapidly without experiencing major losses. Most, however, must make tough choices among competing interests and priorities. Will the organization aim, above all, to maximize market share, asset quality, or profitability? What level of losses will it tolerate? How predictable must its performance be? How should it maximize shareholder wealth?

Businesses can learn to be comfortable—and profitable—with levels of risk that may seem high to outsiders. One of the authors of this book was active in the derivatives market at an earlier stage of his career.

On one occasion, I explained what I did to an oil executive who was seated opposite me at a dinner. "You do interest-rate swaps and currency swaps? That's risky stuff. How do you sleep at night?" the oil executive asked.

"And your company spends hundreds of millions of dollars drilling holes in the bottom of the ocean," I replied. "You bet money on what your geologists tell you, and they don't know exactly what's down there!"

The oil executive was not alarmed by this seemingly high-risk activity. It fell within his company's comfort zone. His entire organization was culturally attuned to this risk, which was viewed as a normal aspect of its business. My own derivatives organization, likewise, was comfortable with the risks that it was taking.

A cultural attitude toward risk is critical in a credit-granting organization. P. Henry Mueller defines credit culture in the following terms:

> Credit behavior has its own cycle, ranging from defensive conservatism to irresponsible aggressiveness. Overlaying each credit system is a stratum of linked attitudes, responses, and behavioral patterns emanating from the CEO and infiltrating the organization. Institutional philosophies, traditions, priorities and standards are additional factors to consider. Personalities of line officers play a role, as do their personal attributes—knowledge, abilities, and biases, together with frailties. These are the seeds from which credit cultures grow, and it is bank culture that influences individual lending behavior. The CEO and the board of directors are its designated guardians. (Mueller 1997, 8)

Senior lenders must begin by deciding what the company's risk profile ought to be—taking into account the realities of the business they are in. Anyone who is uncomfortable drilling holes in the middle of the North Sea probably does not belong in the oil exploration business. Likewise, anyone who is unprepared to take credit risk should not be a banker.

In both businesses, there are, of course, gradations of risk. As there are very speculative drilling opportunities, there are speculative credit opportunities. Calibrating the amount of risk an organization will take is a fundamental strategic issue that must be resolved directly by its CEO. Having established a strike zone for risk taking, senior management must then explain the dynamics and parameters of that zone to people throughout the firm. If the firm is to be a low-risk player, the CEO needs to identify low-risk places to play.

Inconsistent signals and vague statements about what is permitted and what is not generally do more harm than good. Either the policy will be so loosely interpreted that it lacks any teeth, or senior management will have to be consulted for its input every step of the way.

An organization may establish complicated policies and procedures as checks and balances to control its risk taking, but if it lacks a strong cultural core, these will be of little avail. If drivers on a highway simply do not believe in the speed limit, the police can never succeed in enforcing it. But if the drivers basically accept the speed limit, then the job of the highway patrol becomes the manageable one of preventing rogue individuals from causing harm. Institutions generally fail not because they lack credit systems, policies, and procedures, but because they have a prevailing credit culture that makes the deployment of these systems, policies, and procedures meaningless.[1] In some organizations, credit culture is an integral part of a risk culture and is facilitated by a strong and clear sense of purpose. Nowhere is this more evident than in money management firms. Here is Howard Rubin, director at Standish, Ayer and Wood, a fixed-income money manager:

> We seek to enhance return to the client over time . . . everything that we attempt is related to adding value to a specific portfolio relative to client objectives. Taking less of a big picture look, we roll up our sleeves and get very much into the individual security selection—more so than other fixed income managers. Utilizing a team approach brings people with different skills to the table. Using the collective wisdom of the team creates a portfolio with a very favorable risk-return to the client.
>
> We have built a culture where taking risk is accepted and where people can feel comfortable taking risks within their individual specialized area without, for example, the penalty that if you are wrong you are going to be fired. We have nurtured this risk-taking attitude. You are still being prudent, still doing the research, and the collective judgment will be supportive of the decision that has been reached.

If a credit culture has truly entered an organization's bloodstream, then its various policies and procedures can provide powerful support. In this chapter we will consider some contrasting models of credit culture: Morgan Guaranty Trust and Banc One.

MORGAN GUARANTY— MANAGING THROUGH CREDIT CULTURE

At Morgan Guaranty Trust, new employees absorb the bank's strong credit culture from the people around them. In years past, a career at Morgan began with a lengthy training process. "After the formal classroom part, everyone spent several years as a bag carrier," explains William R. Barrett, Jr., managing director and Morgan's senior lending officer, North America. "You would sit in on meetings without talking—watching how things were done and writing memos. The culture seeped in. You learned what is and is not acceptable." The bank's senior managers had been through the process themselves. "Going back as far as I remember, our senior officers were all career Morgan people. They had different styles and different technical skills, but they were all identical in terms of culture."

Today, as young Morgan employees are moved along at a faster pace, they have a shorter exposure to the bank's history and fewer opportunities to develop the informal mentoring relationships that evolved more naturally

---

[1] In bank after bank that one of the authors was involved in resolving during the savings and loan crisis, it was quite commonplace to come across elaborately prepared credit policies, procedures, and credit committee minutes for the failed organization. What was apparently lacking was the practice rather than the appearance of a credit culture.

in years past. At the same time, the bank has entered new businesses, and it has begun to hire significant numbers of people in midcareer—professionals who got their training elsewhere.

Transmission of Morgan's credit culture now begins with a very rigorous screening process at the time of hire. In the case of seasoned professionals, Morgan looks for technical skills, communication skills, client impact, teamwork, and revenue production skills. In the case of one midcareer hire, the candidate was even asked to make a credit presentation. The team evaluating a candidate must reach a consensus before an offer is extended.

To assure cultural continuity, the bank is establishing a formal mentoring system under which new hires are matched with experienced Morgan people. The system is important for seasoned employees as well as for novices. "Morgan can be a lonely place for people who come in at reasonably senior levels," notes Ann E. Darby, vice president. "People here are very connected with each other—they have known each other for years, and they have networks of friendships and relationships." Informal communication helps sustain Morgan's credit culture. "There are many unspoken rules here," says Darby. "People tend to know when someone acts in a way that's inconsistent with those rules—even if their action seems appropriate."

"It's generally understood here that you don't do anything stupid," Bill Barrett adds. "The bank has never had financial pressures for current income that would require us to take silly risks." And how do people know what is an appropriate risk? "They look and see what risks we have taken in the past," says Barrett. "They run into someone who has been around here for a while. Most people reach out as a reality check, even if they don't have to, technically. On paper, people may have a certain degree of lending authority, but they generally don't take that too literally. We tend to work by consensus. Open discussion and communication are highly prized. Most of us would rather set up decision making in a way that incorporates more people. We'd prefer to hear dissenting voices raised at the beginning, so there will be less second-guessing later on."

Should a loan begin to deteriorate, officers at Morgan are generally ready to blow the whistle on themselves. This is a key ingredient of a strong credit culture. "When people have known that something was wrong and raised it, we have managed to reward them for that kind of behavior," says Barrett. "We've had only a small number of credit situations that turned into losses without someone knowing about it in advance. Our record is pretty good."

To sum up, Morgan Guaranty's credit culture appears to have the following notable characteristics:

- Any new entrant to the group has to be accepted by the whole group.
- People are hired based on a balance of traits and skills—people skills are valued as much as technical skills.
- The informal and interdependent network is heavily used to guide decision making.
- Tradition and precedent are valued as guides to the future.

BANC ONE—SMALL IS BEAUTIFUL

Superficially, Banc One could not be more different from Morgan Guaranty Trust. A Midwestern bank with its roots in consumer and small business lending, Banc One has achieved much of its growth through acquisitions. In 1994, in fact, it owned 88 separate banks. Morgan, by contrast, has traditionally served very large corporate and government clients and has made no major acquisitions in years. Although Morgan has recently begun to hire people from the outside, it is clearly a far more insular place than Banc One, where employees started their careers in a wide range of local, regional, and money center banks.

Despite these differences, both institutions are permeated by a credit culture emanating from a strong founder—J. P. Morgan in the case of Morgan Guaranty Trust and the father/son team of John G. McCoy and John B. McCoy at Banc One. "What John wants" shapes everyday business decisions at Banc One and sustains a strong and cohesive credit culture. The McCoys have emphasized a few simple but powerful principles. The first is a strong customer orientation—an emphasis on utility to the customer.

The second is a preference for small exposures. "The philosophy articulated from day one by McCoy is that he wants us to be a middle-market lender," says Chief Underwriting Officer Jim Lavelle. "We avoid extremely large exposures where you have the problem of event risk." When customers such as The Limited or Wendy's have grown beyond a certain size, Banc One has happily passed them along to money center banks like Morgan Guaranty Trust. Banc One has no more than 20 loans of more than $50 million, and all but one of them were acquired through purchases of other banks. Even in acquisitions, Banc One steers clear of any company that is more than a third of its size. As the dominant partner, it can be sure that its own culture will not be diluted.

The preference for small exposures has caused some cultural clashes. "We bought one Texas bank that defined a small business as one with at least $100 million in sales," says Chief Communications Officer John Russell. "We define it as one with no more than $5 million in sales. They had some very good guys that were corporate bankers and would not adjust to the culture of small business lending. You'd explain to them and they'd understand, but then they'd be off on the golf course trying to do $50, $75 or $100 million loans. Finally, we got rid of them. They were not willing to change. They're very competent, and I'm sure they're working in the financial services industry somewhere. But this is the culture at Banc One, and McCoy wants us to stick with the plan."

Another McCoy principle is understanding the business you are lending to. The senior McCoy, John G., was once approached by his son, John B., who wanted to make a loan to Sweden. McCoy responded by asking him to write down ten things he knew about Sweden. John B. realized how little he knew about Sweden, and no loan was made.

This is not to imply that Banc One is risk averse. "In the consumer lending area, we're willing to take on risk so long as we can price it correctly and make a decent profit," says Jim Lavelle. "Some other organizations say, 'This is our risk tolerance, and we won't go beyond it.' We come from the opposite direction. We say, 'This is our profit goal—can we afford to take on this risk and still meet that goal?' "

Like Morgan Guaranty Trust, Banc One rewards employees who come forward when things go wrong. "One part of the culture," John Russell remarks, "is that if you're in trouble, McCoy wants to know immediately. If you're in trouble but don't tell McCoy so he can help you, you'll be out of here if it blows up. Even if you solve the problem yourself, you're in trouble if you don't tell him. When luck helps you, your only hope is that he doesn't find out. But I guarantee you that he does find out."

Avoiding problem loans is not regarded as a sign of good performance. "McCoy pays close attention to people who have no bad news," says Russell. "If you have absolutely no bad news, you're not running your business right—you're not doing what you ought to do. I remember 25 years ago the guy running our mortgage loan business said, 'I haven't had a bad loan in four years.' McCoy said, 'You're not lending enough money!' "

In 1996, Banc One undertook a major strategic shift. For 25 years, the bank followed the elder McCoy's strategy of creating an Uncommon Partnership—a highly decentralized structured that allowed each acquired bank to manage its own business with a high level of autonomy. In 1994, however, the younger McCoy recognized that decentralization was leading to gridlock in decision making. After extensive consultation with his senior staff, he decided to steer Banc One into a 180 degree turn that would create a National Partnership—a centralized structure to run major lines of business. The switch has been accompanied by a massive reengineering effort. This is work still in progress; it is too early to tell how Banc One will emerge at the end of the transition. A single dominant leader (some may call it *one-man rule*) may often prove hazardous to an organization. Banc One takes pains to achieve a genuinely participative management to avoid this pitfall.

The bank's open and direct communication with employees about this change says a great deal about its culture. Rather than delaying the release of information that would undoubtedly trouble many employees, Banc One opted to stage a National Communications Day. Everyone learned at the same time which jobs were going to be closed down and which opened up. As early as possible, people learned what was going to happen so that they, in turn, could make their own decisions. Banc One's senior management clearly understood that open and direct communication is a two-way street.

Knowing that labor-intensive underwriting practices can drive up the cost of making small loans, Banc One invests heavily in credit-scoring models. This contrasts with Morgan Guaranty, which exhibits a cautious attitude toward black boxes that purport to foretell the future. Banc One also understands that to stay competitive it needs to risk differentiate in its pricing. In all segments of its portfolio, the bank has been a pioneer in tiered pricing. Banc One's credit losses tend to resemble the claims experience of a life insurance company: They are actuarially based and may be estimated with reasonable accuracy. Morgan Guaranty's credit loss experience would be more akin to a casualty insurer's: Events are rare, but they are extremely severe.

Morgan Guaranty and Banc One may be on different playing fields, but they share one key element: a management that understands the value of credit culture and takes pains to imprint it on the rank and file.[2]

WHAT MAKES CREDIT CULTURE WORK?

In the real world, financial service organizations cannot afford to make risk management their sole priority. If a bank or insurance company were always to put its own interests first, its customers would soon realize what was happening and move on to other banks and insurers. In a successful organization, customer service and profitability must also occupy an important place within the culture. The challenge to senior management is to strike the right balance among them.

Problems arise when risk management takes a back seat to other priorities. Senior bank managers may say, "We're focused on our customers—we're going to do what they want us to do." This attitude may be admirable as far as customer relations are concerned, but it sends a message to people throughout the organization that customer service is the highest priority of all. In the long run, putting risk management in second or third place behind customer service or short-term profitability can be extremely hazardous. Credit culture also means avoiding a one-size-fits-all or a zero-loss view of the world. Credit emphasis should go hand in hand with product pricing; it is an ingredient of pricing and not just something to protect the organization against losses.

Credit culture is also likely to suffer if the CEO declines to take personal responsibility for establishing and maintaining it. For a time in the 1980s and early 1990s, it became fashionable to think that senior bank executives needed, above all, to be managers and that they could delegate the credit function to people below them. But if the credit function is delegated in its entirety, it is placed in the hands of people who are under pressure both from a competitive marketplace and from senior managers anxious to see their business grow.

Every individual in the credit-granting chain needs to understand a firm's credit culture:

> The behavior of lenders within a strong credit culture is connected with the values of the bank. The behavior of bank personnel must exemplify the bank's risk-taking attitudes and its commitment to excellence. (Mueller 1994b, 81)

Managers' actions often speak louder than their words.

Management must not only firmly believe in the culture it wishes to achieve, it must live and breathe it. Management establishes the credit culture through its behavior, attitudes, responses, verbal and nonverbal signals, and the heroes it creates. These signals, no matter how inconsequential or inadvertent, are

---

[2]On April 13,1998, Banc One announced that it will merge with First Chicago NBD, joining the two biggest banks in the Midwest.

assimilated by loan managers and lenders and dictate their behavior. (Morsman 1994, 21)

A firm's compensation system is one of the most effective tools it has for shaping its credit culture. Employees pay attention to what their leaders say, but they generally pay even closer attention to what their leaders do—constantly trying to discern what the senior team *really* cares about. If employees who find business and take risk are paid significantly more than people who manage risk, then this sends a message throughout the firm. If someone who breaks the rules but succeeds is subsequently rewarded, this also sends a message. People in the organization conclude that as long as you win, everything else is okay.

Relatively few organizations reward individuals who spot a high risk and protect the firm against it. In most cases, dodging a bullet also means avoiding a revenue opportunity. Far too many organizations actually penalize people for doing this by reducing or eliminating their bonus, and other employees are quick to notice this aspect of their company's culture. An incident from the career of one of this book's authors illustrates this point.

I was a senior manager in an organization that was considering transactions in a real estate market that was overheating. At the time, other organizations' underwriting standards were hard to justify. Deals were being done on the assumption that they could be refinanced in the future—not because of their intrinsic value. Many transactions provided no second way out—a violation of a fundamental banking rule.

People in the market were bringing us deals similar to those our competitors had already done. We had a budget goal for the year, so turning these deals down was not easy. But the manager of our real estate department felt these transactions were too risky. She said, "I don't think this is a place we want to be right now. We probably shouldn't be playing in this market." We accepted her recommendation and turned down everything we saw.

At that time, our company was a subsidiary of a larger firm that was focusing primarily on its earnings growth and market share. When the end of the year arrived, I wanted to reward our real estate department head for keeping us out of trouble. But our parent company was very reluctant to pay her a bonus because she had not brought in any revenue. She did ultimately receive a small bonus, but not nearly as much as she deserved. Within 24 months after our decision, we knew with absolute certainty that she had saved us a great deal of money.

Another good test of an organization's credit culture is the way it handles transactions that lie outside its normal comfort zone. In *The Wealth of Nations*, Adam Smith ([1776] 1976, 2:279) wrote:

Though the principles of the banking trade may appear somewhat abstruse, the practice is capable of being reduced to strict rules. To depart from these rules, in consequence of some flattering speculation of extraordinary gain, is almost always extremely dangerous, and frequently fatal to the banking company which attempts it.

Henry Mueller recommends that banks think long and hard before approving deals outside their usual strike zone:

1. Determine the purpose of the credit and the quality of the risk. Is the transaction an appropriate use of the bank's funds? How will it be repaid? Should the funds be obtained from sources other than a bank?
2. Concentrate on the underlying economics of the deal. Is the structure appropriate? Does the transaction and its terms make sense for the bank as well as for the borrower?
3. Evaluate risk and reward. Is it worth it to the bank to make an exception to time-tested policies? Is there more than one way out? Can the bank better employ its funds elsewhere? (Mueller 1994b, 82)

Credit culture, then, is the collection of principles, actions, deterrents, and rewards that exist within a lending organization. The CEO must serve as a primary example of these principles:

- A person cannot innovate or take risks unless he or she is disciplined.
- All employees must know the boundaries of acceptable risk.
- The firm must take a consistent approach to quantifying and pricing that can generate an adequate return on the shareholder's risk capital.

Today, advances in the technology of credit risk management are providing banks and other lenders with better tools of the trade. Effective as they are, these tools must be used in concert with a sound risk culture. Learning from the lessons of the last two decades, senior managers in many lending institutions are paying close attention to the design, establishment, maintenance, and, when necessary, transformation of risk culture. Citibank's decision to establish a bankwide system of consistent risk ratings is an example of the latter. Michael J. Horgan, Citibank's recently retired chairman of credit policy, describes how the bank transformed itself in order to meet the challenge of portfolio management:

> Ten years ago, Citibank did not have a bankwide, risk-rating system. We relied on relationship management and very close attention to the customers. We always prided ourselves on being quick to recognize problems and to pay attention to them very early. We had an intense loan classification system, which recognized problems quickly, and a tight credit audit system that backed that up. We couldn't convince ourselves that there was value to be added by risk rating everything and then by keeping it current. It takes a lot of time, effort, and review resources to put that kind of system in place and then to keep it up-to-date. For us, portfolio management meant setting up industry limits and staying within them. Continental Illinois had one of the early rating systems. I remember talking to them years ago, and I remember when that bank went down, the reaction was, "It didn't do much for them, and they had everything risk rated!"
>
> But once we decided that we were going to be serious about portfolio management, we changed the entire credit management process at the bank. That is, we had to have a risk-rating system using debt-rating models. These

models had to be credible and reliable. Like everything else, when Citicorp does something, it puts tons of people and money against it, and it catches up in a hurry. I think the risk-rating system today at Citicorp is probably as good as anybody's out there.

I would say the process is still in its rudimentary stages, but I think important steps have been taken in managing risk on a portfolio basis. The bank has identified a certain number of industries for which limits have been set for both investment and noninvestment grade exposure. On a regular basis—at least once a year—there is a full-blown industry review where the credit side reviews the industry with the seniors: what's going on and what they see ahead. They'll talk about what they'll need for next year. That's a discipline that clearly wasn't there before. The bank is also looking at credit derivatives and other new tools but is moving cautiously in changing things around.

The Bank of Montreal provides another example of cultural transformation. Traditionally, the bank relied exclusively on its own in-house credit skills, and it subjected all its credits to an annual review. But times have changed. Today, The Bank of Montreal bolsters its own analysis with cross-checks to the equity and debt markets, and it supplements its annual cycle credit reviews with more frequent reviews commensurate with risk and loan size. According to Brian Ranson, senior vice president:

> For many years, owning a declining quality loan was like watching a sunset—there was nothing you could do except to wait for it to go down. So all the analytic emphasis was concentrated on the front end of a transaction—everything was done to prevent a bad loan from being booked. The creation of the syndicated loan market has changed all that.
>
> Once the syndication market grew to vast size, the amount that you held of a loan suddenly became an option, not a requirement, and so the need for a completely different type of credit management arose. We decided we did not need to emphasize a credit culture but an *investment* culture. You've got to think that every use of the bank's risk capital is an investment choice: You can invest in a loan, in a bond, in a sector, or in various different things, but you're making an investment decision. And that decision is conditional upon the portfolio that you have today. So for every loan, you ask two basic questions: First, is the price being paid to bear risk sufficient? If it is, then, given the size of the bank and the existence of the current loans in the portfolio, what is the appropriate size that should be invested in this particular transaction?
>
> Our objective is to continue to manage credit risk after the loan is booked. For example, anything that has a default risk of more than 200 bps we monitor daily. Every month we prepare a report on the top 25 capital users. Every week we identify those companies where we see the largest change in risk.
>
> We use the Internet daily; we go to the SEC database to find out who has filed what. We have a daily bond feed and run it against our portfolio to seek opportunities and review market pricing. We set internal covenants for asset risk. And when the covenant is breached, we *act*. Often, when a company deteriorates, your worst source of information is the customer, and so we must think as investors, not just as relationship managers.

An effective risk culture is not something cast in stone. It must be adapted to fit changing business realities. Despite this flexibility, a strong risk culture must also reflect constancy of purpose.

REFERENCES

Morsman, E. 1994. Analyzing Credit Culture. In *Credit Culture*. Philadelphia: Robert Morris Associates.

Mueller, P. H. 1994a. Notes on the Credit Culture. In *Credit Culture*. Philadelphia: Robert Morris Associates.

———. 1994b. Risk Management and the Credit Culture—A Necessary Interaction. In *Credit Culture*. Philadelphia: Robert Morris Associates.

———. 1997. Cycles and the Credit Culture. *Journal of Lending and Credit Risk Management*, Special Edition, June, 6–12.

Smith, A. [1776] 1976. *An Inquiry into the Wealth of Nations*. Chicago: University of Chicago Press.

Chapter 3

Classic Industry Players: Banks, Finance Companies, Insurance Companies, and Industrial Companies

Accidents that arise from common causes will continue to happen with their expected frequency and variations until the system is corrected. The split is possibly 99 per cent from the system and 1 per cent from carelessness.

—W. Edwards Deming, *Out of the Crisis*

The traditional providers of credit include banks, finance companies, life insurers, industrial companies, and the government. These diverse players have somewhat different objectives and constraints, and their approach to the credit process has differed in matters of detail. As a consequence, their overall experience as creditors has varied as well. Nevertheless, all share the same fundamental strategy: they focus on custom-tailoring the credit decision to the individual borrower. In this sense, they can all be classified as cottage industry players. We use the term *cottage industry* to suggest that each participant takes a unique approach to every single credit. Apart from the residential mortgage and fixed-income securities markets, there are few areas where all participants utilize the same credit language.

BANKS

Since the origins of modern banking in medieval Europe, the distinguishing characteristic of a bank has been its deposit-taking function. To this day, most banking regulations continue to define a bank by this function. Thanks in large part to deposit insurance and aided by the operation of the payments system, deposits continue to flow into banks.[1]

Having agreed to act as a storage facility for a fungible commodity, early bankers quickly began to consider what they could do with deposits until their customers returned to retrieve them. They began to make short-term loans in support of trade. Bankers tended to lend to customers they knew well—oftentimes the very same customers who had deposited money with them.

Many early banks sprang up around groups of industrial enterprises. A number of related companies might join together to establish a bank and then look to it to fund their subsequent activities. Most of America's money

---

[1]See, for example, Merton (1977) for a discussion of the rationale for deposit insurance.

center banks have industrial roots of this kind. In Europe, where banks had similar origins, this pattern is still in evidence: Deutsche Bank, for example, may well be the largest owner of industrial companies in Germany. A similar pattern can be seen in Japan, where major banks are leading members of *keiretsu*—groups of hundreds, if not thousands, of interconnected companies that are the banks' primary customers.

The earliest bankers often charged customers a fee for warehousing their funds. It was not long, however, before bankers recognized that by lending the proceeds of deposits to others, they could create a profitable business. To attract additional depositors, they began paying a fee for the rental of their money—a fee now known as interest. Bankers paid one fee to depositors, charged a higher fee to borrowers, and then lived on the spread between these two fees. For many years, the interest rate that the banks had to pay on consumer deposits was not market determined, and credit risk fell within a narrow band. It used to be said that American bankers operated by the rule of 3-6-3: pay depositors 3 percent interest, lend money at 6 percent, and get to the golf course by 3 P.M.

TRADITIONAL CREDIT ANALYSIS

Traditionally, banks have managed credit risk almost exclusively by adopting procedures for credit analysis—the process of inquiry prior to making the decision to lend. Credit analysis focuses on two distinct but interrelated issues: the borrower's *willingness* and *ability* to repay a loan. Analyzing willingness to pay is, essentially, a matter of investigating the borrower's character. Analyzing the ability to pay is a matter of investigating the borrower's economic prospects.

Research into a borrower's character may begin with an exploration of the individual's position in society and of the mores of the society itself. Is the person a member of the establishment? a radical? Does the society generally consider it important that people repay their debts? A banker might interview a prospective borrower and others who know the individual well to glean as much information as possible about the person's moral fiber.

Evaluating the *ability* of an individual or corporation to pay is a different process. Bankers typically start by looking at macro issues and then working their way down to specifics. What are the prospects for the economy as a whole? Is it heading into a period of prosperity or recession? What is the outlook for the borrower's industry? Is it expanding? mature? dying? What about the borrower's business? Is it thriving? overextended? losing or gaining share? Is the borrower well organized in its affairs?

Both forms of analysis require information, and, generally speaking, the more information available and the greater its accuracy and timeliness, the better the lending decision will be. While both types of inquiry are critical to credit analysis, the economic issues are, on balance, the more important of the two. Historically, more money has been lost because borrowers were unable to pay than because they were unwilling to do so.

In addition to developing techniques for credit analysis, bankers also learned how to manage their risk through such mitigation techniques as down payments and collateral that increase the likelihood of repayment. A borrower who is faced with the loss of a home, farm, factory, or car is highly motivated to make payments in full and on time.

The banking industry has changed rapidly in the last 50 years. For example, banks traditionally took the view that, because their deposit base was short term, they should lend only on a short-term basis. Term loans beyond a year were not introduced until the 1930s and did not become common until after World War II. Banks did not begin to offer personal and mortgage loans until the 1960s.[2] Leases, credit cards, liquidity products, trust services, private banking services, and cash management have likewise become important bank offerings only in the last three decades (Klebaner 1990). Some of these products do not entail credit decisions.

Equally important, as banks have grown larger, the distance between the depositor and the borrower has increased—so much so, in fact, that the relationship between depositor and borrower may be hard to discern.

COMPETITION, CONCENTRATION, AND DECLINE

Meanwhile, in the United States and other industrialized countries, banking has become, by every measure, a mature business. As deposit-taking institutions, banks have lost out in the competition for investable funds. Even as the economy and population continued to grow in the 1960s, banks entered a secular decline. More efficient operators—particularly mutual funds—offered customers a more attractive haven for their savings.[3] Depositors discovered that they could earn more interest from a money-market fund than from their local bank. Meanwhile, borrowers—especially the banks' best commercial customers—discovered that they could borrow more efficiently by going directly to the capital markets. At the same time, because of competition from foreign banks, spreads began to narrow in the core business of U.S. banks—lending to corporations of better credit quality. This forced the banks to move down market, and this, in turn, led to a decline in average credit quality.

The decline in its core business was the primary cause of the banking industry's recent travails. Because federal banking law restricted them from entering such businesses as investment banking and insurance, commercial banks had few alternatives to achieve growth. They could either expand the noncredit aspects of their business or they could lend into situations offering greater spreads.

---

[2] In 1995, the mortgage debt held by commercial banks was $1,072 billion. In 1964, the comparable figure was $28 billion. Likewise, total consumer credit in commercial banks was $505 billion. In 1960, the consumer installment credit extended by commercial banks was a mere $16 billion (Statistical Tables 1970, 1996).

[3] There is a big difference in the cost and tax structure between mutual funds and banks. Mutual funds do not pay taxes; the taxes are paid by the shareholders. Banks have to pay income tax and their dividends are taxed as well. Unlike mutual funds, banks have to maintain a fraction of their deposits (funds) as noninterest-bearing reserves with the Federal Reserve. Unlike mutual funds, banks also have to pay a deposit insurance premium for the protection of the depositors.

Few people, it must be acknowledged—bankers included—are able to see very far beyond the present. Bankers were well acquainted with the credit cycle, and many concluded, despite evidence to the contrary, that this decline was another instance of it. Typically, the credit cycle is linked to the four stages of the business cycle: *boom, bust, recession,* and *recovery.* In the *boom* period, capacity and labor utilization are high, and inflationary pressures build up. Lenders fuel the growth, often forgetting the mistakes of the past. When the boom *busts,* capital asset prices retreat because the Fed applies the brakes to arrest inflation. Economic activity slows down, and banks become defensive. The bust is followed by a period of *recession,* during which there is idle capacity and high unemployment. Interest rates drop while spreads widen. Liquidity increases. In the *recovery* period, economic growth and excess liquidity bring aggressiveness in lending. Consumer demand, inventories, and corporate acquisitions all increase. Lenders resume their lending with gusto, and institutional memories of bad times fade away (for a discussion of the credit cycle, see Mueller [1995]).

But the decline that started in the 1960s was not simply another manifestation of the credit cycle. There were more powerful forces at work.

LATIN AMERICA AND COMMERCIAL REAL ESTATE

Many banking professionals tried desperately to offset declining margins by developing new areas of business, such as lending to Latin America, Poland, Rumania, and other countries . When historians look back on this aspect of the 1970s, they will very likely see it as yet another instance of the madness of crowds. There is no other easy way to account for the fact that a group of seemingly intelligent professionals with large amounts of money at stake were able to convince themselves that Latin American countries could power their way out of a mountain of debt. As Table 3.1 indicates, the trickle of bank lending to this region prior to 1970 turned into a veritable flood, only to end up in round after round of debt reschedulings in the mid-1980s.

Having performed elaborate analyses of country risk and risk limits, banks proceeded to override the country limits they themselves had estab-

Table 3.1 External Financial Flows to Latin America, 1951–1983

Annual averages	Net noncompensatory loans (billions of dollars)
1951–65	0.5
1966–70	1.8
1971–75	7.7
1976–80	20.1
1981	40.6
1982	22.6
1983	2.0

Source: Devlin (1989).

lished because the seemingly attractive risk/reward ratio (on a single entity basis) could be obtained only in places like Latin America.

The 1980s might be described as a period when banks iterated their way to acceptance of their situation. The commercial real estate fiasco followed closely on the heels of the Latin American debt crisis. The circumstances were similar in some ways, but, in this case, duplicity probably played a larger role. Many real estate promoters and developers simply took advantage of the banks by withholding key information about their own financial condition. Thousands of bankers had been trained in the fundamental rules of good credit analysis: know your client and back the people who you think will succeed. And that is what they did.

Banks loaned enormous amounts of money on the assumption that they would later be taken out by insurance companies. The lending decisions were based on optimistic projections of rental income growth, which would lead to appreciation in asset value. On the theory that the buildings would ultimately be needed, construction—especially of office towers—was allowed to outstrip current demand. Total loans grew at an annual rate of 3.7 percent during this period, but real estate loans grew at 8.6 percent per year. As the commercial real estate market started to cool off, the banks believed that, with a little patience, they could expect to be made whole. When the bubble burst, banks had to charge off $34 billion in real-estate-related loan losses for the period 1989–1994 (see Table 3.2).[4]

In part, the Latin American debt and commercial real estate crises reflected a failure on the part of banks to establish and sustain an effective credit culture. The CEO plays the most important role in setting a bank's tone—determining whether it will be aggressive or cautious, expansionary or inclined to stick to its knitting. In the 1980s, senior executives at many large banks were more focused on opportunities and business objectives than on questions of risk. When a CEO says, "We're going to earn a billion dollars in commercial real estate," the message travels throughout the organization. If the financial target has been risk-adjusted, then it may be appropriate. If it has not been, then the message the organization receives is, "Just do it! Find a way!"

PORTFOLIO CONCENTRATION

The banking crises of the last 20 years also reflect a breakdown in the traditional techniques of credit analysis. Banks were lending into markets that were inherently much riskier than those for which the traditional techniques were designed. In addition, the traditional approach—built around customers and relationships—has an inherent tendency to produce concentrations of risk. The problem is compounded when there are significant correlations

---

[4]It should be noted, however, that the effects of the lending market cycle were caused, or at least exacerbated, by government actions. The change in the tax code changed the profit dynamics of real estate investment. Capital requirements were changed for the thrift industry, and when Resolution Trust Corporation liquidated the failed thrifts it dumped huge volumes of real estate into an already soft market.

Table 3.2 Commercial Bank Real Estate Loan Losses (in $ millions)

	1986	1987	1988	1989	1990	1991	1992	1993	1994
Loans and leases, net	1,727,747	1,779,825	1,885,797	2,004,451	2,054,638	1,997,609	1,977,497	2,096,978	2,306,088
Real estate loans	515,317	599,904	675,038	761,526	829,446	851,129	868,309	922,643	997,677
Past-due loans									
(90 days or more)	3,522	3,155	3,173	3,452	4,380	5,005	4,170	3,217	2,386
Nonaccrual loans	10,400	13,479	12,903	18,984	31,586	34,012	29,634	21,230	14,602
Charge-offs, net	1,935	2,448	2,431	3,460	6,382	8,374	8,888	6,677	4,206
Ratio past-due/loans	0.68	0.53	0.47	0.45	0.53	0.59	0.48	0.35	0.24
Ratio nonaccrual/loans	2.02	2.25	1.91	2.49	3.81	4.00	3.41	2.30	1.46
Ratio charge-offs/loans	0.38	0.41	0.36	0.45	0.77	0.98	1.02	0.72	0.42

Source: FDIC

between different borrowers. To the extent that Argentina and Brazil are floating in the same economic tide, for example, a bank that has made loans to both may, in effect, have doubled its risks. Similarly, loans made in the 1980s within the energy-based economies of Texas and Louisiana all suffered in tandem when oil prices fell.

In the modern world, making good credit judgments on a case by case basis is simply not enough. Today, a borrower's financial health may change abruptly in ways that cannot be foreseen at the time a loan is made. A corporation with good credit may be acquired and quickly leveraged to the sky. In short order, it may be teetering on bankruptcy. As a result, the company's bank may suffer a loss because of events over which it has no control.[5]

Likewise, in 1979, Brazil may have been a reasonable credit. (Its Euromoney Risk Rating was 47.)[6] Bank A made loans to Brazil at that time but stopped by 1981 when the country's credit was downgraded. (Its Euromoney Risk Rating was 62, a 31.9 percent drop). Meanwhile, banks B, C, and D went on lending to Brazil. At the end of the day, bank A was hurt just as badly as banks B, C, and D—but through no fault of its own. However rigorous its original credit analysis, bank A suffered a loss because of the actions of other parties. Lacking a market in which to sell its loan, it was unable to act on its risk outlook as Brazil's credit deteriorated.

As W. Edwards Deming has observed (and as was proved yet again in 1997 in the Asian financial collapse), "Accidents that arise from common causes will continue to happen with their expected frequency and variations until the system is corrected" (1986, 479).[7] The only way for banks to safeguard themselves against such losses is to adopt a more sophisticated approach to credit risk than making decisions case by case. They must correct their system and begin to look at groups of credits as portfolios with expected loss norms. They also need to create conditions that will stimulate the emergence of a liquid market for bank loans. These conditions include the standardization of pricing and terms, development of loan servicing standards, and the accumulation of historical data on losses, workout costs, and recoveries.

SOME LESSONS WERE LEARNED

A portfolio approach is not foreign to banks. In fact, it is precisely the approach they have taken, over the last three decades, in building their con-

---

[5] Apart from monitoring the credits in a more proactive manner, banks now have more tools such as asset sales, diversification, and credit risk hedges. These ideas are developed further in later chapters.

[6] The Euromoney country risk assessment is a ranking of the countries in the world based on a country risk score. The country risk score is derived from individual scores on nine categories with the respective weightings as follows: economic outlook (25%), political risk (25%), debt indicators (10%), debt in default or rescheduled (10%), credit ratings (10%), access to bank finance (5%), access to short term finance (5%), access to capital markets (5%), maximum tenor available (5%). A lower number means a better credit risk. In 1997, Luxembourg was ranked first, the United States second, and Yugoslavia was last ranked, as 124th. See Dobson (1997).

[7] W. Edward Deming's work led Japanese industry into principles of management and revolutionized their quality and productivity. His work is the precursor to the TQM (total quality management) precepts.

sumer lending business. In residential real estate lending, too, banks have adopted a portfolio approach, using diversification as a powerful tool to manage their risks. The results have been excellent. It helps, of course, that in this market, individual losses are not terribly severe. Because of the growth of the syndicated loan market, banks are also adopting a portfolio approach to commercial lending.[8] Thus far, a portfolio approach has yet to be applied to commercial real estate lending, but this, too, is about to change.

Recognizing the risks in a situation tends to focus the mind. Ironically, in the commercial sector, banks have done especially well in lending to companies of relatively low credit quality. That is because they have adopted asset-based lending and leasing techniques, which have enabled them to move down the credit spectrum and fund companies that would not qualify for loans on a credit basis. In the process, they have charged properly for the risk. For similar reasons, banks fared reasonably well in lending to leveraged buyouts in the 1980s. They knew that they were dealing with fire so they brought plenty of fire retardant. They insisted on receiving assets as collateral, and they spent a good deal of time analyzing those assets. They priced their loans correctly, and they structured them well. Their approach—and their results—provide a dramatic contrast to their experience with Latin America and commercial real estate. Indeed, in 1992, the regulators decided to do away with the reporting requirement for leveraged buyouts, which fall under the rubric of highly leveraged transactions (HLTs). Appearing before the House Ways and Means Committee, the Comptroller of the Currency noted:

> Most of the banks surveyed have established limits on both their aggregate HLT exposure and on individual transactions. The banks tend to place strict limits on the amount of a given transaction they will hold for their own portfolio: they sell down their initial commitment position, using networks to redistribute portions of the transaction to other investors. The banks also reported, based on their internal credit classification system, that the credit quality of the HLT loan portfolio has generally been satisfactory to date; classified and problem loans have not been excessive, and losses have been minimal. (House 1989)

With regard to loan portfolio, banks have clearly started to move in the direction of active management. According to a survey sponsored by Robert Morris Associates and conducted by the consulting firm First Manhattan Consulting in 1997, 59 percent of a survey sample of 64 institutions with assets of more than $5 billion practice some form of active portfolio management, including the use of portfolio risk analysis, risk classification of loans, loan syndication and trading, geographic and industry diversification, and credit derivatives (Robert Morris Associates 1997).

LIQUIDITY—A RESOURCE UNIQUE TO BANKS

Banks have also fared well as providers of liquidity—whether in the form of lines of credit or of backups for commercial paper. This aspect of the

---

[8] According to an estimate by Loan Pricing Corporation, the U.S. syndicated loan volume in 1996 was $887.60 billion, up from $137.1 billion in 1987, an annual growth of 23 percent.

industry is not widely understood or appreciated, but it is likely to be increasingly important in future years. As providers of liquidity, banks have a natural advantage over all other types of financial institutions: They have access to the discount window at the central bank. Table 3.3 shows the growth in commitments outstanding in the commercial banking system.

Historically, liquidity has been a major concern for the banking industry. Through the period of the Great Depression, banking crises invariably revolved around the issue of liquidity. Bad publicity would prompt depositors to withdraw their funds, causing a run on the bank. Because of this history, bank managers focus sharply on maintaining their liquidity, and central bankers view their discount window as the heart of their regulatory support of the banking industry.

The provision of liquidity is a core strength of the banking industry. It is also a relatively safe business, because if a borrower is no longer creditworthy, the bank can find some way to back away from its commitment to lend or, more likely, to refuse to recommit to it at its maturity. Banks have the ability to scale back or make adjustments in their lines of credit because these lines are periodically reviewed and because most companies take some time to deteriorate. However, many banks make use of this ability only on

**Table 3.3   Commercial Bank Commitments
(in Millions of Dollars)**

Year	Financial and performance standby letters of credit	Total commitments[a]
1986	169,746	769,622
1987	169,891	832,603
1988	170,560	895,436
1989	179,410	984,973
1990	126,400	1,111,993
1991	174,811	1,184,815
1992	162,519	1,273,481
1993	162,967	1,455,217
1994	175,994	1,777,248
1995	189,752	2,157,359

Source: FDIC

[a]From 1990 this figure consists of
  Revolving, open ended lines secured by 1 to 4 family properties
  Credit card lines
  Commercial real estate, construction, and land development
  Securities underwriting
  Other unused commitments
Before 1990 this figure consists of
  Commitments to purchase loans
  Standby contracts and other option arrangements
  Standby letters of credit and foreign office guarantees

relatively rare occasions. They generally continue to lend to a borrower in difficulty—either because they view the borrower as an important customer having value as a going concern, or because they have already lent a significant amount of money. Nonetheless, banks occasionally do refuse to honor their lines of credit. The classic instance of this was when Drexel, Burnham, Lambert was forced into bankruptcy because it was unable to draw on its lines of credit.

In future years, banks are likely to focus on product areas where the credit-risk outlook is favorable or at least the risk/reward ratio is in their favor. Consumer lending should continue to be a major business, as should asset-backed lending, which enables banks to tackle higher-risk segments of the commercial markets while retaining the ability to securitize the assets they originate. Liquidity products should also continue to be an important area of activity for commercial banks. At the same time, the increasing tendency of regulators and the courts to accept relatively broad interpretations of banks' permissible securities activities has enabled many large bank holding companies to become major players in the underwriting of investment-grade bonds, junk bonds, and asset-backed securities. More banks will view their role as an arranger, warehouser, and, finally, a distributor of loans that they would have just booked in the past. Commercial banks have also become important managers and brokers of mutual funds, both in the United States and abroad (Benston and Kaufman 1997). In these areas, banks are likely to continue to play the active roles that they have recently assumed.

FINANCE COMPANIES

Finance companies are basically banks without deposits. Unable to raise low-cost funds by taking deposits, they do not try to compete with banks in what the latter have traditionally viewed as their core customer base—prime commercial clients. And lacking access to the Federal Reserve's discount window, they do not offer liquidity products. Instead, finance companies specialize in higher risk/higher return forms of lending, which they have generally managed quite well.

The traditional business of a finance company has been lending to working class individuals and small entrepreneurs. Over time, however, these borrowers often graduate from finance companies to banks and other less expensive sources of money. Recently, in pursuit of growth, companies such as Household Finance and Beneficial Finance have begun to widen their horizons, attempting to move up the credit ladder to more substantial customers and to expand into leasing and other forms of commercial credit.

The past few years have also seen the launch of many new specialty finance companies. In earlier decades, it was difficult to establish a new entrant in this industry because a company needed to be of significant size in order to access the capital markets on the strength of its own balance sheet. Today, however, the development of the asset-backed securities market has made it possible for even relatively small finance companies to acquire capital. As a result, professionals who used to work for banks—for example, running the auto loan department—are now able to obtain financial backing and re-create their department as an independent company. They can then raise further money from the capital markets and, in time, go public. Examples of this phenomenon include the Money Store (which specializes in second mortgages for B and C credits) and Mercury Finance (which specializes in acquiring and servicing subprime automobile retail installment contracts—car loans—on late-model used cars).

Specialty finance companies outsource virtually everything—including capital—and operate on relatively thin margins. As a result, they are generally attentive to credit risk. Recently, questions have been raised about whether some finance companies are managing credit risk well or simply passing it along to others. Nonetheless, the phenomenon of the specialty finance company is clearly here to stay. New companies are being organized to finance everything from pharmacists' receivables to franchise loans for fast-food restaurants to cosmetic surgery.

Although finance companies have no natural advantage over banks, they can attract professional talent with the prospect of much greater financial rewards. Furthermore, unlike banks, they focus exclusively on one or two niche markets. The stock market clearly loves finance companies. While banks trade at 8–10 times earnings, finance companies trade at multiples closer to 25.[9] One reason for this may be that, as single product companies, they are easier to evaluate than banks. Another reason may be that banks' investment-banking activities lead to more volatile earning streams.

INSURANCE COMPANIES

Life insurance companies and property and casualty insurance companies are alike in that their fundamental mission is protecting clients against risk, but they serve different markets and have developed different investment philosophies.

Life insurers offer products based on life expectancy and health. They absorb mortality risk for a fee, which becomes their primary source of earnings. They also sell products such as life annuities that combine investment and insurance features. Their long-term, fixed-income products—annuities and life insurance policies—have, historically, provided them with predictable cash flows. Consequently, they have specialized in investing in long-term, fixed-rate loans—private placements to corporations and mortgages on commercial real estate. Since they do not have access to the central bank's discount window, they do not offer liquidity products.

Life insurance companies also offer retirement products such as single premium deferred annuities (SPDAs), guaranteed investment contracts, and universal life policies. All of these products require a life insurer to forecast cash flows accurately. They also expose an insurer to the risk that the implicit

---

[9]With the bankruptcy of Search Capital in 1995 and Jayhawk Acceptance in 1997, downgrading of Olympic Financial, and the well-publicized difficulties of Mercury Finance in 1997, Wall Street's ardor for at least the subprime segment of the finance company universe has waned somewhat recently.

promised return will not be earned. Lack of investment opportunities may force a life insurance company to assume more and more risk, even when regulations might appear to make it difficult or impossible to do so.

The credit process at a life insurance company is similar to that at a bank: Lending decisions are made on an individual basis and tailored to the borrower's circumstances and needs. However, life insurers differ from banks in one important respect: The companies to which they lend are not generally their clients. Banks build extensive relationships with their major corporate customers, supplying services from lockboxes to cash management to foreign exchange, in addition to credit. By contrast, when an insurance company lends money to a company, the relationship may go no further than that. Life insurers are therefore somewhat more disciplined lenders who base their decisions on credit analysis alone and are not hampered by relationship profitability concerns. In this respect, they are closer to finance companies than to banks.

As lenders, life insurers—like banks—have had a long history of relative stability followed by greater troubles in recent years, when they have been hurt by concentrations in their real estate and junk bond portfolios. Also like banks, they have been challenged by fundamental changes in their industry. Life insurers serve customers in two basic ways. As providers of life insurance, they spread mortality risk out over a large population of policyholders. As providers of investment opportunities, they help customers build their long-term savings. In this second role, the life insurance industry, like the banking industry, is currently meeting sharp competition from more efficient operators, such as mutual fund companies, that offer attractive alternatives for customers' savings.

Life companies are hard pressed to meet these competitive pressures because their traditional system of distribution is very costly. Life insurance products are typically sold by independent agents. This system was useful in more stable times, but today it is a burden. A customer can buy an annuity from a fund supermarket or a large mutual fund company at a fraction of the price that a life insurer has to charge for the same product. Life insurers cannot fire their agents, because they are not employees. Today, the telephone or the Internet might actually be the best distribution channel for life insurance products and annuities, but the industry has been slow to leave behind the agency system that supported it for so many decades.

Like banks, life insurers have been slow to recognize that the shifts in their environment are secular in nature and require fundamental changes in their operations. Companies in this industry have long been accustomed to business cycles, and this, in itself, has made it harder for them to discern secular change. Rather than transforming themselves, most companies have tried to make tactical adjustments. To cover the high costs built into their distribution systems, they have tried to create higher-yielding products. Since risk and reward generally go hand in hand, this means that they have been driven into riskier types of lending. Once a life insurer sells a guaranteed investment contract (GIC) at 8 percent, it has to create an investment portfolio yielding more than 8 percent. In pursuit of higher yields, many life insurers became overextended in commercial real estate and junk bonds.

Although the life insurance industry's exposure to commercial real estate was even greater than that of banks, its experience in this sector was not quite as disastrous. Life insurance companies do not originate the majority of the loans they make, but instead use correspondents to originate assets or rely on third parties such as investment banks. In commercial real estate lending, this has kept them from entering the riskiest segment of the market—construction lending. In addition, since life insurers are not required to mark their portfolios to market, they were able to ride out the down swing in the real estate market. As long as they could keep a commercial real estate holding current, they did not have to take a loss. Jan Nicholson, managing director at CapMAC, notes that insurance companies largely avoided major real estate losses because they did not lend against dreams and were not taking as much leasing risk—both of which are inherent in the construction lending that banks pursued.

In comparison to other kinds of institutional fixed-income managers, however, life insurance companies have been underperformers. They are basically term lenders. (Indeed, until recently, they were unable to sell private placements on the secondary market.) Unlike mutual funds, life insurers generally have a buy-and-hold mentality, and they pay relatively little attention to the ongoing management of their loans. This tendency to stick with a declining credit has diminished their returns.

Property and casualty (P&C) companies offer products that insure personal or real property against damage as a result of accident, fire, natural causes, or malfeasance. Their product lines may include automobile and home insurance, product liability insurance, officers and directors liability insurance, and medical malpractice insurance. Because natural events are random and the outcomes of legal proceedings are unpredictable, these companies' cash and investment return requirements are less predictable than those of life insurance companies.

P&C companies employ reinsurance to spread the risks that they assume in the course of their business. The quantity of insurance ceded to the reinsurer may itself be reinsured by the reinsurer, creating a chain of insurance coverage. The revenues of a life insurer benefit its policyholders, but those of a P&C company go directly to its bottom line and are taxable. For this reason, P&C companies have traditionally favored tax-exempt investments such as municipal bonds. Howard York was executive vice president and chief investment officer of ITT-Hartford Insurance Group, which grew into a leading full-line P&C company before entering the life insurance business. He explains the P&C company's investment philosophy in the following terms:

> You have hard and soft markets in this business. In hard markets, the demand is very high, and you can pretty much price a policy where you want it. In a soft market, demand and supply conditions are not favorable to the industry, and you can run into negative cash flow when there are huge claims. So the biggest concern of a property and casualty company, until recent years, was to have enough liquidity. Hartford had about ten billion dollars in assets dedicated to the P&C business. It was equivalent to maybe a hundred billion in the life company.

You get a storm, and within three or four weeks, you can have five or six hundred million dollars in claims. So the investment bias there was always toward liquidity rather than toward income return. Most investment groups were never really given any credit for improving returns. The biggest issue was whether or not we had liquidity for service purposes.

As long as you had a positive earnings environment, you always stayed in tax-exempt securities. The only time that *The Hartford* ever maneuvered away from tax exempts was in 1983–1984 when ITT had significant tax losses, which they wanted to obviate by having taxable income. Then we switched over from municipal to corporate bonds.

Like banks, insurance companies are heavily regulated institutions. In 1993, the National Association of Insurance Commissioners introduced risk-based capital requirements. The need to meet regulatory requirements has slowed the industry's pace of change. Nevertheless, insurance companies are managing their business in new ways. *The Hartford*, for example, has moved closer to managing its investment portfolio for total returns. Total return accounts, which are known in some companies as *separate accounts*, are generating much of the industry's revenue growth.

Companies like *The Hartford* are paying closer attention to the asset allocation decision. They are analyzing the relative value of different asset classes—including corporate bonds, mortgage-backed securities, private placements, and real estate—and they are amalgamating multiple liability streams to match up with the cash flow from these assets. This is a major departure from their traditional practice. In the past, insurance companies started with their liability cash flow and then went looking for asset cash flows to match up with it.

While formal portfolio optimization techniques are being tried for asset allocation, Howard York observes that insurers primarily use informal means to diversify their portfolios from a credit perspective. They may, for example, invest in securities with built-in diversification, such as a private placement by a multinational such as Procter and Gamble or a security backed by diversified automobile receivables. York credits *The Hartford*'s significant progress to its recognition that success in investing is as important as it is in underwriting and marketing.

To the extent that book value accounting is still the norm in the industry, most insurers pursue a *buy and hold* strategy and conduct in-depth credit analysis before making an investment. Gradually, however, insurance companies are moving closer to a total return strategy, which relies less on detailed analysis and more on exiting from the credit at the first sign of trouble.

INDUSTRIAL COMPANIES

Credit risk has always been embedded in the business of an industrial company. Receivables are full of credit risk—and, in some ways, it is the most dangerous kind. Selling goods or services is the primary objective at most companies; inquiring whether a buyer can afford them or not is a secondary consideration. In other words, the sales department is typically far more powerful than the credit department. Ultimately, however, every business-person learns that credit is a critical issue.

Historically, industrial companies have often managed or eliminated credit risk by obtaining letters of credit from banks or by selling their receivables to factors, who then take responsibility for managing the collection process. The trouble with these approaches is that outside financial institutions often have a very different perspective on clients than do the companies themselves. It has therefore been part of the natural growth cycle of industrial companies that when they reach a certain size, they begin to take responsibility for their own credit exposure. However, managing credit is beyond the core competency of most industrial companies, which typically have not developed a credit culture. General Electric is one of the few industrial companies to have seen credit as a business in its own right and to have entered it successfully. General Motors and Ford, likewise, have financial operations whose size and sophistication rivals that of all but the largest banks. Westinghouse, on the other hand, is a company that lost a great deal of money in attempting to manage credit risk.

Although industrial companies are generally not well organized in the credit area, their potential losses have been mitigated by the fact that their risks are relatively low. Trade receivables are generally high-quality assets because companies are very reluctant to jeopardize their relationships with their suppliers. Most businesses would sooner fall behind in paying rent or salaries to employees than in paying bills to suppliers. In addition, trade receivables are relatively short-term in nature. It is much easier to manage credit that can be canceled every 30 days than it is to make 15-year term loans. In prior years, when banks were the primary providers of working capital loans to finance receivables and inventories, their loss ratios in this area were very low.

Because, for the most part, they are not comfortable with credit risk and do not view it as an integral part of their business, industrial companies tend to be conservative in their credit policies. Like the banks and other cottage industry players, they have generally made credit judgments on an individual basis, with little consideration for how a particular decision will impact their overall credit portfolio. This is not surprising since, more often than not, credit departments at industrial companies are headed by professionals who were trained at banks. When industrial companies have perceived risks that exceed their established norms, they have generally mitigated them by demanding collateral, deposits, or up-front payments. By adopting a conservative stance and making extensive use of these mitigation techniques, industrial companies have, on the whole, had better credit experience in recent decades than have banks.

However, new challenges are emerging. As business becomes increasingly global, industrial companies are introduced to potential customers they do not know—customers who are subject to pressures and events they cannot readily understand. In addition, the products being sold are increasingly complex, with payments extended over a longer period of time. Selling a dump truck on a 30-day basis is one thing. Selling a highly sophisticated petrochemical plant that will be repaid over a three- or four-year construction period is quite another. If, for example, the buyer is located in China, then new elements of risk are introduced.

In global competition, companies are discovering that in order to sell major products, they need to arrange credit facilities for buyers. In the major industrial countries, export credit agencies have been an important source of help for such companies. On some occasions, however, industrial companies find that they need to accept some credit risks that they cannot easily lay off onto third parties. For this reason, their credit officers have to be more thoughtful and skilled than in the past.

Industrial companies have also begun to realize that credit risk is not restricted to their receivables book. As a growing number of businesses enter into strategic alliances and turn to outsourcing and just-in-time inventory control, they become increasingly dependent on others to supply needed raw materials or to provide essential services. This dependence introduces an element of counterparty risk. In selecting their strategic partners and suppliers, many companies spend little time qualifying these organizations from a credit perspective. The process used in granting a buyer 30-day credit for purchases is clearly not adequate for evaluating a company being considered for a 10-year supply agreement. Industrial companies may also be inattentive to deterioration in the credit quality of their allies, suppliers, and banks, and, therefore, slow to respond.

Nonfinancial companies are also being drawn, increasingly, into the types of derivative transactions that are normally associated with financial institutions. These transactions may have a serious impact on a company's credit profile. The early 1990s saw many episodes in which industrial companies such as Procter & Gamble, Marion Merrill Dow, Gibson Greetings, and Dell Computer lost money on off-balance-sheet transactions. While none of these companies was mortally wounded, others may be less fortunate.

These incidents underscore the role derivatives now play in commercial activities. Because derivatives entail credit risk, companies must pay closer attention to counterparty risk in their financial transactions and provide appropriate disclosures in their financial statements to investors.[10] By the same token, because market participants now have the potential to hide additional risks assumed through the synthetic leverage of derivatives, lenders and stockholders must scrutinize a company's credit exposure more closely than they did in the past. Derivatives allow companies not only to increase their leverage but also to engage in exotic transactions that become public only when they unravel. As a banker is said to have remarked, "A derivative is like a razor—you can use it to shave, but you can also cut your throat with it."

It is reported that Gibson Greetings, certainly not known for its prowess in financial engineering, sold exotic options like *knockouts* and *digitals* in the course of its now famous $27 million loss in derivatives in 1994. None of the risks of these transactions were disclosed by Gibson Greetings in its 1992

---

[10] "To mitigate the credit risk associated with the ten-year swap transactions, the Company entered into margining agreements with its third party bank counterparties. Margining under these agreements does not start until 1997. Furthermore, these agreements would require the Company or the counterparty to post margin only if certain credit thresholds were exceeded" (Apple 1996, 24).

annual report. Other creditors to the firm, including its suppliers and its investors, were kept in the dark about the magnitude of the company's exposure. For a lender to Gibson Greetings, the company's risk had escalated because it had taken on financial market risk. The reasons for doing so had nothing to do with its primary business (Chew 1996, 38).[11]

Global competition will only become more intense in the coming decades, and credit issues will inevitably become an increasingly important element in decision making. If they are excessively conservative in their credit approach, companies will put themselves at a competitive disadvantage. In all likelihood, banks will be of less assistance in credit areas in the years ahead. Industrial companies will therefore need to acquire more tools for evaluating credit risk and for determining how best to hedge it.

The finance operations of large corporations such as General Electric rival those of major financial institutions. Both as credit risk takers and as credit risks themselves, industrial firms will, increasingly, face the same challenges as banks in understanding and managing credit risk.

REFERENCES

Apple Computer Inc. 1996. *Annual Report.* Cupertino, Calif.: Apple Computer Inc.

Benston, G. J., and G. G. Kaufman. 1997. Commercial Banking and Securities Activities: A Survey of Risks and Returns. In *The Financial Services Revolution: Understanding the Changing Role of Banks, Mutual Funds and Insurance Companies,* edited by C. Kirsch. Chicago: Irwin Professional Publishing.

Chew, L. 1996. *Managing Derivative Risks.* New York: John Wiley & Sons.

Deming, W. E. 1986. *Out of the Crisis.* Cambridge, Mass.: Massachusetts Institute of Technology, Center for Advanced Engineering Study.

Devlin, R. 1989. *Debt and Crisis in Latin America: The Supply Side of the Story.* Princeton, N.J.: Princeton University Press.

Dobson, R. 1997. Country Risk: Switzerland Takes a Tumble. *Euromoney,* March.

FDIC (Federal Deposit Insurance Corporation). *Statistics on Banking.* Washington, D.C.: Federal Deposit Insurance Corporation. Annual Issues, 1986–1995.

Klebaner, B. J. 1990. *American Commercial Banking: A History.* Boston: Twayne Publishers.

Merton, R. C. 1977. An Analytical Derivation of the Cost of Deposit Insurance and Loan Guarantees. *Journal of Banking and Finance* 1:3–11.

Mueller, P. H. 1995. Cycles and the Credit Culture. *Journal of Commercial Lending,* September, 41–47.

Robert Morris Associates, Inc. 1997. *State of Play in Credit Portfolio Management.* Philadelphia: Robert Morris Associates, Inc.

Statistical Tables on Consumer Credit and Mortgage Debt Outstanding. 1970. *Federal Reserve Bulletin,* December, A54.

Statistical Tables on Consumer Credit and Mortgage Debt Outstanding. 1996. *Federal Reserve Bulletin,* August, A35–36.

U.S. House. 1989. Committee on Ways and Means. *Hearings on Highly Leveraged Transactions.* 102d Cong. sess. 31 January.

---

[11]It is worth noting that Gibson Greeting, which had reported a healthy EPS of $2.61 in 1991, had an EPS of $–0.95 in 1993, $–2.86 in 1994, and $–1.77 in 1995. Companies suffering from intense profit pressures are perhaps easier prey for such desperate maneuvers.

Chapter 4

The Portfolio Managers: Investment Managers, Unit Trusts, Mutual Funds, and Pension Funds

Even if you put your eggs in different baskets, as long as you are long in eggs you can not escape systematic risk.

—Not attributed to Harry Markowitz

Over the past two decades, professionally managed investment funds such as unit trusts, mutual funds, and pension funds have emerged as major sources of credit. Total mutual fund assets in the United States increased from $42.2 billion in 1975 to $3.5 trillion in December 1996 (ICI 1997, 1996; see also Goldman Sachs 1995), and private and public pension plans grew from $241 billion in 1970 to an estimated $5.27 trillion in 1996 (EBRI 1995, Table 6.9). A substantial share of the assets under professional management is invested in fixed-income—or debt—securities (26.9 percent of corporate pension assets, 35.8 percent of public pension assets, and 38.5 percent of union pension assets [*Pension and Investments,* January 20, 1997, p. 34]).

AGING POPULATIONS

Demographic trends in the United States and other industrialized countries suggest that professionally managed assets will continue to grow for some time to come. Around the world, individuals are recognizing that government pension systems are unlikely to provide them with a secure and comfortable retirement. As the large baby-boom generation ages, unfunded pay-as-you-go pension arrangements such as Social Security in the United States will fall short of meeting retirees' needs. In 1980, when there were 3.2 workers for every retiree in the United States, Social Security payroll taxes on the employed raised sufficient funds to provide substantial benefits to retirees. By the year 2040, when there will be just 2.0 workers for every American retiree, benefits will clearly be reduced (House 1993, 109). A comparable demographic pattern is evident in Europe. In Japan, where the trend is even more pronounced, the proportion of the population aged 65 or older is expected to double from 12 percent to 24 percent between 1990 and 2025 (Dorsey and Turner 1996).

Cognizant of the approaching strains on government pension systems, societies around the globe are trying to spur the growth of prefunded retirement plans. At the same time, many individuals are taking responsibility for their own retirement by investing in mutual funds, unit trusts, and other long-term savings vehicles. Yet another trend is adding to the total volume of assets under professional management: individual investors are increasingly inclined to buy mutual funds, unit trusts, and the like rather than to construct their own portfolios by selecting individual securities. Clearly, pension funds and mutual funds will account for a large percentage of investable funds for many years to come.

In the United States, the last decade has seen particularly rapid growth in 401(k) and other types of defined-contribution pension plans. These plans appeal to employers because they relieve them of the fiduciary and financial burdens associated with traditional defined-benefit plans. In 1993, there were an estimated $1,134 billion in private, single-employer, defined-benefit plan assets and $834 billion in private defined-contribution plan assets. In the year 2000, these assets are projected to rise to $1.5 trillion each (EBRI 1995). Defined-contribution assets are typically invested in mutual funds, while defined-benefit assets are managed in institutional portfolios. Both, however, add to the available pool of professionally managed capital.

FIXED-INCOME PORTFOLIO STRATEGY

As trillions of dollars have accumulated in pension funds and mutual funds, an entire industry has sprung up to manage and invest this money. Professional money managers compete with one another on the yields they can produce for investors as well as on the price of their services. In both respects, the differences between individual managers may be quite small.

Money managers can invest in a wide range of instruments from equities to real estate, but they really have just two basic ways to make money. To the extent that they are able to buy low and sell high, they can earn money through price appreciation. To the extent that they are able to lend money at a reasonable rental, they can earn money by taking credit risk. The latter strategy places them in a position very similar to that of a bank, finance company, or insurer.

It is in their approach to handling credit risk that professional money managers differ dramatically from the cottage industry players such as banks and insurance companies. While a bank or insurer focuses primarily on the individual risk, a money manager focuses on *both* individual risk and portfolio risk—constructing a diversified group of investments and trying, as quickly as possible, to sell any holdings that are not performing well or are not expected to perform well. This approach is generally known as total return portfolio management. While some money managers select securities through a fundamental value/bottom-up process, others combine a top-down view of the economy with a bottom-up view of relative values.

Money managers make use of industry and company research in attempting to select the best investments possible. Let us take for example, Standish, Ayer and Wood, a successful investment management firm based in Boston. This firm is historically known for its successful track record in sector/security selection (65 percent of its historic returns are attributed to security selection and the other 35 percent to the firm's interest-rate outlook). In its investment approach, Standish, Ayer balances classic credit analysis, collective credit judgment, and constrained optimization. It looks, in particular, for companies whose credit rating may be upgraded. As Howard Rubin, director at Standish, Ayer, explains:

> From a sector perspective we are comfortable in all sectors of the marketplace and do not base our decisions on just a select few. Based on the perceived relative value of these broad sectors, we buy the cheapest securities, hoping their value would be recognized by the market place and enhanced—thereby filtering down in terms of performance to the client.

Here is how David Stuehr, another of the firm's directors, describes the bond acquisition process:

> The initial theory can come from many sources. It can be triggered from the trading desk—say, an A rated bond is trading like a BB ... There is always some reason things are trading out of whack. Another example is the current tobacco litigation. How is that going to affect the billboard companies used by the tobacco companies? The idea could come out of screening from our data warehouse. Here we maintain company financials, yield spreads, and company analyses such as ratings and S&P plus, minus, and watch list. We can slice and dice company data coming from many diverse sources. Any of this gets you focused on a fundamental idea.
>
> We look at financial ratios such as traditional interest coverage and free cash flow. Are they improving? We construct a *pro forma* model. We want to know what the downside is. We try to relate the company to the overall state of the economy. In some cases, such as a paper company, the management will tell you the sensitivity of their revenue steams to external variables so we can come up with our own scenario. For others, such as a conglomerate, this is more difficult. Take Koppers for example. As a conglomerate, that company is into many things: treating railroad ties and telephone poles, supplying industrial coke for steel. You cannot even talk about sector sensitivity with their management; they may not know it. In this case, we will try to assess the revenue and profit impact of a 5–10 percent recession.
>
> We also look at market capitalization. We learned early that the equity analyst knows the company better than the bond analyst. It is not that they are smarter than bond analysts, but just that they have to follow the companies more closely and have fewer companies to follow. We then rate the companies based on the chances that they will get upgraded. We set sector limits based on qualitative and subquantitative judgment.
>
> We then assess the credit positives and the credit negatives for the company, including its size and leverage, both financial and operational. Then we analyze relative value; sometimes you will find that the security is not available at the price that was indicated. ... The individual analyst will set up the idea and then build support for it. We build consensus and once it is reached, the decision has our collective support.

The decision to buy/hold/sell does not stop there. Every security has to satisfy what Howard Rubin calls "the capital rationing criterion"—that is, is the investment in the security the best use of capital? Securities in each rating tier are continually ranked according to spread, duration, and potential for a credit quality upgrade. Collaborative decision making does not seem to slow the process. Caleb Aldrich, director at Standish, Ayer, notes:

> But we will not hesitate to challenge each other. Over time, we have built up a level of mutual confidence and respect as we have sought to enhance return to the client. It is understood that everything that we attempt is related to that. For this reason we will not hesitate to challenge each other if necessary to maintain the leading edge we have. That does not mean that we will dismiss ideas out of hand, but we do turn down an idea if it does not fit in with our risk/return perspective.

Professional investment management firms operate with far less manpower than do banks, and, in general, they have less confidence in their ability to select the right borrowers. Disciplined selling is therefore a critical aspect of their approach. The practitioners of total return portfolio management measure their success not only by the skill with which they identify good investments, but also by the speed with which they recognize and jettison bad ones. As Caleb Aldrich observes, "We do have the benefit of having liquidity and marketability on our side. We can afford to make mistakes because we can exit quickly—before the market realizes that it is a mistake. In a lending situation, a bank does not always have that option."

For the vast majority of professional portfolio managers, diversification is the key to managing credit risk. Following the precepts of modern portfolio theory, money managers try to structure a portfolio that is diversified by every conceivable variable—sector, geography, duration, and type of instrument. In doing so, they are careful to avoid excessive portfolio concentrations. If any one security should begin to lose value, it will be counterbalanced by a great many others that have retained their value.

As a corollary to the diversification axiom, money managers generally stay invested in all segments of their chosen market. If they do not like the immediate prospects, say, for mortgage-backed securities, they will lighten their allocation to this segment rather than exiting from it altogether. Professional managers generally stay within the context of the market in which they are investing, observing the relative weightings of its various segments in the index against which their performance is measured. When, for example, they decide to overweight a portfolio in corporate bonds, they regard the decision as a conscious bet on this sector. Their focus is on relative rather than absolute performance: The primary objective is to outperform the index and other money managers.

Although the benefits of diversification have, by now, been well documented, it does remain true that, in diversifying, a manager typically passes up some investment opportunity in order to reduce risks, and he or she may invest in some things that he or she probably would not select in an undiversified pool. At the extremes, a few money managers, such as hedge funds, may ignore the principles of diversification in an effort to maximize returns. However, the experience of professional investment managers has generally been quite good. It is demonstrably true that modern portfolio theory helps to mitigate investment risk and to dampen portfolio volatility.

Practitioners of total return management effectively avoid one of the fundamental flaws of the banking industry—the tendency to hold on to bad loans for too long. When a borrower gets into trouble, a banker may well take the time to hear the company explain its situation and plan of action. Under some circumstances, a bank may even agree to lend additional money. They do this because bank loans have generally been hard to sell in the public markets. If a loan deteriorates in quality, a bank may have few alternatives to participating in its restructuring. A portfolio manager, by contrast, will generally try to get out of a deal at the earliest sign of weakness. As a result, pension funds and mutual funds have rarely suffered the kinds of large losses that banks experienced in recent decades.[1] While banks emphasize their relationship with the customer through good times and bad (with varying results), fixed income portfolio managers never lose sight of where they stand relative to the investment they have made.

Money managers are able to take this tack because they do not allow portfolio concentrations to become so great that the liquidity and marketability of their securities would be affected. Selling any one holding will cause only a small loss, and the proceeds of the sale can then be used to purchase other securities. Portfolio managers typically have no interest in learning how a stressed credit plans to get back on its feet. Such loyalty to the borrower would make little strategic sense. A fixed-income security provides a relatively small stream of interest income. Investing in such securities at 100 cents on the dollar is an activity that offers relatively little upside. Typically, a fixed-income manager has few opportunities to recover a large loss. It is therefore more rational to sell distressed securities as quickly as possible. At the right price, there will always be buyers. Other investors will be willing to pay 60 or 70 cents on the dollar for such bonds because for them, there is an upside—a chance to see their investment appreciate.

Fixed-income portfolio managers differ from bankers in other important respects, as well. They invest in publicly rated securities for which there is generally a liquid market, and they are required to mark their investments to market. When a credit deteriorates, a portion of their portfolio will decline in value. This market discipline strengthens a money manager's motivation to sell. Bankers, by contrast, do not mark loans to market; as long as they continue to receive current payments, they classify a loan as performing— even if the borrower is barely staying afloat.

Banks and pension funds also operate under different regulatory regimes. Indeed, society looks to them to serve somewhat different purposes. While both kinds of institutions are expected to safeguard people's savings, banks are also expected to provide financing to meet the legitimate needs of businesses and individuals. For many people, banks are, above all, a source of liquidity, mortgages, and working-capital loans. When banks tighten their credit policies and slow the flow of financing, some Americans promptly contact their representatives in Congress to complain about the resulting credit crunch. By contrast, virtually no one expects pension funds to carry the burden of financing American enterprises. When a pension fund declines to buy a

---

[1]Mutual funds, for example, have far outperformed banks and insurance companies in lending to BB credits.

particular company's bonds, the firm's executives do not call Congress to complain. Indeed, under the terms of the Employee Retirement Income Security Act of 1974 (ERISA), pension plans are legally bound to put the interests of their participants first. If the officers of a plan allow other interests to intrude, they may be guilty of breaching their fiduciary responsibility to plan participants.

Despite the generally positive record, some professionally managed, fixed-income funds have encountered problems. In the case of certain junk bond funds and real estate funds, for example, diversification has been ineffective because the portfolios were too concentrated within a specific segment of the market. Economic problems affecting the entire segment caused large losses. Funds that are highly concentrated in a particular geographic region (such as country funds) have also experienced sizable losses.

More generally, it should be noted that portfolio diversification has largely been a matter of intuition and common sense rather than of hard science. To date, relatively little serious analytic work has been done on the correlations among different industries and among various types of securities. Lacking these tools, portfolio managers have been unable to realize all the potential benefits of diversification. Pension funds, mutual funds, and unit trusts may therefore gain a great deal from future advances we expect to see in portfolio theory. These are discussed at length in Chapters 17–22.

A second problem for portfolio managers derives from the security selection process itself. Most money management firms are overmuscled in portfolio theory and undermuscled in security selection—as evidenced by the number of analysts they employ relative to the size of the market place they have to address on a name-by- name basis. As a result, they are liable to purchase securities that may potentially lose value because of declining credit quality. While disciplined selling generally protects them against catastrophic losses, fixed-income funds may nonetheless be accepting an unnecessary volume of small losses.

To address this problem and also to take advantage of investment opportunities in the growing market for banks loans, high-yield corporate debt, and the debt of emerging countries —all of which involve credit risk (and yield) of higher than customary magnitude—some large investment firms have begun to incorporate credit skills that are normally associated with banks. Companies like Fidelity Investments, for example, have begun hiring professionals trained at banks to help them design credit systems that combine individual credit analysis with portfolio management skills. Banks, meanwhile, are acquiring some of the portfolio skills normally associated with money managers. Whether in the hands of a bank or a money manager, the combination of the two approaches should lead to much more effective management of credit risk.

REFERENCES

Dorsey, S., and J. A. Turner. 1996. Social Security, Pensions, Disability, and Retirement: An International Perspective. In *Handbook on Employment and the Elderly,* edited by W. H. Crown. Westport, Conn.: Greenwood Press, 1996.

EBRI (Employee Benefit Research Institute). 1995. *EBRI Databook on Employee Benefits.* 3d ed. Washington, D.C.: Employee Benefit Research Institute.

Goldman Sachs Investment Management Industry Group. 1995. *The Coming Evolution of the Investment Management Industry: Opportunities and Strategies.* New York: Goldman Sachs.

ICI (Investment Company Institute). 1996. *Monthly Statistics of Open-end Companies.* Washington, D.C.: Investment Company Institute. September.

———. 1997. *Mutual Fund Fact Book.* 37th ed. Washington, D.C.: Investment Company Institute.

U.S. House. 1993. Committee on Ways and Means. *Green Book: Overview of Entitlement Program.* Washington, D.C.: GPO.

Chapter 5

Structural Hubs: Derivative Dealers, Clearinghouses, and Exchanges

The synthesizing of custom financial contracts and securities is for financial services what the assembly-line production process is for the manufacturing sector. Options, futures, and other exchange-traded securities are the raw 'inputs' applied in prescribed combinations over time to create portfolios that hedge the various customer liabilities of financial intermediaries.

—Robert C. Merton, *Financial Innovation and Economic Performance*

Banks, derivative dealers, and other financial institutions that engage in a high volume of transactions with one another take on credit risk in the course of their daily interactions. Clearinghouses, exchanges, and derivative contracts are structural means of mitigating these risks.

Although derivatives have attracted a great deal of public attention in the last decade, they are not a new phenomenon. For many years, traders have bought and sold pieces of paper representing pork bellies, corn, gold, or oil rather than buying and selling the commodities themselves.[1] Whenever a standard unit of trade can be established, an instrument can be created to reflect this basic transaction. Derivatives are easier to deal with than physical goods. While most futures contracts are closed out in cash before the maturity date, on occasion goods are actually delivered in accordance with the terms of the contract.

It is financial derivatives, which represent rights or options in a variety of financial instruments, that have made headlines in recent years. The overall volume of trading in financial derivatives has increased from $618.3 billion in 1986 to $9,884.6 billion in 1996 (IMF 1997, Table 9). This explosive growth has created substantial risks of several kinds: counterparty risk, settlement risk, and systemic risk, to name a few. Someone buying a stock option from a dealer depends upon the dealer to make good on what it has sold. At the same time, the seller depends upon the buyer to make the payment agreed upon.

Derivative dealers are specially organized companies that are typically affiliated with a commercial bank or an investment bank. A sizable portion of their business involves trades with other dealers. As a result, in addition to

---

[1] The first recorded case of organized trading is said to have occurred in Japan during the 1600s. See Teweles and Jones (1987).

having exposure to the credit risk of their customers, these organizations are also exposed to the credit risk of other dealers. Since the total number of dealers is limited, these risks may become quite concentrated.

When the financial derivatives market was in its infancy, dealers knew one another and felt comfortable that there was little risk of nonperformance. Growth in the derivatives markets, a general decline in the creditworthiness of financial institutions, and the rapid demise of such companies as Barings Securities have combined to create sharper awareness of counterparty risk. Market participants who trade over-the-counter derivatives such as swaps, options, swaptions, caps, and collars are increasingly concerned about managing these risks. Indeed, many observers believe that the management of such counterparty risk is one of the major themes for the financial markets in the 1990s (see, for example, House [1996]).

EXCHANGES

An exchange is an institutional means of reducing counterparty risk. Futures exchanges, for example, facilitate the trading of derivatives ranging from grain and fruit to foreign currencies, bonds, and insurance contracts. These exchanges have virtually eliminated counterparty risk from futures trading.

Anyone buying a contract on a futures exchange—whether an individual or an institution—is required to put up margin. Because the buyer has posted margin, the seller knows that money will be available to pay for the contract. Since the seller is likewise obliged to post margin, the buyer has the same assurance about receiving the purchased goods or their monetary equivalent. The margin requirement effectively eliminates counterparty risk between buyer and seller. The only remaining credit risk is overnight credit risk—the possibility that a counterparty will not put up tomorrow's margin.[2] When this occurs, a player relinquishes any rights to margin or to the underlying contract. The margin requirement allows small players, such as individual investors, to trade on an equal basis with the largest financial institutions. Many participants consider this equality of access one of the great advantages of an exchange. Another advantage of an exchange is that it standardizes the terms of contracts, thereby reducing transaction costs.

CLEARINGHOUSES

Clearinghouses are developed to allow institutions that do a lot of business with each other to offset their transactions. New York banks, for example, formed a clearinghouse to clear checks and other obligations they have to one another. Instead of exchanging millions of bits of paper and billions of dollars in cash, the banks use a clearinghouse as a central place to meet and sort out their transactions electronically.

---

[2]In some cases, there may also be intraday risk in a clearinghouse as, for example, in CHIPS, the system used by New York banks to clear money transfers.

An associated clearinghouse is an important component of a derivative exchange. Institutionally, the credit risk of this clearinghouse substitutes for the credit risks of the multiple counterparties transacting business on the exchange. Every trade executed on the exchange spawns two trades: one between the buyer and the clearinghouse and the other between the clearinghouse and the seller. At the end of the day, the clearinghouse has a perfectly matched book of contracts and thus incurs no market risk. However, the clearinghouse is now exposed to the risk of the clearing members, who in turn are exposed to the counterparty risk of their own customers. Figures 5.1 and 5.2 illustrate how a clearinghouse provides a structural hedge for a member.

Figure 5.1 depicts the operation of the trading in the absence of the clearinghouse. Dealer A is long 2 contracts with dealers B and F, and short 2 contracts with dealers C and E. Because the short positions exactly offset the long positions, dealer A is market neutral, that is, immune to changes in the market value of the positions. But dealer A is exposed to the credit risk of either *B and C* or *E and F* because one of these pairs will to owe money to A if there is a market move up or down. In Figure 5.2, dealer A is again market neutral, but a clearinghouse has been interposed between A and the other dealers. In this case, the clearinghouse assumes the credit risk of the counterparties: If the market moves against B and C, the clearinghouse covers the position as far as A is concerned. By serving as a hub, the clearinghouse eliminates the crisscrossing of credit exposure between every dealer and every other dealer. Since the exposure of the clearinghouse to each dealer is net of that dealer's long and short positions in an instrument, the existence of the clearinghouse enlarges the liquidity of the market—enabling dealers to execute trades in greater number and dollar volume. Since the clearinghouse monitors the credit of each dealer, the dealers themselves no longer need to monitor one another. This is a more efficient arrangement. The telephone ex-

Figure 5.1   Exposure without a Clearinghouse

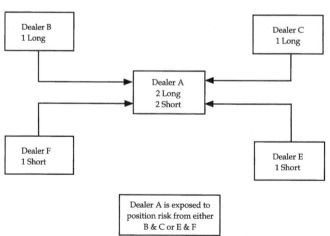

Figure 5.2 Exposure with the Clearinghouse

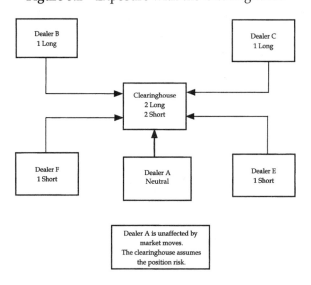

change serves the same function for facilitating communications among people. Instead of connecting every phone to every other phone with individual lines, all lines are connected to the hub, and the connection between phones is made when needed.

NETTING, COLLATERAL, AND DOWNGRADE TRIGGERS

Netting—the practice of setting off payments in one direction against those in the opposite direction—is the primary risk management technique of a clearinghouse or exchange. Netting enables market participants to get an accurate view of their exposure to other players. In reality, the flows between particular institutions are not even. Most players are comfortable accepting each others' credit up to a certain point, but beyond this limit, they want some form of reassurance before they will engage in further business.

Reassurance typically comes in the form of collateral. If dealer A is uncomfortable when its exposure to dealer B exceeds a given threshold, dealer A may ask dealer B to post collateral as a condition for continuing to trade together. Under some circumstances, dealer B's collateral will remain at dealer A on a permanent basis. Dealer B may also insist on collateral from dealer A.

The collateral requirement creates a kind of handicapping system that effectively sets limits for trading. Clearinghouses and exchanges provide the recordkeeping needed to track and mitigate counterparty risk through collateralization.

Since the value of derivatives may be highly volatile, time is a critical aspect of counterparty risk. Exchanges and clearinghouses require participants to mark their portfolios to market, using the market price at the close of the business day to determine the value of each instrument they hold. In this way, margins and collateral can be adjusted on a daily basis. Knowing the value of an instrument on any given day focuses both buyer and seller on their responsibilities to one another. In addition, exchanges have membership requirements including surety bonds, credit surveillance, and monitoring of members.

Clearinghouses also invest in processing systems to assure high reliability, develop procedures to deal with default by a member and with market emergencies, and establish financial resources to withstand stresses from major disruptive events. They maintain relationships with regulatory bodies and may arrange for government support in times of financial distress. They create systemic linkages with other clearinghouses to manage the risk exposures connected with them. Should their resources be depleted as a result of losses sustained, some clearinghouses have the power to impose an assessment on their members (Moody's 1995).

Time can affect a counterparty's creditworthiness. That is why structural hedgers make use of downgrade triggers. A contract between dealers typically specifies that if the credit of one party is downgraded beyond a certain point, that party must post collateral in order to continue trading. This assures other players that money will be available to satisfy the downgraded company's obligations.

The combination of these structural hedges—netting, margins, collateralization, marking to market, and downgrade triggers—has proved highly effective. The record here has been outstanding: Derivative dealers have lost very little money because of their exposure to credit risk. Even where many small players are involved, clearinghouses and exchanges have seen very few losses attributable to credit risk.

It is therefore likely that structural hedging techniques will ultimately be applied to other areas of credit risk management. Clearinghouses, for example, have been proposed for trading in several kinds of derivatives.

LIMITATIONS OF STRUCTURAL HUBS

There are, however, significant limitations on the application of structural hedging techniques. To begin with, they require the existence of a market sufficiently large and liquid that the value of items in every player's portfolio can be marked to market. Prices are posted daily for corn and silver, for example, but not for corporate loans. Banks, in fact, generally resist proposals to mark their loans to market because doing so may publicize the fact that a great many of these loans are under water. Their reluctance makes it very difficult to implement structural hedges in traditional credit areas. The difficulties are compounded by other factors: first, it is hard to get a fair value for these assets; second, the effect of the market value of funding of the assets has to be taken into account; and lastly, unlike the issuer of a bond, a bank customer is likely to be reluctant to have its loan arrangements made public or placed in other transactions.

In addition, netting is meaningful only where there is two-way flow between parties. In the loan market, where the bank is always the lender, netting may be relevant only to the limited extent where there is a right of offset. Some degree of netting might become possible where a company has money on deposit at the same bank from which it has taken a loan. However, the situation is inherently more complicated than that between two derivatives dealers settling trades with one another.

Structural hubs are inflexible systems that work best for standardized products that are traded in volume. For some less common types of derivatives, for example, these techniques may turn out to be more trouble than they are worth. In addition, transparency is critical to the establishment of clearinghouses or exchanges: Every aspect of a transaction must be perfectly visible to regulators and other players. Transparency quickly leads to commodity-like pricing.

Organizations that have financial strength tend to resist joining a clearinghouse unless there are operational, economic, or competitive reasons for doing so. If a triple-A player is required to post collateral, for example, it loses one of its advantages as a counterparty. Strong players will not readily participate in an arrangement if they believe it helps only the weak. In periods when financial institutions are generally under stress, clearinghouses inspire greater interest. At times when financial institutions are in relatively good health, interest in clearinghouses declines.[3]

Nonetheless, there is growing recognition that risk concentrations are a serious issue for financial institutions. As the banking industry consolidates, interbank risk is on the rise. Prior to 1996, for example, Citibank had two separate credit lines for Chemical Bank and Chase Manhattan. Now that these two banks have merged, Citibank has a single line and a greater concentration of risk. As a result of the merger, credit risk may have been reduced, but the increased concentration creates the potential for greater loss severity. Likewise, derivative dealers are increasingly aware that they have enormous exposures to one another. Structural methods are the ideal ways to mitigate these risks.

Clearinghouses and exchanges are complex organizations that cannot be developed overnight. It is only when concerns about credit risk exceed a fairly high threshold that the establishment of such an institution becomes feasible. However, once an exchange has been created, it is comparatively easy to add new products and new types of players. That is why a number of futures exchanges have expanded in recent years.

Structural hubs are powerful techniques with a proven record of success. In all probability, the coming years will see them applied to many areas where they have never been used before. As Merton (1992) notes, structural hubs are the key element in the construction of special purpose, risk-management structures out of general-purpose components.

---

[3]Some organizations have set up bankruptcy-remote SPDVs (special purpose derivative vehicles) to gain the AAA rating that is desired by major financial institutions as minimum for entering into derivatives transactions in the over-the-counter market. These are well-capitalized, stand-alone entities that ring-fence the transactions and are protected from their parent's bankruptcy. Please refer to Chapter 20 for more details.

REFERENCES

IMF (International Monetary Fund). 1997. *International Capital Markets: Developments, Prospects, Key Policy Issues.* Washington, D.C.: International Monetary Fund.

Merton, R. C. 1992. Financial Innovation and Economic Performance. *Journal of Applied Corporate Finance* 4 (1): 12–22.

Moody's Investors Service. 1995. *Credit Risks of Clearinghouses at Futures and Options Exchanges.* New York: Moody's Investors Service.

Teweles, R. J., and F. K. Jones. 1987. *The Futures Game.* 2d ed. New York: McGraw Hill Book Co.

U.S. House. 1996. Committee on Banking and Financial Services. *Hearings on Committee on Banking and Financial Services.* 104th Cong., 13 March.

Chapter 6

The Rating Agencies

All that glitters is not Gold
Often have you heard that told.

—Shakespeare, *The Merchant of Venice*

Rating agencies specialize in evaluating the creditworthiness of corporate, municipal, and sovereign issuers of debt securities. It is their job to inform investors about the likelihood that they will receive all principal and interest payments as scheduled for a given security. What, in other words, is the probability of default? And if default should occur, what level of recovery can be expected?

In some markets—the United States for example— the capital markets have replaced banks as the primary source of debt capital, and rating agencies have assumed enormous importance in the management of credit risk. Prospectuses for fixed-income mutual funds, for example, invariably express the credit quality of a portfolio in rating agency terms, and many investors pay careful attention to this information. Many corporations rely on the rating agencies to establish their creditworthiness as borrowers or guarantors in the financial markets. Although used primarily by investors, bond ratings have also been incorporated into state and federal regulations as a means of ensuring that banks, insurance companies, and pension funds will maintain fixed-income portfolios of sufficient credit quality. The primary regulatory uses of rating agency information are summarized in Table 6.1.[1]

AGENCIES AROUND THE WORLD

The four major U.S. rating agencies are Moody's Investors Service, Standard & Poor's (S&P), Fitch IBCA, and Duff and Phelps Credit Rating Co. Moody's is a subsidiary of Dun and Bradstreet, a commercial credit-rating agency, and Standard & Poor's is a division of the publisher McGraw-Hill. Fitch IBCA and Duff and Phelps, which are smaller rating agencies, are independent companies. There are, in addition, several American agencies that focus ex-

---

[1] This table is based on information from Baron and Murch (1993).

Table 6.1   Uses of Ratings by the Regulators

Securities laws	The rating from an NRSRO (nationally recognized statistical rating organization) may be included in the registration without obtaining the NRSRO's written consent.
	Disclosure burdens are minimized by using abbreviated forms and incorporation of information by reference for rated securities.
	Mortgage securities receiving one of the two highest ratings are treated as U.S. government securities for purposes of state blue-sky laws unless the state acts to override this.
	Calculation of broker-dealers' net capital requirements are based on the ratings of the securities held.
	Exemption from certain reporting requirements on rated securities transactions.
	Permission to trade future contracts on non-U.S. sovereign governments.
	Purchases of investment grade municipal securities during underwriting.
	Eligibility for investment by taxable money market funds, including aggregate risk limits, single risk limits, and downgrades linked to bond ratings of NRSROs.
	Exemption from registration and regulation of certain mortgage- and asset-backed securities of investment grade.
	Permission for a company to acquire securities of persons deriving more than 15 percent of the gross revenue for securities-related activities.
Savings associations	Eligibility for investment in any of the 4 highest rating categories.
	The 4 highest rating categories qualify as liquid assets.
	Additional capacity to lend to highly rated borrowers.
	Favorable risk weighting for capital requirements.
FDIC	Eligibility for investment by FDIC-insured banks.
	Capital calculations of state-chartered banks.
	Eligibility and valuation of assets to be pledged by foreign banks whose deposits are insured by FDIC.
OCC and the Fed	Investment eligibility of assets and valuation for capital determination, and margining requirements are based on agency ratings.
NAIC	Valuation of securities held for investment purposes for reserve requirements and for capital adequacy.
DOL	Eligibility for pension fund investments.
States	Eligibility for investment by state-regulated entities such as insurance companies, public retirement funds, state chartered banks, and thrift institutions.
Other	Self-regulatory organizations such as NYSE, PHLX, and NASD set margin requirements based on the type of security pledged to secure a loan.

clusively on financial institutions and a number of agencies based in Canada, Great Britain, and Japan. Since credit ratings are gaining importance in markets outside the United States, Moody's, Standard & Poor's, Fitch IBCA, and Duff and Phelps have all established operations or joint ventures abroad, where U.S. rating agencies are viewed as highly credible. In this chapter, we concentrate on Moody's and Standard & Poor's, the largest of the agencies. Table 6.2 shows some of the major rating agencies in existence today.

In the United States, bond rating agencies evolved from firms that evaluated the creditworthiness of merchants. Robert Dun and John Bradstreet were among the nineteenth-century pioneers in this business, and their companies would ultimately merge in 1933 to form Dun and Bradstreet. In the first decade of this century, John Moody extended the credit-rating concept to securities—focusing first on railroad bonds and, soon after, on utility and industrial bonds. Today, the agencies rate asset-backed securities, preferred stock, commercial paper, medium-term notes, municipal bonds, and govern-

Table 6.2 Selected Ratings Agencies around the World

Agency name	Year founded	Market orientation	Short-term rating symbols	Long-term rating symbols
Australian Ratings (S&P)	1981	Local	A.1+ to C.1	AAA to C
Canadian Bond Rating Service (CBRS)	1972	Local	A-1 to A-4	A++ to D
Dominion Bond Rating Service (DBRS)	1976	Local	R-1 to U	AAA to C
Agence d'Evaluation Financiere (S&P)	1986	Local	T-1 to T-4	AAA to D
Credit Rating Services of India Ltd.	1988	Local	P-1 to P-5	AAA to D
Japan Bond Research Institute	1979	Local	—	—
Japan Credit Rating Agency	1985	Local	J-1 to J-5	Aaa to D
Mikuni & Co	1975	Local	N/A	AAA to D
Nippon Investors Service	1985	Local	A-1 to D	AAA to D
Korean Investors Service	1985	Local	A1 to D	AAA to D
International Bank Credit Analysis (UK)	1979	Banks	—	A to E
Duff & Phelps	1932	Local	Duff-1+ to Duff-3	1 to 17
Fitch IBCA	1913	Global	F-1 to F-4	AAA to D
Moody's Investors Service	1909	Global	P-1 to P-3	Aaa to C
Standard & Poor's	1922	Global	A-1+ to D	AAA to D

Source: Moody's Investors Service (1995b), p. 62.

ment bonds, as well as corporate bonds. They also rate counterparty risk, the claims-paying ability of insurance companies, the price volatility of mutual funds, and other kinds of risk in the financial markets.

GROWTH IN ISSUERS RATED

The growing importance of the rating agencies is reflected in the rapid increase in the number of ratings that they issue. In 1997, for example, Moody's rated a total of 3841 issuers—substantially above the 2593 rated in 1990 and 912 in 1960 (see Figure 6.1).

In rating long-term debt, each agency uses a system of letter grades that locate an issuer or issue on a spectrum of credit quality from the very highest (triple-A) to the very lowest (D), as seen in Table 6.3. Standard & Poor's describes AAA rated debt with the words, "Capacity to pay interest and repay principal is extremely strong." By contrast, an obligation rated 'D' is in payment default. The 'D' rating category is used when payments on an obligation are not made on the date due even if the applicable grace period has not expired, unless Standard & Poor's believes that such payments will be made during such grace period. The 'D' rating also will be used upon the filing of a bankruptcy petition or the taking of a similar action if payments on an obligation are jeopardized (Standard & Poor's 1997a, 8).

The lower the grade, the greater the risk that interest and principal payments will not be made. All debt rated Baa3 or BBB- and above is considered to be of investment-grade quality, while issues rated Ba1 or BB + and below are viewed as speculative or noninvestment grade. The rating agencies apply separate grading systems to commercial paper.

Figure 6.1   Issuers Rated by Moody's, 1920–1997

Source: Moody's Investors Service (1997a). Reprinted with permission.

Table 6.3 Long-Term Senior Debt Rating Symbols

Investment grade ratings			Speculative grade ratings		
S&P and others	Moody's	Interpretation	S&P and others	Moody's	Interpretation
AAA	Aaa	Highest quality; Extremely strong	BB+	Ba1	Likely to fulfill obligations; ongoing uncertainty
			BB	Ba2	
			BB−	Ba3	
AA+	Aa1	High quality	B+	B1	High risk obligations
AA	Aa2		B	B2	
AA−	Aa3		B−	B3	
A+	A1	Strong payment capacity	CCC+	Caa1	Current vulnerability to default
A	A2		CCC	Caa2	
A−	A3		CCC−	Caa3	
			CC		
BBB+	Baa1	Adequate payment capacity	C	Ca	In bankruptcy or default, or other marked shortcoming
BBB	Baa2		D		
BBB−	Baa3				

Notes: The other agencies listed in Table 6.2 use the rating symbols of the first column, with the exception of DBRS (H and L symbols in place of + and −) and CBRS (H and L symbols in place of + and −, and + symbols that correspond to second and third letters). The agencies follow a variety of policies with respect to the number of ratings symbols given below B−.

Source: Cantor and Packer (1994); updated by the authors to include new grades introduced in 1997.

Since the credit quality of a company, municipality, or sovereign government may change dramatically over time, ratings are subject to revision. Unlike banks and insurance companies, rating agencies update and publish their credit outlook on a continuing basis.[2] To do so, they maintain contact with issuers they have rated and review not only their earnings releases but also a host of other relevant financial and economic data. When there is an important development whose rating impact has not yet been determined, an agency notifies both the issuer and the market of this fact—Standard & Poor's by placing the issuer on its *Credit Watch,* and Moody's on its *Rating Review List.*

Although their primary commitment is to serving the investment community, the rating agencies are, in fact, paid primarily by issuers. Prior to 1970, the agencies provided their ratings free of charge and then sold their analytic publications to investors. Absence of fees from issuers gave the rating agency independence in rating them. Earnings from investor subscriptions, however, were insufficient to support the agencies' operations. During the recession of 1970, investor confidence was seriously shaken by Penn Central's default on $82 million of commercial paper obligations. In the aftermath of this debacle, issuers needed to reassure investors that they were sound credits. Ratings were an effective way to do so. In this environment, the agencies were able to institute charges for their ratings because by then they had a large institutional following.

According to a study recently published by the Federal Reserve Bank of New York, this payment arrangement has not, for the most part, eroded the agencies' credibility:

> While the current payment structure may appear to encourage agencies to assign higher rating to satisfy issuers, the agencies have an overriding incentive to maintain a reputation for high-quality, accurate ratings. If investors were to lose confidence in an agency's ratings, issuers would no longer believe they could lower their funding costs by obtaining its ratings. As one industry observer has put it, "every time a rating is assigned, the agency's name, integrity, and credibility are on the line and subject to inspection by the whole investment community" . . . Over the years, the discipline provided by reputational considerations appears to have been effective, with no major scandals in the ratings industry of which we are aware. (Cantor and Packer 1994, 4)

Although they are paid for their services, the rating agencies generally behave more like academic research centers than like businesses. Analysts, for example, never discuss the price of a rating. They are engaged in pure analysis, and they do not even have to concern themselves with a budget. Their position is far from that of a bank account officer, who is part of a profit center and who is always constrained by a budget.

Policies vary from agency to agency regarding which securities they will rate. Both Standard & Poor's and Moody's, for example, rate nearly every taxable security in the U.S. market that has been registered with the Securities and Exchange Commission (SEC)—whether or not the issuer has requested a rating. Frequently, Moody's also rates structured securities and foreign

---

[2]It is rare for the agencies to monitor ratings of private placements.

bonds on an unsolicited basis. Standard & Poor's does not. There are circumstances under which Standard & Poor's will provide an unsolicited rating, but only if it believes that there is sufficient quantity and quality of information on which to base a rating decision. Ratings issued by Standard & Poor's based on public information are identified by a "pi" suffix to the rating, for example, BBBpi. Fitch IBCA and Duff and Phelps do not issue unsolicited ratings. In making an unsolicited rating, of course, an agency may not meet directly with the issuer's management and may conduct its analysis on the basis of information, both private and public, from sources other than the issuer; however, the agency does inform the issuer of the impending opinion and gives it an opportunity to participate in the rating process. In this situation, according to Moody's, the management of an issuer frequently does meet with the agency, but still may not be satisfied with the rating that is ultimately assigned.

> Moody's and Standard and Poor's usually receive fees for ratings they would have issued anyway because companies want the opportunity provided by the formal rating process to put their best case before the agencies. Moody's unsolicited ratings of issuers of structured securities and foreign bonds are more controversial because such assessments are not part of an overall policy to rate all such securities. Unsolicited ratings in these areas are often substantially lower than the solicited ratings and can affect the yield paid at issuance. Proponents claim that unsolicited ratings provide a powerful check against rating shopping, the practice of hiring only those agencies that offer favorable ratings. Critics complain that unsolicited ratings are based on incomplete information, because communication with the issuer is limited. Although an agency assigning unsolicited ratings may appear to have an incentive to be unduly conservative so as to reward those firms that pay for its ratings, this incentive may be offset by the need to maintain a reputation for analytical credibility. (Cantor and Packer 1994, 5)

THE RATING PROCESS

In evaluating credits, the rating agencies use many of the same tools normally applied by equity analysts, but their approach differs in one key respect—the rating agencies have a much longer time horizon. Equity analysts approach the analysis (understandably) from the perspective of shareholders, while the rating agencies are looking out for the interests of bondholders, other creditors and/or counterparties, and, in the case of insurance companies, policyholders.

Some of the agencies have been more forthcoming than others in describing the procedures they follow in assigning or reviewing a rating. Standard & Poor's explains that in rating an industrial bond, it focuses on the following areas:

Business Risk

- Industry characteristics
- Competitive position
  (e.g.) Marketing

(e.g.) Technology

(e.g.) Efficiency

- Management

Financial Risk

- Financial characteristics
- Financial policy
- Profitability
- Capital structure
- Cash flow protection
- Financial flexibility

Of these categories, Standard & Poor's claims that industry risk—their analysis of the strength and stability of the industry(ies) in which the firm operates—probably receives the highest weight in the rating decision. Moody's personnel have also indicated that they focus on "business funda-mentals such as demand-supply characteristics, market leadership, and cost positions." According to an official at Duff and Phelps, the company's pre-sentation to their rating committee is the most important element of their rating process. At Standard & Poor's, the industry risk analysis often sets an "upper limit" on the rating attainable by any firm in that industry.

In analyzing an issuer's financial strength, Standard & Poor's computes a number of financial ratios and tracks them over time. These include mea-sures of debt coverage, leverage, and cash flow. Moody's, by contrast, has not divulged the financial factors on which it places the greatest emphasis, although it has published its general approach to the determination of rat-ings (Moody's 1995b). This has led some market participants to conclude that "S&P is statistical, but Moody's is mystical"—a viewpoint that may actually overstate the differences. While split ratings between Standard & Poor's and Moody's do occur, these agencies agree with one another in the great majority of ratings, at least at the letter grade level. Long-term default rates among issues with like grades (at least between Moody's and Standard & Poor's) are quite similar, as is evident from comparison of cumulative default rates presented in Table 15.5.

With respect to sovereign ratings issued by the agencies, Cantor and Packer (1995) found that the ratings are very similar in the high-investment-grade area but differences of opinion are greater in the below-investment-grade area. A comparison of the differences is presented in Table 6.4. While agencies need to consider only the factors affecting solvency in the case of corporates, with sovereigns they need to consider other qualitative factors such as the "the stability of political institutions, social and economic cohe-sion, and integration into the world economic system." Cantor and Packer attribute the disagreement between agencies on sovereign ratings to the dif-ferences of opinion on these subjective factors.

The internal rating process at the rating agencies is punctuated by vig-orous questioning and debate, to the point of seeming adversarial: After extensive research, an analyst recommends a rating and then must defend this recommendation before a committee and face some intensive grilling. If

Table 6.4 Comparison of Sovereign Foreign Currency Ratings and U.S. Corporate Bond Ratings

	Share of total		Rated same by Moody's and Standard & Poor's	
Broad rating categories	Sovereigns (%)	Corporates (%)	Sovereigns (%)	Corporates (%)
AA/Aa or above	44	12	67	53
Other investment grade	27	48	56	36
Below investment grade	29	40	29	41

Note: The sample consists of 48 sovereigns rated jointly by Moody's and Standard & Poor's as of June 1995, and 1,168 corporations rated jointly by Moody's and Standard & Poor's as of year-end 1993.

Source: Cantor and Packer (1995).

the recommended rating is Aa, the company will be compared to a range of other Aa rated companies both from within its industry and from without.

At both agencies, an interview with company management is an important component of the credit-rating process. At Moody's, in particular, senior managers are often questioned closely about their company's past performance and future plans. Such meetings, which may carry considerable weight in the rating process, inevitably introduce an element of subjectivity. A CEO with celebrity status may get the benefit of the doubt from a credit-rating agency, while an unknown executive may be treated with greater skepticism. A business leader who has already appeared in the past and made projections that withstood the test of time may receive a more sympathetic hearing than one who has not. This may result in some bias against new CEOs or new issuers of debt.

Despite these caveats, the rating agencies have, for the most part, performed their job extremely well. Major agencies take seriously the proposition that "all that glitters" in a borrower's view of the future is not "gold," and are parsimonious in their assignment of ratings. Both Moody's and Standard & Poor's publish historical data comparing their ratings to the occurrence of default.

RATINGS PERFORMANCE

As Figure 6.2 demonstrates for corporate bonds, default rates are, indeed, inversely related to credit ratings. From 1970–1993, the one-year default rate for Aaa bonds was zero, but it was more than 8 percent for B rated bonds. Likewise, for each of the given time horizons, the most abrupt increase in default probability occurred between Baa and Ba ratings—the dividing line between investment-grade and noninvestment-grade bonds. This distinction, in other words, makes good statistical sense.

The marketplace tends to corroborate the accuracy of the rating agencies' work. The riskier a fixed-income security, the higher the yield investors will require before they will buy it.

As Figure 6.3 shows, bond yields are, indeed, closely correlated with ratings. Although the actual yield differential between, say, triple-A and

Figure 6.2 Default Rates Based on 1970–1993 Experience

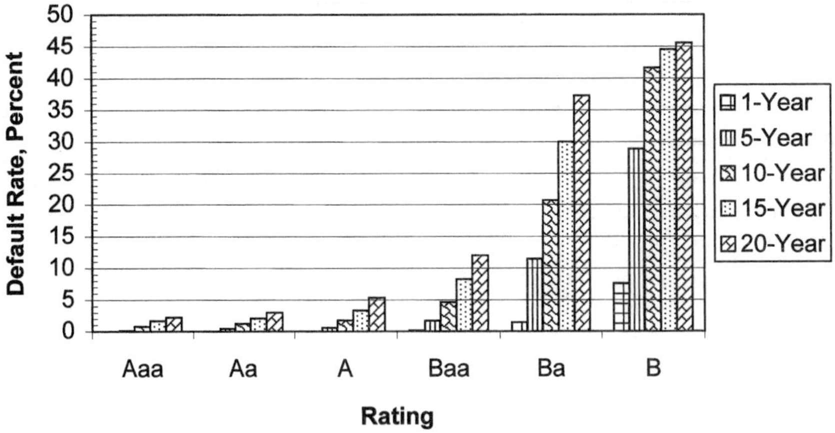

Source: Moody's Investors Service (1996a). Reprinted with permission.

double-A rated bonds may vary widely over time, the relationship remains constant: Investors consistently believe that triple-A rated bonds are more secure than double-A rated bonds.

The achievements of the rating agencies are all the more impressive given the types of credits that they evaluate. The agencies are able to state with confidence, for example, that the People's Republic of China and Pennzoil are both BBB credits, and that the United States Government and General Electric Co. are both AAA.[3] At each rating level, the risk of default is the same. Thanks to a combination of methodology, technology, and culture, the agencies succeed in giving investors a relatively reliable guide to credit risk.

This is not to say that their performance has been flawless. The agencies, for example, are more reliable in measuring relative risk than in measuring absolute credit risk. Over time, the rate of default associated with a given rating is subject to drift, as is evident from Figure 6.4.

Figure 6.4 demonstrates that default rates for noninvestment-grade credits rose substantially between 1971 and 1989, and the default rate for A-rated and Baa-rated credits rose from 1971 to 1989. In retrospect, the rise in default rates is unsurprising given the general deterioration in credit ratios within rating classes that began in the mid-1980s.

Figures 6.5 and 6.6 show that the median fixed-charge coverage and leverage ratios of industrial firms with BBB, BB, and B credit ratings from Standard & Poor's generally worsened between 1985 and 1991. These data suggest that a relaxation of credit standards may have occurred, perhaps as a result of the view commonly held in the late 1980s that even healthy corporations should increase their leverage. In sum, the experience since 1970 indicates that the correspondence of ratings to default probabilities is subject to substantial change over time (Cantor and Packer 1994, 12).

[3] As of January 1997.

Figure 6.3   Bond Yield Spreads over 30-Year Treasury Bonds

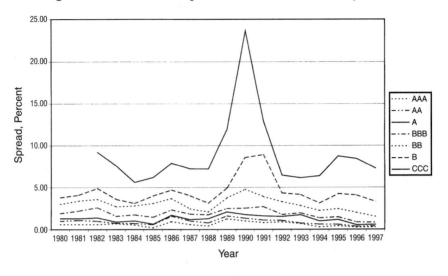

Data for Figure 6.3

Year	AAA	AA	A	BBB	BB	B	CCC
1980	0.60	1.00	1.30	1.90	3.00	3.80	
1981	0.60	1.10	1.30	2.20	3.40	4.10	
1982	0.60	1.00	1.40	2.60	3.60	4.90	9.20
1983	0.70	0.75	0.90	1.57	2.70	3.60	7.60
1984	0.55	0.73	1.04	1.75	2.80	3.10	5.60
1985	0.20	0.58	0.65	1.46	3.10	4.00	6.20
1986	0.95	1.59	1.70	2.33	3.70	4.70	7.90
1987	0.58	1.02	1.18	1.82	2.43	4.03	7.23
1988	0.42	0.79	1.29	1.75	2.07	3.12	7.22
1989	1.28	1.61	2.08	2.49	3.76	4.95	11.91
1990	1.02	1.34	1.77	2.52	4.78	8.57	23.65
1991	0.82	1.13	1.61	2.71	3.92	8.93	12.95
1992	0.90	1.08	1.54	1.77	3.29	4.34	6.46
1993	0.70	0.76	1.74	1.96	2.82	4.15	6.15
1994	0.29	0.62	1.01	1.37	2.23	3.12	6.38
1995	0.43	0.60	1.17	1.49	2.45	4.25	8.75
1996	0.25	0.35	0.54	0.88	2.00	4.08	8.43
1997*	0.28	0.39	0.57	0.83	1.53	3.30	7.29

*1997 data is of 3rd Quarter

Source: Authors' compilation.

Figure 6.4 Trends in 5-Year Default Rates by Original Credit Rating

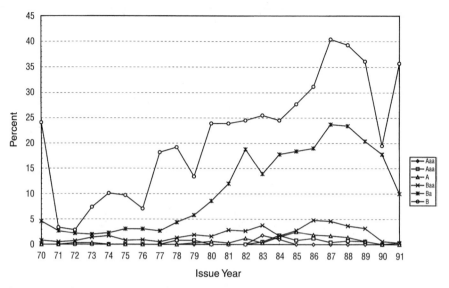

Source: Moody's Investors Service (1996a). Reprinted with permission.

Figure 6.5 Coverage Ratio: Earnings to Fixed Charges

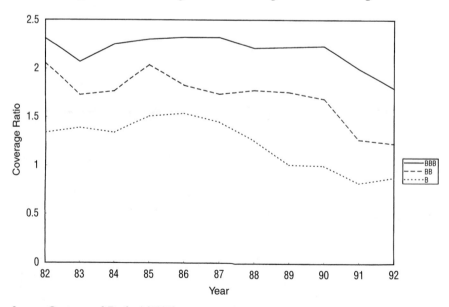

Source: Cantor and Packer (1994).

Figure 6.6   Leverage: Debt to Assets

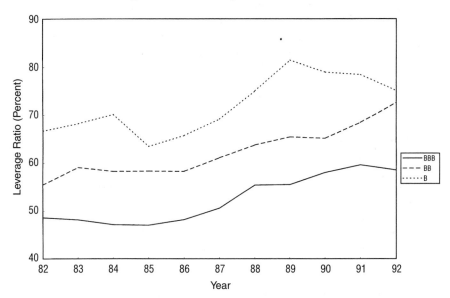

Source: Cantor and Packer (1994).

RATINGS AND REGULATORS

Regulations that make use of bond ratings are based on the assumption that a given rating has a fixed meaning that will not vary over time. Although this assumption is demonstrably false, regulators have yet to adapt to the phenomenon of rating inflation and the differences in average rating levels between rating agencies. Moody's has expressed concern that the use of ratings by the regulators is tending to change, and perhaps undermine, the objectivity of the rating process. Forced to obtain a rating because an institution may not otherwise invest in their securities, issuers pay for the rating not to establish credibility with investors but to obtain what is, in effect, a license from regulators. Thomas McGuire, executive vice president of Moody's, cites the example of the National Association of Insurance Commissioners (NAIC)'s high capital charge against noninvestment-grade bonds in describing this effect:

> To avoid that capital charge, the insurance companies want investment-grade ratings assigned to the bonds they buy, and issuers of high-yield bonds are happy to pay fees to any nationally-recognized rating agency willing to inflate their ratings to investment grade.
> By lowering its quality standards to accommodate them, the rating agency collects a fee, the investment banker who hires it collects a fee, the issuer gets to sell its debt, the insurance company is able to invest in junk bonds without inordinate capital charges—no one loses. The counter-balance to the pressures of issuer fees has been removed from the system because there is no investor discipline in the process. (Moody's 1995a, 8)

Another set of problems arises when different rating agencies disagree about a particular credit. Six rating agencies have currently been designated by the SEC as "nationally recognized statistical rating organizations," or NRSROs—the four mentioned above as well Fitch IBCA and Thomson BankWatch, which both rate financial institutions. On average, ratings from Moody's and Standard & Poor's are highly correlated with each other, but ratings from Fitch IBCA and Duff and Phelps are, on average, higher.[4] Although methodologies and standards differ from one NRSRO to the next, regulators generally do not make distinctions among the agencies: in their eyes, a BBB rating from Duff and Phelps is as good as a BBB from Standard & Poor's. Investors, however, do seem to distinguish between the two identical-sounding ratings.

State and federal regulatory bodies have woven bond ratings into their rules for various types of financial institutions. Banks and thrifts, for example, are forbidden to own any noninvestment-grade bonds in amounts issued by any one obligor held by the bank in excess of 10 percent of the bank's capital and surplus.[5] Mortgage-related securities and foreign bonds must be rated AA or above to qualify as collateral for margin lending. Under rules established by the NAIC, the lowest capital charge is assigned to bonds in an insurance company's portfolio that are rated A or better. Bonds with ratings above these various thresholds become substantially more valuable to the institutions that own them, and their yields can be correspondingly lower. As a result, an issuer can often save a great deal of money in interest costs by obtaining a higher rating.[6]

Most regulations require that a security carry just one rating by an NRSRO. Where ratings are split, some rules state that the highest or second-highest rating will be accepted. The greater the number of rating agencies, the greater the probability that a marginal borrower will be able to obtain a rating above a given threshold.

Split ratings are especially common in the noninvestment-grade or junk sector of the bond market. Standard & Poor's and Moody's disagree far more often here than they do in general, and Duff and Phelps and Fitch IBCA, on average, rank junk bonds substantially higher than do Moody's and Standard & Poor's. Frequently, issuers with borderline ratings from Standard & Poor's and Moody's are able to achieve investment grade status by obtaining a third or fourth rating from the smaller agencies.

Competition among the agencies for market share may also drive them to lower their credit standards. In the case of mortgage-backed securities

---

[4]This comment is to be interpreted carefully. Unlike S&P and Moody, Fitch IBCA and Duff & Phelps, for example, do not supply unsolicited ratings. According to Fitch IBCA, it is not uncommon for an issuer to withdraw from the rating process if it believes that it will receive a less than favorable rating. Thus the Fitch IBCA's rated population may have some self-selection resulting in an apparent surfeit of better ratings.

[5]Investment grade means a security that is rated in one of the four highest rating categories by (1) two or more NRSROs; or (2) one NRSRO if the security has been rated by only one NRSRO.

[6]While most agree that there is an economic value to obtaining a rating, there are others who disagree. See, for example, Do Bond Ratings Matter (1997). There are few studies in the academic literature examining this issue for the corporate market.

(MBS), for example, the standards applied by various agencies have fallen markedly over time.

> Clearly, MBS credit enhancement levels have declined over the history of the market. Analysts and agencies note that this in part reflects a progression along the learning curve: more information has become available over time about the performance of such securities, reducing the degree of uncertainty. Skeptics remark that competitive pressures can lead to increased pressures to review standards. (Cantor and Packer 1997, 21)

EMERGING TRENDS

The rating agencies have acquired enormous power as watchdogs of the capital markets. If they were to fail to do their job well, investors would surely be poorer for it. Clearly, strong checks and balances—in the form of sound regulatory policies—are needed to assure that the rating agencies' power is not abused.[7] Furthermore, investors need to exercise vigilance through interactions with the agencies and through the price mechanism in ensuring that the rating process is not unduly compromised by mercenary pressures. But all these caveats do not detract from the rating agencies' fundamental achievement. The agencies are committed to approaching credit risk in a systematic, disciplined, and conservative fashion, and in the great majority of cases, their ratings are accurate. In a recent instance, at least, the agencies appear to have reacted late and, having done so, may have overreacted. According to the *Economist* (Rating Agencies 1997),

> Asia's financial crises have cost investors dear. As always on such occasions, the search is on for somebody to blame. Among the leading suspects are the firms that rate the creditworthiness of bond issuers. The raters, firms such as Moody's Investor's Service, Standard & Poor's, Duffs & Phelps and IBCA, are supposed to be the financial market's early warning system. Instead, the agencies have spent the past few months belatedly reacting to events.

The *Economist* notes that the rating agencies downgraded the bonds of Korea and Thailand to below investment grade respectively only after the press had reported that Korea's central bank was nearly out of foreign currency reserves and Thailand's baht collapsed. Likewise, according to the *Economist*, ratings of Japanese financial institutions were downgraded for reasons that have been widely commented upon for months. The article goes on to analyze the reasons for this phenomenon. The first is that raters prefer to err on the side of caution because if they reacted too harshly, it would make it harder for the issuer to raise the money to resolve the problem. Another reason is that by centralizing the decision making in New York or London the raters miss the developments at the local level. Whatever the reasons may be, the important lesson for the market participants is that rat-

---

[7]This is not a call for new regulation but for active vigilance on the part of regulators using laws that are already in place. Laws against the willful manipulation of securities markets, insider trading rules, and other securities fraud, as well as slander and libel, when applied judiciously, can effectively regulate behavior.

ing agencies are not infallible, and ratings should not be relied on as the *exclusive* measure of credit risk.

The new developments in the credit market, such as structured financings and credit derivatives, are benefiting from the functions performed by the rating agencies. For example, CreditMetrics, a product released by J. P. Morgan in 1997 to measure portfolio credit risk and value, extensively uses bond-rating data provided by Moody's and Standard & Poor's. Standard & Poor's has recently announced CreditPro, a Windows 95–based software and data package providing default and ratings transition data by industry and static pool (Standard & Poors 1997b).[8] This package is useful in generating portfolio credit risk profiles based on industry, sector, and time periods that closely reflect the securities held. The rating transition and default database in CreditPro spans the period 1981–1996 for 6000+ obligors. The CD-ROM contains marginal and cumulative default rates and transition matrices. Companies are identified by the Standard & Poor's 12–industry classification. This data may be merged with other investor-maintained data used to evaluate the impact of rating transitions and cumulative defaults on an investor's portfolio.

The rating agencies have also responded to the fact that the distinction between loans and securities is being blurred. Moody's now issues ratings for loans. As of 1997, it had rated 891 facilities of 494 companies with an aggregate value of over $200 billion—more than double the $90 billion in loans it had rated by the beginning of 1996 (Moody's 1996b, 1997b). Standard & Poor's had ratings on 620 companies, with an aggregate value of $368 billion.

REFERENCES

Baron, N. D., and L. W. Murch. 1993. Statutory and Regulatory Uses of Ratings in the United States and Other Jurisdictions. Fitch Investors Service, January. Mimeographed.

Cantor, R. and F. Packer. 1994. The Credit Rating Industry. *Federal Reserve Bank of New York Quarterly Review* 19 (2).

———. 1995. Sovereign Credit Ratings. *Current Issues in Economics and Finance, Federal Reserve Bank of New York 1 (3)*.

Do Bond Ratings Matter to High Yield Buyers? 1997. *Investment Dealer's Digest* 16 April.

Moody's Investors Service. 1995a. *Ratings in Regulation: A Petition to the Gorillas*. New York: Moody's Investors Service.

———. 1995b. *Global Credit Analysis*. London: IFR Publications.

———. 1996a. *Corporate Default Rates, 1970–1995*. New York: Moody's Investors Service.

———. 1996b. *Bank Loan Ratings: Pricing Implications*. New York: Moody's Investors Service.

---

[8]The term *static pool* refers to the population of all bonds outstanding at a point in time, regardless of original issue date. The other approach is to track issued by the period of issue. This is known as the cohort analysis method and is used by Moody's, Altman, and others. Please see Chapters 15 and 16.

———. 1997a. *Moody's Rating Migration and Credit Quality Correlation, 1920–1996.* New York: Moody's Investors Service.

———. 1997b. *Bank Loan Ratings Update: Two Years and $200 Billion Strong.* New York: Moody's Investors Service.

Rating Agencies: Risks beyond Measure. 1997. *Economist,* 13 December, 68–69.

Standard & Poor's Corporation. 1997a. *Standard & Poor's Corporate Ratings Criteria.* New York: Standard & Poor's.

———. 1997b. CreditPro. New York: Standard & Poor's.

ADDITIONAL READING

Cantor, R., and F. Packer. 1996. Discretion in the Use of Ratings: The Case of NAIC. *Journal of Insurance Regulation* Winter.

———. 1997. Differences of Opinion in the Credit Rating Industry. *Journal of Banking and Finance,* 21 (10).

Chapter 7

Classic Credit Analysis

From a drop of water a logician could infer the possibility of an Atlantic or a Niagara without having seen or heard of one or the other. So all life is a great chain, the nature of which is known whenever we are shown a single link of it. Like all other arts, the Science of Deduction and Analysis is one which can only be acquired by long and patient study; nor is life long enough to allow any mortal to attain the highest perfection in it.

—Sir Arthur Conan Doyle, *A Study in Scarlet*

The taking of credit risk is a fundamental function of banks. It is the willingness of banks to take credit risk that laid the foundations of the companies that have become the great engines of American industry today. Even though banks have recently lost market share to other institutions and instruments in meeting borrowers' credit needs, they continue to play a primary role in the evaluation of corporate credit risk. Banks are also the only institutions to have developed a formal approach to lending money. Classic credit analysis, a system carefully nurtured by banks over many years and at great expense, provides a model that nonbank financial institutions continue to emulate. To this day, money managers and insurance companies that lack core credit skills turn to bankers to supply the missing expertise. This chapter describes the salient features of the classic credit analysis methodology. Valuable as it is, we argue that this system has two flaws: it is expensive and it can be myopic.

CREDIT ANALYSIS AS AN EXPERT SYSTEM

"Credit decisions are the reflection of personal judgment about a borrower's ability to repay," according to Roger Hale's *Credit Analysis: A Complete Guide* (1983, vii). Classic credit analysis is an expert system that relies, above all, on the subjective judgment of trained professionals. Individuals are turned into credit experts over the course of their careers, gaining additional authority as they acquire experience and demonstrate skill. Within the hierarchical structure of a bank, the more senior an officer, the greater his or her decision-making power. Like umpires in baseball, credit officers are authorized to call them as they see them. "It is your decision, and you must feel comfortable with it according to your own judgment," Hale stresses. "Credit decisions are personal. They can not be made solely on the basis of guidelines or analytic techniques. Each lending officer must exercise common sense and good judgment" (1983, 215).

In this system, the experience of the senior lender is valuable for several reasons:

- The senior lender is in tune with the boundaries of what is possible and what is not in the institution's tradition. Every senior credit officer is a veritable repository of war stories that often shape the character of the credit culture. Culture influences behavior: Junior lenders take their cues from the seniors.

- The senior lender is a source of rules of thumb. Although these are rarely published, they are generally—but not always—reliable. A credit analyst must apply a rule of thumb to set the parameters of a transaction. In valuing a borrower's inventory, for example, obsolescence, ease of handling, perishability, quality level, and inventory turn are among the variables that must be considered. After analyzing all these factors, the credit analyst must ultimately place a value from 0 to 100 percent on the book value of the inventory. In this situation, there is no substitute for the experience-based perspective of a senior lending officer.

- Banks rely on their senior lending officers to zero in on the most important issues—whether they are interpreting industry trends, assessing a borrower's financial condition and direction, or designing the credit structure (e.g., pricing and covenants) under which the bank will make the loan.

SHIFTING EMPHASIS FROM THE BALANCE SHEET TO CASH FLOW

Classic credit analysis evolved in response to fundamental changes in the banking business. Historically, the primary mission of a bank was to finance working capital and trade, and bankers generally made loans that were secured by assets or other forms of acceptable collateral. Working capital loans, for example, were typically made against the borrower's inventories and receivables. The pledge of these assets in no small way protected the bank from possible loss if the company were to run into financial difficulty. Deciding whether or not to make a secured loan was largely a matter of deciding whether the proposed collateral was sufficiently valuable.

In addition, banks traditionally made loans with a term of one year or less—typically to enable their commercial customers to meet their seasonal needs. Bankers focused on a borrower's working capital, trying to determine whether there would be sufficient assets to repay the loan if the business had to be liquidated. Balance sheets were carefully reviewed, but income statements were largely ignored.

In the last 50 years, however, banks have moved beyond financing working capital to financing their customers' fixed assets. This shift made collateralization virtually irrelevant to the credit process. No liquid market exists for collateral such as hospital supplies, automotive parts, or chattel mortgages on farm machinery. If a borrower were to fail, the bank could not readily realize much value for such assets. In addition, starting in the 1950s, banks began to meet their customers' need for longer-term loans.

Since debt must be repaid in cash, bankers gradually recognized that they needed to focus, above all, on a borrower's cash flow.[1] Cash flow from operations defines the company's liquidity, that is, whether it is able to generate sufficient cash from internal operations to service its debt. Cash flow lending replaced secured lending as the principal activity of a commercial bank. At the end of the day, the value of a firm and its creditworthiness were estimated from the amount of cash that it generated in its businesses.

Of course, future cash flows cannot be predicted with absolute certainty. The greater a bank's confidence about a company's future cash flow, the more it is willing to lend against it. Part of a credit officer's job is to make judgments about the relative risks to a company's cash flow posed by unforeseen events in such areas as production, marketing, personnel, finance, and government action.

CREDIT ANALYSIS—GOD IS IN THE DETAILS

Analyzing a credit is a structured and labor-intensive process that includes the following steps:

1. A banker begins by finding out why the company needs the loan. Using his/her preliminary knowledge of the company, the banker will test this need against the bank's current policy and appetite. If there is a tacit green signal from a senior lending officer, a credit analyst will proceed to the next steps.

2. The company's balance sheet and profit and loss statements are analyzed to highlight period-to-period trends and any volatility in its business. A company's business segment level operating results, budgets, and business plans are also helpful in gaining a perspective on its profit dynamics. A banker also needs a clear understanding of how the company adds value in deriving its profits. This includes having a knowledge of the real processes that underlie the financial statements.

3. The trial balance is analyzed.[2] The trial balance of the company is useful in establishing the integrity of the financial statements, the supporting schedules, and the footnoted items.

---

[1] "Cash flow analysis is a powerful tool. It is powerful because it almost unfailingly succeeds in exposing the key mechanism by which a company lives or dies. Cash flows cannot be manipulated by accounting convention and there is virtually no way in which a company can hide significant flows from an analyst who knows how to use cash flow analysis skillfully, except by outright fraud. Cash flow analysis is for these reasons not much liked by companies or their accountants and there is considerable hostility to it in most published work on corporate finance" (Boyadjian and Warren 1987, 158).

[2] The trial balance is the basic source for compiling the financial statements. It is difficult to hide unusual financial transactions as easily from a trial balance as from a condensed balance sheet

4. Accounts are adjusted to bring them into the standard format used by the bank in trending and projections (spreading). Accounting principles are analyzed to state the numbers in a consistent fashion.

5. The purpose of the loan is evaluated relative to the projected cash flows. Lenders look for a first way out and a second way out.[3]

6. Hard and soft assumptions are identified and stress-tested.

7. The industry's structure is analyzed—in particular, emerging trends, the company's position within the industry, and the potential impact of regulatory actions.

8. The company's executive management and operating strategy are evaluated. The managers responsible for its production, inventory, pricing, and distribution functions are also evaluated.

9. Loan and security documentation is prepared, covering such issues as conditions for draw; restrictions on debts, liens, and investments; financial ratios and covenants; parent/subsidiary guarantees; and conditions for default.

A flow diagram of the entire process is presented in Figure 7.1.

One universal assumption in the traditional credit process is that the credit officer should examine the evidence as if he or she were a detective, questioning the information the borrower has supplied, looking for possible weaknesses or inaccuracies in the story, and trying to anticipate problems that might occur in the future.[4] Sherlock Holmes would have made a good lending officer.

In reaching their subjective judgments, credit officers are assisted by a number of standard analytic techniques for evaluating the likelihood that a company or individual will meet a given debt obligation. The classic three Cs of credit—character, capacity, and capital—were and are the three legs of the credit tripod. The analytic techniques themselves have evolved over time, but they continue to focus on the characteristics of the borrower.

FINANCIAL RATIOS—YOU CAN NEVER HAVE TOO MANY

Account officers are trained in the details of cash flow analysis—a process that relies heavily on financial ratios and comparative analysis of similar companies. Table 7.1 is a sampling of the ratios typically generated by the computer program used to spread a company's financial statements.

---

and income statement. It also provides a way to check the integrity of the most recent financial statements.

[3] George Scott, of the First National City Bank (now Citicorp) expressed these concepts in a more direct way: "I have been up and down this business, and there is still no substitute for 'What do you want the loan for? How are you going to pay it back? And what are you going to do to pay me back if your theory doesn't work?' " (Quoted in Mayer [1974], 240)

[4] "After ascertaining what physical asset a particular item represents, the loan officer must go beyond the dollar value to determine the actual value of the asset. . . . This process often leads to a maze of fascinating but quite relevant by-paths as a particular asset may actually be worth more or less than the balance sheet value." (Prochnow and Foulke [1963], Chapter 6).

Figure 7.1   Credit Analysis Process Flow

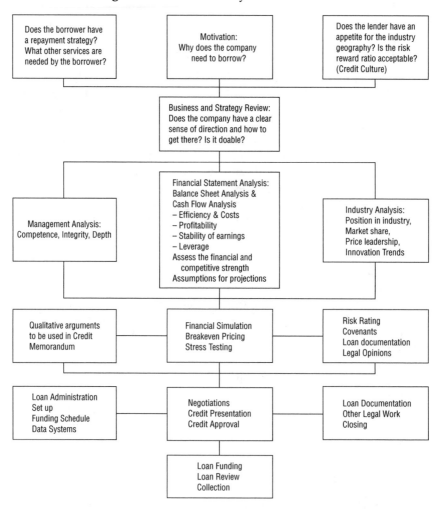

Each ratio imparts information in an absolute and comparative sense. A company's return on equity, for example, is a ratio that provides evidence about its profitability; its debt service coverage ratio is a measure of its capacity to carry its leverage; its ratio of working capital to current assets is a clue to its liquidity. The ratios in Table 7.1 are merely a small subset of the ratios actually produced. There are, in addition, ratios and statistics that are unique to specific industries. In analyzing a utility, for example, the ratio of purchased power to revenues is of interest; in the case of an airline, the passenger load factor is a key ratio. Bankers have evolved their own jargon for speaking about these ratios. They talk about EBITDA (Earnings before taxes, interest, depreciation, and amortization) and cash flow coverages as enthusiastically as baseball fans discuss their favorite player's batting aver-

Table 7.1   Commonly Used Financial Ratios

Category	Ratio
Operating performance	EBITDA/sales Net income/sales Effective tax rate Net income/net worth Net income/total assets Sales/fixed assets
Debt service coverage	EBITDA/interest Free cash flow − capital expenditure/interest Free cash flow − capital expenditure − dividends/interest
Financial leverage	Long-term debt/capitalization Long-term debt/tangible net worth Total liabilities/tangible net worth (Total liabilities − long-term capital)/(long-term capital) Long-term capital = total net worth + preferred + subordinated debt Current liabilities/tangible net worth
Liquidity	Current ratio Quick ratio Inventory to net sales Inventory to net working capital Current debt to inventory Raw material, work in process and finished goods as percentages of total inventory
Receivables	Aging of receivables: 30, 60, 90, 90+ days Average collection period

age. Everybody knows that if EBITDA to interest falls below 1.5, an account is going to need special attention.

INDUSTRY ANALYSIS FOR TERM LENDING

In addition to the financial ratios, modern credit analysis also relies heavily on a subjective view of the prospects for the industry in which the company operates and of the quality of its management. Strategic analysis, as it is sometimes called, goes beyond the balance sheet and cash flow analysis of the firm. According to Joseph Rizzi:

> Strategic analysis concerns the assessment of a firm's long-term prospects within its industrial environment. The analysis is based on three premises. First,

a firm must achieve a competitive advantage to remain profitable. Second, the ways and means of achieving a competitive advantage vary by industry. Finally, as industries evolve, the ways of achieving competitive advantage change. The analysis involves three steps: environmental assessment, firm assessment and strategy evaluation. (1984, 4)

Each industry has its own unique structure and dynamics. A firm's position is affected by the relative level of maturity of its industry. A mature industry, for example, is characterized by market saturation, lack of technological opportunity, and a trend toward a competitive floor rate of return.

A firm attempting to prosper within any industry has to contend with potential entrants, existing rivals, suppliers, buyers, and substitute products. Its competitive weapons may include barriers to entry, cost control through economies of scale, control of distribution channels, favorable government policies, retaliatory pricing (actual or threatened), product differentiation, and product innovation.[5] In analyzing a company's current and evolving position, the analyst must understand how it intends to use its competitive tools in the context of its industry. He or she must then make judgments about whether this strategy will succeed, to what extent the company should be supported in its strategy, which variables should be monitored, and what the fallback position should be. These are personal decisions made by the individual banker, and he or she will be expected to articulate and defend them.

Bankers consider it very important to meet with a borrower's senior leaders in order to hear their story and evaluate them. As a general rule, the greater a bank's exposure to a given enterprise, the more senior the banker who meets with its management.

The entire credit-granting system resonates with principles and checklists and guidelines and procedures, all intended either to train the uninitiated or to make certain that the expert—the credit officer—has in fact thought through all the relevant issues. The nature of the banking business has emphasized respecting tradition, maintaining relationships, avoiding innovation,[6] and striving for consensus.

Thoughtful bankers now realize that they have to re-examine the intensity of their credit analysis process, the techniques that they employ, and the monitoring frequency. Here is Brian Ranson, senior vice president at The Bank of Montreal:

> You cannot use the same traditional credit analysis for evaluating Kellogg's and Joe's Diner. Intense analysis probably will not teach you much about the risk of a AAA company. Moreover, a AAA borrower does not pay enough to cover the cost of all this analysis. On the other hand, if you don't do it (credit analysis) with Joe's Diner, you're going to have some severe disappointments. So we need a credit process that is flexible, that we can tailor to the nature of the customer.

---

[5]The ideas on industry analysis are drawn from Porter (1975).

[6]"The leading edge can easily become the bleeding edge" (a banker quoted in Rogers [1993], p. 221).

Bankers realize that while financial statements do provide consistency in financial disclosure, they do not adequately address risk issues that are of paramount concern to their own institutions as well as to investors. Ranson recommends that, for every credit, the lender should identify five key risk factors that truly take the pulse of this particular borrower and then monitor them on a continuing basis. These factors may vary depending upon a company's type, size, and industry, but they are generally the very same factors that the company's CEO considers most crucial. In the case of a company whose product is perishable or fashion-driven, for example, excess inventory is a key measure of its financial position. In the case of a finance company, the delinquency rate (accounts 30 days past due) is a key indicator of the company's status. The fact that a banker focuses on these vital signs does not mean that the loan structure or the financial disclosures should be ad hoc (i.e., nonstandard); it does mean that a banker cannot rely exclusively on accounting statements. "The context here is uncertainty. Very few bankers make bad loans. Loans *turn* bad, and traditional credit analysis makes a hold-to-maturity assumption. Tracking risk factors is one means of ex post management and it helps focus the lender on what truly drives the obligor's business," concludes Ranson.

CREDIT ANALYSIS IS VALUABLE BUT PROBLEMATIC

Classic credit analysis has proved to have a number of serious flaws. To begin with, an expert system of this kind is extremely expensive to maintain. By definition, it requires significant redundancies. At all times, a bank must have enough experts available to handle its business volume, and it must also have a large number of people in training to become experts. Banks also tend to view one another's experts with suspicion.[7] When several banks join together on a syndication, for example, each will underwrite the credit on its own. Slapping your own bank's approval sheet on top of a competitor's write-up would be considered highly unprofessional. There are legal reasons as well for undertaking an independent analysis. The resulting redundancies and inefficiencies contribute to serious cost problems at many banks. The redundancies prevail even within the same organization: The head office will often have a parallel set of credit analysis requirements over and above what is submitted by a distant subsidiary.

Furthermore, classic credit analysis has often lulled banks into a false sense of security, failing to protect them against many of the systemic risks embedded in their business. If so many experts have been so thoroughly trained for so many years, then why have banks repeatedly encountered such severe credit problems?

The question has several answers. While some institutions have succeeded in creating very strong and effective expert systems, others have un-

---

[7] "We will make our own mistakes, thank you" (J. P. Morgan banker in an interview, November 1996).

derinvested in the training and development of their experts because they faced more pressing organizational needs. Some banks have invested significantly in the credit training only to have their trainees leave for greener pastures elsewhere.[8] Intensified competition in the banking industry has exacerbated this problem. Furthermore, many banks have found it hard to maintain their customer base and market share without increasing the level of risk in their business simply because the better-quality customers have found cheaper sources of financing.

In some cases, credit problems have resulted from poor execution. An expert system is only as good as the experts who make it up. Like any human system, it can perform in very erratic ways. Credit officers take a company's financial statements—which were prepared by an expert—and rewrite them in the format their institution prefers. Five bankers analyzing the same documents might come to five very different conclusions. Training can only go so far. If a bank hires loan officers who lack the basic talent or character required, it invites major trouble—however fine its training program may be. As Citicorp's Walter Wriston is said to have remarked, "If you have the right person in the right place, there is almost no way that you can get hurt. If you have the wrong person in that place, there is NO way you can save yourself."

The larger the institution, the larger the risk posed by this irreducible human factor. One hundred years ago, a strong person sitting in the senior credit officer's chair could probably keep tabs on every credit decision of significance to a bank. Today, a bank may have 75,000 employees[9]—many of them making credit decisions. If the enterprise has grown through acquisitions, these people may have been trained in organizations with very different standards, technology, cultures, and reward systems. Furthermore, when the credit process itself becomes extremely detailed, people may spend more energy complying with its requirements than they do actually thinking about the credit. And when an institution requires too many approvals on a loan, no single individual may take responsibility for the decision that is made. This leads to a perception that banking is a low-risk business, and because low risk is associated with lower compensation levels, until the recent years banking did not attract high-quality (high-priced) talent.

Classic credit analysis is closely associated with a heavily bureaucratic way of doing business. Because of their hierarchical structure, banks are best prepared for conventional ground warfare. In today's markets, however, guerrilla warfare is increasingly the order of the day. The financial world now rewards agility, sophistication, and flexibility.

The disjunction between traditional bank practices and financial reality is nowhere sharper than in the annual review process. Most banks continue

---

[8]"Our training program was ... equal to an outside M.B.A. Our problem has been we lose people to business schools after a few years, competing as we do with Harvard and Stanford. We put up to $50,000 into their education and then we lose them" (a banker quoted in Rogers [1993], p. 213).

[9]The estimated head count at Chase after the merger with Chemical to become the largest bank in the United States, as reported in the *New York Times*, 29 August 1995.

to rely on an annual review of each credit, basing their analysis upon the company's published financial reports. Unfortunately, these reports are often obsolete by the time they arrive at the bank. Furthermore, the reported numbers may provide little insight into the true risks that the company faces and into its probable future fate. Clearly, banks need to tailor the intensity and frequency of their credit monitoring process to the size of an exposure and its riskiness.[10] But in most institutions, tradition carries the day.

Under these circumstances, making an expert system work can be a major challenge.

PORTFOLIO CONCENTRATION IS HARD TO AVOID

Many of the recent credit losses suffered by banks have resulted from excessive portfolio concentrations in particular sectors. Classic credit analysis is based on the notion that each loan should be made against some norm. Prudent bankers have long endeavored to build strong loan portfolios by carefully extending credit to individual borrowers, each of which was expected, on its own merits, to represent an acceptable risk. Concentration risk was generally addressed by limiting the size of exposures to individual borrowers. Recently, however, this method has proved inadequate to the task of limiting credit risk. Supposedly distinct borrowers in particular sectors have experienced similar problems at the same time:

- Real estate and REITs, both in recent business cycles and in earlier ones
- Loans to developing countries in the 1980s and 1990s
- Loans to borrowers in particular industries (e.g., energy and shipping) that had explosive popularity with bankers, followed by quick reversals of their industries' fortunes

What may be termed the credit cycle exacerbates a tendency toward concentration. In any given period of time, banks may find only a few market areas attractive. On a loan-by-loan basis, these areas offer better opportunities than are available elsewhere. To take advantage of this situation, banks may rush into these areas en masse—in the process allowing their portfolios to become highly concentrated. Portfolio concentration is difficult to define. Furthermore, concentration limits are easily breached when a given transaction looks more attractive than the competing transactions available at the same time in other sectors. As a result, the problem becomes deeper. Ultimately, when the entire borrowing sector undergoes a contraction, the banks are often left with serious losses.

Portfolio concentration is also amplified by human factors. To become an expert, an individual must focus on a relatively narrow set of companies within a single industry. From this platform, it is impossible to construct a diversified loan portfolio. Inevitably the individual credit officer follows names that are highly correlated with one another. In a downturn, most

---

[10]See Boyadjian and Warren (1987) for a discussion of the pitfalls a banker faces in relying only on accounting statements.

companies in a given industry will suffer from the same fundamental problems. Foreseeing a downturn, an industry specialist really has just one alternative—to stop lending. For anyone running a profit center, this is a very difficult thing to do.

Banking mostly tends to be a local business—the community bank or a regional bank. Good marketing strategy usually favors concentrating on certain niche areas but this becomes a problem when it comes to portfolio concentration.

PORTFOLIO MANAGEMENT—NEEDED BUT SCARCE

It is conceivable, of course, that an expert system would include experts in portfolio diversification as well as in specific industries. Unfortunately, most banks have been very reluctant to embrace this concept to any large degree. This is not hard to understand. A bank's senior credit officers are homegrown experts who started off with a narrow focus. They have risen to senior positions by demonstrating their ability to concentrate on a relatively small group of companies or activities. As they advanced in their careers, their organization may have shifted them from one specialized industry group to another so that they could gain broader perspective. But perspective and portfolio theory are two different things.

To introduce portfolio management techniques, banks must accept the necessity of selling some of their loans. Until recently, proposals to sell bank assets ran into a kind of Catch 22. If the interest margins on the assets were attractive, the bank would not want to give up a high-yielding asset and possibly jeopardize its relationship with the borrower. If the margins were unattractive, the bank would be reluctant to take a current-period loss when marking the loan to market. When a bank needs to reduce a large exposure, it does not hesitate to share the revenues with other banks—as it does when it syndicates a loan. However, once it has booked the retained piece of the loan, a bank is generally very reluctant to sell it. For these reasons, it has been difficult for banks to apply portfolio theory by selling assets that are less than optimal. Because of this self-inflicted inertia, bank loans remained illiquid until external agents, including investors in bank stocks, started pressuring banks to change their ways.

Furthermore, banks rarely analyze a borrower's business outlook in a way that would lend itself to portfolio analysis. The application of such standardized quantitative terms as the percentage of borrower's income from domestic sales, the percentage from foreign sales by country, or the percentage of current assets in receivables would make it far easier to roll up data and generate a top-level evaluation of a portfolio with respect to macro variables. Such an analysis would make it possible for a lender to evaluate what risks it would face, for example, if the Thai baht were to be devalued. But few banks can readily make such an evaluation.

Portfolio theory would suggest that, to avoid concentration risk, a bank would need to adopt an approach dramatically different from classic credit analysis. Trying to pick the winners from the losers is a very difficult process. According to portfolio theory, breadth of activity—that is, diversification for its own sake—is more important than the selection of individual risks. Translated into banking terms, this might require an institution to make loans into industries in which it has no expertise, or into geographic regions where it has no office, or to people who are not its customers.

To the typical banker, each of these steps would be anathema. Instead of taking them, banks have responded to bad performance by tightening their expert systems—focusing on the customers they know well, excluding those they know less well, and closing offices and exiting from businesses that have not performed well. These are all sensible responses, but bad portfolio theory.

YOU *CAN* HAVE YOUR CAKE, BUT ONLY A SLICE OF IT

Not surprisingly, many commercial banks are beginning to embrace investment-banking activities. Instead of booking loans on their own balance sheets, they are increasingly inclined to syndicate, securitize, or otherwise sell the assets they have originated. In a contingent world, this is much more sensible than holding a loan portfolio over the long term when it contains excessive concentrations. To the extent that the buyer of a bank's loans is creating a diversified portfolio of assets, the credit system can, through this process, successfully restore itself to equilibrium.

In fact, classic credit analysis is well suited to an enterprise whose fundamental business is originating and selling assets. The expert system developed by banks is a very good one for selecting risks. However, the standards that must be applied in originating assets for a third party are actually higher than those that banks traditionally applied when they intended to retain the assets on their own balance sheet. Any bank that hopes to sell assets in volume therefore needs to establish a reputation as a good originator. Developing strong skills in classic credit analysis is one of the best ways to do so. As Federal Reserve governor Susan Phillips (1996, 131) points out:

> That banks can originate and securitize loans enables them to more fully exploit their special expertise in analyzing the creditworthiness of borrowers. Credit analysis, the intermediation function that banks have traditionally performed so well, can sometimes be difficult for the capital markets. By eliminating the need to provide the financing for all of its loans, securitization enables banks to apply their credit analysis expertise on many more loans. This can boost earnings and lower the cost of accumulating capital.

Banks are beginning to respond to this challenge. NatWest Bank, for example, successfully securitized $5 billion of its corporate loans in 1997 with the purpose of freeing up capital so that it could continue to remain in the corporate lending business. The transaction set aside capital for *expected* losses on a pound-for-pound basis and effectively shifted the risk of *unexpected* losses to the investors.[11] By foregoing some earnings in the short term and focusing on long-term benefits, NatWest established a model in which a bank becomes the originator and servicer—but only *temporarily* the inves-

---

[11]It is argued that to the extent that there may not be complete credit risk transference to the investor, these transactions do not free up capital (Moody's 1995). While this is true, risk trans-

tor—in all of its assets.[12] In recent months more banks have constructed similar programs, and it seems quite likely that this will soon become a significant market development (see Chapter 24 for a discussion of some of these deals).

The ultimate suppliers of debt capital will insist that credit analysis, whether classic or any other kind, take place *somewhere*. The key for banks is to perform this function well and to be adequately compensated for it.

Thus far, we have described the institutional settings in which credit risk is analyzed. In recent decades, innovations have altered the classic credit analysis process in two fundamental ways. With respect to transactions, the development of asset-based lending has paved the way for the emergence of structured finance and securitization. With respect to credit management, a series of advances has been made in the quantification of credit risk. Credit scoring models, internal risk-rating systems, market-value-based credit risk models, credit migration models, and portfolio models are all examples of this second type of progress.

It was long believed that credit risk management was an *art*. The new techniques have more of the look and feel of *science*. As we shall see, however, they still lack the precision and certainty that this term implies. Perhaps, at this stage of its development, credit risk management can best be described as a form of *engineering*, where models and structures are created that either prevent financial failure or provide safeguards against it.

References

Boyadjian, H. J., and J. F. Warren. 1987. *Risks: Reading Corporate Signals*. New York: John Wiley & Sons.

Hale, R. 1983. *Credit Analysis: A Complete Guide*. New York: John Wiley & Sons.

Mayer, M. 1974. *The Bankers*. New York: Weybright and Talley.

Moody's Investors Service. 1995. *Can Asset Securitization Squeeze Any Juice Out of Your Capital Structure?* New York: Moody's Investors Service.

Phillips, S. M. 1996. The Place of Securitization in the Financial System: Implications for Banking and Monetary Policy. In *A Primer on Securitization*, edited by L. T. Kendall and M. J. Fishman. Cambridge, Mass.: The MIT Press.

Porter, M. E. 1975. Note on the Structural Analysis of Industries. HBS Case Services 376–054. Boston: Harvard Business School.

Prochnow, H. V., and R. A. Foulke. 1963. *Practical Bank Credit*. New York: Harper & Row.

Rizzi, J. 1984. Strategic Analysis—The Neglected Element in the Term Credit Decision. *Journal of Commercial Lending* 66 (11).

Rogers, D. 1993. *The Future of American Banking*. New York: McGraw Hill, Inc.

Additional Reading

Basu, S. M., and H. L. Rolfes, Jr. 1995. *Strategic Credit Management*. New York: John Wiley & Sons.

---

ference in these transactions gradually does increase as investors become more familiar with the underlying assets. For example, complete credit risk transference is common in mortgage-backed securities.

[12]See Chapter 24 for more details on this transaction.

Chapter 8

Asset-Based Lending

Simply put, asset-based lending may be looked at as no more than account receivable, inventory or equipment lending but with a much more due-diligence approach on the bank's part to set up proper lending and monitoring programs depending on the collateral. Therefore, I feel such loan secured by most balance sheet assets should fall into the generic category of asset-based lending. But many lenders have broadened or strictly used the asset-based term to include a more exotic and high-risk type of loan such as those perhaps involving higher-leveraged borrowers or borrowers who may have assumed ownership of a company by way of a leveraged buyout by putting little or no equity in the deal.

—Peter S. Clarke, *Asset-Based Lending*

Lending against collateral is hardly a new phenomenon. British moneylenders introduced the concept of a mortgage in the seventeenth century to better secure debts by conveying the land in *fee simple* to the lender subject to a *subsequent condition*. A significant innovation over the *pledge,* by which the lender took possession of the land, the mortgage permitted the borrower the continued use of the asset; the fee simple was reconveyed upon the redemption of debt. Over the centuries, bankers have advanced money to farmers against the collateral of their land, livestock, and equipment; to railroads against the collateral of their rolling stock; and to oil companies against the collateral of their petroleum reserves. Indeed, bankers have long debated whether they should focus more attention on the value of a borrower's collateral or on the strength of its business enterprise as a whole.

Over the past four decades, however, the rapid spread of asset-based lending has given new life to the concept of collateral. Modern asset-based lending is founded on the notion that a company's assets (e.g., its receivables, equipment, lease revenues, or inventory) can have a substantial life of their own, independent of the company itself. The technology of asset-based lending is important in its own right, but it is also significant because of its critical contribution to the success of asset-securitization and structured finance.

Asset-based borrowing has exploded in response to fundamental shifts in the U.S. economy. Earlier in this century, a considerable number of small and midsized business enterprises could still be financed within the scope of the wealth their founders had amassed—sometimes with assistance from family and friends. Leverage was unnecessary. In today's much larger economy, however, businesses must achieve much greater critical mass in order to succeed. Firms have grown so large that their financing needs can be met only through a pooling of resources. Relatively few individuals are wealthy enough to finance an enterprise of any size entirely on their own. According to one estimate, for example, only 11.7 percent of U.S. firms with external capital needs exceeding $1 billion could be funded, without pooling, with the wealth of single U.S. families (Sirri and Tufano 1995). Today, credit is as critical to the growth of a business as water is to the growth of a garden. Many companies, however, do not qualify for unsecured loans.

Starting in the 1950s, commercial finance companies became an increasingly important source of funding for American businesses. In the early days, these companies invented the concept of warehouse financing. Before the creation of the Uniform Commercial Code (UCC) in 1952, there was no standardized way to place a lien on a company's inventory, equipment, or finished goods. Physical possession of an asset was therefore the key to controlling it. To obtain warehouse financing, a manufacturer would physically move an asset into the lender's warehouse and then receive a receipt. Once the receipt was presented to the finance company, the latter would make a loan collateralized by the asset. The establishment of the UCC made it possible to put a lien on any kind of property. As a result, warehouse financing of this kind became less necessary.[1]

The Uniform Commercial Code is a common set of regulations that were passed by Pennsylvania in 1953 and subsequently enacted by all the other states (with the exception of Louisiana). Its aim was to simplify, clarify, and modernize the law governing commercial transactions. Making the law uniform among various jurisdictions facilitated the continued expansion of commercial practices through custom, usage, and the agreement of parties. The security agreement, perfection of security interest, priorities of proceeds, and the rights of lien creditors including trustee in bankruptcy are some of the important elements of the code that are applicable to all secured commercial transactions (Henson 1979).

Despite the waning of warehouse financing, commercial finance companies continued to grow because they provided a vital service to small and midsized enterprises—especially those that were growing rapidly. These borrowers were able to finance themselves in return for a pledge of their receivables or inventory. Finance companies would determine how much the assets were worth and then lend at some loan-to-value ratio. They paid less attention to the quality of the enterprise than to the quality of the assets. Typically, these lenders focused on higher-risk customers who may have had few, if any, alternative sources of financing. They were able to charge these customers substantially more than the banks were charging.

In the 1970s and 1980s, many banks discovered that the commercial finance companies had invented an attractive business. The loans on their books performed as well as or better than the banks' own loan portfolios, and they also paid higher spreads. Many commercial banks therefore de-

---

[1]Of course, filing a lien does not give the lender as much control over the collateral as physical possession, as some companies learned at great cost.

cided to enter the asset-based lending business—either by acquiring existing players or by establishing their own organizations. Since asset-based lending was a more bare-knuckled business than the typical work of a banker, it was normally housed in a separate subsidiary rather than in the bank proper.

Competition heated up as more and more regional and money center banks were drawn to asset-based lending. As spreads began to decline, lenders were forced to improve their risk-management techniques in order to remain profitable.

MANAGING THE RISKS

Asset-based loans include additional risk considerations when compared to unsecured loans. Asset-based lending exposes a lender to at least four different types of risks. The first of these is obligor risk.

A secured loan, like an unsecured one, subjects the lender to obligor risk. As Clarke (1996, 15) notes:

> The nature of the collateral being offered does not alleviate the need for a thorough investigation of the integrity, moral character, debt-paying habits, and ability of the proposed borrower. Next to unsecured credit lending, which does not involve collateral, no other type of loan is as dependent on the honesty and integrity of the borrower. Just having an assignment of the collateral is not a substitute for the absence of any of the above factors.

The second type of risk is collateral risk. Should the firm prove unable to generate cash to repay the loan, quality collateral will be of the utmost importance. Asset-based lenders investigate whether receivables are collectible, inventory is obsolete, inventory controls are adequate, and so forth.

Collateral illiquidity is the third type of risk. If the lender must liquidate or foreclose on collateral, the necessary time and costs may detract from the ultimate returns. The longer it takes to liquidate assets, the more expensive the process is likely to become because of the increased administrative costs and the difficulties associated with consummating a distressed sale.

The fourth type of risk is legal risk. Asset-based financing requires complex documentation, public filings, strict compliance with the UCC, and certain borrower impositions. As a result, costly legal mistakes are easy to make. There are hundreds of cases in which secured lenders attempted to liquidate collateral and collect the proceeds only to be enjoined by courts of law, particularly bankruptcy courts, owing to inadequate legal documentation or mismanagement of the loan facility (Stock 1988, 17).

To manage these risks, asset-based lenders have developed a great deal of expertise in the valuation of collateral. When a loan is backed by trade receivables, for example, they must deal with the issue of dilution. Not every receivable a company books is ultimately paid. Some losses occur because the buyer is unable to pay. Dilution also occurs when the buyer is no longer required to pay because the goods have been returned or because they have spoiled. Department stores, for example, know what proportion of goods is likely to be returned at different seasons of the year. Asset-based lenders take this into account by adjusting their loan-to-value ratios. A lender who would ordinarily be willing to finance receivables at 80 cents on the dollar at most times of the year might drop down to 60 cents on the dollar in the period just after Christmas, when returns are especially high.

A company that makes cookies can anticipate a certain level of returns from supermarkets because of spoilage. This is a mature business with a long history, and asset-based lenders can readily establish an appropriate loan-to-value ratio. A company that makes cigarettes, on the other hand, would probably be accorded a higher loan-to-value ratio because cigarettes are less perishable and are sold through small distributors who are required to pay their bills promptly. Receivables are more valuable when they turn over rapidly and when the company can exercise a high level of control over them.

Because asset-based lenders normally deduct expected dilution and losses, they almost always lend at a discount to the actual amount of receivables being financed. A loan-to-value ratio of 80 to 85 percent is considered normal.

When assets are illiquid or hard to value, it is more difficult to finance against them. A company's inventory, for example, is generally more difficult to value, monitor, and liquidate than its accounts receivable, which are fungible. Automobiles or other commodity-like inventories may be relatively easy to deal with. But suppose, instead, that a company manufactures speedometers under contract to an automaker. If the company itself cannot sell its inventory, then how can a lender expect to do so? Lending against inventory requires a substantial amount of industry-specific knowledge.

Exposure on inventory is approached by gaining knowledge of the following (Iannuccilli 1988, 63–64):

- Product and industry
- Stability and perishability of the product
- Supply and demand considerations
- Obsolescence and style considerations
- Trade creditor's posture to acceptance of an inventory lien
- Priority liens
- Secret liens
- Effect of private label merchandise
- Whether the product is bought or manufactured for shelf (speculation) or against firm orders.

Lending against a company's plant and equipment likewise requires a considerable amount of additional analysis. Typically, such loans are structured as term loans based on the liquidation value the assets would have in a forced sale. An objective, professional appraisal by a reliable firm is normally a key element in the decision to lend. Methods have been developed to determine, for example, what an aircraft with a 20-year life might be worth 15 years hence. Residual value insurance companies, which specialize in making such predictions, may help to facilitate an equipment financing. In valuing receivables, by contrast, a lender simply needs to know how they develop and what dilution to anticipate.

Over time, asset-based lenders have accumulated an enormous body of knowledge about seasonal build-ups, trading and cash cycles, working capital and inventory ratios, cyclical production patterns, and the development of losses and dilution in various industries. At the same time, borrowers have learned how to organize their affairs so that they can borrow more money against their collateral. The better their record keeping and administration is, the more comfortable a banker will feel about accepting their assumptions. Lending on a revolving basis against collateral requires constant policing and monitoring of collateral by the lender: loan documentation, collateral reports, accounting, cash flow reports, warehouse reports, and UCC filings are required to control and manage the credit risk.

GROWING RESPECTABILITY

In its early days, asset-based lending was clearly regarded by the mainstream financial world as something that took place on the other side of the tracks. Asset-based borrowers were assumed to be desperate companies not terribly far from bankruptcy court, and asset-based lenders were viewed as little better than loan sharks. All this has changed. As long ago as 1982, John B. Logan, a senior vice president at Barnett Bank in Florida, asserted, "First, let's talk about what asset-based lending is *not*. It is not lending of last resort. I am sure that from time to time we have all heard that if a company has pledged its accounts receivable or inventories for loan purposes, the company must be in serious financial difficulty of some form or another and is using a last ditch effort to raise quick cash. As one who has been involved in the asset-based lending business for the last 11 years, I can assure you this is just not so" (1988, 38).

In the years since 1982, the respectability of asset-based lending has only increased. A company that finances its receivables is no longer stigmatized for doing so. As the costs of asset-based lending have come down, many financial professionals have come to view it as a perfectly acceptable financing alternative that may make good sense for their company under the right circumstances. Two decades ago, a company with a choice between secured and unsecured borrowing would invariably choose the latter because it was less expensive and less complicated. Today, the choice may not be so obvious. An asset-based financing is still more complicated, but it may in fact be cheaper than an unsecured loan. Furthermore, banks today are less interested in making unsecured loans at low spreads to companies that have other alternatives. In deciding between a secured and unsecured loan, a borrower today must make a cost/benefit judgment, and outside observers can no longer assume that a company that finances its receivables is either a first-time borrower or a fallen angel. Rather, they may conclude that such a borrower is a savvy player that knows how to make good use of its assets.

ALTERNATIVES TO ASSET-BASED LENDING

Factoring and credit insurance are two alternative approaches that are closely related to asset-based lending. Factors, which generally are finance companies or bank subsidiaries, are in the business of purchasing receivables rather than of lending against them. In essence, factoring is asset-based lending plus administration. A factor values receivables by subtracting expected losses and the cost of carry from their face value. Historically, factoring has been most important in the apparel industry, where business is highly seasonal and where fashion-oriented executives in smaller companies have been eager to let someone else take over the hassles and risks of collecting receivables. As companies grow larger, however, they often become less satisfied with factoring because it effectively gives an outside party the power to decide who their customers should be. At a certain point in their development, many companies therefore decide to bring the collection of their accounts receivable in-house.

A conservative company that wants to monetize its receivables can also purchase credit insurance, which provides protection against the risk that a customer will become bankrupt. Credit insurance has not become prevalent in the United States, but it has played a very important role in Europe, where companies do a great deal of cross-border business with customers they do not know well. In an environment where banks may have little knowledge of companies beyond their own locality and where credit bureaus such as Dun and Bradstreet do not exist, credit insurers provide a very valuable service. They maintain huge databases on companies in many different countries, and they greatly facilitate cross-border trade. As the European Union (EU) moves toward closer monetary and economic union, however, their business is likely to be challenged.

THE ROOTS OF SECURITIZATION AND LBOS

Asset-backed securities are simply the capital-markets version of asset-based finance, and the same techniques developed by asset-based lenders for evaluating assets and companies have been appropriated by securitization teams. The capital markets require greater precision in the application of these techniques than do the banks because the securities created must be analyzed by the rating agencies and then distributed to investors. Nonetheless, the same fundamental concepts are applied in both markets. In addition, there are times when specific transactions move to the capital markets from asset-based lenders because they are very large or because securitization leads to a lower cost structure. The overlap between these two markets remains very strong.

Asset-based lending methodology also spawned the leveraged buyout (LBO) market. During the 1980s, financial professionals recognized that a technique developed for growing companies could also be applied to companies that had deliberately been leveraged. And if a small company could borrow on the basis of its assets, then why not a large one?

A company like RJR Nabisco might be able to borrow billions of dollars on an unsecured basis, but it could borrow even more on the strength of its assets. By pledging a company's assets as collateral, acquirers were able to borrow a major share of the money needed to purchase it. Asset-based finance techniques—whether executed in the capital markets or through the syndicated bank market—accessed the untapped borrowing power inherent in the target company's receivables and other assets.

FAVORABLE RESULTS

Asset-based lenders have tended to view their business as a risky one, and they have managed it accordingly—underwriting their loans carefully and monitoring them closely. They have also been quite aggressive in realizing the value of their collateral. They focus on the assets rather than on their relationship with the borrower. They may be willing to negotiate with a borrower because they prefer not to own the collateral, but they are less likely than typical bankers to show much forbearance. As a result, their performance has generally been good.

REFERENCES

Clarke, P. S. 1996. *Asset-Based Lending: The Complete Guide to Originating, Evaluating, and Managing Asset-based Loans, Leasing and Factoring.* Chicago: Irwin Professional Publishing.

Henson, R. D. 1979. *Secured Transactions.* 2d ed. St. Paul, Minn.: West Publishing Co.

Iannuccilli, J. 1988. Asset-Based Lending: An Overview. In *Asset-Based Lending: A Special Collection from the Journal of Commercial Bank Lending,* edited by C. Weisman. Philadelphia: Robert Morris Associates.

Logan, J. B. 1988. Clearing up the Confusion about Asset-Based Lending. In *Asset-Based Lending: A Special Collection from the Journal of Commercial Bank Lending,* edited by C. Weisman. Philadelphia: Robert Morris Associates.

Sirri, E. R., and P. Tufano. 1995. The Economics of Pooling. In *The Global Financial System.* Boston: Harvard Business School Press.

Stock, K. 1988. Asset-Based Financing: Borrower and Lender Perspectives. In *Asset-Based Lending: A Special Collection from the Journal of Commercial Bank Lending,* edited by C. Weisman. Philadelphia: Robert Morris Associates.

Chapter **9**

Introduction to Credit Risk Models

The grand aim of all science is to cover the greatest number of empirical facts by logical deduction from the smallest number of hypotheses or axioms.

—Albert Einstein

The previous chapters were concerned with the institutions that manage credit risk and the techniques that they have traditionally employed. We now turn our attention to techniques that have evolved over the last 20 years. These innovations were prompted by a number of secular forces, including the following:

- Deregulation, which has stimulated financial innovation and enabled new entrants to provide services
- The broadening of the credit markets to encompass new borrowing sectors, both domestically and internationally
- A continuing shift from balance sheet lending to cash flow lending
- An increase in off-balance-sheet risks
- Shrinking margins on loans, which have forced banks to explore less costly ways of measuring and managing credit risk
- Securitization, which has prompted the development of more efficient (and standardized) credit risk tools
- Advances in finance theory, which have provided new ways of looking at credit risk[1]

Tools from statistics and operations research, such as survival analysis, neural networks, mathematical programming, deterministic and probabilistic simulation, and game theory, have all contributed to the progress in credit risk measurement. So, too, have advances in our understanding of financial markets, such as arbitrage pricing theory, option pricing theory, and the capital asset pricing model. The new tools for measuring credit risk have been applied to a wide range of financial products—consumer loans, residential real estate loans, commercial real estate loans, and commercial loans, as well as swaps, credit derivatives, and other off-balance-sheet products. Notwith-

---

[1]For example, see McKinsey & Co. 1993 for a discussion of some of these forces.

standing all this progress, we should point out that current credit risk models are more in the nature of pioneering efforts to seek better solutions, rather than the culmination of the search. Some of the results of these efforts may fall away completely, but most will be incorporated into models that are yet to be constructed. In that sense, all of our models are bridges to the future. In this chapter we provide an overview of credit models and their areas of application.

MODELS: WHO NEEDS THEM?

Classical economists characterize capital as the *produced means of production*, by which they mean that capital represents the accumulation of wealth generated from the use of labor and land—the two other factors of production. Financial models represent mental labor and capital, and they may be regarded as the *produced means of problem solving*. They represent, in other words, an accumulation of human insight, experience, and experiment that can be applied to explaining the way that people behave or things work. A model greatly facilitates our understanding of a phenomenon and, eventually, its exploitation. Models for measuring credit risk are no exception. With a credit model we seek to determine, directly or indirectly, the answer to the following question: Given our past experience and our assumptions about the future, what is the value of a given loan or fixed-income security? Equivalently, what is the (quantifiable) risk that the promised cash flows will not be forthcoming?

Models are often constructed on theories. The theory of options, for example, might suggest an approach to measuring credit risk. It might be possible to assess the riskiness of a home loan by assuming that the borrower will exercise the option to default if there is no longer any equity in the home. A simple model of default may then be built that uses the loan-to-value ratio as a predictor of default. The higher the loan-to-value ratio, the less equity the owner has in the home and the higher the probability of default. Today, this simple model provides a foundation for home mortgage lending.

To generate a more accurate prediction of the probability of default, additional variables can be added to this model. The second variable might be the size of the debt service relative to the borrower's cash flow or disposable income. This is known as the income ratio. The higher this ratio, the greater the likelihood that the individual will default. Adverse life events such as divorce, illness, or death are additional factors affecting the probability of default. A model that can anticipate these life events will assess credit risk with even greater precision.

A variety of tools are used in building financial models, including econometrics, simulation, optimization, or a combination of all three. Neural networks, for example, may be viewed as a simulation technique that includes an element of optimization (finding the lowest error rate or the highest accuracy).

VARIETY IN MODELS

Ratios, option theory, econometrics, expert systems—these are all attempts to isolate a problem in a construct that can be studied, refined, tested, and if effective, profitably implemented. Many separate elements go into the construction of a credit risk model. First, relationships must be postulated among the variables that seem to affect the risk of default; this is where theory enters in. Then, to derive a formal model, a set of tools must be employed to estimate or simulate outcomes. A body of data is crucial at this point, because a model cannot be created in a vacuum. Lastly, a series of tests must be applied to establish that the model does, indeed, perform as expected. There are also times when the only way to unearth new relationships is to *mine* data without having any particular theory in mind.

In the measurement of credit risk, models may be classified along three different dimensions: the techniques employed, the domain of applications in the credit process, and the products to which they are applied.

TECHNIQUES

The following are the more commonly used techniques:

- *Econometric techniques,* such as linear and multiple discriminant analysis, multiple regression, logit analysis, and probit analysis model the probability of default, or the default premium, as a *dependent* variable whose variance is explained by a set of *independent* variables. The independent variables include financial ratios and other indicators as well as external variables that are used to measure economic conditions. Survival analysis refers to a set of techniques used to measure the time to response, failure, death, or the occurrence of an event (see Lee [1980]).

- *Neural networks* are computer-based systems that we use to try to mimic the functioning of the human brain by emulating a network of interconnected neurons—the smallest decision-making units in the brain. They use the same data employed in the econometric techniques but arrive at the decision model using alternative implementations of a trial and error method.

- *Optimization models* are mathematical programming techniques that discover the optimum weights for borrower and loan attributes that minimize lender error and maximize profits.

- *Rule-based or expert systems* are used to try to mimic in a structured way the process that an experienced analyst uses to arrive at the credit decision. As the name indicates, such a system tries to clone the process used by a successful analyst so that his or her expertise is available to the rest of the organization. Rule-based systems are characterized by a set of decision rules, a knowledge base consisting of data such as industry financial ratios, and a structured inquiry process to be used by the analyst in obtaining data on a particular borrower.

- *Hybrid systems using direct computation, estimation, and simulation* are driven in part by a direct causal relationship, the parameters of which are determined through estimation techniques. An example of this is the KMV model, which uses an option theoretic formulation to explain default and then derives the form of the relationship through estimation. Migration probability matrices are data summaries that help to predict the tendency of a credit to migrate to lower or higher quality based on historical migration patterns. Such matrices are derived by using the *cohort component analysis,* that is, observing a group of bonds or companies through time from inception to end.

DOMAIN OF APPLICATION

Financial models are applied in a variety of domains:

- *Credit approval.* Models are used by themselves or in conjunction with a judgmental override system for approving credit in the consumer lending business. The use of such models has expanded to include small business lending and first mortgage loan approvals. They are generally not used in approving large corporate loans, but they may be one of the inputs to a decision.
- *Credit rating determination.* Quantitative models are used in deriving "shadow" bond ratings for unrated securities and commercial loans. These ratings in turn influence portfolio limits and other lending limits used by the institution. In some instances, the credit rating predicted by the model is used within an institution to challenge the rating assigned by the traditional credit analysis process.
- *Credit pricing.* Credit risk models may be used to suggest the risk premiums that should be charged in view of the probability of loss and the size of the loss, given default. Using a mark-to-market model, an institution may evaluate the costs and benefits of holding a financial asset. Unexpected losses implied by a credit model may be used to set the capital charge in pricing.
- *Financial early warning.* Credit models are used to flag potential problems in the portfolio to facilitate early corrective action.
- *Common credit language.* Credit models may be used to select assets from a pool to construct a portfolio acceptable to investors or to achieve the minimum credit quality needed to obtain the desired credit rating. Underwriters may use such models for due diligence on the portfolio (such as a collateralized pool of commercial loans). Triggers for reserve levels may be tied to model performance.
- *Collection strategies.* Credit models may be used in deciding on the best collection or workout strategy to pursue. If, for example, a credit model indicates that a borrower is experiencing short-term liquidity problems rather than a decline in credit fundamentals, then an appropriate workout may be devised.

RELEVANCE OF CREDIT RISK MODELS TO THE DECISION MAKER

Credit risk models are important today because they provide the decision maker with insight or knowledge that would not otherwise be readily apparent or that could be marshaled only at prohibitive cost. In a marketplace where margins are fast disappearing and the pressure to lower costs is unrelenting, models give their users a competitive edge. In any large financial institution that has a wide variety of exposures, operates in many geographic regions, and has a large and varied workforce, quantitative models can inject a useful degree of objectivity.

Increasingly, credit risk models are also used to assist in releasing the value of financial assets that would otherwise be hidden from equity investors. For example, structured finance products reallocate credit risk in such a way that the subordinated pieces offer a combination of equity risk and equity return. Credit risk models may be used in the stratification or construction of such portfolios.

Credit risk models have been built for large corporate commercial and industrial loans (Fortune 500 companies), commercial real estate loans, small business loans (up to $500,000), residential first mortgages (up to $1 million), home equity and consumer loans, loans to financial institutions, and loans to sovereign governments.

Experience shows that the market penetration of credit models varies with the size of the borrower, as shown in Figure 9.1. Consumer sector lenders were the first to use credit risk models in decision making. The use of these models has spread to large corporate, upper middle market, and residential real estate lending. In these sectors, the models provide key inputs for credit approval and review. Recently such credit models have been applied to small business lending. Today, lower-middle market and private borrowers and commercial real estate are the sectors with the smallest use (or potential for use) of credit models.

PORTFOLIO MANAGEMENT MODELS

Closely related to credit risk models are portfolio models. Historically, lenders have viewed a loan portfolio as an accumulation of individual credit decisions. Portfolio management refers to a controlled process of both acquiring and retaining assets. Using criteria that take into account the impact of adding an asset to the risk-return profile of the overall portfolio, an institution can control the composition of its portfolio. Once an asset has been added, portfolio management tools may be used to identify assets that are no longer desirable because of changing economic or industry conditions. One simple measure of portfolio impact is concentration.

An optimization model may be used to construct a portfolio of loans or securities from a large universe, based on the relative profitability and credit risk of the assets. *Optimization* refers to a set of tools available from operations research that expresses the relevant trade-offs and constraints as an objective mathematical function to be maximized or minimized. An optimization problem is characterized by a set of *decision variables,* which are unknowns that may be determined by means of the algorithm. The decision variables for the construction of an optimum portfolio are the *weights* or the percentages of the individual assets that portfolio will include. The decision variables are used to define an *objective function,* which is the sum of the value

Figure 9.1   Range of Possible Application of Quantitative Credit Risk Models

Large Corporate Borrowers	Middle Market Borrowers	Middle Market and Private Borrowers	Small Business	Commercial Real Estate	Residental and Real Estate	Consumer
Publicly traded. Extensive disclosure. Many institutional investors with research capabilities.	Publicly traded. Moderate disclosure. Little or no publicly traded debt.	Stock not publicly traded. No public debt. More information problems.	No stock. Even financial statements are unaudited. Information problems.	No publicly traded stock. Approval based on cash flow projections and collateral value.	Reliance on collateral value. Greater use of financial data. Increasing use of credit scoring models.	No financial statements. Fewer information problems because of credit bureaus.
Low monitoring, (annual cycle)	Low use of credit scoring models. Greater emphasis on management.	Reliance on financial statements. Close monitoring. Reliance on Collateral and Covenants.	Reliance on individuals. Close Monitoring. Collateral. Covenants. Moderate use of credit scoring models.	Moderate monitoring. More reliance on collateral. Less reliance on covenants.		Reliance on demographic variables. Collateral only for consumer durables. No Covenants. Heavy use of credit scoring models.
Potential for higher use of credit scoring models because of better data.		Limited use of credit scoring models.				

added by the decision variables to the overall benefit to be derived. The objective function of a portfolio may be expressed as a combination of the portfolio return, which is made up of the returns from the individual assets multiplied by their portfolio weights. The optimization problem always involves constraints. For example, the investment in any single asset may not exceed the institution's lending limit.

Once an optimization problem has been specified, generalized computational techniques such as the simplex method from Operations Research are used to arrive at the optimal solution (for example, see Hillier and Lieberman [1973]). Computer software packages are readily available to solve optimization problems. The composition of the "optimal" portfolio is derived from a set of assumptions about the risk and returns from a universe of securities. Harry Markowitz's portfolio approach (as described in Chapter 17) is an implementation of an optimization problem.

When the interrelationships among variables are so complex that they preclude a direct mathematical or statistical solution, a simulation may be employed to derive the statistical distribution of the outcomes from a set of decisions. An example of this approach is the preparation of earnings projections for a company based on assumptions about sales and cost of sales. Stress testing the structure of an asset-based security to assess whether the structure can withstand an economic downturn (e.g., will there be claims on the financial guarantee) is another case in which simulation is used to understand risk. To produce results that genuinely add value to the decision process, the economic scenarios developed should be internally consistent. For example, if a product price increase is modeled, it should typically be accompanied by a drop in unit sales. Unless care is exercised, simulations may simply generate the results the decision maker wants to see.

One of the difficulties with simulations is that it is very difficult to incorporate uncertainty into these calculations. In ordinary simulation models, the probabilities of the independent variables and the joint probabilities among them (sometimes expressed as the correlations) may be modeled only in a qualitative fashion. A Monte Carlo simulation, by contrast, is a procedure in which the input variables are not single values but are drawn from a prespecified statistical distribution. Rather than specifying, for example, a short-term interest rate of 6 percent, interest may be normally distributed, with a mean of 6 percent and a standard deviation of 3. In selecting this input, an analyst is saying that although he or she believes that the mean of the interest rate is still 6 percent, there is a 34 percent probability that it will be less than or equal to $6 + 3 = 9$ percent, and an equal probability that it will be greater than or equal to $6 - 3 = 3$ percent.[2] In an ordinary simulation, the entire calculation is performed only once, so for a given set of initial assumptions there is only one result. In a Monte Carlo simulation, the computer will run the calculation many times—in some cases, millions of times.

---

[2]This is based on the property of the normal distribution, which states that 68 percent of the realized values will fall within $\pm$ 1 standard deviation and 96 percent will fall within $\pm$ 2 standard deviations.

Each time, a sample (a value of the variable) will be "drawn" from the specified distribution. Thus the result from the simulation is not a single value, but a *distribution* of outcome values (see Palisades [1996]).

As a Monte Carlo simulation is run more and more times, the resulting output distribution may gradually converge, in other words, change less and less with additional iterations. Of course, if the model has only one independent variable, the simulation will, by definition, converge on a simplistic outcome: a distribution value that has a one-to-one correspondence with the independent variable's distribution. But the power of this technique comes into play when the problem has more variables and interactions—specifically, when more independent variables are added, and uncertainty is to be modeled in the time dimension as well. When more variables are added, each is assigned its own distribution function. In addition, the interrelationships among the variables are specified in the form of pairwise correlation coefficients. A growth term is added to the variable to model a random variation around a trend over time. This is typically how the interest rate path is represented.

The first step in constructing a Monte Carlo simulation is to develop an ordinary simulation model that employs the same variables. When this simulation is run, the important variables—those having an effect on the outcomes—will become clearer. The next step is to examine each variable and make a hypothesis about how it is distributed. The shape of the distribution is obtained by talking to the people most knowledgeable about the variable, and by consulting the published literature. For example, stock prices are believed to have a log-normal distribution.[3] The parameters of the distribution functions are set by fitting one of the many available distribution functions to the hand-drawn representation of the distribution. The next step is to input the correlation coefficients among the variables. These coefficients are based on experience and off-line statistical analysis of relationships among the independent variables.

Once the distributions of the independent variables and their correlations are established, the Monte Carlo simulation may begin. The end result of the simulation is a probability distribution of outcomes. An advantage of Monte Carlo simulation is that it makes it possible to model complex relationships without having a mathematical solution. You need not be a mathematician to analyze a risk problem. A simulation may be used to test the validity of direct solutions because in a simulation it is necessary to define all the variables being used and their distributions, all of which may have been hidden or assumed away in the direct solutions. Monte Carlo simulations are used in CreditMetrics (see Chapter 19).

A disadvantage of the Monte Carlo approach is that it may not be able to handle optionality that may be present in the financial structures being

---

[3] A variable has a log-normal distribution if the natural logarithm of the variable is normally distributed. Saying that stock price is log-normally distributed is equivalent to saying that the rate of return from a stock, which is a function of the logarithm of stock price, is normally distributed.

evaluated. For example, if an asset may be sold advantageously in any one of several periods, the system will sell it in the first logically permitted period without trying to optimize the timing of the sale. Simulation, by definition, is forward looking, and the algorithms cannot go back and change a decision made in a prior period based on a realization in a subsequent period.

Optimization and simulation models are useful in understanding the risk-return dynamics of an institution. Although they may or may not provide a precise answer to a problem, the mere process of going through the exercise will contribute to developing a better understanding of the profit dynamics. These models will become even more useful when pooling assets to stratify, shift, or hedge risk because, as Marc Intrater, Director at Oliver, Wyman, Inc. points out, investors are typically more interested in assuming a systemic risk (buying a consumer portfolio whose risk is driven by macro factors) than an idiosyncratic risk (buying exposure to a single name).

COMING ATTRACTIONS

In the following chapter we introduce credit risk models starting with Altman's Z-score model and Altman, Haldeman, and Narayanan's (1977) ZETA model, both of which are applied to the default risk of corporations. These models use accounting *and* market value measures in deriving the likelihood of financial distress. Next, we describe neural networks, which are computer-based adaptive learning systems that *train* themselves to measure credit quality and are then implemented in various parts of the credit management process. In Chapter 11 we discuss models that employ the volatility of equity prices to predict default probability in debt instruments. In Chapter 12, we describe the use of credit risk models in consumer lending. Default prediction models for other applications such as small businesses, financial institution risk, and real estate lending are reviewed in Chapter 13.

Considerable detail accompanies these models. Although not every reader may need to understand all of the intricacies, most will want to grasp the essential ideas that underlie each model. To make it easier for readers to choose an appropriate level of detail, we open each chapter with an overview of its contents.

Chapter 14 concludes the section on credit risk evaluation models with a discussion of model implementation and unresolved issues. Chapters 15 and 16 provide some important tools and data on default and credit risk migration that are useful in the pricing and management of credit products. Chapters 17–22 consider portfolio management tools and techniques that make use of optimization and simulation.

REFERENCES

Hillier, F. S., and G. J. Lieberman. 1973. *Introduction to Operations Research*. San Francisco: Holden-Day.

Lee, E. T. 1980. *Statistical Methods for Survival Data Analysis*. Belmont, Calif.: Lifetime Learning Publications.

McKinsey & Co. 1993. Special Report on *The New World of Financial Services. McKinsey Quarterly* 2:59–71.

Palisades Corporation. 1996. *@RISK—Advanced Risk Analysis for Spreadsheets.* Newfield, NY: Palisades Corporation.

ADDITIONAL READING

Mallios, W. 1989. *Statistical Modeling: Applications in Contemporary Issues.* Ames, Iowa: Iowa State University Press.

Trigeorgis, L. 1996. *Real Options: Managerial Flexibility and Strategy in Resource Allocation.* Cambridge, Mass.: MIT Press.

*Chapter **10***

Credit Risk Models Based on Accounting Data and Market Values

[John Stuart] Mill's Methods of Inquiry are useful only if we have rival hypotheses and must choose between them. The hypotheses come first. This point is made more concisely by some dialogue from a Sherlock Holmes story:

Colonel Ross:	*Is there any other point to which you wish to draw my attention?*
Holmes:	*To the curious incident of the dog in the night-time.*
Colonel Ross:	*The dog did nothing in the night-time.*
Holmes:	*That was the curious incident.*

The circumstance noted by Holmes was to Colonel Ross not a circumstance at all, yet this nonfact was the key to the solution: the crime was committed by someone known to the dog.

—M. Goldstein and I. F. Goldstein, *How We Know*

Other than the U.S. government, the nonfarm, nonfinancial corporate sector is the largest borrower of funds in the capital market. In 1996, the volume of debt outstanding in this sector stood at $4.1 trillion—a substantial share of the $19.8 trillion for all sectors combined. Figure 10.1 shows the growth in volume of bank loans and corporate and foreign bonds, respectively, in the period from 1963 to 1996. Clearly, the corporate debt market is enormous.

HUMAN EXPERT SYSTEMS AND SUBJECTIVE ANALYSIS

Twenty years ago, most banks relied exclusively on subjective judgment—classic credit analysis of the kind described in Chapter 7—to assess the credit risk of a corporate borrower. Essentially, bankers used information on various borrower characteristics—such as character (reputation), capital (leverage), capacity (volatility of earnings), and collateral—in deciding whether to make a given loan. Developing this type of expert system is time-consuming and expensive. That is why, from time to time, banks have tried to clone their decision-making process. Even so, in the granting of credit to corporate customers, many banks continue to rely primarily on their traditional expert system for evaluating potential borrowers.

Figure 10.1 U.S. Credit Market Debt

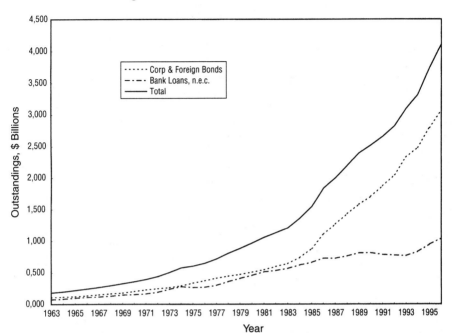

Year	Corp. and Foreign Bonds	Bank Loans n.e.c.	Total	Year	Corp. and Foreign Bonds	Bank Loans n.e.c.	Total
1963	109.0	74.3	183.3	1980	508.4	458.5	966.9
1964	116.6	82.7	199.3	1981	543.7	512.2	1055.9
1965	123.1	98.8	221.9	1982	595.8	532.8	1128.6
1966	135.7	109.6	245.3	1983	642.5	564.2	1206.7
1967	152.5	117.0	269.5	1984	739.7	621.0	1360.7
1968	167.1	130.4	297.5	1985	883.1	662.6	1545.7
1969	181.1	148.3	329.4	1986	1105.6	729.3	1834.9
1970	204.3	154.8	359.1	1987	1270.4	728.2	1998.6
1971	228.8	166.0	394.8	1988	1432.5	763.1	2195.6
1972	249.4	191.8	441.2	1989	1580.6	812.7	2393.3
1973	264.9	239.8	504.7	1990	1703.7	815.0	2518.7
1974	293.9	281.5	575.4	1991	1870.6	785.9	2656.5
1975	337.4	265.8	603.2	1992	2046.8	776.6	2823.4
1976	375.7	272.9	648.6	1993	2327.6	768.0	3095.6
1977	415.9	301.8	717.7	1994	2481.2	830.8	3312.0
1978	447.6	360.4	808.0	1995	2793.0	943.8	3736.8
1979	472.1	411.5	883.6	1996	3066.5	1039.56	4106.6

Source: Board of Governors of the Federal Reserve System 1997a, 1997b, 1997c, 1997d, Table L.5.

Accounting-Based Credit Scoring Systems

In recent decades, however, a number of objective, quantitative systems for scoring credits have been developed. In univariate[1] accounting-based credit-scoring systems, the credit analyst compares various key accounting ratios of potential borrowers with industry or group norms and trends for these variables. Today, Dun & Bradstreet, Standard & Poor's, Moody's, Robert Morris Associates, and data vendors such as DRI/McGraw Hill can all provide lenders with industry ratios. The univariate approach enables an analyst starting an inquiry to determine whether a particular ratio for a potential borrower differs markedly from the norm for its industry. In reality, however, the unsatisfactory level of one ratio is frequently mitigated by the strength of some other measure. A firm, for example, may have a poor profitability ratio but an above-average liquidity ratio. One limitation of the univariate approach is the difficulty of making trade-offs between such weak and strong ratios. Of course, a good credit analyst can make these adjustments. However, some univariate measures—such as the specific industry group, public versus private company, and region—are categorical rather than ratio-level values. It is more difficult to make judgments about variables of this type.

From Univariate to Multivariate Methods

Although univariate models are still in use today in many institutions, most academicians and an increasing number of practitioners seem to disapprove of ratio analysis as a means of assessing the performance of a business enterprise. Many respected theorists downgrade the arbitrary rules of thumb (such as company ratio comparisons) that are widely used by practitioners and favor instead the application of more rigorous statistical techniques. In some respects, however, these latter techniques should be viewed as a refinement of traditional ratio analysis rather than as a radical departure from it.

One of the classic studies of ratio analysis and bankruptcy was performed by Beaver (1967). Beaver found that a number of indicators could discriminate between matched samples of failed and nonfailed firms for as long as five years prior to failure. In a subsequent study, Deakin (1972) utilized the same 14 variables that Beaver analyzed but applied them within a series of multivariate discriminant models. Although Deakin achieved a high classification accuracy in the development sample (more than 95 percent for the first three years prior to failure) there was substantial deterioration in the classification accuracy in the hold-out sample one year prior, a result that Deakin noted "cannot be explained by the presence of any unusual events peculiar to the sample used" (1972, 176). The significance of this finding is that it is premature to conclude from test results from a development sample that a valid empirical relationship has been detected.

In general, ratios measuring profitability, liquidity, and solvency appeared to be the most significant indicators in univariate studies. The order of their importance was unclear, however, because almost every study cited

---

[1] *Univariate* literally means pertaining to one variable.

a different ratio as the most effective indicator of impending problems. An appropriate extension of the univariate studies, therefore, was to build upon the findings by combining several measures into a meaningful predictive model. In constructing a multivariate system, the key questions are (1) Which ratios are most important in detecting bankruptcy potential? (2) What weights should be attached to these selected ratios? (3) How should the weight values be objectively established?

We begin this discussion by presenting Altman's (1968) Z-score model and its extensions. Zeta, which is an update and improvement of the original Z-score model, is presented next. This is followed by a description of other developments including neural networks, artificial intelligence, market premium–based models, and mortality models.

ALTMAN'S Z-SCORE MODEL

Altman's Z-score model is a multivariate approach built on the values of both ratio-level and categorical (Altman 1968, 1993a) univariate measures. These values are combined and weighted to produce a measure (a credit risk score) that best discriminates between firms that fail and those that do not. Such a measure is possible because failing firms exhibit ratios and financial trends that are very different from those of companies that are financially sound. In a bank utilizing such a model, loan applicants would either be rejected or subjected to increased scrutiny if their scores fell below a critical benchmark. Altman based his multivariate model on the financial ratios shown in Table 10.1. The basic Z-score model has endured to this day and has also been applied to private companies, nonmanufacturing firms, and emerging market companies.

The Z-score model was constructed using multiple discriminant analysis, a multivariate technique that analyzes a set of variables to maximize the between-group variance while minimizing the within-group variance. This is typically a sequential process in which the analyst includes or excludes variables based on various statistical criteria. It should be noted that if the groups are not very different at the univariate level, a multivariate model will not be able to add much discriminatory power. (See Table 10.1 for univariate results.)

To arrive at a final profile of variables, the following procedures were utilized: (1) observation of the statistical significance of various alternative functions, including determination of the relative contributions of each independent variable; (2) evaluation of intercorrelations among the relevant variables; (3) observation of the predictive accuracy of the various profiles; and (4) judgment of the analyst. From the original list of 22 variables, the final Z-score model chosen was the following 5-variable model. (Note that this equation is equivalent to the one shown in Table 10.1. When expressed in this form the ratios X_1 through X_4 are expressed as decimals and not percentages. The fifth ratio is measured in number of times, and its coefficient is unchanged from the equation shown in Table 10.1):

$$Z = 1.2X_1 + 1.4X_2 + 3.3X_3 + 0.6X_4 + 0.999X_5$$

Table 10.1   Z-Score Model Variable Group Means and F Ratios

Variable	Bankrupt group mean[a]	Nonbankrupt group mean[a]	F ratio[b]
$X_1 = \dfrac{\text{working capital}}{\text{total assets}}$	−6.1%	41.4%	32.60
$X_2 = \dfrac{\text{retained earnings}}{\text{total assets}}$	−62.6%	35.5%	58.86
$X_3 = \dfrac{\text{EBIT}}{\text{total assets}}$	−31.8%	15.4%	26.56
$X_4 = \dfrac{\text{market value of equity}}{\text{book value of liabilities}}$	40.1%	247.7%	33.26
$X_5 = \dfrac{\text{sales}}{\text{total assets}}$	1.5 Times	1.9 Times	2.84

[a]Sample size is 33.

[b]The F ratio is significant at the .001 level for all variables except sales/total assets. This ratio tests for the statistical difference between the means of the two groups.

The resulting discriminant function is

$$Z = 0.012(X_1) + 0.014(X_2) + 0.033(X_3) + 0.006(X_4) + 0.999(X_5)$$

Altman found a lower bound value of 1.81 (failed) and an upper bound of 2.99 (nonfail) to be optimal. Any score in the 1.81 to 2.99 range was treated as being in the zone of ignorance, that is, where errors were found in the original sample.

Source: Altman (1968).

X_1, Working Capital/Total Assets

The working capital/total assets ratio (WC/TA), frequently found in studies of corporate problems, is a measure of a firm's net liquid assets relative to its total capitalization. Working capital is defined as the difference between current assets and current liabilities. Liquidity and size characteristics are explicitly considered. Ordinarily, a firm experiencing consistent operating losses will have shrinking current assets in relation to total assets.

X_2, Retained Earnings/Total Assets

Retained earnings (also known as earned surplus) is the total amount of reinvested earnings and/or losses of a firm over its entire life. The retained earnings account is subject to manipulation via corporate quasi-reorganizations and stock dividend declarations. Whereas these occurrences are not evident in this study, it is conceivable that a bias could be created by a substantial reorganization or stock dividend. Appropriate readjustments would then have to be made to the accounts. The age of a firm is implicitly considered in this ratio: a relatively young firm, for example, will probably show a low RE/TA because it has not had time to build up its cumulative profits. It may therefore be argued that this analysis discriminates against the young firm. In reality, however, this bias is perfectly reasonable because the incidence of failure is much higher in younger firms. In 1996, for example, approximately 45 percent of all firms that failed did so in the first five years of their existence (Dun & Bradstreet 1997).

X_3, Earnings before Interest and Taxes/Total Assets

The ratio of earnings before interest and taxes to total assets (EBIT/TA) is a measure of the productivity of the firm's assets, independent of any tax or leverage factors. Because a firm's ultimate existence is based on the earning power of its assets, this ratio appears to be particularly appropriate for studies dealing with corporate failure. Furthermore, insolvency occurs when a firm's total liabilities exceed a fair valuation of its assets, as determined by the earning power of those assets.

X_4, Market Value of Equity/Book Value of Total Liabilities

Equity is measured by the combined market value of all shares of stock, preferred and common, whereas liabilities include both current and long-term items. The ratio of market value of equity to book value of total liabilities (MVE/TL) shows how much a firm's assets can decline in value (as measured by market value of equity plus debt) before its liabilities exceed its assets, and it becomes insolvent. For example, a company with $1,000 of equity market value and debt of $500 could experience a two-thirds drop in asset value (which is $1,000 + $500 = $1,500, thus ⅔ of the assets is $500) before insolvency. However, the same firm with $250 in equity value will be insolvent if assets drop only one-third in value. This ratio adds a market value dimension that other failure studies did not consider. Since the model's inception in 1968, Altman suggested adding capitalized leases, both operating and financial, to the firm's total liabilities (Altman 1976).

X_5, Sales/Total Assets

The capital-turnover ratio is a standard financial ratio illustrating the sales generating ability of the firm's assets. It is one measure of management's capacity to deal with competitive conditions. Based on the univariate statistical significance measure, it would not have appeared at all in the model. However, because of its unique relationship to other variables in the model, the sales/total assets ratio (S/TA) ranks second in its contribution to the overall discriminating ability of the model. Still, there is a wide variation among industries in asset turnover. An alternative model without this ratio was constructed and is described later in this chapter.

As seen in Table 10.1, the means for the two groups for four of the five variables differed sharply. For a model to predict effectively, the within-group standard deviations should be relatively small.[2] In Altman's sample, the failed group consisted of 33 bankrupt manufacturing firms, and the non-

---

[2]The use of averages to distinguish between two groups is a decision process that is common in credit analysis. For instance, in commercial real estate, the coverage ratio should exceed 1.5, as a general rule.

**Table 10.2   Classification Results—Development Sample
(1 Year Prior to Bankruptcy)**

Actual group	No. of cases	Predicted group membership	
		1	2
Group 1 (bankrupt)	33	31	2
		94.0%	6.0%
Group 2 (nonbankrupt)	33	1	32
		3.0%	97.0%

Overall classification accuracy: 95.0%

**Classification Results—Development Sample
(2 Years Prior to Bankruptcy)**

Actual group	No. of cases	Predicted group membership	
		1	2
Group 1 (bankrupt)	33	23	9
		72.0%	28.0%
Group 2 (nonbankrupt)	33	2	31
		6.0%	94.0%

Overall classification accuracy: 82.0%
Source: Altman (1968).

failed group comprised a paired sample of manufacturing firms chosen on a stratified random basis.[3] Firms in the nonfailed group were still in existence at the time of the analysis.

The Z-score model's classification accuracy is shown in Table 10.2. The model's overall classification accuracy was 95 percent one year before bankruptcy on the development sample, and 82 percent two years before. Classification accuracy is one of the outputs examined in ascertaining whether a model will perform well in practice. This accuracy is expressed as Type I accuracy (the accuracy with which the model identified failed firms as weak) and Type II accuracy (the accuracy with which the model identified healthy firms as such). Overall accuracy is a combination of Type I and II accuracy. Generally, Type I accuracy is viewed as more important than Type II, because the inability to identify a failing company (Type I error) will cost the lender far more than the opportunity cost of rejecting a healthy company as a potential failure (Type II error). To stretch the analogy of the barking dog just

---

[3]Stratification was achieved by matching a failed firm with a healthy firm of comparable size from the same industry. Because there could be several healthy firms fitting the criteria, the pairing firm was randomly chosen from this subgroup.

a little, Type I error is the case of the dog not barking at the sight of the criminal; Type II error is the case of a dog that barks at a harmless passerby.

Because the results based on the development sample suffer from sample bias, secondary sample testing is extremely important. One type of testing is to estimate parameters for the model using only a subset of the original sample and then classify the remainder of the sample based on the parameters established. A simple t-test is then applied to test the significance of the results.

Five different replications of the suggested method of choosing subsets (16 firms) of the original sample were tested. The five replications include (1) random sampling; (2) choosing every other firm, starting with the first firm; (3) the same test, but starting with the second firm; (4) choosing firms 1 through 16; and (5) choosing firms 17 through 32. All the results showed that the discrimination function was statistically significant. Additional tests using secondary samples (completely independent of the development sample) were performed. Type II errors (classifying healthy firms as bankrupt) ranged from 15 to 20 percent in the secondary samples.

Z-Scores and Bond Ratings

One of the primary uses of credit-scoring models is to assign a bond rating equivalent to each score. This enables the analyst to assess the default probability of an applicant by observing the historical experience of each bond rating. These default probabilities are discussed in detail in Chapter 15.

Table 10.3 shows the average Z-score for bonds of different bond rating classes. Note that the average Z-score in 1995 ranged from about 5.0 for AAA bonds down to 1.67 for B bonds. The average score for B-rated firms actually falls in the Z-score's distress zone. Indeed, the firms issuing B bonds do have distressed firm characteristics. For example, the average B-rated interest coverage (EBIT/interest expense) is actually below 1.0 (Standard & Poor's 1997).

Private Firm Z′-Score Model

In order to score privately held companies, Altman (1993a) revised the original Z-score model by substituting book value for market value when calculating the ratio X_4. He arrived at the following Z′-score model:

$$Z' = 0.717X_1 + 0.847X_2 + 3.107X_3 + 0.420X_4 + 0.998X_5$$

The univariate F-test for the book value of X_4 (25.8) is lower than the 33.3 level for the market value, but the scaled vector results show that the revised book value measure is still the third most important contributor. Indeed, the order of importance (i.e., X_3, X_2, X_5, X_4, and X_1) was retained in the private firm model.

Table 10.4 lists the classification accuracy, group means, and revised cutoff scores for the Z′-score model. The Type I accuracy (correct identification of bankrupt companies) of the Z′-score model is only slightly less impressive

Table 10.3 Average Z-Score by Standard & Poor's Bond Rating S&P 500 (1991–1995)

Rating	Number of firms[a]	1995 Avg.	1995 Std. dev.	1994 Avg.	1994 Std. dev.	1993 Avg.	1993 Std. dev.	1992 Avg.	1992 Std. dev.	1991 Avg.	1991 Std. dev.
AAA	11	5.020	1.603	4.376	1.380	4.506	1.499	5.263	2.194	6.357	3.433
AA	46	4.296	1.911	4.047	1.832	4.032	1.893	4.226	2.088	4.386	2.357
A	131	3.613	2.259	3.472	2.007	3.607	2.180	3.923	3.255	3.736	2.570
BBB	107	2.776	1.493	2.701	1.580	2.839	1.741	2.601	1.535	2.550	1.543
BB	30	2.449	1.623	2.276	1.694	2.185	1.626	2.102	1.544	2.219	1.448
B	8	1.673	1.234	1.876	1.517	1.964	1.716	1.962	2.333	1.887	2.038

[a]Number of firms for 1995 data only.

Source: Compustat Data Tape, Standard & Poor's.

Table 10. 4   Revised Z'-Score Model: Classification Results, Group Means, and Cutoff Boundaries

Actual group	No. of cases	Predicted group membership	
		1	2
Group 1 (bankrupt)	33	30	3
		90.9%	9.1%
Group 2 (nonbankrupt)	33	1	32
		3.0%	97.0%

Note: Mean of the bankrupt group = 0.15; mean of the nonbankrupt group = 4.14. $Z' < 1.23$ zone I (no errors in bankruptcy classification); $Z' > 2.90$ = zone II (no errors in nonbankruptcy classification); Gray area = 1.23 to 2.90.

Source: Altman (1968).

than that of the Z-score model (91 percent vs. 94 percent), and the Type II accuracy (correct identification of nonbankrupt companies) is identical (97 percent). The nonbankrupt group's mean Z'-score is lower than that of the original model (4.14 vs. 5.02). The distribution of scores is therefore tighter, with greater group overlap. The gray area (or ignorance zone) is wider, however, because the lower boundary is now 1.23 versus 1.81 for the Z'-score model, and the upper boundary is 2.90 versus 2.99 for the original Z-score model.

Nonmanufacturers' Z-Score Model

The next modification of the Z-score model was used to analyze the characteristics and accuracy of a model without X_5 (i.e., sales/total assets). This was done to minimize the potential industry effect, which is more likely to occur when an industry-sensitive variable such as asset turnover is included. The book value of equity was used for X_4 in this case.

The classification results are identical to the revised five-variable model (Z'-score). Following is the new Z'-score model:

$$Z' = 6.56 \ (X_1) + 3.26 \ (X_2) + 6.72 \ (X_3) + 1.05 \ (X_4)$$

The coefficients for variables X_1 through X_4 are changed, as are the group means and cutoff scores. This particular model is useful in industries where firms finance their assets in very different ways and where adjustments such as lease capitalization are not made. In the emerging market model discussed below, a constant term of + 3.25 was added so as to standardize the scores with a score of zero (0), equivalent to a D (default) rated bond. This model has also been used to assess the financial health of non-U.S. corporates. In particular, Altman, Hartzell, and Peck (1995) have applied this enhanced Z'-

score model to emerging markets corporates—specifically Mexican firms that had issued Eurobonds denominated in U.S. dollars.

EMERGING MARKET SCORING MODEL AND PROCESS

Emerging markets credits may initially be analyzed in a manner similar to that used for traditional analysis of U.S. corporates. Once a quantitative risk assessment has emerged, an analyst can then use a qualitative assessment to modify it for such factors as currency and industry risk, industry characteristics, and the firm's competitive position in that industry. It is not often possible to build a model specific to an emerging market country based on a sample from that country because of the lack of credit experience there. To deal with this problem, Altman, Hartzell, and Peck (1995, 1996) have modified the original Altman Z-score model to create the emerging market scoring (EMS) model.

The process of deriving the rating for a Mexican corporate credit is as follows:

1. The EMS score is calculated, and equivalent rating is obtained based on the calibration of the EMS scores with U.S. bond-rating equivalents.

2. The company's bond is then analyzed for the issuing firm's vulnerability concerning the servicing of its foreign currency–denominated debt. This vulnerability is based on the relationship between the nonlocal currency revenues minus costs, compared with nonlocal currency expense. Then the level of nonlocal currency cash flow is compared with the debt coming due in the next year. The analyst adjusts the rating downward depending on the degree of vulnerability seen.

3. The rating is further adjusted downward (or upward) if the company is in an industry considered to be relatively riskier (or less risky) than the bond-rating equivalent from the first EMS result.

4. The rating is further adjusted up or down depending on the dominance of the firm's position in its industry.

5. If the debt has special features such as collateral or a bona fide guarantor, the rating is adjusted accordingly.

6. Finally, the market value of equity is substituted for the best value in variable X_4, and the resulting bond-rating equivalents are compared. If there are significant differences in the bond-rating equivalents, the final rating is modified, up or down.

For relative value analysis, the corresponding U.S. corporates' credit spread is added to the sovereign bond's option-adjusted spread. Only a handful of the Mexican companies are rated by the rating agencies. Thus, risk assessments such as those provided by EMS are often the only reliable indicators of credit risk to overseas investors in Mexico. Altman, Hartzell, and Peck report that the modified ratings have proven accurate in anticipating both downgrades and defaults (Grupo Synkro in May 1995 and 1996) and upgrades (Aeromexico in July 1995).

ZETA CREDIT RISK MODEL

In 1977, Altman, Haldeman, and Narayanan (1977) presented a second-generation model with several enhancements to the original Z-score approach. Their purpose was to construct a measure that explicitly reflected recent developments involving business failure. Because the average size of bankrupt firms had increased dramatically, the new study focused on larger firms, with an average of $100 million in assets two years prior to failure. The data employed was timely: 50 of the 53 bankrupt firms in the sample had failed within the last seven years. Appropriate analytical adjustments were made so that it became possible to analyze retailing companies—a particularly vulnerable group—on an equal basis with manufacturers. In addition, the new study reflected the most recent changes in financial reporting standards and accepted accounting practices. It also incorporated refinements in discriminant statistical techniques.

Principal Findings

The new model, which was named ZETA, was effective in classifying bankrupt companies up to five years prior to failure, with over 90 percent accuracy one year prior and over 70 percent accuracy up to five years prior to failure. The inclusion of retailing firms in the same model as manufacturers did not appear to affect the results negatively.

Variables Analyzed

Twenty-seven variables were selected for inclusion in the analysis, based on their widespread use in credit analysis. The variables were classified as measures of profitability, coverage and other earnings relative to leverage, liquidity, capitalization ratios, earnings variability, and miscellaneous.

Reporting Adjustments

The capitalization of leases was the single most important and pervasive adjustment made to the firms' reported data. A capitalized lease amount was added to the firms' assets and liabilities, and an interest cost was imputed to this added liability. Other adjustments were made regarding reserves, minority interests on the balance sheet, nonconsolidated subsidiaries, goodwill and intangibles, and capitalized research and development costs.

The Seven-Variable Model

The model not only classified the test sample well but also proved the most reliable in various validation procedures. These are its seven variables:

X_1 *Return on assets,* measured by earnings before interest and taxes/total assets. This variable had proved to be extremely helpful in assessing firm performance in several prior multivariate studies.

X_2 *Stability of earnings,* indicated by a normalized measure of the standard error of estimate around a 5- to 10-year trend in X_1. Business risk is often expressed in terms of earnings fluctuations, and this measure proved to be particularly effective.

X_3 *Debt service*, measured by the familiar interest coverage ratio, that is, earnings before interest and taxes/total interest payments. This is one of the primary variables used by fixed-income security analysts and bond-rating agencies.

X_4 *Cumulative profitability*, measured by the firm's retained earnings (balance sheet/total assets). This ratio, which imputes such factors as the age of the firm and dividend policy as well as its profitability record over time, was found to be quite helpful in the Z-score model. Without a doubt, this was the most important variable—whether measured univariately or multivariately.

X_5 *Liquidity*, measured by the familiar current ratio.

X_6 *Capitalization*, measured by common equity/total capital. In both the numerator and the denominator, the common equity is measured by a five-year average of the total market value, rather than book value. This five-year average was used to smooth out possible severe, temporary market fluctuations and to add a trend component (along with X_2, above) to the model.

X_7 *Size*, measured by the logarithm of the firms' total assets. This variable was also adjusted for financial reporting changes.

CLASSIFICATION ACCURACY

Table 10.5 compares the classification accuracy of ZETA to that of the Z-score model. Not surprisingly—in view of the improvements made in developing the model—ZETA is more accurate than the Z-score, especially in the more distant years preceding bankruptcy.

GROUP PRIOR PROBABILITIES, ERROR COSTS, AND MODEL EFFICIENCY

If the model is used as part of a credit approval process, the setting of the cutoff value will necessitate certain trade-offs. If the cutoff score is set too high, then weaker credits will be excluded (increased Type I accuracy), but some good credits will be turned away (lower Type II accuracy). If the cutoff is set too low, then the reverse will occur. Intuitively, the cutoff score should be a function of the cost of a Type I error (loan loss sustained by accepting a bad credit) and the cost of a Type II error (income lost by not lending to a good credit risk due to model error). In addition, the cutoff will be influenced by the prior probability that a credit will be a bad one. If the odds are equal that an incoming credit will be good or bad and if the Type I and Type II costs are equal, then the prior probability is 0.5 and the cutoff score is 0.

But only a small proportion of the borrower population will actually default. Thus, the prior probability will be lower than 0.5. Of course, bad credits are not just those that result in charge-offs. Nonjudicial arrangements,

Table 10.5 Classification Accuracy and Comparison of Zeta with the Z-Score Model

Years prior to bankruptcy	ZETA model		Altman 1968 model		Altman's 1968 model with ZETA sample		Altman's 1968 variables, estimated using ZETA sample	
	Bankrupt (%)	Nonbankrupt (%)	Bankrupt (%)	Nonbankrupt (%)	Bankrupt (%)	Nonbankrupt (%)	Bankrupt (%)	Nonbankrupt (%)
1	96.2	89.7	93.9	97.0	86.8	82.4	92.5	84.5
2	84.9	93.1	71.9	93.9	83.0	89.3	83.0	86.2
3	74.5	91.4	48.3	NA	70.6	91.4	72.7	89.7
4	68.1	89.5	28.6	NA	61.7	86.0	57.5	83.0
5	69.8	82.1	36.0	NA	55.8	86.2	44.2	82.1

extreme liquidity problems that require the firm's creditors to take over the business or agree to a distressed restructuring, and bond defaults may also be viewed as equivalent to bankruptcy. In the final analysis, the prior probability of bankruptcy cannot be known with precision. In the development of this model, the prior probability estimate was assumed to be in the 1–5 percent range.

The optimal cutoff score, $ZETA_C$, is then equal to

$$Zeta_C = \ln \frac{q_1 C_1}{q_2 C_2}$$

where q_1, q_2 = prior probability of bankrupt (q_1) or nonbankrupt (q_2), and C_1, C_2 = costs of Type I and Type II errors. Based on the first study of the recovery experience of commercial banks and opportunity cost of foregone income, Altman, Haldeman, and Narayanan estimated the cost of a Type I error C_1 to be $62 per $100 in loans, and that of a Type 2 error C_2 to be $2 per $100 in loans per year. The latter amount assumes a spread of 2 percent and a one-year maturity. With these assumptions, the critical or cutoff score $ZETA_C$ was found to be

$$ZETA_C = \ln \frac{q_1 C_1}{q_2 C_2} = \ln \frac{0.02 \times 62}{0.98 \times 2} = \ln (0.63) = -0.458$$

With this cutoff score of -0.458, the number of Type I errors increased from two (3.8 percent) to four (7.6 percent), while the Type II errors decreased from six (10.3 percent) to four (7.0 percent).

ADJUSTMENTS TO THE CUTOFF SCORE AND PRACTICAL APPLICATIONS

In addition to their use in assessing comparative model efficiency, the prior probability of bankruptcy or default and cost estimates of classification errors could prove valuable in practice. For instance, a bank lending officer or loan-review analyst might want to adjust the critical cutoff score in the light of his or her own estimates of group priors and error costs and/or to reflect current economic conditions. One could imagine the cutoff score falling (thereby lowering the acceptance criterion) as business conditions improve and the banker's prior probability of bankruptcy estimate falls from, say, 0.02 to 0.015. Or, a rise in cutoff scores could result from a change (rise) in the estimate of the Type I error cost vis-à-vis the Type II error cost.

STABILITY OF THE RATIOS IN ZETA

When ZETA was developed, the ratios that were included in the model were carefully chosen as ones that would not be expected to change over time. With respect to their ability to identify distressed companies, Table 10.6 shows the means and F ratios of the model variables in the development sample, and the same ratios for 480 bankruptcies over the period 1981–1993 compared with randomly paired companies that did not fail. It is seen that

Table 10.6 ZETA Ratio Statistics—Development Sample (1977) and 1981–1993 Sample

Variable	1977 data			1981–1993 data		
	Bankrupt group mean	Nonbankrupt group mean	*F* ratio	Bankrupt group mean	Nonbankrupt group mean	*F* ratio
Return on assets	−0.0055	0.1117	54.3	−0.08223	0.09253	316.36
Stability of earnings	1.6870	5.7840	33.8	0.88471	3.83302	247.28
Debt service	0.9625	1.1620	26.1	0.87261	1.09928	156.72
Cumulative profitability	−0.0006	0.2935	114.6	−0.21484	0.21139	559.55
Liquidity	1.5757	2.6040	38.2	1.13783	2.20532	190.48
Capitalization	0.4063	0.6210	31.0	0.47803	0.58802	44.69
Size	1.9854	2.2220	5.5	1.63024	2.01598	40.07

Source: ZETA Services, Inc., 5 Marine View Plaza, Hoboken, NJ 07030. Reprinted with permission.

the ratios continue to demonstrate consistency and contrast between failed firms and nonfailed firms. The ratio means are of the same order of magnitude, and the *F* ratio continues to be statistically significant at the .001 level for all of the variables. *F* ratios in the latter period are much higher, which reflects the much greater sample size (480 vs. 53 in 1977).

REESTIMATION OF COEFFICIENTS

A criticism that may be leveled against Zeta and the Z-score model is that they may have lost their ability to discriminate between good and bad credits because the coefficients have not been continuously reestimated. However, models that progressively drop older data points and pick up more recent data points may suffer from a serious shortcoming: a model may become more sensitive through the addition of newer observations, but it may lose its ability to predict long-term changes because experience from the distant past has been erased.

Lovie and Lovie (1986) provide insight into why the Z-score model and Zeta have continued to be as effective as they have been. For building sturdy models, they offer the following suggestions:

1. Choose the dominant predictor variable/s—usually those with the largest weights as estimated from learning set data. This will at least guarantee that the system produces an above-chance level of discrimination, whatever the weighting scheme used subsequently.
2. Choose the minimum, optimal subset of remaining predictor variables, that is one which produces the largest R^2.
3. Align all predictor variables in the same direction, preferably positively, with respect to the criterion variable to avoid the effects of "suppresser" variables.

4. Choose a dichotic or dichotomizable criterion variable in order to maximize the discrimination power of the model.

If all the above are satisfied, then *"it don't make no nevermind"* which weighting scheme is chosen when the models are used in prediction. (161)

When the Z-score and Zeta models were developed, a great deal of attention was given to choosing the ratios to be used. This may account for the continued stability of their predictive power and to the models' robustness.

CONCLUDING REMARKS: Z-SCORE AND ZETA

Both the Z-score and ZETA models have been applied in a variety of situations:

1. *Credit policy.* An institution lacking an internal risk-rating system may use the rating system developed by relating ZETA's score ranges to actual default experience. This ZETA equivalent rating (ZER) provides an objective and consistent way of dealing with variations in region, size, and ownership. If the ZER is compared to the institution's own rating, any anomalies can be analyzed to validate the assigned rating,

2. *Credit review.* As the credit quality of borrowers improves or declines in a fundamental way, these models provide an early warning system to the institution.

3. *Lending.* These models provide a low-cost and quick assessment of risk for prospecting. Target credit spreads and unexpected losses may be factored into the pricing equation by taking advantage of the consistent relationship between the score and the default rate.

4. *Securitization.* By providing a credible and consistent credit language, these models can facilitate the stratification and structuring of commercial loans for securitization. Indeed such models may prove to be an efficient and responsible way to meet the challenges facing the credit markets in the 1990s and beyond.

NEURAL NETWORKS

A relatively new approach to the problem of credit risk classification is the application of neural network analysis. Neural network analysis is similar to nonlinear discriminant analysis in that it drops the assumption that variables entering into the distress prediction function are linearly and independently related. Neural network models of credit risk explore potentially "hidden" correlations among the predictive variables, which are then entered as additional explanatory variables in the nonlinear distress prediction function. Applications of neural networks to distress prediction analysis include Coats and Fant's (1993) application to corporate distress prediction in the United States, and Altman, Marco, and Varetto's (1994) application to corporate distress prediction in Italy; Trippi and Turban (1996) discuss other applications of neural networks to credit risk, including consumer loans, home mortgages, banks, and thrifts.

A neural network is a collection of simple computational elements that are interconnected. The human brain is a collection of interconnected neurons. In the brain, electric signals passed between neurons are either inhibited or enhanced, depending on what the neural network has learned in the past. In a similar fashion, artificial neurons may be constructed using either hardware or software to behave in a manner similar to the biological neuron. The network's behavior derives from the collective behavior of the interconnected units. The links between the units (neurons) are not rigid but can be modified through the learning processes generated by the network's interaction with the outside world. A simple implementation of a neural network is shown in Figure 10.2.

Each unit, receives an input, X_j, from the outside. The input may be a financial ratio, a market trend, or any other input variable. The input may also be the output signal from another neuron to which this unit is linked. Each X_j is associated with a weight, W_{ij}, indicating that there are j different inputs coming to the unit, where $j = 1, \ldots, n$. In addition to the X_j inputs, the unit receives S_i, a constant input value termed the *excitation threshold value* or *bias*. The overall input to neuron i is termed potential, P_i, which is equal to

$$P_i = \sum_{j=1}^{j=n} nW_{ji}X_j - S_i$$

Figure 10.2   General Scheme of Neural Unit

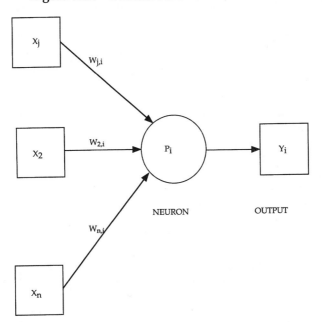

Source: Reprinted from *Journal of Banking and Finance*, Vol. 18, Altman, Marco, and Varetto, "Corporate Distress Diagnosis", pp. 505–529, 1994, with permission of Elsevier Science.

The purpose of S_i is to limit the neuron's degree of response to the stimuli X_i received. For example, S_i may be set such that the neuron gives a response signal only if the total input exceeds the value of S_i. To eliminate S_i from the above equation, set a dummy input X_0 equal to 1, and set W_{0i} equal to $-S_i$, thereby obtaining the general expression

$$P_i = \sum_{j=0}^{j=n} n W_{ji} X_j$$

Notice that P_i is simply a linear combination of weights for the inputs X_j to the neuron.[4] The next aspect of the network is the use of a transfer function by the neuron that converts the potential P_i to an output Y_i. One such function is the logistic or the sigmoid function according to which

$$Y_i = \frac{1}{1 + e^{-P_i}}$$

Y_i is a value between 0 and 1 and may be either a final output or an input to further neuron units. The transfer function gives the capacity to respond nonlinearly to an impulse. For example, it is believed that if a financial ratio such as the coverage ratio exceeds a certain minimum level (say for a AAA rating), the incremental value beyond this threshold does not add to credit quality. Linear regressions cannot limit the response in this manner, but the transfer function in a neural network can.

The network may learn either in a *supervised* mode (where the outcomes are known; this is the equivalent of the a priori groups in discriminant analysis) or in an *unsupervised* mode (this is equivalent to factor analysis, where the prior groupings are not known). The network is given a set of inputs and generates a response, which is then compared with the required (or correct) response. If the error rate exceeds a certain tolerance level, revisions are introduced to the weightings, and the learning starts again. After a large number of cycles, the error is reduced to an acceptable level. Once the hold-out accuracy level is attained, the learning ends and the weightings are locked. Thus, the process is not dissimilar to the traditional models, with the only difference being that the weights are arrived at by trial and error rather than through a closed-form solution.

One implementation of a neural network is a *multilayer perceptron* (see Figure 10.3). In this model there are three layers of neurons, an input layer, a hidden layer, and an output layer. Each of the neurons in the input layer is connected to each neuron in the hidden layer. The input layer provides the external input to the network. The hidden layer receives inputs from the input layer or another hidden layer and provides the input to the output layer. The output layer receives the inputs from the hidden layer and then produces the output. The output in the case of a credit model is a determination of good or bad credit. Depending on the correctness of the prediction, the weights are adjusted.

The input layer neuron sends a signal to the hidden layer that represents

---

[4]Linear discriminant analysis is a special case of a neural network that consists of a single neuron that receives signals from a set of indicators and generates an output (the discriminant score).

Figure 10.3 Multilayer Perceptron

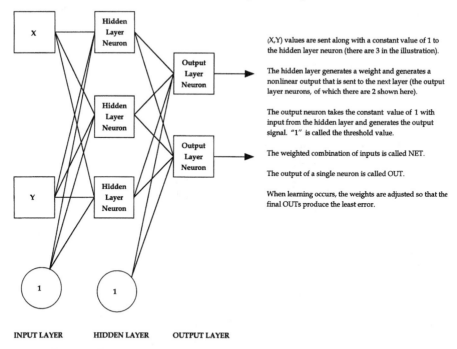

INPUT LAYER   HIDDEN LAYER   OUTPUT LAYER

Source: Berry and Trigueiros (1993) from Trippi and Turban, *Neural Networks in Finance and Investing,* Irwin Professional Publishing. Reproduced with permission of The McGraw Hill Companies.

the value of the input variable associated with itself. The input variable value may be a ratio-level value or a categorical value and may be any of several input variables. A weight is assigned to the connection from the input neuron to the hidden layer neuron. The hidden layer neuron applies weight on the input value, using a nonlinear transformation to generate a signal Y_i, such that $0 \le Y_i \le 1$. This transformation is called a transfer function.

Each output layer neuron receives its input from each hidden layer neuron in the same fashion, that is, using a combination of weights and transfer function. The circles in the illustration are not neurons. They are signal generators that send the constant value 1 along the weighted connections to the hidden layer and to the output layer neurons. This signal becomes a part of the P_i representing a threshold value for each receiving neuron. Beyond the threshold value, Y_i rises rapidly. The outputs from the output neurons in the case of a two-group problem will be 0 for one neuron and 1 for the other. The network learns to generate these values by adjusting the interconnection weights, W_{ji}, during the training process, using a feedback loop containing the error, which is the output value minus the (expected) target value. The training takes place repeatedly until a preset performance level, expressed as the maximum percent of prediction errors, is reached.

If the network is unable to reach the target accuracy rate, the number of hidden layers may be increased. In some instances, the hidden layer is also

changed dynamically by the solution algorithm used to adjust the interconnection weights. Once the training phase is completed, the network may be
used for predictive purposes.

The learning mechanism involves a number of problems:

- The learning stage may be very prolonged, in other words, it may
  require a huge number of cycles.
- The system might lock into a *local* minimum error without ever attaining the *global* (or attainable) error rate.
- The system may oscillate between one or two minimum error points.
- The system may not work well if the actual conditions differ significantly from the test conditions.
- The analysis of the weightings is complex and difficult to interpret. It
  is also difficult to know beforehand if the system is robust, that is,
  insensitive to small variations in input values. Lack of robustness may
  result if the neural network has been "overfitted."

CASA's Neural Network Model

CASA[5] has developed a neural network–based default prediction model.
Compustat[6] data for the time frame 1985–1995 was used in the development
sample. Traditional financial ratios, equity prices, and BARRA factors were
some of the inputs presented to the network. The validation of the neural
net model was performed using a k-group cross validation approach,
whereby the sample was divided into k groups, with $k - 1$ groups providing
the training data and the kth group the test data. The sample consisted of
nonfinancial firms with annual sales exceeding \$600 million. Predictions
were based on the period preceding the date of financial failure, which was
variously defined. A backward propagation algorithm was used to develop
the models.

Camilo Gomez, Director of CASA's Investment Analytics group, observes that, when compared against a benchmark model based on linear
discriminant analysis, the mean classification error (MCE) performance of
the neural network model was superior. "One of the advantages of neural
nets is that they can model nonlinearity through the use of the transfer functions," notes Jose Hernandez, an analyst at CASA. He found that the final

---

[5]CASA stands for Center for Adaptive Systems Applications and is based in Los Alamos, N.M.
The authors gratefully acknowledge the inputs from Drs. Camilo Gomez and José Hernadez on
the neural network model described here.

[6]Compustat is a company that provides quarterly and annual financial statement data in
machine-readable form for publicly traded companies. BARRA factors are fundamental drivers
of security returns. In the fixed income world, they include parallel shifts of the yield curve, as
well as yield curve twists and butterfly movements. In addition, they include various security-
specific factors such as credit quality, industry sector, call features, and so forth. These factor
weights are estimated from historical return data. The basic idea is that for each security, you
can statistically estimate its sensitivity to each of the fundamental factors. Then if you can predict
which way the factors will move, you can estimate price behavior of each security and of the
overall portfolio. BARRA is based in Berkeley, Ca.

models exhibited a "weakly nonlinear" tendency. Although it is possible to combine a set of linear models together (one model for each of k groups), it is more difficult to integrate a set of nonlinear models constructed this way. "Preparing the data properly to present it to the networks and using robust statistics to handle outliers are important elements of building neural network models," adds Hernandez.

Cost of misclassification was incorporated in the implementation segment, yielding interesting results. Industry groupings, the BARRA factors, and equity prices did not add significantly to the predictive ability of the model. According to Camilo Gomez, the results indicate that accounting statement financial ratios have information about corporate failure.

EXPERT SYSTEMS

Expert systems, also sometimes known as artificial intelligence (AI) systems, are computer-based decision-support systems. Expert systems make inferential and deductive judgments about a credit based on three components:

1. A consultation module that interacts with the user by asking questions, providing intermediate answers and hypotheses, and asking further questions until enough evidence has been collected to support a final recommendation.
2. A knowledge base containing static data; algorithms for financial simulation, optimization, and statistical forecasting; and a set of "production rules" that tell the system "what to do if."
3. A knowledge acquisition and learning module that generally consists of two components. The first creates production rules based on inputs provided off-line by an expert. For example, the system will extract from the lending officer the importance of customer background information relative to the business potential. The second component generates additional rules on its own.

Although AI systems appear to hold promise in the credit evaluation area (e.g., Chorafas and Steinmann 1991), they have yet to live up to this promise—apart from a few specialized applications in selected instances.[7] One reason for the limited success of AI is that the nature of credit risk itself is changing in the global financial system. Even human experts become obsolete quickly, and an automated expert runs the same risk. AI models may need frequent retooling and redesign. New technology has made a stronger contribution to progress in other aspects of the banking business, making it possible for institutions to increase their vigilance on credit exposure[8] and to be more flexible in extending credit because of better information sys-

---

[7]This is not to say that AI has been a failure in this area; just that it has not been absorbed by the credit management community as rapidly as one would have expected. For some examples, see Duchessi, Shawky, and Seagle (1988), Srinivasan and Kim (1988), and Shaw and Gentry (1988).

[8]For example, following the failure of Herstatt bank, money center banks implemented systems to monitor daylight overdraft.

tems.[9] It is fair to say that expert systems are still in a development stage, and that they currently play the role of a lending assistant and an automated checklist that forces an analyst to go through a disciplined process. We anticipate further innovations in this area as loan products and risk-rating criteria become more standardized and quantitative.[10]

CRITICISM OF MULTIVARIATE MODELS

The multivariate models presented here are sometimes criticized for being "fitted" or "associative," that is, they are empirical models lacking a theory. The theory behind most failure-prediction models is the same as the options theoretic framework for corporate failure: an overly leveraged firm will fail if unable to generate sufficient earnings. Scott (1981) compared a number of these empirical models with a theoretically sound approach using a bankruptcy construct. He concluded that the ZETA model most closely approximates his theoretical model.

While in many cases, multivariate accounting-based credit-scoring models have been shown to perform quite well over many different time periods and across many different countries (see Altman and Narayanan 1997), they have also been criticized for other reasons. Because they are based primarily on book-value accounting data (which in turn is measured at discrete intervals), these models may fail to pick up more subtle and fast-moving changes in borrower conditions, for example, those that would be reflected in capital market data and values. In addition, the world is inherently nonlinear. As a result, linear discriminant analysis and linear probability models may fail to forecast as accurately as models that relax the underlying assumption of linearity among explanatory variables.

Insofar as accounting data gives an incomplete picture of a firm's true condition and prospects, any model based on this data must, inevitably, suffer from certain limitations. Because the accounting profession has yet to come up with a good way to report on off-balance-sheet risk, such models cannot handle these risks well. Furthermore, for reasons having to do with resource valuation, balance sheet structure, or regulation, these models are unable to measure the risk of utilities, financial companies, new companies, and companies in extraction industries such as oil and mining.

The neural network approach may be criticized for its ad hoc theoretical foundation and its use of data mining to identify hidden correlations among the explanatory variables. In a comparison test, Altman, Marco, and Varetto (1994) concluded that the neural network approach did not materially improve upon the linear discriminant structure in predicting firm failure. Notwithstanding this finding, neural networks have profound potential to im-

---

[9]Credit, debit, and Smart cards are examples of technology as an enabling agent for extending credit.

[10]A major New York bank is in the process of implementing an AI-based credit system for lending to small business and professional corporations. The system is being built by Brightware, Inc., based in San Francisco, Ca.

prove upon past results. Indeed, significant success has been observed in tests run by Finance FX (a bond-rating replication firm based in Atlanta, Ga.) in the replication of Standard & Poor's bond ratings.

MODELS BASED ON MARKET RISK PREMIUMS

Models based on market risk premiums are used to impute implied probabilities of default from the term structure of yield spreads between default-free and risky corporate securities. An early version of this approach can be found in Jonkhart's work (1979), and a more elaborate version in Iben and Litterman's work (1989). These models derive implied forward rates on risk-free and risky bonds and use these rates to extract the market's expectation of default at different times in the future. This approach is based on the assumptions that (1) the expectations theory of interest rates holds; (2) transaction costs are small; (3) calls, sinking fund, and other option features are absent; and (4) discount bond yield curves exist or can be extracted from coupon-bearing yield curves. Recent models for defaultable loans include the effect of default risk, term structure risk, and market risk (see for example, Grenadier and Hall [1996], Longstaff and Schwartz [1995], and Das and Tufano [1996]).

MORTALITY MODELS

The mortality rate model of Altman (1989) and the aging approach of Asquith, Mullins, and Wolff (1989) are both based on the capital markets. These mortality–default rate models seek to derive actuarial-type probabilities of default from past data on bond defaults by credit grade (Moody's or Standard & Poor's) and years to maturity. All of the rating agencies have adopted and modified the mortality approach (e.g., Moody's 1990, Standard & Poor's 1991–92) and now routinely utilize it in their analysis of structured financial instruments (e.g., Duff & Phelps; McElravey and Shah 1996). Mortality–default rate models are discussed in greater detail in Chapter 15.

Mortality models may, potentially, be extended from bonds to loans, but efforts to do so have thus far been hampered by the lack of a loan default database of sufficient size. For example, McAllister and Mingo (1994) estimate that to develop stable estimates of default probabilities, an institution would need some 20,000 to 30,000 names in its database. Very few institutions worldwide come even remotely close to approaching this number of potential borrowers. Recently Altman and Suggitt (1997), summarized in Chapter 15, measure the mortality rate experience of large, syndicated bank loans for the 1991–1996 period.

Having presented models based on accounting and market value data, we now turn to models that rely entirely on market data to derive the credit risk of a borrower.

REFERENCES

Altman, E. I. 1968. Financial Ratios, Discriminant Analysis and the Prediction of Corporate Bankruptcy. *Journal of Finance* 23:189–209.

———. 1973. Predicting Railroad Bankruptcies in America. *Bell Journal of Economics and Management Science* 4:184–211.

———. 1976. Capitalization of Leases and the Predictability of Financial Ratios: A Comment. *Accounting Review* 2:408–412.

———. 1989. Measuring Corporate Bond Mortality and Performance. *Journal of Finance* 44 (4): 909–922.

———. 1993a. *Corporate Financial Distress and Bankruptcy,* 2nd ed. New York: John Wiley.

———. 1993b. Valuation, Loss Reserves and the Pricing of Corporate Loans. *Journal of Commercial Bank Lending* 75 (12): 56–62.

———. 1995. Predicting Financial Distress of Companies: Revisiting the Z-score and ZETA Models. Paper presented at the Korean Institute of Finance Conference on Bank Credit Risk Management, 28–30 June, Seoul, Korea.

Altman, E. I., R. G. Haldeman, and P. Narayanan. 1977. ZETA Analysis: A New Model to Identify Bankruptcy Risk of Corporations. *Journal of Banking and Finance* 1:29–54.

Altman, E. I., J. Hartzell, and M. Peck. 1995. *Emerging Markets Corporate Bonds: A Scoring System.* New York: Salomon Brothers. Reprinted in *Emerging Market Capital Flows,* edited by R. Levich. Amsterdam: Kluwer Publishing, 1997.

———. 1996. *Emerging Markets Corporate Bond Scoring System: Mexican Mid-Year 1996 Review and Outlook.* New York: Salomon Brothers, Inc.

Altman, E. I., G. Marco, and F. Varetto (1994. Corporate Distress Diagnosis: Comparisons Using Linear Discriminant Analysis and Neural Networks. *Journal of Banking and Finance* 18 (3): 505–529.

Altman, E. I., and P. Narayanan. 1997. An International Survey of Business Failure Classification Models. In *Internationl Accounting and Finance Handbook,* edited by F. D. S. Choi. New York: John Wiley & Sons.

Altman, E. I., and H. J. Suggitt. 1997. Mortality Rates on Large Syndicated Corporate Bank Loans. Working paper S-97-39, NYU Salomon Center, New York, N.Y.

Asquith, P., D. W. Mullins Jr., and E. D. Wolff. 1989. Original Issue High Yield Bonds: Aging Analysis of Defaults, Exchanges and Calls. *Journal of Finance* 44 (4): 923–953.

Beaver, W. 1967. Financial Ratios as Predictors of Failures. *Journal of Accounting Research* 4 (suppl.): 71–111.

Berry, R. H., and D. Trigueiros. 1996. Applying Neural Networks to the Extraction of Knowledge from Accounting Reports. In *Neural Networks in Finance and Investing,* edited by R. R. Trippi and E. Turban. Chicago: Irwin Professional Publishing.

Board of Governors of the Federal Reserve System. 1997a. *Flow of Funds Accounts of the United States 1963–1972.* Washington, D.C.: Board of Governors of the Federal Reserve System.

———. 1997b. *Flow of Funds Accounts of the United States 1973–1981.* Washington, D.C.: Board of Governors of the Federal Reserve System.

———. 1997c. *Flow of Funds Accounts of the United States 1982–1990.* Washington, D.C.: Board of Governors of the Federal Reserve System.

———. 1997d. *Flow of Funds Accounts of the United States 1991–1996.* Washington, D.C.: Board of Governors of the Federal Reserve System.

Chorafas, D. N., and H. Steinmann. 1991. *Expert Systems in Banking: A Guide for Senior Managers.* New York: New York University Press.

Coats, P., and K. Fant. 1993. Recognizing Financial Distress Patterns Using A Neural Network Tool. *Financial Management* 22 (3): 142–155.

Compustat Data Tape. Standard & Poor's Corporation, New York, N.Y.

Das, S. R., and P. Tufano. 1996. Pricing Credit-Sensitive Debt When Interest Rates, Credit Ratings and Credit Spreads Are Stochastic. *Journal of Financial Engineering* 5 (2): 161–198.

Deakin, E. B. 1972. A Discriminant Analysis of Predictors of Business Failure. *Journal of Accounting Research* 10 (1): 169–179.

Duchessi, P., H. Shawky, and J. P. Seagle. 1988. A Knowledge-Engineered System for Commercial Loan Decisions. *Financial Management* (Autumn): 57–65.

Dun & Bradstreet. 1997. *The Failure Record*. New York: Dun & Bradstreet.

Grenadier, S. R., and B. J. Hall. 1996. Risk-based Capital Standards and the Riskiness of Bank Portfolios: Credit and Factor Risks. *Regional Science and Urban Economics*.

Iben, T., and R. Litterman. 1989. Corporate Bond Valuation and the Term Structure of Credit Spreads. *Journal of Portfolio Management* 26:433–456.

Jonkhart, M. 1979. On the Term Structure of Interest Rates and the Risk of Default. *Journal of Banking and Finance* 3 (3): 253–262.

Kao, D. L., and J. Kallberg. 1994. Strategies for Measuring and Managing Risk Concentration in Loan Portfolios. *Journal of Commercial Bank Lending* 76 (5): 18–27.

Lachenbruch, P. A. 1967. An Almost Unbiased Method of Obtaining Confidence Intervals for the Probability of Misclassification in Discriminant Analysis. *Biometrics* 23:639–645.

Longstaff, F. A., and E. S. Schwartz. 1995. A Simple Approach to Valuing Risky Fixed and Floating Rate Debt. *Journal of Finance* 50 (3): 790–819.

Lovie, A. D., and P. Lovie. 1986. The Flat Maximum Effect and Linear Scoring Models for Prediction. *Journal of Forecasting* 5:159–168.

McAllister, P., and J. J. Mingo. 1994. Commercial Loan Risk Management, Credit-Scoring and Pricing: The Need for a New Shared Data Base. *Journal of Commercial Bank Lending* 76 (9): 6–22.

McElravey, J. N., and V. Shah. 1996. Rating Cash Flow Collateralized Bond Obligations. *Special Report, Asset Backed Securities*. Chicago: Duff & Phelps Credit Rating Co.

McKinsey & Co. 1993. Special Report on the New World of Financial Services. *McKinsey Quarterly* 2:59–106.

Moody's Investors Service. 1990. Corporate Bond Defaults and Default Rates. In *Moody's Special Reports*. New York: Moody's Investors Service.

———— 1996. Corporate Bond Defaults and Default Rates. In *Moody's Special Reports*. New York: Moody's Investors Service.

Ohlson, J. 1980. Financial Ratios and the Probabilistic Prediction of Bankruptcy. *Journal of Accounting Research* 18 (1): 109–131.

Scott, J. 1981. The Probability of Bankruptcy: A Comparison of Empirical Predictions and Theoretical Models. *Journal of Banking and Finance* 5 (3): 317–344.

Shaw, M. J., and J. A. Gentry. 1988. Using an Expert System with Inductive Learning to Evaluate Business Loans. *Financial Management* (Autumn): 45–56.

Srinivasan, V., and Y. H. Kim. 1988. Designing Expert Financial Systems: A Case Study of Corporate Credit Management. *Financial Management* (Autumn): 32–43.

Standard & Poor's. 1991–92. Corporate Bond Defaults Study. Parts 1–3. *Credit Week*, 16 September; 15 September; 21 December.

Trippi, R. R., and E. Turban. 1996, ed. *Neural Networks in Finance and Investing*. Chicago: Irwin Professional Publishing.

ADDITIONAL READING

Altman, E. I. 1983. *Corporate Financial Distress*. New York: John Wiley.

Beaver, W. 1968. Alternative Accounting Measures as Predictors of Failure. *Accounting Review* 43:113–122.

Dawes, R. M., and B. Corrigan. 1974. Linear Models in Decision Making. *Psychology Bulletin* 81:95–106.

Fisher, L. 1959. Determinants of Risk Premiums on Corporate Bonds. *Journal of Political Economy* 67.

Frydman, H., E. I. Altman, and D. L. Kao. 1988. Introducing Recursive Partitioning Analysis For Financial Classification: The Case of Financial Distress. *Journal of Banking and Finance* 7:197–223.

Moody's Investors Service, 1997. *Historic Default Rates of Corporate Bond Issuers 1920–1997*. In *Moody's Special Reports*. New York: Moody's Investors Service.

Orgler, Y. 1980. A Credit Scoring Model For Commercial Loans. *Journal of Money, Credit, and Banking* 2: 435–445.

Zavgren, C. V. 1983. Corporate Failure Predictors: The State of the Art. *Journal of Accounting Literature* 2.

Zmijewski, M. E. 1984. Methodological Issues Related to the Estimation of Financial Distress Prediction Models. *Journal of Accounting Research* 22 (suppl.): 59–86.

Chapter *11*

Corporate Credit Risk Models Based on Stock Price

The manifest function of financial markets is to allow individuals and businesses to trade financial assets. An additional latent function of the capital markets is to provide information useful for decision-making. . . . As the diversity of financial markets has increased during the past two decades, so too have opportunities to extract useful information from the prices of financial instruments.

—Robert Merton and Zvie Bodie in *The Global Financial System*

The stock market can be viewed as a vast mechanism for valuing publicly owned companies. Information about economies, industries, and companies travels at high speed to investment analysts and investors both large and small. As a result, stock prices fluctuate throughout the business day. To the extent that variations in a company's stock price provide reliable evidence of changes in its creditworthiness, lenders have an opportunity to tap a ready-made credit risk management tool of immense scope and power.

The leading example of stock market–based credit measures is the expected default frequency (EDF) model of KMV.[1,2] KMV initially began with the measurement of expected default frequency and has now extended into portfolio management.[3]

To understand the KMV model, we begin with the developments in modern finance that led to options pricing methods. For a more detailed description of these developments, we refer the reader to standard texts on finance theory (e.g., Haugen 1997). The notion that options pricing methods can be used to assess credit risk may at first seem improbable, but the logic of this approach becomes clearer as we trace the evolution of corporate finance theory. After describing and critiquing the KMV model, we contrast it with Zeta, because these models for measuring credit risk are the best known today.

---

[1] KMV is a San Francisco based firm that sells credit analysis software and information products to financial institutions.

[2] A similar option theory–based model to measure credit risk, called Helix, is marketed by Helix Investment Partners, L.P. Los Angeles. It employs the same inputs as KMV's model and produces a risk score for corporate bonds. See also Newton (1993).

[3] Please see Chapter 19 for a discussion of portfolio management.

PREDECESSORS OF OPTIONS THEORY

In the 1950s, Franco Modigliani and Merton Miller began an exploration of the determinants of a corporation's capital structure that ultimately led to a radical revision in corporate finance. A firm's capital structure is the particular mixture of debt, equity, and other liabilities that the firm uses to finance its assets. Until Modigliani and Miller, the prevailing view was that the market place required more return on a firm's debt as its leverage increased, with the natural result that at some level of leverage, the additional required return would make the use of more debt undesirable. In part, this view was based on the notion that the firm's investment policy was related to capital structure. The required yield on a debt issue would depend on how the firm intended to use the proceeds. As the firm tried to invest more, its return on investment would fall. The overall implication was that there existed a certain level of leverage that would minimize the firm's overall cost of capital. What Modigliani and Miller showed was that, under certain simple conditions, the overall cost of capital was independent of the particular mixture of debt and equity. They also showed that this was the case, even though increasing leverage led to higher required returns on both the debt and equity of the firm.

This was a startling result because it meant that there had to be an additional factor or factors, in addition to leverage alone, in order to explain a firm's capital structure. The search for the additional factors continues today, with some consensus but still much disagreement on the relative importance of various factors.

Equally important to their specific results was their mode of analysis. Their approach was to consider the investment decision and the financing decision separately. A given investment plan implied a stream of expected cash flows for the firm, and that implied a current market value for the firm. This made the market value of the firm into the underlying firm characteristic. The market value of the firm's debt, equity, and other liabilities derived from the overall value of the firm and, taken together, added up to the firm's value.

In essence, the expected operating cash flows of the firm determined its overall value; the capital structure merely represented the division of those cash flows to providers of capital. For instance, more debt meant that debt holders provided more capital and received more of the firm's cash flows. However, more debt did not intrinsically raise or lower the value of the firm, because it was considered separately from the investment program. Subsequent to their original 1958 paper, Modigliani and Miller issued an important correction (Modiglianai and Miller [1963]), in which they noted that if the tax treatment of corporate interest expense was taken into account, the firm's value was no longer independent of leverage. Indeed, a firm's value could be enhanced by increasing leverage. Since in the real world firms employ only a moderate amount of debt, additional variables are needed to explain a firm's optimal capital structure. Of these, bankruptcy costs and differential *personal tax* treatment between interest and dividend are the most significant (see Ross, Westerfield, and Jaffe [1993]).

Unfortunately, at the time that Modigliani and Miller wrote, there was no known way to separately determine the debt and equity values. By the rules of debt, debt holders are paid before equity holders; debt has seniority. No method existed for determining the value of the debt as a senior claim on the firm's cash flows, nor equity as a junior claim. The world had to wait for the development of options pricing theory. As will become clear from what follows, the option theoretic model of default addresses bankruptcy cost by equating all, or part of it, to the value of equity. Bankruptcy here is taken to mean that stockholders relinquish the firm to the creditors when default occurs.

OPTION PRICING

There are three basic types of financial contracts: spot transactions, forwards, and options. A spot transaction is one that occurs "on the spot," namely, where an asset is sold for the current price and is paid for immediately in cash. A forward transaction is one in which the price is agreed today, but the delivery of the asset and the payment actually occur at an agreed future date. An exchange-traded futures contract is a type of forward transaction.

An option contract is like a forward except that the buyer of the option does not have to carry out the transaction. The option can be either an option to buy (call option) or an option to sell (put option). The option usually has a maturity and sometimes can be exercised before maturity.

Both forward and option contracts are considered derivatives because their values can be derived from the value of the spot transaction. Perhaps the major development in finance in the last 30 years is options pricing theory. This theory is the result of work by Fisher Black, Myron Scholes, and Robert Merton, and allows one to derive options prices, including formulas for special cases. The fundamental idea behind options pricing is a generalization of how forward contracts are priced.

A forward purchase contract involves specifying the terms of a transaction that takes place at a later date. The same result achieved by buying an asset forward can be achieved by borrowing money to buy the asset today and repaying the borrowing at the maturity date. In this case, one has ownership of the asset at maturity, by making a payment specified today. Because this yields the same payoff as the forward purchase contract, it must have the same value. Thus, the forward price today must be the cost of buying the good today times one plus the rate of interest one must pay on the borrowing at maturity. In essence, the payoff to the forward contract can be mimicked by buying the asset today and borrowing.

The payoff to a call option can also be mimicked by buying the asset and borrowing. However, instead of making a single transaction, as in the case of the forward transaction, it is necessary to make an initial transaction and then adjust it as the spot price of the asset changes through time and the maturity decreases. Black and Scholes derived a method for constructing the initial transaction and subsequent adjusting transactions so that the option payoff is mimicked and no additional cash is required or produced (Black and Scholes 1973). This means that the value of the option must be the same as the cost of the initial transaction.

In order to make their derivation, however, they needed to know one additional piece of information: the volatility of the underlying asset. The volatility measures the likely percentage range of variation of the spot price of the underlying asset. Generally, greater volatility implies a larger purchase transaction and thus a larger value for the call option.

EQUITY IS A CALL OPTION

The option pricing work of Black, Scholes, and Merton neatly dovetailed with the capital structure theory of Modigliani and Miller. Junior and senior capital structure claims can be understood as options. Thus, one can determine the value of a firm's equity by reference to the underlying market value of the firm. Options pricing supplied the valuation technique that was missing a decade earlier when Modigliani and Miller realized that equity and debt were derivatives.

How does this work? Consider a very simple holding company whose only asset consists of shares in a publicly traded company, say, IBM. Let us assume that the holding company has debt and equity, and the debt consists of a single discount note due in one year. Let D be the face value of the note. This means that the firm must make a single payment of D in one year, or it must default. If it defaults, it will turn over its assets to the lender, and its equity will be worthless.

Under what circumstances will the firm default? If the value of its asset, the IBM stock, is worth more than D in one year, then the firm will not want to default and will not have to. By selling enough IBM stock, it can repay the debt and still retain the difference between the value of the stock and D. On the other hand, if the IBM stock is worth less than D, then the firm will want to default because it would rather give the lenders the stock than have to come up with additional money to pay off the debt. If it did come up with the additional money, it would get nothing for it because the money would just go to repay the debt. On the other hand, if the firm defaulted, then it could use the additional money to capitalize a new firm. In short, the firm will default and the equity will be worthless if the assets are worth less than D in one year; and the firm will not default and the equity will be worth the difference between the asset value and D if the assets are worth more than D in one year.

The equity of the holding company in this example has exactly the same payoff as a call option on the same amount of IBM stock as held by the firm, with an aggregate exercise price of D. In that case, the option would be exercised when the IBM stock was worth more than D, and the payoff would be the difference between the IBM stock value and D; otherwise the option would be worthless. In other words, the equity of the firm is a call option on the assets of the firm, where the exercise price and maturity are given by the face value and maturity of the debt.

We could explicitly value the equity of this firm if we knew the face value and the maturity of the debt, the value of the assets today, and the volatility of the assets. For this simple example, we could actually use the Black-Scholes option pricing formula (Merton 1974). For more complicated cases, we could not use the Black-Scholes formula, but we could use its general approach to obtain a value for the equity of the firm.

From the standpoint of credit analysis, the interesting point is that default can be thought of as the failure to exercise an option. Equity holders "optionally" own the firm, but if the firm does poorly enough, they do not exercise their option, but rather allow the firm's ownership to pass to the debt holders in lieu of paying the debt service.

DEBT IS LIKE SELLING A PUT OPTION

This circumstance can also be recast using the so-called put-call parity theorem. It says that purchasing a call option with an exercise price of D is equivalent to owning the underlying asset, borrowing with a required repayment of D, and holding a put option with an exercise value of D. At maturity, if the asset is worth less than D, one sells the asset for D using the put option and uses the proceeds to pay off the debt, with nothing left over. On the other hand, if the asset is worth more than D, one sells it and uses the proceeds to pay the debt and does not use the put option. Both methods result in the same payoff as the call option, thus the equivalence.

Using this result (because the equity is a call option) we have the following interpretation: The equity holders own the asset, have borrowed D, but own a put that enables them to sell the assets for D. In essence, the debt holders of the firm, at the same time that they lent to the firm, by recognizing the possibility of default, have also sold a put option to the equity holders. The put enables the equity holders to "put" them the assets in lieu of paying off the debt. Thus the firm's debt is like a default-risk-free loan of amount D less a put option. In this case, the event of default is identical to exercise of the put option by the equity holders.

The firm's debt is always worth less than default-risk-free debt, because it is short a put option. The greater the default risk of the firm, the more valuable the put option, and the less valuable the debt, because it is short the put option. Debt subject to default risk can be decomposed into default-risk-free debt and a put option. In doing credit analysis, the focus is on understating the value of the put option and the probability of it being exercised.

THE EDF MODEL

KMV Corporation (1995) has created an approach for estimating the default probability of a firm that is based conceptually on Merton's (1974) approach. In three steps, it determines an EDF for a company. In the first step, the market value and volatility of the firm are estimated from the market value of its stock, the volatility of its stock, and the book value of its liabilities. In the second step, the firm's default point is calculated from the firm's liabilities. Also, an expected firm value is determined from the current firm value. Using these two values plus the firm's volatility, a measure is constructed that represents the number of standard deviations from the expected firm value to the default point (the *distance to default*). Finally, a mapping is determined between the distance to default and the default rate, based on the historical default experience of companies with different distance-to-default values.

In the case of private companies, for which stock price and default data are generally unavailable, KMV uses essentially the same approach by estimating the value and volatility of the private firm directly from its observed characteristics and accounting data. These estimates, however, are based on public company data.

The starting point of the KMV model is the proposition that when the market value of a firm drops below a certain level, the firm will default on its obligations (Figure 11.1).

In Figure 11.1, the value of the firm, projected to a given future date, has a probability distribution characterized by its expected value and standard deviation (volatility). The area under the distribution below the line representing the book liabilities of the firm is the probability of default. As can be seen, this probability value depends on the position of the liabilities line and the shape of the asset value distribution. The following is a detailed description of the methods used to implement the steps described above to obtain an empirical estimate of this default probability.

For a firm with publicly traded shares, the market value of equity may be observed. Using the previously described option approach, the market value of equity may be expressed as the value of a call option, as follows:

$$\text{Market value of equity}^4 = f \text{ (book value of liabilities,}$$
$$\text{market value of assets,} \qquad (1)$$
$$\text{volatility of assets, time horizon)}$$

KMV uses a special form of the options pricing approach that they do not disclose. To make their approach more concrete, the Black-Scholes options formula can be substituted for the function f. This results in the following expression:

$$E = VN(d_1) - De^{-\tau}N(d_2) \qquad (1a)$$

where E = is the market value of equity (option value)
  D = is the book value of liabilities (strike price)
  V = is the market value of assets
  τ = is the time horizon
  r = is the risk-free borrowing and lending rate
  σ_a = is the percentage standard deviation (volatility) of asset value
  N = is the cumulative normal distribution function whose value is calculated at d_1 and d_2, where

$$d_1 = \frac{\ln\left(\frac{V}{D}\right) + \left(r + \frac{1}{2}\sigma_a^2\right)\tau}{\sigma_a \sqrt{\tau}}$$

$$d_2 = d_1 - \sigma_a \sqrt{\tau}$$

---

[4]Strictly speaking, this function should also include the riskless rate of return for borrowing and lending.

Figure 11.1 KMV Model Schematic

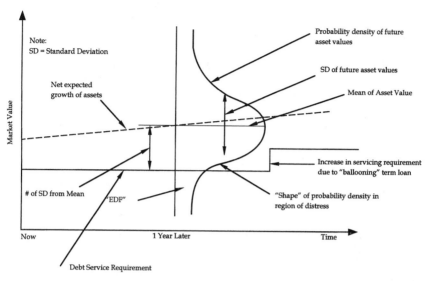

Source: McQuown (1993). Copyright by KMV Corporation. Reprinted with permission.

In equations (1) or (1a), there are two unknowns: the market value of assets (V) and volatility of asset value (σ_a). However, it is also possible to derive another equation from equations (1) or (1a), by taking the mathematical expectation after differentiating both sides of the equations.

Volatility of equity (σ_e) = g (book value of liabilities,
market value of assets, $\quad$ (2)
volatility of assets, time horizon)

Again, this equation can be understood by using the Black-Scholes formula as an example. By taking the first derivative on both sides of (1a), and applying the *expectation* operator, one obtains the following expression[5]:

$$\sigma_e = \frac{N(d_1)V\sigma_a}{E} \qquad (2a)$$

In equations (1a) and (2a), the known variables are the market value of equity (E), volatility of equity $(\sigma_e$, estimated from historic data), book value of liabilities (D), and the time horizon (τ). The two unknowns are the market value of the assets (V) and the volatility of the assets (σ). Because there are two equations with two unknowns, a solution can be found. This completes the first step.

Next, the expected asset value at the horizon and the default point are determined. An investor holding the asset would expect to get a payout plus a capital gain equal to the expected return. The expected return is related to the systematic risk of the asset. Using a measure of the asset's systematic

---

[5]Private communication with Steve Kealhofer and Peter Crosbie, KMV Corporation.

risk, KMV determines an expected return based upon historic asset market returns. This is reduced by the payout rate determined from the firm's interest and dividend payments. The result is the expected appreciation rate, which, applied to the current asset value, gives the expected future value of the asset.

In the previous analysis it was assumed that the firm would default when its total market value reached the book value of its liabilities. At that point, its value would just be sufficient to pay off its obligations. Based upon empirical analysis of defaults, KMV has found that the most frequent default point is at a firm value approximately equal to current liabilities plus 50% of long-term liabilities.

Given the firm's expected value at the horizon, and its default point at the horizon, KMV determines the percentage drop in the firm value that would bring it to the default point. For instance, if the firm's expected value in one year was 100, and its default point was 25, then a 75% drop in the asset value would bring it to the default point. The likelihood of a 75% drop depends on the volatility of the firm. By dividing the percentage drop by the volatility, KMV controls for the effect of different volatilities. Thus, if the firm's volatility was 15% per year, then a 75% drop would correspond to an event equal to five standard deviations.

The number of standard deviations that the asset value must drop in order to reach the default point is called the distance to default. Mathematically, this can be expressed as

$$\text{Distance from default} = \frac{(\text{expected market value of assets} - \text{default point})}{(\text{expected market value of assets})(\text{volatility of assets})}$$

The distance-from-default metric is a normalized measure and thus may be used for comparing one company with another. A key assumption of the KMV approach is that all the relevant information for determining relative default risk is contained in the expected market value of assets, the default point, and the asset volatility. Differences due to industry, national location, size, and so forth are assumed to be subsumed in these measures, notably the asset volatility.

Distance from default is an ordinal measure akin to a bond rating; it still does not tell you what the default probability is. In order to extend this risk measure to a cardinal or a probability measure, KMV uses historical default experience to determine an expected default frequency as a function of distance from default. It does this by comparing the calculated distances from default and the observed actual default rate for the same group of firms. A smooth curve fitted to those data yields the EDF as a function of the distance from default.

PRIVATE COMPANY KMV MODEL

Since the EDF model relies on market prices to predict default, it cannot be applied directly to private companies. For these, KMV uses data from public firms to develop an estimation model for the market value of assets and the asset volatility. It updates the parameters for these models frequently as a way of connecting current market information to private firms. However, these models must rely on the private firm's reported characteristics and accounting data, which may not be as timely or accurate as would be ideal.

The market value of the firm is modeled as shuttling between two values, the operating value and the liquidating value. The operating value is calculated as EBITDA[6] times a multiplier. The multiplier is estimated by stratifying the public companies by country and industry. The liquidating value is based on the firm's book liabilities. When EBITDA is high, the market value approaches the operating value; when it is low, it approaches the liquidating value. The effect of this formulation is to estimate a larger value than if the operating value were used alone. The liquidating value serves to hold up the value of the firm when its cash flow performance is bad.

The asset volatility of the firm is modeled as a function of sales size, industry, and asset size. Because the asset volatility has already been estimated for publicly traded firms, the contribution made by sales size, industry group, and asset size is determined by a multivariate statistical technique. This relationship is then applied to a private firm's characteristics to obtain an estimate of its asset volatility.

Using the market value and volatility thus estimated, the EDF is estimated for the distance-from-default ratios on the basis of the public firm default experience, in a manner similar to that described earlier.[7] However, the mapping between distance to default and EDF is slightly different for the public and private models as a result of the information lost in using estimated rather than actual market data.

In all cases it is worth noting that the model for firms with nontraded equity is derived from the data for firms with publicly traded equity. Nontraded firms are assumed to behave identically to traded firms, once one takes into account the effects of size, industry, and country.[8]

KMV AND OTHER APPROACHES

The EDF model has two fundamental differences when compared with other approaches. First, it relies on the information in equity prices. Second, it does not try explicitly to be predictive. Whereas agency debt ratings are based on trying to forecast future events, there are no real future forecasts in the EDF model. It simply relates the current value of the firm to its default point and historical volatility. Thus, if it has predictive power, it is because the current value of the firm is a good predictor of future values. Because this value is derived from the firm's equity market value, the EDF model is totally dependent on stock prices for its information content.

---

[6] Earnings before taxes, interest, depreciation, and amortization.

[7] KMV maintains a large database of defaulted public firms and reports to have records of upwards of 2,500 defaults.

[8] The authors benefited from discussions with Stephen Kealhofer and Peter Crosbie of KMV Corporation, and Jan Nicholson of CapMAC in the exposition of the model and also received written comments from them on an earlier version of this chapter. However, the authors take responsibility for any remaining errors or omissions.

The starting point for all models is observation and human reasoning. The EDF model comes from a conceptual model of firm value and its relation to debt and equity values, using options theory. The conceptual approach tells us which variables should be important and how they should be combined mathematically. Statistical approaches identify important factors based on experience and consider structural assumptions and alternative relationships before settling on the most robust one. More general statistical approaches, such as neural nets, make few structural assumptions, but at the expense of requiring large amounts of data to be fit appropriately. All methods, KMV included, have an element of fitting. The difference is at what point the process of fitting to empirical experience is introduced.

There are costs and benefits with any approach. No conceptual approach provides a true ex ante specification of which variables to include and exclude, and historical testing of different alternatives is conceptually the same as statistically fitting a model. By narrowing the range of possible variables and the types of interactions, the conceptual approach results in less likelihood of overfitting bias; but there is a possibility of underfitting (excluding what may be an important variable). Both overfitting and underfitting can result in less than satisfactory performance.

The stability of the conceptual approach relies on the concept being correct and being correctly applied, and on the stability of the estimates going into the model. The stability of the statistical approach relies on having correctly identified the important variables, the structural specification of the relaionship, transformations to satisfy distributional assumptions, and rigorous testing on independent samples. Both approaches leave open the possibility of refinement over time as the fundamental forces at work become better understood.

Ultimately, however, the real issue is how well the models work and to what extent their use contributes to improved financial performance of the institution. A conceptual model that does not perform has no advantage over a statistical model that does. Unfortunately, there are no published comparisons of the different approaches, and until such studies are made, the jury must remain out on the advantages or disadvantages of the different approaches.

However, rather than emphasizing the differences, it is interesting to note the similarities. To assess similarities, the Spearman coefficient[9] was calculated for the 1995 EDF and the Zeta score based on book value of equity on a sample of 865 firms. The value of the coefficient came out to be 0.7031 and was significant at the .001 level. This indicates a fairly strong association between the two systems. Approximately half the variance in EDF ranks can be explained by Zeta score ranks, and vice versa.

---

[9]The Spearman rank correlation is similar to the more commonly known Pearson correlation coefficient, both of which are used to measure the degree of association between pairs of numerical values. Spearman's correlation is used for comparison where the numerical value is more indicative of rank than of any absolute measure. Both Zeta and KMV values, though expressed in numerical quantities, indicate the relative likelihood of default of a set of companies rather than the absolute likelihood. For more details on rank correlation see Lehmann (1975).

The distance to default value contains two primary types of information: leverage and volatility. The relationship between the market value of the firm and the firm's liabilities is a leverage relationship, albeit based on market rather than book values. This leverage is judged against the volatility of the firm, based again on market rather than book values. Looking at Zeta's variables, there is also extensive leverage information conveyed by book leverage and coverage ratios, as well as volatility information conveyed by earnings stability and size. It should not be surprising that there is a significant correlation between the two measures.

As noted above, the most distinguishing feature of the EDF measure is that it imposes such a direct connection between market values and default probabilities. Historically, there is a close connection between changes in EDF values for a given firm and changes in the equity value of the firm, a much closer connection than exists for any extant statistical models. In KMV's view, this is a desirable feature because it represents a translation of the information in equity prices into credit information.

PREDICTIVE ABILITY OF DEFAULT MODELS

Most predictive models draw attention to their effectiveness by pointing to recent corporate defaults or bankruptcies that they correctly anticipated. Although this is impressive and necessary, it is rare to see instances publicized in which the model predicted financial difficulties but nothing adverse happened subsequently. In looking at predictive models, one therefore must look beyond examples and anecdotal evidence to stronger statistical tests of effectiveness. The discussion that follows, although concerned with aspects of the KMV model, is applicable to other models as well.

The simplest test of the predictive accuracy of a model is to compare a specific prediction with the actual outcome. For example, if a model were to say that the unconditional probability[10] of default is .25 for a group of firms over a period of one year, and 25 percent of the firms in that group *actually defaulted* in the ensuing one-year period, then the model would be 100 percent accurate and have 0 percent forecast error. The forecast error calculated from ex ante value (estimate) and ex post value (realization) is the best test of performance. If the predicted value of default probability were 25 percent and the realization 35 percent, then the model error would be 40 percent (35 minus 25 divided by 25). If the predicted probability were 25 percent and the realized default was 15 percent, then the error would still be 40 percent (25 minus 15 divided by 25). However, an error of the first kind (not anticipating failure) would cost many, many times more than an error of the second kind (overanticipating failure). It should be noted that the forecast error is calculated not by applying it to a single firm, but to a group of firms with similar values of default probability.

The best test of predictive power begins by assembling data on the largest possible set of firms, including firms that subsequently defaulted and

---

[10] *Unconditional* means that no other conditions must be attached, for example, industry membership or bond rating, that is, no other information other than what the model uses as input.

firms that did not default. For each firm, the model value is calculated at preset times prior to the event of default (for subsequent defaulters, or contemporaneously to the defaulters for the nondefaulters). For each possible level of model value, one can pretend that firms falling below that level are predicted to default, and firms above that value are predicted not to default. These predictions can then be compared with subsequent outcomes.

As noted above, there are two possible types of error: predicting default when it did not occur, and failing to predict default when it did occur. One can determine the error type for each level of model value. The resulting relationships provide a complete characterization of the default predictive power of the model.

The absolute results of such tests are dependent on the particular samples used. In general, it is not appropriate to compare results from one population with results on a different population. To compare two different models, it is important to use exactly the same sample population and include only firms for which both model values were simultaneously available.

The limitation of such tests is that they concentrate solely on default prediction. For higher-quality segments of the population where defaults are rare, it is difficult to draw conclusions strictly from default prediction power. It is particularly in the higher quality ranges where one often wants to use a model to rank firms' risks for purposes of pricing or portfolio management. Models may exhibit similar default prediction power for higher-quality firms but provide surprisingly different rankings of default risk, simply because the predicted default rates are small and there are few subsequent defaults to validate one approach versus the other.

In an ideal world, one could test rankings on higher-quality firms by looking at the agreement of the default-risk rankings with the market pricing of the firm's debt instruments. In practice, the relative low quality of reported bond price data makes it difficult to perform such tests.

As a final point, it can be argued that comparisons of alternative models are meaningful only in the context of portfolio risk *and* reward. There is a natural distribution of credits in the world (there are far fewer AAA credits than BBB credits, for example), and there is a market-determined risk premium for each of these credits. Rather than comparing prediction error rates among models, a more direct evaluation could be carried out by means of a trading simulation based on consistent decision rules and constraints. The resulting profit and loss numbers could then be compared. Unfortunately, this method also relies on better-quality debt price data than are currently available.

DEFAULT PREDICTION RESULTS FOR THE KMV MODEL

KMV's published results indicate that its model is a more powerful default predictor than S&P. For example, using an EDF hurdle that excludes 72 percent of the subsequent defaulters eliminates only 20 percent of the nondefaulting population. Using an S&P hurdle that excludes the same 72 percent of the defaulters excludes almost 30 percent of the nondefaulters. Although agency debt ratings provide a convenient benchmark for judging performance, it should be noted that the markets do not view bond-rating changes as conveying *timely* information (Wakeman 1990). Outperforming the rating agency is thus a necessary but by no means a sufficient condition, because bond yields appear to lead the rating agency changes as well.

The performance of the Helix model, another market-value-based approach, in anticipating rating changes by S&P illustrates this point (see Table 11.1). It reinforces the proposition that it *is* possible to anticipate rating changes. Even if the bond rating is not the ultimate arbiter of credit risk, the publication of comparative tables by KMV, Zeta, and others will be helpful to the users of these models.

Promising results have been reported on the extent to which the EDF model is able to anticipate yield changes of publicly traded bonds, but a definitive study has yet to be published.[11]

APPLICATIONS

Historically, banks have ignored stock market prices in their lending decisions. To the extent that models such as those of KMV or Helix bring market capitalization into the lending equation, they should certainly add to the quality of the decisions made by banks. The actual uses to which financial institutions (mostly commercial banks) put the KMV model vary widely. At one end of the spectrum, some banks use a company's EDF as one more piece of information among the general sources it consults. Other institutions have formally added EDF values as supplemental information to the traditional credit analysis. Still others use the EDF as way of assigning internal risk ratings to their credits.[12] Some use EDF as an early warning tool in the

---

[11] Using the option-adjusted yield spreads on a universe of 108 bonds, KMV has found that forming portfolios using EDFs to determine under- or overpricing generates significant excess returns. However, the authors caveat the results due to potential error in the reported bond prices and spreads (Vasicek 1995).

[12] The EDF may often signal frequent changes to the risk ratings, which may be viewed as a negative; KMV's position is that indeed the credit risk of the borrower continually changes.

Table 11.1 Performance of the Helix Model in Anticipating S&P's Rating Changes, 1993–1997

		Instances Where Helix			
	Total	Led	Coincided	Followed	Disagreed
Upgrades	408	317	10	9	72
Downgrades	391	261	17	21	90
Total	799	578	27	30	162
Upgrades	100%	77.7%	2.5%	2.2%	17.6%
Downgrades	100%	66.8%	4.3%	5.4%	23.0%
Total	100%	72.3%	3.4%	3.8%	20.3%

Source: Helix Investment Partners, L.P. (1997). Reprinted with permission.

portfolio review group to alert loan officers about changes in a company's risk profile. And at least one institution uses EDFs as the sole indicator of credit risk in loan pricing as well as in valuation related to the trading of bank debt.

KMV usually recommends that banks use the model in the manner most suited to their circumstances. For some, the EDF may serve as a tool to prioritize credit decisions. It may also help to minimize the time spent in assessing default risk so that greater resources can be focused on structuring a deal to maximize recovery in the event of default. In nearly all cases, the EDF model tends to act as a change agent in stimulating management thinking on credit risk.

CONCLUDING REMARKS

In conclusion, the EDF model represents an innovative approach to utilizing stock market information in the valuation of debt. Banks can no longer ignore equity market information. They need to monitor equity market valuations constantly and interpret the implications for credit risk. If a model is able to do so objectively and consistently, it is, as Brian Ranson of Bank of Montreal puts it, "another arrow in your quiver." Clearly, as he goes on to point out, an institution cannot rely exclusively on the signals from one model—nor can it ignore them. John Hopper, Director of Structured Finance at Barclays Capital, agrees that KMV-type models are very useful but points out that their conclusions have to be used along with other information and sometimes modified to suit the unique structure of a particular financing, as for example, funded subparticipations.

Innovative approaches such as KMV's model and Zeta provide decision makers with additional tools to be used in addressing credit risk management in a changing world. In conclusion it is well to note Jules Henri Poincaré's admonition:

> To doubt everything or to believe everything are two equally convenient solutions; both dispense with the necessity of reflection.[13]

It is probably prudent neither to accept nor to reject these approaches in toto but to subject them to objective examination and use them in combination with other sources of information in making credit risk decisions.

REFERENCES

Black, F., and M. Scholes. 1973. The Pricing of Options and Corporate Liabilities. *Journal of Political Economy* 81:637–659.

Haugen, R. A. 1997. *Modern Investment Theory*, 4th ed. Upper Saddle River, NJ: Prentice Hall.

Helix Investment Partners. 1996/1997. *The Credit Ranker* (December/January). Los Angeles: Helix Investment Partners.

---

[13]Quoted by Bertrand Russell in Science and Method (1913).

Helix Investment Partners. 1997. *Credit Rankings, October 1997*. Los Angeles: Helix Investment Partners.

KMV Corporation. 1995. Introducing Credit Monitor, Version 4. San Francisco: KMV Corporation.

———. Undated. Empirical Analysis of EDF as a Predictor of Default. Unpublished memorandum. San Francisco: KMV Corporation.

Lehmann, E. 1975. *Nonparametrics: Statistical Methods Based on Ranks*. San Francisco: Holden-Day.

Merton, R. C. 1974. On the Pricing of Corporate Debt: The Risk Structure of Interest Rates. *Journal of Finance* 29:449–470.

Modigliani, F., and M. Miller. 1958. The Cost of Capital, Corporation Finance, and the Theory of Investment. *American Economic Review* 48:261–297.

———. 1963. Corporate Income Taxes and the Cost of Capital: A Correction. *American Economic Review* 53:433–443.

Newton, B. 1993. Modeling Credit Risk. Paper presented at the Bank Loan Portfolio Management Conference, IMI, October 27–28, New York.

Ross, R. A., R. W. Westerfield, and J. F. Jaffe. 1993. *Corporate Finance*. Homewood, Ill.: Irwin.

Vasicek, O. A. 1995. *EDF and Corporate Bond Pricing*. San Francisco: KMV Corporation.

Wakeman, L. M. 1990. The Real Function of Bond Rating Agencies. In *The Modern Theory of Corporate Finance*, 2nd ed., edited by C. W. Smith. New York: McGraw Hill.

ADDITIONAL READING

Arditti, F. D. 1996. *Derivatives: A Comprehensive Resource for Options, Futures, Interest Rate Swaps, and Mortgage Securities*. Boston, MA: Harvard Business School Press.

Black, F. 1986. Noise. *Journal of Finance* 41:529–543.

Bodie, Z., and R. C. Merton. 1995. The Informational Role of Asset Prices: The Case of Implied Volatility. In *The Global Financial System*. Boston, MA: Harvard Business School Press.

Fridson, M. S., and J. G. Jónsson. 1997. Contingent Claims Analysis Does Not Cover All Contingencies. *Journal of Portfolio Management*. 23:30–43.

Galai, D. 1982. A Survey of Empirical Tests of Option Pricing Models. In *Option Pricing: Theory and Applications*, edited by M. Brenner. Lexington, MA: Lexington Books.

Jarrow, R. A., and A. Rudd. 1983. *Option Pricing*. Homewood, IL: Dow-Jones Irwin.

Kealhofer, S. 1996. Managing Default Risk in Portfolios of Derivatives. KMV Corporation, San Francisco. Photocopy.

Kliger, D., and S. Oded. n.d. The Information Value of Bond Ratings. Forthcoming.

KMV Corporation. 1992. Credit Monitor II Overview. San Francisco: KMV Corporation.

Markowitz, H. 1952. Portfolio Selection. *Journal of Finance* 7 (1): 77–91.

McQuown, J. A. 1993. *A Comment on Market vs. Accounting Based Measures of Default Risk*. San Francisco: KMV Corporation.

Merton, R. C., and Z. Bodie. 1992. The Management of Financial Guarantees. *Financial Management* 21 (4): 87–109.

Roll, R. 1993. What Every CFO Should Know about Scientific Progress in Financial Economics: What Is Known and What Remains to be Resolved. Keynote Address at the Annual Meeting of the Financial Management Association, October 12, Toronto, Ontario. Reprinted in *Financial Management* 23 (2 [1994]): 69–75.

Sharpe, W. F. 1964. Capital Asset Prices: A Theory of Market Equilibrium under Conditions of Risk. *Journal of Finance* 19 (3): 425–442.

Chapter *12*

Consumer Finance Models

If Advanta's in trouble, it's safe to assume that the canary just died in the coal mine.

—B. J. Philips in the *Philadelphia Inquirer,* March 19, 1997

Advanta Corp.'s announcement that it will be reporting a loss of about $20 million for the first quarter of 1997 is an example—albeit an extreme one—of the pressures facing the credit card banks.

—Standard & Poor's *Structured Finance,* May 1997[1]

According to the Federal Reserve Board's definition, consumer credit includes short- and intermediate-term credit that is extended through regular business channels to finance the purchase of commodities and services for personal consumption, or to refinance debt incurred for such purposes (Sullivan 1984, 11–15). Automobile loans, home equity loans, secured and unsecured revolving credit, and mobile home loans are among the major types of consumer credit. As shown in Figure 12.1, total consumer credit outstanding in the United States has grown from $9.8 billion in 1946 to $1,226.3 billion in 1996.

The markets and policy makers pay close attention to consumer credit outstanding as a variable that predicts turns in the business cycle. The ratio of the change in consumer installment credit outstanding to disposable personal income (the *credit change ratio,* which has ranged in value from 2 to 3 percent) leads the peak in the business cycle by about eight months and turns up slightly in advance of a business cycle trough (Sullivan 1987, 11–15). A slightly different measure of consumer debt is the *debt service payment ratio,* which is tracked by the Federal Reserve. This is the ratio of scheduled payments on mortgages, credit cards, auto loans, and other household loans as a percentage of personal disposable income. Figure 12.2 shows this statistic for the period 1971–1996. Downturns in this ratio coincided with recessionary trends in 1974, 1980, 1982, and 1990.

As consumer debt has soared in recent years, so too have consumer bankruptcies and delinquencies. The United States has seen a record number

---

[1] Hurt by large loan losses, Advanta, one of the largest issuers of credit cards in the United States, decided to retreat from the business and announced the sale its consumer credit card business to Fleet Financial Group in October 1997.

Figure 12.1 Consumer Credit 1946–1997

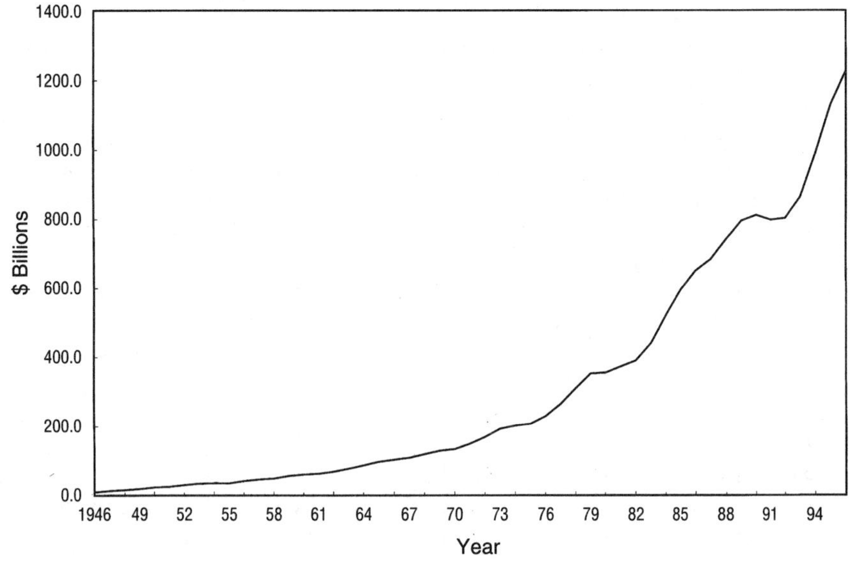

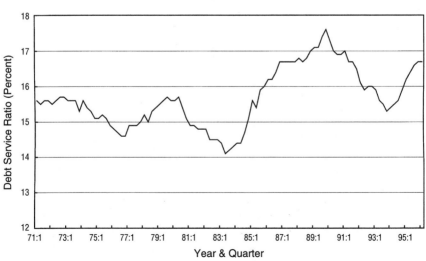

Source: Board of Governors of the Federal Reserve System 1998, Table I.222. Series are seasonally unadjusted.

Figure 12.2 Debt Service Payments Ratio

Source: American Bankers Association. Reprinted with permission. All rights re-served. For more information, contact ABA Surveys & Statistics at (202) 663-5177.

of bankruptcies in the consumer sector. Table 12.1 makes it clear that consumer bankruptcies account for the surge in the overall volume of bankruptcies that began in 1985.

Recent experience with consumer delinquencies, which are the precursor to eventual credit losses, point unmistakably to unwelcome trends. These are evident in Figure 12.3.

Consumer lending has had a curious history; in many financial institutions, the consumer loan department has been regarded as unglamorous but profitable—less prestigious than the upscale world of wholesale banking, where banks have made large but relatively unprofitable loans to corporations. One look at New York's money center banks confirms this strange phenomenon. With the exception of Citibank and, later, Chase, most major New York banks have tried over the years to be more like J. P. Morgan—a premier corporate lender. Elsewhere in the country, institutions such as BancOne have specialized in consumer and small business lending—often with significant success. Retailers, gasoline companies, and auto manufacturers have also been providers of consumer credit for a very long time.

Consumer lending is a volume business in which credit losses may be high but need not be so. For low-cost producers who can manage the losses, the pricing margins are attractive. It is not surprising that many nonbank financial institutions—such as AT&T with its Universal Card and Sears Roe-

Table 12.1   U.S. Bankruptcy Filings, 1980–1996 (Business, Nonbusiness, Total)

Year	Total Filings	Business Filings	Nonbusiness Filings	Consumer Filings as a Percentage of Total Filings
1980	331,264	43,694	287,570	86.81
1981	363,943	48,125	315,818	86.78
1982	380,251	69,300	310,951	81.78
1983	348,880	62,436	286,444	82.10
1984	348,521	64,004	284,517	81.64
1985	412,510	71,277	341,233	82.72
1986	530,438	81,235	449,203	84.69
1987	577,999	82,446	495,553	85.74
1988	613,465	63,853	549,612	89.59
1989	679,461	63,235	616,226	90.69
1990	782,960	64,853	718,107	91.72
1991	943,987	71,549	872,438	92.42
1992	971,517	70,643	900,874	92.73
1993	875,202	62,304	812,898	92.88
1994	832,829	52,374	780,455	93.71
1995	926,601	51,959	874,642	94.39
1996	1,178,555	53,549	1,125,006	95.46

Source: American Bankruptcy Institute, Washington, D.C., 1997.

Figure 12.3   Delinquency Rates

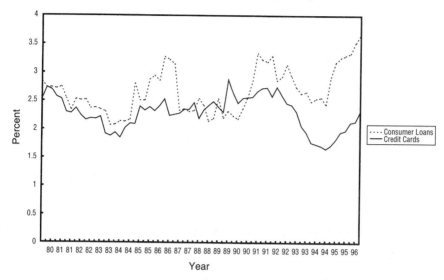

buck & Co. with its Discover Card—entered this lucrative market. There are few barriers to entry because almost all aspects of the lending process— brand identity, origination, underwriting, servicing, and funding—may be outsourced instead of being managed in-house.

Consumer credit risk management systems are applied to a wide range of retail products, such as retail installment credit, home equity loans, auto loans and leases, and time shares. These systems employ a variety of techniques: human judgment, credit scoring, decision tree analysis, mathematical programming, and more recently, neural networks. According to Rajat Basu, managing director, consumer finance at CapMAC, the underwriting of consumer loans for less than $5,000 has traditionally been more automated, whereas that of loans in the range of $5,000 to $10,000 has generally been more judgmental. Companies often use a hybrid of computer-based systems and judgmental systems, with the latter providing an override of the computer model where this is deemed appropriate.

JUDGMENTAL SYSTEMS

Judgmental systems resemble the expert systems used in commercial lending. The rules used in making credit judgments are often home grown and are a function of an institution's credit culture. Such systems are in wide use both in the United States and abroad. Table 12.2 shows the criteria employed by a Japanese lender using a judgmental system.

Table 12.3 is another example of a judgmental credit approval system used by a U.S. finance company specializing in auto loans.

Table 12.2   Credit Screening Criteria

Maximum debt to salary ratio of 60 percent
Must be 25 or older
Length of time on current job 2 years
Type of industry in which employed, for example,
   No show-business people
   No taxi drivers.

Table 12.3   Judgmental Credit Approval Criteria

At least one year at current residence; phone number required; proof of
   residence required.
Three years of verifiable residence history on borderline cases.
At least one year in the current job.
Three years of verifiable employment history on borderline cases.
Length of employment requirement waived for recent college graduates.
Minimum $1500 per month income with proof of income.
Self-employed must provide copies of 1040.
Debt ratio of 50 percent based on auto payment, mortgage, insurance, current
   loans, and other fixed obligations.
Clean credit bureau rating.

Different credit screening approaches are applied when a loan is secured. Home equity line of credit (HELOC) lenders rely more on the appraised value of the home and the loan-to-value ratio and less on the attributes (including cash flow and job stability) of the credit applicant. Subprime lenders, such as finance companies lending to the used auto market, rely almost completely on the collateral. They make up for lower credit quality by adjusting the car price and relying on their ability to repossess the automobile in case of default. For instance, Arcadia, an auto finance lender, does not use credit scoring models and relies entirely on judgment.

Nonetheless, in the vast majority of cases, consumer lending decisions are made by evaluating the applicant's creditworthiness as reflected in such characteristics as home ownership, income, job category, and credit history rather than by evaluating collateral.

QUANTITATIVE CREDIT SCREENING MODELS

Credit risk models fall into two broad categories—*credit approval models* and *behavioral scoring models*. The former are used in reaching a decision concerning whether to extend credit. Typically, they include such variables as shown in Table 12.4.

Behavioral scoring models, by contrast, are used to improve the profitability of accounts by subjecting them to different treatments with regard to credit lines offered and collection methods used. These are based on a statistical

Table 12.4   Credit Scoring Variables and Impact on Score

Variable	Impact
Rent or own	Own = +
Years at current address	High = +
Income per dependent	High = +
Marital status (single, married, divorced, separated)	Married = +
Occupation	Varies
Credit bureau inquiries[a]	Fewer = +
Other credit cards	Yes = +
Oil company credit cards owned	Yes = +
Number of adverse remarks on credit history	Fewer = +
Number of serious derogatory entries	Fewer = +
Number of inquiries in past 6 months	Fewer = +
Telephone number (yes or no)	Yes = +
Years on current job[b]	Higher = +

[a]Credit bureau reports have been shown to have considerable predictive value. See Chandler and Parker (1989), p.47–54.
[b]This is becoming less valuable because creditors now believe that income stability is more important than job stability.

analysis of account use and payment behavior and include variables such as the following.

Simple Criteria

- Number of recent credit inquiries
- Worst credit reference from the bureau

Detailed Criteria

- Number of times 30, 60, or 90 days past due in the last year
- Number of derogatory items
- Transaction volume
- Average line utilization

Models employed to generate so-called preapproved lists use ingredients of both credit approval and behavioral scoring models, as well as data that has been reported to credit bureaus by lending institutions. Credit bureaus, such as TRW, Trans Union, Equifax, and CBI, are information clearinghouses for participating member companies. In summary form, member companies report information on account activity to their bureau, which gathers these statistics and makes them available for a fee to any member requiring a credit profile on an individual. For example, credit bureaus provide lenders with charge-off/bankruptcy prediction indices[2] that rely heavily on variables descriptive of past account activity.

---

[2]CBI: Delinquency Alert System; TRW: Gold Report; TRW: FICO; TU: Delphi;., TU: Empirica; Equifax: Beacon; Equifax: DAS.

DESIGN OF CREDIT SCORING MODELS

Traditional credit scoring models assign statistically predetermined weights to selected applicant attributes to generate a credit score. If this score compares favorably to a cutoff value, then the application is approved. Optimization or multivariate statistical techniques such as discriminant or regression analysis (which are discussed in detail in Chapter 9) are typically used in the development of such models. An institution that wishes to institute a scoring system generally must choose between purchasing a generic system from a vendor or developing statistical samples based on its own previous credit experience. If it chooses a generic product, the population demographics used to develop the system may well differ from the institution's own demographics. As a result, the performance of the system (i.e., its ability to eliminate bad credits) may be unsatisfactory. Typically, an institution will use such a system as a stopgap until it has generated a sufficient sample size to build a system based on its own client population.

The presumption underlying credit scoring models is that there exists a metric that can divide good credits and bad credits into two distinct distributions, as shown in Figure 12.4. There will, however, be some overlap between the two populations. Given that for every 100 accepted applicants some percentage will cause credit losses, the objective is to set the loan approval rate such that net income *after* loan losses is maximized.

The development of a credit scoring system typically proceeds as follows. A representative sample of good and bad credits is developed,[3] based on the institution's actual credit experience. Bad credits may be defined as accounts that were charged off. Good accounts are those that have not ever been severely delinquent, *and* have been profitable.[4] It is assumed here that

---

[3]Sample design to eliminate sample bias is an extremely important step to ensure that the model designed is statistically valid. Among other factors, there may be groups exhibiting differences based upon geography, age, and sex. It may be noted that some variables are prohibited group identifiers for the purpose of credit scoring. The sample size may be equal for the good, bad, and the rejected applicants. The sample size for each group ranges from 1,000 to 3,000. The sample should be as close to random as practical.

[4]One of the realities of consumer lending is that the really good credits seldom borrow, and whereas they may result in low credit losses, they are also not very profitable in terms of interest income. Such accounts may offer other profit opportunities such as an annual fee income or the

Figure 12.4   Distribution of Credit Scores of Good and Bad Accounts in a Credit Scoring Model

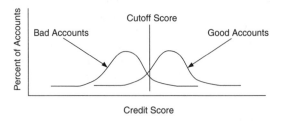

the lender has a credit application form, even if the data in the form is not currently used in a quantitative model.

A metric or scaling system is developed for each attribute in the credit application. For example, it is often more convenient to deal with income in categories (under \$15,000, \$15,000–\$30,000, \$30,000–\$50,000, etc.) rather than as a single continuous variable. Many of the variables, such as *Own or Rent*, are categorical rather than numerical. Usually, each candidate variable is individually analyzed to develop a scaling system that is effective in separating good from bad accounts and that also makes the credit application process less burdensome. Univariate statistics such as t and F statistics are employed to identify the important variables. Some analysts recommend the use of principal component analysis to eliminate highly correlated variables. The latter produce multicollinearity, which results in estimation problems.

The account performance information (good vs. bad) is available only for the population that was accepted by the lender. This leaves out the rejected population, which may contain many good credits that were turned away because of the previous (possibly flawed) credit policy. To adjust for this rejected population, a model is sometimes constructed that distinguishes between the accepted population and the rejected population. Using this model, the probability of acceptance, P_a, may be derived for any accepted account. By definition, this implies that for every accepted individual account fitting this profile, there were $(1 - P_a)$ accounts that were rejected. This account is weighted by the quantity $1/P_a$ to make the sample resemble the population that actually sought credit. This weighting is done for every account in the sample of accepted accounts (good and bad). For example, if the probability of acceptance for an account in the sample is 0.5, it means that one out of every two who applied was accepted. So this account receives a weighting of 2. If another case has a probability of acceptance of 0.1, it means that only 1 out of 10 such applicants was accepted. This account then receives a weighting of 10. Key assumptions here are that (a) the rejected population does not contain subgroups that would not qualify for credit under *any* circumstances (for example, individuals who have filed for bankruptcy); (b) the accepted population does not contain subgroups that were accepted simply *because* of membership in the subgroup (for example, employees of the institution); and (c) an acceptable level of classification accuracy has been attained for the accept/reject model.

A multivariate technique is used to select the best variables and weights to separate the two groups with the greatest efficiency. The techniques may be optimization (objective function: minimize classification error), discriminant analysis, logit analysis, probit analysis, or survival analysis.[5] The equation developed should be able to separate the good accounts from the bad

---

purchase of other products. These are marketing strategies that are outside the scope of this book.

[5]For a technical discussion of these methods, see Altman, Avery, Eisenbeis et al. (1981).

accounts. The less overlap that exists between the score distributions, the better the model is able to distinguish a good credit from a bad one.[6]

TESTS FOR MODEL ADEQUACY

The model is then tested for statistical validity. The weighting of the variables in the scoring model should make intuitive sense, for example, the income variable would be expected to have a positive sign. Furthermore, the variables should not run afoul of laws against discrimination in lending. For example, age may be used as a variable as long as it does not award negative points to the score. One commonly used test compares the score distribution of the good and the bad samples. If the tests of significance show that score distributions are statistically different,[7] then the model can be further analyzed for acceptability. Nonetheless, it is important to bear in mind that a model that behaves well diagnostically may not necessarily be the best predictive model.

This may be demonstrated by an example of the Kolmogorow-Smirnow (K-S) test, which is often employed in evaluating credit scoring models. The K-S statistic is the greatest observed ordinate difference between two empirical distribution functions. With equal class limits applied to both samples, the cumulative frequencies F_1 and F_2 are divided by the corresponding sample sizes n_1 and n_2. The K-S statistic D is given by

$$D = \max \left| \left(\frac{F_1}{n_1} - \frac{F_2}{n_2} \right) \right|$$

In the following example, a sample of 10 yielded the scores shown in Table 12.5.

To calculate the statistics, these scores are sorted in ascending order, as shown in Table 12.6.

As shown in Table 12.7, the frequencies of the score values are then placed in class intervals. There are, for example, four scores in the range 2–2.9 for bad credits, and 2 for good credits.

---

[6]Statistical manuals published by SPSS, Inc. (1997) and SAS, Inc. (1997) discuss many of these techniques with examples.

[7]Two test statistics that are used are the Kolmogorow-Smirnow two-sample statistic and the Chi square statistic. For a description of these methods, please see Sachs (1984).

Table 12.5   Raw Data

Bads	2.1	2.9	1.2	2.9	0.6	2.8	1.6	1.7	3.2	1.7
Goods	3.2	3.8	2.1	7.2	2.3	3.5	3.0	3.1	4.6	3.2

Table 12.6   Data Arranged in Ascending Order

Bads	0.6	1.2	1.6	1.7	1.7	2.1	2.8	2.9	2.9	3.2
Goods	2.1	2.3	3.0	3.1	3.2	3.2	3.5	3.8	4.6	7.2

Table 12.7 Calculation of the K-S Statistics

Region	0.0–0.9	1.0–1.9	2.0–2.9	3.0–3.9	4.0–4.9	5.0–5.9	6.0–6.9	7.0–7.9
f_1	1	4	4	1	0	0	0	0
f_2	0	0	2	6	1	0	0	1
F_1/n_1	$\frac{1}{10}$	$\frac{5}{10}$	$\frac{9}{10}$	$\frac{10}{10}$	$\frac{10}{10}$	$\frac{10}{10}$	$\frac{10}{10}$	$\frac{10}{10}$
F_2/n_2	$\frac{0}{10}$	$\frac{0}{10}$	$\frac{2}{10}$	$\frac{8}{10}$	$\frac{9}{10}$	$\frac{9}{10}$	$\frac{9}{10}$	$\frac{10}{10}$
$\dfrac{F_1}{n_1} - \dfrac{F_2}{n_2}$	$\frac{1}{10}$	$\frac{5}{10}$	$\frac{7}{10}$	$\frac{2}{10}$	$\frac{1}{10}$	$\frac{1}{10}$	$\frac{1}{10}$	0

The highest value of the absolute difference is $7/10$, which is the critical value for the given sample size.[8] Thus, the score distributions are significantly different (or more correctly, the homogeneity hypothesis is rejected). But consider how sensitive this statistic is: If just *one* of the scores happened to be *slightly* different, the statistic would no longer be significant. In the example given, if one observation in the bad group had a score of 3.0 instead of 2.9, then the test statistic would become $6/10$, indicating that the homogeneity hypothesis for the two distributions cannot be rejected. Thus a change of 0.1 in value in 1 out of 20 observations can swing the model from statistical significance to statistical insignificance.

This model performs more effectively if the score cutoff is set at 3.9: at any score of 3.9 or higher, all bad credits are excluded. However, if the applicant population is heavily in the 2.0 range and the cutoff has to be reduced to, say, 2.0, then 5 bad credits will be accepted for 10 good credits. Clearly, this is not a particularly good outcome. A statistically significant model can thus result in unacceptable results. Although this is a very simplified example using a very small sample, it does illustrate the pitfalls of relying exclusively on statistical tests of significance.

OUT-OF-SAMPLE TESTING

Classification results on the development sample will almost always be good because of the sample bias of the model, because the model, by definition, was constructed to maximize in-sample discrimination. A more valid test of the model is carried out on an independent sample. The test consists of classifying good and bad credits based on the calculated probability of group membership and then looking at the error rate. Type I accuracy is the percent of the bad credits correctly identified; this is indicative of the ability of the model to minimize credit losses. Type II accuracy is the percent of the good credits correctly identified; this is indicative of the model's ability not to deny credit to truly creditworthy customers.[9] Type II accuracy is essential in mak-

---

[8] The D statistic is nonparametric, that is, it is distribution free. For a table of critical values see Sachs (1984, 291–292).

[9] "Truly creditworthy" is a conditional definition. Even the truly creditworthy may go to charge-off if impacted by severe adversity. Here the term is taken to mean that these accounts exhibited

ing sure that the profit side of the equation is not sacrificed in the process of controlling the loss side. To prevent *data mining,* this sample should not be mixed with the development sample, and its population characteristics should *not* be analyzed.

Although the credit score is normally used only for a go/no go decision, it is also used by some institutions to set the size of the credit. Others use the scoring model for credit approval but set the line on the basis of income or some other measure of size. The current trend seems to be to let the market set the line. That is why, on any given day, many Americans may receive two or three unsolicited offers in the mail for a preapproved $10,000 line of credit.

DECISION TREE MODELS

The statistically developed credit scoring model has a counterpart in operations research. In the decision tree approach, an applicant's attributes are partitioned off successively, from most important to least important. An applicant population may be divided into two main branches, say, those who own their residence and those who rent. The owners may then be subdivided into different income levels, and each income level may be subdivided according to the number of years at the current address. The entire population is thus divided into mutually exclusive "buckets." The credit decision can then be made based on the probability of delinquency in each of the stages or buckets. This is graphically illustrated in Figure 12.5 for a two-variable system (*own/rent* and *income level*). In the example, as the tree branches are created, the probability of selecting a bad (or a good) account is moved away from 0.5 (a fifty-fifty chance) to a number closer to 0 or 1, thus increasing the likelihood of being correct.

---

no delinquency in the period of observation. The *good* sample is called a *censored* sample because its long-term outcomes are unknown.

Figure 12.5   Credit Screening Decision Tree

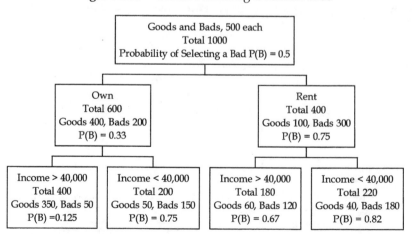

The proponents of the decision tree approach claim that it deals more effectively with the interaction of variables than do credit scoring models. Decision tree models can also generate a credit score even when some of the variables are missing. However, there are some drawbacks. Some of the lower level cells, for example, may have too few entries to provide credit managers with the level of comfort they get from the more common statistical models.

NEURAL NETWORK MODELS

Neural network technology has recently been applied to credit scoring models.[10] Neural networks are artificial intelligence systems that are designed to crudely mimic human thought processes and methods of learning. Neural network algorithms are a set of inputs (in this case the variables used in the credit application) that are mathematically transformed through a transfer function to generate an output (in this case a prediction of whether an applicant will be a performing credit or a charge-off). During the learning or training phase, the weights are modified to reduce the difference between the desired output (correct prediction) and the actual output (generated prediction). The specifications for a neural model generally include type of model (feedforward or feedbackward), number of hidden layers, number of processing elements in each hidden layer, number of variables in the input layer, transfer function, and learning rule for modifying the weights. A more detailed description of this technique is presented in Chapter 10.

Richeson, Zimmermann, and Barnett (1996) report classification accuracy of 78 percent for performing accounts, and 70 percent for nonperforming accounts. Although the results are encouraging, it is by no means clear that models based on neural networks will be acceptable from a regulatory standpoint because it is very difficult to explain the predictions in terms of the inputs. Regulators view a credit analyst's qualitative judgment as an acceptable basis for a credit decision, but they still expect that machine-based credit decisions will satisfy the standard of *tractability*, that is, the ability to explain which variables produced an adverse credit decision. For this reason, neural networks are more useful in the back end of credit management (postapproval processes such as credit review, line increases, collection strategies, etc.) rather than in the front end (credit granting). Neural networks have been applied in behavioral scoring systems and fraud detection models. In these situations, the accuracy of the result obtained is the primary criterion, rather than the theory behind the method. It is more important to detect fraud with acceptable accuracy than to be able to explain what variables were considered and how they were used.

ADVANTAGES AND DISADVANTAGES

Credit scoring models offer many advantages. They are objective and consistent, which are desirable characteristics for any institution, and especially

---

[10]In work by Jensen (1996) and Richeson, Zimmermann, and Barnett (1996), classification accuracy ranged from 76 to 82 percent.

so for those lacking a strong credit culture. If properly designed, they can eliminate discriminatory practices in lending. They tend to be relatively inexpensive, fairly simple, and easy to interpret. Installation of such models is relatively straightforward. The methodologies used to build these models are common and well understood, as are the approaches used to evaluate them. Regulators approve of well-designed, statistically based models. A institution is able to render better customer service by its ability to approve or deny a loan request speedily. This is an important factor in today's fast-paced world.

However, these models do suffer from some drawbacks. In most cases, they simply automate the prevalent credit practices of the bank. They do little, in other words, to eliminate an institution's historical screening biases. Furthermore, if the variables do not satisfy underlying assumptions, such as a multivariate normal distribution, the statistical validity of the models may be questionable. The statistical tests commonly used to whet these models are weak and may mislead the user into overestimating their efficacy.[11] Models are typically tested against a static criterion. For example, the approval rate for various cutoff scores is weighed against the corresponding bad rate. The problem with this approach is that approval is a one-time event, whereas charge-offs accumulate over a long period. Charge-offs do not all occur early in the credit cycle; on the contrary, experience suggests that the charge rate tends to hold steady over time, as shown in Figure 12.6. The "expected charge-off" line in the chart below peaks early and flattens as time passes; the "actual charge-off" does not flatten, which means that losses continue to occur as the portfolio ages. It has been found that even with more stringent acceptance criteria, the slope of the curve does not change; it simply shifts downward. For this reason, any credit screening model should be evaluated in conjunction with the account balances and the cumulative charge rate over the life of the portfolio. With so much consumer finance being securitized, the charge-offs over time are now tracked by issuers and rating agencies. Standard & Poor's (1997), for example, uses ex post information (called a *loss curve*) as the foundation for the amount of credit support needed for a given rating category: both magnitude and timing of losses are important in sizing the credit support.

A credit scoring model may degrade over time if the population against which it is applied diverges from the original population used to build the model. If the population demographics are different, the model may not be very predictive. If, for example, a lender decides to offer credit cards to students but uses a model that did not include students, then the chances are quite good that the model will provide poor discrimination between good and bad credits in this population. A recent communication by the Federal Deposit Insurance Corporation observes, "Lenders encounter trouble when their credit scoring models or other loan selection methods produce unreliable or erroneous results, and they are unable to quantify or differentiate

---

[11] As previously noted, the Kolmogorow-Smirnow test, which is often relied on to accept the models, is not sufficient from a business perspective.

Figure 12.6 Charge-off Rate over Time

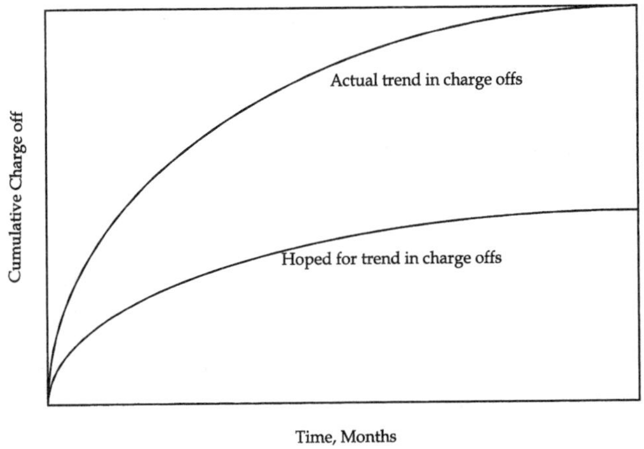

Actual trend in charge offs

Hoped for trend in charge offs

Cumulative Charge off

Time, Months

between relative risk levels accurately. As a result, these lenders are not appropriately compensated for the assumed risks, and losses exceed expectations. To address this problem, credit scoring models should be *continually tested and evaluated to ensure that actual performance approximates initial projections* [emphasis added]" (FDIC 1997, 2). The ability to discern the degradation of a model is especially important in subprime lending, which is the extension of credit to consumers with incomplete or somewhat tarnished credit records. This segment may be very attractive to lenders because of higher yields and servicing fee income.

DYNAMIC CREDIT RISK MANAGEMENT SYSTEMS

There are many who believe that the act of accepting or rejecting an applicant pretty much determines whether an account will ultimately perform as agreed or will become a charge-off. There are others who maintain that a lender can alter the odds of incurring a credit loss by changing the way it treats an individual borrower after studying his or her credit use and payment behavior. This latter philosophy underlies dynamic systems for credit risk management. Such systems are usually developed from a data warehouse that includes monthly billing history for every account—either at the transaction level or at a summary level. Behavioral models generally fall into the following four categories:

- Line increase/re-issue models
- Collection models
- Account cancellation models
- Fraud detection models

Line increase models recognize the fact that the level of line utilization is inversely related to the quality of the credit. In order to encourage better quality credits to use their credit lines, lenders approve line increases with additional inducements such as tiered pricing. Line increase models are constructed by incorporating line usage and timeliness of payments into the credit score, thereby identifying customers who may be targeted for a line increase without significantly increasing the probability of delinquency.

Collection models deal with the other end of the credit spectrum. When there is high risk that an account may migrate to a charge-off, accelerated collection action may be taken. Experience shows that early intervention helps to minimize delinquencies and also reduces the loss in those accounts that do, indeed, become charge-offs. Collection models are used for frequent monitoring of charge and payment activity in order to identify emerging patterns. Variables used in collection models include the credit score, account source (or the mailing list source), pattern of line utilization, monthly payment as a percent of balance, and delinquency history. Although institutions generally do not obtain periodic credit bureau reports on such borrowers, they are known to do so in selected situations. Some customers must ultimately be classified as *skips,* which means that they have skipped town and cannot be found. The ability to predict future problems is predicated on warning signs such as slow payments and low payments (see Cole and Mishler [1995] for causes of consumer deliquency).

According to one report, bankers are losing the ability to predict problem loans because "more and more, borrowers are simply stopping problems and declaring bankruptcy" (Di Stefano 1997). If this is true—and there is no reason to believe otherwise—new strategies have to be devised for managing credit losses. Frequent requalification of borrowers and a more thought-out approach to setting credit limits may be the answer. Some experts believe that there has been a paradigm shift in the way people view credit and that social mores have diluted the stigma attached to declaring bankruptcy. In some areas of the country today, lawyers actively advertise the benefits of declaring bankruptcy and walking away from one's debt obligations.

Stephen Coggeshall, Director, Consumer Analytics Division at CASA, Inc., believes that one key to developing insights into a consumer's behavior is to analyze the credit transactions and all available auxiliary data. He believes that lenders have tended to view the entire process of credit approval, credit monitoring, and collection management in a highly compartmentalized fashion. In order to be more effective, he favors developing strategies that integrate customer selection, product pricing, and credit management in a holistic way. In his view, account activity is just one element in an integrated model of financial product usage that is based on an individual's broad economic and life-cycle profile. An additional challenge is to discover logical relationships without running afoul of the consumer laws and the individual's right to privacy.

Cancellation models are used to limit further draws on an account or even to cancel an account if, barring such action, the customer will borrow more and more and eventually become a charge-off. Cancellation models resemble collection models, but are generally brought into play after a new portfolio has been acquired and has been found to contain less than stellar credits. If there are no legal barriers, cancellation can be a viable way to cap and front-load losses in order to obtain relief under a portfolio repurchase clause.

Fraud detection models attempt to identify fraudulent charges by looking for patterns in previous frauds experienced. For example, if account charges just slightly below the line limit come up for approval, this may be a sign that a card has been stolen. Indictors of fraud are not well publicized by lenders, for obvious reasons. Intuitively, fraud may be traced to specific geographic areas, certain store and merchandise categories, and unusual charging patterns involving successive big-ticket purchases at unusual times. A neural network model may profile the charging pattern of a normal account and send an alert if there is a significant deviation from this pattern, especially if the deviation is associated with a sale category with high fraud potential such as jewelry or a major consumer purchase. Consumer fraud may also be a prelude to a bankruptcy filing. Concealment and/or transfer of assets prior to bankruptcy filing is a common abuse in fraudulent bankruptcies. Computerized records of the applicant's credit history, including the loan application itself, may be helpful in anticipating and analyzing fraudulent bankruptcies.

OTHER QUANTITATIVE CONSUMER MODELS

Today, lenders compete intensely for credit customers. Some institutions have taken an aggressive approach that combines credit risk savvy with marketing in what has come to be called *mass customization* (Hansell 1995). For example, by targeting the middle and lower ends of the markets, where credit needs are more pressing, Providian Bancorp attracts customers with offers of high credit lines, and then *negotiates* a combination of interest rate, credit limit, and other product features that is customized to the individual borrower. In order to be able to do this, the bank needs both a good credit screening tool and a model of long-term account profitability that can predict line utilization, repayment rate, and account life.

Often, secondary variables such as the dealer code for indirect originations or the school code for student loans will give indications about the credit quality of the underlying loan. Although these may not directly influence the primary credit decision, they are nevertheless extremely important for measuring portfolio risk. As in most credit risk models, data quality lags behind technique. With the current emphasis on data warehousing and data mining, we can expect to see even more innovative approaches to consumer credit management.

When new entrants to the business decide to acquire new loans to build up volume, they are increasingly inclined to rely on credit bureau scores rather than on their own independent application data. One of the risks in this approach is that the lender is, in effect, substituting the credit bureaus' systems for its own credit culture and judgment. The explosive growth in consumer installment credit, the fact that an individual may have multiple lines of credit totaling far more than his/her debt-carrying capacity, and the record number of personal bankruptcies in the United States (over one million in 1996) should be enough to alert any prudent banker or investor. According to one study, potentially recoverable debt amounts to just one-fourth of the total debts listed in the average personal bankruptcy filing (Johnson 1989). Put differently, even if a repayment plan is put in place, lenders will recover, at most, 25 percent of the amount owed. Thus, regardless of the leniency or lack thereof of bankruptcy law, it is the credit granting decision that appears to be responsible for mushrooming credit losses.

When portfolio growth declines and can no longer subsidize losses from credit decisions, credit risk models may be the first (and perhaps the only) line of defense against substantial credit losses. Consumer credit models are also making inroads into small business lending (Hansell 1996).[12] A credit risk manager can therefore no longer simply regard credit risk models as black boxes but should instead become familiar with their design philosophy and their strengths and weaknesses.

One question that is frequently asked is why are credit scoring models so effective in consumer lending and not as effective in commercial lending? This question has three explanations: institutional, analytical, and economic. Institutionally, corporate lenders have adamantly maintained that corporate lending is a highly complex, multidimensional process requiring expert judgment that simply cannot be handled by quantitative models. Consumer lenders, on the other hand, have generally been more receptive to modeling approaches, perhaps because they have viewed their product in merchandising terms rather than in lending terms. Analytically, it is somewhat easier to build consumer models because a fixed amount of information is provided on the credit application and a large statistical base of credit experience is available to test and refine credit models. The third reason is economic: Losses in a consumer portfolio tend to be relatively large in number but small in size. Losses from a corporate portfolio are infrequent but much greater in size. Many believe that corporate defaults are less predictable and that reliance on a model may therefore be imprudent. Whatever the reasons, it is certainly true that quantitative credit risk models have not been accepted as widely in corporate lending as they have in consumer lending. But the trend toward greater acceptance has accelerated in recent years.

REFERENCES

Altman, E. I., R. B. Avery, R. A. Eisenbeis, and J. F. Sinkey, Jr. 1981. *Application of Classification Techniques in Business, Banking and Finance*. Greenwich, CT: Jai Press.

Board of Governors of the Federal Reserve System. 1998. *Flow of Funds Accounts of the United States 1945–1997*. Washington, D.C.: Board of Governors of the Federal Reserve System.

Chandler, G. G., and L. E. Parker. 1989. Predictive Value of Credit Bureau Reports. *Journal of Retail Banking* (winter): 47–54.

---

[12]According to the article Hibernia National Bank, Wells Fargo Bank, and Chemical Banking Corporation, now Chase, are using computer models to approve small-business loans for as much as $250,000. Most variables in these models are of the same kind as used in consumer credit models because business financial statements are the exception rather than the rule in loans of this magnitude, and applicant financial strength is what is being scored.

Cole, R., and L. Mishler. 1995. *Consumer and Business Credit Management*, 10th ed. Chicago: Richard D. Irwin.

Di Stefano, J. N. 1997. Debt Soars in Credit Craze. *Philadelphia Inquirer*, 11 May, sec. D.

FDIC (Federal Deposit Insurance Corporation, Office of the Director, Division of Supervision). 1997. Report FIL-44-97, Federal Deposit Insurance Corporation, Washington, D.C.

Hansell, S. 1995. Merchants of Debt. *New York Times*, July 2, sec. 3.

———. 1996. Loans Granted by the Megabyte: Computer Models Change Small-Business Lending. *New York Times*, 18 April, business sec.

Jensen, H. 1996. Using Neural Networks for Credit Scoring. In *Neural Networks in Finance and Investing*, edited by R. R. Trippi and E. Turban. Chicago: Irwin Professional Publishing.

Johnson, R. W. 1989. The Consumer Banking Problem: Causes and Cures. *Journal of Retail Banking* (winter): 39–44.

McCarthy, J. 1997. Debt, Delinquencies and Consumer Spending. *Current Issues in Economics and Finance* 3 (3): 1–6.

Richeson, L., R. A. Zimmermann, and K. G. Barnett. 1996. Predicting Consumer Credit Performance: Can Neural Networks Outperform Traditional Statistical Methods? In *Neural Networks in Finance and Investing*, edited by R. R. Trippi and E. Turban. Chicago: Irwin Professional Publishing.

Sachs, L. 1984. *Applied Statistics*, 2nd ed. New York: Springer-Verlag.

SAS, Inc. 1997. *Statistical Manual—Multivariate Statistical Analysis*. Cray, N.C.: SAS, Inc.

SPSS, Inc. 1997. *Statistical Manual—Advanced Statistics*. Chicago: SPSS, Inc.

Standard & Poor's Corporation. 1997. *Structured Finance* (May): 19–25.

Sullivan, C. A. 1987. Consumer Finance. In *Handbook of Financial Institutions and Markets*, edited by E. I. Altman. New York: John Wiley & Sons.

Chapter **13**

Credit Models for Small Business, Real Estate, and Financial Institutions

Prediction is very difficult, especially of the future.

—Niels Bohr

In the preceding three chapters, we considered credit risk models that have been developed for corporate and individual borrowers. This chapter deals with credit risk models created for other classes of borrowers. Those applied to small-business and residential mortgage lending are very similar to the consumer risk models we have described. Those developed for commercial real estate lending tend to be closer to expert systems. The credit (or solvency) risk of financial institutions themselves is another important area of concern. Regulators, correspondent banks, and even nonbank institutions use models to assess the risk of banks because any bank, as a depository institution, is a borrower. It may also be a counterparty in a derivative transaction or a structured finance deal.

SMALL-BUSINESS MODELS

Public companies generally provide structured and timely disclosures about their operations through earnings reports and SEC filings. In addition, continuous monitoring of their stock prices provides a mechanism—perhaps too volatile for some—for observing their condition. As we have seen, credit risk models have been built to take advantage of both these sources of information. In the case of small private companies, however, one clearly has to look at other means for making a credit risk assessment. Carey, Prowse, Rea, and Udell (1993) suggest that small firms are *information-problematic* to lenders because they enter into fewer externally visible contracts with employees, customers, and suppliers. Such firms also tend to be younger. Incentives to engage in behavior that expropriates wealth from lenders are more acute in such observably riskier firms. For this reason, lenders typically employ tight financial covenants, more frequent monitoring, and relatively short maturities with these clients.

Table 13.1 lists the variables used in a commercial credit scoring model for loans up to $250,000.

In the case of some small businesses, especially proprietorships, it may be difficult to use financial ratios because personal and business activi-

Table 13.1 Commerical Small Business Loan Credit Scoring Model Variables

	Points for Worst Value	Points for Best Value
Credit characteristics and points	0	10
Number of years in business	Less than 1 year	More than 5 years
Current ratio	Less than 1	More than 1.80
Total debt/net worth	Over 2.0	Under 1.2
Profitability	Loss in most recent year	Profitable for 3 consecutive years
Loan/accounts receivable	1.25	<0.5
Acceptable financial data	Interim financial statement	Latest 3 annual
Accounts payable	More than 20 percent over 60 days	20 percent credit; rest cash/discount

ties are combined. This is also true of businesses that operate on a cash-flow basis. Small service businesses that are people- rather than equipment-intensive may be less suited to ratio-based scoring.

In general, small-business models use a combination of personal install-ment credit and financial statement items. For example, as shown in Table 13.1, the model may use financial ratios such as debt service coverage, lev-erage ratio, and negative or excessive growth in revenues for the business side of the risk. At the same time, credit bureau data is used to generate a personal credit score for the principal owner(s) of the business. The RMA/ Fair, Isaac model (Asch 1995) is an example of this approach.

According to Paul Ross, a consultant with Oliver Wyman, Inc., New York, lenders, increasingly, are applying the approaches developed in con-sumer lending to small businesses for several reasons. First, many of the scoring variables applied to consumer lending are effective in differentiating risk in small-business lending, where the credit standing of the principal is key. Second, the economics of small-business lending require an efficient, inexpensive process for data collection and credit evaluation, which is better met by consumer credit scoring processes. Finally, in many cases, borrowing that is used to finance small businesses is actually accomplished through a consumer vehicle, such as the credit card of the principal. Some of the recent innovations in this market are standardized loan products and documenta-tion. Pre-approved solicitation by mail as is done for consumer loans is also becoming more common.

Franchise loans are small-business loans ranging from $500,000 to $700,000. Loan approvals are based on the analysis of qualitative and quanti-tative factors about the franchise. Lending is cash-flow based, with fixed charge coverage being the most important criterion. This ratio varies around 1.5.

RESIDENTIAL REAL ESTATE MODELS

The residential real estate loan market is a significant user of funds in the U.S. financial markets. As shown in Figure 13.1, the balance outstanding was $3.85 trillion in 1996. This is an innovative market in which originators such as mortgage bankers deliver loans to investors who may, in turn, securitize them. FNMA and FHMLC are two entities that securitize huge volumes of residential mortgage loans.

As applied to mortgage analysis, credit scoring is a relatively recent phe-nomenon. Firms use credit scoring in a variety of ways:

- As an underwriting tool to accept or reject applications
- As a way to determine documentation requirements
- As a means of assessing property appraisals
- As support for servicing operations such as collection (Moody's 1996)

Historically, residential mortgage loans were underwritten in much the same way that commercial loans were. Classic credit analysis included a de-tailed analysis of the borrower's financial ability, combined with an appraisal of the property. More and more, however, quantitative credit models are being

Figure 13.1   Residential Mortgages Outstanding 1973–1995

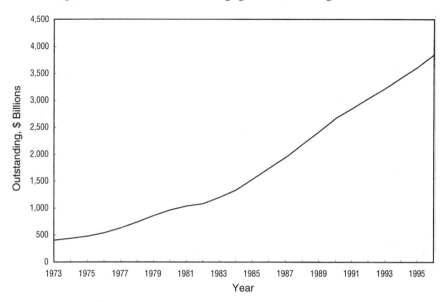

Source: Board of Governors of the Federal Reserve System 1998, Table I. 218.

used—partly because data and computing technology are more readily available and partly because these models help to cut origination costs.

A mortgage default model based on options theory has long identified the size of a borrower's equity in a home as a fundamental determinant of default. The borrower's equity is expressed as the difference between the current value of the home (after adjusting for sales costs) and the current market value of the debt. The model is modified by two other groups of variables. The first measures the borrower's ability to pay—for example, the size of the income cushion represented by the debt ratios and savings, and the borrower's earnings stability as evidenced by his/her credit bureau history. The second group is a set of triggering events such as divorce, unemployment, illness, or business failure that will stress the borrower financially. Even under these conditions, however, a borrower is likely to sell the property and repay the loan rather than to default and potentially lose all equity. This is precisely why the borrower's equity in the home is an extremely important variable in the decision to default.

In home mortgages, as in commercial lending, many institutions rely exclusively on judgmental credit screening. The following factors have been found to be important indicators of credit quality:

- Borrower's sources of income
- Debt ratios with and without nonmortgage debt obligations
- Asset holdings
- Employment history
- Credit bureau reports
- Economic conditions in the area

As shown in Table 13.2, comparisons of key underwriting ratios in a sample of mortgages held by a large Pennsylvania bank lend support to such underwriting practices.

In Table 13.2, mortgages were classified as delinquent if they were at least 90 days past due, were in foreclosure, or were closed out through deed in lieu of foreclosure. The performing loans were those that were never more than 30 days delinquent. Both groups were seasoned, with age in the 7-year range. Note that the geographic location (state) was also significant, reflecting the effect of regional economic conditions. Van Order and Zorn (1995) has confirmed that the severity of the loss is also higher at higher loan-to-value ratios (Table 13.3).

In one of the earliest studies to identify the determinants of default in residential mortgages, Campbell and Dietrich (1983) used an optimization model of consumer choice. The borrower choice set consisted of (1) default, (2) delay payment, (3) prepay the mortgage, and (4) continue to service the mortgage.[1] The explanatory variables used were current loan-to-value ratio, current payment-to-income ratio, rate of unemployment in the area of the residence, ratio of mortgage interest rate to prevailing mortgage rate, age of the mortgage at the beginning of the year, age of the mortgage squared, and New/Not-new Home dummy.[2] A logit function was used to model the probability of choice *i* available in each year to the borrower as a function of the

---

[1]Campbell and Dietrich (1983) point out that delaying payment and default are really sequential events (not mutually exclusive ones) and account for this in the classification procedure.

[2]A dummy variable is one that will take on a value of 1 or 0. For example, the New Home dummy will be 1 for a new home, and 0 for a preowned home.

Table 13.2   Group Means of Key Ratios—Residential Mortgage Loans

Variable	Delinquent mortgages	Performing mortgages	F ratio
Loan to value	.87	.77	33.77
Debt ratio 1	.24	.19	17.08
Debt ratio 2	.33	.28	11.90
Total no. of derogatory remarks in credit report	1.94	0	37.52
State	3.45	2.28	56.99

Table 13.3   Proportion of Selected Mortgages Defaulting by Year-end 1993 and Resulting in Loss

| Performance measure | Loan-to-value ratio ranges | | | | |
	10–70	71–80	81–90	91–95	All
Proportion defaulted	0.24	1.11	2.74	6.20	2.16
Average loss severity	22.3	29.2	34.4	47.9	39.2

Source: van Order and Zorn (1995).

explanatory variable vector X in the beginning of the year. This equation is written as an odds ratio:

$$\log \frac{P_i}{P_4} = - \beta_i X$$

P_4 is the probability of continuing to make mortgage payments and P_i is the probability of making one of three choices i, and β_i is the vector of estimated coefficients. The data used consisted of 2.5 million first mortgages insured between 1960 and 1980. Three regression equations were estimated for the three P_i. The results were found to be consistent with the inverse relationship between initial loan-to-value ratio and default rate. Because the age variables were found to be highly correlated, equations were estimated both with and without these variables. The authors found the regression results to be generally consistent with their hypothesis for prepayment and default decisions. However, the decision to delay payments could not be explained in a satisfactory manner.

FNMA and FHMLC, which are key players in the mortgage market, have encouraged thousands of lenders from whom they purchase loans to consider indexes from credit bureaus such as Beacon and TRW-FICO, as well as the Empirica credit history scores, in their loan underwriting. The credit bureaus base their credit history scoring systems on an applicant's record of bankruptcy, current credit lines, and history of account delinquency. Lenders combine this score with traditional underwriting factors such as the loan-to-value ratio, the debt ratios, and employment stability. They use credit-screening models to identify applicants for streamlined underwriting and to verify the reported information and the evaluation of the collateral. Those that cannot pass the model screen are processed in the conventional manner. Private mortgage insurers are also using such models to determine if a loan is insurable. In one instance, a credit-scoring model was used to stratify a portfolio of seasoned loans for sale in the secondary market.

Extensive analysis to test the predictive ability of such models was performed by Avery et al. (1996) on a large sample of loans for which proprietary data was provided by Equifax Credit Information Services. The credit score was found to be a good predictor of loan performance across all score levels, both for prospective mortgage borrowers and for those with existing mortgages. The proportion of problem loans increased as credit scores decreased. While the industry is slow to catch on to these systems, it does appear that the trend is toward greater use. These scoring models share the same limitations as commercial and consumer models, the most important of which is the relative inability to be forward-looking. They are not very good, for example, at anticipating an economic downturn.

COMMERCIAL REAL ESTATE MODELS

Judgmental methods—especially *appraisal* of the collateral—continue to dominate in commercial real estate lending. Prevailing market indexes for commercial property and simulations to project cash flow are used to estimate collateral value. Quantitative credit risk models are used rarely, if at all, in this market. The following variables, taken from an expert system that identifies potential problem borrowers, seem to impact the ongoing credit risk of commercial real estate projects:

- Debt coverage ratio below 1.2 and dropping
- Prospective criteria (e.g., major tenant not renewing lease)
- Real estate tax delinquency
- Revenue growth that is flat or worse
- Expense growth that is high relative to revenue
- Recent change in ownership
- Presence of secondary financing
- Refinancing
- Complicated financing structure
- Signs that property is neglected
- Financial statements that are late or not credible (not prepared by a CPA or signed by a senior representative of the owner)
- Property that is not near a strong economic center

These variables have proved to be surprisingly accurate in anticipating borrower problems.

BANK MODELS

Because banks perform an important public function by operating the payment system and acting as the vehicle for the exercise of monetary policy, they are highly regulated. Consequently, they are required to submit detailed financial reports to the regulatory agencies. Over the course of years, these reporting requirements have become more sophisticated and streamlined. Large banks are now required, for example, to disclose extensive information about their interest rate risk exposure, derivative risk, and loan portfolio quality. Bank solvency is of interest not only to regulators but also to other financial institutions and to borrowers. A borrower with a liquidity line, for example, will want to make sure that funds will be available to draw when needed.

The following elements are used in assessing a bank's solvency:

- Asset quality
- Management
- Exception via critical ratios—outlier/peer group comparison
- Multivariate or composite measurements
- Market-value-based measurements

ASSET QUALITY

Asset quality is the primary focus for both regulators and investors. Indeed, risk-based capital standards for banks are expressed in terms of asset quality (i.e., the credit quality of various asset classes). A bank's risk assets are examined and classified into several categories of risk, that is, loss, doubtful, and substandard. These categories are assigned equal weights and the bank's capital is reduced to the extent that losses will be experienced. The ratio of the available capital cushion to risk assets, or the net capital ratio, is a measure of a bank's risk of insolvency. Another measure of risk, the adjusted capital ratio, is somewhat more lenient in that it applies a weight of .5 to doubtful loans and of 0 to substandard loans in calculating the numerator. Both of these ratios assess the degree to which a bank will be able to withstand earnings stresses after losses from the nonperforming, substandard, doubtful, and loss categories have been taken into account.

Banks face risks because of both internal and external factors. Quality of management personnel, cost controls, and risk appetite are internal factors over which a bank's management can exercise some control. The state of the economy and the actions of competitors are external factors over which a bank has no control. While the above ratios do not appear to take any note of the external conditions faced by a bank, examiners do take external factors into account tacitly when they classify loans. This is most noticeable in recessionary periods. When the economy is fragile, examiners tend to be overzealous in labeling institutions as problem banks. They prefer erring on the side of caution to missing a problem bank by being too liberal.

MANAGEMENT

A different perspective on bank risk is provided by Graham and Horner (1988) of the Office of the Comptroller of the Currency (OCC), who lay responsibility for bank risk and, by implication, bank failure entirely on internal management factors. While the economy plays an important role in bank failure, many banks in economically distressed areas are able to withstand the adverse economic conditions. OCC studied 171 failed banks, most of them small (under $50 million in assets), 51 rehabilitated banks, and a control group of 38 healthy banks. The study agreed with others that poor asset quality is the major cause of a bank's decline, but it also attempted to trace the factors that *led* to poor asset quality. It identified the following:

- Uninformed or inattentive board of directors, evidenced by
  Nonexistent or poorly followed loan policies
  Inadequate systems to ensure compliance
  Inadequate control or supervision of key officers
  Inadequate systems to identify problem loans
  Decisions by one dominant individual
- Overly aggressive activity by board or management as evidenced by
  Inappropriate lending policies
  Excessive loan growth in relation to the abilities of management
  Undue reliance on volatile liabilities
  Inadequate liquid assets for secondary liquidity
- Insider abuse or fraud
- Economic environment

Based on organizational theory, this model of risk assessment examines an institution's processes and systems for early signs of deterioration.

EXCEPTION VIA CRITICAL RATIOS—OUTLIER/PEER GROUP

This approach is based on establishing critical values for important financial ratios, then using these values to identify outliers. If a bank exhibits financial ratios that fail the critical test, it becomes a candidate for the exception list. Clearly, the success of this approach depends on identifying the right ratio and assigning the correct critical value. The tendency with this approach is to set critical values at relatively tolerant levels so that only pathological cases are selected, but they are sometimes selected too late to do any good. The risk in peer group analysis is that exceptions may mask systemic deterioration.

MULTIVARIATE OR COMPOSITE MEASUREMENTS

Multivariate financial ratio models draw upon the extensive information that banks periodically disclose about their financial condition. However, many analysts believe that present accounting policies give a distorted picture of important aspects of a bank's balance sheet and income statement, and provide a picture of risk that, at best, is incomplete. Accounting principles are indeed unable to capture many dimensions of risk, both embedded and evolving: interest-rate risk, off-balance-sheet items such as letters of credit and interest rate swaps, and differing standards for classifying performing assets. In spite of these deficiencies, there is enough accumulated evidence to indicate that, when properly analyzed, accounting information can indeed be used for prediction.

Of the best-known multivariate models, the CAMEL system is used by three federal regulatory agencies. CAMEL stands for Capital adequacy, Asset quality, Management, Earnings stability, and Liquidity. Weights are applied to the ratios in each of the categories to arrive at a final score and, thereby, a rating. The weights are not statistically developed, however. The CAMEL rating for a bank ranges from 1 = best to 5 = worst. The agencies do not appear to use this system for bank holding companies, nor have they agreed on a uniform system to be used in the surveillance process (Putnam, 1981). In the surveillance process, the Federal Reserve and the OCC use a composite score, that is, an aggregation of financial ratios, while others use critical ratios.

Regardless of methodology, defining the a priori groups of failed and nonfailed banks must be the first step in the construction of a multivariate model. Since it is theoretically possible for the regulators to keep a bank from failing for an indefinite period of time, some arbitrary definitions must be made. It is customary to define failed banks as those that required outlays from the Deposit Insurance Fund, including closed banks as well as all assistance cases. Other definitions may rely on examiner determinations such as the potential payoff, serious problem, and other problem categories. Sometimes the euphemism *vulnerability potential* is substituted for various stages of a bank's demise.

Failed banks are then matched with healthy banks in a random fashion and models are constructed using methods similar to those described in Chapter 10. Important models on bank soundness have been developed by Meyer and Pifer (1970); Martin (1977); Bovenzi, Marino, and McFadden (1983); Lane, Looney, and Wansley (1989); Pantalone and Platt (1987); Santomero and Vinso (1977); and Spahr (1989). Sinkey (1979) gives a good summary of the prior work done in this area. Trippi and Turban (1996) contains three examples of neural network techniques applied to the prediction of failures in banks, thrifts, and credit unions.

MARKET VALUE–BASED MEASUREMENTS

According to the efficient market hypothesis, the intrinsic value of a firm is represented in its stock price, which quickly and accurately reflects any new information regarding its condition. If investors perceive that a bank's risk has increased, they will require a higher rate of return. To compensate the investor for the increased risk, the stock price will drop to a lower level. A decline in the price of a bank's common stock may therefore precede regulatory awareness that its financial condition has deteriorated significantly.

This hypothesis has been tested. Since the decline in the bank's stock may coincide with a general decline in the stock market, the bank-specific changes must be assessed by means of the capital asset pricing model, using a parameter called Beta, which is a measure of the relative risk of the bank stock. If the actual return differs from the expected return indicated by the bank's Beta, which is measured by a quantity called cumulative average residuals, then it may be concluded that the market has signaled an increase in the bank's risk. Shick and Sherman (1980) found support for this hypothesis. A negative residual pattern could be used to anticipate an adverse examination rating change by at least 15 months. A limitation of these market value models is that only a small number of large money center banks and regional banks rely on equity and debt markets. Further, as Eisenbeis and Gilbert (1985) note, market behavior is conditional on the creditors' assessment of the likelihood of government bailout.

The survey of quantitative models that we have presented is by no means exhaustive. It is intended merely as an overview of the types of tools currently available. The next chapter takes up questions that typically must be answered in the process of selecting and implementing a credit risk model.

REFERENCES

Asch, L. 1995. How RMA/Fair, Isaac Credit-Scoring Model Was Built. *Journal of Commercial Lending*, June, 10–16.

Avery, R. B., T. M. Belton, and M. A. Goldberg. 1988. Market Discipline in Regulating Bank Risk: New Evidence from the Capital Markets. *Journal of Money, Credit, and Banking* 20 (4): 597–610.

Avery, R. B., R. W. Bostic, P. S. Calem, and G. S. Canner. 1996. Credit Risk, Credit Scoring and the Performance of Home Mortgages. *Federal Reserve Bulletin* (July): 621–648.

Board of Governors of the Federal Reserve System. 1998. *Flow of Funds Accounts of the United States 1945–1997*. Washington, D.C.: Board of Governors of the Federal Reserve System.

Bovenzi, J. F., J. A. Marino, and F. E. McFadden. 1983. Commercial Bank Failure Prediction Models. *Economic Review* 68 (11): 14–24.

Campbell, T. S., and K. J. Dietrich. 1983. The Determinants of Default on Insured Conventional Residential Mortgage Loans. *Journal of Finance* 38 (5): 1569–1581.

Carey, M., S. Prowse, J. Rea, and G. Udell. 1993. The Economics of the Private Placement Market. Staff Study 166. Washington, D.C.: Board of Governors of the Federal Reserve System.

Eisenbeis, R. A., and G. G. Gilbert. 1985. Market Discipline and the Prevention of Bank Problems and Failures. *Issues in Bank Regulation* (winter): 16–23.

Graham, F. C., and J. E. Horner. 1988. Bank Failure: An Evaluation of the Factors Contributing to the Failure of National Banks. In *Proceedings of the 24th Conference on Bank Structure and Competition*. Federal Reserve Bank of Chicago.

Lane, W. R., S. W. Looney, and J. W. Wansley. 1989. An Application of the Cox Proportional Hazards Model to Bank Failure. *Journal of Banking and Finance* 8:511–531.

Martin, D. 1977. Early Warning of Bank Failure: A Logit Regression Approach. *Journal of Banking and Finance* 1:249–276.

Meyer, P. A., and H. W. Pifer. 1970. Prediction of Bank Failures. *Journal of Finance* 25 (4): 853–868.

Moody's Investors Service. 1996. *A Guide to Credit Scoring of Mortgage Loans*. New York: Moody's Investors Service.

Pantalone, C. C., and M. B. Platt. 1987. Predicting Commercial Bank Failure since Deregulation. *New England Economic Review,* July/August.

Putnam, B. 1981. Early Warning Systems and Financial Analysis in Bank Monitoring. *Economic Review* 68 (11): 6–13.

Santomero, A. M., and J. D. Vinso. 1977. Estimating the Probability of Failure for Commercial Banks and the Banking System. *Journal of Banking and Finance* 1:185–205.

Shick, R. A., and L. F. Sherman. 1980. Bank Stock Prices as an Early Warning System for Changes in Condition. *Journal of Bank Research* 11 (3): 136–146.

Sinkey, J. F., Jr. 1979. *Problem and Failed Institutions in the Commercial Banking Industry.* Greenwich, Conn.: Jai Press.

Spahr, R. W. 1989. Predicting Bank Failures and Intertemporal Assessment of Bank Risk. *Journal of Business Research* 19: 179–185.

Trippi, R. R., and E. Turban, eds. 1996. *Neural Networks in Finance and Investing*. Chicago: Irwin Professional Publishing.

van Order, R., and P. Zorn. 1995. Income, Location, and Default: Some Implications for Community Lending. Paper presented at the Conference on Housing and Economics, Ohio State University, Columbus, Ohio, July.

ADDITIONAL READING

Altman, E. I., R. B. Avery, R. A. Eisenbeis, and J. F. Sinkey Jr. 1981. Application of Classification Techniques in Business, Banking, and Finance. Greenwich, Conn.: Jai Press.

Cates, D. C. 1985. Bank Risk and Predicting Bank Failure. *Issues in Bank Regulation* (autumn): 16–24.

Pettway, R. H., and J. F. Sinkey, Jr. 1980. Establishing On-site Bank Examination Priorities: An Early Warning System Using Accounting and Market Information. *Journal of Finance* 35 (1): 137–150.

Chapter **14**

Testing and Implementation
of Credit Risk Models

Begin at the beginning . . . and go on till you come to the end: then stop.

—Lewis Carroll, *Alice in Wonderland*

We are now at the end of the discussion on credit risk models. The question left to be answered is, how can these models be implemented? Banks and other financial institutions clearly need tools that can

- Reinforce a strong credit culture
- Reduce the high fixed costs associated with credit analytics
- Establish consistency in assessing and pricing credit risk
- Assist in active portfolio management

Most banks have now developed a credit-rating system. But in many instances the system is not given a high priority and has inadequate resources. As a consequence, it does not yield objective, reproducible results. Indeed, many of these systems reflect the subjective preferences of account officers and their superiors rather than the underlying credit risks that are actually associated with each customer. Often, the system is applied selectively by different branches of the same bank, and it is therefore not unusual for credit officers within a single bank to assign different credit ratings to the very same customer. Even the definitions of ratings tend to be couched in vague generalities that leave substantial room for interpretation.

Bank credit-rating systems produce a fuzzy, ordinal risk ranking of customers. A rating of two in a typical nine-grade rating system is obviously superior to a three and worse than a one, but it usually conveys little that would help account officers, central credit departments, or senior credit executives to assess expected losses or to price their loans. In the case of companies that have public debt outstanding, internal ratings do tend to correspond to the public bond ratings, which give banks an external point of reference. However, the risk gradings of private companies are subject to very wide and sometimes arbitrary variations. In some instances, credit professionals are uncertain whether a given risk rating applies to a company as a whole or simply to one among many of its business units.

Subjective systems make it difficult for a lender to recognize the deterioration of its borrowers. Of course, banks have good reason to avoid false alarms in ratings: Bankers know that if they lower their rating on a given borrower, their relationship with this customer will probably suffer. Banks prefer to give customers the benefit of the doubt—waiting to see if they can work things out on their own. Unfortunately, if real deterioration takes place, this reluctance to recognize the truth about a borrower can lead to a loss.

AN INTRINSIC VALUE APPROACH

The first tool that banks require is a standardized way of measuring the inherent risk of each borrower. Grounded in history and unaffected by fads, this tool would measure the risk of default and generate consistent ratings across time for a wide range of borrowers. Such a system could serve as the anchor for a bank's credit policy—providing a common credit language and a feedback mechanism for quality control. Borrowers that did not measure up to this yardstick would be investigated with care. Whenever the system produced a warning that could not be explained by other information, the bank would act on this signal. Such a tool would not supplant the human element in managing risk, but it would—by providing an objective measure of risk—challenge subjectively held beliefs.

Intrinsic value credit models estimate the similarity of any individual company to the hundreds of other companies that have compromised their creditors. Such models focus on a borrower's financial statements. Concepts such as profitability, liquidity, and capital structure are important components of the system. These various indicators are combined into a single measure of corporate vulnerability. This approach provides the benchmarks and feedback needed for rational credit grading and loan pricing.

The intrinsic value approach provides a sound foundation for stabilizing a bank's credit culture because it is rooted in accounting fundamentals and in time-tested principles of credit analysis. It is one of the best ways to measure a borrower's intrinsic risk. If enough data exists for empirical validation, this risk can be quantified in the form of an estimate of the probability of default. However, as we have noted in Chapter 10, accounting statements fail to capture many aspects of an enterprise that contribute to its credit risk. They are neither timely nor forward-looking. In view of these limitations, an approach based on accounting standards can prove its worth only by demonstrating an outstanding ability to predict declines in credit quality and/ or defaults.

Unfortunately, many published firm-intrinsic models appear to be constructed on the same principles that cooks use in making a stew. Variables or ratios are thrown into a pot and stirred about until they seem to predict something in a test sample. Few of the existing models have been subjected by their creators to rigorous testing. This is a serious shortcoming. If it is truly to anchor a bank's credit process, a scoring system must be both objective and well tested—*objective* in the sense that it follow a statistical or mechanical process to arrive at a rating that is independent of human opinion, and *well tested* in the sense that it has been carefully evaluated not only during the design phase but also after it has been put into operation. Building a robust model is akin to engineering. Among other things, it requires that pragmatic decisions be made about drawing up the control samples and model evaluation criteria, about handling outliers and missing data, and about making replicable adjustments to the raw data to make it consistent across the sample. These are the actions of an engineer rather than of a scientist who seeks theoretical purity.

INGREDIENTS OF AN EFFECTIVE SYSTEM

A satisfactory credit evaluation system should have five key attributes:

1. Sensitivity of ratings to real changes in credit quality
2. Lead time with respect to recognized real changes in quality
3. Stability of ratings where no fundamental change has occurred
4. Graduated tiering of risk assessment that facilitates rationality in the pricing of credit and the setting of loan terms
5. Consistency of ratings across industries, company sizes, and locations

Let us examine the different dimensions of the credit evaluation models. These observations are relevant not only to firm-intrinsic models but also to other market value or econometric models. They apply to models developed for individuals, small businesses, and financial institutions, as well as to those tailored to corporate borrowers.

DEFINITION OF THE RISK EVENT

The first step in evaluating a model is discovering what it actually measures. To achieve sensitivity to real changes in credit quality, most models use conditions such as bankrupt/nonbankrupt or default/nondefault as their criterion. Less useful—but still relevant—are models that are designed to classify companies into bond rating grades or bank loan grades. A criterion such as bankruptcy/nonbankruptcy is preferable because this classification is less subjective than a rating or grade. Bankruptcy is a fact, whereas a bond rating or loan grade is a subjective opinion. We know that leading rating agencies disagree with each other in a surprisingly large number of cases and that bankers often disagree with one another on loan grades. Models that are designed to duplicate expert opinion (such as the judgments of rating agencies) must inevitably accept their highly subjective decision criteria.

If a model will be used in prediction, it is also important to define the time frame. To say that a company will default some time in the indefinite future really tells us nothing. The prediction should be made over some time horizon, such as one, two, or three years before the event, and the prediction error should be tracked.

TARGET POPULATION

Credit-scoring models are generally built for different segments of the borrowing population—rightly so because risk parameters are not the same everywhere. Credit-scoring models use different variables for manufacturing and nonmanufacturing corporations, for financial institutions, and for individuals borrowing to purchase a home or car. It is important to map out the scope of the market covered by the model, including geography, company size, and industry. The model's market should be compatible with the institution's market coverage. Even within the same borrowing universe, some models function better in one segment (e.g., large corporates) than in another (e.g., middle market). When looking at test results, it is important to look at the size distributions and industry composition of the test population.

QUALITY OF MODEL DEVELOPMENT

The process of developing a credit-scoring model generally involves statistical testing. Many statistical techniques are available, but the actual technique chosen is less important than the definition of risk events selected and the care with which the explanatory variables are defined, the data is collected, and the model is tested.

In the case of models based on the criterion of bankruptcy/nonbankruptcy, performance is usually measured in terms of two error rates. Type I errors occur when the model classifies bankrupt companies as nonbankrupt. Type II errors occur when the model classifies nonbankrupt companies as bankrupt. Error rate measurement is generally intended to evaluate the sensitivity of ratings to real credit quality changes.

For testing purposes, a second group of companies is held out of the development sample for use in testing the model. The errors reported on the hold-out test are much more representative of a model's expected performance than are errors in the development sample.

While most credit-scoring models work on binary choices (e.g., default vs. no default), the real world of credit seldom presents a clear accept/reject situation. Typically, a borrower is assigned to one of several credit grades. A bank with a 9-level grading system, for example, might decide to accept borrowers graded 1–5 and reject those graded 6–9. At each grade, there will be a different set of Type I and Type II errors. To calculate the different error rates, enough information must be accumulated about nonbankrupt and eventually bankrupt companies in each credit grade for a number of years before bankruptcy. Although it is important to evaluate the success of a credit model over the full range of the credit scale, few models have accumulated enough data to make this possible.

When an institution relies on a vendor to provide statistics of this kind, it is very important to insist on and understand the representations made about the quality, accuracy, and completeness of the data employed in constructing the accuracy tests. Vendors may not necessarily be dishonest in omitting unwelcome results, but they can certainly be expected to put their best foot forward in promoting their model. It is up to the institution to ask the right questions and to exercise due diligence in unearthing the weaknesses of a model. The worst thing an institution can do—other than doing nothing—is to accept a third party model on faith.

MODEL STABILITY

A legitimate concern about mechanical, objective rating systems is that they may be *too* volatile. Will a score change when, in fact, no fundamental change has occurred in the company? Sometimes it will. Short-term, dramatic fluctuations in credit ratings when no fundamental change has occurred result in noise. Noise is a subjective quantity. In trading, for example, individual traders may have a time horizon ranging from a day to a week to many months. What looks like a trend to one class of trader may just be noise to another. Random fluctuations undermine the credibility of the pricing and credit approval process and play no productive part in ongoing credit relationships. The ideal model changes only when the underlying facts about the company also change. It is critically important either to minimize noise or to recognize the level at which a message from the model is truly a signal rather than noise. Testing for noise should play a central part in the process of selecting a credit-scoring model.

Noise may be a particular concern in models based on stock prices. Some would argue that the volatility exhibited by these models reflects the fact that the credit profile has actually changed. While there is no question that the stock market valuation of a company tends to be appropriate over the long term and market value is already being incorporated in the lending thought process, linking credit pricing to short-term market fluctuations may be unsustainable by a bank, unless this becomes an industry-wide practice.

PROBABILITY OF DEFAULT

The credit-scoring model should allow users to associate a probability-of-failure estimate with each credit-rating category. These probability estimates should be based on more than one or two credit cycles of actual experience regarding ratings and defaults. Actuarial techniques are needed to estimate the probability of failure and the uncertainty (volatility) in the estimate associated with a given credit score. If a probability of default is generated, then this may be used to test the prediction versus reality by following a cohort of companies in the same probability bracket over time. If the scoring model is accurate, the forecast accuracy will be better than 80 to 90 percent over its forecast horizon. The probability of default also can be an extremely useful tool for pricing and capital allocation. However, alternative methods of price discovery—such as market pricing—may actually be more helpful.

TRACK RECORD

Every creator of a new model is understandably excited about it. However, even if the statistical work has been thorough, the model has only made its predictions based on hindsight. A good credit model must perform well over time, in good business climates as well as in bad. It must continue to perform well through changes in accounting rules, macroeconomics, stock market

P/E ratios, inflation, and other conditions affecting it. It should make risk assessments with enough lead time for action to be taken.

A model's performance should be verified and validated on a continuous basis. Validation tests take advantage of predictions the model has made subsequent to its initial development. The kinds of tests required are similar to model development tests in that they are intended to measure changes in credit quality and the lead time within which real changes are recognized. There should be a rigorous program to keep track of bankrupt and defaulting borrowers and to monitor a model's success rate.

A considerable amount of data and testing is required to analyze error rates, develop probability of bankruptcy (or loss) functions, and instill confidence in the model. Once a model has been seasoned through exposure to new companies and new economic scenarios, it can be tested with greater validity than is possible in the laboratory.

To be worthy of consideration, a credit model should have been tested with at least several hundred companies over a 10-year test period encompassing more than one credit cycle. Particularly if the model is applicable to privately held entities, it can make predictions for many thousands of companies over the course of 10–15 years. Predictions can then be compared with reality, and this performance can be compared with other credit measures (such as bank rankings or bond ratings). The data eventually become rich enough to permit the estimation of loss functions and even of the timing of the loss. Such experience allows bankers to develop much more confidence in the meaning of credit ratings.

Ultimately, the proof of the pudding is in the eating—in the model's performance—not in its construction or in the elegance of its mathematics. Here again, the burden is on the financial institution to sift through the representations of outstanding model performance made by a vendor. Type I and Type II accuracy, forecast horizon, missing companies and missing data, performance in the private company universe, relationship of the risk rating with market yields—these are all legitimate issues to examine.

APPLICABILITY TO PRIVATE COMPANIES

Due to practical considerations of data accessibility, most model builders limit their efforts to public companies. Databases for public companies are usually more reliable and more extensive than those developed for private companies. This allows for more rigorous initial testing. The public/private test is necessary to assure that classification or predictive results for private and public companies are comparable if the same model is to be used for both. Because of information and moral hazard problems, risk assessments are more difficult to make with respect to private companies.

MODEL RECOGNITION

A good indicator of a model's potential is whether its ratings have credibility in the financial community. Building a model is not difficult; regulators, banks, insurance companies, students, and academics have developed hundreds of them. Only a few have been able to stand up to public scrutiny, and fewer still have been *used*—and not abandoned—by regulators and financial institutions.

IMPLEMENTATION

Whether it has been developed internally or purchased from a vendor, a credit-scoring model should be treated as a major system. Installation involves integration with a bank's loan-accounting systems, database spreadsheets, and report-writing software. It also involves establishing procedures, designing systems, and training bank personnel so that the institution can act on warnings and avoid defaults. A good system should be flexible enough to adapt to changes in the type of information it captures.

Implementing a model requires a strong support staff with a variety of skills:

- *Credit and finance.* The basis of a model is the underlying experience of its builders in credit and financial analysis. Those who understand the variables should build the model from the ground up.
- *Statistics.* Objectivity is assured by strict application of statistical principles. Continuing application of those principles amounts to quality control.
- *Actuarial.* Actuarial methods provide the tools to translate credit information into risk-based pricing and portfolio management information.
- *Systems and programming.* Professionals who have had experience with installation problems can save endless frustration when a credit system is implemented.

PILOT TESTING

The pilot test should be the litmus test for accepting a model. It should be performed on a bank's own data covering a period of 5–10 years. It should be designed to measure the three key aspects of risk measurement: sensitivity to real change, lead time in recognizing change, and stability in the absence of real change.[1] It must also compare model performance with the institution's performance in each area. Test samples must be carefully selected so that results can be compared for large companies and small, for public companies and private ones. Sufficient defaulted loans should be included, and the full range of the institution's credit grades should be covered. Even the largest banks may not have sufficient data on defaults by large corporate borrowers to attain a reasonable sample size. However, a bank does not need to depend on its own experience for financial information on large companies. Moreover, with the help of proxies such as rating changes and yield

---

[1]Real change is defined as a material change, either positive or negative, in the financial condition of the borrower determined on an ex post basis.

changes, tests may be carried out not merely on defaults but also on shifts in credit quality.

Of course, good models should anticipate credit problems that are either unrecognized by the lender or not sufficiently recognized to warrant closer scrutiny. If a model is really effective, it will motivate a reassessment of the loan and perhaps trigger a change in the credit grade assigned by the bank, doing so early enough to avoid a loss.

PROBLEMS AND UNRESOLVED ISSUES IN CREDIT RISK MODELING

There are many unresolved issues in credit risk measurement, not the least of which is the absence of good data. While banks and other institutions have been gathering historical data on corporate financial statements, defaults, and recoveries, they have not, for the most part, kept good cross-sectional and time series data. In the case of industry correlations, SIC groupings at the one-digit level are too coarse to provide meaningful correlations. However, at the two-digit level, the number of data points for calculating correlation coefficients tends to be very small.[2] This problem of data scarcity can be resolved only over time. Indeed, companies that have accumulated reliable data on defaults and recoveries will find themselves able to put them to good competitive use.[3]

Vendors of credit risk models maintain their own data on defaults, but these may be problematic. Since the default data is proprietary, it is impossible to determine whether it is reliable and complete. The default data may not include private firms, for example, or particular industries or areas. In addition, recovery data is unavailable in most instances. The rating agencies (Moody's [1990–1996], Standard and Poor's [1991–92, 1997], and the Society of Actuaries [1996]) have recently started publishing recovery data (see Chapter 15 for more on recoveries). The rating agencies document recoveries at default and also upon emergence from Chapter 11 bankruptcy. These public, bond-market studies observe recoveries stratified by bond seniority. For commercial loans, the most likely equivalents to the public bond market are the straight (nonconvertible) senior secured and senior unsecured classes. Using bond data, Altman and Eberhart (1994) and Altman and Kishore (1996) provide statistics on this important variable by seniority and industry group. Chapter 15 mentions additional sources of data on recoveries.

Another key issue regarding credit risk models remains to be resolved: to date, there has been more emphasis on predicting default than on predicting value. To predict value, one must have a better understanding of the

---

[2]There are other problems with the calculated correlations; for one thing, they tend to be unstable.

[3]This may explain a number of current initiatives in the United States, among the larger banks, to develop a shared national data base of historical mortality and loss rates on loans (a current project of Robert Morris Associates, Philadelphia, Penn.). Loan Pricing Corporation also has a database on corporate loans.

effects of such variables as correlations, covenants, embedded options, bankruptcy, and tax laws on the value of an asset. Thus far, nobody has developed an effective and efficient model to measure and price credit risk. Classic credit analysis involving simulation, stress tests, and offline forecasts will continue to be part of the tool set employed in measuring and managing credit risk.

Credit risk models have not evolved to a point where risk at the micro-level of the firm or individual has been linked to factors at the macro-level of the economy. Most models that have been built rest on historical data and cannot take advantage of macro-economic forecasts such as those for inflation, GDP growth, or unemployment. In other words, the insights into business failure from economists and financial analysts have yet to be integrated. While some attempts have been made to link the micro and macro variables, these are still in the laboratory stage and have not found practical application in the valuation of fixed-income assets.

Lastly, while proper ways to evaluate credit risk models are available, presentations of model results often omit important details regarding methodology, data, test statistics, Type I and Type II errors, and holdout results. Until universally accepted standards are developed, decision makers must exercise due diligence before accepting a model for use inhouse. To the extent that every single credit risk model is a prediction (of what the value of an asset should be or what the likelihood of default is), it is useful for an organization to track the prediction *versus* realization on a continuing basis. This may be done by plotting actual outcomes versus predictions over time, or by plotting the directional error and percent error over time.[4] It is useful to obtain the confidence band around the forecast rather than use a point value. Frequent re-estimation of the model may be advisable if it can be shown that this will improve its performance.

The instruments on the control panel of an aircraft provide measurements of its motion and the space in which it is traveling. They make flying safer and facilitate air travel at high speeds and in adverse weather conditions. But whatever they do, they do not replace the skill and judgment of the pilot. Credit risk models may be viewed in a similar fashion. Pilots, however, are urged to attend to the readings of their instruments, which have been placed in the cockpit because of their demonstrated value and reliability. Credit risk models have not yet achieved the same level of respect—or, for that matter, of reliability. The judgment of the analyst therefore remains critically important in the evaluation and pricing of credit.

REFERENCES

Altman, E. I., and A. C. Eberhart. 1994. Do Seniority Provisions Protect Bondholders' Investments? *Journal of Portfolio Management* 20:67–75.

---

[4]Another name for directional error is turning point error, e.g., when a positive change was predicted whereas the actual change was negative.

Altman, E. I., and V. M. Kishore. 1996. Almost Everything You Wanted to Know about Recoveries on Defaulted Bonds. *Financial Analysts Journal* (November/December):57–63.

Moody's Investors Service. 1990. Corporate Bond Defaults and Default Rates. *Moody's Special Reports*. New York: Moody's Investors Service.

——— 1991. Corporate Bond Defaults and Default Rates. *Moody's Special Reports*. New York: Moody's Investors Service.

——— 1992. Corporate Bond Defaults and Default Rates. *Moody's Special Reports*. New York: Moody's Investors Service.

——— 1993. Corporate Bond Defaults and Default Rates. *Moody's Special Reports*. New York: Moody's Investors Service.

——— 1994. Corporate Bond Defaults and Default Rates. *Moody's Special Reports*. New York: Moody's Investors Service.

——— 1995. Corporate Bond Defaults and Default Rates. *Moody's Special Reports*. New York: Moody's Investors Service.

——— 1996. Corporate Bond Defaults and Default Rates. *Moody's Special Reports*. New York: Moody's Investors Service.

Society of Actuaries. 1996. *1986–1992 Credit Risk Loss Experience Study: Private Placement Bonds*. Schaumburg, Ill.: Society of Actuaries.

Standard & Poor's. 1991–92. Corporate Bond Defaults Study. Parts 1–3. *Credit Week*, 16 September; 15 September; 21 December.

———. 1997. *Ratings Performance 1996: Stability and Transition*. New York: Standard & Poor's.

Chapter 15

Default Rates, Losses, and Recoveries

"Data! data! data!" he cried impatiently. "I can't make bricks without clay."

—Sir Arthur Conan Doyle, *The Adventures of the Copper Beeches* (Sherlock Holmes)

The key ingredient in credit risk is clearly the risk of default. Whether debt instruments are considered on a stand-alone basis or on a portfolio basis, default probabilities and adjustments for recoveries play a critical role in risk assessment and valuation. The CreditMetrics™ approach (Gupton, Finger, and Bhatia 1997) shown in Figure 15.1 is the most recent system developed for these purposes.

By far, the most comprehensive default statistics available today are stratified by company bond ratings. Moody's (1998), Standard & Poor's (1998), Altman (1989), and Altman and Kishore (1997) have all measured and reported statistics on this basis. Standard & Poor's uses a *static-pool* technique, Moody's uses a *cohort analysis,* and Altman computes an actuarially based mortality rate measurement that is somewhat different from the other two. Each of these approaches leads to slightly different empirical findings. In this chapter, we focus on bonds because the default statistics currently available on loans are far less comprehensive and reliable. We will, however, also report on a new study that examines default rates on large, newly issued syndicated corporate bank loans.

TRADITIONAL DEFAULT RATE MEASURES

Prior to 1988, analysts concentrated on measuring the default rate on an initial population of bonds for a finite period of time, such as one year. The populations consisted of either the entire corporate bond universe or, more frequently, just low-grade or junk bonds. While default rates can be computed in many different ways based on different definitions of the underlying populations, defaults, and time periods (see Fridson and Jónsson 1991), two time series are most commonly used. These are Altman's domestic straight (nonconvertible), high-yield debt compilation of defaults divided into the *market value* of outstanding high yield bonds (Altman and Kishore 1997), and Moody's (1990, 1997, 1998) number of defaulting *issuers* (all defaulting issuers including foreign and convertible) where a bond rating was

Figure 15.1   CreditMetrics™ Schematic.

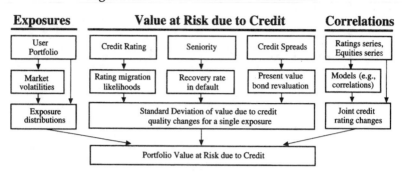

Source: J. P. Morgan CreditMetrics™ Technical Document, April 1997.

observed divided by the number of issuers with bonds of a certain rating. Defaults are defined as bond issues that have missed a payment of interest, filed for bankruptcy, or announced a distressed-creditor restructuring. Moody's also has published a dollar-weighted default rate time series.

Tables 15.1 and 15.2 show the total corporate bond default rate from 1971 to 1997 and the high-yield, straight-debt default rate from 1971 to 1997 (third quarter), respectively. Since relatively few managers invest in the total spectrum of bond ratings, the latter junk bond default rate statistics are the most relevant to a diversified portfolio of low-grade bonds. The weighted average (by dollar amount outstanding) annual default rate was 3.61 percent for the period 1971–1996, and it was slightly higher from 1985 to 1996 (3.82 percent). The unweighted mean was 2.67 percent and the median annual default rate was only 1.61 percent. The large difference between the median and weighted mean rate can be explained by the twin-towers of 1990 and 1991, when annual default rates were over 10 percent from mid-1990 to mid-1991. Indeed, in the 26-year period covered, only five years saw default rates greater than 4.0 percent. In the case of 1987, the rate would have been much below 4 percent if not for one huge default (Texaco). Between 1993 and 1996, the rate was below 2 percent a year. We expect that this recent downward trend in defaults will reverse itself and that the default rate will migrate back toward the mean in future years. Since there were more than $300 billion in junk bonds outstanding in mid-1997, even a 2 percent rate would mean over $6 billion in defaults in 1997. Through the third quarter of 1997, the default rate was 1.3 percent based on $3.9 billion of defaults.

As measured by Moody's, the comparable average annual default rates for the period 1971–1996 were 3.42 percent, (unweighted percentage of issuers) and 3.21 percent (by face value amounts). Standard & Poor's unweighted mean, by issuers, was 3.2 percent for the period 1981–1996.

MORTALITY (DEFAULT) RATES BY RATING AND BY AGE

While the traditional approach to measuring default rates is appropriate for gauging average annual rates for a broad cross section of high-yield bonds,

Table 15.1   Corporate Bond Default Rates, 1971–1997 (All Domestic Corporate U.S. Bonds)

Year	Amount Outstanding Beginning of Year ($ Billions)	Default Amount Straight Debt Only ($ Billions)	Default Amount Converts Only ($ Billions)	Par Value of all Public Bond Defaults ($ Billions)	Default Rate (%)
1997	1,684.59	4.12	0.74	4.86	0.29
1996	1,430.01	3.34	0.35	3.68	0.26
1995	1,238.90	4.55	0.33	4.88	0.39
1994	1,093.69	3.42	0.37	3.78	0.35
1993	982.48	2.29	0.29	2.57	0.26
1992	864.32	5.55	0.33	5.87	0.68
1991	762.27	18.86	0.78	19.64	2.58
1990	711.11	18.35	0.95	19.31	2.72
1989	645.94	8.11	1.00	9.11	1.41
1988	580.31	3.94	0.57	4.51	0.78
1987	528.94	7.49	1.75	9.24	1.75
1986	458.13	3.16	0.30	3.46	0.75
1985	413.20	0.99	0.31	1.30	0.32
1984	372.90	0.34	0.28	0.62	0.17
1983	352.30	0.30	0.11	0.41	0.12
1982	331.40	0.75	0.42	1.17	0.35
1981	311.90	0.03	0.05	0.08	0.03
1980	281.70	0.22	0.03	0.26	0.09
1979	258.60	0.02	0.01	0.03	0.01
1978	248.30	0.12	0.07	0.19	0.08
1977	229.10	0.38	0.07	0.45	0.20
1976	209.90	0.03	0.08	0.11	0.05
1975	183.50	0.20	0.12	0.32	0.17
1974	162.90	0.12	0.17	0.29	0.18
1973	154.40	0.05	0.15	0.20	0.13
1972	143.00	0.19	0.08	0.27	0.19
1971	125.50	0.08	0.04	0.12	0.10
			Average default rate—1971 to 1997:		0.53
			Average default rate—1978 to 1997:		0.67
			Weighted average default rate—1971 to 1997:		0.66
			Weighted average default rate—1978 to 1997:		0.70
			Median default rate—1971 to 1997:		0.26

Source: Author Compilation

it falls far short for measuring bonds or loans of a specific rating. Furthermore, the rates given in Table 15.1 say nothing about the age of the bond. In order to be more precise about the expected default rate for a given credit rating, Altman (1989), Moody's (1990), and Standard & Poor's (1991–92) all identified the relevant cohort group for measurement as the bond rating at

**Table 15.2   Historical Default Rates—Straight High-yield Debt Only[a]
1971–1997 ($ Millions)**

Year	Par value outstanding	Par value defaults	Default rates
1997	$335,400	$ 4,200	1.252%
1996	$271,000	$ 3,336	1.231%
1995	$240,000	$ 4,551	1.896%
1994	$235,000	$ 3,418	1.454%
1993	$206,907	$ 2,287	1.105%
1992	$163,000	$ 5,545	3.402%
1991	$183,600	$18,862	10.273%
1990	$181,000	$18,354	10.140%
1989	$189,258	$ 8,110	4.285%
1988	$148,187	$ 3,944	2.662%
1987	$129,557	$ 7,486	5.778%
1986	$ 90,243	$ 3,156	3.497%
1985	$ 58,088	$ 992	1.708%
1984	$ 40,939	$ 344	0.840%
1983	$ 27,492	$ 301	1.095%
1982	$ 18,109	$ 577	3.186%
1981	$ 17,115	$ 27	0.158%
1980	$ 14,935	$ 224	1.500%
1979	$ 10,356	$ 20	0.193%
1978	$ 8,946	$ 119	1.330%
1977	$ 8,157	$ 381	4.671%
1976	$ 7,735	$ 30	0.388%
1975	$ 7,471	$ 204	2.731%
1974	$ 10,894	$ 123	1.129%
1973	$ 7,824	$ 49	0.626%
1972	$ 6,928	$ 193	2.786%
1971	$ 6,602	$ 82	1.242%

				Standard Deviation
Arithmetic average default rate	1971 to 1996	2.666%	2.588%
	1978 to 1996	2.933%	2.856%
	1985 to 1996	3.953%	3.094%
Weighted average default rate (b)	1971 to 1996	3.613%	3.357%
	1978 to 1996	3.655%	3.384%
	1985 to 1996	3.819%	3.429%
Median annual default rate	1971 to 1996	1.604%	

[a] Excludes prior defaulted issues from par value outstanding.
[b] Weighted by par value of amount outstanding for each year.
Source: Altman and Kishore (1997).

some point in time. As will be shown, however, Altman's mortality measure examines bonds with the same original rating for a period of up to ten years after issuance. Moody's and Standard & Poor's assess default rates of all bonds of a given bond rating, regardless of their age. Moody's is of the view that macro phenomena are more important than vintage effects. It should also be noted that Moody's uses the issuer as the basic unit of account.

Altman (1989) retains the notion that default rates for individual periods—yearly, for example—are measured on the basis of defaults in the period relative to some base population in that same period. The calculation, however, becomes more complex when we begin with a specific cohort group such as a bond-rating category and track that group's performance for multiple time periods. Because the original population can change over time as a result of a number of different events, Altman (1989) considers mortalities in relation to a survival population and then inputs the defaults to calculate mortality rates. Bonds can exit from the original population because of at least four different kinds of events: defaults, calls, sinking funds, and maturities.

The individual mortality rate for each year (marginal mortality rate, or MMR) is calculated using the equation

$$MMR_{(t)} = \frac{\text{total value of defaulting debt in the year } (t)}{\text{total value of the population of bonds at the start of the year } (t)}$$

The cumulative mortality rate (CMR) is measured over a specific time period $(1, 2, \ldots, T$ years) by subtracting the product of the surviving populations of each of the previous years from one (1.0); that is,

$$CMR_{(T)} = 1 - \prod_{t=1}^{T} SR_t$$

where $CMR_{(T)}$ = cumulative mortality rate in (T),
$SR(t)$ = survival rate in (t); $1 - MMR(t)$.

The individual year marginal mortality rates for each bond rating are based on a compilation of that year's mortality measured from issuance. For example, all of the one-year mortalities are combined for the sample period to arrive at the one-year rate; all of the second-year mortalities are combined to compute the two-year rate, and so on.

The mortality rate is a value-weighted rate for the particular year after issuance rather than an unweighted average. If we were simply to average each of the year-one rates, year-two rates, and so on, our results would be susceptible to significant specific-year bias. If, for example, few new bonds were issued in a given year and the defaults emanating from that year were high in relation to the amount issued, the unweighted average could be improperly affected. Altman's (1989) weighted-average technique correctly biases the results toward the larger-issue years, especially the more recent years.

Starting in 1988, Altman measured and updated corporate bond defaults and mortality rates from each of the major Standard & Poor's rating categories (AAA, AA, A, etc.) from 1971 to the present (Altman and Kishore 1997). The most recent estimate is for the period 1971–1996 and is given in

Table 15.3. It is likely the rates would be similar if Moody's original issuance were used instead of Standard & Poor's. Note the marginal (yearly) as well as the cumulative mortality rates for up to ten years after issuance. The hierarchy of cumulative mortality rates is as expected, with the higher rating categories experiencing lower rates—except for the AA category, which has a higher default rate than single-A. This is due to the massive Texaco Chapter XI bankruptcy filing in 1987, which involved over $3 billion of AA rated bonds. The expected hierarchy returns to normal when we observe default losses. The loss rates for AA bonds are lower than those for single-A bonds because Texaco's bonds recovered over 80 percent of their face value just after default—far above the average recovery of 40 percent of face value for all bonds. Within one year, the company's bonds were again selling at par value. We will discuss recovery rates in greater depth later in this chapter.

There are several noteworthy aspects to the mortality rate table. First, we can observe that the marginal rates in the first three years of a bond's life rise each year and then tend to level off for several years thereafter. This is particularly true for the BBB, BB, and B categories. Hence, we do note an aging effect, which can be observed only by tracking default rates from original issuance. The aging effect is intuitively sound, since most companies have a great deal of cash just after they issue a bond. Even if their operating cash flow is negative, they are usually able to meet several periods of interest payments. Indeed, in 1996 an increasing number of high-yield bonds were issued with guarantees of several years' interest payments. For these bonds, the issuers pre-funded or escrowed the cash required for the relevant interest payments. As an alternative structure, an underwriter might guarantee several years of interest payments for its client. For bonds of these types, we should expect a flat, near zero, default rate and then, depending upon refinancing opportunities, a significant increase in the marginal mortality rate after the pre-funded period has ended.

It should be noted that the lower-rated categories, such as single-B, have default rates that appear to be very high. Cumulative defaults are nearly 25 percent by the fifth year and close to 35 percent by the tenth year. But these rates are not so high when viewed in relation to promised yield spreads, which averaged nearly 5 percent per year over the sample period. Factoring in average recovery rates of at least 40 percent (and higher of late), a 25 percent five-year default rate results in an 18 percent cumulative loss rate, or a loss of about 3 percent per year, and a return spread (over the risk-free rate) of about 2 percent per year. Indeed, high-yield bonds, of which single-B's have been the dominant category, returned about 2.3 percent per year above the risk-free rate in the 1978–1996 period (2.5 percent on a compound average annual return basis [Altman and Kishore, 1997]). The investor should also factor in the volatility of returns as well as the average spread.

COMPARING CUMULATIVE DEFAULT RATES

We have mentioned the major differences between the rating agencies' reported default rates and Altman's. These different methodologies, which are summarized in Table 15.4, include (1) face value dollar amount (Altman)

Table 15.3 Mortality Rates by Original Rating—All Rated Corporate Bonds (1971–1996) Years after Issuance

		1	2	3	4	5	6	7	8	9	10
AAA	Yearly	0.00%	0.00%	0.00%	0.00%	0.06%	0.00%	0.00%	0.00%	0.00%	0.00%
	Cumulative	0.00%	0.00%	0.00%	0.00%	0.06%	0.06%	0.06%	0.06%	0.06%	0.06%
AA	Yearly	0.00%	0.00%	0.47%	0.27%	0.00%	0.00%	0.01%	0.00%	0.04%	0.04%
	Cumulative	0.00%	0.00%	0.47%	0.74%	0.74%	0.74%	0.74%	0.74%	0.78%	0.82%
A	Yearly	0.00%	0.00%	0.05%	0.15%	0.08%	0.16%	0.06%	0.17%	0.12%	0.00%
	Cumulative	0.00%	0.00%	0.05%	0.19%	0.27%	0.43%	0.50%	0.67%	0.79%	0.79%
BBB	Yearly	0.03%	0.39%	0.41%	0.67%	0.40%	0.54%	0.21%	0.10%	0.10%	0.46%
	Cumulative	0.03%	0.42%	0.82%	1.49%	1.88%	2.41%	2.62%	2.72%	2.81%	3.27%
BB	Yearly	0.44%	0.98%	3.41%	1.78%	2.80%	1.33%	2.75%	0.29%	1.69%	4.22%
	Cumulative	0.44%	1.41%	4.77%	6.47%	9.09%	10.30%	12.76%	13.01%	14.49%	18.09%
B	Yearly	1.41%	4.31%	7.27%	6.93%	7.06%	6.24%	3.76%	1.96%	1.26%	1.64%
	Cumulative	1.41%	5.65%	12.51%	18.58%	24.33%	29.05%	31.72%	33.06%	33.90%	34.99%
CCC	Yearly	2.46%	16.57%	17.69%	12.17%	4.50%	12.98%	1.63%	5.71%	0.00%	4.41%
	Cumulative	2.46%	18.62%	33.02%	41.17%	43.82%	51.11%	51.91%	54.65%	54.65%	56.65%

Note: Rated by S&P at issuance based on 630 issues.
Source: Altman and Kishore (1997).

Table 15.4   Methodologies and Data in Cumulative Default Rate Calculation

Altman and Kishore (1997)	Moody's/Carty and Lieberman (1997) and S&P (1997)
1. Face value–weighted basis	1. Issuer, unweighted basis (S&P and Carty and Lieberman) and market value (Carty and Lieberman)
2. Domestic, straight bonds	2. Domestic straight and convertible and foreign bonds—considered at the issuer level
3. Based on actual rating from original issuance up to 10 years	3. Based on implied senior unsecured rating from cohort or static-pool groups, combining bonds of all ages up to 20 years (Carty and Lieberman) and 15 years (S&P)
4. Mortality default calculation adjusting for calls, maturities, and defaults	4. Default rate based on percentage of original cohort group (Carty and Lieberman) or static pool (S&P). Carty and Lieberman adjusts for withdrawn ratings in marginal default rate calculations
5. Based on full rating class categories, AAA to CCC (no subgrades)	5. Based on full rating class categories and also sub-grades, Aaa to Caa (Carty and Lieberman); no subgrades for S&P
6. Sample period 1971–1996	6. Carty and Lieberman's sample period 1970–1996 for full grade and 1983–1996 for subgrades; S&P 1981–1996

versus issuer basis, (2) actual ratings versus implied senior-unsecured ratings, (3) domestic straight debt only versus domestic (including convertibles) and foreign, (4) original issuance versus cohort grouping regardless of age, (5) mortality versus default rates, and (6) sample periods.

Table 15.5 shows the one- to ten-year cumulative rates from the three primary sources of data. The primary empirical difference between the mortality/original issuance approach, the *static-pool* method used by Standard & Poor's, and the *dynamic cohort* method used by Moody's is the observed default rates in the first several years—particularly in the lower-grade classes. For example, Altman's first-year rate for single-B bonds is 1.41 percent, while Moody's and Standard & Poor's are 7.27 percent and 4.92 percent, respectively. These relative differences persist until the fourth year, after which the results are quite similar. For example, the fifth-year Moody's rate is approximately 29.5 percent versus 24.3 percent for Altman. Standard & Poor's rate is actually lower (20.5 percent) than Altman's in the fifth year due to a much lower marginal rate in that year. This difference is difficult to explain. As noted earlier, the main reason for these differentials is the aging effect, which manifests itself only in the Altman data.

Which method is best to use probably depends upon the age distribution of relevant portfolio or individual bonds. For new issuance analysis, which is often the perspective for investors in corporate bonds, the mortality rate approach would seem to be more relevant. For portfolios of seasoned bonds, the rating agency approach would perhaps be more relevant. All of the methods include sample periods that cover many business cycles.

Altman's marginal rates could also be used, but only for assessing the one-year marginal default rates for bonds which have survived up to that point. A portfolio manager's strategy regarding the weighting of bonds could also influence the choice of approach. Altman weights the larger issues more than smaller ones, while the rating agencies weight each issuer equally.

DEFAULT RATES ON COMMERCIAL LOANS

A significant asset class that has heretofore remained unanalyzed with respect to default rates is commercial bank loans. The major stumbling blocks for measuring default risk on various levels of loan credit quality are the private nature of the market and the lack of ratings, until just recently. A new study by Altman and Suggitt (1997) has, for the first time, measured defaults using the mortality approach discussed earlier. Utilizing a combination of actual ratings applied to syndicated bank loans by Moody's since 1995 and assigned ratings based on the ratings of publicly traded bonds of the same company, they calculate mortality rates on new loan facilities from 1971–1996.

Table 15.6 shows the marginal and cumulative mortality rates on the full spectrum of ratings for both bank loans and public bonds over the same sample period. The results show cumulative rates that are remarkably similar for both loans and bonds. For example, the five-year bank loan cumulative mortality rate is 9.97 percent, versus 9.24 percent for the bonds. Note that these rates are considerably lower than the mortality rates on bonds covering the 1971–1996 period (Table 15.5). This is certainly due to the benign credit cycle in recent years in the United States. The authors estimate that the bias due to this unusually low default period is between one-third to one-half of the long-term rate.

DEFAULT LOSSES NET OF RECOVERIES

The expected default probability and the severity of default are the two most critical analytical factors determining the required yields on risky corporate debt. In assigning their ratings, bond rating agencies focus almost exclusively on the probability of default and the timeliness of payment of interest and principal. There is, however, a fairly standard rule of thumb that lowers a firm's subordinate bond issues by two notches, compared to its senior issues, if the senior bond is noninvestment grade, and by one notch if it is investment grade. This ad hoc approach is more than likely based on the expectation that, in the event of default, the junior bonds will recover less than

Table 15.5 Cumulative Default Rate Comparison (in % for up to 10 Years)

	1	2	3	4	5	6	7	8	9	10
AAA/Aaa										
Altman	0.00	0.00	0.00	0.00	0.06	0.06	0.06	0.06	0.06	0.06
Moody's	0.00	0.00	0.00	0.04	0.13	0.22	0.33	0.45	0.59	0.74
S&P	0.00	0.00	0.06	0.13	0.21	0.39	0.58	0.92	1.05	1.21
AA/Aa										
Altman	0.00	0.00	0.47	0.74	0.74	0.74	0.74	0.74	0.78	0.82
Moody's	0.03	0.05	0.10	0.25	0.40	0.57	0.73	0.91	1.04	1.13
S&P	0.00	0.02	0.11	0.22	0.38	0.59	0.78	0.03	1.02	1.12
A/A										
Altman	0.00	0.00	0.05	0.19	0.27	0.43	0.50	0.67	0.79	0.79
Moody's	0.01	0.07	0.22	0.39	0.57	0.76	0.96	1.18	1.44	1.73
S&P	0.05	0.14	0.24	0.40	0.60	0.79	1.02	1.31	1.61	1.92
BBB/Baa										
Altman	0.03	0.42	0.82	1.49	1.88	2.41	2.62	2.72	2.81	3.27
Moody's	0.12	0.39	0.76	1.27	1.71	2.21	2.79	3.36	3.99	4.61
S&P	0.17	0.42	0.68	1.22	1.72	2.28	2.81	3.27	3.64	3.97

	1	2	3	4	5	6	7	8	9	10
BB/Ba										
Altman	0.44	1.41	4.77	6.47	9.09	10.30	12.76	13.01	14.49	18.09
Moody's	1.36	3.77	6.29	8.88	11.57	13.87	15.69	17.55	19.23	20.94
S&P	0.98	3.19	5.54	7.86	9.94	11.99	13.10	14.18	15.14	15.89
B/B										
Altman	1.41	5.65	12.51	18.58	24.33	29.05	31.72	33.06	33.90	34.99
Moody's	7.27	13.87	19.94	25.03	29.45	33.26	36.34	39.01	41.45	44.31
S&P	4.92	10.32	14.98	18.22	20.49	22.03	23.33	24.55	25.50	26.53
CCC/Caa										
Altman	2.46	18.62	33.02	41.17	43.82	51.11	51.91	54.65	54.65	56.65
Moody's	—	—	—	—	—	—	—	—	—	—
S&P	19.29	28.58	31.63	35.94	40.06	41.04	41.93	42.28	43.14	43.72

Source: Altman, Market value weights, by numbered years from original Standard & Poor's issuances, 1971–1996, based on actual ratings (Altman and Kisnore 1997, Exhibit 10).

Moody's, Issuer weighted, cohort analysis, 1971–1996, based on actual or implied senior unsecured ratings (Moody's Investors Service 1997).

S&P, Issuer weighted, static-pool analysis, 1981–1995, based on actual or implied senior unsecured ratings (Standard & Poor's 1996, 1997a)

Table 15.6 Comparison of Syndicated Bank Loan versus Corporate Bond Mortality Rates Based on Original Issuance Principal Amounts (1991–1996)

		1 Year		2 Years		3 Years		4 Years		5 Years	
		Bank	Bond	Bank	Bond	Bank	Bond	Bank	Bond	Bank	Bond
Aaa	*Marginal*	0.00%	0.00%	0.00%	0.00%	0.00%	0.00%	0.00%	0.00%	0.00%	0.00%
	Cumulative	0.00%	0.00%	0.00%	0.00%	0.00%	0.00%	0.00%	0.00%	0.00%	0.00%
Aa	*Marginal*	0.00%	0.00%	0.00%	0.00%	0.00%	0.00%	0.00%	0.00%	0.00%	0.00%
	Cumulative	0.00%	0.00%	0.00%	0.00%	0.00%	0.00%	0.00%	0.00%	0.00%	0.00%
A	*Marginal*	0.00%	0.00%	0.12%	0.00%	0.00%	0.00%	0.00%	0.00%	0.00%	0.05%
	Cumulative	0.00%	0.00%	0.12%	0.00%	0.12%	0.00%	0.12%	0.00%	0.12%	0.05%
Baa	*Marginal*	0.04%	0.00%	0.00%	0.00%	0.00%	0.00%	0.00%	0.54%	0.00%	0.00%
	Cumulative	0.04%	0.00%	0.04%	0.00%	0.04%	0.00%	0.04%	0.54%	0.04%	0.54%
Ba	*Marginal*	0.17%	0.00%	0.60%	0.38%	0.60%	2.30%	0.97%	1.80%	4.89%	0.00%
	Cumulative	0.17%	0.00%	0.77%	0.38%	1.36%	2.67%	2.32%	4.42%	7.10%	4.42%
B	*Marginal*	2.30%	0.81%	1.86%	1.97%	2.59%	4.99%	1.79%	1.76%	1.86%	0.00%
	Cumulative	2.30%	0.81%	4.11%	2.76%	6.60%	7.61%	8.27%	9.24%	9.97%	9.24%
Caa	*Marginal*	15.24%	2.65%	7.44%	3.09%	13.03%	4.55%	0.00%	21.72%	0.00%	0.00%
	Cumulative	15.24%	2.65%	21.55%	5.66%	31.77%	9.95%	31.77%	29.51%	31.77%	29.51%

Source: Author's computations for loans, and a special run of data collected and computed from Altman and Kishore (1997) for bonds.

the more senior issues. Lately, the rating agencies report that they have explicitly incorporated severity expectations in their private placement and structured finance analytics—for example, Standard & Poor's (1997b)—and in their corporate bond ratings (Moody's Structured Finance 1991).

Using the traditional default rate calculation discussed above, we can calculate the annual and average annual default loss by factoring in the average recovery at default and adding an amount equal to the lost coupon payment on that proportion of the market that defaulted. Table 15.7 shows this calculation for 1996. Note that to assess the loss, the 1996 default rate is reduced by the average bond price just after default (51.9 percent of face value). This results in a loss of principal from defaults in 1996 of 0.59 percent (1.23 percent × 0.519).

When we add the loss of one-half (six month) of the average coupon (8.92 percent) on the 1.23 percent of the market that defaulted to calculate the default loss of coupon, we arrive at an additional 5.5 basis points to be included, which raises the 1996 default loss to 0.64 percent. The arithmetic average default loss for the period 1978–1996 was 1.90 percent per year, with a weighted average (by amount outstanding) of 2.41 percent per year. Default losses for individual years have varied from as low as 0.14 percent (1979) to as high as 8.42 percent and 7.16 percent in 1990 and 1991, respectively. The median default loss rate over the last 19 years was 1.24 percent, and in three of the last four years (1993–1996) the loss rate was below 1.0 percent.

MORTALITY LOSSES

To continue the progression from the traditional calculations of default to the more informative mortality/aging approach, we present mortality losses

Table 15.7   1996 Default Loss Rate

Background data	Weight calculation
Average default rate 1996	1.23%
Average end-of-month rate after default	51.91%
Average loss of principal	48.09%
Average coupon payment	8.92%
Default loss computation	
Default rate	1.23%
× Loss of principal	48.09%
Default loss of principal	0.592%
Default rate	1.23%
× Loss of 1/2 coupon	4.458%
Default loss of coupon	0.055%
Default loss of principal = 0.647%	

Source: Altman and Kishore (1997), Exhibit 4.

by original rating for the period 1971–1996 in Table 15.8 (Altman and Ki-shore, 1997). Note that the expected hierarchy of losses by original rating holds true, even for the AA and A classes. One can conclude from this analysis that the expected cumulative default loss (adjusting for recoveries and lost coupon) is as little as 0.1 percent for AAA bonds over 10 years. For high-yield junk bonds, cumulative losses are 11.5 percent, 25.9 percent, and 44.6 percent for BB, B, and CCC original issuance.

When cumulative losses for, say, single-B original issuance bonds, are annualized, the result is less than 2.5 percent per year, which is very close to the 2.4 percent per year traditional calculation of the weighted average result discussed above. Hence, an average annual promised yield of close to 5.0 percent per year for B-rated bonds is sufficient, for many investors, to offset expected losses of 2.0 to 2.5 percent per year.

RECOVERIES BY SENIORITY

In addition to arithmetic and weighted average default losses, analysts have further refined the data to consider the critical element of seniority. Indeed, Standard & Poor's (1991–92), with Altman and Eberhart (1994), examines recovery rates on defaulted debt by seniority at the default date and also upon emergence from the distressed corporate restructuring (in most cases upon emergence from a Chapter 11 bankruptcy reorganization). These studies find that recovery rates and loss rates are very much a function of the debt's seniority, as expected, but also that realized returns during the bankruptcy reorganization period are considerably more favorable for the senior-secured and senior-unsecured priorities than for the more junior classes. This situation is perhaps surprising, since one would expect that the market would properly discount the junior bonds at default and that the post-default return experience would be about the same for junior and senior bonds—especially since the variance of returns was about the same for each class.

The term *recovery* can refer to the price that bonds can be sold for at the time of default (or within one to three months, as is typical in credit risk derivative contracts) or the value at the end of the distressed-reorganization period. In this chapter, we examine the experience at default. The industry affiliation of the defaulted debtor and the seniority of the issue both affect the recovery. For a more detailed discussion of recovery by industries, see Altman and Kishore (1997).

The type of business an enterprise is engaged in will dictate the types of assets it holds and the competitive conditions under which it operates. Other factors being equal, the more tangible and liquid the assets, the higher their liquidation value and, hence, the greater the expected price of the debt securities in a distressed situation. In addition, the more certain the future earnings of a distressed entity, the higher the enterprise value and its debt component. Because of their asset structure and regulatory environment, for example, public utilities may have a better recovery rate than companies with few tangible assets operating in highly competitive environments. Since these factors need to be assessed in the pricing of debt securities throughout their duration—whether at the time of issuance or in a distressed situation—

Table 15.8   Mortality Losses by Original Rating—All Rated Corporate Bonds (1971–1996)

		Years after issuance									
		1	2	3	4	5	6	7	8	9	10
AAA	Yearly	0.00%	0.00%	0.00%	0.00%	0.01%	0.00%	0.00%	0.00%	0.00%	0.00%
	Cumulative	0.00%	0.00%	0.00%	0.00%	0.01%	0.01%	0.01%	0.01%	0.01%	0.01%
AA	Yearly	0.00%	0.00%	0.09%	0.10%	0.00%	0.00%	0.00%	0.00%	0.02%	0.02%
	Cumulative	0.00%	0.00%	0.09%	0.19%	0.19%	0.19%	0.20%	0.20%	0.22%	0.24%
A	Yearly	0.00%	0.00%	0.03%	0.10%	0.06%	0.12%	0.02%	0.10%	0.07%	0.00%
	Cumulative	0.00%	0.00%	0.03%	0.12%	0.18%	0.30%	0.33%	0.42%	0.49%	0.49%
BBB	Yearly	0.02%	0.23%	0.22%	0.35%	0.12%	0.31%	0.19%	0.06%	0.06%	0.33%
	Cumulative	0.02%	0.25%	0.47%	0.83%	0.95%	1.26%	1.44%	1.51%	1.57%	1.89%
BB	Yearly	0.29%	0.61%	2.58%	1.35%	1.46%	1.03%	1.45%	0.17%	0.94%	2.18%
	Cumulative	0.29%	0.90%	3.46%	4.76%	6.15%	7.12%	8.47%	8.63%	9.49%	11.47%
B	Yearly	0.73%	2.84%	5.76%	5.16%	5.31%	3.96%	2.38%	1.45%	0.67%	1.06%
	Cumulative	0.73%	3.55%	9.11%	13.80%	18.38%	21.61%	23.48%	24.59%	25.09%	25.89%
CCC	Yearly	1.20%	13.51%	13.04%	7.34%	2.74%	8.93%	1.46%	4.54%	0.00%	3.45%
	Cumulative	1.20%	14.55%	25.69%	31.14%	33.03%	39.01%	39.89%	42.62%	42.62%	44.60%

Note: Rated by S&P at issuance based on 630 issues.

Source: Altman and Kishore (1997).

the actual recovery experience by industry and priority is likely to be useful information.

The ability to sell bonds at significant values just after default has always been an attractive feature of publicly traded, liquid securities. Average prices at default have been calculated for decades with the venerable overall rule-of-thumb of 40 cents on the dollar. Indeed, this average overall recovery rate still persists today. We find that the arithmetic average recovery rate on a sample of over 750 defaulting bond issues from 1978–1996 is $40.11 (Altman and Kishore 1997). Table 15.9 shows the average recovery by seniority for 1978–1996. Seniority does play its expected role—with senior-secured debt averaging about 58 percent of face value, senior-unsecured 48 percent, senior-subordinate 35 percent and junior-subordinate about 32 percent. Note that we interchange dollar and percentage recoveries, since the average issue price is very close to par ($100).

Carty and Lieberman (1997) of Moody's find that the average recovery rate for the period 1970–1995 is 41.25 percent. Their data reveal very high volatility (standard deviation is 26.55 percent) in the yearly recovery rates. Our data confirm this finding with standard deviations of 21–26 percent for various seniorities (Table 15.9 and Table 15.10). Hickman (1958) found an average recovery of 34 percent for the period 1930–1943. Perhaps the finding that secured debt recovers *only* 58 percent of its face value is surprising. It should not be surprising, however, if one considers that the assets serving as collateral vary from factories, buildings, and rolling stock to less tangible guarantees. In addition, the economic value of a distressed firm's assets will typically depreciate as its earning power erodes. Since we observe that secured bonds earn over 20 percent per year during the bankruptcy/reorganization period (Altman and Eberhart 1994), the price at default should be about what we observe in order for the post-reorganization price to approximate par ($100)—which it does. The relatively high returns observed for the reorganization period can perhaps be explained by the uncertainty that surrounds the results and duration of a Chapter 11 proceeding.

Summary statistics from Altman and Kishore (1997) are, for the most part, quite similar to Moody's (1997) findings (Table 15.10). Both studies utilize the price of bonds just after default, or at the close of the default month. Moody's averages these prices with equal weighting for each issuer. Altman and Kishore weight their data by the size of the defaulting issue.

RECOVERY RATES BY SENIORITY AND ORIGINAL CREDIT RATING

Does a bond's original rating play any role in the recovery rate following default? One might expect that since a bond issue is almost always noninvestment grade just prior to default, its original rating would play only a minor role in determining recoveries (no role at all in the return of principal, and some role, perhaps, in the return of accrued interest). On the other hand, if firms affiliated with certain industries (such as utilities) have a greater preponderance of higher-rated, senior-secured and senior-unsecured original debt, then one might expect higher recoveries.

Table 15.9 Weighted Average Recovery Rates on Defaulted Debt by Seniority per $100 Face Amount (1978–1996)

Default year	Senior secured No.	$	Senior unsecured No.	$	Senior subordinated No.	$	Subordinated No.	$	Discount and zero coupon No.	$	All seniorities No.	$
1996	4	$59.08	4	$50.11	9	$48.99	4	$44.23	3	$11.99	24	$51.91
1995	5	$44.64	9	$50.50	17	$39.01	1	$20.00	1	$17.50	33	$41.77
1994	5	$48.66	8	$51.14	5	$19.81	3	$37.04	1	$5.00	22	$39.44
1993	2	$55.75	7	$33.38	10	$51.50	9	$28.38	4	$31.75	32	$38.83
1992	15	$59.85	8	$35.61	17	$58.20	22	$49.13	5	$19.82	67	$50.03
1991	4	$44.12	69	$55.84	37	$31.91	38	$24.30	9	$27.89	157	$40.67
1990	12	$32.18	31	$29.02	38	$25.01	24	$18.83	11	$15.63	116	$24.66
1989	9	$82.69	16	$53.70	21	$19.60	30	$23.95	—	—	76	$35.97
1988	13	$67.96	19	$41.99	10	$30.70	20	$35.27	—	—	62	$43.45
1987	4	$90.68	17	$72.02	6	$56.24	4	$35.25	—	—	31	$66.63
1986	8	$48.32	11	$37.72	7	$35.20	30	$33.39	—	—	56	$36.60
1985	2	$74.25	3	$34.81	7	$36.18	15	$41.45	—	—	27	$41.78
1984	4	$53.42	1	$50.50	2	$65.88	7	$44.68	—	—	14	$50.62
1983	1	$71.00	3	$67.72	—	—	4	$41.79	—	—	8	$55.17
1982	—	—	16	$39.31	—	—	4	$32.91	—	—	20	$38.03
1981	1	$72.00	—	—	—	—	—	—	—	—	1	$72.00
1980	—	—	2	$26.71	—	—	2	$16.63	—	—	4	$21.67
1979	—	—	—	—	—	—	1	$31.00	—	—	1	$31.00
1978	—	—	1	$60.00	—	—	—	—	—	—	1	$60.00
Total/average	89	$57.94	225	$47.70	186	$35.09	218	$31.58	34	$20.81	752	$40.11
Median		$53.42		$41.99		$30.70		$32.91		$17.50		$36.69
Std. dev.		$23.12		$26.60		$25.28		$22.50		$17.76		$25.84

Source: Altman and Kishore (1997), Exhibit 6.

Table 15.10 Default Recovery Rates on Public Bonds and Private Bank Loans by Seniority (% of Face Value)

Seniority	Moody's (1989–1996)			Altman (1978–1996)		
	No.	Mean (%)	Standard Deviation	No.	Mean (%)	Standard Deviation (%)
Senior secured bank loans	59	71.18	21.09	—	—	—
Senior secured public bonds	57	63.45	26.21	89	57.94	23.12
Senior unsecured public bonds	156	47.54	26.29	225	47.70	26.60
Senior sub. public bonds	166	38.28	24.74	186	35.09	25.28
Subordinated public bonds	119	28.29	20.09	218	31.58	22.50
Jr. (disc.) sub. public bonds	8	14.66	8.67	34	20.81	17.76
All bonds	506	41.25	26.55	752	40.11	25.84

Source: Moody's Investors Service (1997), Exhibit 5; Altman and Kishore (1997).

Table 15.11 shows the average recovery price for high-rated, investment-grade original issues versus low-rated, noninvestment grade issues. Once seniority is accounted for, the broad distinction between investment grade and noninvestment grade ratings has no effect on recoveries. While this result may be consistent with intuition and expected values, it is counter to what Altman observed when the original rating was not stratified by seniority.

DEFAULT RECOVERIES ON BANK LOANS

Carty and Lieberman (1996) assessed the recovery rate on a small sample of defaulted bank loans and found that it averaged over 71 percent. These were all senior-unsecured loans. Although the sample is different from the senior-unsecured bonds analyzed by both Altman and Moody's, the result is higher than expected (Table 15.10). Asarnow and Edwards (1995) analyzed a sample of Citibank defaulted loans, including 831 C&I loans and 89 structured loans, over the period 1970–1993. They found that the average recovery was 65 percent on C&I secured and unsecured loans and as much as 87 percent on structured loans. The latter were all highly collateralized with many restrictive covenants. Almost half of the loans had no principal loss, however. The data on recoveries on defaulted loans is clearly incomplete. While we are aware of several initiatives to add to the knowledge base in this critical area, the lack of aged data on bank loan defaults and recoveries remains an obstacle to the development of a comprehensive treatment of loan valuation.

RECOVERY RATES BY INDUSTRY

Altman and Kishore (1996) stratified a sample of 696 defaulted bond issues (which they were able to categorize by industrial sector) into three-digit Standard Industrial Classification (SIC) Codes. A firm is assigned an SIC code corresponding to the product group that accounts for the greatest value of its sales. The original stratification resulted in 61 sector groupings. The arithmetic and weighted average (by amount outstanding in each industry) and median recovery price at default for these categories are shown in Altman and Kishore (1996). Many of the sectors include 20 or more observations, but the majority of SIC codes had under 20, and many had fewer than 10 observations. With so few data points, the summary averages or the measures of variance may not be meaningful.

Altman therefore combined a number of three-digit SIC codes to arrive at a reduced number of reasonable aggregations. Table 15.12 shows the recovery price aggregated into 18 categories, most of which have over 20 observations, and some over 50. The highest arithmetic average recoveries came from public utilities (70 percent) and chemical, petroleum, and related products (63 percent). These two sectors reversed themselves in terms of weighted average recoveries. The recovery rates for these two industrial aggregations differ substantially (and to a statistically significant degree) from all other industry groups. Next came heavy machinery and electrical instruments, services, food, wholesale and retail trade, conglomerates, and casino and hotel/recreation (all over 40 percent). The remaining industrial sectors,

Table 15.11 Recovery Price by Seniority and Original Bond Rating (1971–1995)

Seniority	Rating class	No. of observations	Average price	Weighted price	Standard deviation	Median price
Senior secured	Investment	16	$54.80	$48.58	$15.11	$55.82
Senior secured	Noninvestment	58	$56.42	$56.82	$24.93	$50.50
Senior unsecured	Investment	49	$48.20	$41.34	$30.63	$40.00
Senior unsecured	Noninvestment	175	$48.73	$55.61	$25.64	$42.50
Senior subordinated	Investment	26	$32.74	$37.26	$20.43	$29.75
Senior subordinated	Noninvestment	136	$39.93	$35.01	$25.67	$32.00
Subordinated	Investment	63	$31.89	$33.97	$18.75	$30.00
Subordinated	Noninvestment	136	$31.67	$27.58	$21.07	$28.40
Discount and zero coupon	Investment	7	$24.14	$23.57	$10.79	$23.50
Discount and zero coupon	Noninvestment	30	$24.42	$17.21	$19.14	$19.90
Total		696	$41.00	$39.11	$25.56	$36.25

Source: Altman and Kishore (1996).

Table 15.12 Recovery Rates by Industry and Seniority, Defaulted Bonds, 1971–1995

Industry	Number	Recovery rate average	Recovery rate weighted
Mining and petroleum drilling			
Senior secured	1	71	71.03
Senior unsecured	9	43.6	37.37
Senior subordinated	12	37.78	36.51
Subordinated	21	25.41	27.48
Discount and zero coupon	2	17.75	19.84
Construction and real estate			
Senior secured	1	40	40
Senior unsecured	12	41.91	39.16
Senior subordinated	10	37.31	24.59
Subordinated	12	26.52	22.79
Food and kindred products			
Senior secured	6	54.42	48.27
Senior subordinated	6	31	36.22
Subordinated	6	50.42	36.88
Textile and apparel products			
Senior unsecured	8	34.47	36.24
Senior subordinated	14	31.65	36.56
Subordinated	6	28.25	24.8
Discount and zero coupon	3	31	32.51
Wood, paper and leather products, publishing			
Senior unsecured	3	47.33	58.54
Senior subordinated	8	36.63	27.32
Subordinated	5	44.33	47.14
Discount and zero coupon	3	15	8.27
Chemical, petroleum, rubber, and plastics			
Senior secured	6	75.04	89.17
Senior unsecured	16	71.91	81.71
Senior subordinated	7	63.07	77.81
Subordinated	6	25.54	31.46
Building materials, metals, and fabricated products			
Senior secured	7	48.33	47.66
Senior unsecured	20	44.23	36.55
Senior subordinated	9	44.08	33.02
Subordinated	28	35.39	31.83
Discount and zero coupon	4	6.31	7.15

continued

Table 15.12   (Continued)

Industry	Number	Recovery rate average	Recovery rate weighted
Machinery, instruments, and related products			
Senior unsecured	11	47.55	51.36
Senior subordinated	8	58.41	35.4
Subordinated	15	44.75	41.6
Discount and zero coupon	2	46.5	50.52
Diversified manufacturing			
Senior unsecured	3	85.71	82.37
Senior subordinated	7	36.73	29.33
Subordinated	10	33.16	21.58
Transportation and transportation equipment			
Senior secured	14	55.72	58.12
Senior unsecured	22	30.83	36.28
Senior subordinated	8	45.81	48.02
Subordinated	8	21.6	15
Services—business and personal			
Senior secured	6	56.61	54.37
Senior subordinated	6	35.18	47.96
Subordinated	2	48.25	43.06
Communications, broadcasting, and movie production			
Senior secured	2	36.88	38.64
Senior unsecured	12	34.97	53.73
Senior subordinated	13	39.77	38.1
Subordinated	21	33.16	35.56
Discount and zero coupon	9	36.61	38.16
Public Utilities			
Senior secured	21	64.42	59.64
Senior unsecured	32	77.74	71.53
Subordinated	2	44	43.99
Discount and zero coupon	1	17.75	17.75
Wholesale and retail trade			
Senior unsecured	2	39	33.5
Senior subordinated	2	76.45	69.18
Subordinated	7	37.88	47.17
Discount and zero coupon	1	32	32

continued

Table 15.12   (Continued)

Industry	Number	Recovery rate average	Recovery rate weighted
General merchandise store			
Senior unsecured	26	44.55	45.59
Senior subordinated	27	36.37	30.20
Subordinated	26	25.95	28.83
Discount and zero coupon	10	13.67	10.18
Financial institutions			
Senior secured	6	49.20	52.70
Senior unsecured	37	38.68	42.70
Senior subordinated	12	29.70	30.78
Subordinated	11	24.81	21.28
Lodging, hospital, and nursing facilities			
Senior unsecured	4	20.50	19.39
Senior subordinated	8	26.75	15.49
Subordinated	9	28.08	18.63
Discount and zero coupon	1	34.00	34.00
Casino, hotel, and recreation			
Senior secured	10	40.78	37.18
Senior unsecured	1	100.00	100.00
Senior subordinated	5	34.20	44.59
Subordinated	4	26.13	26.22
Discount and zero coupon	1	60.00	60.00
TOTAL	696	41	39.11

Source: Altman and Kishore, Working Paper #S-96-6, NYU Salomon Center, Stern School of Business and *Financial Analysts Journal,* Nov./Dec. 1996.

with the exception of lodging, hospital, and nursing facilities (26 percent) had recovery rates in the 30 to 40 percent range. Weighted average recoveries produced similar results, with a few exceptions (the lowest category, for example, had recoveries of under 20 percent).

While the remaining industrial categories listed in Table 15.12 may appear to be fairly tightly clustered in the 30 percent-40 percent recovery range, in reality recoveries at the high 40 percent level differ markedly from those in the low 30 percent. Companies in the machinery, instruments and related products, services, and food products sectors have recovered considerably more than, for example, retailers, drilling companies, and textile and apparel firms.

The standard deviations of the average recovery rates are listed. Most are in the 20 percent-30 percent range. Interestingly, public utilities, which have the highest recovery rates, are among the lowest in terms of variance. Textile and apparel manufacturers and mining and petroleum drilling have low average recoveries and relatively low variance. In general, the variability is quite high relative to the mean, indicating that knowledge of specific issuer characteristics is still very important.

REFERENCES

Altman, E. I. 1989. Measuring Corporate Bond Mortality and Performance. *Journal of Finance* (September): 909–922.

Altman, E. I., and A. C. Eberhart. 1994. Do Seniority Provisions Protect Bondholders' Investments? *Journal of Portfolio Management* 20:67–75.

Altman, E. I., and V. M. Kishore. 1996. Almost Everything You Wanted to Know about Recoveries on Defaulted Bonds. *Financial Analysts Journal* (November/December): 57–63.

———. 1997. Defaults and Returns on High Yield Bonds: Analysis through 1996. Special report, New York University Salomon Center, New York, N.Y.

Altman, E. I., and H. J. Suggitt. 1997. Mortality Rates on Large Syndicated Corporate Bank Loans. Working paper S-97–39, New York University Salomon Center, New York, N.Y.

Asarnow, E., and D. Edwards. 1995. Measuring Loss on Defaulted Bank Loans: A 24-year Study. *The Corporate Loan Investor* (March): 8–17. Also published in *Journal of Commercial Bank Lending*, January, 1996.

Carty, L., and D. Lieberman. 1996. Defaulted Bank Loan Recoveries. *Moody's Special Report*. November.

———. 1997. Historical Default Rates of Corporate Bond Issuers, 1920–1996. New York: Moody's Investors Service.

Fridson, M., and J. Jónsson. 1991. Everything You Ever Wanted to Know about Default Rates. *Journal of Fixed Income* (July/August).

Gupton, G. M., C. C. Finger, and M. Bhatia. 1997. *CreditMetrics: The Benchmark for Understanding Credit Risk*. New York: J. P. Morgan Inc. 3 April.

Hickman, W. B. 1958. *Corporate Bond Quality and Investor Experience*. Princeton, N.J.: Princeton University Press.

Moody's Investors Service. 1990. Corporate Bond Defaults and Default Rates. *Moodys' Special Reports*. New York: Moody's Investors Service.

———. 1997. Corporate Bond Defaults and Default Rates. *Moodys' Special Reports*. New York: Moody's Investors Service.

———. 1998. Corporate Bond Defaults and Default Rates. *Moodys' Special Reports*. New York: Moody's Investors Service.

Moody's Structured Finance. 1991. Rating Cash flow Transactions Backed by Corporate Debt. New York: Moody's Investors Service.

Standard & Poor's. 1991–92. Corporate Bond Defaults Study. Parts 1–3. *Credit Week*, 16 September; 15 September; 21 December.

———. 1996. *Ratings Performance 1995: Stability and Transition*. New York: Standard & Poor's.

———. 1997a. *Ratings Performance 1996: Stability and Transition*. New York: Standard & Poor's.

———. 1997b. *Structured Finance*. New York: Standard & Poor's.

———. 1998. *Ratings Performance 1997: Stability and Transition*. New York: Standard & Poor's.

ADDITIONAL READING

Altman, E. I., and S. Nammacher. 1984. The Default Rate Experience of High Yield Corporate Debt. *Financial Analysts Journal* (July/August): 25–41.

———. 1987. *Investing in Junk Bonds*. New York: John Wiley & Sons.

Chapter 16

Credit Risk Migration

The Moving Finger writes; and having writ,
Moves on: nor all your Piety nor Wit
Shall lure it back to cancel half a Line
Nor all your Tears wash out a Word of it.

—The *Rubháiyát* of Omar Khayyam, stanza 71 (translated by Edward FitzGerald)

As we discussed in Chapter 6, the rating agencies typically rate public debt when it is issued and then periodically review it in subsequent years. If a company's credit quality has improved or deteriorated significantly over time, such a review will prompt the agency to raise or lower its rating. Since the market considers bonds with high ratings to be more valuable than those with low ratings, an upgrade or downgrade is generally accompanied by a change in the price of an issue. In the majority of cases, however, the bond market has already observed a change in the issuer's credit quality before the rating itself is changed, and the price has already moved accordingly. While there is some debate about how much residual price movement still takes place at the time of the actual rating change, there is no doubt that credit risk migration, or drift, affects value. With the finality implied by Khayyam's moving finger, a bond rating that has drifted down seldom goes up to its original level.

Migration in credit quality and ratings can affect fixed-income investors in a number of ways. When the price of a bond changes, investors clearly gain or lose. The impact on the overall credit quality of a portfolio may be equally important. Some institutions have explicit policies regarding the quality of the instruments that they may hold, and rating migration may cause them to exceed these established limits. A bank, for example, may have a policy of holding no more than 5 percent of its portfolio in loans with ratings below the equivalent of a BB rating. Likewise, an investment-grade, fixed-income mutual fund may have rules that allow it to continue to hold 5 percent of its portfolio in securities that have fallen below investment grade but that require it to sell any security with a rating that has dropped below B. Rules of these kinds may be self-imposed, or they may reflect regulatory constraints.

Certain fixed-income investment strategies are predicated on assumptions about credit migration. Recently, for example, as yield spreads on corporate debt have generally narrowed, some investment-grade investors have adopted a crossover strategy, purchasing some bonds that have split ratings (investment grade from one agency and noninvestment grade from the other) or that are at the high end of the noninvestment grade spectrum. The first of these possibilities is called a 5-B strategy because the bonds carry one triple-B and one double-B rating. The second approach is called a 4-B strategy because the bonds carry two double-B ratings. Some fixed-income managers are known to take positions on corporate bonds based on predictions about an upgrade or downgrade.

One argument for crossing over is that these bonds have acceptable credit risk but offer significantly greater yield than those that are 6-B (i.e., have investment grade ratings from both agencies). Should the agency that presently assigns the noninvestment grade rating eventually upgrade the issue just one notch, the spread will narrow considerably and the price will rise significantly.[1] Many of these bonds also have substantial call potential—either from high cash flows available to pay off the existing bondholders or from mergers and acquisitions.

Is crossing over a rational investment strategy? Over a relatively short-term horizon, in other words, what are the chances that a 5-B bond will become 6-B or better or 4-B or worse? The question can be answered only with a systematic understanding of credit risk migration and an examination of historical transition patterns.

Apart from the specific needs of fixed-income investors, the analysis of rating migration plays an integral part in broad-gauge strategies for credit risk management (see Lucas [1995]). Indeed, the recently publicized CreditMetrics methodology utilizes credit migration analysis as one of its centerpieces (Gupton, Finger, and Bhatia 1997).[2] While credit risk migration analysis is not a completely new focus for banks, most institutions that are aware of its importance are struggling to find methods and data sources that will allow them to evaluate rating drift in a sound and comprehensive way.[3]

METHODS FOR TRACKING RATING MIGRATION

Thus far, three sets of studies have been published on the rating migration phenomenon. The first is a series of articles by Altman and Kao (1991a, 1991b, 1992a, 1992b) that utilizes data from all Standard & Poor's rating changes over the period 1971–1989. The second is a group of special studies from

---

[1]See Salomon Brothers, Inc. (1996a, 1996b). These reports document the strong relative performance of double B's and split-rated triple B's.

[2]This report emphasizes that upgrades and downgrades cause market-pricing reactions that result in immediate gains and losses in a mark-to-market accounting environment. Failure to recognize the impact of these events on both individual security and portfolio values will miss a significant component of risk.

[3]See Oleksin (1997) for a description of a recent survey of credit migration procedures of the 100 largest U.S. bank holding companies. Oleksin's objective was to learn which institutions were conducting credit migration analysis and how they were doing it. Out of the 100, 80 responded, with the majority of banks analyzing migration in some manner on all loans or only on loans that have been charged off.

Moody's, first published as a special comment in 1991 and reproduced in Lucas and Lonski (1992), Carty and Fons (1993), and Carty (1997).[4] Finally, Standard & Poor's periodically examines rating migration, and its latest report (1997) covers its rating changes over the period 1981–1996. In addition, Altman and Kao (1991b) report on migration patterns of industrials, finance companies, and public utilities. They, as well as Carty and Fons (1993), also examine the autocorrelation of the rating changes (Altman and Kao 1992b). Standard & Poor's (1997b) has now released a product named CreditPro that makes available the default and migration data for over 6000 obligors for the period 1981–1996.

There are some basic differences among these three sets of studies. While all look at the rating migration of credit quality for up to ten years (and more) from some initial level, Altman and Kao assess the changes from the initial bond rating, usually at issuance, for a period of up to ten years post-issuance. Moody's and Standard & Poor's, by contrast, assess rating changes from some initial period, regardless of the age of the bonds constituting the initial rating class. Moody's and Standard & Poor's include newly issued bonds as well as seasoned bonds of all ages in their static pool as of some date (e.g., 1981), and then follow the ratings of the pool for up to 15 years from that date.[5]

This distinction is important because an aging effect is observable in the early years after issuance—one that disappears within four to five years. Older bonds appear to have a greater short-term tendency to be upgraded or downgraded than do newly issued bonds.

Altman and Kao differ from the two rating agencies in another respect, as well. Their method is issue-based, whereas the agencies assess the senior bond equivalent of each issuer, regardless of the size of a particular issue or of the number of issues outstanding from that issuer. In addition, Altman and Kao present several Markov chain models for estimating migration patterns.[6]

Furthermore, it is significant that the various studies cover somewhat different time periods. Moody's now covers the longest period (1938–1996), Altman and Kao include the 1970s in their analyses and end at mid-1989, and Standard & Poor's data start in 1981 and end in 1996. In fact, the relative likelihood of upgrades and downgrades has varied over time. For all rating classes, the decade of the 1970s was typified by more upgrades than downgrades, but the period from 1981 to 1995 saw more downgrades than upgrades in every single year.

One final difference between the rating agency methodology and that of Altman and Kao is that the two former studies include the category *rating*

---

[4]Carty (1997) is an update and covers Moody's rating changes from 1938–1996.

[5]This is also true for both rating agencies' cumulative default analyses, for example, Carty and Lieberman (1996a) and Standard & Poor's (1997a). Altman and Kishore's (1997) mortality rate results trace the cumulative default/mortality rate of all bonds from initial issuance. This is consistent with their rating migration method discussed in this chapter.

[6]A Markov chain is a stochastic process where the conditional probability of a future event given any past event and the present state, is independent of the past event and depends only on the present state of the process.

withdrawn. This usually means that a bond has been called or redeemed for some other reason, such as a call or an acquisition of the issuing firm. It may also mean that there was insufficient information to rate the bond. This is quite an important distinction. After one year, anywhere from 2–3 percent of issuers may fall into the rating withdrawn category, and after five years, as many as 25–40 percent of the issuers may be placed in this classification. Since most redemptions result in the return of 100 percent (or more) of principal to the bondholders, one might choose to include the withdrawn-rating proportion in the same rating class the issuers initially occupied. In calculations of the impact on returns, the rating withdrawn category might also reflect the average price at call or redemption, which is typically 1–5 percent above par value for calls and par value for redemption at maturity. We will return to this factor at a later point.

RATING MIGRATION RESULTS COMPARED

Tables 16.1, 16.2, and 16.3 compare the one-year, five-year, and ten-year transition matrices of the three studies noted earlier. The Altman and Kao results are adjusted somewhat for more complete default statistics. Their findings differ strikingly from those of the two rating agencies, primarily because of the aging effect and the impact of the rating withdrawn (RW) category.

What is the best reference point to use for bonds/loans of different ages? A new or very young loan or bond is likelier to conform to the Altman and Kao results, since their reference point is newly issued bonds. For an existing or seasoned bond, the appropriate reference point is less clear. The more seasoned the issue, the less likely that Altman and Kao will be the relevant reference. While Moody's and Standard & Poor's would probably be better references for more seasoned bonds, it is not clear which of the two is superior.

The three sources generate radically different results. In the case of B rated bonds, Altman and Kao show that 93.7 percent of newly issued bonds are still B rated after one year, and 53.3 percent are after five years. Moody's and Standard & Poor's, however, show that only 76.3 percent and 72.8 percent (after one year) and 31.2 percent and 16.6 percent (after five years) retain their ratings. While Altman and Kao do not specify a rating withdrawn (RW) category, it is not likely that many bonds will be called after just one year since most issues have at least a 3- or 5-year no-call provision. Moody's and Standard & Poor's, on the other hand, indicate that 10.5 percent and 12.2 percent of the issuers, respectively, have their ratings withdrawn after one year, and as many as 38.2 percent and 45.4 percent after five years. It is obvious, in these cases, that the initial baskets included issuers of seasoned bonds. These comparisons are fairly strong evidence of an aging effect with respect to rating drift—similar to the documented aging effect with respect to defaults that we discussed in Chapter 15. The rating withdrawn category deserves further analysis. In his most recent work, Carty (1997) provides important evidence on this phenomenon, first observed by Altman (1997). He shows the one-year migration patterns including the rating withdrawn possibility and, in addition, the patterns conditional upon no rating (Carty

Table 16.1 Rating Transition Matrix—One-Year Horizon (All Numbers Are %)

	Aaa AAA	Aa AA	A A	Baa BBB	Ba BB	B B	Caa CCC	Def. C/D	RW
AAA (A/K)	94.3	5.5	0.1	0.0	0.0	0.0	0.0	0.0	—
Aaa (M)	88.3	6.2	1.0	0.2	0.0	0.0	0.0	0.0	4.3
AAA (S&P)	88.5	8.1	0.7	0.1	0.1	0.0	0.0	0.0	2.6
AA (A/K)	0.7	92.6	6.4	0.2	0.1	0.1	0.0	0.0	—
Aa(M)	1.2	86.8	5.8	0.7	0.2	0.0	0.0	0.0	5.4
AA (S&P)	0.6	88.5	7.6	0.6	0.1	0.1	0.0	0.0	2.4
A (A/K)	0.0	2.6	92.1	4.7	0.3	0.2	0.0	0.0	—
A (M)	0.7	2.3	86.1	4.7	0.6	0.1	0.0	0.0	6.0
A (S&P)	0.1	2.3	87.6	5.0	0.7	0.2	0.0	0.4	3.6
BBB (A/K)	0.0	0.0	5.5	90.0	2.8	1.0	0.1	0.3	—
Baa (M)	0.0	0.3	3.9	82.5	4.7	0.6	0.1	0.3	7.7
BBB (S&P)	0.0	0.3	5.5	82.5	4.7	1.0	0.1	0.2	5.7
BB (A/K)	0.0	0.0	0.0	6.8	86.1	6.3	0.9	0.0	—
Ba (M)	0.0	0.1	0.4	4.6	79.0	5.0	0.4	1.1	9.4
BB (S&P)	0.0	0.1	0.6	7.0	73.8	7.6	0.9	1.0	8.9
B (A/K)	0.0	0.0	0.2	1.6	1.7	93.7	1.7	1.1	—
B (M)	0.0	0.0	0.1	0.6	5.8	56.3	3.1	3.5	10.5
B (S&P)	0.0	0.1	0.2	0.4	6.0	72.8	3.4	4.9	12.2
CCC (A/K)	0.0	0.0	0.0	0.0	0.0	2.8	92.5	4.6	—
Caa (M)	0.0	0.0	0.0	0.3	1.3	5.3	71.9	12.4	8.8
CCC (S&P)	0.2	0.0	0.3	1.0	2.2	9.6	53.1	19.3	14.2

Source and Key:

A/K = Altman and Kao (1971–1989) from Altman and Kao (1992a)—newly issued bonds.

M = Moody's (1938–1996) from Carty (1997)—cohort groups of bonds.

S&P = Standard & Poor's (1981–1996) from Standard & Poor's (1997a)—static pools of bonds.

RW = Rating withdrawn.

Table 16.2 Rating Transition Matrix—Five-Year Horizon (All Numbers Are %)

	Aaa AAA	Aa AA	A A	Baa BBB	Ba BB	B B	Caa CCC	Def. C/D	RW
AAA (A/K)	69.8	23.5	2.9	3.6	0.1	0.0	0.1	0.1	—
Aaa (M)	60.8	15.2	4.3	1.0	0.5	0.1	0.0	0.2	18.0
AAA (S&P)	54.0	23.5	6.0	1.7	0.5	0.2	0.0	0.2	13.8
AA (A/K)	2.4	67.1	22.5	5.0	1.0	0.3	0.1	1.7	—
Aa (M)	3.4	54.1	15.9	3.4	1.2	0.2	0.0	0.6	21.1
AA (S&P)	2.4	53.4	24.4	4.0	0.9	0.8	0.1	0.4	13.7
A (A/K)	0.4	9.2	72.0	15.1	1.9	0.7	0.0	0.7	—
A (M)	0.3	5.9	55.7	10.3	2.6	0.7	0.1	0.6	23.4
A (S&P)	0.2	7.0	53.4	14.9	3.0	1.8	0.3	0.7	18.7
BBB (A/K)	0.4	1.6	19.6	65.4	7.6	1.7	1.9	1.8	—
Baa (M)	0.1	0.9	10.0	47.1	8.0	2.0	0.3	2.3	29.3
BBB (S&P)	0.2	1.3	15.5	41.5	9.6	3.4	0.8	2.0	25.7
BB (A/K)	0.0	0.0	7.7	20.4	40.8	16.5	7.8	6.8	—
Ba (M)	0.1	0.3	1.9	10.4	36.5	8.1	1.3	5.9	35.6
BB (S&P)	0.1	0.4	2.9	13.4	19.9	9.6	1.7	11.4	40.2
B (A/K)	0.1	0.0	2.3	4.0	7.7	53.3	11.8	20.8	—
B (M)	0.0	0.1	0.5	2.4	10.3	32.2	3.5	12.9	38.2
B (S&P)	0.0	0.1	0.6	2.8	9.5	16.6	2.5	22.5	45.4
CCC (A/K)	0.0	0.0	2.6	3.6	2.6	30.7	26.5	34.0	—
Caa (M)	0.0	0.0	0.0	1.6	4.0	7.8	29.6	28.0	29.0
CCC (S&P)	0.2	0.0	0.9	2.4	3.5	6.1	5.4	42.0	39.5

Source and Key:

A/K = Altman and Kao (1971–1989) from Altman and Kao (1992a)—newly issued bonds.

M = Moody's (1938–1996) from Carty (1997)—cohort groups of bonds.

S&P = Standard & Poor's (1981–1996) from Standard & Poor's (1997a)—static pools of bonds.

RW = Rating withdrawn.

Table 16–3 Rating Transition Matrix—Ten-Year Horizon (All Numbers Are %)

	Aaa AAA	Aa AA	A A	Baa BBB	Ba BB	B B	Caa CCC	Def. C/D	RW
AAA (A/K)	52.1	35.6	7.1	4.6	0.0	0.4	0.0	0.2	—
Aaa (M)	41.6	19.0	6.1	2.1	0.8	0.2	0.0	0.6	29.6
AAA (S&P)	30.7	24.7	12.0	6.5	0.5	0.0	0.0	1.1	24.6
AA (A/K)	3.5	45.7	27.1	19.0	2.4	0.2	0.0	2.1	—
Aa (M)	4.5	33.4	19.8	4.9	2.2	0.6	0.1	1.5	33.1
AA (S&P)	3.1	30.3	29.2	6.4	1.5	0.4	0.2	1.8	27.1
A (A/K)	0.8	17.3	60.9	20.0	3.4	0.9	0.6	1.1	—
A (M)	0.3	6.5	38.6	11.1	3.3	1.1	0.2	2.2	36.7
A (S&P)	0.5	7.5	33.5	15.8	3.9	1.7	0.2	2.4	34.5
BBB (A/K)	0.0	2.8	36.1	42.3	8.2	4.6	1.9	4.1	—
Baa (M)	0.8	1.3	11.7	30.0	6.4	2.1	0.3	4.1	43.8
BBB (S&P)	0.3	1.7	14.6	24.5	6.1	1.9	0.1	5.2	45.7
BB (A/K)	0.0	0.0	10.3	25.5	20.6	12.5	17.2	13.9	—
Ba (M)	0.1	0.3	3.0	10.1	17.1	6.1	1.3	9.9	52.1
BB (S&P)	0.1	0.1	3.7	10.3	6.6	3.8	0.5	20.0	54.8
B (A/K)	0.0	0.0	5.7	8.6	6.7	40.9	6.6	31.5	—
B (M)	0.0	0.1	0.8	2.7	7.8	13.8	2.1	18.6	54.1
B (S&P)	0.0	0.1	0.7	2.9	4.7	2.2	0.6	28.6	61.2
CCC (A/K)	—	—	—	—	—	—	—	—	—
Caa (M)	0.0	0.0	0.0	2.1	3.2	5.1	13.5	36.9	39.2
CCC (S&P)	0.0	0.0	0.6	2.3	4.6	2.9	0.0	36.2	53.5

Source and Key:

A/K = Altman and Kao (1971–1989) from Altman and Kao (1992a)—newly issued bonds.

M = Moody's (1938–1996) from Carty (1997)—cohort groups of bonds.

S&P = Standard & Poor's (1981–1996) from Standard & Poor's (1997a)—static pools of bonds.

RW = Rating withdrawn.

1997, 11, Exhibit 8). For example, he finds that the Aaa class increases its retention percentage from 88.3 percent to 92.2 percent if the withdrawn category is not included. This result is now closer to Altman and Kao's 94.3 percent. Analyzing over 35,000 withdrawn debt ratings, he finds that 92 percent were withdrawn because an issue had matured or had been called and that, of the remaining 8 percent of cases, one-half were withdrawn for unspecified reasons. He concludes that as many as 95 percent of the ratings were withdrawn for reasons other than credit deterioration. Hence, their impact should be positive, or neutral at worst, when considering the effect of the Moody's and Standard & Poor's transition matrices on bond valuation.

It is not completely clear why Moody's and Standard & Poor's results diverge so much after five years. More than likely, the different study periods have impacted their results. One could also make the case that differences in the rating criteria employed by the two agencies contributed to the differences in their rating changes, but the systematic effects of the differences are not apparent.

Altman and Kao diverge from the other two sources for all rating classes, with the difference most pronounced at the lower end of the credit spectrum. In every case, Altman and Kao find a higher proportion of bonds that retain their ratings—after one year, the figures are 94.3 percent (AAA), 92.6 percent (AA), 92.1 percent (A), 90.1 percent (BBB), and 86.1 percent (BB).[7] Standard & Poor's shows that 88.5 percent (AAA), 88.3 percent (AA), 87.6 percent (A), 82.5 percent (BBB), 73.8 percent (BB)—down to 53.1 percent (CCC)—retain their rating.

Most likely, Altman and Kao find a lower migration pattern because of the rating process itself, the rating withdrawn category, and the aging effect. With respect to the latter, rating agencies and bank loan review groups do not begin to review most bonds or loans for at least one year. The change in the credit quality of the issuer would have to be substantial to motivate a change in the early years. On the other hand, a seasoned bond may have deteriorated (or improved) slowly for several years before the agencies decide to change its rating.

IMPACT ON RETURNS

When a company's credit quality migrates and its ratings change, the holders of its securities experience an increase or decrease in the value of their investment. How large is the shift? There are at least four possible ways to determine the price impact of a rating change.

One possibility is to multiply the change in yield spread between the initial rating and the new rating by the modified duration (the percentage change in price associated with a 100 basis point move in interest rates) of the bond. This methodology utilizes either the average yield-to-maturity or the option (primarily call option) adjusted spread, by bond rating class. Table 16.4

---

[7]The correlation between credit quality and rating retention does not hold for Altman and Kao's B and CCC categories, however.

Table 16.4 Average Yields and Spread by Rating Class, 1985–1996

Years	AAA Avg. YTM b.p. (Std. dev.)	AAA Spread (Std. dev.)	AA Avg. YTM b.p. (Std. dev.)	AA Spread (Std. dev.)	A Avg. YTM b.p. (Std. dev.)	A Spread (Std. dev.)	BBB Avg. YTM b.p. (Std. dev.)	BBB Spread (Std. dev.)	BB Avg. YTM b.p. (Std. dev.)	BB Spread (Std. dev.)	B Avg. YTM b.p. (Std. dev.)	B Spread (Std. dev.)	CCC Avg. YTM b.p. (Std. dev.)	CCC Spread (Std. dev.)
1985	11.09	21.31	11.54	33.26	11.81	52.53	12.45	122.75	13.91	303.58	14.71	400.00	16.58	570.42
	0.62	7.01	0.57	10.26	0.54	13.27	0.56	13.43	0.83	34.36	0.52	33.03	0.72	45.80
1986	8.81	52.60	9.43	81.75	9.78	113.86	10.55	205.70	11.97	410.33	13.04	530.50	15.65	789.83
	0.52	23.42	0.44	26.71	0.45	29.17	0.41	39.54	0.31	47.38	0.41	40.09	0.83	121.72
1987	8.97	43.99	9.47	63.12	9.71	83.08	10.26	145.41	11.87	345.92	13.21	492.58	16.75	836.08
	0.69	14.14	0.45	14.45	0.57	11.66	0.54	17.93	0.62	44.97	0.83	61.56	0.77	86.14
1988	9.34	47.05	9.69	51.25	9.85	69.66	10.39	118.31	11.89	296.75	13.70	488.08	16.67	789.08
	0.29	13.34	0.25	12.44	0.24	10.29	0.20	20.89	0.23	42.29	0.27	42.00	0.89	70.39
1989	9.35	39.90	9.59	48.65	9.79	72.60	10.30	112.58	11.68	303.50	13.98	543.42	20.77	1221.42
	0.46	13.00	0.49	14.40	0.45	16.90	0.40	21.26	0.27	40.32	0.53	97.51	3.05	347.42
1990	9.28	67.89	9.52	72.27	9.78	101.90	10.52	163.54	11.91	334.00	16.58	804.50	31.58	2304.08
	0.23	10.26	0.22	11.54	0.22	18.00	0.31	37.00	0.37	28.70	1.23	117.58	5.01	499.29
1991	8.35	86.41	8.79	72.16	8.98	114.00	9.79	168.96	12.09	484.75	16.09	778.17	22.07	1668.67
	0.49	9.44	0.34	14.41	0.45	19.67	0.53	40.64	0.79	54.24	2.33	147.81	4.93	363.86
1992	6.82	86.85	7.78	69.71	7.79	104.24	8.58	150.34	9.71	360.58	11.50	546.42	14.10	875.50
	0.44	10.86	0.34	7.55	0.37	9.68	0.35	15.20	0.59	59.28	0.65	62.77	0.91	153.83
1993	5.76	74.03	6.72	75.43	6.75	100.10	7.45	150.64	8.36	307.58	10.08	491.67	12.70	807.75
	0.34	6.41	0.39	3.77	0.37	5.67	0.42	9.28	0.43	25.96	0.46	33.10	0.48	37.03
1994	6.82	51.18	7.54	58.49	7.60	78.10	8.19	123.43	9.21	253.83	10.97	431.42	13.53	699.75
	0.83	3.94	0.69	5.21	0.71	5.55	0.67	7.55	0.87	12.35	0.88	18.97	1.51	87.47
1995	7.01	44.08	7.39	51.69	7.45	69.27	7.93	109.26	9.16	253.83	11.43	484.92	15.54	900.25
	0.66	3.22	0.64	4.32	0.67	5.60	0.67	7.49	0.64	15.24	0.37	39.50	0.38	46.05
1996	6.66	40.06	7.01	44.96	7.05	60.24	7.54	99.87	8.75	245.50	10.85	459.90	14.66	840.90
	0.45	1.76	0.41	1.87	0.43	2.43	0.41	4.17	0.32	23.83	0.18	49.42	0.46	58.13
1985–96 Average	8.21	54.82	8.73	60.44	8.89	85.31	9.52	139.79	10.91	326.13	13.04	538.73	17.59	1027.91
Std. dev.	1.58	22.22	1.44	18.42	1.53	24.52	1.54	36.81	1.76	76.18	2.20	140.23	5.50	520.48

YTM, Yield to maturity (%); average based on 12 (months) observations.

YTW, Yield to worst (%); average based on 12 (months) observations.

Spread, average option – adjusted spread over U.S. Treasury Bonds (basis points, b.p.).

1985–96 averages = monthly observations.

Source: Salomon Brothers, Inc.; Prof. Edward I. Altman, New York University Salomon Center.

Table 16.5 Average Modified Duration by Rating Class, 1985–1996

Years	AAA Duration (Std. dev.)	AA Duration (Std. dev.)	A Duration (Std. dev.)	BBB Duration (Std. dev.)	BB Duration (Std. dev.)	B Duration (Std. dev.)	CCC Duration (Std. dev.)
1985	5.91	6.11	6.18	5.75	6.35	5.87	5.41
	0.20	0.17	0.15	0.14	0.18	0.19	0.11
1986	6.66	6.85	6.70	6.19	6.51	5.32	5.44
	0.15	0.19	0.13	0.09	0.09	0.22	0.26
1987	6.30	6.54	6.67	6.27	6.30	5.34	5.28
	0.36	0.33	0.25	0.18	0.23	0.21	0.13
1988	5.84	6.21	6.27	6.17	6.16	5.40	5.02
	0.19	0.13	0.17	0.09	0.08	0.09	0.12
1989	6.15	6.01	6.13	6.16	5.48	4.90	4.21
	0.15	0.08	0.10	0.09	0.13	0.10	0.30
1990	5.56	5.99	6.03	5.95	5.32	4.41	3.39
	0.42	0.10	0.14	0.14	0.13	0.18	0.34

1991	4.88	6.64	5.86	5.92	4.40	4.60	3.71
	0.19	0.22	0.06	0.10	0.39	0.34	0.14
1992	4.46	6.85	6.04	6.34	4.47	3.94	2.76
	0.05	0.10	0.07	0.15	0.17	0.28	0.34
1993	4.50	6.85	6.45	6.67	4.86	4.23	2.94
	0.06	0.11	0.23	0.13	0.27	0.22	0.46
1994	4.29	6.62	6.25	6.44	5.37	4.94	4.62
	0.16	0.23	0.29	0.20	0.12	0.18	0.37
1995	4.46	6.57	6.12	6.37	5.37	4.75	4.42
	0.19	0.17	0.15	0.14	0.09	0.10	0.09
1996	4.75	6.51	6.20	6.43	5.28	4.55	4.48
	0.10	0.25	0.11	0.16	0.06	0.08	0.17
1985–1996							
Average	5.32	6.48	6.24	6.22	5.49	4.86	4.30
Std. dev.	0.84	0.36	0.29	0.28	0.71	0.57	0.94

Note: 1985–1996 averages = monthly observations.

Source: Salomon Brothers, Inc., Prof. Edward I. Altman, New York University Salomon Center.

contains this data for the period 1985–1996. Table 16.5 presents modified duration data for different bond grades. An example of how this information may be used is shown in Table 16.6.

A second method for calculating the impact of rating migration on a bond's value is to estimate the possible rating change for the next period, e.g., one year, and then discount the remaining cash flows from that period to maturity using the forward zero coupon curve for bonds in the new rating class. Rather than trying to estimate the forward interest rate curves, the first method (above) assumes no change in rates. If, however, we are simultaneously estimating the impact of all possible rating migration patterns on a portfolio of many securities, then a type of forward-yield-curve-simulation analysis would appear to be a reasonable approach.[8]

A third method for analyzing the price impact of a rating change is direct observation of the price changes of a large sample of bonds of different rating classes. The main difficulty in this technique is the need to determine the correct date to measure the price change. It is obviously too late to measure the change at the exact time of the rating change since most, if not all, of the change has already occurred by then. An alternative possibility is to use the date when the rating agency first placed the bond on its watch list and published this event (e.g., in Standard & Poor's *Credit Week*). The price changes over time will not always be the same since market conditions are constantly changing. This type of event-study analysis is an elusive methodology.

A final possibility is to decompose the observed market spreads of bonds in various rating classes so that we can isolate the impact of expected rating drift. Combined with historical rating drift patterns, these observed spreads can reveal the expected economic consequence of a change in rating. Problems in such decomposition are formidable, however.

A complete analysis of the impact of credit risk migration on returns must go beyond the assessment of individual assets to evaluate the probabilities that different fixed-income assets in a portfolio will migrate in the same direction over time. This involves calculating migration correlations

---

[8]This is the approach suggested by CreditMetrics (Gupton, Finger, and Bhatia/J. P. Morgan Inc., New York, 1997).

Table 16.6   Example of the Price Impact of Migration for BBB Bond

	AAA	AA	A	BBB	BB	B	CCC
Average spread from table 16–4	54.8	60.4	85.3	139.8	326.1	538.7	1027.9

Average modified duration for a BBB bond (from Table 16.5): 6.2 years

Average expected price change because of upgrade to A = 6.2 × (139.8 − 85.3) = 338 b.p.

Probability of migrating from BBB to A (from Table 16.2 : A and K values) = 19.6 percent

Expected impact of the migration = (0.196) (338) = 66 b.p.

and their total portfolio effects. In Chapter 19, we discuss the CreditMetrics (Gupton, Finger, and Bhatia 1997) methodology for evaluating migration patterns across all major rating class categories, including default status. One of the key issues in analyzing these correlations is selecting a basis for determining the correlation matrix. Three candidates have been identified: the historical rating series itself, equity prices, and models that explain equity prices. We lean toward the first of these approaches.

IMPLICATIONS FOR CROSSOVER INVESTING

The underlying assumption for most crossover investors is that they will be able to choose 5-B or 4-B bonds that have a good chance for an upgrade and little chance of a downgrade. Either no change in rating (higher yield) or an upgrade (higher yield plus price appreciation) would be an acceptable result. The downgrade to unambiguous junk status is definitely undesirable, although the impact on total return has never been assessed rigorously.

A study published in Moody's (Carty and Fons 1993) and updated in Carty (1997) is relevant to the analysis of crossover strategy patterns with intra-rating notch criteria (e.g., Ba1, Ba2, Ba3). For example, we can observe from Moody's that the one-year transition probability from Ba1 to Baa3 (one notch upgrade) is 5.7 percent and from Ba1 to Baa2 (two notch upgrade) is 3.0 percent. On the negative side, the probabilities that a Ba1 will fall to Ba2 or Ba3 are 4.2 percent and 4.3 percent, respectively. Working through a strategy that includes selling any bond that falls from Ba2 to B1, including specific assumptions as to the impact of a withdrawn rating result, would leave the investor with a +33.8 basis points expected benefit.[9]

CREDIT RISK MIGRATION AND LOAN LOSSES

A fair amount has been written about estimating both the expected and unexpected losses from bank loan portfolios. With the increased importance of mark-to-market price disclosure, gains and losses due to deteriorating credit risk patterns should now be included. The impact of these changes, discussed by Austin (1992) and others, can now be quantified more precisely by an expected price change methodology.

FUTURE DIRECTIONS

We have highlighted some rather great differences between the various published reports on rating migration. These differences are based on different sample methodologies, rating systems, and periods of observation. We have also explored a number of direct applications for this data, including expected returns for various types of investors. Organizations buying and selling credit derivatives (see Chapter 20), especially total-return derivatives,

---

[9]This is derived based on the method that utilizes yield-spread differences between ratings, average durations, and transition probabilities.

have an especially great need to understand rating migration. We encourage even more in-depth studies on rating migration patterns, covering all relevant time periods as well as the entire spectrum of rating notch differentials.

REFERENCES

Altman, E. I. 1997. *Rating Migration of Corporate Bonds—Comparative Results and Investor Implications.* New York: Salomon Brothers, Inc. 13 May. Earlier version published as working paper no. S-97–3, NYU Salomon Center, New York University, New York, February 1997.

Altman, E. I., and D. L. Kao. 1991a. *Corporate Bond Rating Drift: An Examination of Rating Agency Credit Quality Changes.* Charlottesville, Va.: AIMR (Association for Investment Management and Research).

———. 1991b. Appendices to the AIMR Report on "An Examination of Rating Agency Drift over Time." Working paper no. S-91–40, NYU Salomon Center, New York University, New York, N.Y.

———. 1992a. Rating Drift of High-Yield Bonds. *Journal of Fixed Income* (March): 15–20.

———. 1992b. The Implications of Corporate Bond Ratings Drift. *Financial Analysts Journal* (May/June): 64–75.

Altman, E. I., and V. M. Kishore. 1997. Defaults and Returns on High Yield Bonds: Analysis through 1996. Special Report, New York University Salomon Center, New York, N.Y.

Austin, D. 1992. Use Migration Analysis to Refine Estimates of Future Loan Losses. *Commercial Lending Review* (spring): 34–43.

Carty, L. 1997. Moody's Rating Migration and Credit Quality Correlation, 1920–1996. *Moody's Special Report.* July.

Carty, L., and J. Fons. 1993. *Measuring Changes in Credit Quality. Moody's Special Report.* November. Also published in *Journal of Fixed Income* (1994, June): 27–41.

Carty, L., and D. Lieberman. 1996a. Corporate Bond Defaults and Default Rates, 1938–1995. *Moody's Special Report.* January.

Gupton, G. M., C. C. Finger, and M. Bhatia. 1997. *CreditMetrics: The Benchmark for Understanding Credit Risk.* New York: J. P. Morgan Inc. April.

Lucas, D. 1995. The Effectiveness of Downgrade Provisions in Reducing Counterparty Risk. *Journal of Fixed Income* (June): 32–41.

Lucas, D., and J. Lonski. 1992. Changes in Corporate Credit Quality: 1970–1990. *Journal of Fixed Income* (March): 7–14.

Oleksin, I. M. 1997. Using Risk Migration Analysis for Managing Portfolio Risk: Results of a Study. *Journal of Lending and Credit Risk Management* (February): 49–56.

Salomon Brothers, Inc. 1996a. *Bond Market Roundup: Strategy.* New York: Salomon Brothers, Inc. 13 September.

———.1996b. *Bond Market Roundup: Strategy.* New York: Salomon Brothers, Inc. 18 October.

Standard & Poor's. 1997a. *Ratings Performance 1996: Stability and Transition.* Special Report. New York: Standard & Poor's.

Standard & Poor's. 1997b. CreditPro. New York: Standard & Poor's.

ADDITIONAL READING

Altman, E. I. 1989. Measuring Corporate Bond Mortality and Performance. *Journal of Finance* (September): 909–922.

Carty, L., and D. Lieberman. 1996b. Defaulted Bank Loan Recoveries. *Moody's Special Report.* November.

Chapter 17

Introduction to Portfolio Approaches

Even though many economic and financial variables fall into distributions that approximate a bell curve, the picture is never perfect. Once again, resemblance to truth is not the same as truth. It is in these outliers and imperfections that the wildness lurks.

—Peter Bernstein, *Against the Gods*

This chapter introduces portfolio theory as applied to managing the fixed-income assets of banks and insurance companies. In the recent past, these institutions suffered the consequences of having paid insufficient attention to portfolio management. Because they focused on analyzing individual loans with little regard for the portfolio implications, they created excessive concentrations and experienced excessive losses. *Concentration* has now become a buzzword both for the financial institutions themselves and for their regulators. The development of the secondary loan market, of structured finance products, and of credit derivatives are all direct results of the desire on the part of banks and insurance companies to address this problem.[1]

Broadly stated, concentration results when a financial institution has a level of exposure to a single name, product, sovereign, or sector such that adverse developments in this exposure would seriously hamper the institution's ability to continue functioning. A Federal Reserve report sums it up as follows:

> Concentration of credit risk may generally be characterized as inordinately high levels of direct or indirect exposures to a single or related groups of borrowers, credit exposures collateralized by a single security, or securities with common characteristics, or credit exposures to borrowers with common characteristics within an industry or similarly affected group. (Board of Governors 1993)

One level of protection against concentration is the single obligor limit (legal lending limit) set by regulators and by the financial institution's own credit policy. Other controls that exist are industry, country, and collateral limits,[2] which are generally based on judgment. This chapter and the next deal with the questions of how portfolio concentrations can be measured

---

[1]Chapters 18–24 describe the industry's responses.

[2]Collateral limits are common, for example, in commercial real estate. A bank may set limits on office buildings, shopping malls, light-manufacturing buildings, warehouses, and so on.

objectively and how a value or cost can be assigned to them. After introducing the classic portfolio theory, we will consider the problems that arise in adapting it to banking and insurance assets. Then we will review the alternative approaches that have been taken.

DIVERSIFICATION IS GOOD, OTHER THINGS BEING EQUAL

The very mention of a portfolio approach brings to mind Harry Markowitz and the theory of diversification (Markowitz 1959). The idea behind Markowitz's theory is the notion that the *riskiness* of the return from a security may be characterized by its *variance*. This variance, in combination with the co-movement or *covariance* among a group of securities, determines the return from the portfolio comprised of these securities. Using the historical variance-covariance matrix of equity returns as representative of the future, Markowitz formulated the classic quadratic optimization problem, where the objective function is couched in terms of the resulting portfolio's expected return and the variance of return, subject to the constraint that the weights invested in the securities add up to one. The procedure led to finding the portfolio with the highest return for a given level of risk, or the portfolio with the least risk for a given level of return.

Although this is a highly simplified depiction of the investment model, it is introduced here because, from a conceptual viewpoint, it makes intuitive sense. Variability in investment returns may be minimized by investing in assets that are *negatively correlated* with one another. One classic pedagogical example is the notion of investing in a company that manufactures tobacco products and in another that manufactures physical fitness equipment. Since it is unlikely that both companies will do equally well in the same market, the combination of these investments will minimize overall earnings variability. Indeed, even the mere *absence* of correlation can be shown to be beneficial in diversifying a portfolio.

A NUMBER OF SMALL BETS VERSUS A SINGLE LARGE BET

It is better to make a series of small bets than one large bet because as the number of bets is spread out over a fixed amount of capital, the variance of the results is reduced.

This concept may be illustrated with an example involving shipowners.[3] Imagine a group of risk-averse merchants, each of whom owns one ship with the following risk profile. If the ship returns safely, the merchant will make a profit of $100,000. However, there is a 0.2 probability that the ship will sink, in which case the owner will receive nothing. The expected value of the payoff is $100,000 \times 0.8 - 0 \times 0.2$, which equals $80,000. The riskiness of the investment, measured by the standard deviation is:

$$\sqrt{[(0.2)(0 - \$80,000)^2 + (0.8)(\$100,000 - \$80,000)^2]} = \$40,000$$

---

[3]From Mason (1995).

If the probability that one ship will sink is completely independent of the others (for example, if they ply in different routes), two owners can make an agreement to exchange one-half of the payoff from one ship for one-half of the payoff from the other. Now, the probabilities of outcome are no longer 0.2 for the ship sinking and 0.8 for not sinking. Instead, there are three possible outcomes: that both ships sink, that neither of them sinks, and that one of them sinks. These are shown in Table 17.1.

The expected value is still the same, that is, $80,000, but the volatility has been reduced from $40,000 to $28,864. The standard deviation is now

$$\sqrt{[(0.04)(0 - \$80,000)^2 + (0.64)(\$100,000 - \$80,000)^2 + (0.32)(\$50,000 - \$80,000)^2]}$$
$$= \$28,864$$

The merchant has spread his bet from one ship to two ships. Suppose that more and more shipowners adopt this strategy. It may be shown that if there are 100 shipowners, the standard deviation drops to a mere $4,000. The power of diversification is such that if there are N shipowners, the standard deviation drops to $40,000/$\sqrt{N}$. This result is applicable if and only if the outcomes from the trials are independent. For example, if all the ships were on the same voyage, the risk of many of them sinking would be greatly magnified. Moreover, this is *not* the diversification Markowitz was talking about; he was looking at the existence of *negative correlations*, or very low positive correlations. With negative correlations you need fewer investments to achieve the desired result. *Independent trials*, by contrast, are a special case of zero correlations: as you add more assets, the volatility diminishes. When fixed-income fund managers talk about diversification, they are primarily referring to finding investments that are uncorrelated or weakly correlated— not ones that are negatively correlated.

One method employed by Moody's for measuring diversification in asset-based securities is the *diversity index* for the collateral, where the individual assets are distributed as companies across many industries. Moody's diversity score is based on the concept of low or zero correlation. It assumes that firms in the same industry tend to be correlated and that firms in different industries are less correlated. In other words, industry dispersion is used as a measure of independence. The scoring system for diversity takes account of the number of different risks in the population and their degree of independence based on industry membership. There are 32 industries in Moody's classification system. This index is used to measure the degree of diversification of collateral in structured finance transactions (Moody's 1991, 9). Table 17.2 shows the diversity score for the number of firms in the same industry in a portfolio. The score values appear to be arbitrarily derived, but

Table 17.1 Outcome Probabilities and Payoffs

Probability	Payoff
Both sink: (0.2)(0.2) = .04	0
Neither sinks = (0.8)(0.8) = 0.64	100,000
One of them sinks = 1 − .04 − .64 = .32	50,000

Table 17.2   Diversity Score Calculation Table

Number of firms in the portfolio	Diversity score if the companies are in the same industry	Diversity score if each company is in a different industry
1	1	1
2	1.5	2
3	2	3
4	2.33	4
5	2.67	5
6	3.00	6
7	3.25	7
8	3.5	8
9	3.75	9
10	4	10
>10	Evaluated on a case by case basis	

Source: Moody's Investors Service (1991). Reprinted with permission.

conceptually they are based on the same principle illustrated by our story about shipowners.

The diversity index is calculated as the lower (more conservative) of two calculations. The first assumes that the portfolio has the smallest possible number of companies, given the single company limit. The second assumes that the portfolio has the smallest number of industries, given the single industry limit. Let us assume, for example, that an issuer uses a 2 percent maximum per name and a 5 percent maximum per industry in a portfolio of 100 companies. From the first calculation, this implies that there will be at least 100/2 = 50 companies in the portfolio, each accounting for 2 percent of it. You can only place two companies from the same industry in the portfolio because if you place three, the industry exposure rises to 6 percent. With 2 companies per industry, the diversity score to use is 1.5. (from Table 17.2). With at least 25 industries represented, the diversity index in this example works out to 25 × 1.5 , that is, 37.5. The second calculation indicates that the minimum number of industries is 20, based on a 5 percent maximum per industry. Since there is a limit of 2 percent per name, at least three companies must be included from each industry. If just two are included, they will each be 2.5 percent (half of the 5 percent from the industry), and this will violate the limit. Using the diversity score of 2 (for three companies) from Table 17.2, the diversity index is 20 × 2, that is, 40. The diversity score selected is the lower of 37.5 and 40, that is, 37.5.

The diversity score is one of the factors Moody's uses in deciding whether a structured finance transaction qualifies for a particular rating. In addition to calibrating its requirements to the score, Moody's puts an absolute limit on concentrations: the percentage one risk represents in a pool of risks; and the percentage of one industry present in the total portfolio. These limits are factored into the actual score. The higher the score is, the better the rating.

The diversity score is a simple way to understand the degree of diversification by obligor and industry in any portfolio. It is important to remember, however, that the diversity index makes the assumption that the correlation *among* (or between) industries is zero and the correlation *within* an industry is high. This assumption may not be valid in all instances. Nonetheless, in the absence of any good alternative, the same approach may be used to quantify the degree of geographic diversification.

However, an interesting study of residential mortgages challenges the conventional wisdom that geographic diversification reduces risk (Coopers and Lybrand 1993). Coopers and Lybrand examined the portfolios of 340 operating banks for geographic diversification. Represented in the sample were 7.4 million loans representing $404 billion in principal outstanding. The diversification score was assigned to the portfolio based on the regional distribution of the mortgages, and there were five GNMA regions. Regional loan percentages of 20 percent or more were given a score of 20, and regional loan percentages under 20 percent received a score equal to the percentage itself. The diversification score for a typical loan portfolio is shown in Table 17.3.

Coopers and Lybrand measured the portfolio performance by the ratio DQ3RATIO and its standard deviation. DQ3RATIO is the percentage of loans that are 3 months or more delinquent. The higher this ratio, the higher the delinquency losses. The standard deviation of this ratio measures volatility (portfolio risk). The results of the analysis for a selected portion of the portfolio are shown in Table 17.4.

As the table indicates, greater geographic diversification does not necessarily reduce portfolio risk; in fact, quite the opposite occurs. Of course, there may be other factors at work in this case. Nevertheless, the basic conclusion to be drawn is that simplified index values such as the diversity score may sometimes be very misleading. It also means that more careful attention should be paid to systematic risk (or perhaps more accurately *systemic* risk[4]). Out-of-territory lending may indeed add to diversity, but it may also add to overall risk. Factors that affect systemic risk are those that are apply to the whole portfolio, both in terms of endogenous factors, such as underwriting standards, and exogenous factors, such as future changes in interest rates.

---

[4]The dictionary defines *systematic* as *relating to or consisting of a system*. It also defines *systematic* as *marked by thoroughness and regularity* and *methodical in procedure or plan*. Market risk, another name for systematic risk, is neither regular nor methodical.

Table 17.3   Loan Portfolio Diversification Score

Region	Loan percent	Diversification score
East	43.4	20.0
Midwest	14.3	14.3
South	21.4	20.0
Southwest	6.4	6.4
West	14.6	14.6

Source: Lederman (ed.), *Mortgage Banking*, 1993, Probus Publishing Company. Reproduced with permission of The McGraw Hill Companies.

Table 17.4   Portfolio of 10,000 or More Loans

Diversity score groups	Number of institutions per score	DQ3RATIO	DQ3RATIO standard deviation	Average number of loans	Average diversity score
≥60	71	2.39	1.117	60,956	75
40–59	41	2.47	0.859	25,783	51
20–39	33	2.54	0.982	23,194	26
	145	2.45		42,058	57

Source: Lederman (ed.), *Mortgage Banking,* 1993, Probus Publishing Company. Reproduced with permission of The McGraw Hill Companies.

ISSUES IN IMPLEMENTING THE STANDARD PORTFOLIO APPROACH

Markowitz won the Nobel Prize in economics for his work on portfolio theory, and there is no question that this approach is extremely useful. However, there are practical difficulties in applying the standard portfolio model (mean-variance optimization for asset selection) to investments, and to fixed income or loan asset portfolios in particular. We will discuss some of these problems and then present the solutions that have been proposed. The problems have to do with the following:

- Correlation estimates
- Distribution of returns
- Multiperiod choices
- Lack of price data
- Lack of fundamental data

Portfolio selection as Markowitz originally envisioned dealt with choosing among individual securities. The first problem with this is that the number of correlations to be calculated increases very rapidly as the number of securities being considered increases.[5] For example, a covariance matrix of 30 different assets will have 435 different covariances. Let us say we have time series data for 12 quarters (3 years). We are then estimating 435 unknown values with 12 times 30 = 360 known values. This is absurd. In statistical terms, the data available would result in a matrix of rank 66. This is equivalent to saying that only 66 out of the 435 entries would contain information, whereas the remaining 369 would be noise.[6]

The second issue is that while correlations of *equity returns* are used in applying the theory to equity markets, the variable to be used with regard to fixed-income assets is not so clear. With debt securities, which are the variables among which correlation is calculated? correlation of *returns?* correlation of the *factors explaining returns?* correlation of *default probabilities?* correlation of *rating categories?* correlation of *spreads?* Equity return correla-

---

[5]The number of correlations for an N-asset portfolio is $N(N - 1)/2$.

[6]This example is from Beckers (1996).

tions may be measured, but correlation of the tendency to default is not observable. In the large corporate sector, defaults themselves are infrequent. Sometimes the time series of *forecasted probabilities of default* for different companies are used to calculate *default correlations*. The problem with this approach is that the forecasted probability of default is, as its name implies, merely a forecast. It therefore contains an element of forecast error. A correlation calculated on the basis of a series of forecasts has little or no operational meaning if it turns out that the standard error of the underlying forecast is very high.

Furthermore, every definition of correlation has its own properties and limitations. The correlation coefficient captures only the *linear* relationship between two random variables. If two variables have a nonlinear relationship, the coefficient will be unable to capture the *strength* of this relationship.

The third difficulty with implementation is that most correlations are *unconditional,* in that they are calculated without holding the other structural variables constant. It is difficult to model the change in correlation if the structural variable changes, or if the structure itself changes. A simple example of this problem arises when there is sudden shock to the system (such as the outbreak of hostilities or an oil embargo). In such situations, correlations of risk typically break down, just when they are needed most! These problems with default correlations are not academic. A senior banker alludes to the impact of an unstable correlation estimate on the business of lending:

> We were recently told to amend our correlation matrices very substantially. This is the sort of thing that can have a huge impact internally if you are using this matrix. You have been told all along that your sectoral concentration limit is okay and this is your capital. Suddenly, you are told, "Whoops, you have gobbled up your capital! That particular sector is now okay, but this one is not." You cannot get used to some of that stuff.

DISTRIBUTION OF RETURNS

The standard portfolio model is not directly applicable to fixed-income portfolios because the equations for the portfolio return and variance apply if and only if the individual security return distributions are symmetrical— that is, they may be completely characterized by a mean and a variance. If they are not, then the equations no longer hold. While we do not know the precise shape of the distribution of returns from debt securities, we do know that it is not symmetrical. One possible shape of the returns from fixed income securities is shown in Figure 17.1, but it has not been derived empirically. Intuitively, this distribution says what bankers know only too well: When you make a loan, you get none of the upside and all of the downside. That is, you can lose all or most of your investment, but your upside is limited to the promised yield. In the region of loan loss, probability density is higher than that implied by a normal distribution curve. This is known as the "fat tail" problem. Note that the X-axis measures the magnitude of the loss. The graph will be laterally transposed if the X-axis is the rate of return. The fat tail will then be to the left of the mean.

Figure 17.1   Possible Shape of the Distribution of Credit Loss

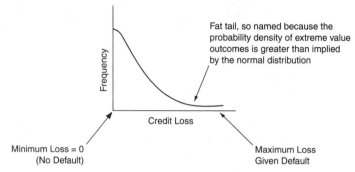

HOLDING PERIOD

The standard portfolio approach is usually stated as a single-period problem. Only if the model is constructed as a multiperiod model can transaction costs come into play as the optimal solution swaps from one asset to another. For securities that are innately illiquid, transaction costs may be so large that they will dominate or even preclude a solution. Of course, a liquid market for credit derivatives will ameliorate this problem.[7] The single-period limitation of the standard model is often handled by running the model repeatedly, that is, the solution is implemented in period t, and when period t + 1 is reached, the model is run again with new inputs. Necessary adjustment can then be made. The drawback of this approach is that while it obviates the need to formulate a multiperiod model, it still does not address completely the issue of transaction costs. Of perhaps greater concern is the fact that there really is no way to know if repeated optimization leads to globally optimum outcomes—that is, whether the results achieved without incorporating intertemporal choices in the model are still optimal.[8]

ABSENCE OF PRICE DISCOVERY

Although equities offer the possibility that returns may be modeled in a smooth continuum, at least in the short run, debt securities are less tractable. There are simply too many variables in the instruments themselves that may affect the magnitude of the outcome. Seniority, covenants, and call options all have an impact on value. In the equity markets, analysts come to a collective judgment on these and other value-impacting variables and total return as measured by (sale price minus acquisition cost) plus dividends may

---

[7]See Chapter 20. Even with credit derivatives, it may be difficult to eliminate basis risk, that is, the relationship between the change in value of the reference asset and the change in value of the asset being hedged.

[8]*Intertemporal* refers to the ability of the algorithm to look forward *and* backward in time when seeking the optimum solution. For example, should a bond be sold in period t or t + 1 or t + 2? The effect of these choices can be modeled only in a multiperiod model.

be measured. However, with the exception of the bonds of large corporations, and, to some extent, high-yield securities, the markets are quite thin and the bid-ask spreads wider than in the equity market. Even when the value of an instrument can be determined from its characteristics, many observers believe that the bond markets lag behind the equity markets in reflecting the true or fair value of a company's securities.

LACK OF GOOD DATA

Added to all this is the fact that, with the exception of the public bond market, good data on variables that can impact the value of a debt security are still difficult to obtain. Even when performing some fairly basic kinds of analysis, the analyst has to resort to elaborate adjustments in order to transform the data into the needed form. The simplest example of this is bond default and recovery data. Defaults by bond ratings are probably the only available database on corporate defaults.[9] If someone has a homegrown risk rating system and wants to use it to project defaults, he/she has to rely on the bond default data. In other words, to analyze a nonbond portfolio, one must go from the homegrown rating system to the implied bond rating and thence to the default probability. If an error is introduced in the mapping process that links the homegrown risk rating to the bond rating, it will be passed on to the estimated probability of default as well. A second problem arises because, despite claims to the contrary by the rating agencies, bond ratings themselves have not been a constant measure of credit risk. An AA-rated company of the 1950's may not be the same as an AA-rated company in the 1990s (see Figure 6.5 and Figure 6.6, Chapter 6). These are important concerns because default probabilities based on bond defaults are the foundation of many of the portfolio approaches currently being proposed.[10]

Data problems are also common with regard to geography and industry identification. With the exception of real estate and consumer loans, it is very hard to pin down the geographic dimension of a borrower. For one thing, the corporate address may have nothing to do with the location of the company's manufacturing operations—which may span many countries—and even less to do with the location of its customers. Consider the shoe manufacturer Nike, Inc. Nike is based in Beaverton, Oregon. In 1994 it employed 700 people there, out of the 9600 people in 86 sites worldwide on its payroll. Chances are that lenders' management information systems (MIS) list Nike as being located in Beaverton and very little else. The company's geographic location is equated with the address of its corporate office. With regard to SIC codes, most MIS systems do not provide for more than one SIC for a given company. In some instances, several SIC categories share the same

---

[9]See Chapter 13 for bond default and mortality data. Robert Morris Associates, Inc. is developing a database of bank loan default and recovery experience for a consortium of banks. This is expected to be available in the year 2000. See also Altman and Suggitt (1997), referred to in Chapter 15, for data on syndicated loan defaults.

[10]CreditMetrics (Gupton, Finger, and Bhatia 1997), a portfolio theory based approach to valuing credit risk, for example, uses the probability of default from bond rating data.

concentration risk. Although they are classified as different groups, automobile battery manufacturers and airbag manufacturers, for example, share common industry risk factors—that is, they behave in the same way.

A company may be in more than one SIC, but a bank's data systems are designed only to capture the primary SIC (see Ranson 1993). It is difficult to decide whether to deal with the SIC code at the 1 digit, 2 digit, or 3 digit level. As industry detail is increased, it becomes possible to pinpoint the economic activity accurately, but there may not be enough data points to create a meaningful summary of the characteristics of an industry group.

Unless a conscious effort is made to profile all of the possible indirect exposures, it is difficult to identify *latent concentrations*. While the link between the fortunes of industries in Louisiana and oil prices is fairly obvious, the dependency of a group of seemingly unrelated customers in the portfolio to a common cause such as export risk is not so apparent. To give an example, if Boeing company starts to depend less on purchases by U.S. carriers and the U.S. government and more on those by overseas buyers, then this shift will mean that events in the foreign economies will have an impact on Boeing's suppliers. Indeed, the entire state of Washington will exhibit behavior that resonates with foreign aircraft purchase trends. It is this *latent* concentration that is more difficult to grapple with. Unless the analyst tags Boeing and its related companies with export risk classification, concentration will not be apparent from routine portfolio analysis.

According to one senior banker, it is difficult to obtain even a baseline database of assets with their risk characteristics:

> The active management portfolio is still in its early days. I suspect you've heard this from others. I don't think we're any different from any other organization. Over the last two or three years, as we've gotten active with portfolio management, the biggest problem of the lot has been getting data of decent integrity. The corporations seem to have management information, but actually getting good quality information in a bank is unbelievably difficult. It's partly because we have some bookkeeping systems that are out of the ark and some that are enormously complicated . . . altogether different systems that don't talk to each other. We have one portfolio in the United States, which has one accounting system. We have another portfolio in the United Kingdom, which has three or four accounting systems—some of them still manual. Then you go to Europe and they've got different accounting systems. So, with all these different accounting systems, we've been trying to develop some systems that can actually go in and pluck out the data.
>
> The problem is that the accounting records are there for a specific purpose, and they were not designed to give all the information and granularity you need to actually undertake all the portfolio management analytics. So, yes, they'll tell us what the drawn balance is. They probably won't tell us what the maturity of the facility is because they don't really need to know that. So we've been trying to develop some records that actually do have the limit, the balance, the product type, all the pricing details, the right maturity, the BIC code, the grading, and the developed severity, and have all this readily available. We're in the throes of introducing a totally new bookkeeping system in the next year, a loan administration system that would be a big step forward. At that stage, we'll be able to go into this system and get most of what we need. And this system will probably need to access one or two other systems to have the

complete picture. The major focus has been getting some data that we actually thought was robust enough to produce some output that's worthwhile.

SOLUTION FOR THE CORRELATION MATRIX

One approach to handling the large size of the correlation matrix is to solve the problem not with individual companies, but with industry average or aggregates or with a representative company as a proxy for an industry. Econometric solutions, notably factor or principal component analysis, have been used to isolate fundamental macro factors affecting corporate financial distress. Failure rate is expressed as a function of external variables such as industry, unemployment , and so on. (Chirinko and Guill [1991]; McKinsey [1997]). The estimate of the failure rate is then equated to the probability of failure of a single firm that fits the profile indicated by the independent variables. Another approach expresses the *return on equity* as a function of a set of index variables (in the spirit of earlier work on multi-index models [see Elton and Gruber 1981] or the later arbitrage pricing theory [see Ross 1984]) and then uses the calculated returns to derive the implied correlation of return among firms. Such frameworks typically are hybrids of econometrics, optimization, univariate time series predictions of exogenous variables, and simulation. This approach may be adequate for broad asset-allocation or sector decisions, but *in the absence of acceptable validation results,* it is probably less applicable to individual asset decisions. But, as the saying goes, getting it broadly right (asset allocation) is clearly better than being precisely wrong (selecting individual assets).

How does one project *future* correlations? Various alternatives have been proposed. Treynor and Black (1973, 66) suggested one of them: Their approach is based on the capital asset pricing model, which, in effect, argues for holding a market portfolio instead of attempting "to translate these insights [of security analysts] into the expected returns, variances, and covariances the algorithms require as inputs." Treynor and Black divide a portfolio into three parts: a riskless part, a highly diversified part resembling the market portfolio, and an active part that has both diversifiable risk and market risk. The latter exists because the portfolio manager has additional insight that the market lacks. Portfolio performance is then measured in terms of how much market risk is taken over the riskless rate, and how much specific risk (called appraisal risk by Treynor and Black) is taken. This approach includes a role for individual risk assessment, and therefore diverges from the capital asset pricing model, which rules it out altogether. To our knowledge, Treynor and Black's approach has not been used in the management of fixed-income portfolios, but it could be applied here because it is able to split market from nonmarket returns, and only the beta of the loan return relative to the market needs to be estimated.

Another way of handling differing expectations about the future, given a correlation matrix, is the scenario approach proposed by Markowitz and Perold (1981). In this approach, the returns are linked to future states of the world (scenarios), and a probability distribution is assigned to each scenario. Equity portfolios are often constructed using the scenario approach. In his loan portfolio analysis, Bennett (1984) suggests that this approach be used in setting the rating impact of factors and thereupon combining the effect of multiple factors constituting a scenario. His work is described in greater detail in Chapter 19.

CURRENT PORTFOLIO APPROACHES

Portfolio approaches used by financial institutions run the gamut from simple to complex. At the simplest level, institutions apply a slicing and dicing approach, whereby they set limits on the various types of concentration and monitor their exposure accordingly. For example, it is common to see banks set limits by state, country (in-country and cross-border), industry, transaction type, and collateral. These limits are primarily based on judgment but employ off-line analysis to support the limits derived. The limits are generally developed based on one or more of the following approaches:

- Historical or recent loss experience
- Standards based on maximum loss tolerance relative to capital
- Risk-adjusted return on capital, where the risk is evaluated relative to the risk either at the transaction level or at the business unit level

Some of the recently introduced concepts are the diversity index, expected and unexpected losses, RAROC, RAROC 2020, Credit Value at Risk, and variants of the Sharpe ratio (Sharpe 1994).[11] Some overlap exists among the items on this list. For instance, RAROC, CreditMetrics, and CreditRisk + use the unexpected loss concept, and all these methods may include migration, security, covenants, and so forth.

EXPECTED VERSUS UNEXPECTED LOSSES

Beset by the difficulties in trying to adapt the approach based on the return and variance of return on individual assets to illiquid fixed-income securities, portfolio analysts have turned to modeling the problem through the notion of unexpected and expected losses. Expected losses are long-run average losses and thus can be reflected in pricing. Unexpected losses are not reflected in pricing but require that capital be set aside to absorb the shock so that the organization is not debilitated by their occurrence. *Unexpected loss* sounds like a contradiction in terms. After all, once a loss is quantified, it can no longer be called *unexpected*. However, the term really means *maximum potential loss*, or the maximum loss at a given level of confidence—say, 95 percent.[12] One rationale behind the concept of unexpected losses is that losses may be incurred because of a joint default that may be attributable to port-

---

[11] The Sharpe Ratio is defined as the ratio of portfolio expected excess return divided by portfolio standard deviation. Excess return is the return in excess of the risk free rate.

[12] Notice that unexpected loss (95 percent value) is simply expected loss + 2 standard deviations for a normal distribution. There is no unexpected *gain;* we do not have a symmetrical term on the positive side. The minimum loss is just zero.

folio concentration or because a single obligor has defaulted with great severity. Another rationale is that the expected loss value may be incorrect, and it is therefore important to know the underlying distribution that produced this value. Because unexpected losses are derived based on default probabilities and recovery rates, this approach is driven more by *intrinsic value* (the so-called *model value*) than by *market value*.

The concept of expected and unexpected credit losses is shown in Figure 17.2. The expected loss is that associated with the mean of the loss distribution of a loan or a portfolio. The unexpected loss is that associated with 95 percent (for instance) of the area under the loss curve. The area to the right is expected with such rarity that it would be uneconomical to hold 100 percent capital against that contingency. Note that this is the graph for a single asset. If all the assets are combined, the resulting area to the right of the 95 percent level is the loss level for which capital is needed. Capital may not be dollar for dollar, but it has to have some relationship to the *value at risk*. Although the term unexpected loss is somewhat recent, the underlying rationale for it has existed for a long period. For example, Vojta (1973, 18) termed the unexpected loss the deviation from average historical loss by "a prudent margin, say a factor of two." Indeed, Vojta's model for capital adequacy considered even concentration, but in a heuristic manner.

The expected loss is represented by the equation:

Figure 17.2   Expected and Unexpected Credit Loss

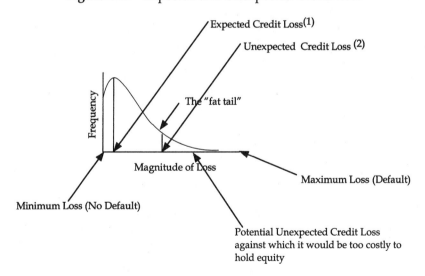

(1) For which reserve should be held; pricing should include this element

(2) For which capital should be held; pricing should include ROE

Source: Adapted from Mark (1996, 282).

$$\text{Expected Loss} = \text{Probability of Default} \times \text{Default Severity}$$

where default severity is defined as a percent of the loan that is lost. For example, if the probability of default is 30 percent and the default severity is 60 percent (which is the same as a recovery rate of 40 percent), the expected loss is 30 percent times 60 percent, or 18 percent of par.

This concept is widely used. Moody's uses diversity scores and the expected and unexpected losses associated with collateral of a particular rating level to come up with the credit protection desired to achieve a certain rating. The higher the diversity score, the lower are the unexpected loss coverage requirements. Table 17.5 (Moody's 1991, 12) illustrates the degree of credit protection (overcollateralization) Moody's requires before it will rate a structured finance transaction as Aaa. The degree of credit protection can also be understood as the level of losses that the pool of assets can withstand.

If the probability of default for a risk class (such as rating) is stable, then we can factor credit losses into the expected value calculations for inclusion in pricing. But, as mentioned earlier, the probability of default itself is an estimate and is subject to uncertainty. The concept of unexpected loss *attempts* to take account of the uncertainty associated with the *ex ante* probability of default. When actual default rates of different bond grades are examined, it becomes clear that they fluctuate over time—to a great extent because of changing economic conditions.[13] The standard deviation of this default rate may be used as a proxy for the unexpected aspect of default. Two standard deviations are added to the mean to derive a *95 percent confidence level* default probability. It is this higher value that is used to derive the unexpected value of the loss to arrive at the capital to be set aside. Table 17.6 shows the one-year default rates experienced by various bond ratings. Based on this historic experience, the probability of default over a one-year period is 1.2246 percent and its standard deviation is 1.354 percent. In Figure 17.3 the horizontal lines are drawn to show the average and average plus 2 times standard deviation. It is worth noting that at least once, the actual default rate crossed over the 95 percent confidence level, that is, exceeded the unexpected level.

OPTIMIZATION OF CAPITAL USAGE

Since economic capital is a scare resource, an optimal portfolio is one that uses it in the most efficient manner. Economic capital is the resource needed to cushion unexpected losses. This reasoning may be used to set up an optimization problem where the objective function is to minimize expected losses in the portfolio, subject to the constraints that (1) the sum of the unexpected losses is less than or equal to the risk capital, and (2) the assets are allocated from among only those available.

Although this approach to portfolio management is on a name-by-name basis, for *strategic* analysis, the problem may be stated in terms of allocation among asset *classes*. The portfolio problem may also be restated as follows:

---

[13] And possibly because the rating criteria themselves have drifted; there is no guarantee that the rating agency criteria are applied consistently because of the human factor and subjectivity involved.

Table 17.5 Structured Secuirty Desired Rating AAA: Losses Required to Be Sustained (%) by Structure for Various Collateral Rating Grades and Diversity Scores

Diversity score	B3	B2	B1	Ba3	Ba2	Ba1	Baa3	Baa2	Baa1	A3	A2	A1	Aa3	Aa2	Aa1
1*															
2	100	100	100	100	100	100	85	71	57	52	49	47	45	42	39
3	99	98	97	95	95	92	75	59	43	38	36	35	33	32	30
4	95	92	91	87	84	80	64	50	36	33	31	29	27	25	24
6	90	87	85	83	76	73	58	44	30	27	25	23	22	21	20
7	81	77	73	69	66	60	49	38	27	24	22	20	19	18	17
10	75	69	65	59	58	51	41	33	25	22	20	19	18	17	17
15	66	60	56	51	46	43	36	30	24	21	19	18	17	16	16
20	62	56	51	46	42	38	33	28	23	20	18	17	16	15	15
25	58	53	48	43	38	35	30	26	22	19	17	16	15	14	14
30	56	51	46	40	35	32	28	24	20	17	16	15	14	13	13
35	54	48	44	38	35	30	26	22	19	16	15	14	13	12	12
40	52	47	42	37	33	29	24	20	17	15	14	13	12	11	11

*Evaluated on a case-by-case basis.

Source: Moody's Investors Service 1991, 12. Reprinted with permission.

Table 17.6   Average One-Year Default Rate by Bond Rating

Rating	1 year default average 1970–1995 (%)	1 year default std. deviation 1970–1995 (%)
Aaa	0.00	0.00
Aa	0.02	0.12
A	0.01	0.05
Baa	0.15	0.30
Ba	1.22	1.35
B	6.32	4.78

Source: Moody's Investors Service (1995). Reprinted with permission.

Figure 17.3   Ba Defaults 1970–1995

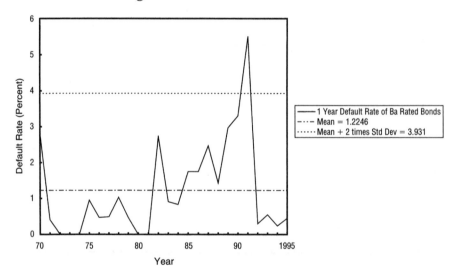

Source: Moody's Investors Service (1995). Reprinted with permission.

$$\text{Minimize} \ - \ \Sigma \ (\text{Unexpected Loss})$$

Subject to

1. Σ (Portfolio Weights)$_i$ = 1
2. Σ (Expected Interest Income − Expected Loss) ≥ Target Return on Equity
3. Total Assets ≤ 100/Capital Ratio

Note that the higher return required to justify higher expected losses is modeled in the second constraint. Given below is an example using a portfolio of bonds. Table 17.7 contains the input data for the portfolio. How much should be invested in AAA, AA, A, BBB, BB, B? Given the information provided, is there an obvious answer for the optimum portfolio?

The objective function is to minimize unexpected losses (expressing all the quantities as fractions):

$$\frac{\sum_{i=1}^{i=6} w_i(p_i + 2^*d_i)(1 - r_i)}{C}$$

In this equation, w_i is the fraction invested in bond rating i. This is multiplied by the term $(p_i + 2 \times d_i)$, which is default probability plus 2 standard deviations. This is multiplied by $(1 - r_i)$ which is the amount of the loan that cannot be recovered. The sum of this quantity taken over all the bond ratings and divided by the capital ratio gives the total value of the unexpected losses from the portfolio, sometimes referred to as the *economic capital*. This value will scale to the true capital that will be needed either dollar for dollar or in some other proportion.

The first constraint is that the portfolio weights add up to 100 percent.

$$\sum_{i=1}^{i=6} w_i = 1$$

The second constraint is that the rate of return on the equity is greater than or equal to a target amount. This constraint captures the leverage, because it is only through leverage that earnings may be magnified.

$$\frac{\sum_{i=1}^{i=6} w_i m_i}{C} \geq \text{target return on ROE}$$

This is a simple optimization problem that may be solved on a personal computer using commercially available optimization software. The solution calculated using various levels of target ROE is shown in Table 17.8.

The results are what one would expect. To increase the margin, you have to go down-market and be prepared for more losses albeit with higher revenues. Note that the losses grow at a very rapid rate. Since probabilities and standard deviations are based on actual bond market experience over a very long period, it does not appear to make economic sense (on a risk-reward basis) to go below BB or equivalent to achieve 15–20 percent ROE. The highest ROE attainable in this portfolio was found to be 21.5 with the available risk-return choices. While these conclusions may be obvious for a small number of securities, the problem soon gets more complicated as further gradations of risk are added and limits are imposed on (a) various segments to reflect the limited number of borrowers of a certain credit quality in that segment, and (b) risk-based regulatory capital. This is where an optimization approach will help reveal the tradeoffs.

We did not consider any covariances or multiperiod choices. Special risk-based capital constraints were not imposed because the capital required is

Table 17.7 Input Data for the Optimization Problem

Symbol	Portfolio weights (%) w_i	Overall capital ratio (constant): capital/total risk asset (%) C	Spread (%) m_i	Probability of default (%) p_i	Standard deviation (%) d_i	Recovery rate (%) r_i
AAA	?	8.00	0.40	0.00	0.00	78
AA	?	8.00	0.65	0.02	0.12	77
A	?	8.00	1.20	0.01	0.05	57
BBB	?	8.00	1.60	0.15	0.30	53
BB	?	8.00	2.40	1.22	1.35	42
B	?	8.00	4.00	6.32	4.78	35

Table 17.8 Optimal Solutions

Target ROE	Optimal solution	Expected loss	Unexpected loss	Net income
5%	100% in AAA	0	0	5.00
10%	49.7% in AAA			
	50.3% in A	0.027	0.297	10.00
15%	98.7% in A			
	1.3% in BBB	0.0644	0.640	15.00
20%	56.7% in BBB			
	43.3% in BB	4.3278	14.798	20.00

the same for all bond grades. Since the bond ratings are considered to apply consistently across all industries, it is quite likely that the correlation of defaults among the rating classes is very low; in other words, there will be some gain in diversifying across bond ratings. The results of the foregoing example should therefore vary if correlations are incorporated and a longer time dimension (say, 5 years) is used.[14]

Portfolio approaches for fixed-income assets are still in the process of evolution. Most portfolio optimization solutions proposed today share the approach just described but may differ in (a) the design of the objective function, (b) the sources of data for correlation and default probability, and (c) the handling of credit migration before an asset reaches one of its final states (maturity of the loan, refinancing, or default).

VARYING OBJECTIVES

Managing a portfolio of assets means different things to different people. Pension plan managers may look at portfolio management as an asset allocation problem—how much to invest in various sectors and how to rebalance the portfolio as expectations change. Capital constraints or taxes are not a part of their investment equation. Brinson, Hood, and Beebower (1986) decomposed the way professional money managers view investment returns and found that they identified three basic components—investment policy (asset mix), market timing, and security selection. Their research indicated that market timing and security selection influenced total plan returns far less than asset allocation policy did. Insurance companies and banks, by contrast, have to take into account regulatory capital and the capital charges applied by the rating agencies. They also have a different liability structure, which must be accommodated by the portfolio strategy. Some of the assets available for investment (such as credit card receivables) come *pre-diversified;* the portfolio model used by an investor should be able to distinguish between these and other single-risk securities such as corporate bonds. For financial guarantee companies, the option feature of the guarantee (there are

---

[14]See Lucas (1995) for data on bond default correlations.

no claims until the transaction-specific first loss levels in the portfolio are exceeded) should be modeled in assessing the earnings variability to be expected from a portfolio of businesses. At the business unit level, default correlation between one transaction and another or between two portfolios may be difficult to estimate. The next two chapters consider the approaches that are available to address these questions.

REFERENCES

Beckers, S. 1996. Survey of Risk Measurement Theory and Practice. In *Handbook of Risk Management*, edited by C. Alexander. New York: John Wiley & Sons.

Bennett, P. 1984. Applying Portfolio Theory to Global Bank Lending. *Journal of Banking & Finance* 8:153–169.

Board of Governors of the Federal Reserve System. 1993. Risks of Concentration of Credit and Nontraditional Activities. Washington, D.C.: Board of Governors of the Federal Reserve System.

Brinson, G. P., L. R. Hood, and G. L. Beebower. 1986. Determinants of Portfolio Performance. *Financial Analysts Journal* (May/June): 51 (1), 40–48.

Chirinko, R. S., and G. D. Guill. 1991. A Framework for Assessing Credit Risk in Depository Institutions: Toward Regulatory Reform. *Journal of Banking and Finance* 15:785–804.

Coopers and Lybrand. 1993. Growth and Diversification: Are the Benefits Always There? In *Mortgage Banking*, edited by J. Lederman. Chicago: Probus Publishing Company.

CreditRisk+ 1996. Credit Suisse Financial Products, New York, N.Y.

Elton, E., and M. Gruber. 1981. *Modern Portfolio Theory and Investment Analysis*. 1st ed. New York: John Wiley & Sons.

Gupton, G. M., C. C. Finger, and M. Bhatia. 1997. *CreditMetrics: The Benchmark for Understanding Credit Risk*. New York: J. P. Morgan.

Lucas, D. J. 1995. Default Correlation and Credit Analysis. *Journal of Fixed Income* 4 (4): 76–87.

Mark, R. M. 1996. Innovative Strategies and Techniques for Pricing Contingent Credit Risk. In *Derivatives Risk and Responsibility*, edited by R. A. Klein and J. Lederman. Chicago: Irwin Professional Publishing.

Markowitz, H. 1959. *Portfolio Selection: Efficient Diversification of Investments*. New York: John Wiley & Sons.

Markowitz, H., and A. Perold. 1981. Portfolio Analysis with Scenarios and Factors. *Journal of Finance* 36: 871–877.

Mason, S. P. 1995. The Allocation of Risk. In *The Global Financial System*. Boston: Harvard Business School Press.

Moody's Investors Service. 1991. Rating Cash Flow Transactions Backed by Corporate Debt. *Moody's Special Report*. March.

———. 1995. Corporate Bond Defaults and Default Rates, 1970–1989. *Moody's Special Report*. April.

Ranson, B. 1993. Rabbit Stew. *Balance Sheet* (spring): 37–40.

Ross, S. A., and R. Roll. 1984. The Arbitrage Pricing Theory Approach to Strategic Portfolio Planning. *Financial Analysts Journal* (May/June): 51 (1), 14–26.

Sharpe, W. 1994. The Sharpe Ratio. *Journal of Portfolio Management* (fall): 49–58.

Treynor, J. L., and F. Black. 1973. How to Use Security Analysis to Improve Portfolio Selection. *Journal of Business* 46 (1):66–86.

Vojta, G. J. 1973. *Bank Capital Adequacy*. New York: First National City Bank.

Chapter *18*

Credit Pricing, Risk-Adjusted Returns, and Allocation of Capital

Essential as it is to put aside "unimportant" features and to stress "important" ones in formulating classes [abstract concepts], the dangers of this intellectual operation are great. A necessary generalization can easily evolve into an overgeneralization. And as a rule we have no opportunity to test in advance whether a concept we have developed has struck the right degree of abstraction or is an overgeneralization.

—Dietrich Dörner, *The Logic of Failure*

Chapter 17 introduced some basic concepts regarding the diversification of assets in a portfolio. In this chapter, we look more closely at the diversification techniques available to financial institutions. We focus in particular on answers that have been given to the following two questions:

1. What kind of "gate-keeping" function is needed such that every incremental asset originated is acceptable from a portfolio perspective? In other words, how should the originator operate?

2. After assets have been acquired, what can be done about the composition of the portfolio? What, in particular, is the right level of diversification? In other words, how should the portfolio manager operate?

Answers to these approaches depend partly on risk-return trade-offs, but even more so on postacquisition strategies available to the institution. Quite clearly, the strategy of "originate and retain" will provide a solution different from a strategy of "originate and retain or hedge or sell."

Because a portfolio is a consequence of a series of asset pricing and approval decisions, we will first consider pricing as a means of managing portfolio composition. After we introduce the reasons for treating capital as a scare resource to be allocated among competing investment opportunities, it will become clear that capital allocation and portfolio management, in the abstract, seek answers to exactly the same question, namely, how should an institution operate to maximize shareholder value? Concepts such as *value at risk* (VAR) address the problem of capital allocation with calculations that are based on the market value of assets. We present examples of different approaches to credit pricing and conclude with observations from practitioners.

USE OF THE PRICING MECHANISM

Some argue that in acquiring assets, an institution should use the pricing mechanism in conjunction with product/geography/industry/tenor limits. For example, if a bank believes that construction loans for suburban malls are unattractive from a portfolio perspective, it can raise the price of these loans to a level that will act as a disincentive to borrowers. This is an instance of marginal cost pricing—the notion that the price of an asset should compensate the institution for its marginal cost as measured on a risk-adjusted basis. The more a product increases a lender's portfolio concentration, the higher its marginal cost to that lender. Marginal cost pricing may not always work. A bank may have idle capacity—a large cost base and capital that has not been deployed. While such an institution clearly would not want to make a loan at a negative spread, it would probably view even a small positive spread as worthwhile as long as the added risk was acceptable.

Institutions tend to book unattractively priced loans when they are unable to allocate their cost base with clarity or to make fine differentiations of their risks. If a bank cannot allocate its costs, then it will make no distinction between the cost of lending to borrowers that require little analysis and the cost of lending to borrowers that require a considerable amount of review and follow up. Similarly, if the spread is tied to a too coarsely graded risk-rating system (one, for example, with just four grades) then it is more difficult to differentiate among risks when pricing than if the risk rating is graduated over a larger scale with, say, 15 grades.

A cost-plus-profit pricing strategy will work in the short run, but in the long run borrowers will balk and start looking for alternatives. Cost-plus-profit pricing will also work when a bank has some flexibility to compete on an array of services rather than exclusively on price. The difficulties with pricing are greater in markets where the lender is a price taker rather than a price leader.

Traditional pricing for credit risk has followed the cost-plus-profit approach as, shown in Figure 18.1.

An illustrative example using the traditional approach is given below. The pricing is based on the borrower's risk rating, tenor, collateral, guarantees, and covenants. A capital charge is applied based on a hurdle rate and a capital ratio. Table 18.1 shows the historic loss rate used for each of the risk-rating categories. This is used in the example to calculate the expected loss allowance to be built into the price.

Based on the yield curve, Table 18.2 shows the cost of funds for various maturities from 1 to 5 years.

The two other inputs needed are the capital ratio (8 percent) and the required rate of return on capital (16 percent). Using these assumptions, the rate to be charged for a 5-year unsecured loan to a customer with a rating of 4 comes to 11.71 percent, or a spread of 1.71 over the cost of funds, as shown in Table 18.3.

This relatively simple approach to credit pricing works well as long as the assumptions are correct—especially those about the borrower's credit quality. This method is used in many banks today. The main drawback is

Figure 18.1   Traditional Loan Pricing Methodology

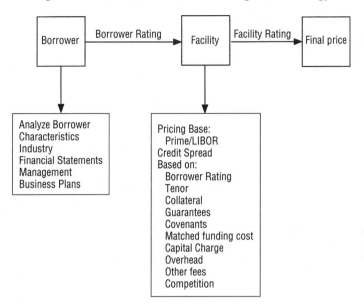

Table 18.1   Historic Loss Rate by Internal Risk Rating

Rating	Historic 5-Year loss rate (%)
AAA ≡ 1	0.01
AA ≡ 2	0.19
A ≡ 3	0.18
BBB ≡ 4	0.85
BB ≡ 5	6.15
B ≡ 6	18.38

Source: Altman and Kishore (1997).

that only "expected" losses are linked to the borrower's credit quality. The capital charge on an 8 percent capital ratio at 16 percent (cost of equity) may not be sufficient, and the capital charge based on the volatility of losses in the credit risk category may also be too small. If the loan were to default, the loss would have to be made up from income from nondefaulting loans. At the rate of $17,100 net income ($117,100 minus funding cost of $100,000) per $1,000,000, the bank will need to book $58.5 million to cover the loss of $1,000,000 in one year. Another drawback of this method is that it implicitly assumes only two possible states for a loan: default or no default. It does not model the credit risk premium or discount resulting from improvement or

Table 18.2   Term Structure of Rates

Maturity (years)	Cost of funds (%)
1	5
2	5.5
3	6
4	8
5	10
10	12

Table 18.3   Price Build-up Based on Cost plus Profit

Item	Calculation	Amount
1. Borrower's risk rating		5
2. Loan maturity		5 years
3. 5-year loss rate (mortality)		6.15%
4. Capital ratio		8.00
5. Hurdle rate		16.00
6. Loan amount		1,000,000
7. Capital required (8 percent of loan amount)	(0.08)(1,000,000)	80,000
Price buildup		
8. Annual capital charge @ 16%	(0.16)(80,000)	12,800
9. Annual funds cost @ 10% fixed	(0.10)(920,000)	92,000
10. Annual loan loss allowance	(0.01)(6.15)(1,000,000)/5	12,300
11. Break-even annual interest income	(12,800 + 92,000 + 12,300)	117,100
12. Loan interest rate (with no funding risk)	117,100/1,000,000	11.71%
13. Minimum spread	11.71–10.00	171 bps

decline in the borrower's financial condition, which is meaningful only if the asset may be repriced or sold at par.

Financial institutions have long struggled to find the best ways of allocating capital in a manner consistent with the risks taken. They have found it difficult to come up with a consistent and credible way of allocating capital for such varying sources of revenue as loan commitments, revolving lines of credit (which have no maturity), and secured versus unsecured lending. One approach is to allocate capital to business units based on their asset size. Although it is true that a larger portfolio will have larger losses, this approach also means that the business unit is forced to employ all the capital allocated to it. Moreover, this method treats all risks alike. Another approach is to use the regulatory (risk-adjusted) capital as the allocated capital. The problem with this approach is that regulatory capital may or may not reflect the true risk of a business. For example, for regulatory purposes, a loan to a AAA-rated customer requires the same amount of capital per dollar lent as one to a small business. Yet another approach is to use unexpected losses in a subportfolio (standard deviation of the annual losses taken over time) as a proxy for capital to be allocated. The problem with this approach is that it ignores default correlations across subportfolios. The volatility of a subportfolio may in fact dampen the volatility of the institution's portfolio, so pricing decisions based on the volatility of the subportfolio may not be optimal. In practical terms, this means that one line of business within a lending institution may sometimes subsidize another. The resulting synergy makes the institution stronger because the direction of the subsidy may reverse at some future time.

Allocating capital is a goal to be attained, but in the absence of adequate data and analytics, most banks have relied largely on approximations such as return on assets in the pricing of loans and the measurement of performance. Covenant-specific step-up or step-down pricing and pricing for migration, or—more generally—for event risk, are rare. It is important for lenders to develop a well-thought-out pricing strategy because, in the eyes of shareholders, this is ultimately what drives the institution's performance. As Marc Intrater, director at Oliver, Wyman & Company observes:

> Typically "the market" is blamed for pricing inadequacies. It is true that market pricing, on average, is insufficient to meet a risk-adjusted hurdle rate in some markets. However, even as a pure *price taker,* a bank can select opportunities for participation based upon whether pricing adequately covers risk and/or leads to sufficient relationship profitability. Furthermore, most banks are not pure price takers in all, or even most, lending situations. In price making situations, a well-designed pricing strategy is obviously critical.

The development of a good pricing strategy is a matter of understanding the loan's component parts: the cash flow sources that make up the total revenue, the term of the loan, the impact of the loan on the risk profile of the portfolio, and the rating/pricing that the loan will obtain in the open market.

RAROC AND ALL THAT

As it became clearer that banks needed to add an appropriate capital charge in the pricing process, the concept of risk adjusting the return or risk adjusting the capital was born. The value-producing capacity of an asset (or a business) is expressed as a ratio that allows comparisons to be made between assets (or businesses) of varying sizes and risk characteristics. The ratio is based either on the size of the asset or the size of the capital allocated to it. When an institution can observe asset prices directly (and/or infer risk from observable asset prices) then it can determine how much capital to hold based on the volatility of the asset. This is the essence of the *mark-to-market* concept. If the capital to be held is excessive relative to the *total return* that would be earned from the asset, then the bank will not acquire it. If the asset is already in the bank's portfolio, it will be sold. Note that the availability of a liquid market to buy and sell these assets is a precondition for this approach. When banks talk about asset concentration and correlation, the question of capital allocation is always in the background because it is allocated capital that absorbs the potential consequences (unexpected losses) resulting from such concentration and correlation causes.

Table 18.4 shows some of the newly coined acronyms and some of the older ones that have appeared in the literature for these ratios. The most important of these, the RAROC, is described next.

Risk-adjusted return on capital (RAROC) was introduced by Bankers Trust in the late 1970s.[1] It is based on a mark-to-market concept. As defined by Bankers Trust, RAROC allocates a capital charge to a transaction or a line of business at an amount equal to the maximum expected loss (at a 99 percent confidence level) over one year on an after-tax basis (Bankers Trust New York Corporation 1995). As may be expected, the higher the volatility of the returns, the more capital is allocated. The higher capital allocation means that the transaction has to generate cash flows large enough to offset the volatility of returns, which results from the credit risk, market risk, and other risks taken. The RAROC process estimates the asset value that may prevail in the worst-case scenario and then equates the capital cushion to be provided for the potential loss. There are four basic steps in this process:

1. Analyze the activity or product and determine the basic risk categories that it contains, for example, interest rate (country, directional, basis, yield curve, optionality), foreign exchange, equity, commodity, and credit and operating risk.

2. Quantify the risk in each category by a market proxy.

3. Using the historical price movements of the market proxy over the past three years, compute a market risk factor, given by the following equation

$$\text{RAROC risk factor} = 2.33 \times \text{weekly volatility} \times \sqrt{52} \times (1 - \text{tax rate})$$

   In this equation, the multiplier 2.33 gives the volatility (expressed as a percent) at the 99 percent confidence level.[2] The term $\sqrt{52}$ converts the weekly price movement into an annual movement. The term 1 − tax rate converts the calculated value to an after-tax basis.

4. Compute the dollar amount of capital required for each risk category by multiplying the risk factor by the size of the position.

---

[1]RAROC was initially applied to the trading portfolio. Bankers Trust used to be a full service bank but in the 1970s withdrew completely from retail banking to concentrate entirely on wholesale banking and trading. It has used this approach in the derivatives market as well. It is notable that the origins of RAROC, RiskMetrics, and CreditMetrics are all in 100 percent wholesale banks (Bankers Trust and J. P. Morgan).

[2]It is assumed that the distribution is normal.

Figure 18.2 gives the risk factors for a sample of seven products: 5- and 30-year Treasuries, Deutsche Mark/Guilder, U.S. dollar/Canadian dollar, U.S. dollar/Yen, FTSE 100, and spot oil.

Establishing the maximum expected loss in each product line and linking the capital to this loss makes it possible to compare products of different risk levels by stating the risk side of the risk-reward equation in a consistent manner. The risk-to-reward ratios thus becomes comparable. To illustrate, let us compare two traders: one trading U.S. government bonds with a US$100 million position, and the other trading Canadian dollars with an average position of US$100 million.

According to Figure 18.2, the government unit trader would require a capital allocation of $14 million, and the Canadian dollar trader would require only $6 million. If both investments made the same profit of, say, $2 million, then the bond trader's RAROC is 2/14 = 14.3 percent, whereas the FX trader's RAROC is 2/6 = 33.3 percent. In an institution that uses RAROC, a business unit does not have a fixed amount of capital. Rather, sufficient capital is allocated to it based on the need to support the desired business volume.

RAROC is an improvement over the traditional approach in that it allows one to compare two businesses with different risk (volatility of returns) profiles. Using a hurdle rate, a lender can also use the RAROC principle to set the target pricing on a relationship or a transaction. Although not all assets have market price distribution, RAROC is a first step toward examining an institution's entire balance sheet on a mark-to-market basis—if only to understand the risk-return trade-offs that have been made.

The astute reader will no doubt have observed that the RAROC for the individual line of business is explicitly neither penalized nor rewarded for correlations. This is one of the potential criticisms of the RAROC approach. This shortcoming becomes apparent as the risk profile of the entire portfolio is considered, because it is here that correlation has its impact.

Figure 18.2   RAROC Risk Factors

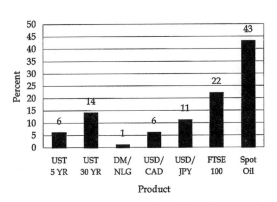

Risk Factors

Source: Bankers Trust Corporation. © 1995 Bankers Trust Corporation and its affiliated companies. Reprinted with permission.

Table 18.4 Risk-Adjusted Performance Measurements

Acronym	Definition	Numerator	Denominator
ROA (return on assets) expressed in bps	This is the venerable ratio that banks have historically used to measure performance. Unfortunately this measure does not account for risk.	Net income after loan loss provision	Average or end-of-period assets (book value)
ROE (return on equity) expressed as a percentage	This is measure does not take risk into account. It also begs the question of what the denominator should be for a single loan or line of business.	Net income after loan loss provision	Average or end-of-period equity (equity capital and retained earnings)
VAR (value at risk) expressed in maximum $ loss at 99 percent confidence level	This is a late arrival on the scene, but the quantity it represents is based on the long-held view that capital allocated should serve as the cushion against all unexpected losses. VAR is a measure of maximum expected loss from an asset. Sometimes VAR = allocated capital. At other times the relationship is governed by the confidence level desired.	Maximum dollar loss expected with probability of 99 percent	Acquisition cost of the asset. (Note that this quantity will account for the premium or discount paid when the asset was acquired. For a bank, most of the time it will be the book value of the asset.)

MTM (mark to market) expressed as a percentage of par (book value)	This is the present market value of an asset. The relationship between VAR and MTM is that MTM is a *realization* of a statistical distribution, whereas VAR is the *value associated with the 99 (for example) percent probability* in the distribution. MTM is a measure of value *as it is*; VAR is a measure of the impact of value *as it could be* under adverse conditions.	Market value of asset	Book value of asset
MTM (mark to model) expressed as a percentage of par (or book value); sometimes also as a distribution	Mark to model is the imputed (or the estimate) of the market value of an asset according to a model. This model will try to capture all the variables that have an impact on market value. Mark to model is sometimes used to derive the VAR.	Market value of asset as estimated by the model	Book value of asset
RORAA (return on risk-adjusted assets)	This is a refinement of ROA, with the denominator adjusted to account for the varying riskiness of the asset classes.	Net income	Assets grossed up or down based on credit risk. For example, AA bonds or credits may have a risk weighting of 2 percent, whereas B rated bonds or credits, a weighting of 0 percent
RAROC (risk-adjusted return on capital)	Return based on capital allocated to the business. The allocation is based on unexpected loans.	Net income	Position size multiplied by the risk factor. Risk factor is based on volatility of market value.

In 1991 Bankers Trust expanded RAROC and named it RAROC 2020. RAROC 2020 includes portfolio concepts, and it assumes that market prices are available for the products in the portfolio. By implication, the market prices include credit risk, so there is little direct emphasis on default as an event that drives asset value. One of the elements of RAROC 2020 is the calculation of daily price volatility (DPV). This is a *value-at-risk* measure that shows the maximum potential economic loss of the portfolio overnight.

CALCULATION OF VALUE AT RISK

The calculation of value at risk for a single asset is relatively straightforward. At the simplest level, if the historic volatility of the asset is known, the future value at risk may be expressed based on the historic volatility. For assets that are combined with derivatives (for example, a floating-rate loan with a cap), the value function is nonlinear, and the change in value of the asset in response to a change in value of the underlying factors is more difficult to measure. For a portfolio, assuming the asset returns are jointly normally distributed, portfolio return is a linear combination of the returns from the individual assets in the portfolio. Portfolio variance (leading to the value at risk) may be calculated based on the variance-covariance matrix using the Markowitz capital asset pricing model concepts (see Chapter 17).

Today, the assets in a bank's portfolio are not simple. Most have options embedded in them—some placed deliberately, and others introduced through custom and practice. A floating-rate loan, for example, may have a rate cap, a corporate bond may have a call option, and a mortgage has a prepayment option. When options are involved, the value of an asset can change in nonlinear fashion with respect to the underlying variables.[3] When there are nonlinearities, the impact on value of future market conditions may be estimated only through simulations (see Chapter 9). Even in simulations, components using "no arbitrage" arguments may prove to be unreliable when there are large price movements and a drop in liquidity.[4]

RiskMetrics is a collection of methodologies and data sets designed to help an institution derive its portfolio value at risk. It provides a set of tools to map its products to standardized risk positions. These positions are fed

---

[3]It is important to distinguish between linear and nonlinear risks. In most cases the pay off (or loss) changes linearly with the asset. For example, if you owned a Treasury bill, a drop of 1 percent in value of the bill will directly equate to a 1 percent drop of the Treasury bill you own. For derivatives and some securities such as mortgages, the value of the product may change by more or less than the change in the underlying risk factor. Additional risk factors with options are change in value due to change in volatility (vega risk) and nonlinear change in value due to change in price (gamma risk). This terminology is associated with market risk, not credit risk, although credit risk may be a contributory factor of these variables.

[4]"No arbitrage" argument is used, for example, in deriving the fair value of an option in the Black-Scholes model. If you cannot arbitrage, such as when there is a discontinuity in the market, the fair value derived is no longer applicable. For comments on pricing model risk see Wilson (1996).

into a variance-covariance matrix to derive the portfolio return and variance. RiskMetrics estimates this matrix using historic data and a multitude of techniques ranging from simple exponential smoothing to autoregressive moving average models and other sophisticated forecasting techniques. This set of tools provides an institution with an easy way to calculate its risk positions directly, without having to invest in the development of databases and software. It may be noted that the value at risk calculated is the daily value and may be calculated only in a mark-to-market world. Where prices are unavailable, *mark-to-model* approaches may have to be used. Indeed, many financial institutions will find that despite the innovations that have been introduced, a large portion of the balance sheet still has to be analyzed in a mark-to-model mode.

Analytically, concepts such as VAR are equally applicable to credit risk. In a market where competitive forces set the price, the value of credit risk will be directly reflected in asset pricing.

ECONOMIC CAPITAL, REGULATORY CAPITAL, AND BOOK VALUE OF EQUITY

How are economic capital, regulatory capital, and book value of equity related, and how do these relationships impact efficient allocation of capital? This basic question may go unanswered in discussions of VAR, RAROC, and so forth. Economic capital is management's internal assessment of the capital cushion to be provided to the asset or the line of business. When this is used in the pricing of assets, there is no a priori reason for the total capital needed to equal the amount of regulatory capital. For example, the regulatory capital needed for a $1 million loan to an A-rated borrower is the same as that need for a $1 million loan to a BB-rated borrower, even though it is clear that much less capital is needed for the A-rated borrower. In order to set optimal allocations of capital, therefore, both economic and regulatory constraints have to be taken into account.[5] By the same token, it is a mistake to use regulatory capital ratios in setting prices because risk-based capital requirements are designed to be applicable to a wide range of institutions. They are, of necessity, blunt instruments (Marvin 1996, 2) requiring simplified assumptions, and their use is intended to achieve consistency at the expense of accuracy.

Risk-based capital standards are the consequence of a political process that was aimed at stemming the erosion of capital among the world's banks, and at minimizing or eliminating the huge inequalities prevalent among these banks that allowed some institutions to price so thinly that they were, in effect, guilty of dumping. These standards are by no means scientific, and they may not lead an institution to optimal capital allocation. It is also important to remember that the regulatory capital includes tier 1 and tier 2 capital definitions, whereas economic capital refers primarily to stockhold-

---

[5]With mathematical programming techniques such as optimization it is readily possible to impose multiple constraints and solve for the optimum mix of assets. A simple example was presented in Chapter 17.

ers' equity. The book value of equity is a component of capital but does not constitute all of it. Regulatory capital requirements also do not take into account the liability side of the balance sheet. For example, what would be the impact on a lending institution if there were an unexpected flight to quality by investors (in its certificates of deposit)? The bank may tide over the problem by going to the discount window, but what are the long-term capital implications? Should retail time and demand deposits be given a lower capital charge than wholesale time and demand deposits? In addition, the problem of capital allocation quickly becomes entangled in the issue of asset-liability management because the profit from an asset is based, among other things, on the nominal rate on the asset minus the funding costs.

Mathematical optimization introduced in Chapter 17 can help in deciding on the right amount of capital to allocate. The regulatory capital ratio, economic capital, and the book value of equity may be modeled as constraints, so that the resulting capital allocated to an asset class satisfies all of them. An institution should have no more capital than it needs (because overcapitalization will result in a lower return on stockholders' equity) and no less capital than is dictated by the risk exposure (unexpected losses) it has assumed. In the optimization process, any resulting excess capital is treated as if it were invested at a riskless rate of return, signaling to the objective function that excess capital is economically unattractive. In practical terms, if an institution discovers that it has more capital than it needs, it may either take on more risk or decide to repurchase its stock. The latter sends a signal to the market that the institution is not prepared to alter its chosen tolerance for risk. *Postoptimality analysis* is helpful in identifying the factors and their marginal cost that constrain the institution from reaching goals superior to those indicated by the optimal solution.

In mathematical optimization, the objective function is set up such that the total profit contribution made by a decision variable increases or decreases with the increase or decrease in the value of the variable. For example, if the decision variable is the percent to be invested in BBB bonds, then as this quantity increases, the total income from the investment in BBBs increases. The increase in the profit may be linear or quadratic, or in the opposite direction, but whatever it is, it is always assumed to be monotonically increasing or decreasing. But what about an investment in the interest rate cap business or an option? The profit contribution will be positive for some values of interest rates, and zero or even negative for others. In the case of options, the payoff is nonlinear in some parts of the profit function and zero or negative in others. Because it is difficult to model such products with the standard optimization techniques, Monte Carlo simulation (introduced in Chapter 9) is perhaps the only way to assess the impact.[6] Of course,

---

[6]The standard portfolio optimization method is called asset-normal because it assumes that asset returns are jointly normally distributed. When the asset returns are not normal, then optimization may be carried out using the delta (small changes in price of assets in response to small changes in the underlying variables). When the payoffs are not linear, then delta-gamma methods are used. These methods are progressively more complex, and yet can not handle event risk. See Wilson (1996).

when Monte Carlo simulation is used, we no longer have the benefit of being able to find the optimum strategy directly because the simulations merely sample the world as we describe it to the computer. The ability to handle options is of concern not only to institutions that deal in derivative products, but also to those that do not because they too have options embedded in traditional products. Prepayments, first loss protection, downgrade triggers—all of these are in reality financial options. The degree of detail to be used in formulating the optimization or simulation model depends on the complexity of the institution and on whether the objective is strategic or tactical. As Dörner (1996) notes in the passage quoted at the beginning of this chapter, what may be a generalization to one institution (e.g., treating all bonds as one category of investment) may be an overgeneralization to another (which would prefer to break them down by sector, maturity, and risk rating).

TRENDS IN CAPITAL ALLOCATION METHODOLOGIES

Marvin (1996), of the Office of the Comptroller of the Currency, examined the current and evolving trends in selected banks and found agreement among them regarding general principles. Banks believe that capital is required as a cushion against the overall risk of unexpected loss and that it is defined as the volatility of earnings and value. The objective of the capital allocation methodology is to produce measures that may be used in both pricing and portfolio decisions. Banks agreed that economic capital may (and generally does not) equal the book capital. Marvin found that where the capital allocation process was effective, it was characterized by the following elements (Marvin 1996, 1):

- It is part of a disciplined management process.
- The focus is on maximizing shareholder value.
- It is consistent with the corporate risk governance framework.
- It is comprehensive (i.e., includes all risks and activities).
- It applies quantitative as well as qualitative analysis.
- It is well understood, effectively controlled, and communicated internally.
- It is embraced as a credible tool (one source of information) by decision makers.

"The strongest processes have a common standard for risk measurement that is based on the company's risk appetite and applied consistently across the company's risks/businesses," Marvin (1996, 7) notes. Management makes a conscious decision on the capital cushion, knowing that to provide for all possibilities of outcomes beyond their expectation would be unjustifiably expensive. The approach taken resembles in large measure the one taken by rating agencies arriving at a rating. In consumer lending, models are used extensively to estimate loss volatility and to determine the capital cushion needed. As banks have come to rely more and more on noncredit products, noncredit risk is also explicitly considered. When credit risk is the primary risk, the model is driven by the concept of expected and unexpected loss (see Chapter 17).

TRENDS IN PORTFOLIO MANAGEMENT

In a recently commissioned survey of 64 banks, Robert Morris Associates found that, of late, banks have been obtaining much better information from their management information systems. These systems are able to characterize risk in more granular (more detailed) grading schemes. Banks have strengthened their traditional portfolio management practices by such measures as installing or improving their risk-rating systems, conducting loss analysis, and analyzing portfolio risk as a whole. Underwriting has been strengthened by process reengineering and the linking of compensation to accuracy in risk grading. The survey found that banks are seeing early "wins" in concentration-risk management, particularly with respect to single obligor and large sector concentrations. Twenty-three percent of the responding banks were found to have progressed to the point where they appeared to be moving to advanced portfolio management, which includes strategies such as taking action on low-return relationships and buying or selling credit risk. Traditional portfolio management actions include early warning systems and watch lists.

Of particular interest is the trend to rate both the obligor and the facility—the former on the probability of default and the later on the basis of loss given default. The KMV portfolio model and scenario analysis were the most widely cited techniques for analyzing portfolio risk, with the KMV model used primarily for large commercial credits. Some banks, but not many, use correlation analysis. Regulatory anomalies that treat AAA-rated and B-rated credits alike have made it uneconomical for banks to hold better-quality credits on their balance sheet. Citibank's response to this regulatory quirk has been to create Oasis, an off-shore vehicle that takes deposits from foreign investors and invests them in high-quality assets with minimal interest rate risk. Oasis operates under a tight set of investment policies and a surety bond from CapMAC. This entity does not have to maintain reserves. It neither pays deposit insurance premiums nor comes under the direct control of bank supervisory authorities. Citibank places into Oasis the assets that are unattractive to hold in its own balance sheet because of regulatory treatment, but which can provide an adequate risk-reward trade-off to investors.

TRENDS IN CREDIT PRICING

Increasingly, banks are using quantitative models such as Zeta or KMV to derive their internal risk ratings, which are the starting point for all pricing. They are deriving allocated capital from the internal risk rating using either judgmental methods or ones based on the volatility of expected default probability. John Hopper, director of structured finance at Barclays Capital, describes the process in these terms:

> If anybody wants to get a deal approved, it comes to the Operations Committee. Risk-adjusted capital technique is applied to see what the deal looks like. Pre-

liminary analysis of the credit is done using KMV (for corporates) or any of a series of other country-specific grading models we have. Based on this assessment, the grading will be 1.1, or 1.2, or 1.3, up to 3, which is the limit for investment grade credits. Each grading equates to an expected default frequency. We have a severity model, which takes seniority and structure into account. The severity analysis culminates in a percentage severity, which, when combined with the expected default rate, produces a risk tendency.

We work out the matrix pricing using a risk adjusted capital model. Cash flows including costs are input to this model and it generates two outputs. The first is the net present value based on a target rate. The second output is the internal rate of return. Though there may be a tendency to view these calculations as highly scientific, we do not conclude, for example, that a negative NPV destroys shareholder value. There is a large element of judgment and subjectivity involved. Nevertheless, we do use this as our core tool.

Our methodology assumes that our portfolio is very large and diversified. It assumes a standard diversification factor and does not take into account asset-to-asset correlation. We would like to come up with a correlated capital figure, but we are not there yet.

Relationship profitability does enter into the deliberative process. John Hopper continues:

> The fact is that we're not a Goldman Sachs. People know that we've got balance sheets and take deposits, and therefore, for the big corporates, they expect us to be there to lend when they need us. And any time we run those facilities through one of these models, much of the time we'll end up with negative NPV's. We're destroying shareholder value just by lending to them. But when people come to the Operations Committees, they have to make the whole business case for these support-lending situations. We will actually have corporate lending people who are presenting the case support it by looking at how much revenue we generated from that name during the previous year and how much will be generated in the current year. In certain cases, people will be required to make promises as to what they expect to make from that name. And then we have the review process and all this information is loaded into a database and out of that spews something called a Promises Register. If we do a bit of support lending, it may come up for review in a year's time or in six months time. People would say, 'You know, if we do this, we're actually going to get this Bond piece of business. We'll go back and review that in six months' time. And if they haven't got it, we have another meeting or follow-up process, and if we conclude that it is possibly destroying shareholder value, we sell the asset.

In the Bank of Montreal, KMV plays a role in the assignment of internal risk ratings to large corporates. Layered on the risk rating are other considerations such as migration risk. Here is Brian Ranson, senior vice president at the Bank of Montreal:

> Loan pricing should never be disconnected from loan structure. For many banks, covenants are seen as necessities for a sound loan whereas we look at them as elements which change the effective term of the risk and must therefore directly impact pricing.
>
> To illustrate, if a customer wants a five-year loan, he must be asked for a higher price than a one-year loan because of migration risk. If we can introduce covenants that are appropriate and tight, then we can arrive at a one-year price. We also value collateral and price according to the extent and nature of the

collateral. All this gives our relationship managers the opportunity to reverse engineer loan agreements—they can start at the price the customer wants and build a structure to accommodate that price.

A relationship manager has, for each customer, a certain amount of risk capital depending on how big of a risk he is managing. His job is to optimize that capital. That can be done through different products, loans, swaps, foreign exchange, cash management, lock box . . . the list goes on. Our aim is to manage that relationship to sell products that use capital in an optimal way. The customer's aim is to try and get most of the products as cheaply as possible. The relationship manager gets credit for every single product sold to that customer and the revenue that comes therefrom. The portfolio manager gets credit for the income from accepting credit risk and the charge for the expected credit loss.

Competition, risk-based capital standards, scale economies attained through industry consolidation, capital allocation techniques, lessons from history—whatever may be the driving factors, innovation in pricing and portfolio management is evident in today's financial institutions. Some of the practical approaches developed in this arena are the topic of the next chapter.

REFERENCES

Aguais, S. D., and A. M. Santomero. 1988. "Incorporating New Fixed Income Approaches Into Commercial Loan Valuation," *Journal of Lending & Credit Risk Management*, February 80(6), 58–65.

Aguais, S. D., L. Forest Jr., S. Krishnamoorthy, and T. Mueller. 1998. "Creating Value from Both Loan Structure and Price: KPMG's Loan Analysis System (LAS)," *Commercial Lending Review*, 13(2), 1–13.

Altman, E. I., and V. M. Kishore. 1997. Defaults and Returns on High Yield Bonds: Analysis Through 1996. Special report, New York University Salomon Center, New York, N.Y.

Bankers Trust New York Corporation. 1995. *RAROC and Risk Management: Quantifying the Risks of Business*. New York: Bankers Trust New York Corporation.

Dörner, D. 1996. *The Logic of Failure*. New York: Henry Holt.

Marvin, S. G. 1996. *Capital Allocation: A Study of Current and Evolving Practices in Selected Banks*. OCC Staff Study 96-1. Washington, D. C.: Office of the Comptroller of the Currency.

RiskMetrics. 1997. 4th ed. Technical document. New York: J. P. Morgan, Inc.

Wilson, T. C. 1996. Calculating Risk Capital. In *Handbook of Risk Management and Analysis*, edited by C. Alexander. New York: John Wiley & Sons.

ADDITIONAL READING

Beckers, S. 1996. A Survey of Risk Measurement Theory and Practice. In *Handbook of Risk Management and Analysis*, edited by C. Alexander. New York: John Wiley & Sons.

First Manhattan Consulting Group. 1997. *Credit Portfolio Measurement and Management Survey Findings*. Philadelphia: Robert Morris Associates.

Jorian, P. 1997. *Value at Risk: The New Benchmark for Controlling Derivatives Risk*. Chicago: Irwin Professional Publishing.

Matten, C. 1996. *Managing Bank Capital: Capital Allocation and Performance Measurement*. New York: John Wiley & Sons.

Chapter *19*

Application of Portfolio Approaches

Previously, banks had only two options with regard to loans: go long or go longer.

—Stephen Thieke, J. P. Morgan, Inc.

In evaluating credit risk, the ultimate measure is the risk of the entire portfolio. The portfolio risk is substantially less than the sum of the stand-alone risks, due to the effect of diversification within the portfolio. The purpose of portfolio management is, however, not just to determine overall risk, but to determine how to achieve the maximal return for the risk that is being taken. Three key points emerge from portfolio analysis:

1. The amount of diversification achievable in a portfolio depends on the correlations between default risks within the portfolio.
2. The amount of risk contributed by any asset to the portfolio's net diversification depends significantly on how much of the asset is held in the portfolio.
3. Improving portfolio performance consists of including large numbers of assets and varying asset holdings to bring each asset's contribution to the portfolio risk into line with its contribution to the portfolio return.

Recent developments in the bank loan, asset securitization, and derivatives markets have made it possible for an institution to shed unneeded concentrations and take on needed exposure. An example is Bank of Montreal, whose approach to managing its $5 billion portfolio is described by Brian Ranson, senior vice president at The Bank of Montreal: "We've built some models that identify in a global portfolio of 17,000 companies the most diversifying assets by company name. We then can go in and find if they've got bonds outstanding. We can then rank order investments in terms of the highest diversification value given expected market pricing and add these to a diversifying portfolio."

Because portfolio management requires transactions, market values play an integral role. Marking to market, or valuing assets and liabilities at market prices, has been adopted by major banking institutions—not only for purposes of selling assets, but also for help in deciding which risks to retain in the portfolio and which markets to emphasize. Valuation is applied to both liquid and illiquid assets. Stephen Thieke, managing director and head of credit and market risk management at J. P. Morgan states the following:

> Management sees the portfolio on a total return basis, adjusted for changes in rating and credit/market spreads. The nature of the valuation is more by way of mark-to-model than mark-to-market because correlations of credit risk cannot be observed, and there is a large judgmental element in credit assessment. The system is driven by the internal risk rating, which is assigned by a disciplined analytic process to reflect all the expectations of the key factors. The default probabilities and recovery assumptions are not changed frequently, but the results are a lot better than those obtained by taking the view that a loss is not a loss until it is written off. The old way meant not coming to grips with the asset value until it was too late.

Marking to market for market risk is more straightforward because the market prices are available every day. Marking to market for credit risk is more difficult because it is very subjective: It is much harder to detect changes in credit quality and even harder to incorporate default correlations. But it is done nevertheless. Blythe Masters, managing director at J. P. Morgan Securities, Inc. adds the following:

> Loan portfolio managers need information about what the true opportunity cost of their business is in order to properly allocate resources. Whether they make a loan at the wrong price for relationship reasons or buy a bond, purely because of its risk-return characteristics—every transaction can be broken into risk buckets—economic/credit risk, spread or default component, relationship qualitative component, balance sheet component, liquidity risk component, regulatory risk component. In the credit derivatives business and increasingly even in the traditional lending business, we try to price all those things separately on a rational basis. The additional rigor of operating in derivatives and trading businesses is that we mark everything to market.

Although these quotes reflect some of the more advanced practices in the market, they are indicative of where credit markets are headed. With more options for adjusting exposure, banks are increasingly focused on understanding the risks within their portfolios and how those risks can be brought into line with returns to produce better performance. This is the subject matter of portfolio management.

PORTFOLIO THEORY

Risk is uncertainty. Looking at an asset on a stand-alone basis, it has a probability of default, and if it defaults, a certain percentage of its value will be lost. If we multiply the probability of default times the loss we expect when default occurs, the result is the asset's expected loss. This is how much we would expect to lose on average over a long period of time on such an asset. This expected loss is not risk; it is what we expect to lose. The risk is the deviation of the actual loss from what we expected, that is, the unexpected.

Expected loss is not subject to diversification. A portfolio's expected loss is simply the average of the expected losses of the assets in the portfolio. However, risk does diversify. The portfolio's risk, or unexpected loss, is much less than the average of the risks of the individual assets. In other words, the loss outcomes associated with a portfolio are much less variable than those associated with individual assets in the portfolio.

The amount of diversification obtainable depends on the degree of relatedness of the risks of the assets in the portfolio. If any one of the assets being in default implies that it is very likely that many other assets will be in default, then there is a high degree of correlation and little diversification possible. On the other hand, if the default risks are relatively unrelated, then considerable risk reduction via diversification is possible.

Portfolio theory, developed by Harry Markowitz (1952) and William Sharpe (1964), is the mathematics by which portfolio risk and return are calculated. The main thrust of portfolio theory, however, is not simply to measure risk, but also to show how, by changing the composition of the portfolio, the return and risk characteristics of the portfolio can be improved. Because expected loss and expected return are simple averages, increasing portfolio return is simple. One merely has to hold assets with higher expected returns. However, changing risk is more complicated because of diversification. Holding less risky assets reduces risk, but holding too much of any single asset increases risk.

Portfolio theory concentrates on the expected return per unit of risk. The ratio of return to risk for a portfolio is called the Sharpe ratio (Sharpe 1994), and efficient portfolios are those with the highest attainable Sharpe ratios. Portfolio optimization refers to a variety of mathematical techniques for determining efficient portfolios.

The main problem in applying portfolio theory to debt or loan portfolios lies in determining the return, risk, and correlation measures that are needed as inputs. Of these, the most difficult are the correlation measures because it is very difficult to infer default correlations directly from historical data.

There have been a number of recent papers describing different portfolio approaches to credit risk; a partial listing is included in the additional reading section at the end of this chapter. We survey some of these approaches and we concentrate on explaining two approaches in detail, those of Altman and CreditMetrics (Gupton, Finger, and Bhatia, 1997; J. P. Morgan, Inc., 1997). In evaluating portfolio approaches, the main issue is how the input data are obtained, particularly the correlations.

Although these approaches are illustrative of the ones being used in banks today, they are not the only models in existence. For instance, Adamidou et al. (1993) present a portfolio optimization technique for fixed-income securities that uses a scenario approach. This technique is driven by a *total return* approach over a specific horizon with a stochastic interest rate path, and it does not consider default, credit drift, or correlation.[1] Table 19.1 shows some of the recently developed approaches. Before going into greater detail, we begin by presenting capsule summaries of the current approaches.

John Morgan suggests a way for a bank to derive the optimal industry composition of a portfolio by using the Markowitz optimization. He uses

---

[1]*Total return* implies a mark-to-market world, which is yet to come for banks and insurance companies.

Table 19.1 Alternative Portfolio Approaches

Technique	Author	Scope	Key assumption	Output
Optimization	Morgan (1989, 1993)	C & I loans	Industry average Zeta is a meaningful quantity for industry default rate. Probability of default correlation exists using this industry average.	Portfolio variance relative to the market efficient frontier
Optimization	Altman (1997a)	Individual high yield bonds	Historic correlations will prevail in the future.	Optimum portfolio weights
Econometric/ simulation	Chrinko and Guill (1991)	C&I loans: industry aggregations	Econometric estimates are reliable for forecasting.	Industry losses

(continued)

Table 19.1 (Continued)

Technique	Author	Scope	Key assumption	Output
Econometric/Monte Carlo	RAROC 2020 (Bankers Trust 1995)	All assets for which market prices may be observed. Includes derivatives. Does not include real estate loans, consumer loans, exotic assets.	Normal distribution of prices. Historical correlations will hold.	Risk-Adjusted Return on Capital, daily price volatility, Risk limit usage
Econometric/Monte Carlo	CreditRisk⁺ (1996)	Loans, derivatives, and bonds.	Volatility of default probabilities incorporates the effect of default correlations.	Expected loss, risk contribution, 99th percentile loss
Econometric/Monte Carlo	CreditMetrics (Gupton, Finger, and Bhatia 1997)	All assets for which market prices may be observed. Includes derivatives. Does not include real estate loans, consumer loans, exotic assets.	Econometric estimates of parameters will continue to prevail in the future. Equity correlations approximate asset value correlations which approximate credit quality correlations.	Portfolio value, standard deviation of value, 1% value, marginal risk
Econometric/Monte Carlo	Wilson (1997)	Applies to all assets, including real estate and consumer loans.	Econometric estimates of relationships will continue to prevail in the future. The number of firms in a segment is a proxy for portfolio diversification.	Portfolio value distribution

ZETA score averages to derive the variance-covariance matrix of default used in the analysis. With this approach, an institution with nonpublicly traded assets could arrive at a portfolio with the desired level of industry diversification.

Altman initially derives an optimum bond portfolio using two approaches: (1) mean-variance of returns and (2) unexpected losses. For a small set of publicly traded bonds, he builds a correlation matrix of quarterly returns and uses it to construct an efficient portfolio (the portfolio with the highest return for a given variance). In his second approach, because most debt instruments (e.g., bank loans) may not have a rating or total return data, he constructs a scale that links his Z-score model to the public bond rating. He then uses the concept of expected losses given an implied bond rating. He establishes the link to unexpected losses by mapping the score to public bond ratings. The unexpected losses are based on the standard deviation of annual expected losses for the bond ratings calculated at each quarterly interval. Thus, Altman's notion of unexpected loss for a rating is based on historic bond-market default experience and is equal to the standard deviation of the actual default rate experienced annually. The correlation matrix he uses is also based on a time series of annual unexpected loss values given the implied bond grades. Using these data, he constructs an efficient portfolio with the highest expected return (nominal return minus expected losses) and lowest unexpected loss.

Approaches that apply econometric and simulation methods such as CreditMetrics use transition probabilities derived from observed migration from one bond rating to any other rating (including a default state) to derive an expected value for a security over a one-year period. The unexpected loss is estimated by CreditMetrics using an approach similar to the one developed by KMV, namely, distribution of asset value returns. The risk drivers for CreditMetrics are asset values. Correlation of equity returns is used as proxy for asset value correlation. To derive obligor-obligor correlation, the model utilizes index correlations based on country and industry aggregate equite returns. Individual obligors are linked to the industry-country group by the level of participation in the respective segment. RAROC 2020, which is applicable to all types of publicly traded assets, uses correlations based on total returns. It can also handle derivative positions. RAROC 2020 is a simulation model that does not explicitly model default probability or rating migration. McKinsey's (Wilson 1997) approach is applicable to all classes of assets in a financial institution. It is also a simulation model that derives the value at risk after accounting for default losses. Macro-economic factors are the risk drivers for McKinsey's approach. Further details of these models are provided below.

MANAGING A LOAN PORTFOLIO AS
YOU WOULD MANAGE AN EQUITY FUND

In one of the early applications of portfolio theory to bank loans, John Morgan (1989) suggested that banks might use the data on shared national credits as a proxy for a market portfolio. Banks are required to report to the Office of the Comptroller of the Currency (OCC) data on any loans and credits of $20 million or more that are shared with other banks. This is the only publicly available data source on the industry exposure of banks at the two-digit standard industrial classification (SIC) code level.[2] By comparing the SIC composition of its portfolio with that of the Shared National Credits (SNC) data, a bank can assess how closely its holdings resemble the market portfolio, which, by definition, is diversified to the greatest extent feasible. A measure that captures the degree of comparison between an individual bank and the industry is defined as the variance

$$\sum_i \frac{(X_i - \bar{X}_i)^2}{N}$$

where X_i is percent of the bank portfolio in industry i and $\bar{X}_i$ is the same quantity for the industry in the market portfolio. However, beyond giving a measure of diversification, this approach does not provide a prescription for the right portfolio to hold based on an institution's own strategy and current portfolio.

In a subsequent study, Morgan and Gollinger (1993) attempted to do just that, using data from the Compustat database of financial statements to provide a ZETA score for the companies.[3] Morgan and Gollinger calculate an average ZETA score for the industry, which they use as a proxy for the industry risk. Using the historical quarterly ZETA score averages for the industries for the period 1980–1990, the authors calculate the covariance of the score averages between industries. Having obtained proxies for default and covariance of default, Morgan and Gollinger employ an industry return that is based on the Loan Pricing matrix. This matrix, provided by the Loan Pricing Corporation, contains data on posted prices of commercial and industrial (C&I) loans. Return on assets on a generic loan in each industry is then used as a proxy for the industry return. Using the ZETA score average for the industry risk, industry covariance of ZETA average scores, and industry return on assets, Morgan and Gollinger now solve the standard optimization problem of minimizing portfolio variance subject to the constraints that

- portfolio weights add up to 1;
- portfolio return is equal to or greater than the target return; and
- no industry accounts for more than 10 percent of the portfolio, based on the argument that an exposure greater than this would subject the bank to criticism by regulators for excessive concentration.

---

[2]The total reported in the database for May 1987 was $471 billion versus the total commercial and industrial (C&I) loans of $557 billion. According to the author, this database may be obtained from the Industry and Financial Analysis Division of the OCC.

[3]See Chapter 10 for a description of ZETA.

Formally this is written as the following:
Minimize

$$\sum_{i=1}^{N} X_i^2 \sigma_i^2 + \sum_{j>i}^{N} \sum_{i}^{N} X_i X_j \sigma_{ij}$$

Subject to

$$\sum_{i=1}^{N} X_i = 1$$

$$\sum_{i=1}^{N} X_i R_i - R_p \geq 0$$

$$0 \leq X_i \leq 0.10$$

where X_i are the portfolio weights, R_p is the portfolio target return, R_i is the return on assets from industry i, σ_i^2 is the variance of the ZETA score for industry i, and $\sigma_{i,j}^2$ is the covariance of the average ZETA score of industry i with industry j.

Morgan and Gollinger acknowledge that historical covariance may not be representative of the future. A questionable assumption in this methodology is the notion of using the industry average score to characterize industry risk. Even though ZETA has been demonstrated to be an adequate index of default risk, it does not follow that an industry average necessarily generates acceptable results. What is meant by "industry index" will vary, depending on the industry's structure (whether, for example, it contains a few dominant companies or a number of equally sized companies). The ZETA score distribution and the size distribution across industries may not be similar. The second concern follows from the first, which is that the forecast error in historic ZETA values will carry into the covariances as well. Despite these concerns, this study is interesting because it broke new ground in proposing a way to handle default correlations and is among published attempts to use the Markowitz model to calculate the efficient frontier for a commercial loan portfolio. Several subsequent models that use factor models to estimate covariance rely on industry membership as the dominant factor.

ALTMAN'S PORTFOLIO APPROACH

Altman's (1997a) approach focuses on the portfolio's Sharpe ratio, namely, the ratio of expected return to portfolio risk. The measurement of expected portfolio return is actually quite straightforward for fixed-income bond and loan assets. The investor is promised a fixed return (yield-to-maturity) over time and should subtract from this promised yield the expected losses from a default of the issuer. For certain measurement periods, the return will also be influenced by changes in interest rates, but it is assumed, for purposes of exposition, that these changes are random with an expected capital gain of zero.[4]

The expected annual return is therefore

$$EAR = YTM - EAL \qquad (1)$$

where EAR = expected annual return
　　　YTM = yield-to-maturity (or yield-to-worst)
　　　EAL = expected annual loss

The EAL is derived from Altman's prior work on bond mortality rates and losses (Altman 1988, 1989). Each bond in the portfolio is analyzed based on its initial (or existing)[5] rating, which implies an expected rate of default for up to 10 years after issuance. Tables 19.2 and 19.3 list cumulative mortality rates and cumulative mortality losses, respectively, covering the period 1971–1994.[6] Table 19.4 annualizes these mortality rates and losses. So, for example, a 10-year BB (S&P-rated) bond has an expected annual loss of 91 basis points per year. If the newly issued BB-rated bond has a promised yield of 9.0 percent with a spread of 2.0 percent over 7.0 percent risk-free U.S. Treasury bonds, then the expected return is 8.09 percent per year, or a risk premium of 109 basis points over the risk-free rate. If the measurement period were quarterly instead of annual, then the expected return would be about 2.025 percent per quarter. The expected return measure is focused primarily on credit risk changes and not on the yield curve.

The problem of measuring expected returns for commercial loans is a bit more complex. Because commercial loans usually do not have an explicit risk rating attached to them by the rating agencies,[7] the loan portfolio analyst must utilize a proxy measure. Altman advocates using the bank's own internal systems or commercially available systems,[8] as long as each of the ratings is linked with the public bond ratings, for example, those used by Altman, Moody's, or S&P in their cumulative default studies. Only by linking with the public rating systems can a bank utilize the credit migration, default, and recovery experience from a large database of debt securities.

---

[4]One way of handling the holding period problem is to optimize a portfolio of zero coupon securities, representing all the available maturities.

[5]The measurement of expected defaults for existing bonds compared to newly issued ones is basically the same for bonds with maturities of at least five years. Moody's and S&P publish data on existing baskets of bonds by rating without regard to age. Their results and Altman's essentially converge after year four (see Altman 1992).

[6]For updated data through 1995, see Altman and Kishore (1997) and Chapter 15 on mortality rates.

[7]This is changing, however. In 1997, Moody's had rated $200 billion in outstanding bank loans, representing 891 facilities and 494 borrowers.

[8]Systems such as ZETA Services (Hoboken, N.J.), KMV (San Francisco), Helix (Los Angeles) or the new neural network bond-rating replication process from Finance FX (Atlanta, Ga.) are available to assign ratings and/or expected defaults to all companies, regardless of whether they have public debt outstanding. Please see our earlier discussions of these models in Chapters 9–14.

Table 19.2 Mortality Rates by Original Rating: All Ratings of Corporate Bonds

Rating		1971–1994 Years after issuance									
		1	2	3	4	5	6	7	8	9	10
AAA	Yearly	0.00%	0.00%	0.00%	0.00%	0.08%	0.00%	0.00%	0.00%	0.00%	0.00%
	Cumulative	0.00%	0.00%	0.00%	0.00%	0.08%	0.08%	0.08%	0.08%	0.08%	0.08%
AA	Yearly	0.00%	0.05%	1.06%	0.09%	0.00%	0.00%	0.01%	0.00%	0.06%	0.04%
	Cumulative	0.00%	0.05%	1.11%	1.20%	1.20%	1.20%	1.20%	1.20%	1.26%	1.30%
A	Yearly	0.00%	0.19%	0.07%	0.21%	0.06%	0.06%	0.20%	0.19%	0.00%	0.00%
	Cumulative	0.00%	0.19%	0.26%	0.47%	0.53%	0.59%	0.78%	0.98%	0.98%	0.98%
BBB	Yearly	0.41%	0.25%	0.32%	0.55%	0.89%	0.39%	0.09%	0.00%	0.59%	0.23%
	Cumulative	0.41%	0.66%	0.97%	1.51%	2.39%	2.77%	2.86%	2.86%	3.44%	3.66%
BB	Yearly	0.50%	0.58%	4.15%	4.84%	1.13%	0.33%	0.94%	0.23%	0.64%	0.58%
	Cumulative	0.50%	1.08%	5.19%	9.78%	10.79%	11.26%	13.64%	13.87%	14.55%	15.21%
B	Yearly	1.59%	7.12%	6.80%	7.29%	3.40%	3.40%	2.80%	2.13%	2.83%	3.43%
	Cumulative	1.59%	8.60%	14.82%	21.02%	23.71%	28.21%	30.22%	31.70%	33.63%	35.91%
CCC	Yearly	8.32%	10.69%	18.53%	10.26%	9.18%	5.56%	2.49%	2.97%	12.28%	1.35%
	Cumulative	8.32%	18.13%	33.30%	40.14%	45.63%	48.66%	49.94%	51.42%	57.39%	58.31%

Note: Rated by S&P at issuance.

Source: Altman and Kishore (1997).

Table 19.3 Mortality Losses by Original Rating: All Ratings of Corporate Bonds

Rating		1971–1994 Years after issuance									
		1	2	3	4	5	6	7	8	9	10
AAA	Yearly	0.00%	0.00%	0.00%	0.00%	0.08%	0.00%	0.00%	0.00%	0.00%	0.00%
	Cumulative	0.00%	0.00%	0.00%	0.00%	0.08%	0.08%	0.08%	0.08%	0.08%	0.08%
AA	Yearly	0.00%	0.02%	0.21%	0.03%	0.00%	0.00%	0.01%	0.00%	0.04%	0.02%
	Cumulative	0.00%	0.02%	0.23%	0.26%	0.26%	0.26%	0.26%	0.26%	0.30%	0.32%
A	Yearly	0.00%	0.03%	0.02%	0.15%	0.06%	0.03%	0.11%	0.13%	0.00%	0.00%
	Cumulative	0.00%	0.03%	0.05%	0.20%	0.26%	0.29%	0.40%	0.52%	0.52%	0.52%
BBB	Yearly	0.27%	0.10%	0.21%	0.26%	0.36%	0.30%	0.06%	0.00%	0.41%	0.14%
	Cumulative	0.27%	0.37%	0.58%	0.84%	1.19%	1.49%	1.55%	1.55%	1.95%	2.08%
BB	Yearly	0.26%	0.26%	3.34%	2.14%	0.70%	0.33%	0.94%	0.23%	0.64%	0.58%
	Cumulative	0.26%	0.51%	3.84%	5.90%	6.56%	6.86%	7.74%	7.95%	8.54%	9.07%
B	Yearly	0.83%	5.12%	5.02%	5.95%	2.44%	3.93%	2.06%	1.64%	1.98%	1.59%
	Cumulative	0.83%	5.90%	10.63%	15.95%	18.00%	21.22%	22.84%	24.11%	25.61%	26.79%
CCC	Yearly	7.22%	8.87%	15.30%	6.82%	6.76%	3.29%	2.49%	0.91%	8.35%	1.25%
	Cumulative	7.22%	15.45%	28.39%	33.27%	37.78%	39.83%	41.33%	41.87%	47.47%	47.61%

Note: Rated by S&P at issuance.

Source: Altman and Kishore (1997).

Table 19.4 Annualized Cumulative Default Rates and Annualized Cumulative Mortality Loss Rates (1971–1994)

Annualized cumulative default rates (%)

Original rating/year	1	2	3	4	5	6	7	8	9	10
AAA	0.00	0.00	0.00	0.00	0.01	0.01	0.01	0.01	0.01	0.01
AA	0.00	0.00	0.27	0.27	0.22	0.19	0.16	0.14	0.13	0.12
A	0.00	0.05	0.08	0.11	0.10	0.09	0.10	0.11	0.10	0.09
BBB	0.04	0.27	0.26	0.33	0.37	0.40	0.44	0.39	0.35	0.37
BB	0.00	0.35	1.26	1.44	2.10	1.91	2.02	1.81	1.68	1.59
B	0.99	2.14	4.61	5.01	5.14	4.71	4.58	4.25	3.97	4.09
CCC	2.24	8.35	11.75	10.50	9.87	9.78	8.82	8.07	7.21	8.35

Annualized cumulative mortality loss rates

Original rating/year	1	2	3	4	5	6	7	8	9	10
AAA	0.00	0.00	0.00	0.00	0.00	0.00	0.00	0.00	0.00	0.00
AA	0.00	0.00	0.05	0.06	0.05	0.04	0.04	0.03	0.03	0.03
A	0.00	0.01	0.01	0.04	0.05	0.04	0.05	0.05	0.05	0.05
BBB	0.03	0.15	0.15	0.20	0.19	0.20	0.24	0.22	0.19	0.21
BB	0.00	0.20	0.86	1.01	1.22	1.11	1.09	0.98	0.94	0.91
B	0.42	1.23	3.29	3.64	3.81	3.46	3.36	3.12	2.91	2.89
CCC	1.51	7.19	9.79	8.69	7.82	7.57	6.87	6.13	7.06	7.25

Source: Calculation from data from Tables 19.2 and 19.3.

These statistics are more reliable because they are based on a large sample extending over three decades. Data integrity is also not a concern because these securities are tracked by the rating agencies from origination or from a specific pool of bonds at a point in time (*static pool* approach).

The expected portfolio return (R_p) is based on each asset's expected annual return, weighted by the proportion (X_i) of each loan/bond relative to the total portfolio.

$$R_p = \sum_{i=1}^{N} X_i \, EAR_i \qquad (2)$$

The classic portfolio variance framework given in equation 3 is appropriate when a short holding period (e.g., monthly or quarterly) is used, and historical data exists for the requisite period to calculate correlation of returns among the loans/bonds.

$$V_p = \sum_{i=1}^{N} \sum_{j=1}^{N} X_i X_j \sigma_i \sigma_j \rho_{ij} \qquad (3)$$

where V_p = variance (risk) of the portfolio
X_i = the proportion of the portfolio invested in bond issue i
σ_i = standard deviation of the return for the sample period for bond issue i
ρ_{ij} = correlation coefficient of the returns for bonds i and j.

Altman specifies the portfolio optimization problem, given the above measures, in the following standard way, subject to minimum holding constraints and minimum target return:

$$\text{Maximize } \eta = \frac{R_p}{\sqrt{V_p}}$$

$$\text{Subject to } \sum_{i=1}^{N} X_i = 1$$
$$R_p \geq \text{ target return}$$
$$X_i \leq \text{ individual bond investment limit}$$

The portfolio ratio η is the so-called Sharpe ratio, first introduced as a reward-to-variability ratio by Sharpe (1966), later popularized as the Sharpe index or Sharpe ratio by many (e.g., Reilly 1979; Morningstar 1993), and finally generalized and expanded to cover a broader range of applications by Sharpe (1994). Most often applied to measuring the performance of equity mutual funds, it captures the average differential return per unit of risk, where risk is measured as the standard deviation of returns.

With respect to the required correlation values, Altman suggests that meaningful correlations can be calculated if returns on all assets exist for a significant period of time—say, 20 quarters.

The solution to this objective function can be represented by the classic efficient frontier. Figure 19.1 shows an efficient frontier, in other words, maximization of expected return for given levels of risk, or minimization of risk

Figure 19.1   Portfolio Ratio Approach for Risk-Return Assessment

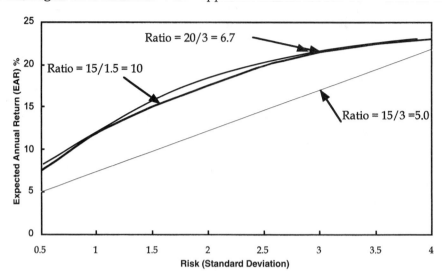

(variance of returns) for given levels of return, for a hypothetical high-yield bond portfolio. Note that an existing portfolio with an η of 5.0 can be improved to 6.67 holding risk constant or to 10.0 holding return constant.

Figure 19.2 shows an efficient frontier for a potential portfolio of 10 high-yield corporate bonds that is based on actual quarterly returns from the five-year period 1991–1995. The return-risk trade-off of the efficient portfolio is considerably better than that of the equally weighted portfolio. For example, the η goes from about 0.67 (2.0/3.0) to 1.14 (2.0/1.75) for the same expected return and to 1.0 (3.0/3.0) for the same variance of return. Note also the link between the risk-free rate at about 1.4 percent per quarter and the tangent line to the efficient frontier, indicating various proportions of risky versus risk-free fixed-income assets. The efficient frontier, calculated without any constraint as to the number of issues in the portfolio, involved investment in 8 of the possible 10 high-yield bonds. When we constrain the model so that no issue can be greater than 15 percent of the portfolio, the actual number of issues is either seven or eight, depending upon the different expected returns (see Table 19.5).

PORTFOLIO RISK AND EFFICIENT FRONTIERS USING UNEXPECTED LOSS

The reality of the bond and loan markets is that there simply is insufficient historical high-yield bond return and loan returns data to compute correlations directly from historical price data as was done above.

Altman analyzed the potential to use returns or durations in the high-yield corporate debt market. Out of almost 600 bond issues that existed as of year-end 1995, fewer than 40 had 20 quarters of historical data. He con-

Figure 19.2   Efficient Bond Portfolio, Using Returns (10 Issues)

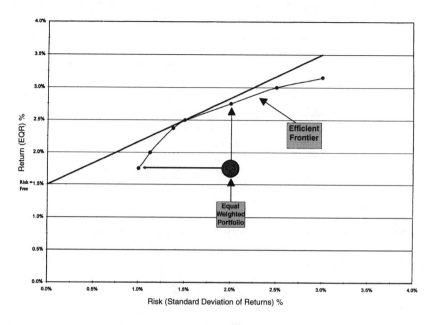

Table 19.5   Relative Weightings of Optimal Portfolios

Company ticker	Weights using Zeta scores	Weights using quarterly returns
AS	0.0000	0.1065
BOR	0.0776	0.0000
CGP	0.1500	0.1500
CQB	0.1500	0.1500
FA	0.0000	0.0000
IMD	0.1500	0.1351
RHR	0.1500	0.1209
STO	0.1500	0.1500
USG	0.1500	0.1500
WS	0.0224	0.0376

Note: For a return of 1.75 per quarter and a 15% maximum weighting constraint.

cluded that it is simply not appropriate to utilize the historical variance of return as the measure of risk for either the individual assets or the portfolio.

An alternative risk measure that is critical to most bank and fixed-income portfolio managers is unexpected loss from defaults. It may be recalled that promised yield was adjusted for expected losses. Therefore, unexpected loss represents the downside in the event that actual losses turn out to exceed expected losses.[9] The notion of unexpected losses is the cornerstone measure in the determination of appropriate reserves against bank capital in the risk-adjusted return on capital (RAROC) method adopted by many banks (see Chapter 18). One possible approach for determining unexpected losses is to utilize a variation of the Z-score model, called the Z'-score model (Altman 1993) to assign a bond-rating equivalent to each of the loans/bonds that could possibly enter the portfolio (see Table 19.6).[10] As noted earlier, these scores and rating equivalents can then be used to estimate expected losses over time. If we then observe the variation (e.g., standard deviation) around the expected losses, we have a procedure to estimate unexpected losses. For example, the expected loss on a BB-rated equivalent 10-year bond is 91 basis points per year (Table 19.4). The standard deviation around this expected value is computed to be 2.65 percent, or 265 basis points per year. The standard deviation is computed from the individual issuance years' results, which are independent observations that were used to calculate the cumulative mortality losses. For example, there are 24 one-year default losses for bonds issued in a certain rating class over the 1971–1995 period (i.e., bonds issued in 1971 that defaulted in 1972, bonds issued in 1972 that defaulted in 1973, etc.). In the same way, there are 23 two-year cumulative loss data points, 22 three-year loss observations, and so on, up to 15 ten-year observations.

The Z'-score risk-rating model, whose form is shown in equation 4, provides a straightforward way of classifying assets into risk categories. Table 19.5 gives a correspondence of Z'-score values to bond ratings. Other bond-rating models such as ZETA, KMV, or Finance FX could also have been used.

$$Z'\text{-score} = 6.56(X_1) + 3.26(X_2) + 6.72(X_3) + 1.05(X_4) + 3.25 \quad (4)$$

where X_1 = working capital/total assets
X_2 = retained earnings/total assets
X_3 = EBIT/total assets
X_4 = equity (book value)/total liabilities

---

[9]This idea is similar to the use of the semivariance measure of returns, whereby the analyst is concerned with only the return below the mean.

[10]The Z'-score model is a four-variable version of the Z-score approach. It was designed to reduce distortions in credit scores for firms in different industries or different countries. We have also found this model extremely effective in assessing the credit risk of corporate bonds in the emerging-market arena (see Altman, Hartzell, and Peck 1995).

Table 19.6 U.S. Bond Rating Equivalent, Based on Z″-Score

Average U.S. equivalent rating[a]	Sample Z″ score	Sample size
AAA	8.15	8
AA+	7.60	—
AA	7.30	18
AA−	7.00	15
A+	6.85	24
A	6.65	42
A−	6.40	38
BBB+	6.25	38
BBB	5.85	59
BBB−	5.65	52
BB+	5.25	34
BB	4.95	25
BB−	4.75	65
B+	4.50	78
B	4.15	115
B−	3.75	95
CCC+	3.20	23
CCC	2.50	10
CCC−	1.75	6
D	0.00	14

[a]Average is based on over 750 U.S. industrial corporates with rated debt outstanding; 1994 data.

Source: Author's computation based on data from Salomon Brothers, Inc., May 15, 1995, and In-depth Data Corporation.

PORTFOLIO RISK USING UNEXPECTED LOSSES

The formula for Altman's portfolio risk measure is given in equation (5).

$$UAL_p = \sqrt{\sum_{i=1}^{N} \sum_{j=1}^{N} X_i X_j \sigma_i \sigma_j \rho_{ij}} \qquad (5)$$

The measure UAL_p is the portfolio unexpected loss, consisting of measures of individual asset unexpected losses (σ_i, σ_j) and the correlation ($\rho_{i,j}$) of unexpected losses over the sample measurement period. The individual asset unexpected losses are based on the standard deviation of annual expected losses for the bond rating equivalents calculated at each quarterly interval, in contrast to the previous definition based on historical return data.[11] All

---

[11]Altman recognized that the measure of covariance is potentially biased in two ways. First, estimates of individual firms' debt unexpected losses are derived from empirical data on bonds

that is necessary is that the issuing firm (or borrower) was operating for the entire sample period (e.g., five years) and had quarterly financial statements. The actual bonds/loans did not have to be outstanding in the period, as is necessary when returns and variance of returns are used. Since the actual bond/loan may not have been outstanding during the entire measurement period, leverage measures will likely also vary over time. Still, it is expected that most of the covariance of default risk between firms will be captured.

EMPIRICAL RESULTS

A portfolio optimizer program[12] was applied to the same 10-bond portfolio analyzed earlier, but this time with the Z'-score bond-rating equivalents and their associated expected and unexpected losses instead of returns. Figure 19.3 shows the efficient frontier compared to an equal-weighted portfolio.

---

from a given bond-rating class and as such will probably understate the risk of loss from individual firm defaults. On the other hand, the covariance of default losses between two firms' debt is based on the joint probability of both defaulting at the same time. If the default decision of each firm is viewed as 0,1, that is, as a binomial distribution, then the appropriate covariance or correlation should be calculated from a joint density function of two underlying binomial distributions. Altman's measure, however, assumes a normal density function for returns, and thus returns are jointly, normally distributed for each firm, which could result in a higher aggregate measure of portfolio risk. As such, the two biases neutralize each other to some extent, although it is difficult to assess the relative magnitude of each.

[12]Using a double precision, linear constrained optimization program (DLCONG).

Figure 19.3　Efficient High-Yield Bond Portfolio, Using Z'' Scores 10 Issues

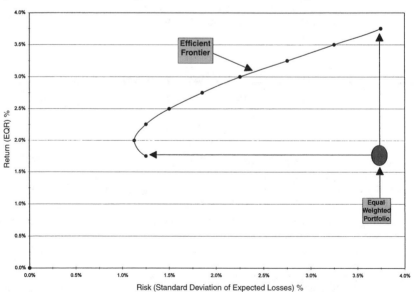

As observed earlier, the efficient frontier indicates considerably improved values of η. For example, the return:risk ratio of just above 0.50 for the equal-weighted 10-bond portfolio can be improved to 1.60 (2.00/1.25) at the 2.00 percent quarterly return level and to about 1.00 for the same risk (3.75 percent) level.

Table 19.5 shows the portfolio weights for the efficient frontier portfolio using both returns and risk (unexpected losses) when the individual weights are constrained at a maximum of 15 percent of the portfolio. This is for the 1.75 percent quarterly expected return. Note that both portfolios utilize 8 of the 10 bonds and very similar weightings. Indeed, seven of the eight bonds appear in both portfolios. These results are comforting in that the unexpected loss derived from the Z'-score model as an alternative risk measure appears to be consistent with the approach based on actual ratings. Test results from this small sample are encouraging and indicate that this type of portfolio approach is potentially quite feasible for fixed-income assets. It should be noted that these are preliminary findings. Subsequent conceptual refinements and empirical tests with larger samples are necessary to gain experience and confidence with this portfolio technique for fixed-income assets (including loans).

CREDITMETRICS

CreditMetrics (Gupton, Finger, and Bhatia 1997) is a set of analytical methods and databases to measure portfolio value and risk released by J. P. Morgan in April 1997. The objective of CreditMetrics is to provide a process for estimating the *value distribution* of any portfolio of assets subject to changes in credit quality (including default). The value distribution is summarized by a mean, standard deviation, percentile level, and marginal risk. Credit-Metrics is described in a 200-page document; what follows is an overview based upon that document.

The centerpiece of CreditMetrics is the notion that asset or portfolio value should be viewed not just in terms of the likelihood of default but also in terms of changes in credit quality over time, of which default is just a special case (or, to use a Markovian term employed by CreditMetrics, an "absorbing state" [p. 75]).[13] This approach is not new. Altman and Kao (1991) and Altman (1997b), for example, examined ratings migration over time. Transition probability matrices have been used to look at a portfolio's credit profile as expressed in delinquency levels. What is new, however, is that CreditMetrics is the first attempt to consider the problem of credit quality drift, default, recovery, and default/rating correlation in a consistent and comprehensive framework. Of particular note is CreditMetrics's approach for handling correlation of credit quality, which is discussed in detail later.

A schematic of the CreditMetrics calculation process appears in Figure 19.4. The left-hand side of the diagram represents the determination of ex-

---

[13]Strictly speaking, default is not an absorbing state because a firm can return to a functioning state even after default.

Figure 19.4   CreditMetrics™ Schematic

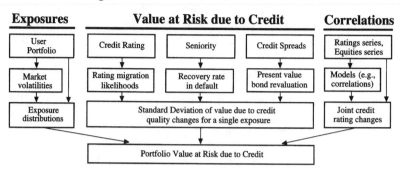

Source: J. P. Morgan CreditMetrics™ Technical Document, April 1995.

posures, that is, the amounts actually at risk should a default occur. The middle section represents the determination of the stand-alone risks per dollar of exposure. The right-hand side of the diagram represents the determination of correlations. The bottom box of the diagram represents the overall portfolio risk calculation, which is arrived at by combining the exposure, stand-alone risk, and correlation values. The following exposition will concentrate on the stand-alone risk and correlation parts of this process. Exposure determination is primarily an issue with respect to off-balance-sheet bank assets.

The initial portfolio is defined in terms of individual assets with the necessary information to project future contractual cash flows. One needs to know, for example, the loan balance, its amortization schedule, and the coupon rate. A bond rating is associated with each asset. If there is no rating, some other grouping may be used, as long as the user has the data to express the probability of default and the probability of migration to other "ratings" in the time interval over which the analysis is performed. In what follows, we will assume that ratings are the grading method chosen.

Beginning from its initial rating, an asset may end up at the horizon of the analysis in one of eight future states, each state representing a bond rating to which it may migrate. The state to which an asset can migrate is characterized by a transition probability. A sample transition matrix for the seven bond-rating grades is shown in Table 19.7.

To explain this table, consider a BBB bond. It has a 0.02 percent probability of being upgraded to an AAA bond, 0.33 percent probability of being upgraded to AA, and so forth. The probability of continuing to be rated BBB is 86.93 percent. Each of the future states has a different credit spread, as represented by a zero coupon forward-yield curve, which is used to discount the promised cash flows to a present value. The value of the bond in each state is determined by discounting its cash flows at the appropriate zero coupon rate. Table 19.8 shows the forward zero coupon rates for various rating grades.[14]

---

[14]The zero coupon rate is used to discount the cash flows because this rate does not have a reinvestment component, and each promised cash flow from the bond may be treated as a zero

Table 19.7   One-year Transition Matrix (%)

| Initial Rating | Rating at year-end (%) | | | | | | | |
	AAA	AA	A	BBB	BB	B	CCC	Default
AAA	90.81	8.33	0.68	0.06	0.12	0	0	0
AA	0.70	90.65	7.79	0.64	0.06	0.14	0.02	0
A	0.09	2.27	91.05	5.52	0.74	0.26	0.01	0.06
BBB	0.02	0.33	5.95	86.93	5.30	1.17	0.12	0.18
BB	0.03	0.14	0.67	7.73	80.53	8.84	1.00	1.06
B	0	0.11	0.24	0.43	6.48	83.46	4.07	5.20
CCC	0.22	0	0.22	1.30	2.38	11.24	64.86	19.79

Source: J. P. Morgan CreditMetrics™ Technical Document, April 1995.

Table 19.8   Example One-year Forward Zero Curves by Credit Rating Category (%)

Category	Year 1	Year 2	Year 3	Year 4
AAA	3.60	4.17	4.73	5.12
AA	3.65	4.22	4.78	5.17
A	3.72	4.32	4.93	5.32
BBB	4.10	4.67	5.25	5.63
BB	5.55	6.02	6.78	7.27
B	6.05	7.02	8.03	8.52
CCC	15.05	15.02	14.03	13.52

Source: J. P. Morgan CreditMetrics™ Technical Document, April 1995.

If the bond defaults, there is no longer any promised cash flow. Instead there are recoveries, which vary by the seniority of the asset. Because the recoveries consist of range rather than point estimates, an adjustment is made to the standard deviation of the value of the asset. The expected value of the asset is unchanged by the fact that recoveries are random.[15] The recovery estimates used to project cash flows upon default are shown in Table 19.9.

Given the present value of the asset in the future states and the probabilities of attaining these states, CreditMetrics calculates the expected value of the asset. To describe the volatility of the value, CreditMetrics uses two alternative measurements. The first is the standard deviation. This measure is sometimes unsatisfactory when the variable is asymmetrically distributed,

---

coupon security. Note that the Treasury yield curve expresses the interest rates on a yield to maturity basis with semiannual coupon payments and a balloon payment for principal. To derive the value of a BBB bond with a 6 percent coupon and five-year maturity, the annual cash flows of $6, $6, $6, $6, and $106 by the zero coupon rate of 0, 4.10, 4.67, discounting by 0, 1, 2, 3 and 4 years 5.25, and 5.63, respectively, results in the value of $107.55.

[15] Although this is the assumption made in CreditMetrics, it may not be true if recoveries are jointly distributed with the rating. Altman and Kishore (1996), however, found that the rating, when adjusted for seniority, has no effect on recoveries.

Table 19.9   Recovery Rates by Seniority Class (% of face value, i.e., "par")

Seniority Class	Mean (%)	Standard Deviation (%)
Senior Secured	53.80	26.86
Senior Unsecured	51.13	25.45
Senior Subordinated	38.52	23.81
Subordinated	32.74	20.18
Junior Subordinated	17.09	10.90

Source: J. P. Morgan CreditMetrics™ Technical Document, April 1995.

which is the case for debt securities. An alternative measure of volatility that captures its essence is the *1 percent value*—the value of the distribution corresponding to a state with a transition probability of 1 percent.[16]

Table 19.10 shows the derivation of the probability distribution of future values of a BBB-rated bond. The expected value of the bond is $107.09, and its standard deviation is $2.99. Looking at the second data column, at the 1 percent probability level the value of the bond corresponds to a B and is 98.10 (see column 3). The 1 percentile value is thus the mean value minus 98.10, that is, $107.09 - 98.10 = 8.99.

---

[16]This is similar to the value-at-risk (VAR) concept. The major difference being that the value at risk is derived from actual observed market prices. Also, VAR does not explicitly deal with defaults. In VAR, all the ramifications of credit migration and default are handled through the observed, realized return. Another difference is that VAR has an overnight horizon, whereas CreditMetrics uses a one-year horizon. See J. P. Morgan (1997).

Table 19.10   Calculating Volatility in Value due to Credit Quality Changes

Year-end rating	Probability of state (%)	New bond value plus coupon ($)	Probability weighted value ($)	Difference of value from mean ($)	Probability weighted difference squared
AAA	0.02	109.37	0.02	2.28	0.0010
AA	0.33	109.19	0.36	2.10	0.0146
A	5.95	108.66	6.47	1.57	0.1474
BBB	86.93	107.55	93.49	0.46	0.1853
BB	5.30	102.02	5.41	(5.06)	1.3592
B	1.17	98.10	1.15	(8.99)	0.9446
CCC	0.12	83.64	1.10	(23.45)	0.6598
Default	0.18	51.13	0.09	(55.96)	5.6358
		Mean =	$107.09	Variance =	8.9477
				Standard deviation =	$2.99

Source: J. P. Morgan CreditMetrics™ Technical Document, April 1995.

To summarize the stand-alone risk determination, CreditMetrics derives the probability distribution of future values on the basis of the promised cash flows, recovery rate, seniority, the probabilities of the future states, and the rating-specific forward-zero curves. The value of the asset pursuant to credit migration is summarized by the transition probability-weighted expected value, and its risk by either its standard deviation or its 1 percent value. Note that so far, no assumptions have been made about credit quality correlations. The analysis is on a stand-alone basis.

TREATMENT OF CREDIT RISK CORRELATION

The next question is how to incorporate the effect of the correlation between the credit quality of the assets in the portfolio.

The CreditMetrics approach is based on the proposition that credit quality transition probabilities are best captured through asset value correlations. This approach, which is based on KMV, assumes that firm's asset value is the variable that drives not only the default likelihoods but also its rating changes.

The asset value distribution represents the range and likelihood of future market values for the borrowing firm. In essence, it summarizes the underlying business risk of the borrower. Under the assumption that this distribution is normal (i.e., bell-shaped), the relationship between the business risks of two different borrowers can be characterized by the correlation between their future market values. Two businesses are related if they both tend to do well at the same time, in other words, if they have positively correlated asset values. The strength of the relationship is reflected by the size of the correlation.

The correlation between the future debt values of these two borrowers can be deduced from the underlying asset correlation between their businesses. Debt values are assigned to asset value outcomes for each borrower, resulting in a specification of the joint debt value distribution. The debt value correlation can then be calculated from this joint distribution.

The following is a description of the debt correlation measurement process. There is assumed to be a future asset value at which the borrower will default. If we imagine the distribution centered at the current value of the firm, with a known variance, then the default point can be inferred by knowing the probability of default from the rating transition matrix.

In fact, we can determine threshold values not just for default, but for any possible rating change because we know the probability for each rating change from the transition matrix. Thus, we can divide the area under the asset value distribution into regions, each with the appropriate probability (Figure 19.5).

An important but more subtle point is that it is irrelevant for the calculation of correlation as to exactly what the mean and standard deviation of the asset value distribution are. In calculating correlation, first one eliminates the effect of the mean, and then one standardizes the variance to one. Thus, we could just as well determine the threshold values using a standard normal distribution because it is only the probabilities that matter.

Figure 19.5   Distribution of Asset Returns with Rating Change Thresholds

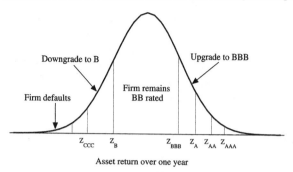

Asset return over one year

Source: J. P. Morgan CreditMetrics™ Technical Document, April 1995.

The threshold values of an A-rated bond, given transition probabilities, are as shown in Table 19.11.

The probability of transition from A to one of the eight other states is taken from actual historical data. The threshold probability according to the asset value model is in the third column. Here is how the values are interpreted. Given the return (μ and σ) for an A-rated obligor, a normalized future firm asset value greater than 1.98 σ will cause an upgrade from A to AA. A normalized future firm asset value of less than -1.51 σ will cause a downgrade from A to BBB.

Thus the rating probabilities have been mapped to the firm's (normalized) future asset values. If we now know the correlation of the asset values, s, between two borrowers, then we can determine the joint distribution of possible future ratings. Technically this is done by integrating the bivariate normal distribution function with the given asset correlation between the upper and lower threshold values for each of the respective rating classes. Assuming a correlation coefficient of 20 percent, the joint distribution of

Table 19.11   Transition Probabilities and Asset Return Thresholds for A Rating

Rating	Probability	Threshold	Value
AAA	0.09%		
AA	2.27%	Z_{AA}	3.12σ
A	91.05%	Z_A	1.98σ
BBB	5.52%	Z_{BBB}	-1.51σ
BB	0.74%	Z_{BB}	-2.30σ
B	0.26%	Z_B	-2.72σ
CCC	0.01%	Z_{CCC}	-3.19σ
Default	0.06%	Z_{Def}	-3.24σ

Source: J. P. Morgan CreditMetrics™ Technical Document, April 1995.

possible future ratings for a pair of obligors currently rated BB and A is shown in Table 19.12. The correlation coefficient of the firms' future asset values drives the calculations.

As previously described, a debt value can be associated with each possible future rating grade for each of the firms, as was done for the stand-alone risk calculations. Thus, a pair of debt values can be associated with each of the cells in Table 19.12. Given that we now know the probabilities for each cell from the previous calculation, we can calculate the correlation between the debt values.

This brings up a key question: How does one derive the asset correlations between two firms? CreditMetrics uses the correlation between equity returns as a proxy for the correlation of asset returns. It uses industry indexes in particular countries to construct a matrix of correlations between the industries. The individual obligors in the portfolio are mapped by industry participation. Using these weights and the industry correlations, the equity correlation between obligors is obtained. The equity correlation is then used as a proxy for the asset value correlation.

To recap, the probability distribution of credit quality migration is obtained by considering the correlation of the firm's future asset values. Assuming equity returns as a proxy for asset value changes, the equity return correlations are estimated based on industry return correlations, country, and company size. CreditMetrics provides users with a spreadsheet of industry returns and correlations.

The exposure amounts, stand-alone risks, and debt value correlations are used to calculate the portfolio's unexpected loss, using the same portfolio equations described earlier in the Altman portfolio model. This characterizes the total risk of the portfolio.

The total risk of the portfolio can also be characterized by means of a simulation approach. In this approach, the indexes used to determine the asset value correlations are simulated, giving rise to a simulated set of firm asset values for all the borrowers in the portfolio. Each asset value implies

Table 19.12   Joint Rating Change Probabilities for a Tuple of BB and A Rated Obligors (%)

Rating of first company	Rating of second company								
	AAA	AA	A	BBB	BB	B	CCC	Def	Total
AAA	0.00	0.00	0.03	0.00	0.00	0.00	0.00	0.00	0.03
AA	0.00	0.01	0.13	0.00	0.00	0.00	0.00	0.00	0.14
A	0.00	0.04	0.61	0.01	0.00	0.00	0.00	0.00	0.67
BBB	0.02	0.35	7.10	0.20	0.02	0.01	0.00	0.00	7.69
BB	0.07	1.79	73.65	4.24	0.56	0.18	0.01	0.04	80.53
B	0.00	0.08	7.80	0.79	0.13	0.05	0.00	0.01	8.87
CCC	0.00	0.01	0.85	0.11	0.02	0.01	0.00	0.00	1.00
Def	0.00	0.01	0.90	0.13	0.02	0.01	0.00	0.00	1.07
Total	0.09	2.29	91.06	5.48	0.75	0.26	0.01	0.06	100

Source: J. P. Morgan CreditMetrics™ Technical Document, April 1995.

a future debt rating, and thus a future debt value for each instrument in the portfolio, and in turn a future portfolio value. The process is repeated thousands of times, and the results summarized in a frequency distribution of portfolio value outcomes. This can then be used to determine the likelihood of extreme outcomes, such as the 1 percent probability point.

CreditMetrics should be viewed fundamentally as an attempt by a key industry participant to address some of the long-standing problems in pricing and unbundling credit risk. By shifting the focus from default to changes in credit quality and the consequent changes in value as the basis for action, CreditMetrics will provoke (and already has) serious thought on what to do about asset concentration. Analytics such as CreditMetrics will hopefully lead to rational ways of measuring changes in value, and for their proponents, opportunities for providing innovative products such as credit derivatives that will add liquidity to the market. As the liquidity in the credit market increases, market participants will have the ability to track market-determined as opposed to model-determined credit pricing.

CREDITMETRICS IMPLEMENTATION: CREDITMANAGER

The methodology in CreditMetrics is implemented in a Microsoft Windows 95– or NT–based software product named CreditManager by J. P. Morgan Securities.

The software produces reports that quantify the credit value-at-risk, broken down by country, industry, maturity, and rating. The asset types modeled by CreditManager are bonds, commitments to lend, standby letters of credit, loans, market-driven instruments (swaps, caps, etc.), and trade receivables. The user constructs an exposure profile of the portfolio by specifying the following components for every asset in it:

- Asset type
- Currency
- Maturity
- Spread curve
- Rate terms
- Seniority
- Recovery rate
- Recovery rate standard deviation
- Exposure amount

The input items vary slightly for individual asset type. For example, for loan commitments, the total drawdown, current drawdown, and expected drawdown are specified.

CreditManager computes each asset's volatility caused by possible upgrades, downgrades, and defaults. The asset's expected value and volatility of value are estimated with a transition matrix. The transition matrix selected should correspond to the risk-rating system used for the assets (Moody's 8-state, Standard & Poor's 8-state, Moody's 18-state or custom). The yield curve by currency and the spread curve by rating is maintained and updated by the system. The system uses a horizon of one year. Default recovery rates may be user specified or based on one of four recovery studies (e.g., Altman and Kishore 1997). Foreign exchange rates are user specified to convert all calculated values to the base currency used for reporting.

Obligor-specific volatility (as a percent) is specified by the user, which defines the extent to which a company's volatility is correlated with the market. The total asset size determines how much the volatility is related to the index and is provided by the CreditManager as default value. The weights of country and industry are specified by the user. These weights will be used along with the respective equity indexes to derive the distribution of asset value. For each obligor the degree to which its asset value is related to equity market indexes is specified through weights in up to three countries and three industries. Suggested weights are provided by fitting the historic stock returns to the returns of equity indexed. Alternatively, the user may purchase data from Dow Jones that produces weights for a firm based on a fundamental analysis of its financial statements. J. P. Morgan Securities provides a time series that is used to derive the correlations between different market indexes used in estimating asset value correlations.

The correlation between each of the events (upgrade, downgrade, or default) is assessed by means of a equity returns and is used to combine the individual volatilities to arrive at the aggregate volatility of value for the portfolio. Either a constant correlation may be used, or one based on the proprietary method developed by J. P. Morgan. The obligor correlation matrix is created by generating an asset value profile based on simulation and calculating the pairwise correlations based on the resulting sets of firm values.

The results of the Monte Carlo simulation are current value by industry and country, fifth percentile loss amount, and the marginal risk by risk category for the portfolio.

By developing an interface with its own asset information database, CreditManager can quickly assess the volatility of value based on the baseline exposure, transition matrix, recovery rates, yield and spread curves, and the country plus industry weights.

OTHER SCENARIO-BASED APPROACHES

Portfolio approaches that use the correlation matrix have been criticized because of difficulties related to the size and stability of the matrix. Also, historical correlation coefficients are unconditional in that they are calculated without controlling for key exogenous variables that are thought to influence market prices. For example, what is the impact of increasing interest rates on the risk profile of a portfolio? Markowitz and Perold (1981) suggested using a scenario approach to optimize the portfolio. Rather than developing an explicit correlation, this approach relates the return on the security to each scenario in a set of scenarios (for example, optimistic, pessimistic, and likely), and each is constructed from an event tree. Every scenario considered encompasses a set of internally consistent assumptions about the state of the economy and returns earned. The scenarios may be assigned a probability of outcome, and an optimal portfolio can be constructed to maximize expected value of return. Bennett (1984) also proposed a scenario approach.

Conceptually, all simplifications of portfolio models share the common goal of expressing the relationship between the security return in a compact manner in terms of a set of external (exogenous) variables so that two goals are met. First, a portfolio may be constructed to be positioned most favorably, given a set of assumptions about the future.[17] Second, the portfolio may be stress tested to analyze the impact of low-likelihood, high-severity events. One can use the capital asset pricing model (CAPM) or the arbitrage pricing model (APT) to relate the portfolio return to the market return. The CAPM is designed to do just this. The arbitrage pricing theory utilizes a set of key factors that are expected to influence security returns. On a rudimentary level, the single index and multi-index models are the practitioner's equivalent of the CAPM and APT approaches. Indeed, these index models existed even before the CAPM and APT were articulated (see for example, King 1966).[18]

One of the early applications of scenario approaches to bank portfolio management was proposed by Bennett (1984). He suggested that to manage the bank's total portfolio, it should stratify its assets in terms of risk ratings. After identifying important factors that can impact the change in credit quality, the bank should assess the portfolio impact by stressing the factors. His approach is illustrated in Table 19.13.

The current portfolio (along with potential customers to be added) is considered on a loan-by-loan basis relative to various external variables (factors). The response of the loan's risk rating to the factor is expressed as a rise or fall in rating. This is referred to as rating drift. A scenario is a collection of selected factors. The total rating impact on an asset for a scenario is a sum of the impact of individual factors. Correlations can be then added for assessing the probability of changes in ratings.

Bennett advocates setting loan pricing to reflect the borrower's contribution to portfolio risk. The methods proposed by him are heuristic rather than empirical. Even so, this paper shows that bank portfolio concentration and scenario approaches to manage it have been a subject of serious study for many years. Indeed, even this simplified approach will serve a bank management well today by providing a basic understanding of portfolio risks and framing the right questions for which answers are needed.

---

[17]The positioning of the portfolio would include decisions to sell selected assets in the portfolio, add other assets, and neutralize certain risk elements in the portfolio through various hedging mechanisms.

[18]A single index model assumes that stocks move together only because of a common co-movement with the market. Multi-index models assume that there are nonmarket factors such as economic factors or structural groups that account for common movement in stock prices beyond that accounted for by the single-index model. These models have evolved to respond to the need for forecasting security returns. See Elton and Gruber (1981).

Table 19.13   Current Portfolio and Possible Impacts

				Potential impacts on ratings			
	Current rating (1 to 5; 5 best)	Current exposure ($000)	Factor 1 ($10 drop in oil prices)	Factor 2 (2% slower OECD economic growth)	Factor 3 (25% dollar depreciation)	Scenario A: (factors 1 and 2)	Scenario B: (factors 1, 2 and 3)
Company 1	4	10	0	0	−1	0	−1
Company 2	5	20	0	−1	0	−1	−1
Company 3	5	30	−1	−1	0	−2	−2
Company 4	3	10	+1	0	+1	+1	+2
Company 5	2	100	+1	0	+1	+1	+2
Company 6	5	60	0	−1	0	−1	−1
Company 7	3	200	−2	−2	+2	−2	−2
Bank 1	4	150	0	−1	+1	−1	0
Bank 2	5	225	0	0	0	0	0
Bank 3	4	25	−1	0	0	−1	−1
Bank 4	5	30	0	0	−1	0	−1
Bank 5	2	10	+1	0	0	+1	+1
Government 1	5	20	−2	0	0	−2	−2
Government 2	2	50	−1	0	+2	−1	+1
Government 3	5	60	0	−1	0	−1	−1
Potential Customer 1	2	—	+2	0	+1	+2	+3
Potential Customer 2	4	—	−1	−1	0	−2	−2

Source: Reprinted from *Journal of Banking and Finance*, Vol. 8, Bennett, "Applying Portfolio Theory to Global Bank Lending", pp. 153–169, 1984, with permission of Elsevier Science.

CHIRINKO AND GUILL'S MODEL

Chirinko and Guill (1991) consider the credit risk problem from the view of macroeconomic and industry variables. A key ingredient in their study is the availability of the Shared National Credits Database (which was mentioned in the discussion of the Morgan and Gollinger study earlier in this chapter). This database provides the industry group associated with a given exposure. The authors use a two-step process to understand industry-specific credit losses by a depository institution. In the first step, loan losses in an industry are econometrically linked to industry revenues, industry cost, the federal funds rate, and gross national product. In the second step, exogenous variables are generated through a large-scale nonlinear econometric model operated by DRI/McGraw-Hill, based on assumptions about exchange rates, fiscal policy, monetary policy, and primary commodity prices. These variables are provided to the results from step one, along with the probability of outcomes.

Chirinko and Guill's study is one of the early attempts to address portfolio concentration and quantify default correlation. By looking at loan losses at the industry level, the authors were able to detect covariance of failure among industry groups.

CREDITRISK$^+$

The CreditRisk$^+$ framework, introduced by Credit Suisse Financial Products (CSFP), is a statistical model of credit default risk employing the default rate as a continuous random variable. It incorporates the volatility of default rates to capture the uncertainty in the level of default rates.

This approach is conceptually similar to the term structure models of the yield curve used in modeling market risk. Pairwise correlation of defaults is handled through dividing the portfolio into homogeneous sectors within which a collection of obligors is presumed to share the same systematic risk factor. Each obligor may be apportioned to more than one sector. Country of domicile is cited as one example of a sector.

The number of default events over a specified time horizon is approximated by a Poisson distribution. The volatility of default rate is incorporated into the Poisson model (whose standard deviation is equal to the square root of the average number of defaults) by dividing the exposure into sectors, each of which is independent of other sectors. The basic premise in CreditRisk$^+$ is that it is possible to obtain a portfolio's risk exposure from the following input data:

- Exposure from individual assets
- Mean default rate
- Standard deviation of the default rate
- The sectors and respective loss percentiles over which each exposure is distributed

The technical document (CSFP 1996) provides a theoretical derivation of the relationships that lead from the default probability and recoveries to the loss distribution estimates.

McKinsey & Co.–Wilson Model

Wilson (1997) has described a recent attempt to analyze portfolio risk and return through econometrics and Monte Carlo simulation. He recognizes many of the realities faced by financial institutions that are often omitted in portfolio solutions. The following are among the refinements his approach offers:

- It explicitly models actual, discrete loss distribution dependent on the number and size of credits in a subportfolio.
- Rather than being based passively and unconditionally on historic averages, the loss distributions are conditional on the state of the economy.
- The losses are measured on a mark-to-market basis both for exposures that may be liquidated and for those that cannot be.
- The approach is applicable to single obligors as well as to collections of obligors such as retail portfolios.
- The approach captures the uncertainty regarding recovery rates as well as losses arising from country risk.

On the basis of historic macroeconomic variables and an average default-rate time series, this approach builds a multifactor model for different country and industry segments. Sample default rate estimates for certain countries are as shown in Table 19.14.

This is a top-down approach in that the model starts with a probabilistic assumption about the state of the world, which is then passed on to a segment model that calculates the conditional probability of default for each customer segment (subportfolio). In predicting defaults and default correlations, the model assumes no further information other than country, industry, rating, and state of the economy. Portfolio diversification within a segment is characterized by the number of companies in the segment. The larger the number of companies, the lower the implied losses for the segment index. Retail portfolios are handled as diversified index portfolios. Default losses are projected based on marginal default probabilities over time and discounted to the present. Liquid positions are marked to market. The output of the simulation is the portfolio loss/gain distribution—a plot of the gain or loss against the probability.

Wilson notes in conclusion that a strong analytic foundation should precede any portfolio management strategy. Portfolio management begins when senior management asks some basic and intuitive questions about an institution's mix of assets and economic prognosis. "The sign of a successful credit portfolio risk management process is therefore not the number of Greek letters used; but rather whether or not your management asks, and

Table 19.14 Default Rate Prediction Equation Coefficients (t statistic in parentheses)

Country	Constant	Unemployment	GDP growth	Gov. disbursements	Long-term interest rates	Exchange rates	Gross savings	R²
Germany	8.41** (30.66)	-0.074** (4.87)	-0.063** (7.74)	0.025** (2.15)	—	—	—	95.7
France	5.37** (29.92)	-0.148** (5.41)	—	—	0.047** (2.36)	0.080** (2.26)	—	89.7
Spain	3.87** (35.43)	-0.065** (17.23)	—	0.027** (9.47)	0.013** (3.25)	—	—	77.5
U.K.	-0.11 (0.12)	-0.12** (4.35)	—	0.08** (3.80)	—	—	0.15** (5.38)	65.5
U.S.	5.48** (32.2)	-0.001 (0.04)	0.03 (1.84)	—	-0.165** (11.28)	—	—	82.6

** Significant at the 95% level.
Source: Wilson (1997).

answers these questions" (Wilson 1997a, 2:14). He points out that any portfolio strategy should be tailored to the specific needs of the institution.

Concluding Remarks

The Modeling Approach and Model Risk

The modeling framework embodies a number of assumptions about the future that may or may not have been tested. Validation of the models to actual experience is therefore critical in minimizing model risk (see Chapter 14 on this point). In practice, it may be impossible to validate certain aspects of models within a reasonable time frame, such as the actual likelihood of extreme losses. The next best approach is to focus on the critical aspects of the model from the standpoint of the specific user, be it input data or modeling assumption.

The risk emphasis differs from one player to the next. A financial guarantor will perhaps be more interested in understanding the structural aspects of the credit risk (covenant triggers, first loss level, issuer financial strength, etc.) and the *current* rating distribution of the insured assets rather than understanding rating migration—even though the latter may be important to the issuer who uses the services of the guarantor. In looking at a portfolio, a consumer bank, on the other hand, would be less concerned about concentration risk and more concerned about systemic risks such as a nationwide recession or changes in the bankruptcy laws. An insurance company will want to model its strategy to take advantage of regulatory arbitrage opportunities (e.g., differing capital charges for rated versus unrated securities), and the pricing/term/seniority/first-loss protection/diversification features implicit in asset-backed securities such as credit card receivables, CLOs, and CBOs.

Commercially offered portfolio solutions/approaches are sometimes the door opener that the sponsoring firms hope will lead to sales of financial advisory services or other products such as derivatives. Such solutions should therefore not be viewed as a silver bullet. However, the mere act of gathering the information needed to feed the model will serve a useful purpose in educating management about the risks being taken.

Some institutions have found it necessary to combine the oversight of credit and market risk. At J. P. Morgan, for example, which has moved more and more into an origination and distribution strategy rather than origination and retention, there is a convergence of credit- and market-risk measurement methodologies. As Allen (1996) points out, integration of the two functions is desirable for three reasons. First, there is a lot of transactional interaction between credit and market risk; second, there is a need for comparability between returns on credit and market risk (for example, emerging-market debt); and third, the emergence of hybrid credit- and market-risk product structures makes this necessary.

It is not even necessary to have a mark-to-market regime for taking advantage of these solutions. Indeed, David Goldman (1998) provides an interesting current perspective on default risk management when *not* marking to market proffers some advantages to entrepreneurs seeking risk capital.

According to Goldman, entrepreneurs, who bet on innovations whose risks are rewards, lie outside the probabilistic distribution of business experience and therefore represent an uninsurable risk. Only very big portfolios with wide diversification and "broad backs" are able to take on such uninsurable risk. However, because of the regulatory restrictions on banks, insurance companies, and others for eligible investments, Wall Street created CBOs so that the investment grade tranches went to the insurance companies and pension funds and the unrated, highly subordinated pieces (some with a sense of humor have called them radioactive or glow-in-the-dark pieces to signify the risk carried) went to the speculators (for example, hedge funds). The hedge funds have now discovered that, in their mark-to-market world, they cannot bear the volatility of the first-loss prices. Coming full circle, it is the big portfolio lenders such as large banks and insurance companies who can finance risky ventures. They can hold on to these credits to maturity and not worry about having to mark to market. Diversification, Goldman notes, has thus become the decisive issue. He notes that CreditMetrics and CreditRisk$^+$ are among the solutions available to measure diversification and to suggest strategies, including the use of credit derivatives.

The determination of value at risk has been criticized because it provides just a single number that does not tell management what to do or where the risks are. In the case of portfolio solutions, management should likewise be wary of single indexes that purport to signify everything. Management should understand the assumptions behind the numbers and be familiar with the analytics so that it is aware of a model's strengths and weaknesses. Although this is a tedious and difficult process, it is a simple fact that management, not the model, must ultimately take responsibility for the organization's operating results.

Data

Even before portfolio analytics are applied, an institution should invest in an information system that makes such analysis possible. Deal structure, product data, industry membership, geography, loss/claim history, borrower's sources of revenue, key borrower-specific indicators, ratings (where available), and stock price (where available) are some of the obvious variables that should be scrubbed and maintained. Reliance on third-party data is acceptable, but management should ensure that the data is of acceptable quality and is applicable to its own environment. For example, bond default recovery data may not apply to bank loans or derivative exposures unless it has been properly adjusted for differences in collateral, seniority, call provisions, industry segment, and so forth. Brian Ranson, senior vice president at Bank of Montreal, likens the process to making rabbit stew according to an old recipe. He says that before getting into the details of the ingredients and the way to make the soup, the recipe directs you to go out and catch a rabbit. "Ironically, it is much more difficult to get a rabbit in your own backyard than one in the forest. For many institutions, the external market provides far better data on lending than do their own systems" (Ranson 1993).

Organization

Portfolio management raises organizational as well as analytical issues. An asset originator in a bank is part of a profit center, but a portfolio analyst tends to occupy a staff position—often in a cost center with power and influence that is more imagined than real. Whereas an asset originator is perceived to be creating value, a portfolio manager's recommendations may be viewed as negative—advising the bank to stop a deal or to sell an asset. Because these roles are often seen as in conflict, the portfolio manager may be reduced to a passive role, or worse still, gridlock may ensue. A senior banker echoes these sentiments:

> I still got the problem of all these originators who are very attached to the asset. They are likely to say, "This is my asset. I originated this and I look after it and I sort of polish it and make sure it is okay." They are emotionally attached to that thing. Even after you struggle to whip the asset away from them, you've got to go through all the relationship concerns. The top of the organization will say, "Yes, you young guy, you've got the right to go out and sell this stuff." But you have to live with these guys. Although changes are happening, it does take time for the culture to change.

Conflicts arise when originators are compensated based on assets under management but do not own the risk. The burden falls on senior management to provide the necessary empowerment through fiat, compensation, and rational transfer-pricing mechanisms. The compensation system for origination should focus on the value and quantity of what is originated, whereas the compensation scheme for portfolio management should focus on maximizing return relative to risk. Brian Ranson explains that at Bank of Montreal, the portfolio manager occupies an influential position:

> The job of relationship management is one of asset origination. They go out and find assets, and negotiate an appropriate price and structure. We [in portfolio management] decide how much we will invest in, and the rest of it is disposed of by loan sales and trading. We actually own the portfolio. The account officer does the credit work. Portfolio management does KMV, comparison with Moody's and S&P, and the market comparisons. If, based on what we see, we want to sell some of it, it is gone.

The Future

Given the rapid advance in market liquidity, transaction vehicles, and measurement technologies, portfolio management of credit risk represents the leading edge of institutional practice. The challenges will be to find practical and workable methods for the day-to-day management of credit risk, given the information and measurement complexities of this problem. The only safe prediction is that we should expect rapid change as organizations move to exploit the new opportunities being created.

REFERENCES

Adamidou, E., Y. Ben-Dov, L. Pendergast, and V. Pica. 1993. The Optimal Portfolio System: Targeting Horizon Total Returns under Varying Interest-rate Scenarios. In

Financial Optimization, edited by S. A. Zenios. Cambridge: Cambridge University Press.

Allen, R. A. 1996. Integrating Credit and Market Risk Management. *Journal of Lending and Credit Risk Management* 78 (6): 14–29.

Altman, E. I. 1988. *Default Risk, Mortality Rates, and the Performance of Corporate Bonds.* Charlottesville, Va.: Institute of Chartered Financial Analysts.

———. 1989. Measuring Corporate Bond Mortality and Performance. *Journal of Finance* 44:909–922.

———. 1992. Revisiting the High Yield Debt Market. *Financial Management* (summer):78–92.

———. 1993. *Corporate Financial Distress and Bankruptcy.* 2nd ed. New York: John Wiley & Sons.

———. 1997a. Corporate Bond and Commercial Loan portfolio Analysis. Working paper S-97-12, New York University Salomon Brothers Center, New York.

———. 1997b. *Rating Migration of Corporate Bonds—Comparative Results and Investor Implications.* New York: Salomon Brothers, Inc. An earlier version was published as working paper S-97-3, New York University Salomon Center, February, 1997.

Altman, E. I., J. Hartzell and M. Peck. 1995. *Emerging Markets Corporate Bonds: A scoring system.* New York: Salomon Brothers. Reprinted in *Emerging Market Capital Flows,* edited by R. Levich. Amsterdam: Kluwer Publishing, 1997.

Altman, E. I., and D. L. Kao. 1991. *Corporate Bond Rating Drift: An Examination of Rating Agency Credit Quality Changes.* Charlottesville, Va.: AIMR.

Altman, E. I., and V. M. Kishore. 1995. Report on Defaults and Returns on High-Yield Bonds: Analysis through 1994. Special report S-95-3, New York University Salomon Center, New York.

———.1997. Default and Returns in the High-Yield Debt Market, 1991–1995. Special report, New York University Salomon Center, New York.

Altman, E. I., and A. Saunders. 1997. Credit Risk Measurement over the Last 20 Years. Working Paper S-96-40, New York University Salomon Brothers Center, New York, and forthcoming in *Journal of Banking and Finance.*

Bankers Trust New York Corporation. 1995. *RAROC and Risk Management: Quantifying the Risks of Business.* New York: Bankers Trust New York Corporation.

Bennett, P. 1984. Applying Portfolio Theory to Global Bank Lending. *Journal of Banking and Finance* 8:153–169.

Chirinko, R. S., and G. D. Guill. 1991. A Framework for Assessing Credit Risk in Depository Institutions: Toward Regulatory Reform. *Journal of Banking and Finance* 15:785–804.

Company and Country Risk Models. 1984. Special issue. *Journal of Banking and Finance* 8(2).

CreditRisk +. 1996. Credit Suisse Financial Products, New York.

Elton, E. J., and M. J. Gruber. 1991. *Modern Portfolio Theory and Investment Analysis.* New York: John Wiley & Sons.

Goldman, D. F. 1998. The Brave New World of Default Risk Management. *Forbes Global Business and Finance* 1 June, 68–69.

Gupton, G. M., C. C. Finger, and M. Bhatia. 1997. *CreditMetrics: The Benchmark for Understanding Credit Risk.* Technical document. New York: J. P. Morgan, Inc.

J. P. Morgan, Inc. 1997. *RiskMetrics,* 4th ed. Technical document. New York: J. P. Morgan, Inc.

King, B. 1966. Market and Industry Factors in Stock Price Behavior. *Journal of Business* 39:139–140.

Markowitz, H. 1952. Portfolio Selection. *Journal of Finance* 7 (1): 77–91.

Morgan, J. B. 1989. Managing a Loan Portfolio Like an Equity Fund. *Bankers Magazine* (January-February): 28–35.

Morgan, J. B., and T. L. Gollinger. 1993. Calculation of an Efficient Frontier for a Commercial Loan Portfolio. *Journal of Portfolio Management* (winter).

Morningstar, Inc. 1993. *Morningstar Mutual Funds User's Guide.* Chicago: Morningstar, Inc.

Ranson, B. 1993. Rabbit Stew. *Balance Sheet* (spring): 37–40.

Reilly, F. 1979. *Investment Analysis and Portfolio Management.* Hinsdale, Ill.: Dryden Press.

Sharpe, W. F. 1964. Capital Asset Prices: A Theory of Market Equilibrium under Conditions of Risk. *Journal of Finance* 19 (3): 425–442.

———. 1966. Mutual Fund Performance. *Journal of Business* (January): 111–138.

———. 1994. The Sharpe Ratio. *Journal of Portfolio Management* (fall): 49–58.

Wilson, T. C. 1997. Measuring and Managing Credit Portfolio Risk, a Two-part series. McKinsey & Co. Mimeograph.

———. 1997. Measuring Credit Portfolio Risk: A New Approach. Paper presented at the IAFE annual meeting, Zurich, 10 June.

ADDITIONAL READING

Jagtiani, J., A. Saunders, and G. Udell. 1995. The Effect of Bank Capital Requirements on Bank Off-Balance Sheet Financing. *Journal of Banking and Finance* 647–658.

Jonkhart, M. 1979. On the Term Structure of Interest Rates and the Risk of Default. *Journal of Banking and Finance* 253–262.

Kealhofer, S. 1995. Portfolio Management of Default Risk. Draft, KMV Corporation, San Francisco.

———. 1996. Measuring Default Risk in Portfolios of Derivatives. KMV Corporation, San Francisco. Photocopy.

KMV Corporation. 1993. *Credit Monitor Overview.* San Francisco: KMV Corporation.

Markowitz, H. 1959. *Portfolio Selection: Efficient Diversification of Investments.* New York: John Wiley & Sons.

Markowitz, H. M., and A. F. Perold. 1981. Portfolio Analysis with Scenarios and Factors. *Journal of Finance* 36:871–877.

McAllister, P., and J. J. Mingo. 1994. Commercial Loan Risk Management, Credit-Scoring and Pricing: The Need for a New Shared Data Base. *Journal of Commercial Bank Lending* 76 (9): 6–20.

McQuown, J. 1994. All That Counts is Diversification: In Bank Asset Portfolio Management. San Francisco: KMV Corporation.

Platt, H. D., and M. B. Platt. 1991. A Linear Programming Approach to Bond Portfolio Selection. *Economic Financial Computing* (spring): 71–84.

Santomero, A., and J. Vinso. 1977. Estimating the Probability of Failure for Firms in the Banking System. *Journal of Banking and Finance* 185–206.

Saunders, A. 1997. *Financial Institutions Management: A Modern Perspective,* 2nd ed. Burr Ridge, Ill: Irwin Professional Publications.

Smith, L. D., and E. Lawrence. 1995. Forecasting Losses on a Liquidating Long-Term Loan Portfolio. *Journal of Banking and Finance* 19(6), 959–985.

Vanderhoof, I. T. 1997. Variance of a Fixed-Income Portfolio. *Contingencies* (September/October).

Chapter **20**

Credit Derivatives

Ah, take the Cash, and let the Credit go,
Nor heed the rumble of a distant Drum!

—The *Rubháiyát* of Omar Khayyám, stanza 13 (translated by Edward FitzGerald)

Credit derivatives are instruments that are used to trade credit risk, which, in the process, is separated from other features of a financial instrument. They were introduced by banks in the early 1990s to help them deal with their paradoxical desire to enjoy the benefits of asset concentration[1] without having to face the attendant risks. Implausible as this may seem at first sight, it is possible, under certain conditions, for banks to resolve this paradox to the benefit of all concerned. The solution depends on the bank finding a counterparty that will assume the credit risk in exchange for a fee, while the bank itself retains the asset on its books. A credit derivative is so named because it is *derived* from the existence of an underlying asset, for example, a loan. Just as a bank is able, today, to swap the fixed rate on an asset for a floating rate, it can now, by paying a premium, swap *the default risk* on an asset for *the promise of a full or partial payout* if the asset defaults. Credit derivatives can be tailored to lay off any part of the credit risk exposure: amount, recovery rate, and maturity. They may even be constructed for events such as a rating downgrade that do not involve default.

Even though credit derivatives appeared on the financial scene after interest-rate derivatives were introduced, they are actually the less exotic of these instruments. Apart from the newness of the name, credit derivatives resemble traditional credit insurance products such as standby letters of credit and loan guarantees. Indeed, the resemblance is close enough that

---

[1]Asset concentration refers to both an unacceptably high and/or unprofitable exposure. The exposure may be to a single obligor or to a group of obligors sharing common risk factors such as industry group or geographic location, such as a country, state, or region. Concentration is the consequence of a bank's desire to specialize in certain industries and/or geographic areas. As to be expected, when concentration increases, there is an increase in the severity of default. The antidote for concentration is diversification, that is, replacing highly correlated assets with uncorrelated or negatively correlated assets. This concept was formalized by Harry Markowitz as modern portfolio theory in the 1950s. Please also see Chapter 17.

regulators see credit swaps as analogous to letters of credit, and total return swaps as equivalent to equity swaps.[2] Lloyd's of London offered reinsurance on trade credit as early as 1893 (Cockerell 1984). The good news is that the pricing analytics used for a letter of credit may be transported to credit derivatives—all other things, such as capital allocated, being equal. The bad news is that problems with default probabilities, correlation, recovery rates, and so on will dog anyone who tries to value a credit derivative. Credit volatility is more opaque than market volatility: the impairment of an obligor's creditworthiness is not as visible as a change in its share price.[3] This adds another layer of complexity to the equation.

CREDIT DERIVATIVES—AN EXAMPLE

Broadly stated, a credit derivative is a bilateral financial contract that derives its value from an underlying index or event that is credit sensitive. The most common form of credit derivatives is an arrangement between two parties by which they agree to exchange predetermined or formula-determined cash flows, contingent on the occurrence of a credit event over the course of a preset future time period. The event must be observable and is generally, but not always, associated with an adverse development such as default, bankruptcy filing, rating downgrade, or a significant drop in market price. The intent of the derivative is to provide default protection to the risk seller and compensation for taking risk to the risk buyer. In credit derivative parlance, the *derivative seller* is the *protection seller*—the party that sells the put (*the right to put the asset back in exchange for cash for par, for example*). Consider this example:

Let us say that Bank A has an exposure of $10 million with Corporation X for five years and wants to reduce it without actually selling all or part of it to another institution. This is a common dilemma for banks in their lending relationships, because borrowers typically are unwilling to have their debt sold. Banks fear that if they sell a loan, they may lose the opportunity for future business with the borrower.

Faced with exposure that it wants to minimize, Bank A can enter into an arrangement with Bank B whereby, in exchange for a fixed periodic fee of 50 basis points, Bank A obtains protection for all or part of its exposure. If Corporation X defaults on its obligation, Bank B will pay Bank A a sum representing the loss that Bank A incurred in the credit event. Bank B may have several different reasons for entering into this transaction. It may wish to gain exposure where, because of barriers to entry, it had none before. It

---

[2]"For guarantor banking organizations, the examiners should review the credit quality of individual reference assets in derivative contracts in the same manner as other credit instruments such as standby letters of credit. Thus the examiners should evaluate a credit derivative . . . based upon the overall financial condition and resources of the reference obligor, the obligor's credit history; and any secondary source of payment such as collateral." (Board of Governors of the Federal Reserve System 1996, 12). Note the similarity to traditional credit analysis.

[3]After creating a credit hedge, the same difficulty applies to the counterparty risk for the credit derivative.

may wish to diversify its portfolio. Finally, it may have better information than Bank A about the creditworthiness of Corporation X, and it may therefore value the risk differently.

Bank B's contingent obligation may be defined in a variety of ways, such as

- Cash settlement for the loss in value of the loan
- A fixed amount (binary)
- Par value of the loan, with the loan delivered to Bank B

and so on. The period for which this arrangement may be in effect also varies. Bank A may obtain protection for just the first two years, on the theory that Corporation X faces the greatest uncertainty during this period: it may, for example, be a pharmaceutical company awaiting regulatory approval of a new drug. The credit event need not be default on the underlying obligation per se.

Credit derivatives are not currently traded on exchanges but are arranged on an over-the-counter basis, in much the same way as reinsurance is arranged. Banks do not like to use the "I" word (insurance) for fear that this product will be legally termed insurance, thereby setting off alarms in the insurance industry and in the offices of insurance regulators.[4] The documentation for credit swaps, which is patterned after master agreements that the International Swaps and Derivatives Association has developed, is still evolving. The salient items in the agreement are the payment terms for the protection buyer, the credit event, and the payout by the protection seller if the credit event occurs.

Today the market for credit derivatives is minuscule relative to the volume of bank debt outstanding. According to Blythe Masters, managing director at J. P. Morgan Securities, Inc., probably $200 billion in notional principal was outstanding at the end of 1997 versus the total loan market size of $1.2 trillion.[5] A typical transaction ranges from $10 to $50 million (U.S. dollars), with a maturity from 1 to 10 years. Reference credits include sovereigns, semigovernments, financial institutions, and corporates (both investment grade and subinvestment grade entities). Transactions commonly fall into three broad categories: (1) swaps of high-quality credits where the protection is bought by banks mainly for diversification purposes; (2) swaps for purposes of hedging developing country credit risk in Brady bonds by stripping the flows not backed by U.S. Treasuries and transferring them to investors; and (3) multicredit baskets in which a credit derivative provides first loss protection. The last category is of interest to hedge funds and others seeking leverage in their credit investments.

---

[4]"Under New York law entities have to be specifically licensed under the Federal Financial Guarantee Insurance Program to write financial insurance guarantee contracts. Only seven institutions are authorized and none of them have any connection with Wall Street" (Credit Derivatives 1996, p. 26).

[5]Some of the material in this chapter is drawn from information gathered at the J. P. Morgan Derivatives Conference in New York City on March 19, 1996. J. P. Morgan is not responsible for any of the material presented here, however.

However, the regulatory treatment of credit derivatives is currently biased against protection sellers other than Organization for Economic Development and Co-Operation (OECD) banks. If the protection seller is an OECD bank, the loan is deemed to be replaced by risk to the counterparty. The new counterparty (i.e., the OECD bank) merits a lower capital allocation (20 percent weighting) than the previous counterparty (100 percent weight). Even so, the regulators will not net out and reduce the reported concentration statistics for the protection buyer. But with more experience with this market, the regulatory treatment may change.

STRUCTURAL FORMS OF CREDIT DERIVATIVES

The types of credit derivatives commonly used, although many other structures are rapidly developing, are as follows:

- Credit swap
- Total return swap
- Credit-linked note
- First-to-default swap
- Index swap

Credit Swap

The "plain vanilla" version of a credit derivative is a credit swap where the protection buyer pays a fixed recurring amount in exchange for a payment contingent upon a future credit event. If this event occurs, then the protection seller pays the agreed-upon amount to the protection buyer to cover the credit loss pursuant to default. The credit swap structure is illustrated in the Figure 20.1. There may also be an intermediary who arranges this structure (not shown here).

Figure 20.1 Credit Swap

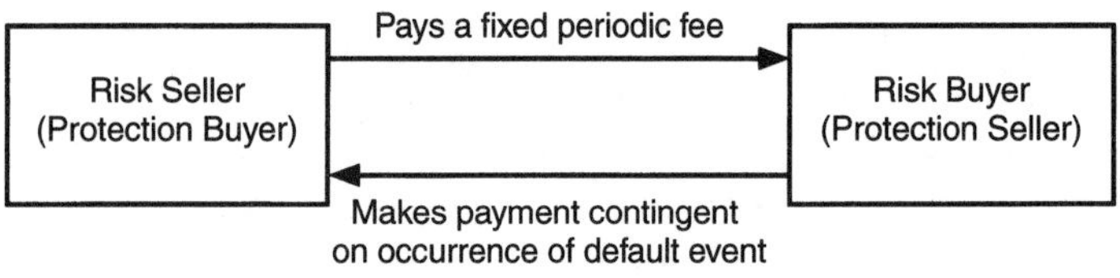

```
                        Pays a fixed periodic fee
  ┌──────────────────┐ ──────────────────────────▶ ┌──────────────────┐
  │   Risk Seller    │                              │   Risk Buyer     │
  │(Protection Buyer)│                              │(Protection Seller)│
  └──────────────────┘ ◀────────────────────────── └──────────────────┘
                        Makes payment contingent
                        on occurrence of default event
```

```
Default:
Based on the default on a reference security by a reference credit
Alternative Settlement Forms:
(1) Fall in market value of the reference security @ months from
    default date
(2) Physical Delivery of Notional Principle in exchange for defaulted security
(3) Binary: Payment of a predetermined fixed amount
Materiality:
There should be a significant deterioration in the price of the reference
security before settlement is triggered.
```

Credit swaps often contain a *materiality* clause that ensures that the credit default is not triggered by minor, nonmaterial, or staged events. Materiality is usually defined as a significant price deterioration based on a dealer poll in a preset period following an apparent credit default event. If there is truly a default event, the reasoning is that its economic effect will be reflected in a change in the price of the reference security. The credit swap resembles a loan guarantee and may in fact be priced using the same methodology.

An alternative way of analyzing this transaction is to treat it as an asset swap. Because of its simplicity, a credit swap is easy to arrange, as long as the parties can agree on the definition of the credit event.

Total Rate of Return Swap

The total rate of return swap (TROR or TR swap) is a bilateral financial contract in which the total return of an asset during the holding period is exchanged for another cash flow. It differs from the credit swap in that the credit swap is credit event–specific, whereas the TROR exchanges the cash flows whether there is a default or not. The schematic diagram for a TR swap is shown in Figure 20.2. The TR swap has the effect of completely removing the economic risk of an asset without the actual sale of the asset.

Credit-Linked Note

A credit-linked note is described in Figure 20.3. A special purpose vehicle is set up to issue notes and/or certificates. The proceeds are invested to acquire cash collateral equal to the amount of protection sought by the protection buyer. The yield from the collateral plus the fees paid the protection buyer are passed through to the investor. If there is a default, the cash collateral is

Figure 20.2 Total Return (TR) Swap

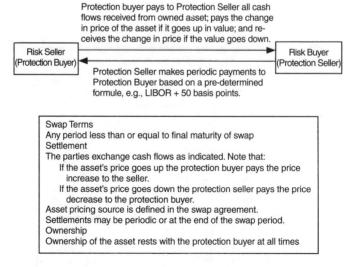

Figure 20.3   Credit-Linked Note

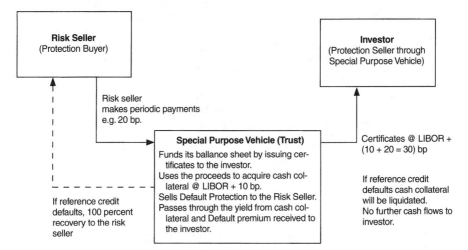

liquidated to satisfy the protection buyer and the remaining proceeds are distributed to the investors.

First-to-Default Swap

In the first-to-default swap, several assets are bundled together, and a credit swap is created on the whole basket. The default event is a default on any one of the assets in the basket.

Index Swap

An index swap is a combination of a bond and a credit option. The bond coupon payments and/or the principal payments are recalculated based on the provisions of the credit option. Suppose, for example, that a finance company has issued a fixed-rate bond to finance its operations. The credit option may provide that the applicable interest rate will decrease by x basis points for every y percent increase in past due loans nationally. Thus, the company is protected from having to continue making high loan repayments if consumer delinquencies increase; it has bought insurance in the form of a credit option.

FEATURES OF CREDIT DERIVATIVES USEFUL TO A RISK SELLER

Banks make their profits by making loans and selling other complementary credit-market services. This inevitably places them in a long position vis-à-vis credit risk. As Blythe Masters observes:

Lending, loan syndication, derivatives intermediation, underwriting, market making, credit enhancement are credit functions which generate systematic credit exposures for banks and financial institutions. In the past, it was impossible to actively manage credit portfolios: you cannot short a loan; there was no repo market for loans. Similarly you could not sell your business concentration risk without getting out of the business. Now, portfolio managers have a set of tailored credit risk management tools. With increasing liquidity we can completely reverse or change or optimize our credit risk profile, which—keeping the future in perspective—is extremely valuable to us at this point of the credit cycle.

Portfolio diversification is a common motivation for a bank to buy or sell a credit derivative. A bank's loan portfolio risk-return profile may be viewed in terms of two parameters:

1. Expected return, calculated from the net interest margin and expected loan losses
2. Unexpected loss, calculated from the maximum possible loss that may be sustained

The expected return will depend on the spread and the credit losses calculated from the probability of default and the recovery rate. The unexpected loss will be calculated based on assumptions about the joint default of many credits at the same time.[6] The unexpected losses are usually associated with correlation of credit default. The ratio of expected return to unexpected loss is an index for a loan portfolio that is analogous to the Sharpe ratio for equities (which is the ratio of expected excess return over the risk-free rate divided by the standard deviation). The expected portfolio performance is improved by improving the Sharpe ratio. This is accomplished by either or both of two strategies:

1. Reducing the assets currently in the portfolio that have relatively lower returns for higher unexpected losses
2. Adding other assets that will make a positive contribution to the Sharpe ratio

Until now, a bank could implement either of these strategies only through buying or selling loans. Although a loan syndication market now exists, it is still relatively small and illiquid. With credit derivatives, however, these strategies may easily be implemented. A bank no longer needs a relationship-building/loan origination/loan syndication infrastructure to acquire exposure. Furthermore, some risk mitigation strategies such as the hedging of commitment risk and the selective hedging of tenor risk cannot be accomplished through the sale or purchase of loans.[7]

---

[6]Unexpected loss may also be adjusted upward by using the "high" estimate of the default probability and the "low" estimate of recovery rate. Unexpected loss is thus influenced not only by the correlation of default risk with other assets but also the degree of ignorance associated with the estimate of the unconditional probabilities of default and recoveries. These are subtle but extremely important points to understand.

[7]Refer to Chapters 17 to 19 for methodologies used in portfolio management, including the development of loan portfolio optimization strategies.

A credit derivative allows a bank to take advantage of arbitrage opportunities such as pricing discrepancies across asset classes, geographic locations, maturity ranges, and investor classes. In money-market assets, for example, there are discrepancies in pricing past the 13-month maturity. Likewise, differing philosophies exhibited by rating agencies present arbitrage opportunities: in assigning a rating Moody's appears to consider both default probability and expected recovery rate, whereas S&P is said to be biased more toward the default probability. According to Blythe Masters, in the past these discrepancies were either interesting or frustrating, but there was nothing that a bank could do because it had no way to execute the short leg of the transaction. Credit derivatives open these possibilities for banks.

Another advantage of credit derivatives is confidentiality. An investor that owns a risk asset can obtain credit protection against its defaulting without the obligor even knowing about it. If the bank decides to use a third party *reference credit,* the protection seller also need not know the identity of the obligor. A bank, for example, that has lent to ABC Corporation in South Korea may obtain a credit derivative whose default provisions are based on South Korea's sovereign debt rather than on ABC Corporation. This will make sense only if the *basis risk* (the relationship between the basis, South Korea, and the underlying risk) is acceptable.

A bank can choose from a wide variety of coverages depending on its tolerance for risk and the price at which credit risk may be laid off. A credit derivative can be customized, for example, to cover a portion of the notional principal, a fraction of the period exposed, or a recovery rate ranging from 0 to 100 percent in the event of default.

Documentation has tended to be quite simple (but generally not very good, according to some), because the more complex it is, the greater the likelihood for disputes in the case of a claim. According to Blythe Masters, it takes just a few hours to set up a credit derivative[8]—in contrast to a loan syndication, which requires 10 days or more to settle.

FEATURES OF CREDIT DERIVATIVES USEFUL TO A RISK BUYER

A buyer of exposure can take on credit risk without having to fund a loan or having to develop any origination capability. This is the credit equivalent of buying a future or an option. Some entities have unique credit-monitoring resources in certain industries or countries that other players may lack. They can use this information advantage to become protection sellers.

Credit derivatives are a special class of *event derivatives* because they contract for a cash flow that is contingent on some event that may or may not occur. Even nonfinancial companies that are concerned about the solvency of their suppliers and customers may find them helpful. Using a credit derivative, a company can also profit from pricing discrepancies in its own

---

[8]It can take much longer than this depending on the complexity and the novelty of the structure for the participants.

capital structure. If, for example, a company's senior unsecured debt is priced more thinly than its secured debt, it can buy its senior unsecured exposure and short its secured exposure.

The speed with which credit derivatives have grown in just one year is indicative of their versatility.

POSSIBLE APPLICATIONS OF CREDIT DERIVATIVES

Credit derivatives are another development in the steady march of the financial markets toward products that are identified less by the institutions that sell them than by the economic function they perform. Banks were traditionally—and still are—regarded as the evaluators of credit risk: they not only *assess* credit risk but also *assume* it.

In the residential mortgage market, GNMA, FNMA, and FHMLC have created uniform underwriting and documentation standards. These have made it possible for separate entities to serve as originators of mortgage assets and as investors in mortgage assets. The same has not happened in the commercial and international loan markets, where loan standardization is more the exception than the rule. Banks custom tailor their loans. They worry that selling loans to free up capacity will endanger their relationships with customers. Credit derivatives offer an unobtrusive way to reduce or increase their credit exposure.

Of course, credit derivatives presuppose the existence of willing buyers and sellers, and of market-clearing prices—bid/ask spreads at which such transactions may be consummated. The market still has very wide bid/ask spreads, and it still takes time to find counterparties and to come to an agreement. But the market will grow.

Credit derivatives thus have the potential to help banks balance their conflicting goals—the goal of focus (achieving comparative advantage[9] in credit evaluation administration by concentrating in selected areas) and the goal of diversification.

For perhaps the first time in history, the investment banker selling this product will have something to offer the corporate lending officer or the bank portfolio manager. Since credit derivatives can eliminate all or part of the credit risk of a transaction, both banks and their regulators will have to learn to look at credit risk not only at the individual transaction level but also at the portfolio level. Indeed, a day may come when regulators may permit a bank to use an internal model to derive the value at risk due to credit risk that will then be used in computing its regulatory capital.

Banks can buy or sell protection or act as intermediaries. They may employ credit derivatives to increase their income by using their unique ability to assess risk without going on to fund the loan. Banks may also benefit from

---

[9] A term made famous by the Hechscher-Ohlin theorem that held that economic welfare is maximized when countries produce things in which they have an advantage in cost and quality and trade these with other countries, who should do likewise.

the chance to spread the fixed costs of their credit analysis infrastructure. Ultimately, banks may divide themselves into pure *credit risk takers* and pure *loan funders.*

Good credit is a valuable and scarce commodity. Obligors are always trying to borrow money at the lowest possible cost with the least impact on their creditworthiness. Special purpose subsidiaries and captive finance companies are two examples of corporate structures aimed at managing credit risk from the obligor's side. The first category insulates the parent from liability by providing a corporate veil; the second category minimizes borrowing costs by putting only high-quality financial assets on the borrowing company's balance sheet—thus making it possible for the subsidiary to access the (lower cost) commercial paper market. It may be recalled that Chrysler Financial enjoyed access to the commercial paper market because of the high quality of its assets even when its parent, Chrysler Corporation, was undergoing financial difficulties in the 1980s.

There is always an unspoken tug-of-war between lenders who want to obtain the greatest amount of protection for a given set of loan terms and borrowers who want to obtain funds with the least encumbrance on their resources. The availability of credit derivatives greatly facilitates the achievement of both of these goals. Even after the loan has been consummated, both borrower and lender can shop credit more easily. Corporate borrowers may fine-tune their debt structure without acquiring or retiring debt, and they may also be able to hedge the credit-risk premium for future borrowing costs.

THE REGULATORY VIEW OF CREDIT DERIVATIVES

Credit derivatives have the potential to provide new insights into credit risk and its management. Just as the futures and options markets help in price discovery, so will credit derivatives help to develop efficient credit pricing, eventually providing the benefits that a free competitive market affords. They will make it possible, for example, to understand the term structure of credit risk premiums.

It is thus reasonable to expect that regulators view the development of the credit derivative market with interest. At the same time, because credit derivatives are off-balance-sheet instruments, they have the potential for increasing the system risk. The current regulatory view on credit derivatives may be summarized as follows:

The bank providing the guarantee should treat it as a direct credit substitute (i.e., put it on the balance sheet) and the notional equivalent should be converted at 100 percent. The regulators view the provision of a loan guarantee by a bank as equivalent to having the loan on its books.

For the protection buyer, the underlying asset will be considered guaranteed for capital purposes as long as the underlying assets and the reference asset are obligations of the same legal entity, have the same level of seniority in bankruptcy, and are subject to mutual cross-default provision. *Basis* risk, the relationship between the underlying asset and the reference asset, is of concern to the regulators. Although it is a real risk, basis poses no major problems to a bank. In most cases, the reference asset is a publicly traded security whose prices can readily be obtained. But there is a risk that the reference asset will not track the real risk being hedged against.

If the guarantor is an OECD bank, then the underlying asset should be assigned to the 20 percent risk category. If the guarantor is an institution other than an OECD bank, it is to be treated at the 100 percent risk category for purposes of risk-based capital. The implication is that regulators view nonbanks, regardless of their creditworthiness, as five times riskier than banks. To the extent that nonbank protection sellers will be unattractive to banks, this rule reduces the liquidity of the credit derivatives market. In reality, many AAA-rated insurance companies would be stronger counter-parties than, say, a highly leveraged bank.

Although the examiners will take note of credit derivative–based guar-antees designed to mitigate asset concentrations, for reporting purposes, the existence of such guarantees is not deemed to reduce asset concentration. If, for example, a bank that has loan concentration in China purchases a credit derivative to protect it, the regulators would note this fact but continue to view the bank as having loan concentration in China.

According to Blythe Masters, the current risk-based regulatory treatment of bank assets is the greatest impediment to the growth of credit derivatives. For example, loans that have been hedged with a AAA-rated counterparty that is an insurance company attract the same capital treatment as an un-hedged loan to an individual consumer.

As Stephen Thieke, managing director at J. P. Morgan observes,

> With credit risk premia contracting, and with a regulatory capital framework that effectively incents pursuit of low-quality credit business, we are sowing the seeds of the next credit cycle problem. Urgently needed before that hits are better markets and tools for proactive portfolio management of credit risks, as well as a more risk-sensitive approach to capital rules. Fortunately, the mar-ketplace is aware of these needs and is hard at work providing frameworks for both.[10]

Within a few years, Thieke expects all banks to move to a mark-to-market approach, which means that they will no longer make an artificial distinction between the loan book and the trading book. Credit derivatives will not only facilitate the mark-to-market approach, they will play a strong role in rede-fining the risk profile of the portfolio.

CREDIT RISK OF CREDIT DERIVATIVES

Counterparty Risk

When an institution has sold exposure to another institution, it has ex-changed the risk of default of the underlying asset for the joint risk of default

---

[10]Comments made by Stephen G. Theike at the International Monetary Conference, Interlachen, Switzerland, June 2, 1997.

by the counterparty and the underlying asset. Clearly if only *one* of the two defaults, then there is no credit risk. The probability of default by *both* depends on the marginal probability of default of either and the *correlation* between the two default probabilities. This may be expressed by the equation:[11]

$$P(A \text{ and } B) = \text{Corr}(A,B) \times [P(A)(1 - P(A))]^{1/2} \times [P(B)(1 - P(B))]^{1/2} + P(A) \times P(B)$$

where A = Default by the underlying obligor
 B = Default by guarantor or protection seller
$P(A \text{ and } B)$ = Probability that both default together
 $P(A)$ = Probability of Default of underlying obligor (assuming a binomial distribution)
 $P(B)$ = Probability of Default of guarantor (assuming a binomial distribution)
$\text{Corr}(A,B)$ = Correlation between the two events A and B

Although this equation is straightforward, it must be borne in mind that it is difficult to obtain dependable estimates for $P(A)$ and $P(B)$, and even more so for the correlation of A and B (which, being a product of two quantities, is the equivalent of squaring one's uncertainty). If the two default events are independent, then the correlation is 0, in which case purchasing the credit protection would have brought the probability of loss from $P(A)$ down to $P(A) \times P(B)$. Generally, however, there will be some degree of correlation between the guarantor and the underlying credit—for example, because they both participate in the same national economy.

Five-year default correlations for various bond ratings were reported by Lucas (1995) as shown in Table 20.1. This table is provided only for the purpose of illustration. The correlation to use would consider not only the rating class of the two names but also other variables such as geography, industry, and size that may impact its value.

MODEL RISK

Major financial institutions use internal models for measuring market risk (such as value at risk [VAR]). Typically these models project a term structure of interest rates and make some assumptions about a statistical process for the movement of security prices. VAR includes credit risk as reflected in the security prices. VAR itself may be criticized because volatility, which drives this measurement, is difficult to forecast. When it is a matter of modeling default *events* rather than *rates*, the VAR model will not be satisfactory. Unlike interest rate or stock price movements, the occurrence of a default significantly changes the value of a debt security. CreditMetrics is a step in the direction of recognizing that it is perhaps more reasonable to model the

---

[11]See Lucas (1995) for the derivation of this relationship.

Table 20.1   Five-year default correlations

	Aaa	Aa	A	Baa	Ba	B
Aaa	0					
Aa	0	0				
A	0	.01	.01			
Baa	0	.01	.01	0		
Ba	0	.03	.04	.03	.15	
B	0	.04	.06	.07	.25	.29

Source: Reprinted from *Journal of Fixed Income,* Lucas, "Default Correlation and Credit Analysis", p. 81, March 1995, with permission of Institutional Investor, Inc.

volatility of returns from credit-risky assets through rating migration, and thence rating-specific values. In spite of the altered view of the value at risk, CreditMetrics, in its current state of development, can provide only an *approximate* view of risk exposure—we stress the term *approximate* because the assumptions built into it make it necessary to constantly review the output. Moreover, it will not give prescriptions for dealing with risk exposure. However, tools like CreditMetrics may yield insights in managing the portfolio through credit derivative products.

VALUATION OF CREDIT DERIVATIVES

In general, the variables that have impact on the *intrinsic value* of a credit derivative are the same variables used to value a credit risk asset. The following is a partial list of the variables that may enter the calculation for intrinsic value:

- Likely probability of default of the underlying credit and the protection seller
- Pessimistic probability of default
- Joint probability of default of the underlying credit and the protection seller
- Timing of default
- Recovery rate distribution
- Workout cost distribution
- Asset's seniority
- Timing of recovery
- Interest rate
- Prepayment probability distribution
- Pricing basis—fixed versus floating
- Amortization structure
- First loss level ("deductible" in insurance parlance)
- Correlation structure for the default, prepayment, recovery interest rates

A probabilistic cash flow approach may be taken to calculate value based on assumptions on these variables. The value so calculated may be compared with the current market spreads to estimate the cost of the protection. Approaches taken to calculate the outcomes may be deterministic (e.g., scenario analysis) or stochastic (Monte Carlo simulation). The limitation of scenario analysis is that the calculations follow a limited number of paths that the analyst has defined. With Monte Carlo simulation, because the variable values are not preset and are drawn from a distribution, calculations may be performed over a larger number of paths, presumably resulting in a range of likely outcomes instead of point estimates (see Trigeorgis [1996] for a summary of standard numerical procedures for solving such problems).

CURRENT PRICING PRACTICE

Although credit derivatives have existed in alternative forms for a long time, their current form is new, and pricing methodologies are still evolving.[12] Here we will describe a practitioner's approach based on information gathered in 1997. Today, the pricing of credit derivatives is based on that of asset swaps. That is because an asset swap is a close substitute for a credit derivative. Let us consider why.

An asset swap is a package consisting of a fixed-income security and an interest-rate or a currency swap. It is constructed by using the price discovery of the swap and options markets to strip out the effect of the noncredit components of the security. Once a fixed-income security is bundled with a swap to remove the interest rate and currency risk, for example, it is turned into a pure credit-based opportunity. A relative value comparison can then be made between this and an existing investment choice.

For example, an investor whose current investment choices are US$ LI-BOR-based may consider a package whose ultimate cash flows are also LI-BOR-based: a Euro Sterling noncallable bond (a fixed-rate Sterling security) on XYZ company combined with a currency swap of fixed GBP (British pounds) at 8.875 in exchange for U.S.$ LIBOR + 20 basis points. The resulting cash flows have no currency or interest-rate risk because both are removed by the currency swap.

Let us see how the transaction works. Initially, the proceeds from the currency swap are used to purchase the XYZ bonds. The exchange rate for the purchase of the XYZ bond is the same as that used for the principal exchange on the currency swap at maturity. The risk assumed is the credit risk of XYZ and the counterparty credit risk for the swap. By buying this package the investor has purchased XYZ exposure. This has the same effect as selling a put: assuming the risk of default in exchange for the credit spread. The only difference is that the buyer of the asset swap *already owns* the XYZ bond, whereas the derivative seller does not. In both instances, there is no interest rate or currency risk.

---

[12]Intrinsic value and price are not the same thing. The former is an estimate of what it is worth, and the latter is what one is willing to pay for it.

Let us say Little Bank wants to buy a put, that is, buy credit protection from Big Bank. The pricing of a credit derivative can start from the pricing of an asset swap. The buyer of the put (say, Little Bank) wants to shed XYZ Corporation exposure, which is now assumed by Big Bank. Big Bank could have taken on this exposure simply by buying a synthetic XYZ security, a fixed-rate bond bundled with an interest rate swap to convert the asset into a LIBOR-based floating-rate instrument (thereby taking on pure credit risk and no market risk[13]). Let us say that the spread over LIBOR for this asset swap for XYZ is 50 basis points. Note that this spread is compensation for pure credit risk of XYZ as priced by the market. Intrinsic value does not enter into the calculation because the institution is taking market pricing as the basis for deriving the "arbitrage-free" price. Arbitrage-free pricing (also known as the law of one price) would dictate that the put and the asset swap are equivalent, all other things being equal. Thus the put should also be priced at 50 basis points.

However, a credit derivative will pay more than an asset swap because of a risk, however slight, about the settlement in case of a default event and greater uncertainty in case Big Bank wants to make a clean exit and close its position. If Little Bank's price for terminating the contract is unattractive, Big Bank has to find some other way of covering its exposure. For this reason, Big Bank, the seller of the put, adds a premium, of say, 25 percent of the risk spread. Thus the derivative will be priced at $50 + 0.25 \times 50 = 62.5$ basis points.

This pricing will apply when the risk of the counterparty selling protection is not an issue. But what if the seller of the put—say, a bank named NoHope Bank—is perceived to be more risky? In this case, Little Bank may not want to buy the put because of the possibility that NoHope Bank may not be able to perform when default occurs. To mitigate this risk, Little Bank will want cash collateral. This is where the credit-linked note comes in. With this instrument, NoHope puts up cash collateral with Little Bank, receiving in exchange an additional premium representing the risk of Little Bank— say, 10 basis points. The net result of this transaction is that NoHope will receive a return of $50 + 12.5 + 10 = 72.5$ basis points over LIBOR from Little Bank. NoHope bank has taken on XYZ risk and also Little Bank risk with respect to return of cash collateral when the put expires unexercised.

In applying this approach we should distinguish between investment-grade and noninvestment-grade credits. For investment-grade credits, because the pure credit spread is already quite small, compensation for illiquidity and structure uses a greater multiplier, say 50 percent as used in the above example. The term structure of credit spreads in the market may be observed in the marketplace (see Table 20.2), which helps to validate the pricing.

For noninvestment-grade names, since the credit spread is already much larger, the illiquidity and structural premiums do not add so much propor-

---

[13] Actually the spread is not pure credit risk; it also includes a spread associated with the counterparty risk in the interest-rate swap.

Table 20.2   Term Structure of Credit Spreads, February 1998

Category	1 Year	2 Years	3 Years	5 Years	7 Years	10 Years
A1 Industrials	47	40	46	48	53	58
A2 Industrials	53	47	50	59	60	71
A3 Industrials	57	51	57	64	69	80
BBB1 Industrials	62	56	63	73	79	87

Source: Bloomberg Financial Markets.

tionally. A name with a spread of 250 basis points may have a default swap spread of 300 (20 percent markup). The increment is greater as the maturity increases. Illiquidity is not as significant an issue in the short term (e.g., one year) as it is for the longer term. These credits are difficult to price because there is not a term structure to observe; it has to be guessed. Noninvestment-grade default swaps tend to be in the one- to three-year range, whereas investment-grade default swaps may be for longer maturities, as much as 10 years.

The next layer of innovation is the *first-to-default swap.* Let us say the basket has four credits, A, B, C, and D, with swap spreads of 30, 35, 40, and 50 basis points, respectively. The asset swap spreads are added up, giving a total of 155 basis points. If the credits are highly correlated, then a lower percentage is applied to the total to arrive at the pricing. The investor may apply, say, 15 percent, and arrive at $155 \times 0.15 = 23$ basis points. If the credits are uncorrelated, then a higher percentage is applied—perhaps 75 percent—to arrive at a price of 116 basis points. The reasoning behind this appears to be that if the risks are correlated, the investor expects the hit to come from a single underlying cause, whereas if they are poorly correlated, the hit may come from *any* of four different causes; therefore the risk is greater. In this exceptional case, correlation is good for the structure.[14]

As the observant reader will have noted, credit derivative pricing depends on the availability of market-based credit spreads. If all assets were marked to market, it is almost a certainty that credit derivatives would gain wide usage. Today, most credit risky assets are not marked to market, but indexing (such as linking delinquencies on a consumer portfolio to regional unemployment rate) makes it possible to use credit derivatives nonetheless.

Thus far, there have been far more theoretical studies on the pricing of debt subject to interest rate risk than on the pricing of assets when credit ratings and spreads are stochastic. Studies of the latter type have just begun. A recent paper by Das and Tufano (1996) provides a good review of the theoretical work and proposes a model for the pricing of credit-sensitive debt when interest rates, credit ratings, and credit spreads are stochastic. As credit derivatives gain wider acceptance, the pricing methodologies will also evolve to handle defaults and credit quality migration.

---

[14]Jan Nicholson, managing director at CapMAC, provided much of the information on current pricing practices.

An institution that wants to reduce its credit risk exposure using derivatives should attempt to answer the following basic questions:

- Will the transaction really reduce the credit risk that is to be reduced? Are the credit event and the time frame linked to the underlying credit in a reasonable way? Does the transaction make sense for the overall portfolio?
- Do the numbers add up? Are the assumptions made about the future states of the world consistent with historic experience, and is there solid reasoning to support the assumptions? Has the analysis dealt correctly with the credit risk and market risk of the asset? Is the price right?
- Is the counterparty risk tolerable? Is there liquidity for the transaction so that it can be closed out during its life?

Credit derivative transactions should be subjected to the same kind of evaluation as other derivatives. It is important that the institution exercise its own independent judgment rather than simply accepting the recommendation of an intermediary. After all, credit data on default, recovery, and correlation of default are generally among the weakest of all financial market data. With regard to pricing, the applicability of these data to the instruments owned by the institution should be carefully examined. The pricing model should be calibrated with live data and thoroughly stress-tested to reveal the financial implications of the transaction.

MARKET ACCEPTANCE OF CREDIT DERIVATIVES

Credit derivatives have caught on because of what appear to be compelling arguments in favor of their use by financial institutions. This is despite the fact that around the time that credit derivatives were introduced, derivatives as a whole were getting bad press because of the well-publicized problems of Gibson Greetings and Procter & Gamble. The motivation to lay off credit risk disappears when the spreads are at a cyclical low, and the bids are at prices above fees. What is more, most concentration risk comes from revolving lines to the better-quality companies in the portfolio: fees on these commitments tend to be very low, rarely enough to cover the cost of getting credit protection.

According to Blythe Masters, regulatory uncertainty about the equitable treatment of credit derivatives and shortcomings in the current risk-based-capital definitions for all banks' assets are the greatest impediments to the wider use of credit derivatives. Finally, documentation has been standardized under an International Swaps and Derivatives Association (ISDA) standard.

In all likelihood, the day will come when credit derivatives are the rule rather than the exception on the balance sheets of financial and nonfinancial institutions.

REFERENCES

Board of Governors of the Federal Reserve System. 1996. Supervisory Guidance for Credit Derivatives SR 96–17 (GE). Washington, D.C.: Board of Governors of the Federal Reserve System.

Cockerell, H. 1984. *Lloyd's of London: A Portrait.* Homewood, Ill.: Dow-Jones Irwin.

Credit Derivatives Come Good. *Risk* 9 (7), 22–6.

Das, S. R., and P. Tufano. 1996. Pricing Credit-Sensitive Debt When Interest Rates, Credit Ratings and Credit Spreads Are Stochastic. *Journal of Financial Engineering* 5 (2): 161–198.

Lucas, D. J. 1995. Default Correlation and Credit Analysis. *The Journal of Fixed Income* 4 (4): 76–87.

Trigeorgis, L. 1996. *Real Options.* Cambridge, Mass.: MIT Press.

Chapter **21**

Credit Risk of Derivatives

Credit risk is the risk that a loss will be incurred if a counterparty defaults on a derivatives contract. The loss due to a default is the cost of replacing the contract, less any recovery. The replacement cost represents the present value, at the time of default, of expected future cash flows. It is important to emphasize that a credit loss will occur only if the counterparty defaults and the derivative contract has a positive mark to market value to the nondefaulting party. Both conditions have to be satisfied simultaneously for a loss to be incurred.

—Global Derivatives Study Group, Group of Thirty

Most derivative transactions are, by nature, highly leveraged. In the futures market, for example, it is possible to speculate on the entire value of a U.S. government bond with just a fraction of the money needed to purchase the bond in the cash market. Counterparty risk can therefore be substantial—indeed, so large that the marketplace imposes strict credit quality requirements on participants. Although defaults figure prominently in the assessment of credit risk in the G-30 definition, a mere change in the credit quality of the obligor can signal a change in the credit risk of a transaction. In this chapter we will consider the approaches that can be used to analyze counterparty credit risk as it relates to over-the-counter (OTC) derivatives. For a discussion of clearinghouses and margining in relation to derivatives, please see Chapter 5.

Derivative volume, both on organized exchanges and in OTC markets has grown tremendously in the last 15 years. Table 21.1 shows the volume over a five-year period for U.S. commercial banks.

Although figures based on notional principal outstanding make derivative volume seem very large, the replacement value (shown in the last line of the table) gives a more accurate sense of the overall size of the exposure. On the basis of this measure, the swaps of U.S. banks had a replacement value of 7.29 percent in 1991 (151/2,071) and 3.7 percent in 1995 (219/5,945). Chew (1996) estimates the replacement values to be in the range 0.6 to 2.4 percent for interest-rate derivatives and 1.1 to 3.8 percent for foreign exchange derivatives.

DERIVATIVE LOSSES

Concern about derivatives has recently been magnified by a series of derivatives-related disasters in the mid 1990s. Japan's Kashima Oil, America's

Table 21.1 Off-Balance-Sheet Derivatives U.S. Commercial Banks Notional Amounts ($ Billions)

	12/91	12/92	12/93	12/94	12/95
Total derivatives	7,339	8,765	11,878	15,773	16,860
Futures and forward contracts	3,876	4,780	6,230	8,110	7,399
Interest rate contracts	1,227	1,738	2,497	3,435	3,063
Foreign exchange rate contracts	2,624	3,016	3,689	4,620	4,221
Other futures and forwards[a]	25	26	44	54	115
Options contracts	1,393	1,588	2,386	2,841	3,516
Interest rate options	854	1,013	1,771	2,039	2,485
Foreign currency options	463	495	518	653	817
Other option contracts	76	60	97	149	214
Swaps	2,071	2,417	3,262	4,822	5,945
Interest rate swaps	1,756	2,122	2,947	4,450	5,547
Foreign exchange rate swaps	306	279	277	331	350
Other swaps	8	16	38	40	49
Memoranda					
Spot FX contracts	NA	NA	NA	NA	305
Number of banks reporting derivatives	612	613	666	625	558
Replacement cost of interest rate and FX Rate Contracts[b]	151	148	143	146	219

[a] Not reported by banks with less than $300 millions in assets.
[b] Reflects contracts covered by risk-based capital requirements. Does not include FX rate contracts with original maturity of 14 days or less or futures contracts.
Source: House (1996).

Procter & Gamble and Gibson Greetings, Germany's Metallgesellschaft, and Great Britain's Barings Securities, to name a few, all suffered spectacular losses in which derivatives figured prominently.

Beder (1996) of Capital Market Risk Advisors reported losses of $16.24 billion in derivatives in 1995. Although the amounts associated with credit losses were not broken out separately, the reasons given for the losses are as follows:

- Insufficient management oversight
- Mark-to-model risk
- Improper hedging techniques
- Unexpected market moves
- Too much risk relative to capital
- Fraud

Losses here mean that the derivative transaction failed to produce the intended result, not that one party lost in a zero-sum game. Credit losses on derivatives are just beginning to emerge. According to Beder, Chase and Bankers Trust recently announced losses due to the nonperformance of certain counterparties on OTC derivative transactions. Because of the decline in the overall credit quality of the banking system, the credit quality of derivative transactions entered into with financial institutions cannot be taken for granted. To undertake derivative-based transactions, counterparties have had to establish AAA-rated special purpose derivative vehicles. After many years of financial innovation, it is fair to say that the critical issue facing the global players today is the control of credit exposure both at the individual deal level and at the portfolio level.

When reference is made to derivative risk it usually pertains to *all* risk associated with using derivatives. Banks (1997) mentions the following risks in the capital markets: operational risk, legal/documentary risk, liquidity risk of the asset or collateral, hedging risk, sovereign risk, counterparty default risk, market risk, delivery risk, position risk, and provisional risk (additional risk exposure due to a weakening credit). All these risks apply to derivatives as well. Here, however, we are concerned with the *counterparty credit risk of derivatives*—the amount of current and future exposure to a counterparty as a consequence of a derivative transaction, the likelihood that the counterparty will default on the financial obligation coming due, and the magnitude of the recovery upon default.

THE ROLE OF COUNTERPARTY CREDIT RISK

The measurement of credit risk is important to the derivatives market for a variety of reasons, of which pricing is the most important. It is only through sensible pricing that a firm can ensure that it is adequately compensated for assuming current and future counterparty credit risk. There are many subtle issues in pricing. For example, the credit risk of a five-year pay-fixed swap is *not* identical to the credit risk of a five-year fixed-rate loan. In the case of a loan, the borrower does not need to go to the market for five years, but in the case of the swap, the borrower needs to roll over the principal every three to six months because the underlying financing will be three to six months floating. Second, both principal and interest are at risk in a loan, whereas an interest swap involves interest alone. Moreover, because the periodic cash flows are based on the difference between two interest rates in the swap, they are smaller in magnitude to those on a comparable loan.[1] Third, a default in a swap requires two events to occur jointly: that the party to the swap is in distress *and* the value of the contract to the party is negative (i.e., money is owed). Fourth, a swapper can more easily put collateral and credit triggers onto a swap. These variables, taken together, can influence the credit spread to be applied, which may generally be lower for a swap than for a loan.

Once counterparty risk is understood, it can be mitigated through deal structure or hedging. Banks have a unique advantage here over the exchange-traded derivatives markets, where standardization prevails. Banks, by contrast, can be more flexible in meeting the needs of the borrower.

An understanding of counterparty risk is also necessary for purposes of setting aside an appropriate level of capital to weather adverse outcomes. This, in turn, makes it possible to evaluate the profitability of a derivatives operation on a rational basis.

DERIVATIVE EXPOSURE

In the case of a derivative, the amount at risk is not the notional principal and will vary based on what assumptions are made about the financial variables. Generally, the exposure is expressed as the *current exposure*—the current cost of finding a replacement for the existing counterparty; the *potential exposure*—based on what might happen to interest rates in the future; and the *peak exposure*—the replacement cost in a worst-case scenario. Why replacement cost? In the case of an interest-rate swap, the contract calls for exchanging cash flows in every reset period. The amount of the cash flow represents the difference between the fixed and floating interest rates multiplied by the notional principal. Suppose the counterparty defaults and files for bankruptcy. This has a financial impact only if money was owed by the counterparty because the interest-rate difference was against it for the remainder of the contract. The counterparty will no longer be available to hold up its end of the bargain, so a replacement must be found. If rates have moved, replacement will be based on the current interest-rate differential and on expectations about rates. The important point to remember is that the estimate of this exposure is influenced by a number of exogenous variables that themselves cannot be determined in advance.

Another key feature of derivative credit risk is that it may be nonlinear. For example, if you have purchased an interest-rate cap, your counterparty

---

[1]The risk in currency swaps is greater, though it tends to remain constant.

credit risk increases as interest rates increase beyond the cap. However, if rates are below the cap, the counterparty risk is zero.[2] In the case of the holder of an over-the-counter call option, the current exposure is equal to the current payoff, but only if the option is in the money. If the option is out of the money, the current exposure is zero.

INTEREST-RATE SWAPS

The intermediary in an interest-rate swap between two counterparties faces exposure because if either party defaults, the intermediary will have to step in and fulfill the terms of the contract with the nondefaulting counterparty. As summarized in Table 21.2, the impact of default on the intermediary is determined by the direction of the rate change and by which party defaults. The intermediary's exposure is equal to the replacement cost of the swap, or the loss sustained by selling the remainder of the unmatched swap in the secondary market. The replacement cost is found by simulating a scenario of rates and projecting the period net cash flows to the party at risk. This

---

[2]In some instances the increase in short-term rates may flatten or invert the yield curve, thereby indicating lower future short-term rates. Typically this sort of behavior is modeled in the interest rate scenarios used to estimate exposure.

Table 21.2   Interest Rates and Exposure in Interest Rate Swaps

Interest rate environment	Effect on the Intermediary	
	If the fixed payer (floating receiver) defaults	If the fixed receiver (floating payer) defaults
Interest rate unchanged	None	None
Interest rates increase	Intermediary gains because the replacement cost of finding a new fixed payer is lower.	Intermediary incurs loss because the nondefaulting unmatched fixed pay swap is now worth less in the marketplace.
Interest rates decline	Intermediary incurs a loss. Loss corresponds to the increase in price of lower fixed rate for remainder of swap.	Intermediary gains. Gain corresponds to increase in price of the nondefaulting, unmatched fixed pay swap.

Source: Das (1994). Reprinted with permission.

notion of replacement cost is applicable not only to interest-rate swaps but also to currency swaps, forward-rate agreements, caps, collars, and floors.

An example may clarify the concept of potential loss. Let us assume that a bank enters into a $100 million, five-year swap with a company. The bank will receive a fixed rate of 10 percent against six-month LIBOR. Initially, the exposure is zero. Let us assume that the swap rate then declines to 9 percent. At the end of the first year the market value of the receive-fixed swap will go up by an amount equal to the present value (PV) of an annuity of $1 million for four years (1 percent of $10 million). This is the replacement cost of the swap at the end of the first year under this scenario. At the end of the second year, if the rates go up by another 100 basis points, the replacement cost will be the PV of an annuity of $2 million for three years, and so on, returning to zero at the end of the fifth year. The nominal (undiscounted) value of the exposure for the expected interest-rate scenario is shown in Table 21.3. It is seen that exposure is subject to two effects: changes because of the amortization (passage of time) and volatility (changes in interest rates).

In any year, the current exposure will equal the potential exposure estimated for that year to maturity. The peak exposure in the preceding example is $6 million. Note that the credit exposure on the swap can vary dramatically, depending on the divergence in interest rates. The changing exposure results in the familiar "inverted cup" graph associated with the modeling of interest-rate scenarios adverse to the party at risk (Figure 21.1). The exposure in future time periods may also be expressed in present-value terms by discounting at the prevailing interest rate.

The potential exposure for other derivatives such as futures and options may be similarly derived by postulating a future financial scenario and projecting cash flows, which then may be translated into a replacement cost. If the counterparty has a bilateral netting arrangement, then the exposures should be netted out before arriving at the exposure at the institution level. If there is no netting, only the positive (in the money) exposures should be added up. For futures, the exposure will increase linearly. For some options, the presence of an exchange will eliminate the need to calculate counterparty exposures, but some institutions may want to do it for tracking purposes.

Table 21.3   Example Showing Increasing *Potential* Credit Exposure in a Swap

Beginning of year	Volatility effect (rate increase from year 1, basis points)	Amortization effect (time remaining, years)	Exposure ($MM)
1	0	5	0
2	100	4	$4
3	200	3	$6
4	300	2	$6
5	400	1	$4
6	NA	0	$0

Figure 21.1   Potential Swap Exposure

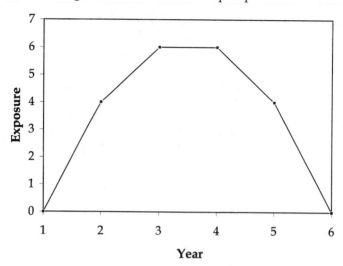

CALCULATION OF EXPOSURE AND EXPECTED LOSS

Although most people agree on the constituents of credit risk, the actual calculation of it is subject to wide variation. At the rudimentary level, as we have just seen, exposure is calculated by using worst case scenarios to derive a value to use in conjunction with the credit limits. At a more-advanced level, yield curve and default probability models may be used in a Monte Carlo simulation to develop a distribution of exposure and losses. The detailed method for calculating the future credit exposure in an interest-rate swap may be summarized in two steps: the calculation of exposure and the calculation of losses.[3]

Calculation of Exposure

Distributions of future credit exposure are estimated at many discrete points over the life of the instrument or portfolio. These distributions are conditioned on the current state of the financial variables (such as the prevailing yield curve and credit spreads), but not on the probability of counterparty default. The future state of the financial variables is specified through a Monte Carlo simulation employing an interest-rate term structure model that has been calibrated with historical data. The interest-rate model will, at the minimum, contain a volatility component to model the random behavior of interest rates. The replacement value of the contract (mark to market) is calculated at each point along each time path. The replacement value assumes riskless replacement. The resulting exposures are used to calculate the average and maximum exposures.

---

[3]This section draws from Duffee (1996).

Calculation of Losses

After the exposure is measured, other elements affecting credit risk must be evaluated, including the counterparty's financial condition, which will influence the probability of default, and the seniority structure of the borrower's liabilities, which will influence the recovery. The probability of default and expected recovery rate are then applied to the replacement value of the contract to obtain the average loss and the maximum loss given default. Having opened up this line of reasoning, we can also apply the concepts of expected and unexpected losses and correlation of defaults (see Chapters 17 and 18). In particular, the transition probability from one risk category to the next may be applied in deciding on the correct pricing to be used or in recouponing should there be a downgrade or upgrade during the life of the contract.

Let us illustrate the calculations by a simple example. Bank X enters into an interest rate swap with company Y. It receives semiannual payments at an interest rate of 8 percent against payment of six month LIBOR for a period of three years. Assuming a notional principal amount of $1,000,000, we can calculate X's exposure for two scenarios: (1) the swap rate goes down to 6 percent, and (2) the swap rate goes up to 10 percent.

There is exposure to bank X when the swap rate falls (if Y defaults) because X now must replace the existing swap at (and receive thereafter) *lower rates*. The exposure is the present value of the remaining payment differential in the swap discounted at the new (replacement) swap rate. For a swap rate of 6 percent, the replacement cost is $45,797 at the end of the first interest payment and gradually drops to zero, reflecting the reduction in the number of interest payments for the remaining life of the swap (Table 21.4). (The exposure is shown as negative values). There is no exposure to Y for X when the swap rate goes to 10 percent, because X will now make an additional profit if it has to replace the swap at a higher prevailing rate.

If company Y is BBB rated, then the bank's implied credit spread in the swap would be the equivalent of 200 basis points on the exposure (based on the credit spreads shown in Table 21.5). Put differently, entering into this swap transaction is the equivalent of making an amortizing loan of $45,797 to Y at a 200 basis point credit spread, and this is built into the percent fixed rate on the swap. The implied credit margin for the swap, spread over the notional principal amount of $1,000,000 is then $.08 \times 45,797/1,000,000 = 37$ basis points.

This analysis assumes that company Y remains a BBB throughout the life of the swap. But what if it gets downgraded or defaults sometime along the way? And what is the likelihood that it may happen? Table 21.6[4] gives one-year transition probabilities for a BBB-rated company. Based on this table, the probability that Y will be downgraded to a BB is 5.30 percent. The probability that it will worsen to BB, B, or CCC is 5.30, 1.17, and 0.12 percent, respectively. Corresponding to these ratings, the incremental credit spread,

---

[4]The credit spreads and default probabilities shown in Table 21.4 and Table 21.5 are merely illustrative.

Table 21.4 Calculation of Swap Exposure

Interest period	Fixed rate payment @ 8 percent	Fixed rate payment @ 6 percent	Fixed rate payment @ 10 percent	Cash flow differential @ 6 percent to X	Cash flow differential @ 10 percent to X	PV of remaining cash flows discounted at 6 percent	PV of remaining cash flows discounted at 10 percent
1	40,000	30,000	50,000	(10,000)	10,000	(45,797)	43,295
2	40,000	30,000	50,000	(10,000)	10,000	(37,171)	35,460
3	40,000	30,000	50,000	(10,000)	10,000	(28,286)	27,232
4	40,000	30,000	50,000	(10,000)	10,000	(19,135)	18,594
5	40,000	30,000	50,000	(10,000)	10,000	(9,709)	9,524
6	40,000	30,000	50,000	(10,000)	10,000	0	0

Table 21.5 Credit Spreads

Rating	1 year	2 years	3 years
AAA	50	100	150
AA	65	105	155
A	75	110	170
BBB	100	150	200
BB	250	280	350
B	300	380	480
CCC	1200	1200	1100

Table 21.6 Transition Probabilities

Rating	Probability
AAA	0.02
AA	0.33
A	5.95
BBB	86.93
BB	5.30
B	1.17
CCC	0.12
Default	0.18

taken from Table 21.5, is 150 (that is, 350 − 200), 280 (that is, 480 − 200), and 900 (that is, 1100 − 200) basis points. This equates to a fixed-rate basis of 9.5, 10.8, and 17 percent, from the base value of 8 percent for the company. Using this amount, the downgrade premium applicable to this credit may be calculated by the expected value of the incremental interest based on the transition probability for the exposure amount (in this case $45,797). In Table 21.7, this comes out to $298, which translates to 3 basis points on the notional principal. Thus in this arrangement, the credit spread for the swap is 37 basis

Table 21.7 Effect of Rating Migration on Spreads

Downgrade from BBB to:	Incremental credit spread (basis points)	Transition probability (%)	Incremental expected value of loss (on exposure of $45,797)
BB	150	5.3	231
B	280	1.17	58
CCC	900	0.12	9
			Total = $298

points along with an additional 3 basis points to protect bank X against the downgrading risk of Y.

Another example of incorporating migration and default likelihoods is provided in Gupton, Finger, and Bhatia (1997, 47). Bond market default and migration data (discussed in Chapters 15 and 16) are useful to the analyst in extracting alternative market value based credit spreads.

Although we utilized a single value for the swap rate in the example, in practice, institutions use stochastic models to generate the trajectory of the interest rates, and Monte Carlo simulations are employed to derive the swap exposures. For institutions unable or unwilling to perform Monte Carlo simulations, the Bank for International Settlements has provided an add-on factor that is based on asset type and remaining maturity. To derive the potential exposure, this factor should be multiplied by the notional amount of the contract and added to its current replacement value. The add-on factors provided by BIS and Standard & Poor's are presented in Table 21.8. These add-ons are applicable to the portfolio as a whole and not to an individual counterparty. It may be noted that an institution cannot use the figures derived from these factors to set prices any more than it can use regulatory capital to price its loans. These are merely rules of thumb.

Currency Swaps

From the point of view of exposure, currency swaps resemble interest-rate swaps, but with two exceptions. First, the cash flow projections are affected not only by the two interest rates but also by the currency exchange rate. Second, at maturity there is an exchange of principal between the two parties. The general impact on an intermediary for a default in a fixed A$ to fixed US$ currency swap is summarized in Table 21.9. A fixed A$—floating US$ swap may be analyzed by splitting it into two swaps: Fixed A$—Fixed US$ and Fixed US$—Floating US$.

Table 21.8   Add-on Factors for Calculating Potential Exposure

BIS add-on (July 1994 and April 1995 amendment) remaining maturity (years)	Interest rates	Currencies	Equities
< 1	0.0	1.0	6.0
1–5	0.5	5.0	8.0
> 5	1.5	7.5	10.0
S&P risk factors			
Futures and forwards	0.3	3.0	15.0
Options	2.0	4.0	15.0
Swaps	2.5	10.0	15.0

Source: L. Chew (1996), *Managing Derivatives Risks*, p. 129. Copyright John Wiley & Sons Limited. Reproduced with permission.

Table 21.9   Effect of Counterparty Default on Intermediary

	Effect on intermediary	
	Default by fixed A$ payer	Default by fixed US$ payer
Interest rate environment		
Rate same as contract rate	No effect	No effect
A$ rate higher than contract rate	Intermediary gains	Intermediary loses
A$ rate lower than contract rate	Intermediary loses	Intermediary gains
US$ rate higher than contract rate	Intermediary loses	Intermediary gains
US$ rate lower than contract rate	Intermediary gains	Intermediary gains
Currency rate environment		
Rate same as contract rate	No effect	No effect
A$ appreciates against US$	Intermediary loses	Intermediary gains
A$ depreciates against US$	Intermediary gains	Intermediary loses

Source: Das (1994). Reprinted with permission.

MANAGEMENT OF DERIVATIVE CREDIT RISK

Derivatives are executed either on an exchange or in the OTC market. In the exchanges, the process of margining (see Chapter 5) provides credit risk management. By serving as a hub, an exchange is able to add up and net out all of a member firm's exposures. It thus makes it possible to manage the exposure on an aggregate single-risk basis. In comparison to the OTC approach, this is not only safer from a credit risk perspective, but also more economical. Currently, no mechanism exists for knowing, on a current basis, the total value a counterparty has at risk in the OTC market. Most institutions rely on the counterparty's public bond ratings and their own internal "house limits" to manage credit risk exposure. Default prediction models such as ZETA or KMV may also be used to assess a counterparty's financial condition. Portfolio management methods based on these tools may be applied to portfolios of derivatives. Published and proprietary models also exist for assessing the solvency risk of banks.[5]

In response to criticism by the U.S. General Accounting Office (1994) of regulatory gaps in the derivative markets, representatives of OTC dealers have developed a voluntary code of conduct intended to guide conduct between participants in the wholesale OTC financial markets. It is hoped that, among other things, this code will produce better disclosure to participants about counterparty risk.

MASTER NETTING AGREEMENTS

Adoption of master netting arrangements allow a bank to net out all its exposures to a given counterparty rather than having the exposure from each

---

[5]Please refer to Chapter 13 for more on financial institution risk.

individual transaction stand on its own. The netting includes both payments and balances.[6] When a bilateral "closeout netting" arrangement has been signed, a counterparty that is defaulting on derivative contracts on which it owes money cannot simultaneously demand payment on contracts on which it is owed money.[7]

- *Time puts* in swap agreements give a party the option to get out of all deals after a preset period.
- *Collateral arrangements* require the counterparty to post collateral in support of the transaction. These were quite common with capital-poor thrifts that entered into interest-rate swaps in the late 1980s. The collateral would be topped up to keep up with changing exposures.
- *Creation of a cash buffer* may be used to mitigate settlement risk with a weaker counterparty by altering the timing of the cash flows between the amount to be received and the amount to be paid out.
- *Rating downgrade triggers* allow a bank the option to presettle outstanding transactions should a counterparty's grade fall below a certain level (Lucas 1995).

STRUCTURED FINANCE SOLUTIONS TO DERIVATIVE CREDIT RISK

Some organizations have set up bankruptcy-remote SPDVs (special purpose derivative vehicles) to gain a AAA rating. Major financial institutions require that nonbank counterparties such as securities firms establish SPDVs to enter into derivatives transactions in the OTC market with them. SPDVs are well-capitalized, stand-alone entities that "ring-fence" the transactions and are protected from their parent's (the securities firm's) bankruptcy (Derek 1995). Three types of structures have been set up: joint ventures, separately capitalized vehicles (SCVs) with a continuation structure, and separately capitalized vehicles (SCVs) with a termination structure.

In the joint venture structure, a derivatives firm teams up with a stronger partner to enhance its credit rating, presumably in exchange for a share of the profits in the joint venture or some other quid pro quo. Goldman Sachs's joint venture with Mitsui is an example of this structure.

In the SCV with a continuation structure, a contingent manager is appointed to step in to continue the transactions through the maturity of the open deals. The parent posts sufficient collateral to the subsidiary to obtain a top rating. This approach was pioneered by Merrill Lynch and appears to have greater market acceptance than the termination structure.

---

[6]For example, the International Swap Dealers Association (ISDA) has a standard master agreement to separate deal-specific confirmations that are added. The U.S. bankruptcy code has been amended expressly to permit the exercise of rights of termination, and in particular, closeout netting. This was to allay concerns that a bankruptcy trustee would cherry pick the contracts to continue depending on financial impact (Hendricks 1994).

[7]It is assumed here that the closeout netting is consistent with the legal jurisdiction relevant for the counterparty.

In the termination structure, which has been pioneered by Salomon Brothers, existing derivative transactions are terminated at agreed-upon termination values. Thereupon the SCV is liquidated.

EVALUATING THE CURRENT METHODS FOR ASSESSING DERIVATIVE CREDIT RISK

Exposure—the amount at risk—is dynamic and subject to variability because of uncertainty about the future of market variables and about their impact on a derivative transaction. Exposure measurements may also be impacted by *model risk*, that is, how the effects of external variables are modeled. There are, for example, many interest-rate models available today, such as the Ho-Lee model (Ho and Lee 1986),[8] the Black-Derman-Toy model (Black, Derman, and Toy 1990),[9] and the Heath, Jarrow, and Morton model.[10] Each of these models makes a set of assumptions based on which the output, that is, time path of the interest rates, is generated. Within the yield curve itself, the mathematical methods for deriving the zero-coupon rates for various maturities are subject to variation depending upon which interpolation technique is used.

Duffee (1996) compared calculations of potential exposure by the Monte Carlo method using three progressively sophisticated models: a Cox-Ingersoll-Ross (1985) model for interest rates with fixed parameters, a Cox-Ingersoll-Ross model with probabilistically selected parameters, and a bootstrap method that directly employed actual historic data. The third method is unconditional in that it uses the actual price paths. He found that the Monte Carlo methods using yield curve models tended to underestimate the magnitude of the exposure relative to the unconditional distributions. His research indicates that model risk may lead to mismeasurement of credit risks for typical derivative instruments and third parties.

Duffee found that stochastic models used in projecting future values are accepted at face value, without proper regard for the behavior of the underlying financial variables. A second problem is that the financial variables driving the interest-rate paths are not used jointly to determine the firm's

---

[8]The Ho-Lee model generates a future interest by modeling it as the previous interest rate plus or minus a random shock. It assumes that at any time the interest rate is normally distributed. It uses only two parameters: interest rate volatility σ and drift term m.

[9]The Black-Derman-Toy model, unlike the Ho-Lee model, allows the short-term volatility to vary over time and makes the drift term a function of the level of rates.

[10]The Heath, Jarrow, and Morton (HJM) model is the most general form of term structure models. It focuses on instantaneous forward rates in the yield curve. A wide variety of volatility structures can be chosen in the HJM model to match either the historical or observable volatility in the term structure. Being able to model each forward rate independently allows each of them to depend on external shocks differently and exhibit a richer correlation structure than was possible with other models. It has been demonstrated that all the previous term structure models are special cases of HJM. HJM is actually an approach, not a model. In many of its variations, it is becoming the standard method of term structure modeling. Please see Baxter and Rennie (1997) and van Deventer and Imai (1997).

credit quality. Third, correlations among derivative instruments are not taken into account either in measuring exposure or in pricing. Specifically, Duffee points out that current derivative credit risk methodologies do not consider adequately the correlations of default and the marginal effect of a derivative instrument on the upper bound of credit losses associated with the portfolio.

COMBINING CREDIT AND MARKET RISK

In traditional credit products, it was relatively simple to separate the credit risk from the market risk. Indeed, the credit function was often functionally separate from the treasury (market risk) function. But as is evident with off-balance-sheet assets, credit risk and market risk are closely interlinked. It is also not uncommon for an on-balance-sheet asset to be bundled with off-balance-sheet assets (a loan combined with a cap, or an asset swap, for example). In such instances, the credit and market functions need to be combined because the credit risk in the transaction depends on market value. Diversification applies both to credit risk and market risk.

If an organization has multiple derivative contracts, the volatility of its portfolio's value will be influenced not only by the volatility of the individual contracts but also by the extent to which the contracts move together in response to changing market conditions. Since domestic and foreign interest rates and exchange rates are closely related, the volatility of the market portfolio is *not* a simple sum of the component volatilities. In some cases, the increase in exposure due to interest rates will be offset by changes in exchange rates. A portfolio that is evenly divided between pay-fixed and pay-floating swaps will exhibit low volatility because when rates rise, the increase in the value of the pay-fixed swaps will be offset by a fall in value of the pay-floating swaps.

Increasingly, large institutions are combining the oversight of market risk and credit risk. According to Steve Thieke, managing director, head of credit and market risk management, J. P. Morgan, Inc., the bank is finding that as it moves away from the classic "buy and hold" strategy to a strategy of "originate-package-and-distribute," it is increasingly exposed to market risk both because of its need to distribute the loan assets and because of its derivatives transactions. In return for transferring market risk, the bank is also taking on counterparty risk. Moreover, the bank finds business opportunities such as credit derivatives that revolve around the concept of credit intermediation. To manage the portfolio on a total return basis, the bank has recognized that it needs to view credit and market risks consistently. In a market populated by a finite number of financial institutions dealing in derivatives, concentration risk (single entity, country, and product type) can reach sufficiently high levels to cause concern. For these reasons, having a view that combines both credit and market risk is considered essential.

Today credit losses are generally projected over the remaining life of the contract assuming that the contract will be retained until maturity. If the market for credit risk becomes more liquid, it will become possible for banks to terminate or assign the contract to other dealers. By means of credit derivatives, a bank may be able to shield itself from the credit risk associated with a derivative contract. Thus, the credit risk of derivatives must be analyzed in the context of an entire portfolio—one that may consist of the combined effect of all the exposures an institution has to a single obligor, currency, country, or product type. This approach may be used to arrive at pricing, selling, or hedging decisions. This is one of the basic goals of tools such as CreditMetrics used to combine default prediction with correlation of default, and correlation of credit quality change.

References

Banks, E. 1997. *Volatility and Credit Risk in the Capital Markets*. Chicago: Irwin.

Baxter, M., and A. Rennie. 1997. *Financial Calculus*. Cambridge, England: Cambridge University Press.

Beder, T. S. 1996. Lessons from Derivatives Losses. In *Derivatives Risk and Responsibility*, edited by R. A. Klein and J. Lederman. Chicago: Irwin.

Black, F., E. Derman, and W. Toy. 1990. A One-Factor Model of Interest Rates and Its Application to Treasury Bond Options. *Financial Analysts Journal* (January-February): 33–39.

Chew, L. 1996. *Managing Derivatives Risks*. New York: John Wiley & Sons.

Cox, J. C., J. E. Ingersoll, Jr., and S. A. Ross. 1985. A Theory of the Term Structure of Interest Rates. *Econometrica* 53: 385–407.

Das, S. 1994. *Swaps and Financial Derivatives*. 2d ed. London: IFR Publishing.

Derek, R. 1995. Special Purpose Derivative Vehicles. *Accountancy* (November).

Duffee, D. 1996. On Measuring Credit Risks of Derivative Instruments. *Journal of Banking and Finance* 20: 805–833.

Global Derivatives Study Group, Group of Thirty. 1995. *Principles and Practices for Wholesale Financial Market Transactions* 1.1. Washington, DC: Group of Thirty.

Gupton, G. M., C. C. Finger, and M. Bhatia. 1997. *CreditMetrics: The Benchmark for Understanding Credit Risk*. New York: J. P. Morgan Inc. 3 April.

Hendricks, D. 1994. Netting Agreements and the Credit Exposures of OTC Derivatives Products. *Federal Reserve Bank of New York Quarterly Review* 19(1), 7–18.

Ho, T., and S. Lee. 1986. Term Structure Movements and Pricing Interest Rate Contingent Claims. *Journal of Finance* 41 (5): 1011–1029.

Lucas, D. J. 1995. The Effectiveness of Downgrade Provisions in Reducing Counterparty Credit Risk. *Journal of Fixed Income* (June).

U.S. General Accounting Office. 1994. *Financial Derivatives: Actions Needed to Protect the Financial System*. Washington, D.C.

U.S. House. 1996. Committee on Banking and Financial Services. Hearings. Cong. sess. 104.

van Deventer, D. R., and K. Imai. 1997. *Financial Risk Analytics*. Chicago: Irwin.

Chapter 22

Country Risk Models

The idea of being fully hedged is a very questionable assumption. If the counterparty is out of business you won't find anyone to cover the position. Small players in the market will have difficulty, only the Triple-A players will survive. We are developing toward the Titanic solution. We only build bigger and bigger ships, but not remembering there are still icebergs.

—Norbert Walter, chief economist, Deutsche Bank

Country risk, a topic that receives added attention in the media whenever there is an international economic crisis, is always a complicated subject for a lender. This is because outcomes from lending decisions not only are uncertain because of the individual obligor but also may be swamped by macro variables that may have nothing to do with the borrower's creditworthiness. In this chapter, we will review the important issues in country risk and risk assessment tools. We analyze the Asian financial crisis of 1997 using many of these tools. We conclude this chapter with a description of a few recent country risk models.

Country risk is the possibility of delayed, reduced, or nonpayment of interest and principal where the outcome is attributable to the country of the borrower. In practical terms, country credit risk requires assessing political risk, social risk, economic risk, environmental risk, regulatory risk including tariffs and taxes, and foreign exchange risk, to name a few, and putting these in the context of the credit risk of the individual obligor. Another dimension of country risk is that of contagion—that right or wrong, what affects one country spreads to others.

Legal risk arises because of diminished legal redress: collateral may be difficult to repossess or liquidate, for example. Political risk may be associated with political upheavals, revolution, and outbreak of hostilities. Social risks may arise from strikes or law and order problems. Economic risks may be magnified by a cyclical slowdown in economic growth, increase in costs or export prices, fall in export demand, or fiscal policy inhibiting growth. Sovereign risk may arise because a nation-state has the option to renege on its debts. Transfer risk may arise if a country imposes exchange controls on remittances even if adequate foreign exchange is available. Indeed, transactions may involve risks because of differences in language, cultural differences, and even time zones. Each of these factors is a complex, constantly evolving topic by itself, even for a single country; space permits us just brief look at their aspects. The references provided at the end of this chapter provide more expansive analyses.

POLITICAL RISK FACTORS

The relationship between the constitution of a country and the way it is enforced gives a fundamental measure of political risk. In some countries the importance accorded to the constitution and its legal precedents is high and provides credibility to the government. In others, the constitution is used, or even frequently amended, to achieve the government's own goals. Depending on the economic system in place, the link between the political leadership and the bureaucracy may be strong or weak. The degree of influence that political leaders in the United States can exert on the bureaucracy, for example, is greater than it is in the United Kingdom. In some countries political risk is defined by a few key players in the political parties because they have personally more impact than the ideologies of the parties. The behavior of the bureaucracy, which is responsible for the day-to-day decision making in the country is also another dimension of political risk. The bureaucracy of some countries greatly influences the speed with which things get done. Corruption also plays a role.

With the conclusion of the cold war, the political leanings of the country are influenced less by ideological concerns. However, the effect of the legacy systems (i.e., the remnants of communism), local geopolitics, and internal ethnic and religious differences have assumed greater importance. In many Asian economies, for example, the state-controlled sector continues to be a dominant factor, with stronger links to the political leadership than the private sector. Lack of transparency and corruption often indicate the political risk of the country.

Literacy rate, degree of urbanization, income distribution, per capita gross domestic product (GDP), and birth rate are some of the quantitative indicators of the underlying social structure that contributes to the assessment of political risk. Although the political risk assessment is most often a qualitative one, trends in the key quantitative indicators are helpful in the assessment process in much the same way as in classic credit analysis.

TRANSFER RISK

Transfer risk refers to the economic and financial factors attributable to the country (as separate from the financial condition of the borrower). When considering the transfer risk associated with a private borrower, it is often very difficult to separate it from the individual entity risk. For example, the exchange rate will influence the operating results of an export-oriented company to a greater extent than, say, a power generation company whose customer base is domestic. To assess the transfer risk of a country, it is customary to analyze the country's balance of payments, that is, the country's current account position, the size and structure of its external debt, and the level of liquid foreign reserves it possesses. Because foreign exchange is critical to a country's ability to service its foreign debt, foreign exchange movements related to the country's international trade in goods and services and capital account flows are crucial to assessing and monitoring a country's credit-worthiness.

Several other economic variables—both domestic and foreign—also influence a nation's balance-of-payments strength, including inflation, exchange rate and monetary policy, fiscal policy, and the relative openness of the economy to both trade and capital. Some of the external macro factors are the imposition of trade barriers (both unilateral and retaliatory), world commodity prices (especially oil price), foreign interest rates, and even weather patterns. Obviously, the relative importance of these factors will vary with the country. Weather plays a greater role in a country dependent on coffee exports, whereas falling metals prices impact a country exporting aluminum ore (bauxite).

In addition to the internal and external factors just mentioned, the current level and mix of external debt and the available credit from major providers of liquidity to the country are the other components of the transfer risk puzzle. Together with foreign reserves, the liquidity and solvency position of a country are influenced by the availability of funds from government and quasi-government entities, International Monetary Fund (IMF), and the World Bank, world capital markets, and direct institutional investors. Rating agencies play an important role as assessors of this risk, both in assigning an initial rating and then monitoring it on a continuing basis (see Chapter 6).

KEY RATIOS

Just as there are key ratios commonly used in analyzing corporate credit, there are counterparts in country risk assessment as well. Of the ratios, one of the most important is the debt service ratio. This is defined for a future period as the ratio of (interest and principal with maturity of more than one year) to (income from exports of goods and services plus unilateral transfers).

A ratio of less than 10 percent is considered very healthy, while anything over 30 percent becomes potentially problematic, depending on the maturity structure of the debt, the degree of access to credit markets and other country-specific factors. It is useful to note that the numerator of the ratio is relatively less volatile than the denominator, and the quantities being used to calculate the ratio may be subject to measurement and timing errors. The debt ratio has many drawbacks, one of which is that it is subject to the volatility of imports or exports. Even if a debt ratio is satisfactory in the current time period, the existence of a large current account deficit may indicate potential future problems. Krayenbuehl (1988) recommends using the ratio of current account balance to debt service. Another widely used ratio to assess the debt burden relative to the size of the economy is the ratio of external private and public debt, excluding short-term debt of one year or less net of liquid foreign assets, to gross national product (GNP).

A ratio of under 30 percent is usually considered acceptable, whereas a value greater than 50 percent is considered to be on the high side. The usefulness of these ratios is enhanced by looking at the trend rather than at a point in time, and also in comparison to other countries. The risk factors are not additive: most often, negative events are triggered by a dominant factor than by a confluence of factors. The collective impact of the factors is usually seen in secular trends in the country's reserve position, which is the reason tracking the ratios over time is so important. Table 22.1 shows some of the other ratios used to do the economic assessments.

Table 22.2 shows the typical quantitative data used to analyze country risk trends (in this case Thailand). Although the trends in the debt burden ratios do indicate a growing problem, it is interesting to note that this trend has been in process for quite some time. Therefore, the suddenness and severity with which the foreign currency markets dealt with the Asian currencies has economists suggesting that the market may have reacted in a manner out of proportion with the condition of the underlying factors.

CHALLENGES IN ASSESSING COUNTRY RISK

According to Belcsak (1995), the heyday for country risk analysis came in the late 1970s and ended on the day in 1982 on which Mexico informed its creditor banks in no uncertain terms that it was unable to repay its loans.

Table 22.1 Country Risk Ratios

Ratio	Definition	Range of values
Interest service ratio	Interest payments due/exports in the same period	This is a liquidity ratio. A value of 4 percent is considered good, and a value of 20 percent is borderline.
Reserves/ imports	Currency reserves/ imports	This ratio is expressed in months of cover and measures the ability to pay for imports. A value of 3 months or more is desirable.
Liquidity gap ratio	One year short-term debt minus current account balance plus availability of funding sources	This is a liquidity measurement.
Current account balance/GNP	Current account balance/GNP	Indicative of medium-term performance. This ratio should be positive. A value of -5 is indicative of potential problems.

Table 22.2 Thailand—Country Data

	1991	1992	1993	1994	1995	1996e	1997p	1998p
Basic data								
Real GDP growth (%)	8.5	8.2	8.5	8.9	8.7	6.4	1.5	–3.0
CPI inflation (per. avg., %)	5.7	4.1	3.3	5.1	5.8	5.8	7.0	9.5
Unemployment rate (%)	3.1	3.0	2.6	2.6	1.7	2.0	3.0	5.5
Fiscal balance—central government (% of GDP)	4.7	2.7	2.1	1.7	2.6	2.5	0.5	1.0
External trade								
Current account balance	–7572	–6304	–6364	–8086	–13555	–14690	–8800	–5200
Total exports	38169	43920	50819	60581	75283	77037	76900	82500
Total imports	–45741	–50224	–57183	–68667	–88838	–91727	–85700	–87700
Current account balance/GDP (%)	–7.7	–5.6	–5.1	–5.6	–8.0	–7.9	–5.9	–3.3
External debt								
Total external debt	36783	43379	53675	67436	88054	98368	101094	106750
Medium/long-term	20574	23553	27927	38194	46644	60419	67900	76233
Short-term	16209	19826	25748	29242	41410	37949	33194	30517
Short-term (%)	44.1	45.7	48.0	43.4	47.0	38.6	32.8	28.6
Of which, public sector	12810	13068	14171	15714	16402	16796		
External assets	20389	23405	30638	36071	45347	44759	27000	22000
Total Official Reserves, excl. gold	17517	20359	24473	29332	35982	37731	22000	20000
Deposit Money Banks	2872	3046	6165	6739	9365	7028	5000	2000

(continued)

Table 22.2 (Continued)

	1991	1992	1993	1994	1995	1996e	1997p	1998p
Net external debt	16394	19974	23037	31365	42707	53609	74094	84750
Debt service	4117	4088	4667	6314	9408	10126	19296	20033
Interest payments	2288	2058	1996	2708	4212	5149	5750	6150
Amortization	1829	2030	2671	3606	5196	4977	13546	13883
Debt burden indicators								
Net debt/GDP	16.7	17.9	18.3	21.7	25.4	29.0	49.4	53.0
Net debt/total exports	43.0	45.5	45.3	51.8	56.7	69.6	96.4	102.7
Debt service/total exports	10.8	9.3	9.2	10.4	12.5	13.1	25.1	24.3
Interest/total exports	6.0	4.7	3.9	4.5	5.6	6.7	7.5	7.5
Short-term debt/liquid reserves	92.5	97.4	105.2	99.7	115.1	100.6	150.9	152.6
Reserves/monthly imports	4.6	4.9	5.1	5.1	4.9	4.9	3.1	
Foreign currency debt/GDP	37.5	38.9	42.7	46.7	52.3	53.1	67.4	66.7
Foreign currency debt/exports	96.4	98.8	105.6	111.3	117.0	127.7	131.5	129.4
Memoranda								
Foreign liabilities of DMBs	4902	6567	13799	31086	46214	48781		
Net foreign liabilities	2030	3521	7634	24347	36849	41753		

Source: Compiled by CapMAC from statistical data from IMF, IIF, and Bank of Thailand.

343

He goes on to suggest that top managements frequently feel that the predictive power of analysts in whom they put their trust has not measured up.

There are several reasons for the fallibility of country risk assessments. For one thing, the interdependencies of the variables are so complex that it is difficult if not impossible to model the outcomes. Paul Krugman (1998), the noted economist, who regarded the Asian economic miracle as less than what met the eye, expected no worse than a longer-term slowdown in growth in these countries. Instead, noting that developments in Asia were far more drastic, he wrote:

> As is all too often the case, we find ourselves playing theoretical catch up—trying, after the fact, to develop a framework for thinking about events that have already happened. Yet this is by no means a pointless exercise. For one thing, this crisis is still unfolding at the time of writing, and policy is being made on the fly; any clarity we can bring to the discussion is bound to be helpful. Moreover, while this crisis did not play exactly in the way posited by standard currency crisis models, nonetheless those models were helpful in providing at least a first-pass framework for both understanding and policy formation—and those who knew those models were better forecasters than those who did not. The point is that while any model we may make of the 1997 Asian crisis will surely miss some crucial features of the next crisis to come along, it will still be helpful.
>
> Anyway, enough apologies. (Krugman 1988, 1)

Methodologically the notion that traditional macroeconomic analysis using national income accounts is sufficient for analyzing the risk and reward for the international investor or lender is open to criticism. Macroeconomists are now accepting the notion that micro factors such as the agency problem[1] and the optionality implicit in guarantees can influence the behavior of foreign (and domestic) financial institutions and result in outcomes not anticipated in conventional macroeconomic constructs. To return to Paul Krugman's (1998, 3) analysis of the Asian problem,

> What all of this suggests is that the Asian crisis is best seen not as a problem brought on by fiscal deficits, as in "first-generation" models, nor as one brought on by macroeconomic temptation, as in "second-generation" models, but as one brought on by financial excess and then financial collapse. Indeed, to a first approximation currencies and exchange rates may have had little to do with it: the Asian story is really about a bubble in and subsequent collapse of asset values in general, with the currency crises more a symptom than a cause of this underlying real (in both senses of the word) malady.
>
> It has long been known that financial intermediaries whose liabilities are guaranteed by the government pose a serious problem of moral hazard. The U.S. savings and loan debacle is the classic example: because depositors in thrifts were guaranteed by FSLIC, they had no incentive to police the lending of the institutions in which they placed their money; since the owners of thrifts did not need to put much of their own money at risk, they had every incentive to play a game of heads I win, tails the taxpayer loses.

---

[1]An agency problem exists when the principals (e.g., owners or stockholders) and agents (e.g., bank management) have a conflict of interest.

The Asian situation is considerably more murky. In general, creditors of financial institutions did not receive explicit guarantees from the governments. However, press reports do suggest that most of those who provided Thai finance companies, South Korean banks, and so on with funds believed that they would be protected from risk—an impression reinforced by the strong political connections of the owners of most such institutions.

It is unfortunate but true that as long as the investment returns are good, no one finds fault with a financial system's vulnerability, corruption, or other inadequacies. Even if these are known, they are noted, but few take the view that the problems are serious enough to withdraw from the market. When there is general prosperity and lack of transparency, then investors and lenders indulge these idiosyncrasies as cultural differences with the saying that "that is the way business is done in that country." Indeed this is true even for domestic obligors—when you are winning, you can do no wrong. Country risk analysts who find themselves swimming against the current usually mute their criticism for fear of sounding alarmist. Only when there is a major downturn does the criticism come out.[2]

The advent of computers and databases has facilitated the construction of country risk models, but these models are also prone to failure because the data used in them may often be suspect and/or stale. Just as any troubled domestic corporate borrower will furnish incomplete or inaccurate data on its conditions or delay it altogether, the same is true of sovereigns and foreign borrowers. According to the *Wall Street Journal* (Foreign Banks 1998), most of Indonesia's private foreign debt was hidden until mounting pressures on the rupiah prompted the central bank to order commercial banks to disclose their exposures. When this disclosure came, the rupiah plummeted even further. Even official reserve statistics are known to be reported incorrectly in some instances: according to the *Financial Times* (Asia in Crisis 1998), Thailand's foreign exchange reserves and the central bank's loan volumes had been hidden from the public for months.

Country-level information is available only after significant delay. Data collected by the agencies such the IMF, the World Bank, OECD, Bank for International Settlements, and the United Nations tend to emphasize the individual needs of the organization, not those of the lenders/investors. Even if the data being fed into the models are of satisfactory quality, model risk—the risk that the structure has shifted away from the model's original premise—can be a problem.

Furthermore, while econometric models may yield nice, neat numerical rankings and default probabilities, political factors can shape the business environments in a dramatic fashion. These are subjective and qualitative variables, less amenable to modeling. Nor are the interactions of these variables self-evident. According to PERC (1996, 1),

> More than numbers, Asia is about people and the systems in which they live. Just as it is much less important to have access to a balance sheet of a typical

---

[2]To see an example of how sanguine the view was about these economies until recently, please see Haggard and Lee (1995).

Asian company than it is to know the dynamics of the families who stand behind these companies, macroeconomic statistics often tell little about the quality of the government that put them together. Yet it is the quality of the government (at the national and local levels) and its policies that often make or break the business environment.

To understand country risk, then, one needs expertise in political risk, macroeconomics, and an understanding of the *structure of the financial system.* Lending decisions made by the financial intermediaries played no small role in the events leading to the Asian collapse. In a portfolio context, it is generally also conceded that data historically failed to reveal the contagion effect—the manner in which the events unfolding in Thailand spread to Indonesia, Malaysia, Philippines, and Korea.

THE ASIAN CRISIS

The Asian financial crisis surprised everyone by its speed and magnitude.[3] According to *The Economist* (Rating Agencies 1997), even the rating agencies could only *react* to market developments in East Asia. All factors leading up to the Asian collapse are yet to be fully understood. Explanations advanced have included both classic macroeconomic factors and structural factors. Although the significantly affected countries (Thailand, Indonesia, Malaysia, the Philippines, and Korea) share some common reasons for the collapse, such as the strengthening U.S. dollar and weakening yen, there are also country-specific factors having to do with poor regulation or the impact of the ruling family. We present here a necessarily brief analysis of the factors leading to the crisis, the broad dimensions of which were described in Chapters 1 and 3. To recap, starting in the middle of 1997, equity prices in these countries collapsed; the exchange rates were under immense pressure, with the respective central banks unable to provide sufficient support, their reserves having been almost depleted. American, European, and Japanese banks found that private obligors (banks, finance companies, and industrial corporations) in these countries were unable to repay their obligations, a great bulk of which were short-term loans that had not been hedged against currency risk by the obligors. The end of the crisis is not yet in sight at the time of this writing. The causal factors that are common to most of the economies were many.

Exchange Rate Regime

The central banks in Indonesia, Malaysia, the Philippines, and Thailand for many years have followed a relatively rigidly fixed to the U.S. dollar in Southeast Asia. This led to a significant real appreciation of regional currencies, contributing to a diminution in regional export competitiveness, slower

---

[3]The authors thank Jack Guenther, formerly senior vice president, country risk in Citibank, for his insights. Kevin Kime, vice president and economist, CapMAC, provided much of the material used in this section.

export growth, large current account deficits, and excessive foreign borrowing by economic entities that believed they were insulated from foreign exchange risk by the various fixed-rate regimes that had been in place for several years.

Decline in the Value of the Yen

The trend appreciation of the yen vis-à-vis the U.S. dollar (which had been ongoing since 1985) ended and reversed course in mid 1995. Because many of the Asian currencies were linked to the dollar in some fashion, the fact that the dollar was now appreciating against the yen reduced their export competitiveness vis-à-vis Japan and increased the cost of imports from Japan. The trend depreciation of the yen also reduced incentives for Japanese firms to shift production to other sites in Asia, negatively impacting foreign direct investment flows to these countries. Although the extent to which the yen/dollar exchange rate affected developing Asia is debated, the adverse terms-of-trade shock stemming from the change in relative currency valuations did coincide with a sharp slowdown in export growth in 1996 that marked the beginning of the end of Asia's asset market bubble (although a fall in the demand for certain electronic products, particularly semiconductors, was also partly responsible).

High Domestic Interest Rates

Domestic interest rates were relatively high and this made it attractive for domestic borrowers (including financial intermediaries) to obtain foreign financing. Foreign banks were only too happy to lend at rates that they could not obtain elsewhere. It is believed that international banks were so anxious to lend that they did not perform due diligence on whether the exchange rate was sustainable or the terms of the loan were consistent with the purpose of the loan. Obligors in these countries also did not hedge their liabilities from exchange rate risk but tried to cover their large short-term foreign liabilities by quickly buying dollars with local currency. This selling pressure on domestic currencies served only to drive the exchange rate down further, exacerbating the negative psychology and keeping these countries on a vicious circle. In addition, of course, the decline in the value of domestic currencies greatly increased the domestic cost of servicing foreign debt—and increased enough in some circumstances to prevent corporate entities from being able to service that debt. Debt defaults are thus occurring currently in Thailand and Indonesia and may well occur in Korea going forward as the Korea economy begins to slow in response to the liquidity crisis in the financial system.

Booming growth and high interest rates in the context of fixed exchange rate systems encouraged overborrowing by domestic residents—particularly banks that could borrow abroad at lower foreign interest rates and relend at higher domestic rates—and overinvestment by foreigners. These capital inflows were, for the most part, not hedged so that they contributed directly to the rapid growth in money supply and credit that fed the asset market boom. Because a substantial portion of these inflows was short-term lending or "hot money," the capital outflows were large and quick to occur once currency problems arose and investor sentiment shifted in mid 1997.

Excessive Investment in Asset Markets and Productive Capacity

Much of the foreign lending was channeled—in the case of Southeast Asian nations—into asset markets (property and equity markets), leading to a classic asset market bubble that was ready to burst at the first sign of trouble (which came in 1996 with the regional slowdown in export growth). In Korea, the process was a bit different, as foreign borrowing was largely channeled into excess productive capacity by highly leveraged conglomerates to whom the nation's banks were highly exposed. As the export slowdown hit Korean firms, their high leverage quickly began to bite, with negative earnings consequences for their banks. In addition, as the won began to depreciate in 1996, the foreign debts of Korean firms become more costly to service.

Structural Factors

The impact of these classic macroeconomic factors are applicable to any economy and there is no question that these fundamental factors had a lot to do with the pessimism that investors exhibited in the second half of 1997. However, other factors contributed to the *severity* of the collapse. Central banks were squeezed and eventually ran out of reserves to counter pressure from the currency speculators and hedgers. The short-term tenor of much of the region's foreign borrowing allowed lenders to withdraw quickly and, in so doing, created foreign exchange liquidity problems for several countries. As reserves became depleted, the ability of the authorities to support the external obligations of private firms—particularly in the all-important financial sector—was degraded. In addition, there were structural factors at work.

Overdependence on Banks for Credit   Based on the Japanese economic model, governments in Asia discouraged the development of independent capital markets in an effort to maintain financial power in the hands of a relatively small group of large banks in each country. By concentrating lending resources with the banking system, governments could more easily influence the allocation and pricing of credit. This approach to finance has been particularly pronounced in Japan and Korea (where governments have been particularly interventionist over the course of the countries' economic development; some have called it the "fear of finance," akin to "fear of flying"). This system supposedly encouraged long-term and strategic thinking. Sheltered by the government, the banks were slow to acknowledge their loan problems.

Credit Culture   The asset market boom was fed by the specific credit culture that exists in much of Asia, whereby lending is often done on a relationship/name basis or on the basis of collateral, with little attention paid to cash flow. Because real estate of some types was typically the only collaterizable asset available, much of the lending in Asia was underpinned in some fashion by real estate. Thus, although direct lending to real estate–related transactions may not have appeared excessive, much of the residual lending for other purposes was backed by real estate assets, thus greatly increasing banks' exposure to this sector. As growth slows, businesses' cash flow is crimped and banks have to try to seize the collateral (a difficult process in these countries). But even if the bank succeeds in seizing collateral, the bursting property market bubble makes this collateral worth far less than when the loan was made, thereby leaving banks with large stocks of nonperforming loans.

Moral Hazard   *Moral hazard* embedded in Asian governments' traditional support of financially troubled firms/banks was an important contributor to the risk-prone borrowing habits of these firms. Governments—particularly in Korea and Japan—have traditionally insulated investors, firms, and employees from financial risk. The problem in recent months was that the buildup of (predominantly short-term) foreign debt was too great for governments to shoulder when it became necessary to bail out the banks and firms encountering difficulties. As investor fear grew, the exodus developed a psychology of its own, negatively affecting the domestic sentiment and causing even residents to prefer to hold foreign currency out of fear that domestic currency depreciations would continue.

Inadequate disclosure on the part of corporations also contributed to the breadth and depth of the crisis, particularly in the case of Korea where there are not yet consolidated financial statements for the major industrial groups (chaebol). It is quite clear that the institutions in these countries have as much if not a greater need for the credit management tools and, more importantly, a credit culture in strengthening their institutions. Both too much regulation (such as setting priorities concerning to whom credit was extended) and too little regulation (failure to regulate speculative real estate lending) contributed to the problem. Japanese and European banks, and to a lesser extent American banks, were caught up in the economic euphoria and failed to perform the required due diligence in lending (*Wall Street Journal*, 1998).

IN EVERY CLOUD A SILVER LINING

The crisis in Asia, although extremely painful to the local economies and international lenders and investors, nevertheless will likely prove beneficial to the countries concerned over the long term. To restore growth in these countries, investor confidence must be restored. This is likely to be accomplished by revamping the regulatory system so that corporate disclosure and the lending and investment practices of financial institutions are improved. Enhancing transparency will also increase liquidity to the marketplace.[4] While mentioning transparency it is useful to remember that the existence

---

[4]PERC (1997) defines transparency in the following way: "The more transparent a country's system or environment is, the easier it is supposed to be to understand the rules of the game and to gain access to the information needed to make decisions and plan for the future. Conversely, the less transparent an environment is, the more company managers have to live with uncertainty and navigate without a map, relying instead on personal connections and experience to know what can and cannot be done and how to do it."

of transparency did not prevent the thrift crisis in the United States nor the financial crises that have occurred elsewhere in the world, most recently in Norway, Sweden, and Finland.[5] Yet transparency, like chicken soup, may do no harm, and will in all likelihood increase the response time for taking proactive steps.

Although the prevailing view in the West seems to be that Asian values are what led to nepotism in credit allocation, an overly intrusive state, and lack of transparency, Fukuyama (1998) offers some arguments why this may not be so. For example, he argues that the problem in Thailand began when the baht's link to the dollar came under attack in the currency markets. It was the very stability of that link that had encouraged foreign banks to lend short-term funds to finance speculation and other questionable ventures. The decision to lend came not from Thailand but from banks in Japan, Europe, and the United States. Also, if there was a failure at the government level, it lay not in excessive interventionism but in insufficient use of regulatory power in dealing with lending practices.

The failure in Thailand was not much different from the regulatory failure in the United States with regard to the savings and loans. With regard to the Japanese *keiretsu* being a culprit of "crony capitalism," Fukuyama notes that, ironically, business-school professors and information-technology gurus have been urging *American* firms to move in precisely the same direction. American companies are told to replace their bureaucracies with smaller, flatter ones linked by informal networks. Many high-tech firms have also adopted a policy of "relational contracting," where alliances are formed based on relationships of trust, not on price and performance. Before rushing to judgment about how the Asian economies should conduct themselves, Fukuyama suggests that it is important to separate fact from fiction.

For the corporations whose approach to these economies is based on long-term fundamentals rather than short-term trends, it appears that there will be many opportunities to contribute to the recovery and eventual growth in the Asian economies.

Credit is opaque whenever institutions follow a "lend and hold" philosophy. Asset securitization makes credit more transparent through the use of consistent underwriting policies, standard loan documentation, and more complete disclosure of risk. Until investor confidence is restored, credit guarantors and rating agencies will see an enhanced role as "gatekeepers" for access to financing. These change agents will also, it is expected, work toward creating legal structures (similar to the Uniform Commercial Code) that facilitate commercial transactions and investing.

COUNTRY RISK ANALYSTS

Today, many organizations have dismantled the resources that they dedicate to analyzing country risk. This is unfortunate because, perhaps more than ever, there is a need for understanding and planning for country credit risk.

---

[5]See Joseph Stiglitz in the *Wall Street Journal*, February 4, 1998.

The rating agencies understand the importance of this and have established or strengthened their presence in many foreign countries. Although country risk analysis is traditionally a staff function in large banks performed by professionally trained international economists, increasingly it requires a multidisciplinary approach and needs to be incorporated in asset-by-asset credit decision making as well as in portfolio management. The key is to make the analysis systematic, objective, and relevant. There are many outside sources that measure country risk (Erb, Campbell, and Viskanta 1996), which may be used to supplement/validate the analysis:

- Bank of America World Information Services
- Business Environmental Risk Intelligence
- Control Risks Information Services
- Economist Intelligence Unit
- Euromoney
- Institutional Investor
- Standard and Poor's Rating Group
- Political Risk Services: International Country Risk Guide
- Political Risk Services: Coplin-O'Leary Rating System
- Moody's Investor Services

COUNTRY RATING SYSTEMS

Rating systems that combine the scores for various criteria are one way to compare the relative risks of various countries. The system used by Credit Risk International is summarized in Table 22.3. Each parameter is scored based on the criteria and subcriteria for that parameter. To assess each criterion, Credit Risk International uses a "Delphi Technique" where a panel of experts arrive at group consensus on the score to be assigned to the criterion. The global rating can be adjusted according to the type of transactions, for example, export, direct investment, or a loan. Although all the inputs to this system use qualitative ranking, the rating system used by Euromoney includes quantitative data in addition to qualitative factors. Twenty-five percent of the weighting is given to economic data based on a survey of leading economists; 25 percent to political risk, also based on a survey; 10 percent to financial data based on ratio analysis from the World Bank debt tables;[6] 10 percent to sovereign debt ratings; and 5 percent each to available sources of external financing (banks, short-term finance, capital markets, and forfaiting). These rating systems are useful in combining the assessments in multiple dimensions by many individuals. However, they do have their drawbacks: the underlying questionnaires may be too simplistic

---

[6]The ratios include debt service to export, current account balance to GNP, and external debt to GNP.

Table 22.3 Credit Risk International's Rating System

Parameter 1: Market prospects and flexibility in coping with changes
Criterion 1: Economic size (weight 30%)
Criterion 2: Level of economic development (weight 40%)
Criterion 3: Standard of living (weight 30%)

Parameter 2: Financial risks
Criterion 4: Financial vulnerability (weight 30%)
Criterion 5: External debt (weight 30%)
Criterion 6: Financial rating (weight 40%)

Parameter 3: Political Instability
Criterion 7: Homogeneity of social fabric (weight 30%)
Criterion 8: Government political regime stability (weight 50%)
Criterion 9: Foreign relationships (weight 20%)

Parameter 4: Business environment
Criterion 10: Management of the economy (weight 40%)
Criterion 11: Foreign investment (weight 40%)
Criterion 12: Working conditions (weight 20%)

Source: Clark and Marois (1996) from Credit Risk International.

to capture the true risk; the averaging process may wash out the impact of a single major development (e.g., a low ratio of reserves to imports may be serious warning signal if it came from, say, Thailand but may be of less concern if it came from Switzerland); the weights themselves are arbitrary and have not been validated; and there may double counting; for example, the bond ratings and default data may be measuring the same underlying quantity.

Clark and Marois (1996) recommend considering the evolution of the ratings across time to capture the trend. Volatility in the rating, as measured by average and standard deviation, adds a new dimension by casting the problem in mean-variance space. Table 22.4 shows the means and standard deviation of credit ratings published by institutional investor. The standard deviation indicates the volatility of the rating, which is a function of the true changes taking place in the country, and the "learning curve" of the analysts.

Analytical techniques are used to compare important ratios across countries and also to track the trends over time. Belcsak (1995) recommends using the "CAMEL" approach, borrowing the acronym from bank regulators (see Chapter 13). CAMEL stands for Current Earnings, Asset Quality, Management Quality, Earnings Potential, and Liquidity.

- *Current earnings* refer to current account balance of payments. To project the balance-of-payment trends, the merchandise and invisibles trade must be analyzed. If the imports exceed the exports, the balance is to be bridged through foreign borrowing or from reserves.

Table 22.4   Mean and Standard Deviation of Country Risk Ratings

	1979–1991		1979	1986	1991	1997
	Mean	Std. Dev.				
Global Average	42.73	5.70	55.7	40.5	37.9	41.0
Algeria	48.99	8.71	58.6	50.4	34.2	24.5
Argentina	32.67	17.26	62.4	24.9	20.2	41.3
Bolivia	13.78	7.49	31.6	8.0	15	26.2
Brazil	37.92	12.54	64.9	35.2	26.5	39.5
Cameroon	33.55	5.04	35.0	38.4	23.1	18.8
Chile	37.64	12.16	54.9	25.1	41.1	63.5
Colombia	45.5	9.93	60.7	39.2	36.6	47.2
Costa Rica	22.05	10.44	44.7	17.0	22.5	36.0
Ecuador	31.1	13.5	53.2	26.7	19.6	26.3
Egypt	30.03	5.92	33.9	29.5	23.4	39.7
Greece	52.66	6.26	62.6	47.6	47.2	53.0
India	47.66	3.6	54.2	50.7	38.4	46.9
Indonesia	50.05	4.57	53.2	47.6	50.4	51.8
Ivory Coast	30.98	9.99	48.2	27.5	17.2	NA
Korea	61.55	5.52	71.2	58.4	68.1	69.7
Malaysia	64.6	6.76	70.3	59.9	62.0	66.7
Mexico	43.89	17.08	71.8	30.8	38.7	43.5
Morocco	29.57	7.32	45.5	23.1	28.3	40.9
Nigeria	32.42	15.17	54.1	22.8	19.5	15.3
Peru	22.86	11.99	30.7	14.9	12.2	33.7
Philippines	30.63	11.08	53.7	21.4	24.5	44.3
Portugal	55.19	5.04	52.0	51.8	63.3	71.2
Sudan	8.43	3.81	18.5	7.3	6.1	9.1
Thailand	55.05	3.96	54.7	53.3	62.5	59.9
Tunisia	42.02	5.72	50.0	39.7	37.5	47.9
Turkey	30.78	11.43	14.8	38.6	42.7	38.6
Uruguay	32.78	5.64	41.0	27.8	31.2	43.4
Venezuela	45.99	15.07	72.4	38.1	37.2	35.4
Yugoslavia	34.87	10.68	57.5	31.4	24.5	10.2

Notes: The range of ratings is from 0 to 100, where 100 represents the most creditworthy country. Credit rating for Cameroon starts in 1982. This rating is shown for the year 1979.

Source: Updated by authors from Clark and Marois (1996).

- *Asset quality's* concerns are the country's natural, human, and economic resources. The GDP, its growth trends, savings rate, investment rate, productivity, and inflation are key factors to be considered.
- *Management quality* refers to the country's government and its policies with regard to monetary targets and revenues as well as actions with regard to social and political unrest.

- *Earnings potential* should be examined to derive a realistic picture of probable balance of payments, factoring in such considerations as terms of trade, external factors such as the weather and world commodity prices, competition in the export markets, technological change, and so on.
- *Liquidity* refers to the country's access to hard, convertible currency from reserves (primary) and other sources such as other central banks, and international organizations such as IMF and the World Bank (secondary).

Given the comparative lack of knowledge about emerging economies, quantitative models of risk are of particular interest to lenders and investors. Firm-specific credit scoring models similar to those used in the United States have been developed for both developed and emerging countries.[7] Altman, Hartzell, and Peck's (1995) emerging market model for Mexico layers the sovereign risk considerations on top of the firm-specific Z-score model adapted to Mexico (see Chapter 10). Examples of country credit risk allocation models using the portfolio (mean-variance) approach are presented in Clark and Marois (1996) and Solberg (1992).

Babbel and Bertozzi (1996) present an extensive bibliography of research relating to external debt management. After a review of the available literature, the authors conclude that the current trend toward converting foreign bank loans into securities presents numerous challenges to anyone trying to deal with external debt management. Macro indicators such as money supply data and inflation may be insufficient for monitoring the stability and integrity of a country's financial system. Even if they appear to have predictive value, explanatory variables such as growth rates in money supply, international reserves, external debt, and inflation are difficult to forecast. Statistical models based on them are therefore of limited use, according to the authors. But this has not stopped anyone from trying to build quantitative country risk models. Feder and Just (1977) have developed a probability of default model using logit analysis with the following variables:

- Debt service ratio
- Imports/reserves
- Amortization/debt
- Income per capita
- Capital inflow/debt service
- GDP growth
- Export growth

More recently, Dym (1997) describes a model used to measure sovereign risk based on the following macroeconomic variables:

- Reserves coverage—number of months that imports can be paid for using existing foreign currency reserves

---

[7]For a review of international credit models applicable to individual firms, please refer to Altman and Narayanan (1997).

TABLE 22.5 Country Expected Default Frequency (EDF) May 1997

Country	SRQ EDF
South Korea	0.01%
Indonesia	0.01
China	0.02
Thailand	0.11
South Africa	0.38
Turkey	0.65
Russia	0.81
Mexico	0.91
Brazil	1.2

Source: Morris (1997)

- Current account deficit to GDP
- External borrowing to GDP
- Budget deficit to GDP
- Real GDP growth, percent
- Inflation rate

These variables are combined to create an overall measure of developing country risk. The overall measure is the sum of the individual Z-scores of the preceding six variables. Dym found a significant relationship between this measure and the yield spread of Brady bonds over U.S. Treasuries of comparable maturity.

Clark (1991) has used the Black-Scholes options theoretic approach to derive the risk-adjusted rate of return for 60 countries. He found that the forecasted risk premium in 1988 was consistent with the outcomes in 1989 to 1992. Morris (1997) has developed a sovereign credit risk model using the methodology similar to the one used by KMV (see Chapter 11). Termed SRQ (sovereign risk quantification), this approach calculated the expected default frequency over short- and long-term horizons. The expected default frequencies (EDFs) for selected sovereigns as published in May 1997 are shown in Table 22.5.

The country risk models that we have presented are by no means exhaustive. The reader is referred to Solberg (1992) for other approaches.

REFERENCES

Altman, E. I., J. Hartzell, and M. Peck. 1995. *Emerging Markets Corporate Bonds: A Scoring System*. New York: Salomon Brothers, Inc.

Altman, E. I., and P. Narayanan. 1997. An International Survey of Business Failure Classification Models. In *International Accounting and Finance Handbook*, edited by F. D. S. Choi. New York: John Wiley & Sons.

Asia in Crisis—A 5 Day Series: The Day the Miracle Came to an End. 1998. *Financial Times*, 12 January.

Babbel, D. F. with S. Bertozzi. 1996. Insuring Sovereign Debt Against Default. World Bank Discussion Paper No. 328., The World Bank, Washington, D.C.

Belcsak, S. 1995. Country Risk Assessment. In *Handbook of International Credit Management*, edited by B. Clarke. London: Gower Publishing Co.

Clark, E. 1991. *Cross Border Investment Risk: Applications of Modern Portfolio Theory.* London: Euromoney Publications.

Clark, E., and B. Marois. 1996. *Managing Risk in International Business: Techniques and Applications.* London: International Thomson Business Press.

Dym, S. 1997. Credit Risk Analysis for Developing Country Bond Portfolios. *Journal of Portfolio Management* 23 (2): 99–103.

Erb, C. B., R. H. Campbell, and T. E. Viskanta. 1996. Political Risk, Economic Risk, and Financial Risk. *Financial Analysts Journal* 52 (6).

Feder, G., and R. E. Just. 1977. A Study of Debt Servicing Capacity Applying Logit Analysis. *Journal of Development Economics* 3.

Foreign Banks Lent Blindly. 1998. *Wall Street Journal*, 4 February.

Fukuyama, F. 1998. Asian Values and the Asian Crisis. *Commentary* 105 (2).

Greider, W. 1997. *One World Ready, or Not.* New York: Simon & Schuster.

Haggard, S., and C. H. Lee, eds. 1995. *Financial Systems and Economic Policy in Developing Countries.* Ithaca, NY: Cornell University Press.

Institutional Investor's 1997 Country Credit Ratings. 1997. New York: Institutional Investor.

Krayenbuehl, T. E. 1988. *Country Risk.* Cambridge, England: Woodhead-Faulkner.

Morris, A. 1997. Quantifying Sovereign Credit Risks: Methods and Issues. *SBC-Prospects* 4–5:8–13.

Krugman, P. 1998. What Happened to Asia? on his home page, January.

PERC (Political and Economic Risk Consultancy, Ltd.). 1996. The Importance of Political Risk. *Asian Intelligence Issue*, #456, Hong Kong, March 6.

———. 1997. Transparency Problems in Asia. *Asian Intelligence Issue* #498, Hong Kong, November 19.

Rating Agencies: Risks beyond Measure. 1997. *The Economist*, 13 December, 68–69.

Solberg, R. L., ed. 1992. *Country Risk Analysis.* London: Routledge.

Sommerville, R. A., and R. J. Taffler. 1995. Banker Judgment versus Formal Forecasting Models: The Case of Country Risk Assessment. *Journal of Banking and Finance* 19 (2): 281–297.

ADDITIONAL READING

Kapstein, E. B. 1994. *Governing the Global Economy.* Cambridge, Mass.: Harvard University Press.

Kindleberger, C. E. 1996. *World Economic Primacy.* Oxford and New York: Oxford University Press.

Chapter 23

Structured Finance

In my experience, securitization was born to a greater extent out of a need for capital than out of a desire for a lower price of capital.

—S. P. Baum, executive vice president, Paine Webber

Asset securitization is a technique for transforming illiquid financial flows such as home mortgages, credit card receivables, and corporate accounts receivable into tradable asset-backed securities (ABS). In the securitization process, a company or financial institution typically sells the good assets it has originated to a special purpose company, which then issues high-quality securities.[1] Interest and principal payments from these securities depend on cash flows from the underlying assets. The burden of repayment is thus not on the originator, but on the pool of assets generating future cash flows and, in the event of a shortfall, on the entity—if there is one—providing credit support. Securitization enables issuers of lower credit quality to tap into the capital markets at more advantageous rates by establishing a structure whose credit risk is better than—and largely independent of—their own. Such a structure can be engineered by means of such techniques as overcollateralization (a form of self-insurance), third-party credit enhancement, and the creation of credit tiers (tranches) with differentiated pricing. Techniques such as these have proved to have applications beyond the securitization of assets. The term *structured finance* encompasses the full range of these applications—asset securitization and considerably more as well.

Many financial institutions, including banks, thrifts, and finance companies, have benefited from structured finance. Commercial banks, for example, were able to become very active home mortgage lenders because FNMA, FHMLC, and GNMA could securitize and sell the mortgage loans they had made. Public corporations have also benefited—most dramatically in the case of Chrysler Financial Corporation (CFC). In 1980–81, Chrysler Corporation was on the brink of collapse, and CFC itself had a CCC rating. After the bankruptcy of Penn Central, commercial paper investors abandoned all firms perceived to be weak, and CFC was unable to fund its activ-

---

[1]In some cases, the institution may also securitize not-so-good assets but wrap them around with various credit enhancements.

ities with commercial paper. It could, however, sell its receivables as securities, and it continued to finance itself by doing so. By 1996, CFC had grown into one of the largest issuers of ABS in the United States (Cantwell 1996).

American taxpayers have also benefited from securitization. In the 1990s, this was one of the principal strategies used by the Resolution Trust Corporation to liquidate assets accumulated in the course of closing hundreds of thrifts. By securitizing single family and commercial real estate loans, the RTC raised approximately $43 billion (Jungman 1996). A significant amount of credit enhancement accompanied these commercial transactions—more, perhaps, than will ever be seen in the nongovernment sector.

Securitization was first developed in 1970, when Ginnie Mae Pool #1 was issued. Subsequently, the issuance of mortgage-backed and asset-backed securities expanded rapidly in the United States. At the close of 1996, there were more than $1.6 trillion in mortgage-backed securities outstanding in the U.S. market (*Mortgage Market* 1997). The growth in the ABS markets in the United States has been meteoric as well, reaching $480.3 billion in 1997 (Figure 23.1). Total ABS volume includes public nonmortgage debt, private debt (Section 144A), and asset-backed commercial paper. In 1996 alone, a record-setting $151 billion was raised in nonmortgage ABS in the U.S. public market. Within Europe, ABS have been issued in the U.K, France, Spain, Italy, Belgium, the Netherlands, and Sweden. They have also been issued in Japan, Canada, Australia, New Zealand, and other countries in Asia and Latin America.

The underlying assets in the ABS market are primarily consumer-oriented loans of varying kinds (credit cards, auto loans, home equity loans, and manufactured housing loans). The market for securities backed by commercial loans (both large and small) is still developing.[2] Figure 23.2 shows the composition of the ABS market by collateral type. Credit cards, home equity loans, and auto loans have equal shares of the market.

USES OF SECURITIZATION

Structured finance techniques assist in the delivery of all four core functions of the financial markets. The first of these is a depository function: people need a place to store their money. The second is an investment function: people need ways to grow their capital by investing in assets that match their preferences with respect to yield, liquidity, maturity, and so on. The third is a credit function: people need a place where they can borrow money. The fourth is a risk-management function: people need a way to transfer financial risks they are not comfortable bearing on their own. These core functions have remained quite stable over time; in 1897 as in 1997, people turned to the financial markets for these same fundamental reasons.

Although the functions themselves have changed little, the institutions providing them have changed dramatically. For many years, banks and in-

---

[2]There does exist a secondary market for syndicated bank loans and the Section 144A private placements that are traded in the over-the-counter market.

Figure 23.1 U.S. Asset-Backed Securitization Market

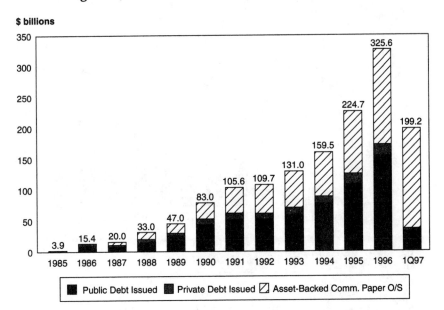

	Public debt issued	Private debt issued	Asset-backed commercial paper outstanding
1985	0.7152	0.14	3
1986	10.0407	1.32	4
1987	9.1159	3.17	7
1988	15.78	5.06	12
1989	25.5	6.18	15
1990	45.08	8.23	30
1991	51.08	9.65	45
1992	51.25	11.60	47
1993	59.96	13.06	58
1994	75.8	12.44	71
1995	107.792	17.68	107
1996	151.443	23.25	152
1997	179.481	56.80	244
1st qtr. 1998	35.5	5.45	285

Source: Merrill Lynch, Dean Witter; Goldman Sachs; MCM Corporate Watch; Securities Data Co., MBIA estimates

Figure 23.2   Composition of the ABS Market

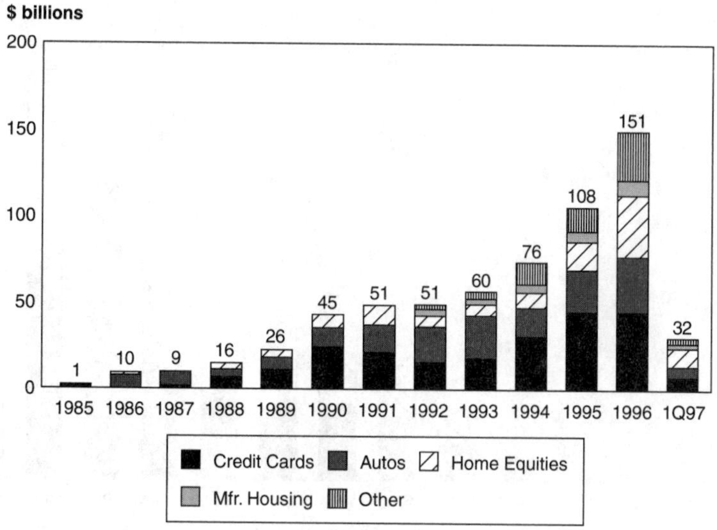

	Credit cards	Autos	Home equities	Mfr. housing	Other
1985	0.00	0.38	0.00	0.00	0.34
1986	0.00	9.66	0.00	0.00	0.38
1987	2.41	6.52	0.00	0.18	0.00
1988	7.80	6.00	0.00	0.85	1.13
1989	12.00	8.00	2.99	2.00	0.51
1990	24.60	13.10	5.70	1.05	0.63
1991	21.80	17.00	10.20	1.32	0.76
1992	15.76	23.24	6.23	2.79	3.23
1993	19.60	24.80	7.09	2.49	5.99
1994	31.90	17.50	10.10	4.30	12.00
1995	47.02	24.75	16.08	5.55	14.39
1996	46.89	32.07	36.26	7.92	28.32
1997	37.87	31.42	63.70	9.29	37.20
1998	7.70	7.18	16.66	3.12	7.78

Source: MCM Corporate Watch

surance companies were the dominant suppliers of depository, investment, credit, and risk management services. Today, specialty finance companies, specialty insurance companies, brokerage houses, pension funds, and mutual fund companies all give these traditional providers stiff competition. Burdened with excess capital and high costs, banks and insurance companies have been losing out to these newer and often more efficiently managed entrants.

Structured finance is an important tool for all these parties. Banks and insurance companies use it to improve their efficiency. Instead of holding all loans to term as they did in the past, many banks now originate certain financial assets with the express intention of selling them off. Banks traditionally worked with other banks in sharing credit risk, but they are now letting other capital market participants (such as guarantee companies, investors, and rating agencies) become involved with their asset origination and sale activities. Meanwhile, specialty finance and specialty insurance companies are using structured finance techniques to fund the clever ideas they are dreaming up and to increase their capabilities. Some specialized companies are applying these same techniques in the capital markets for purposes of risk management, defeasing insurance risk through finite risk products. Investors, too, are beginning to use the tools of structured finance to create the investment structures they want and to obtain the assets they need.

In structured finance, the focus shifts from what the issuer wants to what the investor wants. Rather than generating assets that suit borrowers and then trying to find a home for them, the issuer looks at the available investor classes and structures a security that enough of them will buy. In this way, it generates the cash with which to support the assets. This change in mindset is subtle but crucial.

Structured finance is expanding rapidly because there is something in it for virtually everybody. The asset supplier is able to raise funds to support more originations and retain a spread. The guarantor earns a fee. The servicer earns a fee for asset management. The investor has an earning asset that is tailored to its risk/return preferences. The secondary market maker earns a bid-ask spread by providing liquidity. Most players in the financial markets already benefit in some way, and those that do not benefit today can be expected to do so tomorrow.

Why is this happening now? Information technology is part of the answer. Structured finance demands comprehensive and thorough financial analysis of a kind that would have been impractical before the widespread availability of the computers.

BENEFITS FOR ISSUERS

The following are among the key reasons why issuers choose to securitize assets:

- *Liquidity.* Banks and other issuers can convert their illiquid assets into cash.
- *Reduced borrowing costs.* Independent and captive finance companies have securitized assets to obtain capital at attractive rates.
- *Tax management.* Some jurisdictions charge taxes based on asset size.
- *More efficient use of capital.* Securitization can be used to multiply the assets created without increasing leverage.
- *Regulatory capital arbitrage.* Because of high regulatory capital charges for loans to high-quality borrowers, lenders are unable to earn an attractive return on equity when they hold these loans. It is advanta-

geous for them to securitize these assets, taking them off the balance sheet and placing them in a nonbank special purpose vehicle. Insurance companies, as well, can use securitization to reconfigure the financial assets on their balance sheets to obtain more favorable treatment under risk-based capital rules.

To date, the expansion of structured finance in the United States has been driven largely by the needs of issuers. Banks and insurance companies have had to reduce their costs and gain greater economies of scale by removing assets from their balance sheets—while retaining their franchise. The introduction of risk-based capital standards has been a major factor here. These standards have forever changed the banking and insurance industries. Banks face much higher capital requirements for the loans they hold than for the securities they own.[3] If a bank wants to improve its capital ratio, it can therefore invest in securities—especially when demand for loans is weak and security yields are acceptable. This may explain why the proportion of mortgage-backed securities in bank asset portfolios nearly doubled from 5.3 percent in 1988 to 9.9 percent in 1995 (FDIC 1988, 1995).

For insurance companies, too, the regulatory treatment of securities differs from that for whole loans and real assets. Table 23.1[4] gives the National Association of Insurance Commissioners (NAIC) capital guidelines.

Prior to the imposition of risk-based capital standards, relatively few bankers or insurance executives paid much attention to their return on equity. But under the terms of the Basel accords (for banks) and the NAIC capital standards (for insurance companies) these institutions must allocate specific amounts of capital to specific asset classes on their balance sheets. This means that they must track their ROE and ROA closely. Banks and insurance companies now manage their balance sheets far more actively than they did in the past, using structured finance as their most effective tool for doing so.

SECURITIZING MORTGAGES

The first widespread application of structuring technology occurred in the residential mortgage market. In 1938, the federal government established the Federal National Mortgage Association (FNMA, or Fannie Mae) to ensure

---

[3]The asset weight for a C&I loan is 100 percent, whereas for securities guaranteed by U.S.-sponsored agencies such as FNMA, FHLMC, and SLMA it is 20 percent. For one dollar of capital, a bank can hold five times as much in securities as in C&I loans. Note that within an asset class the capital requirement does not change whether it is a real estate loan or a loan to a major corporation. For life insurance companies, the reserve factors are 10 percent for commercial and other mortgages and 1 percent for BBB-rated securities.

[4]Insurance companies are regulated by states. The New York Department of Insurance, because of the size, experience, stature, and stringent regulations, has led insurers to regard New York as the de facto insurance regulatory authority. To promote a convergence of state regulatory standards, state insurance commissioners formed the National Association of Insurance Commissioners (NAIC) more than a century ago in 1871. NAIC proposes model investment laws, which the states may choose to adopt. See Santamero and Babbel (1997).

Table 23.1 Capital Reserve Factor for Different Asset Types

Asset category	Rating range	Security type	Reserve factor (%)
Securities			
U.S. government	NA	Treasuries, GNMAs	0
NAIC1	AAA–A	Agency debentures, corporate bonds, MBS, ABS, CMBS	0.3
NAIC2	BBB	Agency debentures, corporate bonds, MBS, ABS, CMBS	1.0
NAIC3	BB	Agency debentures, corporate bonds, MBS, ABS, CMBS	4.0
NAIC4	B	Agency debentures, corporate bonds, MBS, ABS, CMBS	9.0
NAIC5	CCC	Agency debentures, corporate bonds, MBS, ABS, CMBS	20.0
NAIC6	Default	Agency debentures, corporate bonds, MBS, ABS, CMBS	30.0
Whole loans			0.5
Single/multifamily residential mortgages			0.1
Guaranteed municipal mortgages			3.0
Other mortgages including commercial real estate			10.0

Source: Jacob and Duncan (1995).

that mortgage capital would be readily available to large numbers of American home buyers. Fannie Mae bought qualified mortgages and issued its own securities. In 1968, the Government National Mortgage Association (GNMA, or Ginnie Mae) was split off from Fannie Mae and authorized to guarantee the principal and interest on mortgage securities from other issuers. This guarantee is backed by the full faith and credit of the U.S. government. Figure 23.3 shows how the securitization process for a GNMA works (Kinney and Garrigan 1985).[5]

---

[5]Once a lender makes a loan to finance a home, the lender prepares the assignments of the interest to GNMA. The underlying loan documents are held by the custodian, and GNMA pool certificates serve as the vehicle the investor purchases through the dealer. Monthly payments received by the servicer are sent to the investor, with the servicer retaining a servicing spread (approximately 12–25 basis points). The servicer maintains the tax and escrow funds in a custodial account. When there is a default, the claim by the investor is paid by GNMA. The servicer will continue with the collection process, including foreclosure or deed in lieu of foreclosure on behalf of GNMA, which now becomes the investor.

Figure 23.3 The GNMA Mortgage-Backed Securities Program

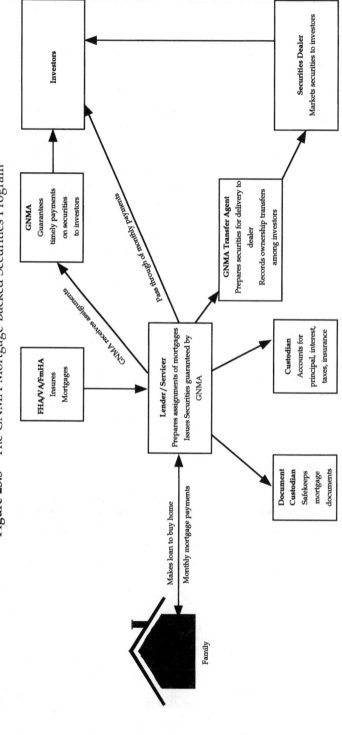

Source: Kinney and Garrigan (1985).

Mortgage-backed issues may take the form of a *pass-through security*, in which the assets are sold to a trust and investors buy shares of the trust, or of a *pay-through security*, in which the assets are sold to a special purpose vehicle that issues debt to finance their purchase. Both types of security include internally generated credit support in the form of accumulated reserves from excess cash flows and of subordinated interest (first loss absorption) on the part of the asset originator. There may also be external credit support in the form of a letter of credit, loan insurance (e.g., a cash collateral account), a corporate guarantee, a surety bond, or cross-collateralization. A trustee responsible for monitoring collateral value and cash distributions helps hold the structure together.

Mortgage securitization has been a resounding success. The proportion of residential mortgages in the United States that are securitized has gradually increased from 1 percent in 1970 to 40 percent in 1996 (Kinney and Garrigan 1985; Board of Governors 1997). Knowing that they can raise capital by selling the loans they have originated, many different players have been encouraged to enter the mortgage market. In the real estate section of their local newspapers, Americans can compare ads from mortgage brokers and mortgage bankers, as well as from commercial banks and thrifts—all of whom are competing to lend them money. No matter which lender the home buyer selects, the mortgage will, in all likelihood, be securitized within a matter of months. Securitization has reduced the cost of a residential mortgage in the United States by about 0.5 to 1.0 percent. In many emerging nations where governments are eager to establish vibrant mortgage markets, the U.S. model has enormous appeal.

Residential mortgages are relatively easy to securitize. To begin with, the mortgage market is large enough to make securitization interesting to financial professionals. In addition, this is a consumer financing activity where the law of large numbers can be applied and an actuarial base readily established. Since record keeping has generally been good, abundant data are available for this purpose. Finally, mortgage documentation in the United States has been standardized over the last 30 years. Whether a mortgage is originated by Citibank in the Bronx or a mortgage banker in Des Moines, the documentation is identical. This makes it easy to collect, maintain, and evaluate data across portfolios and originators. Federal agencies have been the major force behind this standardization.

SECURITIZING OTHER ASSETS

After residential mortgages, the first nonmortgage assets to be securitized were computer leases in 1985. Next came auto loans (certificates of automobile receivables, called CARS). Securitization of other consumer assets, such as credit card receivables, was a natural next step. The first credit card deal was completed in 1986. Here, again, the asset class is sufficiently large to enable structured finance professionals to create mathematical models to predict consumer behavior. Unlike mortgages, however, the documentation for credit cards has yet to be standardized, but there are signs of progress in this direction.

In the course of the transition from mortgages to credit cards, the definition of an asset shifted to some extent. A mortgage, after all, is a legal right to a home. The underlying real asset is the home. But in the case of a credit card, what is the asset—the sweater that the cardholder bought? The semester of college courses that were charged to the card? Clearly not. The asset in this case is the cash flow from cardholders as they pay their credit card bills. Securitization techniques have evolved to the point where cash flow is the primary source of value. When a transaction involves hard assets that can, in fact, be realized, these represent no more than a secondary element in the deal structure—one that serves to mitigate the risks. Today, the absence of such hard assets presents no serious impediment to the securitization process.

Over time, many types of consumer assets have been securitized, including home equity loans, recreational vehicle (RV) loans, boat loans, auto loans, leases, utility payments, and bank-originated student loans. Consumer financing stood at $1226.3 billion in 1996, of which $151 billion—or 12 percent—was securitized in the U.S. public market.

Consumer debt securitization represented 46 percent of total ABS issuance in 1996. Securitizations of corporate assets accounted for the remaining 54 percent of issuance. Corporate assets have been securitized in considerable volume, but the pace here has been somewhat slower. Since corporate assets tend to be "lumpier" (the average loan size is $1 million) than consumer ones (the average loan size is $3,000), they do not lend themselves as readily to the application of actuarial principles. In addition, banks have generally kept less thorough records of their corporate lending experience. When things have gone wrong and a bank has actually experienced a loss, this fact has been recorded. But when things have gone right and a loan has been repaid, banks have generally kept no record of any migration in the borrower's credit quality that may have occurred along the road to this happy outcome. Even if the obligor came perilously close to default at some point, the bank has not normally recorded this fact.[6]

The resulting dearth of information about credit migration has been an impediment to the securitization of corporate loans. Over the past two decades, however, the major credit rating agencies and others have been working to develop default prediction models that make it possible to evaluate corporate credit more effectively. These should allow the securitization market to broaden and deepen. Two approaches are available for modeling default. The first is to study the historical behavior of pools either as cohorts or as static pools and to use the default experience over time to stress portfolios of rated assets. The second approach, which follows from the first, is to risk rate each asset (by means of either agency ratings or a model) and to link the default likelihood and recovery to the rating and seniority. These methods have been discussed in Chapters 15 though 20.

As in the consumer sector, the easiest corporate assets—trade receivables—were the first to be securitized. Trade receivables are relatively low-

---

[6]This is one of the shortcomings of the book-value accounting practiced by banks.

risk, short-term assets. Any ongoing commercial enterprise will pay its suppliers so that it can continue to receive the supplies it requires. A wide range of other corporate assets have also been securitized, including rolling stock leases for utilities, worker compensation insurance premium receivables, real estate tax lien receivables, and the future receivables of a major film studio. Collateralized bond obligations (CBOs) and collateralized loan obligations (CLOs) are additional types of corporate ABS that are discussed in some detail in the chapter that follows.

SEGMENTATION OF RISK

The key to a structured financing is segmentation of cash flow into common risk buckets. Assume for a moment that we have a $100 portfolio of assets with an expected loss ratio, based on past experience, of 10 percent. If we have just one asset in the portfolio, then there is very little we can do except to hope that we have chosen it well and priced it correctly. If we have 100 items in the portfolio, each worth $1, then we have reason to expect that 90 of them will be good and 10 bad. We do not know which are which, but we do know that 9 of every 10 payments are likely to be made on time.

If we decided to give the first 90 payments that came in to some other party and to hold the other 10 back in a reserve, then owning the first 90 payments would be an extremely safe activity and owning the 10 others would be very speculative. If, instead, we said that the first 50 payments would go to one party and that we would keep the last 50, then we would have created two new investment alternatives—the first one extremely secure and the second one more risky than the first but less risky than the 90/10 split. Just by altering the priority of payment, we alter the dynamics of the deal, even though the fundamentals of the transaction remain unchanged.

Suppose, instead, that we split the payments into four tranches: 40/20/20/20. The dynamics of each tranche would differ with respect to earnings as well as risk. The first 40 payments would represent the first bite of the apple—a safe deal. The investor in the next tranche would demand somewhat greater earnings than for the first tranche because the risks are somewhat greater. The holder of the third tranche would want even more yield. The last investor would face a fair amount of risk and would therefore expect an equity-like return.

The lowest or equity tranche of an asset-backed transaction is critical to the entire structure. It is only by concentrating risk in this tranche that it becomes possible to create more highly rated senior tranches above it. If a deal makes sense for the equity holder, then it will generally make sense for everybody else. The key is finding the real risk taker who will accept this lowest tranche. Who is this investor? What are his or her motivations?

There are, generally speaking, two possibilities. In many instances, it is the originator of the assets—often a bank—that retains the equity tranche in order to enable the transaction as a whole to be consummated. In other cases, an outside investor purchases the equity tranche. For someone who is knowledgeable and adequately capitalized, this may be a perfectly reasonable investment decision. For an investor who is highly leveraged or unfamiliar with asset-backed structures, this investment may well lead to a loss the next time the economy turns down. Having been burned once, such an investor will probably avoid such investments in the future.

By calculating the risks of the equity tranche accurately and pricing this investment appropriately, structured finance professionals should be able to expand the universe of investors with an appetite for this vital portion of an asset-backed issue. Consider how investors assess securities backed by home equity loans. Those who purchase the senior classes look at the least creditworthy collateral because it has the greatest prepayment stability. For the B-pieces (low-rated or junior tranches), however, credit quality concerns dwarf prepayment concerns. The key question about the B-pieces is whether the credit enhancement will hold up under the most severe stress. The rating agencies need to feel confident that the B-piece will not be paid off early, since this would expose the senior classes to credit risk. Although this structure was designed for credit reasons, the B-piece actually has less prepayment sensitivity and relatively higher value per unit of risk than does the senior piece (Wagner and Callahan 1997).

Optimization techniques, such as nonlinear, mixed-integer programming may be used to develop alternative strategies. A structured financing is a prediversified portfolio that may be treated as a mathematical programming problem in which constraints of liquidity, rating agency requirements, regulatory limits, and internal capital allocation may be modeled. Once the alternative structures have been developed, the solution may be stress tested in the same optimization scheme using postoptimality analysis. If this proves difficult or insufficient, simulation may be used.

If the assets in question are interest bearing (e.g., junk bonds or residential mortgages), then the timing of defaults becomes a critical issue. Suppose that we have a $100 portfolio with a loss expectation of 10 percent and an earnings expectation of 10 percent. If the portfolio of assets lasts for 10 years, then over that period, without losses, we would earn $100 on a simple interest basis. A 10 percent loss coming in the first year would hurt us much more than one coming in the last year. Today, the structured finance markets are devoting substantial attention to formulating assumptions about the level and timing of defaults (see Table 23.2). A security that is very sensitive to timing—that is, the longer the time before problems develop, the better the overall performance—may attract investors who would otherwise turn it down. By the same token, prepayment risk is also a consideration because ABS generally do not have prepayment protection.

Table 23.2 illustrates some of the financial analyses performed in structuring the security. The first section contains the important assumptions made with respect to the cash flows, defaults, and recoveries. Only the results for years 1, 5, and 10 are shown. An important assumption is the cumulative default rate and its timing. The total default rate is assumed to be 34 percent in the base case scenario. The structure is stressed for default timings of 41, 24, 18, 11, and 6 percent of this total in successive years. In the stressed case, the total default rate is assumed to be 48 percent, and the default timing is accelerated to 50, 33, 8, and 8 percent in successive years. This structure has three tranches—senior, mezzanine, and junior subordinated.

The asset coverage ratio and the interest coverage ratio are set at the required levels and the structure is tested to see whether termination will be triggered because of failure to meet one or both. The second section of the table shows the projected cash flows and distribution to the three tranches. It may be observed that for the junior subordinated piece, the only principal paydown of $52,314,591 occurs in the 10th year in the base case, but it does not occur at all in the stressed scenario. The paydown for all three tranches is shown in the third section of Table 23.2. In both the base and stressed case the senior and mezzanine tranches are paid down in year 10. The junior subordinated tranche is paid down to $32,616,253 in year 10 in the base case but remains at $84,930,844 in the stressed case.[7]

Of course, a good asset selection process or a good portfolio manager can also stack the deck in the investor's favor. A manager who is reasonably knowledgeable should be able to select assets that will perform well for at least the first few years. Uncertainty will come into play only over time. If the portfolio manager is skilled at anticipating problems and has the power to sell assets, then the value of the portfolio can probably be enhanced—as long as assets can be sold for more than 90 cents on the dollar.

FINANCING RISKY CREDITS

One of the great virtues of structured finance is that it makes it possible to finance risky credits as well as strong ones. If a pool of assets is large enough to be actuarially sound (40 to 50 names or more), then it can include some relatively low-rated assets along with better ones. If we want to make a loan to someone whose credit is questionable, this kind of structure provides an excellent way to do so—as long as we price our loan appropriately. The good assets in the structure will offset the bad. This is the very same process that insurance companies use to manage risk in other business segments. Every day, they insure people who may have short life expectancy by pooling them with people who have long life expectancy. The risks are blended out. Moreover, the senior tranche in a structure may be sized so that even at the highest expected stress, cash flow to this tranche will remain within the risk boundaries set by investors in this class and by the rating agencies.

In the financial markets, structured solutions allow lenders to broaden their customer base—mitigating their credit risk by creating portfolios of loans. That is why Americans today receive so many unsolicited credit card offers in the mail. Once the insurance model has been applied to the financial markets, it becomes possible for lenders to offer credit cards, mortgages, and auto loans to people they would not have been willing to finance in the past.

Bear in mind, however, that portfolios are not immune to systemic risk. Advanta is a case in point. Under pressure from rising delinquencies and

---

[7]It should be noted that the data shown in Table 23.2 are meant as an illustration. The assumptions for actual deals may vary.

Table 23.2 Example of CLO/CBO Analysis

	Assumptions, Collateral Balance, and Coverage Ratios					
Assumptions	Base case			Stress case		
Cumulative default rate	34%			48%		
Default timing (% of total per annum)	**41,24,18,11,6**			**50,33,8,8**		
Recovered amount	32%			15%		
Recovery timing	**Immediate**			**One-year delay**		
Asset coverage test	110%			110%		
Interest coverage test	125%			125%		
LIBOR	6%			6%		
Scheduled interest	L + 3%			L + 3%		
Reinvestment period	4 years			4 years		
Year	⟨⟨1⟩⟩	⟨⟨5⟩⟩	⟨⟨10⟩⟩	⟨⟨1⟩⟩	⟨⟨5⟩⟩	⟨⟨10⟩⟩
Collateral balance						
Beginning balance	490,000,000	409,893,105	398,757,266	490,000,000	259,135,912	259,135,912
Principal payments received	0	0	398,757,266	0	0	259,135,912
Defaults on original collateral	68,600,000	9,800,000	0	117,600,000	0	0
Defaults on reinvested recoveries	0	614,656	0	0	0	0
Defaults on reinvested spread	0	721,184	0	0	0	0
Balance after defaults	421,400,000	398,757,266	0	372,400,000	259,135,912	0
Reinvestment of recoveries	21,952,000	0	0	0	0	0
Reinvestment of excess spread	9,621,432	0	0	5,211,432	0	0
Ending asset balance	452,973,432	398,757,266	0	377,611,432	259,135,912	0
Ratios and tests						
Asset coverage ratio[a]	133.25	120.79	111.00	111.93	91.49	111.00
Interest coverage ratio[b]	174.03	164.68	126.00	153.79	124.30	126.00
Reinvestment period	Yes	No	No	Yes	No	No
Termination event occurs[c]	No	No	No	No	Yes	No

Sources and Uses of Cash

Cash flow from assets					
Principal payments received	0	0	0	398,757,266	259,135,912
Cash recoveries	21,952,000	3,136,000	0	0	0
Total principal received	21,952,000	3,136,000	0	398,757,266	259,135,912
Scheduled interest on original assets	44,100,000	44,100,000	44,100,000	44,100,000	44,100,000
Scheduled interest not received	6,174,000	14,994,000	10,584,000	14,994,000	21,168,000
Net interest received on original assets	37,926,000	29,106,000	33,516,000	29,106,000	22,932,000
Interest received on reinvested recoveries	0	4,073,288	0	4,073,288	0
Interest received on reinvested excess spread	0	2,708,866	0	2,708,866	390,232
Total interest received	37,926,000	35,888,154	33,516,000	35,888,154	23,322,232
Total cash sources	**59,878,000**	**39,024,154**	**33,516,000**	**434,645,419**	**282,458,144**
Less uses					
Interest on senior debt	21,793,203	21,793,203	21,973,203	19,266,393	16,811,633
Interest paid on sub debt	6,511,365	6,511,365	6,511,365	5,744,454	6,510,599
Accrued interest paid	0	0	0	0	0
Surety bond reimbursement	0	0	0	0	0
Principal to senior	0	8,804,985	0	293,532,714	256,666,154
Principal to mezzanine	0	1,914,601	0	63,827,267	2,469,758
Reinvestment of recoveries	21,952,000	0	0	0	0
Reinvestment of excess spread	9,621,432	0	5,211,432	0	0
Junior subordinated payments	0	0	0	52,314,591	0
Total cash uses	**59,878,000**	**39,024,154**	**33,516,000**	**434,645,419**	**282,458,144**

Table 23.2 Example of CLO/CBO Analysis (Continued)

	Balance Sheet					
	Base case			Stress case		
Year	⟨1⟩	⟨5⟩	⟨10⟩	⟨1⟩	⟨5⟩	⟨10⟩
Senior debt						
Beginning balance	332,720,660	332,720,660	293,532,714	332,720,660	286,444,913	256,666,154
Principal paydown	0	8,804,985	293,532,714	0	7,500,090	256,666,154
From residual account	0	0	0	0	0	0
End balance	332,720,660	323,915,675	0	332,720,660	278,944,823	0
Mezzanine debt						
Beginning balance	72,348,496	72,348,496	63,827,267	72,348,496	72,348,496	72,348,496
Principal paydown	0	1,914,601	63,827,267	0	0	2,469,758
End balance	72,348,496	70,433,895	0	72,348,496	72,348,496	69,878,739
Accrued and unpaid interest	0	0	0	0	29,777,311	78,274,118
Accrued interest paid at termination	0	0	0	0	0	0
Principal and accrued int. balance	72,348,496	70,433,895	0	72,348,496	102,125,807	148,152,857
Junior subordinated						
Beginning balance	84,930,844	84,930,844	84,930,844	84,930,844	84,930,844	84,930,844
Principal paydown	0	0	52,314,591	0	0	0
End balance	84,930,844	84,930,844	32,616,253	84,930,844	84,930,844	84,930,844
Surety bond						
Beginning balance	0	0	0	0	0	0
Draw	0	0	0	0	0	0
Reimbursement	0	0	0	0	0	0
Interest	0	0	0	0	0	0
Ending balance	0	0	0	0	0	0

[a] Asset coverage ratio (ACR) = (balance after defaults/beginning senior debt)
[b] Interest coverage ratio (ICR) = (interest received/interest on senior debt)
[c] ACR < 110% or ICR < 125%

decreasing revenues from its consumer portfolio, Advanta announced that it would lose $20 million in the first quarter of 1997. Subsequently, Advanta signaled a retreat from the business by announcing that Fleet Financial Group had agreed to acquire its consumer credit card business, estimated to contain $11.5 billion in balances and 6 million accounts. From its modest beginnings in 1951, Advanta had grown into the seventh largest issuer of credit cards in the country and was viewed as one of the best at minimizing losses on credit-card loans. Soaring personal bankruptcies in the United States are one of the reasons cited for Advanta's difficulties (*Philadelphia Inquirer* 1997).

THE ANATOMY OF AN ASSET-BACKED SECURITY

Presented next are two examples of ABS. The first, illustrated in Table 23.3, is structured as a revolving trust using closed end loans. During a fixed revolving period, as long as the performance of the portfolio does not deteriorate beyond established loss levels, a portion of the principal payments will be used to purchase new loans. In the second example (Table 23.4), the security is backed by bullet loans with monthly payment of interest (no call prepayment protection). When the loans are paid off, the life of the security ends. Both securities receive credit support as described.

EVALUATING ASSET-BACKED SECURITIES

When they evaluate an asset-backed issue, structured finance professionals focus on three key areas: the originator (or seller/servicer), the assets themselves, and the structure of the transaction.

Who made the loans? What process did the originator use? How good is it at selecting and sizing credits? What has been its past experience? Why does it want to sell the assets? These are among the key questions to be asked about the originator.

The assets themselves must also be studied. If they are consumer assets, what are the interest rates? What kinds of purchases were they used to finance—homes? boats? recreational vehicles? The quality of an asset is often related to the importance of the item being financed. Under acute financial pressure, most individuals will do everything in their power to avoid defaulting on their home mortgage. Relatively few, however, will feel as strong a compulsion to continue meeting lease payments on a sports car. The characteristics of the asset need to be thoroughly understood. Location and industry concentration should be identified. Other features of the assets should also be studied. In one instance in the authors' experience, the preapproval criteria used in a solicitation systematically drew a disproportionately large number of inferior credits into a portfolio. Even though it had no geographic concentration, the portfolio had a steep loss curve.[8]

---

[8]The loss curve is a graph of cumulative net losses for a portfolio plotted over time. See Chapter 12.

Table 23.3 Example of a Consumer Asset-backed Security

Chevy Chase Home Loan Asset-backed Certificates Series 1996–1

Class	Investor certificate
Description	Senior principal and interest
Amount	$154MM
Coupon	7.15 %
Rating	Aaa
Structure	Surety bond/revolving trust
Credit support	Unconditional and irrevocable guarantee of Capital Markets Assurance Corporation (CapMAC—Rating Aaa) of principal and interest to the investor certificate holders; initial enhancement of 3.10% (0.50% reserve fund and 2.6% overcollateralization); built up to and maintained at 6.25% with overcollateralization
Issuer	Chevy Chase Savings Bank, FSB
Seller	Chevy Chase Savings Bank, FSB
Originator/servicer	Chevy Chase Savings Bank, FSB
Trustee	Norwest Bank of Minnesota N.A.
Underwriter	CS First Boston
Tax election	Debt for tax
Pool summary type	Fixed rate, fully amortizing; simple interest; closed-end home improvement and home equity (debt consolidation) loans

Number of loans	12,966
Principal amount	$11,840
Average loan	$11,840
Maximum loan	$73,425
Seasoning	10 months
WAC	14.15%
WAM	104 months
Coupons	6.00–18.00%
State concentration	55% VA; 31% MD; 6% NC; 5% Wash DC; 1% NJ.
Comments	Aaa rating is based primarily on the CapMAC (insurance financial strength rating of Aaa) surety bond.

Internal credit support is available from excess spread, reserve fund, and overcollateralization. The overcollateralization created by the excess of loan balance over the certificate balance will provide the first loss protection by absorbing loan losses before claims on the CapMAC policy.

Revolving feature of the transaction will allow Chevy Chase to fund new loans using principal collections subject to the delinquency performance level of the portfolio and acceptable quality of new loans.

Potential interest shortfalls could occur as a result of declining interest rates and prepayments. The rating addresses credit risk only.

Table 23.4 Example of a Corporate Loan Asset-Backed Security

CAC-titrisation

Rating	AAA
Issuer	Fonds Common de Créances (FCC)
Amount	FF672m
Seller/Servicer	Société des Bourses Francaises
Management Company	Eurotitrisation
Deposit Pay Agent	Caisse des Dépots et Consignation (CDC)
Arranger	Caisse Autonome de Refinancement (CAR)
Placement	Caisse des Depots et Consignations
Loan Characteristics	Bullet maturity, monthly pay, loans to stock brokerage firms
Interest	Variable (TMP + 0.30%)
Pool Summary	22 loans to 12 brokerage firms
Amount Structure	Varies between FF10m and FF100m

	Tranche 1	Tranche 2	Tranche 3	Tranche 4
Rating	Aaa	Aaa	Aaa	Aaa
Type of shares	Regular	Regular	Regular	Residual
Placement	Public	Public	Public	Private
Interest payments	quarterly	quarterly	quarterly	maturity
Nominal rate	TMP + 0.22%	TMP + 0.05%	TMP + 0.04%	0.175%
Nominal amount	FF214m	FF160m	FF298m	FF2,016m
Maturity	02/09/91	07/09/92	06/09/93	06/09/93
Stated average life	161 days	2 yrs 13 days	3 yrs 53 days	3 yrs 171 days

Credit support: First call guarantees by Aaa-rated CAR (up to FF15m) and by Aaa-rated CDC (the amounts in excess of FF15m up to FF657m). The guarantees do not decline as the loans pay off and are replenished in an amount equal to recoveries. CDC also guarantees a 9 percent minimum reinvestment rate on the funds in FCC's account.

Residual: The residual tranche is a single share priced to cover issuing costs. Nothing is paid on this share until all the other tranches are paid off. The stated average life assumes no prepayments, although the residual tranche is extremely sensitive to prepayments. The ratings do not address the possibility that the shareholder might suffer lower-than-anticipated yields due to prepayments.

Source: Moody's Investors Service (1995), pp. 462–463. Reprinted with permission.

If the assets are corporate receivables, other issues arise. Are there circumstances under which the receivable might be extinguished? A bookseller's unsold inventory, for example, can normally be returned to the publishers. In certain businesses, a high level of returns must be factored into the equation. Are the assets subject to economic cycles? to interest rate shifts? to national catastrophes? If the originator started to experience financial difficulties, would the nature of the assets change? Once a company realizes that one of its suppliers is about to go out of business, it may delay making payments.

Servicing quality is also critical to the valuation of assets. If a portfolio depends on monthly billing, then collection may deteriorate if the loans are not effectively serviced. The staffing levels of the collection departments and the tools for the management of delinquencies must be analyzed. In the subprime auto sector, for example, where the credit quality of the obligor is low, aggressive servicing may be needed to keep the payments flowing in. From the investor's perspective, the servicer should collect and apply the payments promptly and carry out reporting, remittance, and reconciliation on a timely basis. The servicer should be strong enough that bankruptcy is not an imminent risk.

Assets must be evaluated by people who truly understand them—professionals who have worked at rating agencies or bank credit card operations, or who have studied the business and become experts.

Finally, the legal structure must also be evaluated. The key question here is ownership and control of the assets. Has ownership truly been transferred to a special purpose vehicle? If the originator were to become bankrupt, could a court take the assets away?

On all three counts—the originator, the assets, and the structure—evaluating an asset-backed issue requires the close scrutiny of experienced professionals.

IMPACT ON THE BANKING INDUSTRY

The opportunity to securitize assets is gradually transforming the primary role of a bank. Increasingly, banks are in the business of originating, promoting, and servicing assets rather than warehousing them. To fill this role effectively, bankers must become better at creating and pricing assets properly so that they can later be sold off. In the past, banks did not price debt rationally. Saddled with excess capacity in a mature business, they faced a Hobson's choice: either to make loans or to go out of business. To preserve their client base, their first response has been to lower prices and continue making loans.

By separating the holder of a loan from its originator, the structured finance process brings pricing discipline to the debt market. If a loan has not been priced correctly, no one will buy it. An investment fund is not a business; it has no borrower base to preserve. Its decisions are based on relative value, not absolute value. A similar pattern is evident in other dealer markets, such as the art and antiques markets. Collectors who fall in love with works of art are liable to pay any price at all to own them. But dealers are inherently more disciplined in their approach. They are careful to pay a price that will allow them to resell the work with some additional margin for themselves. Unlike principal players, they are in the business of knowing values. They rarely make mistakes.

Structured finance is transforming the banking industry in emerging countries as well as in developed ones. Not long ago, the importance of a nation's banking industry could generally be judged by its stage of economic development: the less developed the country, the more important the banks. As an economy develops, the banking sector generally loses prominence as other institutions, such as pension funds, command a growing share of the investable capital. This pattern would suggest that banking is a mature business in OECD countries but still a growth business in emerging countries.

However, globalization of the financial markets appears to be undermining this truth. Today, a finance company based in Indonesia or Thailand can readily complete a private placement of ABS in the U.S. capital markets. Even in the absence of significant local pension funds or insurance companies, this possibility changes the competitive dynamics for Indonesian and Thai banks. In emerging markets, in other words, banking may prove to be a more mature business than many observers realize.

OTHER APPLICATIONS OF STRUCTURED FINANCE

Although the issuance of ABS remains the single largest application of structured finance technology, other uses are gaining in importance. An insurance company, for example, recently wanted to increase the yield from its investment portfolio but was unable to make further high-yield investments because of regulatory constraints. A portion of the company's existing high-yield portfolio was structured as a $500 million collateralized bond obligation (CBO) and wrapped with a surety bond from CapMAC. The CBO reduced the company's exposure to high-yield investments, enabling it to create additional capacity to purchase high-yield bonds. As a result, the insurer was able to increase the overall effective yield on its investment portfolio. When packaged in this manner, the bonds that originally carried a risk rating of "3" through "6" carry a rating of "1" or "2." The Asset Valuation Reserve (AVR) is correspondingly reduced. This strategy has been dubbed "AVR-bitrage" because it is an arbitrage based on the difference in AVR treatment.

In another example, a major film studio in the United States financed the production cost of recently completed, ready-for-release films through the innovative use of structured finance. Traditionally, this cost would be financed largely through equity, with some additional funding from bank loans. Using off-balance-sheet financing, however, the studio was able to diversify its sources of funding—tapping the capital markets rather than the banking industry. By means of limited-recourse debt, it was also able to raise more money. Gross receipts from the films and the film rights themselves provided the security for this medium-term-note financing. In a traditional asset-backed securitization, the performance of the asset is either delinked from the originator or reserved to protect the creditors and guarantors from the originator's credit problems. In this instance, however, the performance of the asset—the films—still depends on the studio's success in distributing the films and in exploiting film rights through various channels of distribution. How did this financing become possible now?

In the past, banks were the only players who were in a position to extend credit for projects of this type. Flotation costs and other institutional considerations would probably have impeded access to the capital markets. Today, however, two more players have entered the picture: the rating agency and the guarantor. By rating the financing as investment grade, the rating agency threw its weight behind the transaction. This opened the door to investment by institutional investors. CapMAC, which provided the financial guarantee, acted as a key facilitator for the transaction. It offered its guarantee on the basis of both modern portfolio concepts and classic credit analysis. The financing is backed by an entire portfolio of films. A film that generates above-average revenues can therefore make up for one with below-average performance. Classic credit analysis was used to assess the financial viability of the studio and its management over the life of the transaction. The studio's performance relative to the industry, factors in its distribution strategies, and stress tests of the future outcomes were among the components of this analysis. Optionality is built into the financing as well, in the form of trigger events that will cause the structure to liquidate more rapidly if the studio's financial viability should become impaired.

Structured capital markets' techniques are also being used to finance projects in a number of developed and developing countries. One recent example is the refinancing of a power generation company in England. The deregulation of the UK electric supply industry has created opportunities for independent power generation companies. The European Investment Bank (EIB), a financing institution of the European Union, can provide long-term loans to assist in economic development. However, EIB is not permitted to vary its spread to borrowers in step with their varying credit risk. To be eligible for the spread that EIB charges, a financing must therefore be wholly or partly guaranteed. This financing was based partly on the power purchase arrangements that were in place, partly on the stable regulatory environment, and partly on the expected profitability of the power generation system. Rating agencies gave a "shadow rating" of investment grade to the financing, and CapMAC provided a surety bond that guarantees timely payment of principal and interest to EIB and the other lender in the transaction. Here, too, structured finance techniques enabled a borrower to tap the capital markets rather than relying on traditional sources such as commercial banks.

In other parts of the world, as well, there are examples of similarly structured financings in which commercial banks, financial guarantors, and other capital market participants play a role. One is Indonesia's East Java Project, which is jointly owned by Enron and local sponsors. The financing structure is supported by power supply agreement, a power purchase agreement, and the sponsors' base equity investment of 25 percent. The remaining 75 percent of the financing was debt raised through a combination of commercial loans and bonds issued in the Section 144A market. Gaining access to the 144A market required, among other things, that the bonds be rated investment grade. This was made possible by a surety bond from a financial guarantor.

By means of asset-based financings, securitization, financings based on future revenues, and other innovations, the capital markets have been able to bear credit risk that was hitherto borne mainly by commercial banks and government entities such as states, municipalities, and sovereigns.

STRUCTURED FINANCE TECHNIQUES AND INVESTMENT MANAGEMENT

When an investment product is new and unfamiliar to investors, efforts are made to make it look and act like more familiar, established products. One of the obvious ways of doing so is to obtain an acceptable rating from an established rating agency. The rating agencies maintain stringent credit standards and provide a common credit language. They can perform an important service in bringing new credits to the market (please see also Chapter 6).

Structured finance techniques such as pooling, senior/subordinated structures, reserves, and guarantees can transform the risk/return profile of a product so that it qualifies as an acceptable investment. Taken one at a time, all auto loans may not be of investment grade, but structured finance techniques can transform a pool of them into a security that insurance companies are able to buy. An asset may even be turned into a close substitute for the investor's current preferred investment. A good example of this is an *asset swap*—typically, a combination of a long-term fixed-rate bond with an interest-rate swap that converts it to a floating-rate asset. The combined product, sometimes termed a *synthetic bond,* enables an investor to take on the credit risk of the issuer (and thereby earn a credit spread) without taking any interest-rate risk because the asset return floats with LIBOR.[9] Many features of an asset—including its payment frequency—can limit its acceptance by investors. Lewis Ranieri (1996), who is often credited with the invention of the collateralized mortgage obligation (the CMO), notes that when John Hancock Insurance initially bought a mortgage pass-through security, it complained because the security paid monthly instead of semiannually like other bonds.

Last, transparency in pricing and liquidity are two other issues of concern to investors. The more liquid the market, the easier it is to mark the securities to market instead of relying on models. These are some of the considerations that go into the engineering of structured finance products.

REFERENCES

Baum, S P. 1996. The Securitization of Commercial Property Debt. In *Primer on Securitization,* edited by L. T. Kendall and M. J. Fishman. Cambridge, Mass.: MIT Press.

---

[9]The asset swap market is the precursor to the credit derivative market because it allows an investor to take pure credit risk but not interest rate risk. However, it should be noted that an asset swap requires the investor to own the underlying bond, which may not be the case for the credit derivative.

Board of Governors of the Federal Reserve System. 1997. *Federal Reserve Bulletin.* Washington, D.C.: Board of Governors of the Federal Reserve System.

Cantwell, L. T. 1996. Securitization: A New Era in American Finance. In *Primer on Securitization,* edited by L. T. Kendall and M. J. Fishman. Cambridge, Mass.: MIT Press.

FDIC (Federal Deposit Insurance Corporation). 1988. *Statistics on Banking.* Washington, D.C.: FDIC.

———. 1995. *Statistics on Banking.* Washington, D.C.

Jacob, D P., and K. R. Duncan. 1995. Commercial Mortgage-backed Securities. In *Handbook of Mortgage Backed Securities,* 4th ed., edited by F. Fabozzi. Chicago: Probus.

Jungman, M. 1996. The Contribution of the Resolution Trust Corporation to the Securitization Process. In *Primer on Securitization,* edited by L. T. Kendall and M. J. Fishman. Cambridge, Mass.: MIT Press.

Kinney, J M., and R. T. Garrigan. 1985. *The Handbook of Mortgage Banking: A Guide to the Secondary Mortgage Market.* Homewood, Ill.: Dow Jones–Irwin.

Moody's Investors Service. 1995. *Moody's Global Credit Analysis.* London: IFR Publishing.

Mortgage Market Statistical Annual. 1997. Washington, D.C.: Inside Mortgage Finance Publications.

Ranieri, L. S. 1996. The Origins of Securitization, Sources of Its Growth, and Its Future Potential. In *Primer on Securitization,* edited by L. T. Kendall and M. J. Fishman. Cambridge, Mass.: MIT Press.

Samuel, T. 1997. Customers' Debt Is Catching Up to Credit-card Firm. *Philadelphia Inquirer.* 18 March.

Santamero, A. M., and D. F. Babbel. 1997. *Financial Markets, Instruments and Institutions.* Chicago: Irwin.

Wagner, K., and E. Callahan. 1997. B-Pieces on Home-Equity Loan ABS. *Mortgage-backed Securities Letter,* 14 July.

ADDITIONAL READING

Rosenthal, J. A., and J. M. Ocampo. 1988. *Securitization of Credit: Inside the New Technology of Finance.* New York: John Wiley & Sons.

Chapter **24**

A New World Driven by Analytics and Diversifying Agents

Credit risk is moving to the securities market. One of the historic barriers to securitization was that the securities market was reluctant to take real credit risk. Increasingly, the securities market is willing to take real credit risk.

—Lowell Bryan

A growing number of organizations, both old and new, manage credit risk by applying the tenets of portfolio theory. They focus, in particular, on diversification. These organizations devote more of their energy to managing risk than they do to acquiring it—an approach predicated on the existence of a liquid secondary market for loans. Such a market has evolved in recent decades as an outgrowth of the loan syndication activities of commercial banks.

Prior to the 1970s, bank syndication was a kind of club activity. When General Motors wanted to raise a lot of money, it asked its various house banks to arrange a loan. Although one bank would be designated as the agent and lead, in reality, the banks all acted in concert in what was, in effect, an insider's game.

The bank syndication business, which was centered in London and New York, began to expand in the 1970s. After OPEC raised the price of oil from $3.00 to $20.00 a barrel, the global financial system had to readjust so that petrodollars could be recycled effectively. When Japan and Korea purchased oil from countries in the Middle East, the latter transferred the money to banks, which could then lend it to Japan and Korea. It was a zero sum game. As this kind of international oil lending came into vogue, banks needed to spread out their risks. Syndication evolved into a mechanism by which banks could manage their exposures as they originated business.

In the 1980s and 1990s, syndication evolved further, to the point where the buying and selling of loans became a regular practice in the banking industry. By now, most money center banks have established specialized trading desks to buy and sell bank loans, and a secondary market for these assets has emerged—particularly for large loans. Trading of "junk" loans— loans to companies of below investment-grade credit quality—is particularly active. The U.S. syndicated loan market and secondary loan market volumes are as shown in Figures 24.1 and 24.2.

Figure 24.1   U.S. Syndicated Loan Volume

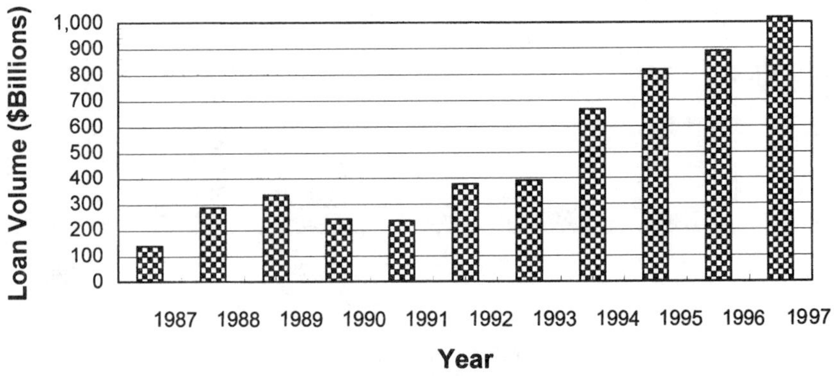

Year	Volume
1987	137.1
1988	284.39
1989	333.19
1990	241.27
1991	234.38
1992	375.48
1993	389.33
1994	665.3
1995	817
1996	887.6
1Q97	189.08

Source: Loan Pricing Corporation (1997). Reprinted with permission.

Typically, U.S. money center banks serve as both originators and traders in this market, whereas regional banks and European banks are the end buyers. Money center banks are usually asset long and liquidity short, but regional banks are typically liquidity long and asset short. Regional banks have a limited number of asset types that they can buy, including government securities, mortgages, and syndicated loans. The latter are attractive because they offer superior yields. Foreign banks have a somewhat different motivation. Those wanting to book U.S. assets may find it difficult to compete directly with American banks as loan originators. As an alternative, they can buy good loans in the marketplace and add them to their portfolios.

Syndicated loans are 5–8 years in tenor and have London Inter-Bank Offered Rate (LIBOR)–based pricing. Term loans are generally divided into A, B, C, and D tranches, with each tranche generally one year longer in maturity than the preceding one. The A tranche is of shorter maturity (3 to 5 years) and generally contains a revolving portion. The other tranches (also called institutional tranches) have a predetermined principal and a longer maturity (around 10 years). There is typically a 25 to 50 basis point premium

Figure 24.2 Secondary Loan Market

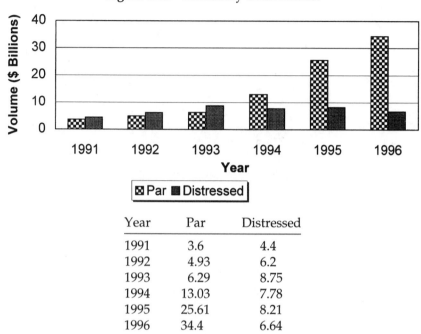

Year	Par	Distressed
1991	3.6	4.4
1992	4.93	6.2
1993	6.29	8.75
1994	13.03	7.78
1995	25.61	8.21
1996	34.4	6.64

Source: Loan Pricing Corporation (1997). Reprinted with permission.

for each additional year. The ownership interest is conveyed either through an assignment (whereby the investor has a direct debtor-creditor relationship) or through a loan participation agreement. In the latter case, the buyer has an undivided interest in the loan but no direct relationship with the debtor.

At first, the purchasers of bank loans came to the market with a buy-and-hold mentality. As the secondary market expanded, however, new players with a different orientation began to enter. Investment management companies hired experts in bank loans and began to buy these assets for their portfolios. Unlike the regional banks and foreign banks, these players are steeped in portfolio theory, and they are inclined to manage their portfolios actively—selling loans as well as buying them. Investment management companies have also developed structures into which these assets can be placed. Eaton Vance, a mutual fund established in 1989, is an early example of a "prime rate" mutual fund.

A variety of special-purpose companies have been established to acquire assets, create diversified portfolios, and then sell off tranches of these portfolios to different investor types. The investors in senior tranche are those who invest in AA-rated floating-rate instruments and structured finance products such as credit card receivables with 4–5 year maturities. They may be arbitrage investors such as Alpha, Beta, or Centauri, or banks, to name a few. The investors in the mezzanine piece are typically insurance companies.

Investors in the equity piece may be institutional investors or high net worth individuals with an appetite for higher yields (with higher risk, of course). The rating agencies have become comfortable rating investments of this kind, focusing on the issues of diversification, liquidity, and active asset management. The most recent examples of this concept are CBOs and CLOs.

CBOs AND CLOs

Collateralized bond obligations (CBOs) and collateralized loan obligations (CLOs) are structured financing backed by bonds (sovereign or corporate) and bank loans, respectively. These structures have the virtue of turning (primarily) below-investment-grade assets into investment-grade securities. Pooling, tranching, diversification, and various forms of credit enhancement combine to work this alchemy. While securities of this kind were issued as early as 1987, the volume of issuance has surged in recent years. Since 1992, for example, Fitch IBCA has rated over $10 billion of such securities (Fitch Investors Service 1997). A number of factors are driving this growth: the arbitrage opportunity created by the disparity in coupon payments between high-yield and investment-grade assets; the need on the part of some banks and insurance companies to lower their capital charges by removing assets from their balance sheets; and investors' appetite for securities offering attractive yields and diversified exposure. Collateralized loan obligations represent the last frontier in banks' ability to manage their balance sheets. If this market takes off, it is conceivable that its impact on the financial landscape will be as dramatic as that had by interest rate swaps.

Figure 24.3 shows a typical CBO/CLO structure. The issuer establishes a bankruptcy-remote special purpose vehicle, which purchases bonds/loans from the portfolio on the basis of pre-set criteria approved by the rating agency. The portfolio manager will manage the assets in the special purpose vehicle. The management activities include loan administration, asset replacement, and receipt and distribution of funds. The special purpose vehicle may enter into an interest rate swap to eliminate interest rate risk, thereby providing the debt holders with a LIBOR plus spread cash flow augmented by any return of principal from prepayments. The redistribution of risk and return is brought about by tranching. This structure creates senior obligations (which may be rated AAA) that have lower expected returns but a higher rating than the overall portfolio. The subordinated debt also earns an investment-grade rating (such as BBB). The junior subordinated tranche, which represents the true equity piece, may be unrated. The structure may include reserve accounts or a liquidity line of credit, and/or guarantees. As investors become more comfortable with the structure and quality of CLOs and CBOs, the need for many of the facilitators in these transactions will diminish over time. The resulting savings will flow to the investor or the borrower, depending on supply and demand conditions.

There are presently two forms of CBOs. In a cash flow CBO, also referred to as an arbitrage CBO, the cash flow generated by the underlying assets is used to pay interest and principal to investors. A market value CBO, by contrast, requires that the market value of the assets in the portfolio always

Figure 24.3 CLO/CBO Structure

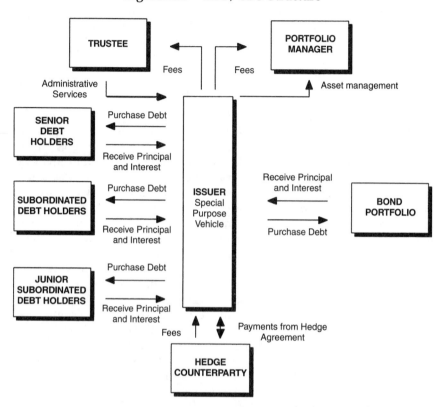

Source: Fridson (1997). Reprinted with permission. Copyright © 1998 Merrill Lynch, Pierce, Fenner & Smith Incorporated.

be sufficient to pay off the liabilities. Portfolio management is based on the total return concept: Cash flows for payments to investors are derived from trading profits as well as from principal and accrued interest received on the underlying bonds.

In both CBOs and CLOs, the real issue is whether the underlying collateral is investment grade. Northstar 1997–1, for example, is a $325 million CBO underwritten by Bear Stearns & Co. and managed by Northstar Investment Management Corporation. The collateral pool consists primarily of U.S. high-yield bonds from at least 47 issuers with an average rating of B. Up to 15 percent of this portfolio can be emerging-markets bonds. No single obligor can account for more than 2.15 percent of the portfolio and no single industry for more than 5.0 percent. The portfolio must meet the following required rating percentages:

- BB− and above, 10 percent
- B+ and above, 25 percent
- B and above, 75 percent
- B− and above, 95 percent

A knowledgeable and experienced manager of high-yield investments actively manages the portfolio. It should be mentioned that in cash flow CBOs such this, the structure approved by the rating agencies severely limits the manager's ability to trade assets.

Northstar 1997–1 issued four classes of debt totaling $340.8 million, as listed in Table 24-1. During a four-year revolving period, any principal proceeds from the collateral can be reinvested in new collateral, so long as all coverage tests and portfolio requirements are met.

The presence of the equity class cushions investors in the senior notes (to the extent of their principal and a low rate of interest) against price declines and defaults on the collateral pool. They enjoy a senior claim on all assets of the CBO, and they are protected by swaps and hedges against most of the impact of interest rate shifts. In addition, structural protections insulate them against prepayment and reinvestment risk. The deal is attractive to the equity holders as well, who gain a higher potential risk/return profile through their exposure to the entire upside potential of the collateral. They do, however, absorb the impact of defaults on the underlying collateral, and their returns may be affected by prepayments, reinvestments, and changing interest rates.

EVOLUTION OF THE CLO MARKET

Until late 1996, most the activity in the securitizing of corporate assets was arbitrage driven. In these deals, either bonds or loans, or both are purchased for a trust from many sources. The specific assets are chosen so that their expected return exceeds the combined cost of the liabilities, which are in turn designed to be as cost effective as possible given the market at the time and given certain requirements driven by the composition of the assets. The difference between the return on the assets and the cost of the liabilities is reaped by the investment banker, the manager/advisor, and/or the equity investor. Arbitrage has worked for high-yield loans and bonds. Investment grade assets have not afforded an arbitrage opportunity.

Table 24-1   Northstar 1997–1 CBO Tranches

Class	Par ($MM)	Yield	Final maturity	Rating
A−1	$15.8	5.75%	February 1998	A−1+/D−1
A−2	$285.0	8.02%	February 2009	A-/A-
B	$21.0	8.925%	February 2009	BBB-(Duff & Phelps only)
Income notes	$19.0	20.7% (Expected)	February 2009	NR
Total	$340.8			

Occasionally these deals have been driven by the equity investor, an entity like a hedge fund, that wants to invest in the high-yield asset class on a highly leveraged, nonrecourse basis. The price that such a borrower pays is not having complete freedom to move in and out of names. The standard CBO or CLO is suitable only for an invest-and-hold strategy. Investors who are trading for a total return will borrow through repurchase agreements, or bank lines, or perhaps market-value CBOs, which are securitizations that rely on the market value of the assets being ample enough to pay off the debt at any time at par, rather than on the cash flow being ample enough to cover the stream of principal and interest payments.

In November 1996, the market took on a new dimension. NatWest, the global British bank, issued a $5 billion CLO. The assets were 197 corporate loans and revolvers with maturities not exceeding five years. These assets were investment grade and were taken out of NatWest's loan portfolio. The deal was driven by NatWest's own goals, not the goals of an arbitrageur, manager, or equity investor.

The size was the first remarkable thing about this deal. Arbitrage CBOs and CLOs tend to range between $300 and $1 billion. The assets are $5 to $30 million apiece. (The transaction size limits the asset size because of diversity requirements for the pool.) NatWest and the banks that followed in its wake have three reasons for making their CLOs larger: (1) they want to lay off large risks because their commitments to companies can be $100 million or more; (2) they are inclined to include a large number of credits to improve the diversity (197 names for NatWest compared with 40 to 70 for the arbitrage CBO/CLOs) in order to increase the economic efficiency of the transaction; and (3) the assets are readily available from the bank's own balance sheet.

When the assets are high in credit quality, another impediment must also be overcome. On the face of it, it may seem that, given the tight pricing on high-grade assets, on a mark-to-market basis there may not be enough margin to make a transaction worthwhile. However, the deals may often make economic sense if the marginal cost of equity capital is taken into account. Moreover, in future years the very fact that banks will have the ability to sell these assets will likely cause changes in their pricing strategies for these credits.

In the case of middle-market loans, other obstacles arise because a loan-by-loan review is costly and because documentation and collateral are not standardized. These problems will be worked out incrementally as more and more commercial loans are securitized.

MORE ON R.O.S.E.: A GROUND-BREAKING TRANSACTION

R.O.S.E. Funding No. 1, NatWest's $5 billion securitization of corporate loans, illustrates how a bank can use asset securitization to provide financing to its clients efficiently and effectively. NatWest is the U.K.'s largest corporate lender. A conduit known as R.O.S.E. Funding No. 1 Ltd. was established to buy subparticipations in loan facilities that the bank had originated and was maintaining on its balance sheet. R.O.S.E. Ltd. is registered in the Cayman

Islands, and its shares are held by a charitable trust. It is authorized to issue floating-rate notes denominated in dollars and sterling (Figure 24.4).

The portfolio of assets securitized in this transaction consists of 218 lines of credit that NatWest had extended to 189 different clients in the United Kingdom (64 percent), other EEC countries (15 percent), the United States (18 percent), and Canada and Australia (3 percent combined). The average exposure to an individual borrower is $27 million. In addition to geography, the loan portfolio is diversified by industry sector, maturity (from one to five years), and credit quality (from AAA to BBB). Approximately half of the pool is rated BBB, one quarter of it is rated A, and the other quarter is rated either AA or AAA. The two largest loans (each of £75 million) are AAA credits. Most of the loans in the portfolio were not rated independently by the rating agencies,[1] which instead studied correlations between NatWest's grading system and their own ratings and analyzed the bank's historical data on defaults and recoveries. The transaction includes a substitution period, during which R.O.S.E. Ltd. may use the funds from redemptions to add new loans to the portfolio.

Investors were offered $2 billion of floating-rate notes (FRNs) with three different maturities, all rated AA, and £1.8 billion of sterling AA paper, also in three tranches. There were also $25 million and £16 million of A-rated notes, $27 million and £18 million of BBB notes and $100 million in unrated notes, which NatWest itself is believed to have retained. The senior tranches are credit enhanced through the subordination of both principal and interest of the tranches below them.

---

[1]S&P emphasized that it did an in-depth review of the credit process applied by NatWest in assigning its risk scores.

Figure 24.4   R.O.S.E. Funding Structure

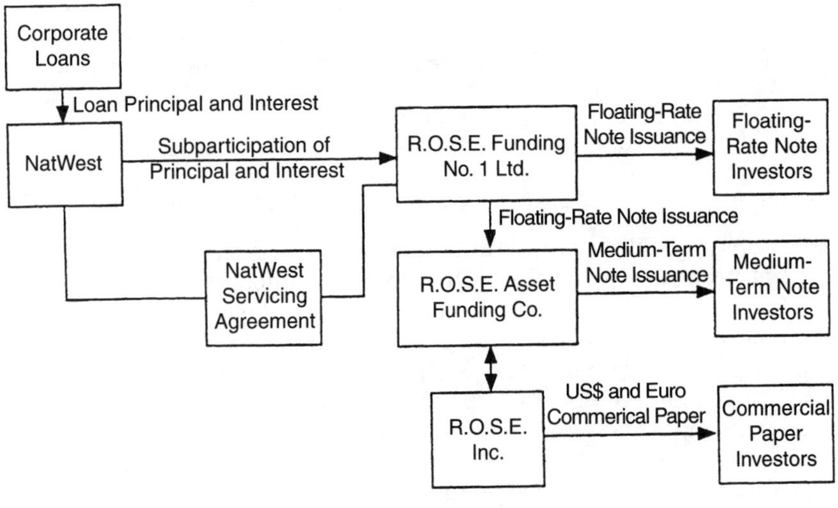

Source: Fitch IBCA.

In the case of revolving credits, NatWest kept all the unused amounts at the outset and absorbed all the pay downs as long as the facility was not in default. If the outstandings dip below the participation amount, the excess cash will be held by R.O.S.E. Funding and invested in a guaranteed income/investment contract (GIC) provided by NatWest at the average loan yield. NatWest also removed interest rate and currency risk by providing swaps. The participations may not be treated as collateral in the event of NatWest's financial failure, which means that NatWest's continued viability is a precondition for the success of this vehicle. In this respect, the transaction differs from conventional securitizations, which de-link the asset from the originator.

NatWest's transaction was a bold stroke that broadened the market for investment-grade corporate loans. Andy Clapham, managing director at NatWest, who was closely involved in bringing the deal to fruition, sheds light on the key factors that were responsible for it:

> Our chairman was on record stating that he wanted to free up the capital from corporate lending. Something had to happen because our choices were either to not renew the loans when they matured or to sell them. Our ambition was to free up capital so we could redeploy it. It so happened that the head of corporate lending, which generated these assets, was also the head of structured finance. Maintaining the revenue from the loans was not a reason to hold the loans any more. We had the backing from the top executives.
>
> When you are taking revenue out of a profit center without really replacing it, you are dealing with a very political issue. The method of funding is also different with securitization. The transaction affects the treasury function as well. Normally the treasury funds the loan assets, whereas when you securitize, the funding comes from the bond market. So this process cuts across many different areas of the organization. We had weekly meetings involving all the affected departments with people from many areas, sometimes 30 at a time. We wanted to keep it operationally simple. The system used to rate the loans was 100 percent quantitative.
>
> Being able to sell the loans is a challenge other banks face because it is such a political issue. It helped that in our case the head of lending was also responsible for structured finance and was willing to give up earnings in the short term for long-term flexibility. We wanted to continue to be in the lending market in Europe for our relationships. Now we can.[2]

CLO MARKET GROWTH

During 1997, $45 billion worth (Bear Stearns' tally) of such CLOs were issued by banks, in about a dozen deals. They occurred almost entirely in the second half of the year because it took the market time to digest what NatWest had accomplished and then gear up to copy and improve on it. This is an enormously significant number. The deals were issued in Europe and privately in the United States under the Security and Exchange Commission Rule 144a. In comparison, asset-backed securities of all asset types issued publicly in

---

[2]In the United States, keeping the 2 percent subordinated interest would cause all the loans to stay on the balance sheet of the bank.

the United States during 1997 totaled $179 billion (CapMAC 1998). Another $104 billion of asset-backed securities was issued in the private and non-U.S. markets (AiC Conference 1998). (Only $30 billion of the $104 billion constituted the CLOs. Not every deal is categorized as an asset-backed issue; the CLOs can take derivative or commercial paper form, which are not included in the market numbers.) There could be another leap in volume in 1998. As of the end of December 1997, Fitch IBCA was already reviewing $40 billion of such deals, and Bob Grossman, executive vice president of Fitch IBCA Inc., said he wouldn't be surprised to see $100 billion of CLOs done worldwide by banks in 1998 (Slicing up Bank Loans 1997).

In truth, the $45 billion of CLOs that appeared in the capital markets in 1997 may be but the tip of the iceberg. Anecdotal evidence makes it plain that CLOs are being arranged and invested in privately in the form of credit derivatives. We do not know the size of that market.

The motivations of the banks that are laying off risk in the form of CLOs have led to important variations in the deals' attributes. To develop this theme, we refer to specific attributes of the NatWest transaction and four, subsequent, publicized CLOs that represent market milestones. These deals, together with their attributes, are presented in Table 24.2.

CAPITAL AND PORTFOLIO MANAGEMENT: THE FUNDAMENTAL FACTORS

The primary driving force for the bank-sponsored CLOs is the reduction of required regulatory capital. For their main books, banks are required to hold 8 percent capital against even high-grade corporate names. Given what they earn for taking the credit risk against these names, the capital requirement is burdensome. Until recently, however, there has been no overwhelming pressure to do something about it because the banks have been awash in capital.

As of 1997, two things changed. First, banks have been instituting management techniques that measure profitability in terms of return on capital employed. They want recognition from regulators and shareholders for the capital they have relative to what they have to have, and they are thinking about how to redeploy the excess to shareholders' benefit. Second, the NatWest transaction showed that senior, investment-grade bank loans could be sold at a cost that is not very much more than the cost of moving credit card receivables off balance sheet.

The NationsBank deal, which was AAA, was priced at 3-month LIBOR + 11 basis points for the three-year tranche, and 3-month LIBOR + 14 for the five-year tranche. At about the same time in September 1997, AAA-rated credit card securities of a representative sample of good issuers traded at 1-month LIBOR + 6, and LIBOR + 9 basis points for the three- and five-year tranches, respectively . At the time, one month LIBOR was worth 1 or 2 basis points less than 3-month LIBOR. Thus, there was a six or seven basis point difference in the cost of the senior securities of a CLO verses that of cards.

This comparison of cards to CLOs is admittedly a simple-minded one. A thorough analysis would take into account the fact that card transactions have smaller senior classes than CLOs—85 percent on average compared to

Table 24-2 Collateralized Loan Obligations Market Highlights

Bank sponsor	Deal name	Date issued	Notional amt*	Capital markets execution	Senior class size	Senior rating	Asset type	Asset ratings
NatWest	R.O.S.E. funding	11/96	$5 bil	FRN's in $, Br. Pounds, half via CP conduit	96%	AA, Aa	Loan and revolver participations	BBB and above (half A and above)
Nations-Bank	Nations-Bank CLO	9/97	$4.4 bil	Master trust floating rate ABS; with seller interest	91.75%	AAA, Aaa	Perfected interests in 100% participations; loans, revolvers	Up to 45% BB+; Up to 90% BB+ to BBB+
SBC	Glacier	9/97	$1.6 bil	Master trust FRNs, backed by SBC credit linked notes (NY MTN program)	91.75%	Aa+, Aa1	Reference names, clients to which SBC has credit risk	95% BBB or up; specific weighted average risk maintained;
Tokyo—Mitsubishi	Merlin or JLS**	9/97	$2.0 bil	FRNs in $, Br. pounds, yen, SFr	90%	Aa2	Loans by assignment	Investment grade
J. P. Morgan	Bistro	12/97	$9.7 bil	Default swap with a trust that privately issued $.7 bil fixed rate notes; cash put in Treasuries	92.50%, + 4.73% senior notes of the trust	AAA, Aaa for trust senior notes	Reference names, to which J. P. Morgan may or may not initially have credit risk	A3 and BBB+ or better

Bank sponsor	Own rating system?	Diversity	Country of obligors	Unrated pct retained	Disclosure of names?
NatWest	Yes	197 names	64% U.K. 18% U.S. 15% EEC	2%	No
Nations-Bank	Yes	$6MM ave. loan size	80% U.S.; up to 20% countries at least Aa2, or Italy	3% plus a 1% reserve fund	No
SBC	Yes	2% of pool name max.	Max. 5% in countries less than AA-; blind pool analysis	Unknown, goal of 45 and 65 bps for 5- and 7-yr notes	No
Tokyo—Mitsubishi	No; Moody's	Less than 100 loans	100% Japan	Unknown	Yes
J. P. Morgan	No; most have both Moody's and S&P	No credit exceeds .38% of pool	80% U.S.; 20% European and Canadian	None, Morgan obligated to fund 33 bps reserve over five years	Yes

* includes subordinate tranches

** Japan Loan Securitization

Source: CapMAC (1998).

the 90 percent to 97 percent for CLOs. This makes the CLOs look better. On the other hand, card transactions can achieve 100 percent capital relief, and CLOs usually cannot; that makes cards look better. There is also a difference in the cost of laying off the mezzanine pieces.

REGULATORY CAPITAL REDUCTION

The NatWest deal appears to have reduced the regulatory capital the Bank must hold against that $5 billion of loans from 8 percent to 2 percent. This is because 98 percent of the portfolio was supported by securities rated investment grade, which were sold into the market, and the capital requirement is capped at the nominal retained exposure. This low, retained percentage was a notable achievement.

The NationsBank, Swiss Bank Corp., Tokyo-Mitsubishi, and J. P. Morgan deals have all done a little less well with regard to the amount of the deal rated investment grade (although had J. P. Morgan chosen to create a BBB-rated tranche they would probably have surpassed NatWest). With regard to retained exposure, J. P. Morgan sold off a BB-rated tranche and reduced its retained risk all the way down to a 33 basis point reserve to be funded over time. SBC intends to retain only 45 basis points of risk on its five-year series of notes and 65 basis points on its seven-year series.

Capital requirements are a more complex issue now that banks can hold assets for sale on "trading books," for which regulators assign different, and generally substantially less onerous, capital requirements. A variation on the CLO theme that might help a bank manage its trading book risks is CLOs where the risks in the pool are expressed as credit derivatives rather than loans. SBC's Glacier and J. P. Morgan's Bistro use credit derivatives. Exactly how much credit derivatives reduce capital requirements for trading books, however, is new territory. Different countries' regulators are not of one mind, and within countries, banks and their regulators are not necessarily clear.

The capital-relief efficacy of selling risk by way of a credit derivative depends on the counterparty, among other things. For the main "banking book," the counterparty has to be an Organization for Economic Co-Operation and Development (OECD) bank, and then the capital requirement on the underlying risk is reduced by 80 percent. (It would be reduced 100 percent for an OECD country.) The counterparty can also be a trust that holds OECD securities in the full amount of the notional risk. Partial funding of the trust would achieve a pro rata capital reduction. For the trading book, a counterparty that is investment grade but not an OECD bank achieves a 50 percent reduction. Payout formulas and tenor are other factors that bear on the suitability of credit derivatives for reducing capital requirements.

PORTFOLIO MANAGEMENT

One of the benefits of a CLO is the exercise of portfolio management. It allows a bank to reduce exposures that are too large. Many bank sponsors may be deceiving themselves, however, if this is what they believe. If the assets are evaluated with their own risk-rating system, if the investor is not given the identities of the credits in the pool, and if the banks are allowed to move names in and out of the pool after the deal is closed, one could argue that these banks bear a responsibility to the investor. If defaults start occurring in a pool, and investors face downgrades or even losses, the sponsor is likely to feel that it must support the transaction if it wants to be able to come to market again. This has been the case with credit card securitizations.

J. P. Morgan, on the other hand, has disclosed its names; almost all are rated by both Moody's and S&P, and the pool is fixed. The investors' risks have therefore been fully disclosed and can be easily evaluated. J. P. Morgan will be in a better position than any other CLO issuer thus far to let a deal stand on its own, come what may, without damage to the bank's franchise. J. P. Morgan has said, in fact, that its transaction was engineered as much as a macrohedge of credit exposures in its banking and trading businesses as a tool for capital reduction.

SBC disagrees with this challenge to the true portfolio-management effectiveness of most of the CLOs, and their disagreement is worth noting. Of all the CLO sponsors discussed here, they have the most control: they use their own risk-rating system, do not disclose the names, and can move names in and out at will. They, moreover, can put a small amount of poor credits in their pool as long as overall average ratings are maintained. To protect the investors, there is an individual at SBC charged with being the portfolio gatekeeper. If credits deteriorate unexpectedly, however, the Bank has every intention of letting the investors bear the consequences. SBC says that the yields on their mezzanine tranches fully reflect the risk of the leveraged position in the pool. The pricing does not incorporate any moral responsibility on SBC's part to fix a problem. The Bank also points out that although the individual names are not known to investors, the guidelines for the pool were disclosed in detail.

ASSET TYPE FLEXIBILITY

Until the NatWest transaction, CBOs and CLOs comprised loans and bonds exclusively. Banks shedding risks, however, also want to sell exposures such as revolving loan agreements, letter of credit obligations, and counterparty risks. NatWest's CLO accommodated revolvers. In fact, 60 percent of the assets were participations in revolvers. What NatWest did was sell a participating interest that was fully funded and likely to remain fully funded. NatWest's retained interest—the balance of the loan commitment—covers any advances and receives all pay downs first, providing the loan is not in default. If the borrower pays down the revolver so far that it intrudes upon the CLO's share, the cash is held by the CLO trust and invested in a guaranteed investment contract with NatWest. These funds are used first if the loan is funded up again. In the event of a default, all recoveries are shared pro rata with NatWest's and the CLO's outstandings at the time of default. This structure represented a breakthrough. It was awkward, however, because it leaves NatWest with a conflict in servicing the CLO's assets. Loans generally do not default without warning. They are usually troubled and under close management before there is a formal default. It would be in

NatWest's self interest—and to the disadvantage of the CLO—to delay a default as long as possible while working the loan down.

NationsBank took another approach for accommodating revolvers. It mimicked the structure used for credit card securitizations. There, the seller of the assets to the master trust retains an interest in the whole trust, called the *seller interest*. The balance, the *investor interest*, is a fixed amount. As the pool size goes up and down with the net funding variation across all the revolving commitments, the seller interest takes up the slack. The seller interest has a minimum percentage size. If it falls below that amount by virtue of there being more pay downs and prepayments than expected, the seller is required to sell more assets to the trust.

The introduction of credit derivatives to CLOs expanded the risks that could be transferred from loans, revolvers, and letters of credit (LCs) to counterparty risks. Glacier was the first derivative-based CLO transaction in the public markets. In this transaction, Swiss Bank Corp. sold individual credit-linked notes (one for each risk) off its medium term note (MTN) desk in New York to a trust. The trust funds the group of notes with the proceeds of a floating rate note (FRN) issue. For a particular counterparty exposure, SBC can estimate the potential loss if the counterparty defaults, decide how much of that it wants to cover, and then imbed the respective notional amount in the credit-linked note.

Name Flexibility

SBC structured their deal to give themselves total flexibility with the pool, so they can move names in and out (irrespective of reductions in the underlying risks) on an ongoing basis. They do it by issuing new notes and retiring notes at will. (The trust can issue additional FRNs.) Other deals have less flexibility to change the mix of names. The earlier deals had initial reinvestment periods, during which any principal pay downs or recoveries in a default could be reinvested in new assets instead of being applied to retire securities. Next came the master trust transactions, which are structurally more complex. They allow for subsequent securities issuances to finance new assets, which are added to the initial pool. Glacier goes yet a step further, and allows SBC to take names out of the pool completely at will. The limitations heretofore had been due to accounting considerations (the ability to take assets out spoils U.S. generally-accepted accounting principles [GAAP] sales treatment) and rating agency reticence to allow unfettered trading in a securitization structured on the presumption that the assets would be held (cash flow structure).

For Bistro, J. P. Morgan entered into a single credit default swap with a trust. The swap referenced 307 names. It represented an absolutely static pool, so J. P. Morgan does not have any ability to change the risk mix later on. The derivative structure still gave J. P. Morgan flexibility, however. It could put risks it did not own into the pool. J. P. Morgan is a credit derivatives dealer. Bistro could have been used to inventory offsetting hedges for future sales of credit protection.

COST

Cost is an issue that has driven the development of CLO structures. NatWest held back half its FRNs and funded them through a commercial paper conduit. This saved about 10 basis points because the all-in commercial paper cost plus the fees for the liquidity backstop is less than the yield on the FRNs.

J. P. Morgan went a step further by eschewing funding altogether. The Bistro trust was capitalized at just 7.5 percent of the notional amount of the transaction. This was more than enough to cover any conceivable loss in the portfolio referenced in the credit derivative; in fact, the top 4.73 percent tranche of the cash raised was rated AAA or Aaa. (Although cost efficient, this deal was not capital-relief efficient for the banking book under strict risk-based-capital rules in effect at the time the deal was done. The Bistro trust, J. P. Morgan's credit derivative counterparty, was not an OECD bank. It held OECD securities—U.S. Treasuries—but only to the extent of 7.5 percent of the notional amount of the swap.)

The yield that the market demands on an FRN is related to the rating on the security and the strength of the sponsor. The rating of many of these deals is capped by the rating of the sponsor, for any of several reasons:

1. The rating is generally capped if the risks are transferred by way of loan participations. The holder of a participation interest could be deemed an unsecured creditor of the bank if the bank became insolvent. NationsBank used participations, but filed liens to get the security interest perfected so its CLO rating would not be held down by its own rating. The Tokyo-Mitsubishi deal was not capped because the Bank sold loan assignments (requiring the consent of the borrower) rather than participations.

2. Glacier is capped by SBC's rating because the assets of the trust are all SBC notes.

3. Many deals depend upon rate maintenance agreements with the sponsor, which can cap the rating. The J. P. Morgan transaction is not capped because the subordinate tranche absorbed not only the credit risk to the pool of names, but also the risk that J. P. Morgan might default on its obligation to make fixed payments representing the reserve and the credit spread on the derivative.

FUNDING

Not having the rating capped was particularly important to Tokyo-Mitsubishi. For them, the ability to raise funds at an attractive price was probably just as important as reducing regulatory capital. In the winter/spring of 1998, a number of CLO's were contemplated by institutions having problems funding at a reasonable cost—and not just Japanese ones. Some of these banks even planned to use below-investment-grade collateral. Below-investment-grade collateral is not very suitable for reducing regulatory capital. The unrated piece is large and difficult to sell, and if it cannot be sold, capital relief is unlikely.

OTHER MOTIVATIONS AND CONSIDERATIONS

Motivations that the banks have for creating CLOs—beyond regulatory capital relief—are funding, portfolio management, and providing business to their own fledgling underwriting departments. There are also several subplots going on at the same time. Banks want to maximize their flexibility, which means they want to be able to (1) handle a breadth of assets (e.g., revolvers, LCs, and counterparty risk, as well as loans); (2) add names over time, and ideally, take names out as well; and (3) use their own rating system for categorizing the risks rather than having to have an agency rating for every one. Disclosure is a big issue. Banks prefer not to reveal the names of the companies whose risks they have sold. But not disclosing the names can affect the cost of the transaction and compromise the goal of portfolio management. It's a balance, and each bank designs its CLO in the way that best meets its goals.

PROPRIETARY RISK-RATING SYSTEMS

Another breakthrough in the NatWest deal was the fact that the rating agencies accepted NatWest's own risk-rating system. This was the first time ever that the agencies had been willing to trust any but their own ratings. Swiss Bank Corp. (SBC) and NationsBank then followed suit in getting their own systems vetted. When these CLO sponsors add new loans to their pools, they won't have to go to the trouble and expense of getting agency ratings. Clearly, however, that is not the choice of everyone. Some banks may not have systems with adequate recorded experience to satisfy the agencies, but there are other reasons to use third-party ratings. Tokyo-Mitsubishi wanted to avoid the pricing stigma that Japanese banks were suffering in the winter of 1997–1998. They therefore needed to distance the pool as much as possible from themselves. Third-party ratings—and full disclosure of the names—do that. J. P. Morgan may have eschewed internal ratings and provided full disclosure for reasons of pure portfolio management.

COUNTRIES

The pool of risks in a CLO can comprise names from any country, but until the Tokyo-Mitsubishi transaction, the expectation was that the companies would be domiciled mostly in the United States and Europe. The Bank of Tokyo–Mitsubishi showed that a CLO could be done even with Japanese companies in the winter of 1997–1998. This was Tokyo-Mitsubishi's second CLO. The first one did not include loans to Japanese businesses. In December 1997, Citibank sponsored a $600 million (Australian dollars) CLO for Australian companies.

THE FUTURE

CLOs will continue to evidence a variety of forms that depend on each sponsor's priorities. As a further development, we may see a fund that will buy risks from multiple sponsors and be run by an independent risk manager—something more akin to an arbitrage fund. Why? Because this is what it may take to allow the sponsors to exercise true portfolio management. Until they can unload risks without entangling the reputation of the institution, they have not really optimized economic capital.

Credit derivatives are a promising medium for transferring risk in a multiseller CLO. There need be no disclosure to the borrower. The transferor, moreover, would have the flexibility to offset any type of bank exposure. The compromise is that these transactions would probably not provide funding. Were the sponsors to receive funds, their obligations to repay would represent concentrations of risk. The whole fund would trade like the weakest sponsor in the pool; or at worst, investors would have no interest in the securities, due to having to review multiple concentrations of risk.

Credit derivative trades for portfolio management are going on right now over the counter. They are happening on a single name basis, in baskets of four to six names, and in large pools. Banks using the over-the-counter market to hedge their credit risks would probably find an AAA-rated fund with no other purpose than to price and trade credit risks an attractive alternative. It could be an exchange, or a derivatives products company, or an investor fund. We have no crystal ball, but we can see the need for the ability of banks and other financial intermediaries to exercise true portfolio management, with flexibility and without disclosure.

THE VIRTUES OF DIVERSIFICATION

These transactions demonstrate the evolution of a new kind of funding operation—one that can have a powerful and very salutary impact on the credit markets. Conduits like R.O.S.E. Funding and Northstar can finance themselves efficiently. At the same time, they can enlarge the circle of acceptable credits. Because this kind of entity can operate in a senior-subordinated structure and can diversify, its sponsor is able to lend to borrowers who might not have qualified for credit in the past.

Up to now, virtually all types of financial intermediation have been designed by people who were asset focused—people who wanted to raise money for their businesses. Diversifying agents, by contrast, are liability focused. They want, above all, to obtain low-cost capital, and they set out to design a structure that will enable them to do so. Having raised this money—actually or hypothetically—they then proceed to obtain assets that will create a diversified portfolio. This pool of assets can then be sliced and diced in various ways to match the requirements of a variety of investor types who have provided the funds.

The pooling of assets has a profound impact on the entire lending process. Under the traditional bank lending system, default was a low probability–high severity type of risk. A lender was unlikely to lose money, but when it lost, it lost a lot. On these terms, a rational lender would naturally avoid putting principal at serious risk when the best it could hope for was a rather modest rent on its money. But under the new system, every loan is ultimately held by a considerable number of investors, so default becomes a low-severity type of risk. Stated differently, when a loan pool is large, the default of a single large loan has a smaller impact on the volatility of returns from the entire pool. Knowing that Bulgaria's sovereign debt has a very low rating, an alert investor would hesitate to purchase $100 million in Bulgarian bonds. But the same investor might gladly invest $100 million in a CBO transaction that included $2 million of Bulgarian bonds as part of a diversified portfolio. The portfolio strategies described in Chapters 17–19 can help investors take advantage of the protection afforded by diversification, just as they can help a bank know which assets it should shed.

The new system includes a concentrated group of loan originators and a diversified group of lenders or investors. Diversifying agents are consolidators who serve as intermediaries between these two groups. Their role is to buy loans in bulk and then redistribute them. They connect the originators to the investors, and in the process they wash the severity out of the system. They may be special-purpose corporations or mutual funds or funding companies or bond insurance companies or investment management companies, but they all use the same fundamental techniques. This is illustrated in Figure 24.5.

The concept of a *connector* is clearly illustrated by Oasis, a special purpose vehicle created by Citibank. The bank faced a dilemma: it had a high capital ratio and was unable to earn a suffcient return on equity from investment-grade assets to justify tying up the required capital. However, plenty of liquidity was available from investors who wanted exposure to high-quality assets but without any of the attendant interest rate risk. Oasis connects the investor to the borrower without taking the traditional path of insured deposits. Instead, Oasis receives funds from investors and places them in a senior-subordinated structure that provides the holders of the se-

Figure 24.5   The Role of Consolidators

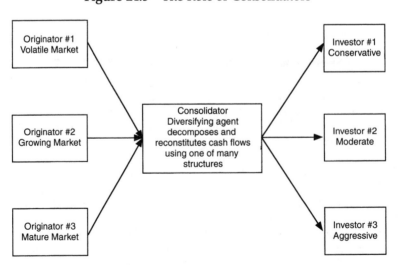

nior notes (the A-piece) with an attractive, above-average yield. Holders of the subordinated notes (B-piece) take credit risk and are rewarded for it. Oasis looks and acts like a bank, but it is not a bank—at least for now. The structure under which it operates successfully replaces the deposit insurance guarantee and the access to the discount window that are characteristic of a bank. Here is how Richard Levinson, group treasurer at Citibank and the person who runs Oasis, explains it:

> Our objective was to create an attractive alternative to bank deposits for substantial clients whose balances exceeded credit insurance limits. We wanted to provide the clients all the benefits of a bank deposit but with higher rates than either a deposit or money market fund. This required a hybrid between a bank and a fiduciary structure.
>
> Oasis senior notes mimic deposits by being issued at any time, in any amount, for any maturity the client desires and by using standard deposit insurance conventions. To protect the clients' investment, assets are professionally managed and diversified according to strict rules across a spectrum of investment grade securities. The assets are then enhanced with a 100% timely principal and interest guarantee provided by CapMAC. The CapMAC guarantee has a small deductible which is absorbed by long term subordinated debt issued to institutional investors. To protect both senior and subordinated noteholders, various reserves and structural protections were built into the Oasis indenture.
>
> In this structure, the CapMAC guarantee and the subordinated debt replace bank capital, the senior notes replace deposits and both carry better yields than bank or money fund obligations. Asset management resembles an investment fund more than a bank, with much stricter rules on diversification and asset quality. We can afford this luxury because we are not driven by commercial bank capital requirements or return objectives.

Because the liability base is positioned as a bank deposit alternative, interest rate and liquidity management borrow heavily from modern bank asset-liability management techniques. Levinson describes Oasis's approach to noncredit risk management as follows:

> Since both assets and liabilities are globally diversified, we encounter currency, interest rate and maturity mismatches that must be carefully managed.
>
> To manage both the interest rate and currency risk, we hedge all assets and liabilities to U.S. dollar floating rates. This reduces these risks to only that normally encountered in a commercial bank's short term gapping book and we treat the residual risk accordingly. We adopted Citibank's "Earnings at Risk" interest rate risk management system which sets limits on interest rate mismatches based on the cost of an instantaneous adverse 3 standard deviation change in rates.
>
> We manage liquidity in three ways. First, and by far most important, we diversify the customer base and we continuously monitor the number of noteholders, their balances and any concentrations of note maturities. Second, a large portion of the asset portfolio is highly liquid. We hold at least 5 percent of assets in cash equivalents and at least another 25 percent in high grade, publicly traded bonds with a maximum investment of $50 MM per issuer. At that level, we don't risk moving the market if we sell the bonds to raise liquidity.

Together the cash and bonds provide at least 30 percent liquid assets, far more than most banks maintain. Finally, we maintain a commercial paper program with syndicated liquidity backstops and can access either the CP market or the backstop in the event of a funding crisis.

Oasis also manages all its risk through the involvement of third parties. The Oasis board includes active, independent accounting, and legal and finance professionals. A risk committee, which consists of program managers and independent directors, oversees the day-to-day management of the company. The program is also subject to ongoing review by CapMAC, the rating agencies, and the liquidity backstop syndicate. Although these parties are primarily protecting their own interests, their cumulative involvement also protects the senior noteholders at least as well as traditional bank regulatory oversight.

By acting as an agent of diversification to Citibank, Oasis has relieved Citibank of having to keep these assets on its own balance sheet and yet provides an attractive return on a deposit-like product to investors.

THE IMPACT OF DIVERSIFYING AGENTS

The emergence of diversifying agents reflects the confluence of a number of forces: maturing of the banking business and the need on the part of banks to sell assets; the shift of investible assets from the hands of banks to the hands of investment managers; the growing comfort of the rating agencies with structured finance; and the revolution that has occurred in information technology. Together, these factors have prompted explosive growth in this new type of credit system.

When different elements of a process are bundled together—as they are in the case of traditional bank lending—costs often rise while quality declines. The new system represents an unbundling and reassembly of the elements of the lending process. The outcome is likely to be lower cost and better quality. That is why many different participants stand to benefit from the new market structure. Banks gain an opportunity to broaden and deepen their origination activities, knowing that they can subsequently sell the loans they have originated. Of course, their pricing of credit risk is now subject to the discipline of the marketplace, because consolidators will not purchase a loan that has not been priced properly. At the same time, investors gain access to attractive securities that meet their risk-return requirements.

For some borrowers, the new system will reduce the cost of funds. By shopping the marketplace, good credits should be able to obtain a better deal for themselves. Poor credits, by contrast, will have to pay more. A company whose loans currently trade at 60 cents on the dollar will not be able to obtain a new loan at 100 cents on the dollar. Consolidators will not pay full price for an asset that they can buy at a substantial discount, and loan originators will be aware of this fact.

For some companies, the new system will require that liquidity be managed with greater care. Companies that become overly dependent on this system may discover that their liquidity has disappeared just when they need it the most. Some borrowers will have to reduce their operating leverage. Many companies will need to build liquidity from a bank or other source into their capital structure so that they can count on being able to finance themselves even under adverse market conditions. Rating agencies are focusing on this issue in their evaluation of specialty finance companies. The latter are dependent on securitization to finance their core business. First USA, MBNA, and other specialty finance companies are now required to demonstrate that they have liquidity facilities in place. If for some reason they are unable to securitize assets, they must be able to obtain funding elsewhere.

Because banks will continue to keep some loans on their books, the new system will not wholly supplant the old. Securitization will probably be most common at the small and large ends of the market: in the consumer and large corporate sectors. A loan of $1 million to a small-cap company will still, in all likelihood, be held by the bank that made it—although this too might change if the lenders can succeed in reengineering the lending process for these credits. Liquidity lines are another vital area of bank activity that may not lend itself to securitization. In most large books of corporate loans, most of the credit risk is contingent; the lines are committed but undrawn. These lines are thinly priced. Thus far, no method has been devised that would enable the capital markets to replace banks as providers of liquidity lines. Banks are willing to extend credit lines largely because they have access to the Federal Reserve's discount window. If other parties are going to provide these lines, a substitute for this access will need to be devised. Some form of financial engineering may solve this problem.

Bank regulators will be concerned about the new lending arrangements, which bring market forces more directly to bear in the granting of credit. Markets are notoriously fickle, and they have been known to evaporate quickly. Regulators are responsible for, among other things, minimizing any disruptions in liquidity. A credit crunch may be no greater danger under the new scheme of things than it was under the old, but it is, nonetheless, a concern.

In the hands of people with the wrong motivations, the new techniques could certainly introduce new dangers to the credit market. When banks lend their own money, they have a powerful interest in making the right decisions. Insofar as a specialty finance company is actually lending other people's money, there is a risk that its managers' economic interests will diverge from those of the other participants. The new system also creates ways that an organization can take on credit risk without ever meeting anyone face to face.

In the new scheme, sound judgment and clear thinking will become even more important than they were in the past. The economic interests of those who manage the process will have to be carefully aligned with those of the other participants. Computers can perform elaborate analytic operations, but only human beings can establish and maintain prudent business practices. As the next chapter explores, the new system calls for renewed attention to something as old as lending itself: credit culture.

REFERENCES

AiC Conference, Inc. 1998. *Asset-Backed Alert.* 12 January.

CapMAC. 1998. *CapMAC ABS MarketWatch.* New York: CapMAC. January.

Fitch Investors Service. 1996. *R.O.S.E. Funding Limited: New Issue, October.* Fitch Research special report. New York: Fitch Investors Service.

———. 1997. *CBO/CLO Rating Criteria.* Fitch Structured Finance special report. New York: Fitch Investors Service.

Fridson, M. S. 1997. *A Guide to Collateralized Bond Obligations.* New York: Merrill Lynch & Co.

Slicing up Bank Loans. 1997. *Investment Dealers' Digest,* 22 December.

Chapter **25**

The Rediscovery of Culture as a Primary Management Tool

There's no art to find the mind's construction in the face.

—William Shakespeare

Managing credit risk was once considered to be the realm of the artist. With time and experience, a banker could master the art of lending and rise to positions of greater and greater authority. A senior lending officer was an expert who—whatever analytical aids might be applied along the way—ultimately made an individual decision about a particular borrower at a particular moment in time.

Today, as we have seen, the number of analytic techniques available for managing credit risk has expanded exponentially. The mathematical symbols that appear in this book might seem to suggest that managing credit risk has become a science. But it is not a science—at least, not yet. The management of credit risk lies somewhere between art and science, in the realm we commonly call engineering.

Today's practitioners clearly have a greater array of systematic techniques from which to choose. They are like drivers who have acquired a late-model car with far greater horsepower than their old one had. Because the new techniques make it possible to distribute risk authority more broadly within the firm, many more individuals are now able to take to the road in their own cars. Thanks to modern information technology, all of these drivers are getting a flood—perhaps an avalanche—of data about the road ahead. Do these sound like the conditions for better highway safety? Not necessarily.

What the practitioners of credit risk management do not have is a black box that will reliably spit out the right answer to each and every question fed into it. Placing unmerited faith in any of the existing systems could be very hazardous to one's financial health. Credit derivatives, for example, enable investors to sign up for credit risk arising in industries and places about which they know virtually nothing—without ever having agreed to make a loan. The danger is that some practitioners will be tempted to conclude—prematurely—that they can now operate with credit risk much greater than anything they would have accepted in the past.

Financial professionals must now add model risk to the other risks—interest rate risk, market risk, credit risk—impacting their business. Model risk arises from the fact that the adoption of new models often leads to fundamental changes in the markets they are designed to represent. "When markets are new, the problem is that advanced practitioners tend to undermine their own models," says Ross Miller, president of Miller Risk Advisors. He explains the phenomenon in these terms:

> In the credit risk world, the models are still too new for us to have any real horror stories. But consider prepayment models in the mortgage market. In the early days of mortgage securitization, consumers were not very savvy about refinancing, and this inefficiency initially drove the market. Mortgage modeling was based on a fixed history regarding prepayments. In fact, though, as the mortgage market became more developed, it caused a shift in the way that prepayments occurred. Parties with better information systems called on consumers to offer them refinancing deals, and the refinancing industry sprang up. As a result, all the existing prepayment models blew up. And derivatives based on mortgages behaved in unintended ways.
>
> By analogy, behaviors in the credit risk world that make sense based on past patterns may no longer make sense in an environment that includes CLOs and CBOs. Opening up this market can, by itself, change the profile of risks you get, so that in a down market, behavior will no longer mimic the old loss rates.
>
> At the highest level, what's going on is that analytics are developed to create new financial institutions and strategies to exploit the inefficiencies in a market. But in the process of financial engineering, you change the environment so that it no longer matches the one you modeled. The existence of complex mortgage-backed derivatives puts you in a world that no longer resembles the pre-derivative world.
>
> Even if we can't rigorously quantify model risk, we know what it looks like in qualitative terms—it is large early in the history of a new market. As more experience develops, it drops. But if things blow up, then spreads widen so much that you can't do business in that market for a while. Over time, a new equilibrium may be reached, as it was in the mortgage market.

Bankruptcy patterns can be a significant element in model risk. Historically, bankruptcies have generally tracked the overall state of the economy— rising when times are hard. In 1996–1997, however, consumer bankruptcies rose even though the overall economy was buoyant. This kind of performance is unprecedented. It results from the facts that more credit has been extended to consumers and that attitudes toward bankruptcy are changing. In some parts of the country, with encouragement from the legal profession, personal bankruptcies are spreading like a contagious disease. Apparently, hundreds of thousands of people now believe that it is all right not to pay their debts. One can easily imagine something similar happening in the corporate world as well. Should this occur, credit risk models based on historical data would mislead practitioners in very dangerous ways.

In a world of shiny but imperfect models, senior leaders in financial services firms must renew their attention to traditional management tools: checks, balances, and controls, and, behind them, a strong risk culture. Recent events in the industry from outside the credit risk arena should be sounding an alarm in executive offices. Among the players in the derivatives markets, for example, most large money-center banks and investment banks have done very well. They have used derivatives to manage their own business, and they have offered market risk services to customers. Through careful positioning, they have found ways to make money over the long term, despite considerable short-term volatility.

There have, however, been some spectacular failures, such as that of Barings. In this instance, a venerable merchant bank became insolvent because of the trading activities of a single individual in Singapore, Nicholas Leeson, regarded by Barings as a rogue trader. It is clear, however, that there was more at work here than an isolated individual who was making unauthorized trades. If Barings' senior managers had been aware that the ranch was being bet day in and day out, they would surely have put a stop to Leeson's activities very early on. Evidently, the firm lacked proper techniques and systems to monitor, manage, and control risk of this magnitude. But the real issue may actually be more subtle. It would appear that Barings' risk-management culture was not appropriate to the activities the firm was engaged in.

Reports on Nicholas Leeson's activities indicate that he had made significant amounts of money in the years prior to Barings' failure. There is no evidence that anybody ever tried to figure out how he was trying to make money from a so-called riskless activity. Leeson appeared to be in what people in the business have dubbed the "trader's option." *Because I am playing with your cards, if I win, we win. But if I lose, you lose.* In the Barings system, Leeson shared in the firm's profits but did not have to pay for any of its losses. As long as he was winning, he had every reason to be public about it. If, on the other hand, he began to lose, he had every reason to double up or do whatever else he could to get Barings' money back. Once he had passed beyond the bounds of reason in the size of his bets, he was better off keeping his activities covered up and hoping that the market would turn in due course.

These are, of course, the very reasons why a firm needs a good reporting system and proper checks and balances. Barings clearly failed to impose adequate controls. Equally important, however, is the fact that when things were going right, his management in London was apparently quite happy to take the profits and ask no questions. It appears that Barings was always something of a swashbuckling place—the kind of organization that did not ask too many questions as long as someone seemed to be making money. Over the long haul, a culture of this type will condemn any organization. In an organization with strong risk culture, control mechanisms are both backward and forward looking. Backward-looking systems may be as simple as timely tracking of cash flows to the trading records. Forward-looking systems would seek out potential risks, not merely in terms of position risk, but also all systemwide risks.

There are parallels to be drawn to the debacle at Sumitomo Metals, where the world's leading copper trader lost billions of dollars in what was subsequently described as a massive cover-up of trading losses. Newspaper reports indicated that this trader, Yasuo Hamanaka, dominated the copper markets for several years. Many observers indicated that they had wondered how he could possibly be making money from some of the positions he was taking, but they quickly concluded that nobody would trade on such a scale without having some angle that made sense. Where were the controls at Sumitomo? Did management in Tokyo know of the positions being taken? Did anybody ask any questions? Apparently not.

This was clearly a failure of both culture and controls. In a business where you can lose billions of dollars, you do not have to be a rocket scientist to realize that you must have some controls to assure that the risks are managed properly. There is no evidence that there were any controls whatsoever. An even more important question is this: What sort of risk management culture operated at Sumitomo Metals? What kind of culture allows a single person the power and authority to trade on that scale?

Whereas risks are embedded in every type of business, they are truly a daily aspect of life at a financial services firm. That is why it is critically important for every financial service organization to create a strong system of checks, balances, and controls, and to support it with a culture that defines the appropriate amount of risk to take. Every employee must know what is right and wrong—what will be rewarded and punished. Good cultures tolerate little ambiguity in these areas.

As Shakespeare noted, *"There's no art to find the mind's construction in the face."* A senior manager cannot tell at a glance what any given employee might be doing. Every organization must establish a culture that reflects the realities of human nature. Our corporate corridors are populated neither by robots nor by angels, but by human beings who sport widely varying personalities—some more honest than others. Even people who are fundamentally honest do not like to admit when they have been wrong. We all have a tendency to paper-over our flaws. In a world of large risks, significant decisions may be quickly proved wrong.

The best time to admit a trading error is surely the moment you discover you have made it. When something you have bought goes down in price, you can, if you admit it, go on to make a clear-headed decision about what you will do next. If you do not admit it, then you may be tempted to try more desperate maneuvers to undo your error. A company's risk culture can create a powerful incentive for employees to admit their mistakes.

J. P. Morgan has tended to select people they feel will be a good fit for their corporate culture. At Bank One, employees come to understand that the chairman does not like surprises. If you neglect to tell Mr. McCoy about a problem and you manage to fix it on your own, you will still be in deep trouble when he finds out. In that kind of setting, covering up is not an option. If Barings had had a similar culture, Nicholas Leeson would probably have seen little advantage in trying to cover his tracks.

Traditionally, banks have operated with an enormous number of rules. In most U.S. banks, for example, managers were expected to take two weeks of consecutive leave every year so that someone else could come in and check their books. Banks assumed that human nature needs a system of checks and balances. This is hardly surprising in a business where the inventory is cash. But banks do, by and large, lack one of the key control mechanisms available to institutions dealing with market risk: marking to market. All securities traders must mark their portfolios to market on a daily basis, and they may not exceed the limits set on how much they may have outstanding at any time. In this setting, a trader cannot deny reality. Unfortunately, credit risk is generally not marked to market at this time. Banks typically make loans and then look at them infrequently, if at all. A loan may be worth a lot less today than it was when it was made, but nobody knows this fact because nobody cares about it. As Bank of Montreal's Brian Ranson pointed out in Chapter 2, the whole world changes once a bank begins to mark its loans to market. If the loan is illiquid, marking it to market will signal the need for some action such as credit protection using derivatives and changing the price on the next transaction to that customer. If the loan is liquid, marking to market will be yet another step toward total return management.

In the current period of transition to new market structures and new techniques for managing credit risk, a firm's risk culture is more important than ever. Companies must carefully consider what kinds of behavior they want to foster and what kind of compensation system they need to establish. If they reward employees for success no matter how that success was achieved, then they are instructing their employees to try to win at any price. If their employees are making decisions that have long-term consequences, then they would be much wiser to peg their compensation to long-term results. To whatever degree they can, firms should also try to mark their portfolios to market on a frequent basis—not for accounting purposes but for reasons of risk management. There is no better way for senior management to convey the message: *We will reward good performance but make sure you play by the rules. We are watching.* These are the building blocks of a strong risk culture.

In our experience, the key to a strong risk culture is to have the CEO make his or her wishes known to every employee. Under these conditions, virtually all employees will fall into line and do what is expected of them. In the absence of a clear message from the top, however, employees will do whatever they themselves think is right. Many will make good choices, but some will not. Risk culture is people *and* systems. By making a real commitment to control mechanisms such as a credit risk rating system, a CEO can create a structure for a consistent credit language that reinforces the credit culture.

Many of the risks we face today will become easier to manage 5 or 10 years hence, when the present shakedown cruise has ended. Today, we still must use proxies for many of the values we want to measure. But once a large, liquid market for credit has been established, it will become possible to mark loans to market on a direct basis. As record keeping improves, professionals will be able to tap far more reliable data about what happened in the past. Better information will lead to better decision making. But this new-found freedom to trade credit risk will probably lead to greater market volatility: In a world full of portfolio managers chanting the *mantra* of total return, the buy or sell actions started by a few could well turn into stampede.

Meanwhile, during the transition to that brave new world, professionals need to apply a good measure of common sense. Fortunately, most practitioners are a skeptical lot when it comes to new techniques. No one we have met thus far is willing to buy or sell a loan strictly on the basis of a KMV or a Zeta score. Even the professionals who are very enthusiastic about these models will say little more than, "It's an important source of information." In the case of consumer lending, where decisions are small and granular, the consequences of model risk may not be overwhelming because there is time to adjust the model. In the case of corporate lending, where $100 million may be at stake, model risk may have a very different profile. Practitioners are well advised to take the existing models with several grains of salt, and to look to several models at once, rather than just one, in reaching their decisions.

Even when better tools become available in the future, someone within each firm will still have to take responsibility for deciding what its risk tolerance should be. The desired results may become easier to achieve—and with fewer people—but a strong risk culture will still remain a critical prerequisite for success.

Sources of Information for Credit Analysts

This appendix summarizes and reviews a large number of information sources related to the analysis of credit risk of individual corporate entities.[1] The analyst engaged in this task has an ever-increasing number of sources available due to the communication industry's explosion. Whereas the electronic media has become the major source of credit information, the print media's importance has not diminished. Indeed, if anything, there are many new sources as well as the venerable ones. Many of the sources listed here may be accessed (or, more accurately, purchased) through the Internet. Almost all major vendors of data have established Web sites and may be contacted very easily. Search engines such as YAHOO also make it possible to obtain data somewhat more readily than in the past. As most people would agree, using the Internet may be either enormously productive or quite useless, depending partly upon the user's agility on the system. *AAII Journal,* in *The Individual Investor's Guide to Investment Web Sites,* contains a list of sites that provide substantial investing information or interactions. These may be of interest also to financial institutions.

We have organized our listings in several ways. First, we proceed from the general macroeconomic and financial sources to industry and sector trend analysis. These aggregated sources are a useful jumping-off point for the analyst, who should try to understand the economic and financial environments that the individual firm functions within. Company-specific sources, while the main focus of our attention, need to be utilized and compared to many benchmarks, including aggregated sector data, market- and product-line-comparable data, and historic time-series data. Another critical benchmark of companies is the aggregated statistics of credit risk categories of bond ratings. The rating agency designations play an important role in both individual credit and portfolio analysis. A second organizing method for credit source discussion is the aforementioned electronic versus print media dichotomy.

The Internet has opened the world of financial information and provides financial statements to the casual as well as the professional observer. In

---

[1]The authors would like to thank Vellore M. Kishore for his assistance on this appendix.

addition, on-line services complement the stored data for a variety of credit-related sources. Most of these on-line services involve four types of databases: (1) directories, (2) indexes, (3) full-text databases, and (4) statistical databases. Some sources are hybrids of more than one of these distinctions. Although much of what is available is oriented toward stock market investors, analysis of credit risk is also relevant in most cases.

Extremely relevant sources of credit risk data are the several reports that document the default risk and loss severity of aggregated credit risk classes, such as credit quality ratings. These default and credit risk migration studies and their sources are noted here but are reviewed in depth in two chapters of this book. Of note is the recent release of a CD-ROM product from Standard & Poor's called CreditPro which makes available default and rating history data for 6,000+ obligors, each identified by one of Standard & Poor's 12 industry groupings.

GENERAL ECONOMIC AND FINANCIAL ANALYSIS

A number of factors such as capacity utilization, monetary and fiscal policies, level of disposable personal income, inflation, interest rates, and GDP growth influence the economy and labor cost. In general, the economy undergoes periods of expansion and contraction, although the length of the periods varies. This business cycle pattern is also a fundamental determinant of the performance of the economy, which in turn affects the performance of the industry and company. Hence, study of the economy is often the starting point in analyzing the expected performance of companies. The following sources provide information on the economy.

Government Publications on Macroeconomic Data

The primary source of macroeconomic information is published by the U.S. government. The following are the most important sources:

Administrative Office of the U.S. Bankruptcy Courts (Washington, D.C.) This agency reports monthly and annual data on corporate and personal bankruptcies throughout the U.S. District Court system. The data are in aggregate form and are sorted by chapter, type, and so on. The data can be used for statistical purposes. This publication does not provide information on individual companies.

Bureau of Labor Statistics (BLS) (Washington, D.C.)   BLS provides information on employment, unemployment, consumer expenditures, prices, productivity, and economic growth. Its most important publication is *Employment and Earnings,* which is published monthly. It covers employment development and provides data on national, regional, and area unemployment, hours worked, and earnings. Following are its other publications:

- *Consumer Expenditure Survey*
- *Consumer Price Index*
- *CPI Detailed Report*
- *Producer Price Indexes*
- *Compensation and Working Conditions*

Economic Indicators **(Washington, D.C.)**   This is a monthly publication prepared by the Council of Economic Advisors and contains monthly and annual data on prices, money and credit, output, income, spending, employment, and production.

Economic Report of the President **(Washington, D.C.)**   In January of each year, the president of the United States presents an economic report on the United States to the Congress. This report discusses the economy in the past year and is published in the *Annual Report of the Council of Economic Advisors.* This report has a wealth of historical information on income, employment, production, inflation, and so forth.

Federal Reserve Banks   There are 12 Federal Reserve banks in the Federal Reserve system. They represent 12 geographical areas in the United States, as shown here:

1. Federal Reserve Bank of Boston
2. Federal Reserve Bank of New York
3. Federal Reserve Bank of Philadelphia
4. Federal Reserve Bank of Cleveland
5. Federal Reserve Bank of Richmond
6. Federal Reserve Bank of Atlanta
7. Federal Reserve Bank of St. Louis
8. Federal Reserve Bank of Minneapolis
9. Federal Reserve Bank of Kansas City
10. Federal Reserve Bank of Dallas
11. Federal Reserve Bank of San Francisco

These banks publish monthly reviews or letters that provide economic data on their region, or commentary on various economic issues, and at times on accounting issues also. The Federal Reserve Bank of St. Louis publishes statistics on various economic factors on a weekly and monthly basis. Statistical data on interest rates and yields of short-term and long-term securities in particular are important to the credit analyst because they serve as benchmarks for the borrowing costs of companies. These banks also maintain Web sites on the internet.

Federal Reserve Bulletin **(Washington, D.C.)**   The *Federal Reserve Bulletin* is published by the Board of Governors of the Federal Reserve System, Washington, D.C. This monthly publication is the primary source for most of the data on the U.S. banking system and for monetary data. It also provides historical data on financial markets, industrial production, assets and liabilities of corporations, and GNP, among other items.

Quarterly Financial Report **(Washington, D.C.)**   This quarterly report provides information on the financial condition of U.S. corporations. It is published by the Federal Trade Commission (FTC). FTC estimates income, expenses, and balance-sheet and related financial statements for all manufacturing and mining corporations. The statistics are classified by industry and size.

Statistical Abstract of the United States **(Washington, D.C.)** This publication, also available on a CD-ROM, is prepared by the Economics and Statistical Administration of the Bureau of the Census and provides statistical data covering all subjects. It provides information on population, employment, earnings, cost of living, purchasing power, and a host of other subjects.

Survey of Current Business **(Washington, D.C.)** This monthly periodical is published by the Bureau of Economic Analysis (BEA) of the U.S. Department of Commerce. It provides raw data on monthly updates on a broad spectrum of economic information such as GNP, manufacturers' shipments, business inventories, the labor market, fixed investment, and gross state product. This periodical provides voluminous data on various industries that are useful to the analyst in studying a particular industry and is perhaps the most important economic publication by the U.S. Government. In addition, BEA publishes *Weekly Business Statistics,* a weekly update. This publication has provided economic statistics for close to 2,000 economic data series on a monthly basis for the past four years, and annual statistics for the last 25 years. The data include general business indicators, production, sales, inventory, and other sources. Additionally, it provides quarterly and annual data on new plant and equipment expenditures.

Nongovernment Macroeconomic Publications

DRI/McGraw-Hill Reports (Boston, Massachusetts) One of the leading sources on the economy and industry information, the DRI/McGraw-Hill reports provide a variety of economic studies and forecast, and regional forecasts. Among others, these include the following:

- *DRI Business Fixed Investment Forecast*
- *DRI Coal Forecast*
- *DRI Commodities*
- *DRI Cost Information Services Forecast*
- *DRI Financial and Credit Statistics*
- *DRI Financial Market Indexes*
- *DRI Housing Forecast*
- *DRI Metropolitan Area Forecast*
- *DRI Plant and Equipment Expenditures Forecast*
- *DRI Steel Forecast*
- *DRI Long-Term Energy Forecast*
- *Platt's Chemical Prices*
- *Platt's Energy Prices*

These publications contain historical and forecast series data in various categories. To illustrate, *DRI Business Fixed Investment Forecast* provides nearly 200 historical and forecast time series on equipment and construction. It covers 23 categories of equipment and 11 categories of nonresidential construction. The data include spending, price deflators, costs of capital, and so on.

Ibbotson Associates (Chicago, Illinois) This service publishes an annual yearbook, *Stocks, Bonds, Bills, and Inflation,* which contains copious amounts of data on returns on stocks, bonds, bills, and inflation since 1926. In addition, the service provides U.S. investment benchmarks on a variety of financial instruments.

Standard & Poor's Statistical Service **(New York, New York)** This publication provides an exhaustive array of statistical data on a monthly and annual basis covering the economy, industries, production, the labor market, and the stock market.

INDUSTRY ANALYSIS

After studying economic and financial conditions, the analyst can examine the relevant industry. The following sources provide information on industries.

Almanac of Business and Industrial Financial Ratios **(Prentice Hall, Englewood Cliffs, New Jersey)** This annual study provides financial data on several industries. It provides 22 financial indicators, and companies are segmented by asset size. The data is derived from tax returns of 4 million companies filed with the Internal Revenue Service.

Annual Survey of Manufacturers This study prepared by the WEFA Group in Eddystone, Pennsylvania, uses government data to provide over 5,000 time series of industry data. The data, based on standard industrial classification (SIC) code, presents raw material cost, value added by manufacturers, value of shipments, employment, payroll, and capital expenditures.

This database is available on a diskette or magnetic tape. The data is available from 1963 and is updated annually.

Business and Industry This database is provided by Responsive Database Services, Inc. and is available on-line from DIALOG. It covers about 500,000 articles on companies and industries from various periodicals since 1994.

Credit Reference Directory of 10 Million U.S. Businesses Published by American Business Information, Inc., this publication provides company ratings of 10 million businesses based on a multivariate analysis. The variables include sales, historical performance, industry stability, and SEC data. It is available in print form and on-line from the publisher.

Industry Magazines Industry magazines provide continuous coverage of particular industries. These magazines provide developments in the industry, performance of companies, products coming to the market, government regulations, and so forth. These are some of the industry magazines:

- *Automotive News*
- *Beverage World*
- *Chemical Week*
- *Coal Age*
- *Electric Utility Week*
- *Modern Plastics*
- *Pulp and Paper*
- *Supermarket News*

McGraw-Hill is a leading publisher of industry magazines.

Industry Norms and Key Business Ratios **(Dun & Bradstreet, Bethlehem, Pennsylvania)**   Dun and Bradstreet provides operating financial norms and key business ratios for more than 800 lines of businesses and over 19 million public and privately owned U.S. companies. It provides industry balance sheet, short income statement and working capital, solvency, and efficiency and profitability ratios for a total of 14 key business ratios for each industry for up to three years. The industry norms are published separately for the following five major industry segments:

1. Agriculture, mining, construction/transportation/communication/ utilities
2. Manufacturing
3. Wholesaling
4. Retailing
5. Finance/real estate/services

The data are provided based on SIC codes as well as geographic region (east, west, north, and south). The publication is available in hard copy, diskette, or magnetic tape. The following publications are available:

- *Industry Norms and Key Business Ratios, Three-Year Edition*
- *Industry Norms and Key Business Ratios, One-Year Edition*
- *Key Business Ratios, One-Year Edition*

D&B can provide industry studies as well as company analysis in comparison with its industry. Its V.I.P. service provides customized service to the client. This service provides an overview of the company's structure and business background, financial analysis compared with its peers, trend and comparative information, and an outlook on the industry. In addition, D&B's Industry Studies provide a full overview of industry specifics and a description of world events that have shaped the industry's past and will impact the future.

Manufacturing, U.S.A.: Industry Analyses, Statistics, and Leading Companies **(Gale Research, Detroit, Michigan)**   Published by Gale Research in two volumes, this set provides data on 458 industries and over 21,000 manufacturing corporations. The presentation includes the following:

- 17-year data, including 4-year projections
- Financial ratios for companies and industries
- More than 21,000 listed companies, ranked by sales volume and other relevant data
- Material consumption for each industry showing volume and raw materials and their cost
- Industry data by state
- Inputs and outputs

Moody's Investors Service (New York, New York)   In addition to providing ratings of bond issues and company information, Moody's performs annual default/mortality studies based on the number of issuers defaulted, and periodic reports on rating migration patterns. This is discussed in a later section.

RMA Annual Statement Studies **(Robert Morris Associates, Bethesda, Maryland)**   This is an annual study of more than 350 industries in terms of 17 financial and operating ratios. The data are presented for total industry as well as stratified by asset size. The studies provide current and historical analysis of an industry's assets, liabilities, and income, classified according to the size of the company assets. The data are provided in six parts as shown:

1. Manufacturing Industries
2. Wholesaling Industries
3. Retailing, Service, Agricultural and Other Industries
4. Contractor Industries
5. Construction Financial Management Association Data (CFMA)— These are excerpts from *Construction Industry Annual Financial Survey*, published by CFMA.
6. The First National Bank of Chicago Consumer and Diversified Finance Company Ratios

The publications provide the balance sheet, condensed income statement, and 16 ratios, which are grouped into three categories: upper quartile, median quartile, and lower quartile. The uquartile ratios are strong ratios in the top 25 percent of the ratios. An explanation of ratios is included.

Bibliography of publications that report composite financial data, including financial and operating ratios for specific industries.

Service Industries, U.S.A.: Industry Analyses, Statistics, and Leading Companies **(Detroit, Michigan)**   Published by Gale Research in two volumes, it provides data on 2,100 services grouped into 151 industries, and over 3,500 service corporations and 700 nonprofit organizations. The presentation includes the following:

- Statistical data by firms, employment, payroll, revenues, and type of ownership by SIC code

- Statistical data by firms, employment, payroll, revenues, and type of ownership by city
- Financial and operating ratios
- List of leading companies
- Occupations employed by the industry

***Standard & Poor's Industry Surveys* (Standard & Poor's Corporation, New York, New York)**   The surveys are published annually and updated every week. The annual study is presented in terms of the following:

- Current environment
- Industry profile
- Industry trends
- How the industry operates
- Key industry ratios and statistics
- How to analyze the industry
- Glossary
- Industry references
- Composite industry data
- Comparative company analysis

In addition, S&P publishes *Industry Surveys Monthly,* which covers performance and valuation statistics for all industries in the S&P 500 Index, industry outlook and charts on various aspects of the industries, and an earnings supplement. The surveys cover 52 industries. The *Trade and Security Statistics* provides historical data on various industries and security prices. In addition to providing ratings of bond issues and company information, Standard & Poor's publishes annual default/mortality and rating migration studies based on the number of issuers defaulted and utilizes a static-pool analysis. This is discussed in a later section.

Trade Associations   These provide a wealth of information on the industry they represent. Some of the trade associations are:

- Steel Institute
- Institute of Life Insurance
- Paper Institute
- American Bankers Association

These associations provide extensive statistical data on the industry and also information that affects the industry. Some of them publish fact books annually, which provide industry shipments, pricing, operating costs, companies in the industry, historical trends, foreign competition, and latest developments. The publication *Encyclopedia of Associations* provides a comprehensive list of associations.

U.S. Department of Commerce (Washington, D.C.)   The department publishes industry studies every five years. Partial updates are published as *Annual Survey of Manufacturers*:

- *Census of Manufactures*
- *Census of Construction Industries*
- *Census of Retail Trade*
- *Census of Service Industries*
- *Census of Wholesale Trade*

Census of Manufacturers provides reports on manufacturing activity every five years. Statistics on the industry are provided by SIC codes and geographic regions ranging from places with a population as low as 2,500 to the entire United States. This is updated annually in the *Annual Survey of Manufacturers*.

Census of Construction Industries provides data on different segments of the industry. The data are reported for the entire United States, states, and selected standard metropolitan statistical areas (SMSAs). The census covers receipts, employment, hours worked, payments for materials and supplies, and other data.

Census of Retail Trade provides data by SIC code. The data include sales volume, operating costs, capacity, operating ratios, and other data of the retail industry. In addition, it provides descriptive data on shopping centers, malls, and neighborhood business districts. The data are extensive and useful to the analyst studying the retail industry. The data are presented by geographic region ranging from places with 2,500 people to the total United States.

Census of Service Industries provides data on service industries arranged by SIC code. The data include the number of service establishments, receipts, payroll, and expenses, and selected operating ratios. The data are presented by geographic region ranging from places with 2,500 people to the total United States.

Census of Wholesale Trade provides data by SIC code. The data include sales volume, operating costs, capacity, operating ratios, and other data of the wholesale trade industry. The data are presented by geographic region ranging from places with 2,500 people to the total United States.

INDEXES

Periodicals indexes make the analyst's job easier. They provide titles of articles published periodically. The analyst can search for appropriate sources and then go to the articles relevant to the analysis.

The Business Periodicals Index **(H. H. Wilson Co., New York, New York)** This index provides publication of articles from approximately 400 periodicals in subjects relating to business, economics, and finance. It is available on-line through WILSONLINE, as well as on CD-ROM and magnetic tape. Although most of the coverage is general, it cites articles on specific industries as well.

F&S (Predicasts) Indexes **(Foster City, California)** These indexes provide approximately 4 million citations on economics, business, industries, companies, and products, covering more than 2,500 publications in all fields related to business. The first part provides indexes on industries and products by SIC code, and the second part provides indexes on companies in alphabetical order. This service is one of the most comprehensive available to the analyst. In addition, *F&S Index Europe* and *F&S Index International* are also available. This service is available on-line through Dialog and DataStar.

F&S Index of Corporate Change, Annual Edition **(Foster City, California)** The annual edition provides information on companies arranged alphabetically as well by SIC code. It contains special tabulations covering name changes, foreign operations, subsidiary name changes, bankruptcies, new companies, joint ventures, reorganizations, and liquidations.

Journal of Economic Literature Index **(Nashville, Tennessee)**   This index contains articles from nearly 300 economics journals. Some have abstracts. This index, a quarterly, is published by the American Economic Association.

New York Times Index **(New York, New York)**   This is an annual index that is updated every two weeks. Subjects are arranged in chronological order. The *New York Times* provides articles on current business topics, and extensive market data.

The Wall Street Journal Index **(New York, New York)**   This index provides reference to articles that have appeared in the *Wall Street Journal*. The index is presented in two parts: corporate news (which lists companies) and general news. In addition, the index references *Barron's* articles also.

DIRECTORIES

America's Corporate Families **(Dun & Bradstreet, Bethlehem, Pennsylvania)**   This directory provides a list of 11,000 U.S. companies. The first volume includes information on the parent, division/branch, and subsidiaries. The following information is published on the parent company:

- Address and telephone number
- State of incorporation
- Principal bank
- Accounting firm
- Description of business and product lines and SIC codes
- Financial data
- Ticker symbol and stock exchange where the stock is traded
- Names and titles of executive officers

Division and bank information is listed alphabetically and includes name and address, SIC code, and executive officers. Data on subsidiaries are listed by hierarchical level within the corporate family, and the following information is provided:

- Address of the subsidiary
- Subsidiary level
- Percentage of ownership
- Sales volume
- Number of employees
- SIC codes and lines of business
- Chief executive

The second volume provides a cross-reference on the ultimate parent, division or branch, and subsidiaries. Another section lists the data in alphabetical order by city, including some of the data just listed. The third section provides businesses by industry classification. The third volume provides information on international subsidiaries, division or branch, and subsidiaries. It covers U.S. multinational corporations and provides information similar to that in the first two volumes.

Directory of Corporate Affiliations **(New Providence, New Jersey)**   This publication by Reed Elsevier lists over 5,000 companies and their divisions, subsidiaries, and branches domestically and internationally. The data includes year founded, lines of business, SIC codes, personnel information, and stock exchange and ticker symbol. The first volume is a master index with company name index, brand-name index, and geographic index. The second volume is another master index with SIC code index and personnel index. The third volume provides listings of public companies. The fourth volume provides listings of private companies. The fifth volume provides listings of international private and public companies.

Dun's Business Rankings **(Dun & Bradstreet, Bethlehem, Pennsylvania)**   This publication ranks public and private companies by sales. The rankings are further broken down by sales in each state and by industry. An additional section ranks private companies by size, and another section ranks public companies by size.

Dun & Bradstreet's Million Dollar Directory **(Dun & Bradstreet, Bethlehem, Pennsylvania)**   This directory is published in five volumes. The first three volumes list nearly 160,000 private and public companies in alphabetical order. The listing for each company includes the following:

- Address and telephone number
- Indication of public ownership
- Company's industry
- SIC code, up to six, with the primary code listed first, and description of lines of business

- Annual sales volume
- Total number of employees
- Names and titles of senior officers
- Names of directors
- Foundation/ownership date
- Other information

The fourth volume presents data from the first three volumes by geography in terms of states and cities. The fifth volume presents data from the first three volumes by industry in terms of primary and secondary SIC codes.

The International Directory of Company Histories **(Detroit, Michigan)** Published by St. James Press, this publication is a 16-volume collection of over 2,650 company histories. The presentation includes historical developments, acquisitions and mergers, and a company perspective.

Market Share Reporter **(Gale Research, Detroit, Michigan)**   This publication provides market share data on over 2,000 products and services. It covers 5,400 companies and 1,650 brands. Data is provided based on SIC code.

Standard & Poor's Register of Corporations, Directors, and Executives **(New York, New York)**   This publication covers over 56,000 companies in three volumes. The first volume, *Corporate Listings,* provides the address, telephone number, officers, directors, lines of business, SIC code, and other relevant data in alphabetical order. The second volume, *Individual Listings,* provides biographies of officers and directors. The third volume is a potpourri of indexes. Companies are arranged by SIC code and geography, and in an index that links parents and subsidiaries.

Thomas's Register of American Manufacturers **(New York, New York)**   This directory is published in 26 volumes. Volumes 1 through 16 list over 150,000 U.S. manufacturers by products and service. Volume 16 contains a product index. Volumes 17 and 18 contain the list of companies arranged alphabetically with the following information:

- Name and address of the company
- Branch offices
- Subsidiaries
- Products
- Brand names of products
- Principal officers

An "American Trademark Index" is included in volume 18. Volumes 19 through 26 provide descriptions of products made by nearly 3,000 of these companies.

Ward's Business Directory of U.S. Private and Public Companies **(Gale Research, Detroit, Michigan)**   This directory is a leading source of information on 120,000 private and public companies. The publication is in seven volumes. The first three volumes present company profiles in alphabetical order. Up to 20 items of information are presented, including the following:

- Financial data
- Number of employees
- Up to four-digit SIC codes, with description of products and services offered
- Executive officers' names and titles
- Year founded
- Ticker symbol and stock exchange where traded
- Name of immediate parent
- Description of products and services
- Import/export status
- Company type: private, public, subsidiary, division, joint venture, or investment fund

The fourth volume is a geographical listing of companies listed in the first three volumes. The companies are organized by state. In addition, it contains a special feature section that presents various tables based on company sales and includes the following information:

- 1,000 largest privately held companies
- 1,000 largest publicly held companies
- 1,000 largest employers
- Analysis of private and public companies by state
- Analysis by revenue per employee of top 1,000 companies
- Analysis of private and public companies by four-digit SIC code

The fifth volume presents companies listed in the first three volumes by the four-digit SIC code and ranks them according to sales. Other financial data are also included. The sixth and seventh volumes derive from the first five volumes, presenting companies by state, then by the four-digit SIC code, and by sales ranking. In addition, there is a special features section that presents the following information:

- 100 largest privately held companies for each state
- 100 largest publicly held companies for each state
- 100 largest employers for each state

In addition, the seventh volume has a list of companies ranked alphabetically, with assigned state rank number, state, and primary SIC code.

In addition to these directories, there are directories based on industries published by associations, individuals, or Dun and Bradstreet:

- *Dun's Industrial Guide: the Metalworking Directory* published by Dun and Bradstreet

- *Corporate Technology Directory*
- *Davison's Textile Blue Book*
- *Thomas Grocery Register*
- *Lockwood-Post's Directory of the Pulp, Paper, and Allied Trades*
- Some trade journals publish "Buyers Guides" issues giving names and addresses of companies, for example, *Chemical Week Buyers Guide*, October issue, and *Textile World*, July issue

PERIODICALS AND NEWSPAPERS

American Banker   This publication provides information on banking and financial services. It is a daily publication concentrating on technology, banking products, mortgages, finance, and various other subjects.

Bank Letter   A weekly publication of Institutional Investors, it publishes articles on the syndicated loan market, loans that are being arranged (with terms and conditions), secondary loan market, borrowing strategies of companies, and corporate loan ratings assigned by rating agencies.

Barron's   This is a weekly publication. Its articles are directed toward the investor. However, there are analyses of companies in a section called "Investment News and Views," which serve the needs of the analyst. The "Market Laboratory" provides copious amounts of statistical data on bonds, stocks, economic and financial indicators, and market statistics.

Bloomberg Magazine   This monthly magazine published by Bloomberg contains articles on market perspective, complex financings, personal wealth, new capabilities on Bloomberg, and interviews with senior officers of companies. *Bloomberg* articles cover a wide variety of cutting-edge subjects.

BondWeek   This is a publication for the institutional investor, containing news on fixed-income and credit markets, the economy, company strategies, new financings, rating changes, and yield curves for bond ratings and treasuries.

Business Week   This is a weekly publication and contains articles on the economy, industries, and companies. The articles cover products, finance, labor, production, and corporate news. It provides earnings of companies on a quarterly basis and presents an annual survey of industry performance. In addition, it includes a weekly update on such economic variables as interest rates, electricity consumption, and market prices. Each quarter, *Business Week* publishes "*BusinessWeek* Corporate Scoreboard" in which it provides financial data on 900 companies in 24 industries. The presentation includes sales, net profit, return on invested capital, return on common equity, growth in earnings per share, market value, and earnings per share. The quarterly earnings appear in the May, August, November, and February issues. The July issue features the "*BusinessWeek* Global 1,000" which provides information on the 1,000 largest companies in the world ranked by market value, share price, price/book value ratio, P/E ratio, sales, profits, and return on equity. All figures are translated into U.S. dollars. The April issue features the *"Business Week* 1,000: America's Most Valuable Companies." Companies are ranked based on market value and the long-term outlook of the companies and their industries. The data provided include market value, sales and profit margin, return on equity and invested capital, recent share price, book value per share, and earnings per share.

Commercial Lending Review This is a publication of the American Bankers Association and provides articles on credit risk management, bank regulations, community banking, and accounting issues related to banking.

The Economist This magazine provides worldwide coverage of politics, business, economics, finance, science, and technology. Its articles on politics are grouped geographically as "American Survey," "Asia," "International," "Europe," and "Britain." It publishes economic and financial statistics on 15 OECD countries and 25 emerging markets. Periodically it publishes surveys on countries, finance, and the economy.

Financial Times **(London)** This international daily provides news and articles on politics, economics, finance, as well as the financial, commodity, and other markets. Periodically it publishes surveys on markets, industries, and countries.

Financial World This magazine is published twice a month and contains about 10 articles on companies, industries, overall stock market performance, and stock market data.

Forbes This biweekly contains 12 to 15 articles on individual companies and industries. It has columnists that write on various subjects relating to business and finance. In its January issue, *Forbes* publishes "Annual Report on American Industry" in which it provides a ranking of companies in 21 industries, based on growth of sales and stock market performance. The report includes profitability, growth in sales and earnings per share, sales, net income, and profit margin.

Fortune This is published biweekly. It contains in-depth articles on the economy, business, individual companies, the stock market, and personal investing. The April issue features the "Fortune 500 Largest U.S. Industrial Corporations" ranked by sales. The list also includes "Who Did Best and Worst Among 500" section, which features companies based on return to investors, profitability, change in sales, sales per employee, and stockholders' equity. The June issue features "Fortune 500 Service Companies," which ranks within each industry.

High Yield Report This is published by *American Banker* and includes news on high-yield markets, personnel changes in various firms, the economy, data on new issues, traded debt, and distressed bond trading.

Journal of Lending and Credit Risk Management   This was formerly called *Journal of Commercial Bank Lending* and is published by Robert Morris Associates, Philadelphia, Pennsylvania. It publishes articles on banking, credit risk, lending strategies, bank regulations, and lending to various industries.

OTC Review   This is a monthly publication that provides analysis of stocks traded on the OTC market. It contains an analysis of an industry traded by many OTC companies, and an analysis of three or four firms.

Turnarounds and Workouts   This bimonthly publication by Beard Group, Inc., Washington, D.C., provides the latest news on defaulted, bankrupt, and distressed companies, a research report on companies that have filed for bankruptcy, including a profile on the officers of the company, members of the committees, the trustee, lawyers, and the judge.

Wall Street Journal   This is the primary daily source of information on business, economics, and finance and is the most widely circulated financial newspaper. It features articles on economy, corporate performance, company news, politics, taxes, and investing. "Digest of Earnings Reports" is a daily feature about updates on quarterly and annual reports of companies.

Wall Street Transcripts   This is a weekly that contains texts of speeches made in security analysts' meetings, copies of brokerage house reports on companies and industries, and interviews with corporate officers. In addition, it provides information on industries through "Round Table Discussion" in which analysts discuss various aspects of an industry.

ON-LINE SERVICES

Bloomberg News (New York, New York)   Bloomberg News is a real-time global news service that provides coverage of the world's governments, corporations, industries, commodities, and most segments of financial markets. The service is available on a dedicated computer terminal. It not only provides financial information like other on-line services but also processes it and presents it in tabular and/or graph form. Bloomberg provides a broad spectrum of data that includes financial news on industries and companies, debt rating actions, EDGAR filings, company analysis, equity, debt, commodities, foreign exchange, and municipal markets. The breadth and depth of coverage by Bloomberg is extensive. Its services are summarized here:

- Bloomberg analytics include beta, moving averages, money flows, volatilities, option sensitivity, deliverability, technical analysis, monitors, montages, option modeling, option-adjusted spread, duration, convexity, derivative evaluation, risk management, and scenario analysis.
- Fundamental data provided include earnings, balance sheets, cash flows, ratio analysis, and EDGAR filings.
- Various securities including stocks, convertibles, warrants, bonds, foreign exchange, interest rates, currency swaps, synthetics, strips, mortgage- and asset-based securities, and structured products.

- Real-time prices for instruments trading on the world's exchanges. These prices include current, historical and projected bond, currency, spot energy, derivative, and over-the-counter.
- The Bloomberg Forum provides in-depth interviews with corporate executives and industry executives.
- Bloomberg Multex Research allows the user to consolidate research from hundreds of providers.
- The Bloomberg fair value model draws on real-time market prices and is based on actual market activity for similar bonds, and option-adjusted methodology provides a theoretical market price for a bond.
- Bloomberg News produces over 3,000 stories a day on companies, industries, and global markets. However, the major weakness of Bloomberg is that the information can only be printed.

Indepth Bond Services **(New York, New York)**　This service provides information on the fixed-income market through the Internet, by subscription. The information includes the following:

- Prices and interest rates of government and private fixed-income instruments
- Detailed terms, covenants, and conditions, both at-offer and current
- Description of the issuer, and financial data and financial ratios on an annual and last-12-months basis
- Market commentary, debt rating actions, exchange and tender offers, and coverage of the 144-A market
- Real-time on-line access to SEC filings
- Watch list, which alerts the analyst of events in the market
- Rating actions by rating agencies
- Economic indicators and survey of expectations of leading economists
- Statistics provided by the Conference Board, University of Chicago, Michigan consumer confidence survey, Johnson Redbook retail sales, Columbia University inflation index, and other reports
- The *Indepth* bond calculator is a useful tool in bond mathematics.

Dow Jones Business and Finance Report **(New York, New York)**　This publication contains financial news, statistics, and information on developments in business and industry, and economic and financial information gathered from the Associated Press, Dow-Jones News Service, and the *Wall Street Journal.* This report is available through Dow-Jones News Retrieval on-line service also.

Dow Jones News Retrieval (New York, New York)　This on-line service contains articles from over 3,000 business, trade, and industry publications, and financial data on more than 1 million companies. In addition, the service provides information on consumer trends, company analyses, industry analyses, economic conditions, and a variety of other subjects.

Dun & Bradstreet (Parsippany, New Jersey)   One of the leading information providers, Dun & Bradstreet has a wide variety of publications. *D&B Dun's Financial Record Plus* provides directory and financial information on private and public companies. The data covers company's history and operation, financial data, and SIC codes.

Business Failure Record provides a comparative statistical analysis of business failures in terms of geographic and industry trends in the United States. *Manufacturing Survey* provides a survey of 1,000 manufacturing companies regarding their production, new orders, unfilled orders, exports, finished goods, and inventories. *Construction Survey* provides a survey of 200 construction firms regarding their current conditions and expectations in the next three months. *U.S. Survey of Business Expectations* provides a nationwide survey of 3,000 business executives regarding their expectations of sales, prices, inventories, exports, employment, and new orders for the coming quarter. *D&B Million Dollar Directory* provides information on public and private companies, such as address, SIC codes, ticker symbols, and in some cases, sales. This directory is a valuable addition to any library. Currently it is available in the on-line Dun's Market Identifier database in addition to the printed book. Dun & Bradstreet United States provides information on public and private companies in the United States. This is similar to the million dollar directory but is available only on-line through Informat Online. Dun's Electronic Business Directory provides the names, addresses, and recent information on more than 10 million U.S. businesses, and the data are arranged into eight groups based on SIC codes, as follows:

1. Construction Directory provides data on contractors.
2. Financial Services Directory provides data on banks, savings and loan institutions, insurance companies, and credit unions.
3. Manufacturers Directory provides data on manufacturers of all types.
4. Professionals Directory provides data on more than 1.2 million professionals in a variety of professions.
5. Services Directory provides data on more than 1.4 million service firms of all types and sizes.
6. Wholesale Directory provides data on over 650,000 wholesale establishments of all types and sizes.
7. Schools Directory provides data on 100,000 schools and libraries ranging from elementary schools to colleges.
8. Retailers Directory provides data on 1.9 million retail establishments of all types and sizes.

The service is available through CompuServe Information Service, AT&T EasyLink, and is part of Dun's Market Identifier. Dun & Bradstreet's Web address is http://www.dnb.com./

InvesText Group (New York, New York)   This service provides three databases, Investext, the PIPELINE, and MarkIntel. The last two are corollaries of Investext. Investext database provides complete text of several hundred thousand international company and 54 industry reports from nearly 320 investment banks, research firms, consulting firms, and brokerage houses. Each report provides an in-depth analysis of companies, industries, products, and geographic regions. In addition, the report provides industry trends, market share, business strategies, emerging technologies, and other relevant data. The database provides financial data and market forecasts for 3,000 large, publicly traded companies, more than 5,000 OTC-traded companies, and more than 2,500 foreign companies. The database provides industry reports on more than 50 industries. The PIPELINE database alerts on-line researchers to newly released information. MarkIntel is the on-line database of industry and market studies. The database is available on-line through CompuServe, DIALOG, and Dow-Jones News Retrieval.

Lexis-Nexis (Chicago, Illinois)   One of the most popular on-line services, Lexis-Nexis provides articles published in various periodicals, company information, and reports written by security analysts. In addition, it has access to the law library maintained by Lexis. Lexis-Nexis Express has a service by which researchers find the information the analyst needs efficiently and send it to the analyst. Another service, Tracker, provides, at the request of the organization, automatic news updates about its clients, competition, and industry.

Securities Data Company (Securities Data Base, New York, New York) SDC provides a database that covers worldwide information on new issues, mergers and acquisitions, joint ventures, venture financing, and corporate restructuring. The database is updated on a daily basis and is one of the most popular. The Global New Issues database includes the following:

- Domestic common stock issues with over 14,000 offerings since 1970
- Domestic preferred stock issues with over 2,200 offerings since 1970
- Debt database with over 22,000 offerings since 1970, inlcuding straight debt, convertible debt, mortgage, asset-backed debt, and taxable municipals
- Private Placement database with information on over 25,000 domestic private placements since 1981, containing information on straight debt, convertible debt, common stock, and preferred stock
- Euroequity and Eurobond databases with information on over 1,700 euro, global, and domestic issue program since 1973, covering public and private debt and common and preferred stock offerings
- Medium Term Note database with information on over 1,700 euro, global, and domestic issue programs since 1973, updated on a daily basis
- Issues withdrawn from registration
- Shelf registrations
- Underwritten calls of convertibles
- Foreign public offerings in the United Kingdom and Canada, and international warrants

- The Worldwide M&A database with coverage of more than 55,000 domestic transactions since 1980 and over 45,000 deals since 1985, covering mergers, acquisitions, partial acquisitions, leveraged buyouts, divestitures, exchange offers, stock repurchases, self-tenders, squeeze outs, tender offers, and spin-offs, updated daily based on SEC filings, tender offers, major financial publications, and company press releases

In addition, SDC offers specialized databases that include the following:

- Joint Venture and Strategic Alliances database provides information on over 19,000 cross-border and intra-nation joint venture transactions since 1988. The database tracks over 75 data items for each transaction in which two or more companies combined existing units or assets to form a new operating business or strategic alliance. Current state of the deal, recent developments concerning the transaction, as well as coverage of the participants involved are included.
- Venture Financing database is based on research by SDC subsidiary Venture Economics and contains business and financing abstracts on more than 17,000 public and private U.S. companies since 1970.

Reuters (New York, New York)   Reuters Holdings PLC supplies the business community worldwide with a wide range of products including real-time financial data, transaction systems, and access to statistical and textual historical databases. Reuters gathers information from over 250 exchanges and OTC markets, from 4,800 subscribers who contribute data directly, and from a network of journalists. Reuters Target News delivers news stories by topic in a timely manner. It provides annual reports of companies, key facts, financial results of a company, and its 11-year history.

Dow Jones Telerate (Jersey City, New Jersey)   Telerate provides access to real-time financial data, analyses, and news of financial markets. This service includes the following: Page Displays provides instant access to over 60,000 pages of live market data, news, commentary, and financial databases containing pricing and terms and conditions on corporate bonds. Quotes provides prices of a broad spectrum of financial instruments. News provides stories and headlines. It conducts searches on the past 180 days of news, based on key words, ticker symbols, company name, or geographic location. Studies provides graphic displays of data. Dynamic Data Exchange helps import live market data to Excel spreadsheets for price/yield calculations, portfolio valuations, and so forth. Telerate II Historical database provides access to nearly 500 time series on financial instruments and commodities.

DIALOG (Mountainview, California)   A Knight-Ridder Information service, DIALOG provides access to over 450 on-line databases related to market research, business planning, and related areas. It provides investment analysts' reports. DIALOG's Bluesheets describe and provide guidelines for searching all databases related to DIALOG.

Company Intelligence, Information Access Company (IAC, Foster City, California) This service provides financial and descriptive information on more than 160,000 public and private companies derived from over 5,000 periodicals and *Ward's Business Directory*. It is available on-line from DIA-LOG, Nexis, and DataStar. Its sister publication, Company ProFile, provides similar information on about 100,000 companies.

Financial Times Business Reports: Business/Finance (London, England) These reports provide complete text of nearly 50,000 commentaries and news articles covering companies, industries, international finance and business, and developing countries.

Find/SVP Market Research (New York, New York) This service provides information on current and historical size, growth trends, and forecasts of various markets, profiles of companies and their competitors, and other relevant information.

ABI/Inform (New York, New York) This is a database on compact disk containing indexes and abstracts of articles from over 800 business and trade journals covering the last five years.

Bridge Information Systems, Inc. (New York, New York) Bridge provides information on equities, fixed-income instruments, foreign exchange, derivatives, and commodities. BridgeNews (formerly Knight-Ridder Financial), a division of Bridge Information System, provides real-time news, in-depth analysis of markets, forecasts and calendars, market-focused government news, and so forth.

University Web Sites Several Web sites provide sources of information on evaluating credit, but the most notable are as follows:

- Department of Finance, Ohio State University, has the Financial Data Finder, which provides an excellent source of data providers and connects to various business libraries, http://www.cob.ohio-state.edu/dept/fin
- University of Texas, http://kiwiclub.bus.utexas.edu/
- California State University, Fresno, http://www.csufresno.edu/Economics/
- University of Delaware, http://www.lib.udel.edu/
- College of Business, Florida State University, http://www.fsu.edu/~finance/press/

COMPANY ANALYSIS

After examining the economic and financial conditions and examining the industry, the analyst may now analyze the company. The following are the most important sources.

Company Reports

The best source on a company is the company itself. A company publishes press releases, which provide information on topics such as earnings and management changes. The senior officers make presentations before security analysts and are interviewed by analysts and the press. In these interviews the officers discuss current performance, company strategy, prospects for the company, business plans, and new product development. In addition, many companies have their own Web site on the Internet.

Annual Reports   By far the most important source of information on the company, the annual report, provides information on the current operations and financial conditions of the company. The annual report contains two parts and must contain the following items:

PART I

- Business. If the company has multiple lines of business, those product lines that account for more than 10 percent of sales must be presented for the last two years. Gross profit or operating profit by product lines must be included.
- Summary of operations.
- Properties, location, type of property at each location, and whether each is leased or owned.
- Parents and subsidiaries.
- Legal proceedings.
- Changes in outstanding securities.
- Approximate number of equity holders.
- Executive officers of the company.
- Indemnification of officers and directors.
- Financial statements including income statements, balance sheets, and detailed footnotes.

PART II

- Principal security holders.
- Directors of the company.
- Remuneration of directors and officers of the company.
- Options granted to management to purchase.
- Ownership of the company by management and others.

Part I must be filed with the SEC within 90 days from the end of the company's fiscal year, and part II within 120 days.

SEC Filings   Pursuant to the Securities and Exchange Commission Act of 1934 all firms that have publicly issued securities have to file various statements with the SEC and also distribute them to the stockholders.

- Form 10-K includes the annual report and presents the company's business and financial information in greater detail.
- Form 10-Q and quarterly reports are are unaudited. Form 10-Q is filed with the SEC on a quarterly basis and must be filed within 45 days from the end of the fiscal year. The quarterly report must contain the operations for the quarter, year to date and comparison with quarter of the previous year. The report must contain an income statement, balance sheet, and funds flow statement, as well as a written analysis of the operations during the quarter.
- The proxy statement discloses information relevant to the stockholder.
- Form 8-K is an interim report filed when there is an important event that affects the corporation, such as bankruptcy filing, changes in control, and resignation of officers or directors.

S-18 REGISTRATION

S-18 registration is a simplified registration used by small companies; the offering of new securities can not exceed $7.5 million. The following statements have to be filed with SEC:

- An audited balance sheet for one year
- An audited income statement and statements of change in financial condition for two years
- No management discussion or analyses of financial condition and no selected financial data

S-1 REGISTRATION

This registration filed with the SEC is more complex and requires more information:

- Details of the offering, underwriting discounts and commission, proceeds from the issue
- Ownership of existing shares
- Presentation of risk factors
- Use of proceeds
- The company's dividend policy and a statement as to how future earnings will be used; the company's capital structure before and after the new issue
- Management discussion of the performance of the company
- Description of the business
- Information about the directors and officers
- Company financial statements and auditor's opinion

Other Sources of Company Analysis

BANK LOAN REPORT (AMERICAN BANKER, NEW YORK, NEW YORK)

This is a weekly newsletter providing information on terms and conditions of newly arranged million-dollar loans. The coverage includes fees, spreads, covenants, and participants. IDD Information Services publishes this report.

BANKRUPTCIES AND DEFAULTS (*SECURITIES DATA COMPANY, NEWARK, NEW JERSEY*)

This publication provides data on reorganization plans and information on companies with assets over $50 million that filed for bankruptcy. SDC publishes this data going back to 1988. The publication is updated monthly.

THE BANKRUPTCY DATASOURCE (*NEW GENERATION RESEARCH, BOSTON, MASSACHUSETTS*)

This publication provides information on companies that filed bankruptcy, asset sales, financing arrangements, law suits, claim transfers, and reorganization plans filed. New Generation Research, Inc., publishes this monthly report. *Bankruptcy Yearbook and Almanac* is published by the same publisher annually. The yearbook contains lists of companies that filed for bankruptcy, companies that came out of bankruptcy, bankrupt companies by industry, private companies that filed for bankruptcy, and other data. New Generation has a Web site on the Internet (bankrupt.com).

BROKERAGE REPORTS

Most large brokerage firms periodically publish industry and company analyses written by security analysts. Stock and bond investors and credit analysts will find these publications extremely useful.

DISCLOSURE SEC DATABASE (BETHESDA, MARYLAND)

Disclosure, Inc., a private company, has a contract with the SEC to reproduce all filings. Although hard copies of SEC filings are available free of charge from the respective company, previous years' filings are hard to obtain. Disclosure maintains SEC filings from 1977, and financial data on more than 12,500 publicly traded companies. The information is obtained primarily from SEC filings. The database includes both current and historical financial data, company summary information such as corporate addresses, officers, directors, institutional and insider ownership, and other relevant information. The information is extracted from the following filings: 10K, 20F, 10Q, 8K, proxy, registration statements, and annual reports. Disclosure reports are available in microfiche, CD-ROM, magnetic tape, and on-line through ADP Financial Information Service, DIALOG, LEXIS-NEXIS, Dow-Jones News Retrieval and Bloomberg.

DUFF & PHELPS FIXED-INCOME RATINGS (CHICAGO, ILLINOIS)

Duff & Phelps rates over 500 major domestic corporations. Commercial paper ratings range from Duff 1 plus (top quality) to Duff 3, and long-term debt is rated on a 17-point scale that ranges from AAA to CCC with plus and minus modifiers similar to those used by S&P. Duff & Phelps is one of four statistical rating organizations fully recognized by the SEC.

EDGAR DATABASE OF CORPORATIONS (WASHINGTON, D.C.)

EDGAR, the electronic data gathering, analysis, and retrieval system, is the fastest growing source that provides copies of SEC filings. Companies have been phased in to EDGAR filing over a three-year period ending May 1996. As of that date all public domestic companies were required to file in ED-GAR. Currently EDGAR is available through the Internet (World Wide Web, Gopher, and anonymous FTP). Any public electronic filings submitted to the SEC can be retrieved.

FITCH IBCA (NEW YORK, NEW YORK)

Fitch IBCA rates debt instruments of industrial, bank, and finance companies, and municipal bonds and structured finance. Commercial paper ratings range from Fitch-1 to Fitch-4, and long-term debt is rated on a 7-point scale that ranges from AAA to CCC. Fitch IBCA is one of four statistical rating organizations fully recognized by the SEC. Fitch IBCA provides the following services:

- Corporate and government bond databases that provide financial information on securities including bond covenants
- Rating database containing all Fitch IBCA–rated issues
- Structured Finance Surveillance features asset-backed securities (ABS) and mortgage-backed securities (MBS) pool information and current key credit indicators
- Market risk ratings to gauge comparative risk for CMO tranches
- Research reports detailing Fitch's IBCA credit opinions
- Real-time rating news

HOOVER'S HANDBOOK OF AMERICAN BUSINESS (AUSTIN, TEXAS; WEB ADDRESS: HTTP://WWW.HOOVERS.COM)

This handbook provides information on 500 of the largest and most influential companies in the United States. It is available through LEXIS, Bloomberg, and America Online. Profiles on 500 companies are presented based on revenues and include an overview, history, key competitors, products and services, brand names, key personnel, five years of financial and stock information, and public visibility. These are summarized in one page. Based on its operating performance, profitability measures, financial strength, innovation, and market share in the industry, the companies are ranked from A to F. The sister publication, Hoover Company Database, provides information on approximately 3,200 foreign and domestic companies, with new entries added each month. It is available on-line through CompuServe Information Service.

MOODY'S INVESTORS SERVICE (NEW YORK, NEW YORK; WEB ADDRESS: HTTP://WWW.MOODYS.COM)

Moody's Manuals. Moody's publishes several financial databases. Its manuals are most valuable sources of information on a company and are divided into several categories as follows: (1) industrial, (2) bank and finance, (3) public utility, (4) transportation, (5) municipal and government, (6) OTC listed, (7) OTC unlisted, and (8) international.

The manuals are published annually in August of each year. They are updated with a twice-a-weel supplement containing quarterly earnings, dividend announcements, mergers, and other financial news. The manuals are comprehensive and supplied in two volumes. The extent of coverage is determined by the level of coverage purchased by the company. The descriptions range from extensive to limited.

The *Industrial Manual* (two volumes) contains reports on publicly held companies that are listed in major stock exchanges. The manual provides information on the history, recent acquisitions, product lines, capital structure, financial statements ranging from 2 to 10 years, location of important properties, officers, and detailed description of securities outstanding. The *Bank and Finance Manual* (two volumes) publishes information on banks, savings and loan associations, investment companies, insurance companies, real estate companies, real estate investment trusts, and other finance-related companies. The presentation is similar to that of the *Industrial Manual*. A "Special Features" section presents summary statistics on the finance industry. The *Public Utility Manual* (two volumes) covers electric and gas utilities, gas transmission, telephone, and water companies. The presentation is similar to that of the *Industrial Manual*. A "Special Features" section presents summary statistics on the public utility industry. The *Transportation Manual* (one volume) covers airline, railroad, trucking, steamship, automobile/truck leasing and rental, oil pipeline, and bus line companies. The presentation is similar to that of the *Industrial Manual*. Moody's presents maps of routes for some companies. A "Special Features" section presents summary statistics on the transportation industry. The *Municipal and Government Manual* (threee volumes) covers federal, state, and municipal government financing. The manual describes pollution control, industrial development, revenue and other related bonds, and financial statistics for each state. The *OTC Industrial Manual* (one volume) covers industrial companies that are traded over the counter. The presentation is similar to that of the *Industrial Manual*. A "Special Features" section presents a geographical index of companies, and a classification of companies by industry and product. The *OTC Unlisted Manual* (one volume) covers OTC stocks that are less actively traded and those companies that are not traded on the NASDAQ. The presentation is similar to that of the industrial manual. It contains a geographical index of companies. The *International Manual* (two volumes) provides information on large international corporations and supranational institutions such as the World Bank. Corporations and institutions are arranged by country. The information includes history, subsidiaries, income statement, balance sheet, principal officers, and plant locations.

Moody's Bond Survey. This publication provides ratings of commercial paper and bonds of issuers, and articles on the economy, credit analysis of companies, and rating changes. The issuer's credit is analyzed for the purposes of rating. The rating spectrum ranges from Aaa to C, with 1, 2, or 3 used as modifiers that are similar to "plus" and "minus" used by S&P for bonds and "P-1" to "P-3" for commercial paper. The market sectors covered are (1) industrials, (2) sovereigns, (3) public finance, (4) structured finance, (5) insurance, and (6) project finance.

Its research activities are broken down into several major components by sector as follows:

- U.S. public finance credit research includes more than 70,000 ratings on both bonds and short-term obligations of some 20,000 municipal entities, covering more than 90 percent of bond volumes in the United States
- Corporate credit research proivdes in-depth analysis of some 400 issuers in industrial, utility, and nonbank finance, and one-page analysis of some 800 issuers
- Bank credit research provides in-depth analysis of banking institutions and security firms worldwide
- Sovereign credit research includes reports on over 50 sovereign nations, and descriptions of economic and political factors that affect ratings
- Speculative grade research includes monthly market commentary on over 500 issuers of non-investment-grade debt
- Structured finance research has reports and updates on ratings of asset-backed and mortgage-backed securities
- Insurance credit research provides credit evaluations of property-casualty companies

Moody's Bond Record. This publication is similar to S&P's *Bond Guide*. This monthly publication provides description of debt security, its month-end price, rating, date of issuance, and price range.

Moody's Handbook of Common Stocks. This publication provides descriptions of stocks traded on the New York and American Stock Exchanges, with each stock described on one page. Approximately 900 stocks are covered. The coverage includes 10-year financial data, shares outstanding, earnings per share, and P/E ratio. Current condition and recent developments of the company are also presented.

STANDARD & POOR'S CORPORATION (S&P) (NEW YORK, NEW YORK; WEB ADDRESS: HTTP://WWW.RATINGS.COM)

S&P has an extensive array of publications that cover most facets of finance. Many of them are discussed here.

CreditWeek. CreditWeek presents analysis of companies, and ratings of debt issued by them. In rating a debt security, S&P takes into account the company's business risk, industry risk, financial risk, default risk, company size, management, and quality of financial statements. While rating a new security, S&P presents a complete analysis of the issuer. S&P incorporates default risk over the life of the security in assigning the rating, but financial conditions change. *Ratings Outlook* and *CreditWatch* address these situations. By placing a security in *CreditWatch*, S&P alerts the financial markets of a forthcoming change in credit rating. S&P may judge the outlook to be positive, negative, or neutral. The rating spectrum ranges from AAA to D, with ratings from AA to CCC being modified with plus and minus signs to show relative standing within the major rating categories. The market sectors covered are (1) corporate finance, (2) sovereigns, (3) public finance, (4) structured finance, (5) insurance, and (6) project finance.

CreditWeek presents feature articles by economists, special reports on topics of interest, selected industry and sector analyses, and assessment of key market trends. Periodically, S&P publishes articles on credit quality, for example, *Ratings Performance,* and *Stability and Transition,* and *High Yield Bond and Bank Loan Ratings.* An offshoot of *CreditWeek,* Electronic Rating Information Service (ERIS) provides the latest database containing the ratings. The database is provided monthly.

Corporation Records. This publication is a seven-volume work with companies arranged in alphabetical order in the first six volumes; the seventh volume is a daily update of companies covered in the first six volumes. *Corporation Records* is a monthly publication that provides history, financial statements, news announcements, earnings updates, and other information. The sixth volume has a statistical section covering new stock and bond offerings on a monthly basis, and a classified index of industrial companies listed by SIC code. This index is very useful in compiling a list of companies in a specific industry.

Stock Guide. This is a monthly publication that provides information on stocks of several thousand companies.

Bond Guide. This is a monthly publication that provides information on bonds, both rated and unrated. The *Bond Guide* lists all the outstanding bonds of the company, with the name of the bond, maturity, interest rate, price at the end of the month, amount outstanding, price range, current and former rating, date of rating change, yield to maturity, and date of issue. It has a section on convertible bonds and a section on foreign bonds. Each month it publishes rating changes, bonds called, and new offerings.

Corporate Reports. One of the most popular publications, the *Corporate Reports* are a three-volume publication describing New York Stock Exchange stocks, American Stock Exchange stocks, and over-the-counter and regional exchange stocks. Current reports are published in a three-ring binder, and the annual is published in a bound form. Data is presented on product lines, 10-year historical performance, current developments, and stock performance.

STANDARD & POOR'S *COMPUSTAT* DATABASE (NEW YORK, NEW YORK)

One of the most popular databases, S&P's COMPUSTAT covers 9,000+ active and 7,000+ inactive companies. The active companies have data with up to 20 years of annual, 12 years of quarterly, 7 years of business segment, and 30 years of monthly stock prices and dividend data. The active companies are divided into 270 industry groups. COMPUSTAT provides income statement, balance sheet, and statement of cash flow items, monthly price data, business segment data, geographic segment data, and company address. COMPUSTAT is estimated to contain analysts' recommendations on more than 4,000 companies. COMPUSTAT provides a more expansive database than COMPUSTAT II, which provides financial data for more companies and with SIC codes. There are specific data files that can be extracted from COMPUSTAT:

- Bank File contains financial data for approximately 150 leading U.S. banking institutions. Available in both annual and quarterly formats.
- Industrial Compustat comprises three files that can be obtained separately or merged together. These files are available in annual or quarterly format.
- Primary Industrial File has financial statement data on approximately 800 companies that include the S&P 400, S&P 40 utilities, S&P 20 transportation companies, and S&P 40 financial companies. These files are available in annual or quarterly format.
- Supplementary Industrial File provides financial statement data on approximately 800 companies traded on major exchanges but of lesser degree of investor interest.
- Tertiary Industrial File includes financial statement data on approximately 800 companies traded on New York and American Stock Exchanges.
- Over-the-Counter File: Financial statement data on approximately 850 companies traded on the OTC. Annual format only.
- Industrial Annual Research File provides financial statement data on companies deleted from the primary, supplemental, tertiary, and OTC files due to acquisitions, merger, bankruptcy, liquidation, going private, or other reasons. Available in annual format.
- Full Coverage File has financial statement data on approximately 4,000 companies that file 10-K reports, primarily companies listed in NASDAQ, trading OTC, and on regional exchanges.
- Business Information Industry Segment File has SIC-code-based data on 6,250 companies for selected data items, with five-year histories.

In addition, S&P provides a back-data companies database and the S&P Industry Index History database that contains over 100 industries and up to 30 years of financial data.

COMPUSTAT is available online from CompuServe, ADP Network, Interactive Data, S&P's Compustat Services, and Bloomberg. The database is updated weekly. COMPUSTAT is so popular that it is a household name in finance!

CREDITPRO

CreditPro is a Windows 95–based software and data package providing default and ratings transition data by industry and static pool. This package is useful in generating portfolio credit risk profiles based on industry, sector, and time periods that closely reflect the securities held. The transition and default database in CreditPro spans the period 1981–1996 for 6000+ obligors. The CD-ROM contains marginal and cumulative default rates and transition matrices. Companies are identified by the S&P's 12-industry classification.

THOMSON BANKWATCH, INC. (NEW YORK, NEW YORK)

This rating agency monitors more than 1,000 banking, securities, and financial firms. It provides ratings on banking companies in over 60 countries, and their debt instruments. Thomson BankWatch is one of four statistical rating organizations fully recognized by the SEC. It offers several types of ratings:

- Issuer ratings. These ratings are based on the overall health and financial condition of a rated company on a consolidated basis. These ratings give an indication of the likelihood that future problems wil arise and the ability of the company to address the problems. Issuer ratings take into account the credit risk and performance risk. They incorporate the performance of the operating units within the consolidated group and the issuer's legal structure. Ratings are based on a nine-point scale from A, A/B, B through E. These ratings are different from Moody's and S&P's in that Thomson rates the issuer and the latter rate the issues.
- Debt ratings. Debt ratings are applied to specific short- and long-term debt issues. Short-term debt ratings are based on a scale from TBM1 (highest) to TBW4 (non-investment-grade/speculative). Long-term debt ratings are based on a scale from AAA, AA, A through D (default). Thomson BankWatch is one of four statistical rating organizations fully recognized by the SEC.

VALUE LINE INVESTMENT SURVEY (NEW YORK, NEW YORK)

This survey is published in two parts. The first part provides analysis of about 1,700 stocks in 91 industries, which are updated on a quarterly basis. The analysis covers historical performance, descriptions of the company's business, current conditions, stock price data, two-year projections, and the beta of the stock. The second part is published weekly and contains stock recommendations and general investment advice.

WALL STREET RESEARCH NET (NEW YORK, NEW YORK)

This site on the Web is a large collection of financial links to other sites on the Web. It connects to the home pages of companies, SEC filings, and so forth. The Web site address is http://www.wsrn.com/, and it has a link with America Online.

DEFAULT/MORTALITY RATES RATING MIGRATION STATISTICS

Of particular reference to the theme of this book are the statistics and analyses performed related to the default and mortality rates of corporate bond issuers and the patterns of rating drift (migration). These statistics are usually keyed to the corporate bond ratings of the major bond-rating agencies (discussed earlier). Structural financial products analysts are particularly interested in these aggregated statistics because of their focus on pools of assets. We have devoted two entire chapters in this book to the discussion of these statistics and their importance, and we summarize their sources and descriptions here

- Altman/NYU Salomon Center, Stern School of Business (New York, New York). Provides an annual report, usually published in January, of the past year's activities, and also data from 1971 to the present on corporate bond default rates, default losses, recoveries at default, bond mortality rates by original bond rating, and performance of high-yield corporate bonds. All data are analyzed on a market-weighted average basis. Only U.S. straight debt is reported. A companion report from the NYU Salomon Center analyzes the monthly market-weighted risk and return performance of portfolios of defaulted bonds from 1971 to the present. A second index on the performance of defaulted bank loans was started in 1996. Since 1996 the center has also combined the two defaulted security indexes into a single index.

- Moody's Investors Service—Global Credit Research Reports (New York, New York). Produces an annual report on "Historical Default Rates of Corporate Bond Issuers," published in January since 1990. The 1998 report covers the period 1990–1997. This report documents default data on issuers rated by Moody's for up to 20 years after the senior unsecured bond equivalent is classified into a specific rating category (subcategories since 1983). Recoveries on default and loss rates are also published. Data is analyzed by corporate issuer, not on a market-weighted or issuer-weighted average basis.

- Moody's also reports its default rate series (moving 12-month average) in its monthly publication "Speculative Grade: Ratings and Analysis." Descriptions of all defaulted issues including, straight debt, convertible, and eurobonds, are presented in both the annual and monthly publications.

- Moody's report, "Rating Migration and Credit Quality Correlation," documents historical ratings movements and the correlation of the movements. The July 1997 report covers the period 1920–1996.

- Standard & Poor's Default and Migration Risk Reports (New York, New York). This rating agency report, like Moody's, concentrates on rates of default by corporate issuer and utilizes a static-pool analysis. Data from 1981 to 1996 was analyzed in their latest report (February 1997) and covers default rates and rating transition for up to 15 years after the pool is formed. At times this report has appeared in *CreditWeek*.

- The 1998 special report "Ratings Performance 1997: Stability and Transition" documents credit quality changes of specific industrial sectors for the past decade in addition to its focus on the past year. Their rating action database tracks activity of investment as well as speculative-grade issues in seven sectors including industrials, telecommunications, utilities, banking, other financial institutions, project finance, and sovereign. Industrials are broken into 17 subsectors. Their rating outlook service focuses on intermediate-term (one to three years) rating considerations. (See also CreditPro, mentioned previously in this section.) This report is published annually.

RATING MIGRATION DATA

The same three services discussed in the default rate section have also reported on rating migration statistics. Altman's work (with Kishore) has appeared in scholarly journals and NYU Salomon Center working papers, and Moody's and S&P report their own rating migration statistics on a regular basis (in the case of S&P, in the same report as their default statistics; in Moody's case, on an irregular, special report basis). These migration publications are of particular interest to analysts of rating stability, specific rating grade investing, credit risk deterioration, and so forth. For an in-depth discussion of the rating migration phenomenon and comparison between the three primary data sources in this area, see Chapter 16 in this book.

Index